ANTHROPOLOGICAL PAPERS

MUSEUM OF ANTHROPOLOGY, UNIVERSITY OF MICHIGAN

NO. 47

THE PREHISTORIC PEOPLE OF THE FORT ANCIENT CULTURE OF THE CENTRAL OHIO VALLEY

BY

LOUISE M. ROBBINS AND GEORG K. NEUMANN

ANN ARBOR

THE UNIVERSITY OF MICHIGAN, 1972

© 1972 by the Regents of the University of Michigan
The Museum of Anthropology
All rights reserved

ISBN (print): 978-0-932206-45-9 (paper)
ISBN (ebook): 978-1-951519-23-0 (ebook)

Browse all of our books at
sites.lsa.umich.edu/archaeology-books.

Order our books from the University of Michigan
Press at www.press.umich.edu.

For permissions, questions, or manuscript queries,
contact Museum publications by email at umma-pubs@umich.edu or visit the Museum website at
lsa.umich.edu/ummaa.

TABLE OF CONTENTS

Acknowledgments v
Foreword By *James B. Griffin* vii
I. Introduction 1
II. Description of Major Physical Varieties in the
    Eastern United States 9
    Lenid 9
    Ilinid 12
    Iswanid 14
    Dakotid 15
    Muskogid 18
III. Description of Skeletal Material by Focus 21
    The Baum Focus 21
    The Feurt Focus 31
    The Anderson Focus 41
    The Madisonville Focus 49
IV. Analyses of Crania Within the Fort Ancient Aspect 71
    Intrafocus Comparisons 73
    Interfoci Comparisons 80
V. Comparisons on the Varietal Level 87
    Varietal Comparisons 88
    Fort Ancient "Varietal" Comparisons 92
VI. The Reconstruction of Fort Ancient Phyletic History 103
References 111
Appendixes 115
    A. Metrical and Morphological Terminology 117
    B. Metrical and Morphological Data for
       Major Physical Varieties in Eastern United States ... 131
    C. Description of Skeletal Material by Focus 177
    D. Analysis of Crania in the Fort Ancient Aspect 465
    E. Comparisons on the Varietal Level 575
    F. Drawings of Sample Crania from
       Each Focus and Variety 649

ACKNOWLEDGMENTS

I would like to take this opportunity to express sincere gratitude to Dr. Georg K. Neumann for making available the wealth of data which he has so laboriously gathered on the Fort Ancient population. There is little doubt that without his encouragement and advice this report would not have been completed, since the mass of material and magnitude of the analyses often seemed overwhelming. The results, however, have more than compensated for earlier apprehensions regarding work with a problem of such proportions.

I also wish to express appreciation to the members of the staff of the University of Kentucky Computing Center who offered every assistance in running the various tests that were needed for the report. Their willingness to help resolve the problems of setting up the programs made the task of running the programs quite pleasant.

A special acknowledgment is given to the many individuals—family, friends, colleagues, and students—who have helped me to complete the report. Many have offered technical assistance; all have offered encouragement.

L. M. R.
Mississippi State University

FOREWORD

James B. Griffin

This study of the Fort Ancient populations in the Central Ohio Valley had its inception in 1936 when Mr. Eli Lilly of Indianapolis wrote to me, asking questions about the physical type of the Fort Ancient people. At that time the only study of the people of Fort Ancient was one by E. A. Hooton on the skeletal material from the Madisonville site near Cincinnati. In my reply to Mr. Lilly, I indicated that there was a considerable amount of skeletal material from other Fort Ancient sites in various museums and private collections and that these should be studied in order to determine the homogeneity or variability of the Fort Ancient people. When this was done, it should then be possible to compare Fort Ancient populations with other prehistoric and historic populations. This proposed study would be parallel to my work, then in progress, on the archaeological remains from various Fort Ancient sites, and to the linguistic and ethnohistorical work of Carl and Erminie Voegelin. Mr. Lilly agreed to underwrite such a study by Georg K. Neumann, and Neumann began his work at the Museum of Anthropology at Ann Arbor in January, 1937. For the next few years he succeeded in acquiring data on much of the skeletal material from sites in the Miami Valley north of Cincinnati, from the Scioto Valley, and from Ohio Valley sites east of Cincinnati. It rapidly became apparent that the Fort Ancient populations show more physical diversity than had been expected and also that there seemed to be a good correlation between archaeological subunits of Fort Ancient and the different physical groupings that Neumann recognized.

Professor Neumann did not complete his study of the Fort Ancient populations, but his collected data formed an important part of Dr. Robbins' study. She has added additional skeletal material and extensively reworked Prof. Neumann's data. In recognition of his work and of his guidance of her preparation of her Ph.D. thesis at Indiana University, his name has been added as a joint author of this publication.

viii   PREHISTORIC PEOPLE OF FORT ANCIENT

When I began my study of the Fort Ancient archaeological material in 1933, I believed there were 5 to 10 sites of this complex. By the time the Fort Ancient study had been essentially completed in late 1939, I knew of some 31 sites; and when the work was finally published in 1943, quite a few other sites were known. In addition to being handicapped in their assessment of the Fort Ancient complex by their incomplete list of sites, anthropologists of the 1930's had a very poor idea of the time depth of prehistoric Indian occupation of North America. The time span of Fort Ancient was viewed as about 300 years—from about A.D. 1400 to close to A.D. 1700. It is now believed, on the basis of radiocarbon dates, that the Fort Ancient complex was initiated about A.D. 1000, and on the basis of historic European trade goods, that many villages were occupied in the Ohio Valley during the seventeenth century. It is my impression that if a really comprehensive survey of the Ohio Valley could have been made in A.D. 1850, hundreds of Fort Ancient sites would have been identified in southeastern Indiana, southern Ohio, northern Kentucky and northern West Virginia.

This view of the Fort Ancient complex as occupying hundreds of sites over 700 years of time means that extensive revisions of my 1939 interpretations are necessary and that more recent interpretations by other archaeologists currently studying Fort Ancient sites will continue to be altered as additional materials appear and are combined with the reevaluation of data now available. While it is gratifying to find that this study of the physical types of the Fort Ancient people identifies a Muskogid variety with the Madisonville focus or phase, I would expect to find that future studies would indicate temporal and areal variations within this cultural division. It is also probable that the Madisonville focus or phase is much too gross and that future studies will recognize more coherent units with significantly different patterns. This study by Dr. Robbins identifies an Ilinid population which occupied the Baum and Anderson focus sites and which was also represented to some degree in the Madisonville focus, presumably in the early part of the temporal span of that archaeological unit. It is her contention that the Ilinid Fort Ancient population is descended from Woodland populations of the general area, and this interpretation is supported, I believe, by the probable slow cultural change from the Late Woodland into the northern Fort Ancient complexes. Furthermore, there is a high degree of similarity between the Ilinid populations of Fort Ancient populations in central Indiana and the Fisher populations of northern Illinois. These could represent prehistoric groups of southern

FOREWORD

Central Algonquian-speaking peoples who were gradually changing their way of life as the Middle Mississippi complexes were developing to the south. If the Fort Ancient people were primarily Shawnee speakers, as seems most likely, this would be compatible with the proposed alignment of marginal late Mississippian populations in Indiana, Illinois and southwestern Michigan with Central Algonquian populations.

A microfilm has been made of the measurements of the individual crania used in this paper. Copies of the microfilm are available from the Department of Anthropology of Mississippi State University and the Museum of Anthropology at the University of Michigan.

Eli Lilly not only is responsible for the initiation of this project and support for much of the work over the years since 1936, but he has provided a major part of the support for this publication by the Museum of Anthropology at the University of Michigan. We are most grateful for his continued interest in this project.

I
INTRODUCTION

THE Middle Ohio Valley has known the presence of man from prehistoric times to the present day. Until the coming of the white settlers, the aboriginal inhabitants of the valley directed most of their time and energies toward obtaining food in sufficient quantities for the survival and perpetuation of their own social group. Some subsistence patterns, such as agriculture, involved a cultural elaboration of material items, whereas less diversity in the array of material traits generally was associated with earlier hunting and gathering populations. In other words, the earlier inhabitants of the Middle Ohio Valley concentrated on practicing their culture and left some of its products in passing.

Although the more recent immigrants to the region, the white settlers, were also interested in populating the area and gaining a living from it, they brought a new interest with them. They were inquisitive about the earlier occupants whose cultural items were frequently found on the surface of the ground or when the soil was cultivated. As a result, considerable attention was and continues to be devoted to the location, description, and identification of the cultures of the prehistoric inhabitants. This interest in extinct cultures has not been confined to the professionally trained investigator, as a perusal of early historic journals illustrates. More frequently, it is the amateur investigator who finds evidence of aboriginal occupations and who calls them to the attention of the trained specialist. Within the last one hundred years, many prehistoric sites have been found and subsequently given particular names in terms of location (name of landowner, town, etc.), of temporal placement (Archaic, Protohistoric, etc.), and of the population who made the material remains found on the site (Hopewell, Adena, Fort Ancient, etc.).

Physical remains of the population are often found in association with items of the material culture, and it then becomes possible to study not only the life ways of the people but the people themselves. For example, the skeletal remains found with the preceramic Southern Archaic shell mound manifestation at Indian Knoll display a combination of physical characteristics which G. Neumann (1952:18) describes as being diagnostic of, and thus serving as, the type series of the Iswanid variety of North American Indians. A population which was responsible for a Middle Mississippi cultural assemblage tends to be representative of the Muskogid (formerly called Walcolid) varietal type (G. Neumann, 1952:21). For the most part, the physical populations who produced the prehistoric cultures have not received the concentrated attention that has been directed toward their material products. Except for some reports such as H. Neumann's (n.d.) investigations of the relationship of the Walcolid (Muskogid) Spoon River Focus population of Central Illinois to the Muskogean-speaking historic Choctaw-Chickasaw tribes and Funkhouser's (1938:243) proposal that some of the Norris Basin people greatly resembled certain Iroquoian groups to the north, few definitive attempts have been made to link the people of late prehistoric or protohistoric archaeological manifestations with historic tribes.

This report is an attempt to reconstruct the history of the people who produced the Fort Ancient archaeological cultural assemblage by using a multidisciplinary approach toward the solution of a historic problem. Specifically, the report is a test to determine to what extent the skeletal data support the conclusions that have been drawn on the basis of archaeological evidence.

During the 1930s Dr. James B. Griffin made a comprehensive analysis of the Fort Ancient archaeological manifestation, and his data form the parameters for the descriptive and comparative analyses of this study. The four foci—Baum, Feurt, Anderson and Madisonville—were established by Griffin on the grounds of artifactual similarities and differences and are accepted here as archaeological subgroups (see Fig. 1). In his work, Griffin outlines the temporal and spacial distribution of the Fort Ancient culture. He presents ideas of cultural origins and traces cultural continuities as they relate to the aspect. He points out external influences upon the culture as witnessed by the diffusion of traits, and he demonstrates the cohesiveness of the groupings on the focus, aspect, and phase levels.

The ethnohistorical identification of the earliest tribes found in the region has been tested against the archaeological distribution in concordance with the temporal position of the Fort Ancient Aspect. While there is the possibility that the earliest historic tribes of the Middle Ohio Valley may have been derived from Siouan-, Muskogean-, or Algonquian-speaking stocks, it is more probable that the Fort Ancient people were Algonquian and

INTRODUCTION

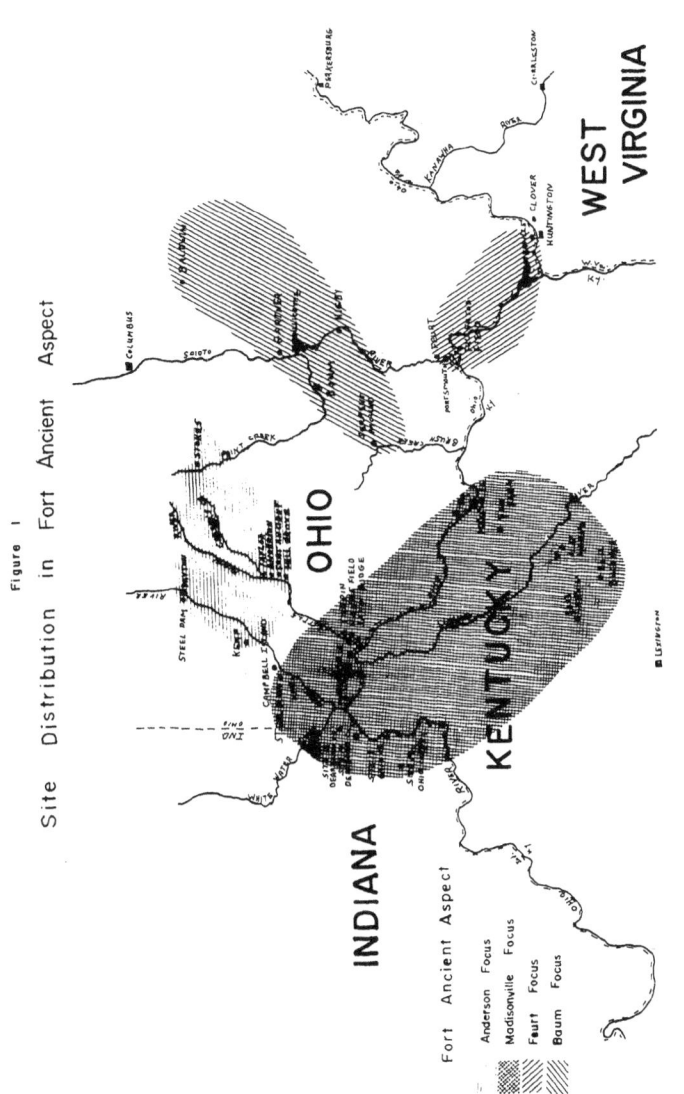

Figure 1
Site Distribution in Fort Ancient Aspect

therefore the ancestors of the historic Shawnee tribal group.

Working with the assumption that the protohistoric people in the area were affiliated with the Central Algonquian linguistic group, the cultural and physical correlations with other members of this division are explored to evaluate the precise temporal and spacial placement of the population. In other words, an attempt is made to determine which, if any, of the Central Algonquian tribes most closely resemble the Fort Ancient peoples in physical and cultural characteristics.

As noted earlier, the cultural grouping, i.e., the archaeological focus, is accepted as the basic unit. In regard to physical traits, the skeletal populations representing each focus are described in terms of their metrical dimensions, indicial values, and morphological features, following the methodology of Martin (1928), see Tables 1, 2, and 3 in Appendix A. Each component within a focus is correlated with every other component of that focus to test the degrees of physical homogeneity within the focus. The populations of each focus are then tested with every other focus to assess the homogeneity of the entire Fort Ancient population. And lastly, the groupings, component and focus, are compared with five established physical groupings on a varietal level—the Lenid, Iswanid, Ilinid, Muskogid and Dakotid type series, as presented by G. Neumann (1960)—to establish phyletic relationships of the protohistoric Fort Ancient people. As a precaution, the Fort Ancient populations are also compared with several geographically adjacent populations to determine the possibility of an admixture of traits between the peoples.

THEORETICAL ASPECTS

When one attempts a broad study of a physical population based on their archaeological background, he is immediately faced with the problem of delimiting an archaeological population. But this may readily be done by grouping the skeletal material according to association with particular assemblages of artifacts. The geographical limitations of an archaeological population are established in a similar manner. If different populations resemble each other in a number of diagnostic characteristics, one is justified in combining them into varietal groupings. Temporal boundaries are defined in terms of differences found in the cultural materials at different stratigraphic levels and from Carbon-14 dating of specific time periods within the complex. Both temporal and spacial delimitation thus provide the framework for the recognition of biophyletic relationships of the population. The

INTRODUCTION

skeletal remains of a specific culture are assumed to constitute an inbreeding population which may be homozygous for a cluster of characteristics and thus form a recognizable stabilized entity. Only after analyzing the physical characteristics of the available remains and comparing the results with other delimitable populations can one identify individuals as being representative of a particular archaeological population or assignable to a well-defined tribal grouping.

Since one purpose of this report is the selection, identification, and evaluation of physical traits having diagnostic phyletic significance for the group rather than the noting of human variability or whether racial groupings are identifiable, attention must be given to the selection of diagnostic traits—traits that have historic meaning at a particular level of differentiation. The premise is that these traits and combinations thereof will best reflect the genetic continuity of the population in accordance with other lines of evidence. Such factors as selection, isolation, population size, and mixture with neighboring populations must be taken into consideration. Once the diagnostic, morphological and metrical traits have been delimited, the population may be compared with a number of contemporary peoples to demonstrate relationships to more ancient physical groups of known identity and to elucidate the history of varietal differentiation.

When attempting to identify an archaeological population, the investigator must of necessity utilize the morphological and metrical data of the skeletal remains available to him. The morphological characteristics serve as basic units since they more readily express the features typical of the group. The metrical dimensions primarily yield data on size rather than form, and the indicial units pertain exclusively to proportions, eliminating the size factor. However, if the morphological, metrical, and indicial traits are used together, and significant correlations between them are noted, the population may be accurately described and identified in terms of trait combinations unique to it. Since all physical traits have a hereditary basis and are modified to varying degrees, it must be emphasized that combinations of traits, rather than individual traits, serve to delimit and identify a group.

STATISTICAL METHODOLOGY

Statistical evaluations are made on approximately 1000 crania, both males and females, of the Fort Ancient Aspect and on a large number of ancestral and related populations of the eastern

United States. The comparisons are made by using Student's "t" test, a statistical device for determining significant differences between small populations and an important step in evaluating which traits would provide the most definitive information if more precise analyses were desired. The assessment of population distance and, inferentially, the problem of local differentiation versus hybridization is given in terms of t-ratios and t-probabilities. An estimate of population distance is obtained from the ratio of significant differences found in the total number of variables for each measurement and index, and is expressed as a coefficient of population distance. Although the coefficients are based on a continuum, they are distributed proportionally in index classes to indicate near identity, close relationship, moderate relationship, and unrelatedness. The different populations are examined in terms of this scale to determine which ones can be combined into larger groupings.

The comparisons are made on three levels of differentiation—an intrafocus, an interfocus, and a varietal level. At the first and second levels, comparisons are made of unit traits, i.e., of the means of the individual traits and indices. However, on the third level, comparisons are made of coefficients, in which case all significant unit traits are treated as a single group. Comparisons at the varietal level are correlated with a scale of nine similar coefficients that, according to G. Neumann (n.d.), are valid for American Indians on the varietal level, see Table 4 in Appendix B. Thus, Fort Ancient groups that can be pooled are tested to determine whether any of the coefficients of population distance attain a varietal magnitude. On a continental scope, the varietal values range from 28 to 74 for the populations used in this study. However, the range of coefficients is valid only for American Indian groups and only on a varietal level; hence, the coefficients must be interpreted in light of the archaeological history of each sample. It is essential to keep this interpretation in mind since some comparisons may be of varieties from quite different time levels, whereas other comparisons may involve two contemporaneous groups (or varieties) that have arisen from hybridization. In effect, coefficients that exceed the value 66 may not necessarily reflect the true nature of varietal relationship. As in the coefficient of racial likeness, the coefficient of relatedness (Table 5) used in this report is meaningful only within a given range and in comparisons of series of related varieties.

THE MATERIAL

The cranial material used in the statistical analyses represent the archaeological population of the Fort Ancient Aspect. During the time that Griffin (1943) was gathering the archaeological data for his report, Georg K. Neumann of Indiana University was collecting the physical data on the skeletons associated with the archaeological remains of the aspect. Since the total skeletal sample recovered from the aspect was very large and since satisfactory statistical tools were not developed until recently, a comprehensive analysis of the physical traits of the people has not, until now, been attempted. Even today such an analysis is feasible only when using computerized facilities. There are a total of 732 individuals in the aspect sample, distributed among the four foci as follows: Baum 40, Feurt 71, Anderson 118, and Madisonville 503. Some components were excavated more completely than others, and some sites are still yielding both skeletal and artifactual material.

The aspect sample contains adults of both sexes, most of whom are within the age range of 25 to 45 years. No attempt has been made in this particular study to establish specific age categories, nor has attention been given to traits that exhibit pathological characteristics, as was done by Hooton (1920:114-15) with the people of the Madisonville component. However, careful note is made of the presence, type, and degree of artificial cranial deformation, as this necessitates particular adjustive procedures to insure the comparability of groups when tracing genetic continuities. Of the various types of cranial deformation noted by G. Neumann (1942:306-10), type 4, or occipital flattening, is most common among the Fort Ancient people; and as Hooton (1920:85-86) found at Madisonville, there is usually only a slight to moderate degree of flatness present. There are some individuals who exhibit deformation resulting from posthumous earth pressure, but they represent a very small percentage of the total population. It is seldom the case that deformation caused by earth pressure or cultural practices eliminates the use of all data on the individual from the sample; however, it may be necessary to omit certain metrical and morphological recordings which are affected by the deformation. Occasionally only limited information may be obtained from some individuals, due to the poor preservation of the remains, acid soil conditions, or postmortem breakage. Conditions such as these account for the absence or paucity of available data from some components in the aspect.

II

DESCRIPTION OF MAJOR PHYSICAL VARIETIES
IN THE EASTERN UNITED STATES

THE Fort Ancient data will be compared with a number of physical varieties from the eastern United States in order to evaluate phyletic relationships with the former and to denote possible varietal admixture within the different foci of the Fort Ancient Aspect. Before beginning the comparative exercises, the metrical and morphological features of the varieties are examined; the geographical distribution of these varietal groups during historic times is presented in Figure 2.

LENID

The Lenid variety is the distinctive physical type found in the Great Lakes Middle Archaic archaeological levels and persists in populations of the Early and Middle Hopewellian periods, see Plate I, Appendix F. Lenid is the predominant physical form in the northeastern Woodland area, and is found in many of the Eastern Algonquian-speaking people, e.g., the Delaware (G. Neumann, 1960:66-68). Living during the Archaic-Early Woodland period, the Old Copper population of Wisconsin and the Black Sand population of Illinois display typically Lenid features, and are used here to exemplify the variety.

In general, Lenid male crania can be described as being large and rather longheaded with a cranial module of 153.1 mm, cranial length of 187.2 mm, cranial breadth of 136.2 mm, and a cranial height of 137.4 mm (Table 6).[1] These measurements yield a cranial index of 71.90 and a length-height index of 72.53 (Table 7), demonstrating dolichocephaly and a moderately high cranial vault. The morphological observations (Table 22) indicate that the crania are long ovoid in form and exhibit a large amount of robusticity with correspondingly large brow ridges,

---

[1] Unless otherwise noted, all tables referred to in this chapter will be found in Appendix B beginning on page 131.

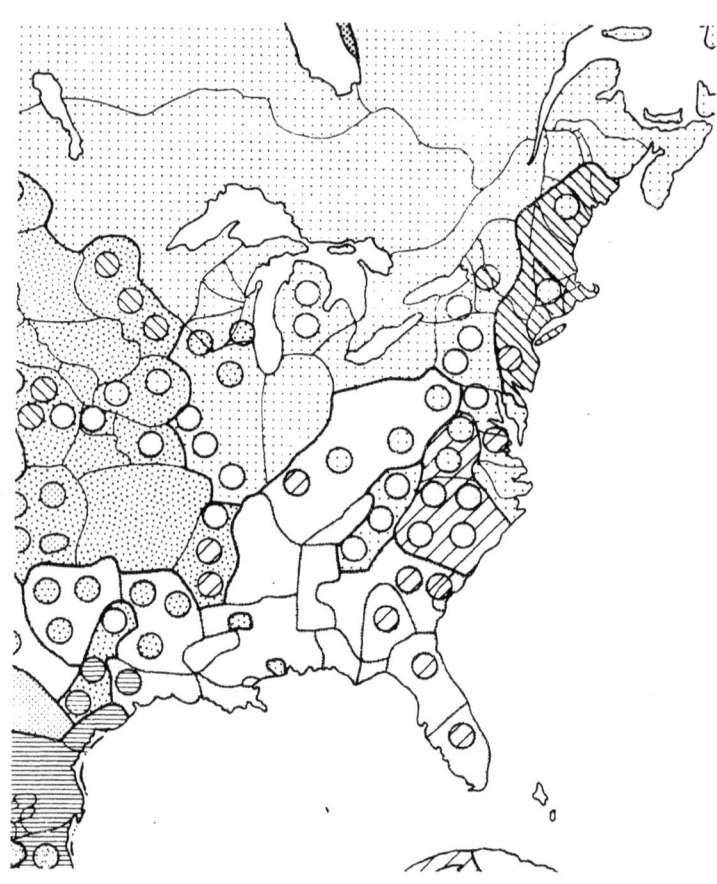

VARIETIES OF AMERICAN INDIANS

THE HISTORIC PERIOD

PALEOAMERIND SERIES
- Lenid
- Iswanid

META-AMERIND SERIES
- Ilinid
- Dakotid
- Muskogid

DESCRIPTION OF MAJOR PHYSICAL VARIETIES

large mastoids, and a high degree of muscular relief. The frontal sloping, frontal breadth, and parietal eminences are in the medium range, with the occiput being low and narrow in placement. There is a frequent occurrence of median cresting of the frontal region and of lambdoid flattening, and a degree of sagittal elevation tends to be present in all skulls (Robbins, n.d.).

The facial size of the male is from medium to large with a total facial height of 129 mm and an upper facial height of 75 mm. These dimensions, plus the facial breadth of 140 mm, reveal a long and rather broad face. The size and projection of the zygomatic bones tend to fall in the medium range. Orbital shape varies from oblong to square to rhomboid, with a small to medium amount of inclination. The nasal height of 57 mm is rather large while the 25 mm width is moderate. The nasal profile is slightly concavo-convex with the dimensions of the nasal root breadth and height giving the impression that the nose is straight with a high bridge. The Lenid males display a submedium amount of total prognathism, but tend to have a medium to large mandible, a large amount of gonial angle eversion, a neutral amount of chin projection, and a bilateral chin form.

The Lenid female series is small in number and may not, therefore, represent the typical Lenid female as closely as might be desired. On the other hand, the standard deviations of the mean measurements and indices indicate a fairly high degree of physical homogeneity among the individuals in the series. Many of the cranial measurements of the females closely approximate the male dimensions except in instances of size, which might be due to sexual dimorphism.

In appearance and in dimension, the Lenid females have a fairly long and large head, as can be noted in the mean measurements of a cranial length of 181.2 mm, a breadth of 135.2 mm, and a height of 135.0 mm (Table 8). A cranial index of 74.63 and a length-height index of 74.56 are derived from the measurements (Table 9), and indicate a slightly dolichocephalic skull with a moderately high cranial vault. Morphologically (Table 23), the crania tend to have an ovoid to pentagonal vault form and show a medium to large amount of robusticity. As in most female crania, they have only a trace or small amount of brow ridge development and a small to medium mastoid size. The slope of the frontal region tends to be slight and rather narrow, or to have some anterior bulging, but the sagittal region shows a moderate amount of elevation, which is characteristic of the high-vaulted Lenids. The parietal eminences of the females are of a medium size and are emphasized by the flatness of the temporal region. There is a pronounced amount of occipital curvature and naturally-occurring lambdoidal flattening. The occipital condyles are largely elevated, demonstrating the complete absence of platybasia.

Facial size of the Lenid female crania is slightly smaller than is found in their male counterparts. A total facial height of 113.4 mm, upper facial height of 69.6 mm, and a total facial breadth of 133.0 mm denote a medium to long face of moderate width, i.e., total facial index of 85.33, upper facial index of 52.36, and midfacial index of 72.96. The zygomatic bones are of moderate size and display a medium amount of lateral projection but only a small amount of anterior projection. The orbits tend to be squarely shaped with little, if any, inclination from the horizontal axis. The nasal height of 49.2 mm and breadth of 23.2 mm yield an index of 47.28, signifying a nasal size of slightly mesorrhine proportions. The height of the nasal bridge is rather low but the breadth is moderately developed; in profile, the nose has a slightly concavo-convex form. There is little midfacial prognathism in the female crania, but a slight to moderate amount of alveolar prognathism is present. The mandibles tend to be of moderate proportions with variable chin forms and degrees of projection but with little eversion of the gonial angle.

It must not be assumed that the Lenid variety remained physically unchanged through time in all geographic areas. G. Neumann (1960:68) observes that during the latter part of the Middle Woodland period, the Lenid populations in the southern margins of the Great Lakes display a gradual change in a number of traits, out of which evolved the Ilinid variety of the Late Woodland and Upper Mississippi periods. It is this latter physical variety that is most often represented in Central Algonquian-speakers such as the Miami and Menominee and in some Iroquoian-speakers like the Seneca.

ILINID

In this report the Ilinid variety is represented by series of male and female crania from Oakwood Mound of the Fisher Focus of northern Illinois, see Plate II, Appendix F. The males tend to have a rather large skull as is demonstrated by the following mean dimensions: length, 181.7 mm; breadth, 140.1 mm; height, 142.0 mm; and cranial module, 154.6 (Tables 10 and 11). The cranial vault is ovoid to ellipsoid in shape. Muscularity, brow ridge size, frontal slope, frontal breadth, size of parietal eminences, and occipital position all tend to be in the medium range

DESCRIPTION OF MAJOR PHYSICAL VARIETIES 13

in degree of development. There is little sagittal cresting, and flattening of the lambdoid region ranges from a small to a medium degree of expression (Table 22).

The typical male Ilinid face displays only slightly more than an average degree of robusticity and appears to be of moderate size relative to the braincase. The facial dimensions demonstrate this moderate tendency: total facial height, 124.1 mm; upper facial height, 73.6 mm; bizygomatic breadth, 140.3 mm. The zygomatic arches display a moderate amount of anterior projection but a medium to pronounced degree of lateral projection. The orbits are oblong to square in shape with a submedium to medium degree of inclination of the transverse axis. The nasal form is described as being mesorrhine, resulting from a mean nasal breadth of 26.4 mm and a mean nasal height of 53.6 mm. The breadth of the nasal root and the nasal bridge tends to be medium in proportion, while the height of the nasal bridge ranges from medium to high in degree of elevation. There tends to be a medium to submedium amount of facial prognathism. The mandible is inclined to be medium to large in size with a narrow bilateral chin form but with only a small amount of gonial eversion.

The Ilinid female crania are moderately large and broad with a fairly high cranial vault as revealed by the following dimensions and indices: cranial length, 174.0 mm; breadth, 135.5 mm; height, 133.3 mm; cranial module, 147.6; cranial index, 77.93; and length-height index, 76.60 (Tables 12 and 13). The cranial vault usually has an ovoid form with a slight to moderate amount of frontal sloping, little sagittal elevation, and varying degrees of lambdoid flattening (Table 23). Brow ridges range from a slight to medium size with little glabellar prominence. The frontal region is of intermediate width and displays small to medium frontal eminences, while the parietal eminences range from medium to large in size. The temporal region displays varying amounts of fullness, but the mastoid processes tend to be small or moderate in size. There is a pronounced to medium amount of occipital curvature with a medium to large amount of elevation of the occipital condyles. In other words, the rear of the skull has a Lenid-like morphology.

The female Ilinid face is slightly broad, as demonstrated by the facial dimensions and indices: total facial height, 112.0 mm; upper facial height, 66.7 mm; total facial breadth, 131.7 mm; total facial index, 85.15; and upper facial index, 50.72. The females have small zygomatic bones which show some lateral projection but little anterior projection. Orbit shape may be oblong, rhomboid, or square, with a small to moderate amount of inclination from the transverse axis. The nose tends to be slightly concavo-convex in profile with a root height and breadth of small to moderate proportions and a moderate development in the height and breadth of the nasal bridge. There is little midfacial prognathism and only a slight amount of alveolar prognathism. The mandible tends to be small in size and have a medium or narrow bilateral chin form with varying degrees of chin projection—negative, neutral, small, medium, or large amounts of anterior projection of the chin.

G. Neumann (1952:24; 1960:68) has demonstrated that the Ilinids (previously called Lenapid) are metrically distinct from the phyletically earlier Otamids, Lenids, and Iswanids. However, there are fewer metrical differences noted when a comparison is made between the Ilinids and the Muskogids, although morphological differences are readily apparent in the two varieties. The spacial and temporal distribution of the series utilized in the comparison, i.e., Spoon River focus and Oakwood Mound, may have permitted intermixture of the two groups.

ISWANID

The Indian Knoll population is used as the type series to designate the Iswanid variety, see Plate III, Appendix F. This population is representative of a preceramic Archaic shell mound culture of the Ohio Valley and is phyletically older than the more recent occupants of the region (Snow, 1948; G. Neumann, 1952:18-19).

In evaluating the physical features of the Iswanid variety, it is found that the male skull is rather small as the following dimensions indicate: cranial capacity, 1367.5 cc; length, 176.9 mm; breadth, 134.8 mm; height, 137.8 mm (Tables 14 and 15). The cranial vault is high relative to the length of the skull and borders on mesocrany. The vault tends to be ovoid in form and displays a medium amount of muscularity (Table 22). The brow ridges are small to medium in size; the frontal breadth is small; and there is a medium amount of frontal sloping. There is a slight degree of sagittal cresting and a medium degree of development of the parietal eminences. There is only a slight amount of flattening of the lambdoid region, with a medium high positioning of the occiput.

The face lacks robusticity and is small relative to the braincase, as demonstrated by the facial dimensions: total facial height, 118.0 mm; upper facial height, 70.8 mm; bizygomatic

DESCRIPTION OF MAJOR PHYSICAL VARIETIES   15

breadth, 135.8 mm. The zygomatic arches tend to be of medium size and display a moderate amount of anterior projection, but they exhibit a pronounced amount of lateral projection. The orbital shape tends to be oblong, although some individuals have square-shaped orbits, with a slight degree of inclination from the horizontal axis. Nasal dimensions tend to be small, e.g., height, 51.2 mm; breadth, 23.9 mm. The root and bridge dimensions are moderate, giving a leptorrhine to mesorrhine nasal form. Facial prognathism ranges from submedium to medium. The mandible tends to be medium in size with a bilateral chin form and a small to medium amount of gonial eversion.

No comparative series has yet been assembled from the Iswanid Indian Knoll females, so information regarding them is based on the data presented by Snow (1948). In brief, Snow found that the females displayed a tendency toward dolichocephaly, having a rather ovoid head shape and a high cranial vault. The frontal region has a medium to small breadth relative to the cranial vault, and the brow ridges tend to be small and divided. A moderate to small amount of sagittal elevation is noted, and the amount of lambdoid flattening ranges from moderate to absent. Parietal eminences are of a moderate to small size while the temporal region displays a small amount of fullness. Mastoid processes tend to be moderately developed. The female face is medium to large in size and displays some degree of robustness. The orbits tend to be rhomboid or oblong in shape with a small to moderate amount of inclination. The nose is concavo-convex in profile and has a low root height with a medium to small root breadth. The bridge of the nose is low to medium in height but moderate to large in breadth. The zygomatic bones tend to be of a moderate to large size with a comparable lateral projection and a small to medium amount of anterior projection. Midfacial and alveolar prognathism are rather pronounced as is the amount of total facial prognathism. The mandible is of medium proportions with a medium to narrow bilateral chin form and a neutral to small amount of anterior chin projection.

The Iswanid variety presents a number of metrical and morphological differences when compared with other varieties of the eastern United States, and it is an easily identifiable variety in the Ohio Valley.

DAKOTID

The Dakotid variety is included as a comparative series in order to examine the possibility of there having been Dakotid influences in the Ohio Valley. G. Neumann (1952:29-31) considers the Dakotid, or Lakotid as he originally termed them, to be of trihybrid origin, stemming from a mixture of Lenid, Walcolid (Muskogid), and Deneid characteristics, see Plate IV, Appendix F. He proposes that this secondary variety has evolved as a result of the distributional pattern of the Plains groups.

The Dakotid male skull is medium in size with a length of 178.3 mm, a breadth of 145.6 mm, and a height of 131.0 mm (Tables 16 and 17). The low dimension of the basion-bregma height is a result of the flattened cranial base, platybasia, a diagnostic trait of the Deneid variety. The cranial capacity of the Dakotid averages around 1490 cc with a cranial module of 151.7, suggesting a fairly high braincase. The cranial vault tends to have an ovoid form, but a substantial number of individuals exhibit the birsoid shape and all individuals display a medium to large amount of robusticity (Table 22). The brow ridge size and frontal breadth dimension range from small to large, and a medium to pronounced degree of frontal sloping is present. There is usually little sagittal elevation, with the parietal eminences occupying a medium position on the parietal bones. There is seldom any lambdoidal flattening, but due to the presence of platybasia, the occiput is often broad and in a low to medium position.

The male face is rather distinctive and appears to be large and rugged due to the high, large, flat zygomatic bones. However, the size of the face is moderate, with a total facial height of 124.9 mm, an upper facial height of 75.6 mm, and a bizygomatic breadth of 141.3 mm. The orbits have a rhomboid shape with a medium to pronounced angle of declination of the horizontal axis. The nasal region of the Dakotid is a diagnostic feature of the variety in that it displays an average nasal height of 54.0 mm and a breadth of 26.1 mm with only a slight nasal depression but with a high to very high nasal root height and a medium nasal root breadth; the nasal bridge is also high and is usually narrow to medium in breadth. The nasal bones tend to be very large and straight or slightly concavo-convex when viewed in profile. The face displays only a small degree of prognathism. The mandible appears rather massive with a wide bilateral chin form and a neutral to medium amount of gonial eversion.

The Dakotid female series, though small in number, is fairly homogeneous in cranial morphology and metrical dimensions. The skull is moderate in size with a slightly mesocephalic shape noted by the following dimensions and indices: length, 175.2 mm; breadth, 134.5 mm; height, 127.5 mm; cranial index, 76.80; and

DESCRIPTION OF MAJOR PHYSICAL VARIETIES

length-height index, 72.78 (Tables 18 and 19). Like the Dakotid males, the females exhibit some platybasia, which is reflected in the lower height and basion-porion dimensions. The vault tends to be ovoid or pentagonoid in form and of a moderate height (Table 23). The crania exhibit little robusticity and only a trace or moderate amount of brow ridge development and glabellar prominence. The breadth of the frontal region is rather narrow, but there is a moderate amount of frontal sloping. Varying degrees of sagittal elevation are found, parietal eminences being small to moderately developed. Fullness of the temporal region ranges from small to large with small to medium development of the mastoid region. There is little flattening of the lambdoid region, but there is a moderate to pronounced amount of curvature of the occiput with slight to moderate elevation of the condyles.

The face of the Dakotid female, unlike that of the male, is long but rather narrow, as indicated by the following dimensions: total facial height, 122.2 mm; upper facial height, 74.8 mm; and total facial breadth, 132.2 mm. The large, flat zygomatic bones of the male are not prominent in the female, which results in a narrow, or leptene, face for the latter, i.e., an upper facial index of 56.69. The orbits have rhomboid or square shapes and display a small to moderate angle of inclination from the horizontal axis. The zygomatic bones tend to be small or moderate in size with varying amounts of anterior projection and usually a moderate amount of lateral projection. However, some females display a rather pronounced amount of lateral zygomatic projection. The nasal region of the female face is morphologically only slightly less distinctive than that of the male. The mean nasal height of 51.8 mm and breadth of 24.3 mm yield an index of 46.99 in the female, which is somewhat narrower or more leptorrhine than the typically mesorrhine form of the male. The nasal root tends to be narrow or moderate in breadth with a moderate height and little, if any, depression. The bridge also tends to be moderately developed in height and breadth, and both portray a straight or slightly concavo-convex nasal profile. The face has little midfacial prognathism, but some individuals display a moderate amount of alveolar prognathism. The females tend to have small mandibles with narrow to wide bilateral chin forms and negative, neutral, or large amounts of chin projection. The variation of chin form and projection is reflected in the small to medium amount of development of the pterygoid attachment processes on the median side of the gonial angle and in some of the slightly everted gonial angles.

In some metrical traits and many morphological traits, the Dakotid appear to be closely related to the Deneid variety; but when combinations of the traits are evaluated, it is found that a number of the Dakotid values vary toward the means of Lenid series. The distinctive features of the Dakotid variety are readily apparent when viewed among crania of the Deneid and Lenid series.

MUSKOGID

Although evidence from the Modoc Rock Shelter in southwestern Illinois indicates that the Muskogid (Walcolid)[2] physical variety evolved during the Middle Archaic period from an earlier Iswanid variety, it is more typically representative of the Middle Mississippi archaeological horizon during late prehistoric times, see Plate V, Appendix F. Following the typology put forth by G. Neumann (1952:21-23) and H. Neumann (n.d.), undeformed male crania from the Spoon River Focus in central Illinois are used to denote the Muskogid variety. A comparative Muskogid female series is unavailable for inclusion in this report.

The Muskogid male skull tends to be rather large, as is indicated by the following dimensions: length, 181.1 mm; breadth, 139.5 mm; height, 144.1 mm (Table 20). The series has a mean cranial module of 154.9. The braincase tends to be high relative to its length and may be classed as mesocephaly, with a cranial index of 77.07 (Table 21). It should be noted that a significant incidence of varying degrees of artificial cranial deformation among Muskogid populations is present. Efforts were made to eliminate any crania displaying deformation, and it is possible that some individuals exhibiting a slight degree of natural deformation may also have been eliminated in making the selection. The cranial index and cranial height are raised slightly if the doubtful crania are included. In either case, the cranial vault displays a short ovoid form with a medium to pronounced degree of robusticity (Table 22). The brow ridges and frontal breadth display a medium degree of development. There is a slight to medium amount of frontal sloping and little, if any, sagittal elevation. The parietal eminences are in a medium position with little or no flattening of the lambdoid region, and the occiput is situated in a medium high position.

The male Muskogid face is rather distinctive in that it appears to be large for the braincase. Facial dimensions are

---

[2] In this report the Muskogid term is used since it more fully reflects the major linguistic affiliation of this physical variety.

DESCRIPTION OF MAJOR PHYSICAL VARIETIES

large, e.g., total facial height, 125.7 mm; upper facial height, 75.6 6 mm; bizygomatic breadth, 139.6 mm, but facial indices tend to fall within the medium size range. The zygomatic bones range from medium to large in size and in anterior and lateral projection. This helps to emphasize the rugged appearance of the face. The shape of the orbits is usually rhomboid or square with a small to medium degree of inclination from the horizontal axis. Nasal form tends to fall in the range of mesorrhine with a length of 53.7 mm and a breadth of 26.2 mm. The nasal root and bridge dimensions are in the medium range. The face displays a submedium to medium amount of prognathism, while the mandible tends to be medium to large in size. The chin usually displays a narrow to medium bilateral development, but there is seldom any gonial eversion of the mandible.

If the metric data of the Muskogid series are compared with those of a Lenid series, distinct differences are not apparent; but when morphological observations are included in the comparison, the diagnostic traits of each series are more readily revealed. The Lenids tend to have a somewhat elliptical cranial vault while the vault of Muskogids has a broad ovoid or spherical form. Additional differences are noted in the larger, broader face and greater chin prominence of the Muskogids. A greater amount of sagittal elevation and lambdoid flattening plus greater prominence and lower positioning of the occiput also serve to distinguish the Muskogid variety.

III

DESCRIPTION OF SKELETAL MATERIAL BY FOCUS

THE archaeology of the Fort Ancient Aspect is widely known from the work of Griffin (1943); hence, reiteration of the material is believed to be unnecessary except for purposes of identification of sites or foci or to stress unique features of particular populations. Many of the sites displaying evidence of the Fort Ancient culture were exposed as land was being cultivated by the early white settlers, and annual plowing has gradually exposed and destroyed upper levels of a number of prehistoric mounds, villages, and cemeteries since that time. The early settlers were most often interested in, and sought, the artifactual material of exposed sites, so it is impossible to evaluate the number of burials destroyed in the process of searching for "relics." Consequently, the number of individuals excavated from each site and available for study is seldom indicative of the total burial population. In some cases, many of the burials were of children of different ages; in other instances, breakage, warpage, or deterioration of the skeletal remains resulted from the method of interment, earth pressure, or composition of the soil, respectively. The remains from each site are given metrical and morphological descriptions in order to evaluate the degree of homogeneity to be found within the various foci and to determine interfoci relationships. Statistical procedures are given in Appendix A.

THE BAUM FOCUS

The Baum mound and village site is the largest single component within the focus (Griffin, 1943:36). The attention given the site has been due mainly to its geographic proximity to a large Hopewellian earthwork located southwest of the Baum site. Baum is located on the first gravel terrace of the Paint Creek valley in Ross County, Ohio, where the creek flows in a northeasterly direction to the Scioto River south of Chillicothe, and it is the only Fort Ancient site found in that immediate vicinity.

There is some disagreement between Griffin and Mills (1906: 49) as to the archaeologist in charge of the excavation conducted by the Bureau of American Ethnology in 1894, but according to the the 12th Annual BAE Report (Thomas, 1894), Mr. Middleton directed the work at the time a circular structure, 36 feet in diameter, was found on the ground surface of the mound. Superimposed upon this structure, but separated from it by layers of sand and burned clay, was a second structure which was similar to the former but which contained an inner circle. Such a structure is an unusual feature in a Fort Ancient site. Of the 17 burials found within the two circular entities, 16 were in an extended position and 1 was interred in a flexed position. Grave goods of pottery, shell, bone, and stone were found with 7 individuals with 2 of the 7 being interred in a wood structure.

Additional skeletal material was recovered from the village during the excavations by Mills in 1899 and 1903. A total of 127 burials, of which 74 were less than 16 years of age, were found in what Mills terms "family groups." It appears that the village site had been erected between the burial grounds and an area containing numerous storage pits. Most of the burials removed by Mills were interred in an extended position with an east or northeast orientation and were usually accompanied with grave goods. One individual had a sandstone slab placed beneath the head, and a second person displayed a copper and shell necklace.

Mills believed that the Baum village exhibited a cultural assemblage that was quite similar to that of the Gartner village site along the Scioto River and to the Fort Ancient and other sites along the Miami River. He maintained that the resemblances supported the proposal that at one time a people sharing a common culture had lived throughout the valleys of central and southern Ohio. For convenience, he called this population the Fort Ancient culture. However, he erroneously placed the Fort Ancient culture at an earlier time period than the Hopewell occupation, since he felt that the artifactual superiority of the latter suggested higher levels of achievement and, hence, were more recent in time. Griffin resolves the temporal problem of the protohistoric Fort Ancient population in his description of the artifactual remains of the Baum component (1943:36-47). The flint artifacts, mainly arrow points, spear points, and knives, are of the triangular shape that is characteristic of the Fort Ancient culture. Some notched and stemmed points were found in the site which seemed to be atypical of Fort Ancient but which were included in the artifactual array. Most of the stone implements

DESCRIPTION OF SKELETAL MATERIAL BY FOCUS   23

consisted of a number of celts, various sorts of hammerstones, some mortars and grinding stones, and a few black slate hoes. Seventeen discoidals are reported to have come from the site, with one displaying the uncommon feature of being made of pottery. Many articles were fashioned from deer and elk antlers—arrow points and larger projectile points, flaking tools, scrapers, and game counters. Bone ornaments in the form of pendants and beads were found in the village area, but the latter were most often recovered from burials. Shell hoes, spoons, knives, and various ornaments have been recovered, with one of the sea shell gorgets showing some similarity to the masklike form found further south. Most of the pottery is what Griffin designates as Baum Cord-marked and Baum Incised types. The most distinctive features of the wares are found in the lug and strap handles and in the surface decorations.

Approximately eighty percent of the cultural material found in the Baum component is also found at the Gartner site in the same focus. However, there are material traits that are unique to the Baum component. It is the only site within the focus that contains any items fashioned from copper. Pipes are found at the other components of the focus, but only Baum displays a wide variety of these items, some of which indicate southern influences.

No radiocarbon samples have been obtained from the Baum component, but dates are available from more recently excavated sites which have been placed in the Baum focus. Two dates have been obtained from the Graham Village Site in Hocking County, near Logan, Ohio, (McKenzie, 1967:63-97). This site is considered to be among the earliest of the Fort Ancient manifestations, with a radiocarbon date of A.D. 1180 ± 145 years from a charcoal sample recovered from a pit about one meter below the surface of the earth. A second date of A.D. 1665 ± 220 years was obtained from a fire hearth about 30 to 35 cm below the surface from which Baum Focus pottery was recovered. McKenzie tends to reject the latter date on the basis of the absence of Madisonville traits and lack of shell tempering in the pottery. He reports the recovery of shell-tempered sherds bearing some resemblance to the Feurt Incised wares of the Feurt Focus; but most of the Graham Village pottery is of the Baum Cord-marked type, with grit tempering. Only one copper item, a rolled copper bead, was found in the site. There are no skeletal remains available from the site which might contribute information regarding the physical characteristics of the people or their foci affiliation.

The skeletal material from the Baum component used in this report is from the collection at the National Museum. The adult population consists of 17 males and 5 females, whose states of preservation range from fair to good. A few of the remains are in such a poor state of preservation that only limited information is obtainable from them. Most of the males and all of the females display metrical and morphological traits that are somewhat characteristic of the Ilinid physical variety, see Plate VI A, B in Appendix F. Crania of both sexes are examined in this report, and since cranial deformation is a significant factor to be considered in the Fort Ancient peoples, the crania of the Baum Focus have been separated into undeformed and deformed groups. The undeformed males tend to have rather large skulls, as can be observed from the mean dimensions listed in Table 24 and the indicial ratios of Table 25[3]—cranial length, 182.0 mm; breadth, 138.8 mm; height, 145.0 mm; and cranial module of 155.2. These dimensions and indices are somewhat different in the deformed crania of Tables 26 and 27, e.g., cranial length, 172.2 mm; breadth, 145.0 mm; height, 137.0 mm; and cranial module, 151.4. Dimensional changes of this sort are to be expected in crania exhibiting simple occipital deformation. However, the deformation is not so great that it changes the predominantly ovoid shape of the cranial vault as shown in Table 46. There is also much similarity in the morphological features of the degrees of muscularity (medium to large) and slope of the frontal region (medium). Divergent tendencies are found in the undeformed and deformed cranial width of the frontal region, sagittal elevation, temporal fullness, occipital curvature, lambdoid flattening, and condyle elevation, all of which would be affected by deformation.

The face appears to be of moderate proportions as observed by the mean dimensions of a total facial height, 126.0 mm; upper facial height, 76.0 mm; and total facial breadth, 143.1 mm, for the undeformed crania, contrasted with a mean total facial height of 126.0 mm; upper facial height of 75.8 mm; and total facial breadth of 140.3 mm for the deformed crania. The narrower facial breadth of the deformed group is unexpected since this is one dimension readily affected by occipital deformation, but the biangular and bicondylar dimensions also suggest a narrower face since each is within a 2 mm range of the undeformed dimensions. It is felt that these dimensions reflect the small degree of deformation of these crania, and it may be that selection of the deformed crania was too rigorous.

Orbital dimensions of the undeformed and deformed crania

---

[3] Unless otherwise noted, all tables referred to in this chapter will be found in Appendix C beginning on page 177.

DESCRIPTION OF SKELETAL MATERIAL BY FOCUS

are nearly identical, e.g., height, 35.2 mm and 34.8 mm; breadth, mf., 43.1 mm and 43.0 mm; breadth, d, 41.1 mm and 41.0 mm, respectively. Orbital shape and inclination of the two groups are not identical, but a high percentage of the individuals have square orbits with only a slight inclination from the horizontal axis.

The two groups display much similarity in the nasal features of a medium root height and breadth and bridge breadth, although some divergence is noted in the bridge height, which ranges from a medium to high degree of elevation. The nasal dimensions of breadth, height, and subtense of nasal arc reflect the homogeneity of the undeformed and deformed crania.

Although the Baum female sample is small, the crania are, like the males, separated into undeformed and deformed categories. Only one individual lacks a moderate amount of occipital deformation and, except for the dimensions affected by the deformation, her cranial features are quite similar to the other females (see Tables 28, 29, 30, and 31). The undeformed female has a fairly long, narrow head but the vault is less high than that found in the deformed females—undeformed: cranial length, 180.0 mm; breadth, 136.0 mm; height, 130.0 mm; and cranial index, 75.56—deformed: cranial length, 160.8 mm; breadth, 144.8 mm; height, 137.2 mm; and cranial index, 90.04. However, there is close agreement between the two groups in dimensions of the facial, nasal, orbital, and mandibular regions of the skull. Morphologically, the female crania exhibit a small to moderate amount of muscularity; they have an ovoid vault form, little brow ridge development, and a frontal region that may be small to large in breadth and may be bulging or have a slight amount of slope (Table 47). The simple occipital deformation less severely affects the frontal breadth and slope, sagittal elevation, temporal fullness, lambdoid flattening, occipital curvature, and condyle elevation of the female crania than the males, but note must be taken of it. The female face is mesene, or of medium proportions, with a total facial height of 118.0 mm, upper facial height of 75.0 mm, total facial breadth of 140.8 mm, and with an upper facial index of 53.19 for the undeformed cranium and 53.30 for the deformed crania. The similarity in the upper facial index of the undeformed and deformed skulls is indicative of a narrower face in the deformed individuals rather than lack of influence of the occipital deformation revealed in the differences found in the degree of curvature of the occiput.

Dimensions and morphology of the orbit are also similar in the undeformed and deformed females, with an orbital height of about 34.0 mm and breadth, at maxillofrontale, of 44.0 mm.

Orbital shape tends to be square although one skull exhibits an ellipsoidal shape and a second skull has round orbits; all the skulls, however, show only a slight angle of inclination from the horizontal axis. The size of the zygomatic bones varies among the crania from small to large, but they project laterally to a large degree and anteriorally to a moderate degree.

While nasal dimensions are nearly identical in the undeformed and deformed females, nasal morphology reveals that the individuals do exhibit some variation. The nasal root tends to be moderate to high in height and small to large in breadth with only a slight depression, while the nasal bridge height may be low or high with a moderate bridge breadth. In profile, the nose appears straight in some individuals and slightly concavo-convex in others. None of the individuals display midfacial prognathism, but they do have a slight to medium amount of alveolar prognathism. The mandibles are small to moderate in size with an intermediate or median chin form and show a negative amount of anterior chin projection.

After examining the crania of the Baum component, even separating the deformed crania from the undeformed, it is apparent that all members belong to the same physical population and differ only in the cranial dimensions and morphological features that would be easily affected by deformation. The presence of the deformation need not imply a closer relationship to the more typical Fort Ancient populations, e.g., Madisonville, since simple occipital deformation is widespread among people throughout the Middle Ohio Valley. It is found in Ilinid populations from the Woodland period in southern Illinois and on into protohistoric times where some degree of occipital deformation is found among the Seneca.

The Gartner mound and village site is found on the high east bank of the Scioto River in Ross County, Ohio, approximately six miles north of Chillicothe. According to the stratigraphy of the component, the mound was constructed in three sections within the confines of the living area some time after the village was first occupied. Subsequent to the mound construction, the village first surrounded and then expanded outward from the mound (Mills, 1904:129-31). While it appears that most of the population were buried in the three sections of the mound, some individuals were placed within the village. On the basis of the artifactual remains, Mills maintains that the same population built both the mound and village (1904:130-47); but some of the burial practices raise the possibility of the site having been occupied by different people at different times or of contact between

DESCRIPTION OF SKELETAL MATERIAL BY FOCUS 27

two populations. Mills noted that section one in the mound was distinctly different from sections two and three, which closely resemble each other. Section one was constructed on top of an earlier habitation site by laying down a prepared clay platform, upon which were placed the cremated remains and associated grave goods of a great many individuals. Unburned animal bone, ornaments, and implements made of stone, bone, and shell were found intermingled with the cremated human remains. An examination of the earlier habitation site revealed no burials below the platform but disclosed refuse pits and artifacts which were similar to those found in the surrounding village. Three burials were found a few feet above the platform, apparently having been placed there prior to the construction of the next section. Section two contained burials above and below the original base line, but none were found on the base line itself. Several of the graves contained pieces of clay mixed with broken quartz pebbles and shell or clay surrounded by small river boulders placed in small niches near the head of the individual. This unusual practice was not found among the village burials. Most of the burials in section three of the mound were adults who had been placed below the original base line level.

Except for one individual, all of the mound burials had been interred in an extended position. The one exception, a flexed burial with no grave goods, was found at the edge of the mound in section two but was considered by Mills to be inclusive in the population on the basis of the artifactual remains in the immediate vicinity. He considers one burial in the upper levels of section two to be intrusive due to the soil disturbance above the burial.

The village burial area resembled that found at the Baum village site (Mills, 1904:181-89). The people tended to bury their dead in an extended position close to, but not within, their habitation area. No evidence of cremated remains was found in the village, except for some fragments in a large crematory. The presence of the crematory and of the cremated remains placed on the platform at the base of section one of the mound suggests that populations utilizing different burial practices occupied the site, but the time of occupation of the earlier group cannot be established from the existing cultural remains, which exhibit homogeneity throughout the site. The subfloor burial practice of Gartner appears to be a survival from the earlier Hopewell-Adena period, while cremation burials are quite characteristic of the Ohio Hopewellians. Griffin (1943:48-49) points out that some of the flint implements resemble types commonly found in

Tennessee-Cumberland Middle Mississippi sites. The ceramic complex of Gartner resembles that found at the Baum component, although some items of the former display variations in design and decoration that are reminiscent of Illinois and Wisconsin Woodland sites. There were several traits found at Gartner that had no counterparts at Baum. The subfloor mound burials are unique to Gartner in the Baum Focus, but this feature is found at the Feurt site in Scioto County, Ohio, and the Clay site in Nicholas County, Kentucky. Triangular points are present at Gartner but some of them display a wide base that is more frequently associated with Woodland sites in the Northeast. This unusual type of triangular point appears in only two other Fort Ancient sites, both of which are in the Anderson Focus. The only other traits present that suggest influence from the Northeast are the roller pestle and stone adze. An adze with a narrow poll is the single trait unique to Gartner in the Baum Focus that suggests influence from the south; the implement is also present at Fox Farm and the type site of the Madisonville Focus.

    The skeletal remains from the Gartner component examined for this report are, like the Baum series, from the National Museum collection. There are 12 males and 4 females in the series, ranging in preservation from poor (which applies to several) to good. Two of the males display some Muskogid physical features as do 2 of the females, but most of the Gartner population appear more closely related to the Ilinid physical variety and seem to be quite similar to the people of Baum component, see Plate VI C, D in Appendix F. The Gartner crania, like the Baum and all component populations used in this study, were separated into undeformed and deformed categories. The Gartner deformed series, though small, demonstrates that dimensions and observations affected by occipital deformation (and some earth pressure) i.e., dimensions of cranial length, breadth, and height and the cranial, breadth-height, and mean height indices, vary to some extent from the undeformed group, as may be observed in Tables 32 through 39. Similar variation is found in the morphology of the crania in the degree of frontal sloping, breadth of the frontal region, temporal fullness, occipital curvature and lambdoid flattening, see Table 46. In most of the male dimensions and observations, the Gartner deformed group closely resembles the Baum deformed group, and the undeformed Gartner group shows a significant correlation with the Baum undeformed series. However, the female crania from the two sites exhibit less uniformity in the dimensional and morphological traits, due to the presence of Muskogid physical characteristics in the small sample. The Gartner females have smaller, more brachycephalic skulls, e.g., cranial length, 169.0 mm; breadth, 136.0 mm; height 136.0 mm; cranial index, 80.50 for the undeformed group, and length, 159.0 mm; breadth, 151.0 mm; height, 138.0 mm; and cranial index, 94.97 for the deformed cranium. Less dimensional dissimilarity is noted in the facial regions of the two series, but the Gartner females tend to have shorter and broader noses and less development and projection of the zygomatic bones (Table 47). In the following chapter, the amount of physical similarity among the populations of the Baum Focus will be evaluated.

There is little information available on the Baldwin component, a small village with several refuse pits and five burials located on a minor tributary of the Hocking River a short distance northeast of Lancaster, Ohio, in Fairfield County (Griffin, 1943:54-56). One burial from this site was a child interred in an extended position and accompanied with unidentified grave goods. The remaining four burials were of adults who had been placed in flexed positions in individual graves in the bottom of an ash pit. Of these four burials, only that of a single female was available for study. From the account given by Moorhead (1897:165-275) of the distribution of flexed burials in the area and of the Late Woodland-early Fort Ancient admixture of traits found in sites more recently excavated, it is probable that the culture at the Baldwin site may have had some contact with cultures in the Northeast, and the female skull lends some support to that supposition.

The skull is undeformed and slightly mesocephalic with a high ovoid vault, having a length of 175.0 mm, breadth of 133.0 mm, height of 135.0 mm, cranial index of 76.00, and a length-height index of 77.14 (Tables 40, 41, and 47). The face is rather narrow, an upper facial index of 55.04, but the nose is moderately broad with a nasal index of 48.00. In morphology, the skull exhibits little muscularity and only a trace of brow ridge development. The frontal region is narrow with a slight amount of slope, a small median crest, and moderate eminence development. There is a small amount of sagittal elevation and temporal fullness, but a medium amount of natural lambdoid flattening and a pronounced degree of occipital curvature are present. The square-shaped orbits exhibit a moderate angle of inclination from the horizontal axis. The zygomatic bones are small but show a medium amount of lateral and anterior projection. The root of the nose is high and narrow while the bridge shows a moderate height and breadth development which presents a concave nasal profile. Midfacial prognathism is absent, and alveolar prognathism is slight. The mandible is small with a median chin form and a neutral amount of chin projection. In general, the Baldwin female looks somewhat like the Seneca females used as a comparative series in this report.

While Baldwin is a northern extension of the Baum Focus, most of the material culture is quite similar to the material found at the Baum site although not as plentiful. The only trait unique to Baldwin is a broken butterfly gorget which Griffin considers to be a non-Fort Ancient trait.

The Brush Creek component of the Baum Focus is found in Adams County, Ohio, as a part of the Serpent Mound complex. The Brush Creek name was given to the protohistoric Fort Ancient occupation to distinguish it from the earlier Adena occupation of the conical mound and adjoining village and of the Hopewellian effigy mound, Serpent Mound, to the north of the habitation and burial area (Griffin, 1943:64). The Fort Ancient occupation was found in the uppermost level of the Adena conical mound, and as far as is known, two intrusive burials were excavated from the area assigned to the Brush Creek site. Both were adult individuals, one male and one female, and were found on the north side of the conical mound; nothing is known of their burial positions or possible artifactual associations. The extent and diversity of the material culture from Brush Creek is not well-known, but the pottery fragments present are mainly Baum Cord-marked types, although two rim sherds resemble a cord-marked ware of the Anderson Focus.

The skeletal specimens from the site are stored in the Peabody Museum collection. The two available individuals are not accepted as representing an entire Fort Ancient component population, but it is worth noting that both the male and the female are in an excellent state of preservation and exhibit typically undeformed Muskogid physical features. The Muskogid affiliation is readily apparent in the male cranium in the dimensions of cranial length, 179.0 mm; breadth, 143.0 mm; and height, 138.0 mm, noted in Table 42, and in the cranial, breadth-height, and mean height indices of 79.89, 96.50 and 85.71, respectively, in Table 43. The Brush Creek female cranial dimensions of length, 172.0 mm; breadth, 140.0 mm; height, 141.0 mm and the cranial index of 81.40, breadth-height index of 100.71, and mean height index of 90.38 (Tables 44 and 45) are more typically found among people to the south who display the Muskogid physical type. It is more difficult to evaluate Muskogid tendencies in the cranial observations of single individuals, but when viewed in a table

DESCRIPTION OF SKELETAL MATERIAL BY FOCUS 31

containing the Baum and Gartner groups (Tables 46 and 47), the Muskogid features become more apparent.

In summary, most of the crania of the Baum Focus display physical features that are associated with Ilinid varietal groups to the north and west. Only the crania from the Brush Creek site exhibit the combination of traits which are typical of the more southern Muskogid variety. By comparing the populations of this focus with groups from adjacent foci and with varietal groupings, it will be possible to determine more definitive relationships.

THE FEURT FOCUS

The four components of the Feurt Focus represent the southeastern geographical extension of the Fort Ancient Aspect, and as is frequently the case in peripheral areas, there is a greater amount of variation in the artifactual material and in the burial manifestation of this focus.

The Feurt mounds and village site are situated on the east side of the Scioto River in Clay Township, Scioto County, a short distance north of the city of Portsmouth, Ohio. Mills (1922) noted that the occupants took advantage of their natural surroundings and placed the mounds and village on a projecting terrace approximately 40 feet above the river bottomland. Local residents have collected material from the surface of the site for many years, and Mills observed that some collections display a much wider variety of artifacts than were found below the plow line during his excavations.

Several unusual features are observed in the construction of the mounds and village and are also found in the artifactual remains. The existence of only a few refuse pits is not often found in a Fort Ancient site, but this is the situation at the Feurt site. Instead of burying their debris in the pits, or throwing it down the hillside, the occupants carried soil from the steep banks and covered the debris in and around their dwellings or "tepees," as Mills terms them. As a result, the present humus layer is from 6 inches to 4 feet above the original surface, and artifactual debris is found throughout the living area. Burials are found in the living area, as well as in three mounds which were constructed within the habitation area. Moorehead (1897:216) observes that the mounds were constructed of sand and gravel brought in from nearby locations; Griffin (1943:70) contends that the burial complex of this component tends to set the Feurt Focus apart from the other foci. In the Fort Ancient Aspect, extended burials are most numerous with an occasional fully flexed burial being found. At the Feurt component, only one of 345 burials removed from the three mounds is listed as being found in an extended position (Mills, 1922:307-30). However, an examination of a number of the burial photographs discloses that Mills does not distinguish between fully and partially flexed individuals as do many authors. Moorehead comments that the skeletons were usually found in the flexed position with no apparent directional orientation of the burials. He adds that in some cases several individuals were "on top of each other," but it is not known whether this refers to multiple burials or soil stratification. Both Griffin and Mills note the extreme scarcity of grave goods with most of the burials, and the fact that no burial was found to have an abundance of grave articles although the soil surrounding and covering the graves would often contain artifactual debris.

From the evidence presented by Mills, Moorehead, et al., there appear to have been slight differences in burial practices among the different mounds and between the mounds and village. Mound 1 was the smallest of the 3 mounds and contained 107 burials. It was constructed by placing the individuals on the original soil surface and was gradually enlarged as additional individuals were placed on the existing ground surface and then covered with soil. Only 1 individual was interred in an extended position, but Mills gives no indication of the placement of this burial in the mound. One individual had apparently died from wounds of arrows found in the skeletal remains. A female had been placed in a grave partly lined with sandstone slabs and was the only example of this mode of burial in any of the mounds, but information relative to the depth or positioning of the burial is missing. Only 2 individuals in Mound 1 were found to have copper grave goods in association with them.

Mound 2 was the highest of the 3 mounds and also contained the greatest percentage of the burials in the site. All interments were placed in flexed positions and were found above and below the original base line. However, only 4 of the 137 individuals were accompanied with grave goods, an uncommon occurrence for a Fort Ancient site.

Mound 3 had been constructed over the site of a circular dwelling, or tepee, having a central fireplace. No burials were found within the tepee circle, but several were found in the strata above the circle. This mound produced evidence of single, double, multiple, and secondary burials which, according to Mills, had been interred in flexed (or partially flexed) positions and

DESCRIPTION OF SKELETAL MATERIAL BY FOCUS

accompanied with a variety of grave goods.

A total of 68 flexed burials were excavated from the village area, but only 4 were found with grave articles. The village burials were mainly of a few aged individuals and many very young children, the latter being placed near tepee sites on the west side of the village.

From the information given, it appears that Mound 2 might represent the earliest burial structure on the site. Mound 1 may have been the second structure to appear, although it contained the only fully extended burial. Nevertheless, it was constructed upon the base line while Mound 3 was constructed above an earlier living site. The presence of grave goods in Mounds 1 and 3 suggests that a change in burial practices had occurred since the erection of Mound 2.

Flexed burials and the separation of adult and child burials appear to be characteristic of Middle Mississippi sites in eastern Tennessee and the Cumberland Valley, respectively, and may represent cultural influences from the south. Griffin (1943:70-80) points out that some of the material artifacts are not usually found in Fort Ancient sites, e.g., a number of large spear points, triangular points with serrated edges showing fine workmanship, a banded slate chisel, and a double-pointed awl. Many of the flint implements are unusually large for Fort Ancient cultures, and some of the shell ornaments found at the site are of a type common to the Tennessee Valley. A few pipes faintly resemble the Iroquois trumpet-shaped pipes while others resemble the Hopewell platform pipes. The effigy pipes at the Feurt site, however, are noticeably different from the Hopewell effigy forms. Griffin also observes that although much of the pottery is a mixture of Baum and Madisonville types, the most numerous ware is the Feurt Incised type, unique to the Feurt Focus. The pottery tempering materials are grit or shell with some Baum Cord-marked sherds displaying the use of both materials. The range of variation in many of the cultural traits may provide partial explanation for the diversity in the burial practices in different parts of the site.

The skeletal material from the Feurt site used in this study comes from the National Museum collection. While nearly 400 burials were excavated from the mounds and village, only 47 adult individuals—32 males and 15 females—are in a state of preservation sufficient for metrical and morphological evaluation. According to catalog records, all of the specimens had been mound burials, but whether they represent a single mound or all three mounds is unknown. Most of the individuals in the population display a strong resemblance to the Ilinid physical variety, but a few males show features more commonly found in the Muskogid variety. Only one female displays an admixture of traits from both varietal groups. The relatively small sample and incomplete documentation of location within the site make the material of little value in helping to explain the unusual features of the Feurt component noted by Grifffin, but there does seem to have been considerable influence from the north.

The Feurt male crania are nearly equally divided into deformed and undeformed series with all of the undeformed crania exhibiting Ilinid-like tendencies and only two of the deformed crania showing Muskogid features, see Plate VII A-D in Appendix F. Both groups tend to have large skulls and exhibit dimensional differences mainly in areas of the skull that are affected by occipital deformation. Measurements for the undeformed crania were: cranial length, 182.4 mm; breadth, 141.0 mm; height, 142.9 mm—yielding a cranial index of 76.42, length-height index of 78.13, and a breadth-height index of 102.42. The deformed crania measurements were: cranial length, 172.4 mm; breadth, 150.7 mm; height, 143.5 mm—yielding a cranial index of 87.90, length-height index of 83.46, and a breadth-height index of 95.16 (see Tables 48 through 51). However, the deformation causes only moderate differences in the morphological traits of frontal breadth, temporal fullness, occipital curvature, and lambdoid flattening, as noted in Table 74. In each observation there is overlap in the range of variation.

The face displays a medium to large amount of robusticity and appears to be above average in facial dimensions, showing little effect of deformation—undeformed: total facial height, 126.7 mm; upper facial height, 77.4 mm; total facial breadth, 141.8 mm; midfacial breadth, 104.5 mm—deformed: total facial height, 127.3 mm; upper facial height, 79.0 mm;. total facial breadth, 141.9 mm; midfacial breadth, 102.6 mm. The zygomatic arches display a pronounced amount of lateral projection and a moderate degree of anterior projection. There is some difference between the two groups in the shape and inclination of the orbits with most of the undeformed group having orbits of an oblong shape with a small to medium degree of inclination from the horizontal axis and the deformed group having orbits of a rhomboid shape with a medium to pronounced degree of inclination. However, dimensions and observations of the nasal region of the two groups are nearly identical. There is much similarity in the mandibular region, although the undeformed group appears to have a slightly larger mandible.

DESCRIPTION OF SKELETAL MATERIAL BY FOCUS

Of the Feurt female crania, only one deformed individual displays definite Muskogid physical characteristics. Some of the crania cannot be assigned a particular physical type which may indicate an admixture of traits of more than a single physical type. The undeformed crania are mesocephalic with a rather high ovoid vault according to the dimensions: cranial length of 173.7 mm, breadth of 137.3 mm, height of 134.2 mm, and the indices: cranial, 79.08; length-height, 77.28; breadth-height, 97.82; and mean height of 86.33 (Tables 52, 53, and 75). They are slightly robust with only a trace of brow ridge development and a small glabellar prominence. The frontal region is narrow to moderately broad with some individuals displaying a slight or moderate degree of sloping while others have a slightly bulging forehead. There is little sagittal elevation on the skulls, but most of them have parietal eminences of a medium size and a small amount of temporal fullness with small mastoid processes. Curvature of the occiput is found in slight to pronounced degrees along with a moderate to no naturally-occurring lambdoid flattening.

The faces of the undeformed females tend to be somewhat narrow with an upper facial index of 55.25, calculated from the dimensions of the upper facial height, 71.8 mm, and total facial breadth, 130.2 mm. The orbits are mesoconchic if dacryon is used, i.e., orbital index of 85.44, and they tend to be rhomboid in shape with only a slight to moderate angle of inclination. Most skulls exhibit a nasal root of medium height and small to medium breadth but a low bridge height with a medium width. According to the nasal dimensions—nasal breadth, 26.2 mm, and nasal height, 51.0—the nose is almost platyrrhine. Most individuals have small zygomatic bones with a medium or large amount of lateral projection and a small amount of anterior projection. No midfacial prognathism is observed, but some alveolar prognathism is present. Mandibles are small with a median chin form and a negative or small amount of chin projection.

The deformed females exhibit a small to pronounced amount of occipital deformation but still retain an ovoid vault form, for the most part. They are brachycephalic with a high and fairly short braincase, according to the dimensions and indices: cranial length, 159.1 mm; breadth, 148.1 mm; height, 131.8 mm; cephalic index, 82.10; and length-height index, 82.89 (Tables 54, 55, and 75). The morphology of the cranial vault is quite similar to that of the undeformed group except for the areas directly affected by the deformation, i.e., frontal breadth, temporal fullness, etc. Facial features and dimensions of the deformed group need not be described here since they would be a reiteration of those presented for the undeformed crania.

The undeformed and deformed male and female crania from the Feurt component, like those of Baum and Gartner, appear to be from a single physical population of Ilinid derivation, with the exception of the few individuals who display Muskogid-like tendencies.

The Fullerton Field site consists of a village, two oval mounds, and a burial ground apart from the mounds. The existence of the site was revealed when the land was being cleared for the development of a subdivision housing project in the town of Fullerton, Kentucky, in Greenup County. The site lies along the west bank of Tygart's Creek near its point of junction with the Ohio River.

Most of the burials came from the mounds, and Funkhouser and Webb (1928:106-19) note that one mound contained only flexed or partially flexed burials while the second mound contained only extended interments. The excavation also exposed two stone-lined box graves similar to those found in the Tennessee-Cumberland region. The skeletal remains removed from the site comprised only 33 persons since much of the site was destroyed before the University of Kentucky archaeologists were called to the scene.

Griffin (1943:80-82) questions the assignment of this component to the Feurt Focus but apparently uses its geographic proximity to the type site for its placement. He finds most of the pottery to be of a Fox Farm Cord-marked (Madisonville Focus) type with a shell tempering somewhat like the Baum Cord-marked ware. Fox Farm salt pans are present at Fullerton Field, but the Feurt Incised pottery is absent in this component. Most of the nonpottery items are similar to those recovered from the Feurt site. A wide variety of implements and ornaments were made from the bones of different animals, and one circular gorget was made from a portion of a human cranium—an unusual trait for the Fort Ancient culture.

The skeletal material from this site is in the University of Kentucky collection. Only 12 adult individuals—8 males and 4 females—are available for evaluation, and many of these are in such a fragmentary condition that few metrical dimensions can be obtained from them. Therefore, greater weight must necessarily be given to the morphological analyses of the material. In most instances, varietal affiliation cannot be precisely determined, but some individuals display Ilinid morphological characteristics; and one male is thought to exhibit some relationship to the Muskogid variety. It is not known in which part of the site the individuals were found, and their present condition offers no help in determining the mound or village burial location.

In order that the Fullerton Field crania may be included in the population of the Feurt Focus, those measurements and observations that are not obtainable from an individual have been supplied by using the means of those measurements or observations which have been made on the other individuals in the population. Thus, the series is a "standardized" series and may appear more homogeneous than might be the case if all traits were present in the original sample.

Since most of the male crania are undeformed and one of the two deformed crania appears somewhat Muskogid, differences in cranial dimensions might be due to varietal differences rather than to deformation. A comparison of the cranial measurements, indices, and morphological observations of the two groups does not reveal any substantial degree of difference in traits that are little affected by occipital deformation (see Tables 56 through 59 and Table 74), nor do the Fullerton Field males differ significantly from the Feurt males.

The Fullerton Field female sample is small and contains but one cranium with a medium amount of deformation resulting from headbinding. Varietal affiliation cannot be assigned to the crania with the exception of one undeformed individual who has Ilinid-like features. The undeformed group have slightly longer heads, slightly broader faces, and narrower noses than the Feurt females; but for the most part, morphologically and dimensionally, they are so much alike that it seems unnecessary to repeat a description already given. The single deformed Fullerton Field skull shows some divergence in measurements and observations that would be affected by a medium amount of occipital deformation, e.g., cranial length, 165.0 mm; breadth, 150.0 mm; height, 139.0 mm; moderate sloping of a broad frontal region; extreme temporal fullness; no occipital curvature (Tables 60 through 63 and Table 75).

Since it is found that the crania from Fullerton Field are quite similar to the population at the Feurt component, it may be concluded that the people of both sites belonged to the same physical population.

The Proctorville site is located in the southeast section of the town of Proctorville in Lawrence County, Ohio, along the north bank of the Ohio River (Griffin, 1943:82-88). The skeletal material was apparently found within the village area with no particular orientation of interment. In a personal communication to Griffin, McCown, the excavator, stated that the skeletal remains of women and children were found within the one foot depth of the habitation level while prepared graves of both sexes were found two to three feet below the habitation line. At least one stone-lined box grave was present, and several graves showed evidence of the use of wood stakes which were slanted to cover the body.

Griffin finds that the cultural material falls well within the range of the Fort Ancient Aspect, but that the ceramic complex includes some wares that are diagnostic of this site, e.g., the distinctive shell-tempered Proctorville Cord-marked pottery and the Proctorville net-impressed type. Other sherds, however, exhibit relationships with the ceramic technology of other sites. When the artifactual inventory of a site contains some material from other sites, note must be taken of it in case the contact with other peoples may have altered the physical characteristics of the population. Evidence of Fox Farm salt pans, Feurt Incised, and Madisonville Incised pottery fragments also exists at the Proctorville component. Some sherds display shapes and surface finishes that are typical for Fort Ancient but which are commonly associated with cultures in western Pennsylvania and the Virginias. Another ceramic type, exceptional in a Fort Ancient site, displays a crushed limestone tempering agent, yet has a cord-marked surface which Griffin relates to an early Woodland pottery group of the Hopewell-Adena period in this part of Ohio. Still another sherd, with a fine-grained texture and mica fragments on both inner and outer surfaces, suggests contact or trade with Appalachian peoples to the south.

Skeletal remains of only 9 adult individuals—3 males and 6 females—from the collection at the National Museum are suitable for study. A few of the specimens are in a fragmentary condition but can be subjected to morphological analyses. Unlike the populations of the Feurt and Fullerton Field components, the Proctorville group shows a stronger physical affiliation with the Muskogid variety; all of the females and the single deformed male are typically Muskogid. This is the only site not in the Madisonville Focus that seems to be strongly influenced by Muskogid varietal groups. While this population may have been influenced by its close proximity to the roundheaded Clover population a short distance to the east on the West Virginia side of the Ohio River, it appears to have been equally influenced by the Muskogid population at Fox Farm in northern Kentucky.

The two undeformed male crania are quite unlike the Muskogid deformed male in cranial measurements although the

DESCRIPTION OF SKELETAL MATERIAL BY FOCUS 39

indices do not reflect this size difference (see Tables 64 through 67). Cranial vault dimensions indicate that the undeformed crania are small i.e., cranial length, 168.0 mm; breadth, 136.0 mm; height, 137.0 mm; length of base, 100.0 mm, with an ovoid shape and display more than an average amount of robusticity. These dimensions are reminiscent of those of the Archaic Iswanid variety. In many dimensions of the face, nasal structure, and mandibular region, there seem to be few significant differences among all of the Proctorville crania. There are also many similarities in the cranial morphologies of the entire male series (Table 74), although percentages obtained from so few individuals may be quite misleading.

As previously noted, all of the Proctorville females show Muskogid physical affiliations and, by the same token, all of the crania exhibit a small to pronounced degree of occipital deformation. The skulls are roundheaded with short, broad braincases and a moderately high ovoid or pentagonoid vault—cranial length, 163.0 mm; breadth, 141.7 mm; height, 129.8 mm; cephalic index, 87.06; length-height index, 79.70; breadth-height index, 91.71 (see Tables 68 and 69). The breadth of the frontal region may vary from narrow to wide with a slight to medium amount of sloping (Table 75). Due to the broadness of the skulls, there is no sagittal elevation, but moderate to large parietal bosses occur with slight to large amounts of fullness in the temporal region. There is little curvature of the occiput or flattening in the lambdoid region. The face is moderately broad, i.e., total facial height, 116.0 mm; upper facial height, 69.0 mm; bizygomatic breadth, 133.0 mm. The shape of the mesoconch orbits may be oblong, square, ellipsoid, or round, but the angle of inclination of all orbits is slight. The nose is broad—breadth, 26.2 mm; height, 51.2 mm—with a medium root height but very narrow to moderate root breadth; nasal bridge height and breadth are of moderate proportions. The zygomatic bones tend to be small in size with a moderate amount of lateral and anterior projection, and some degree of prognathism is found in the midfacial and alveolar regions. The mandible is small, displaying a narrow bilateral or median chin form and a negative, neutral, or small amount of chin projection.

Before more definitive statements can be made of physical relatedness to other groups, it will be necessary to compare the Proctorville crania with other crania of the Feurt Focus and of other foci.

The Gp 1 component is located along the Ohio River in Greenup County, Kentucky, opposite the juncture of the Ohio and

Scioto Rivers. It is only a short distance northwest of the Fullerton Field component (Gp 3) with which it shares many traits.

The Fort Ancient level of occupation at Gp 1 was discovered during excavation of a group of Adena earthworks known as "Old Fort."[4] Although Gp 1 is a multiple component site of Woodland Adena and Fort Ancient, there is no indication of a gradual transition from the former to the latter. Rather there is a definite difference in trait typology between the two cultural levels. On the other hand, the Fort Ancient level does continue on into historical times, which is discernible from the quantity of copper, brass, and iron trade objects removed during excavation, e.g., copper and brass beads, iron hooks and rings, iron knives and bolts, to name a few.

The artifactual distribution is rather characteristic of the Fort Ancient culture with implements of chipped and ground stone, bone, and antler being present. Ground stone discs and pipes and shell beads were also removed from the site. The pottery appears similar to the Proctorville types although, according to the field report, the tempering material was grit rather than shell. Dunnell (n.d.:28) places the site in the "late phase" of Fort Ancient development on the basis of ceramic similarity to the Madisonville Focus. However, in this report Gp 1 is placed in the Feurt Focus on the basis of geographical proximity and artifactual similarity—including ceramics—to Fullerton Field and Proctorville. In addition, the three male individuals removed from the site and now in the University of Kentucky collection share a greater proportion of physical characteristics with the population of the Feurt Focus than with Fox Farm, the nearest component of the Madisonville Focus. Two of the crania exhibit some Muskogid-like features but could not be considered typical of that variety, see Plate VII E, F in Appendix F. The third cranium displays metrical and morphological characteristics most commonly associated with the Ilinid variety.

The cranial dimensions of the undeformed Gp 1 males show them to border on brachycephaly with a cranial index of 79.57, resulting from a mean cranial length of 183.0 mm and a maximum cranial breadth of 145.5 mm (see Tables 70 and 71). However, the high standard deviation indicates that there is some variation between the two individuals. There is less variability found in the facial dimensions of height and breadth—total facial

---

[4]Field notes and photographic records of the excavation and artifacts are on file in the University of Kentucky Museum of Anthropology.

DESCRIPTION OF SKELETAL MATERIAL BY FOCUS 41

height, 126.0 mm; upper facial height, 76.0 mm; and total facial breadth, 141.0 mm, yielding a total facial index of 89.36 and a midfacial index of 73.79. Some variations in nasal breadth, 25.5 mm with a standard deviation of 4.94, is noted between the two crania, but other dimensions of the nasal structure appear fairly homogeneous. Table 74 illustrates the degree of difference between the two crania and their similarity, or dissimilarity, to the other crania in the Feurt Focus.

Some of the cranial dimensions of the single deformed cranium would suggest a greater degree of occipital deformation than is noted in the morphological observations in Table 74—a cranial length of 165.0 mm and a breadth of 157.0 mm—yet the cranial index of 81.14, given in Tables 72 and 73, is in the lower range of brachycephaly. Most of the vault dimensions of the deformed crania are quite close to those of the undeformed group and comparable dimensional similarities may be noted in the other cranial regions of the two groups with the exception of the broad total facial breadth of the deformed skull.

Since the Gp 1 crania are so few in number, only 3 males and no females, it would be premature to place them within any specific varietal grouping until they have been subjected to comparative tests in order to determine more precisely their physical affiliations with other groups.

THE ANDERSON FOCUS

The components of the Anderson Focus are within rather close proximity of each other and are adjacent to a river or creek. The Anderson component is a village site in Warren County, Ohio, on the east bank of the Little Miami River only a short distance north of the Hopewellian Fort Ancient mounds and earthworks. The protohistoric Fort Ancient cultural manifestation is known as Anderson, being named for the former owner, to avoid confusion with the adjacent Hopewellian Fort Ancient complex. The village served as both habitation site and burial ground. The fully extended burial position is the usual pattern, although some individuals are in a partially extended position with the knees flexed. There were few fully flexed burials present, and individuals were seldom placed in refuse pits. The few burials that had grave goods in association tended to be of children. A number of the burials were surrounded by slabs of stone, placed on edge at spaced intervals, which supported a larger stone slab "cover" (Moorehead, 1892:94). The Anderson Fort Ancient stone graves differed from the Tennessee stone graves only in that the former lacked a stone floor and were less well constructed.

There seem to have been three separate levels of occupation in the village, with each level being demarcated by a layer of sterile soil. This may indicate an extended period of occupation for the village, but Griffin (1943:93-95) notes that the artifactual remains and burial patterns of all levels exhibit homogeneity. It is more probable that the sterile layers were deposited as a result of the site being periodically flooded when heavy rains occurred.

The flint implements recovered from the site tend to be triangular in shape with some variability in size of the points and blades. Some flint scrapers were found during excavation, but few flint celts were present. Numerous polished stone celts and hammerstones appeared in the strata while most of the bell-shaped pestles and grinding stones appeared near the surface of the soil. Implements made from animal bone and elk and deer antler were far more numerous than implements made from flint or stone. Mollusk shells were used for making various implements (knives, scrapers, and spoons), as well as being the main source of material used in making ornaments (gorgets, bracelets, necklaces, and perforated discs).

Griffin (1943:97-101) considers the Anderson pottery to be culturally distinct from the ceramics of adjacent foci, especially in the thickened upper rim strip that is diagnostic of nearly all of this pottery, and he places it in separate categories of Anderson Cord-marked and Anderson Incised. A variety of tempering materials were used in making the pottery; some sherds exhibit only grit temper, others only shell temper, and still other sherds contain a combination of both tempers. The shell-tempered wares, with their typically Mississippi designs, suggest some contact between the Anderson and Madisonville foci while the use of grit temper and the numerous examples of cord-wrapped paddling relate to a Woodland influence. The presence of stone slabs in the graves is an additional link between the Anderson and Madisonville sites, and an examination of the skeletal remains from both sites may yield more definitive information about physical similarities between the two populations.

The adult skeletal remains available for study from the Anderson component consist of 46 males and 39 females, nearly all of whom are in a good state of preservation. The specimens are from collections at the Anderson Museum, near the site itself, and at the National Museum. Smail (n.d.) demonstrated the near identity of the Anderson population with the inhabitants of the Oakwood Mound of the Fisher Focus, a known Miami tribal group displaying traits typical of the Ilinid variety. However, the extensive use of stone graves as the predominant burial practice at Anderson is more characteristic of populations located to the south, being widespread in the Madisonville Focus and diagnostic of the Tennessee Stone Grave culture.

All of the male crania in the Anderson population appear to be undeformed and of a moderate size with a cranial length of 179.9 mm, breadth of 138.1 mm, and height of 140.6 mm. These dimensions yield a cranial module of 152.8, a cranial index of 77.07, and a length-height index of 78.36, demonstrating mesocephaly and a fairly high cranial vault, see Tables 76 and 77. The morphological observations indicate that the cranium is ovoid in form with little sagittal elevation and with a medium amount of robustness. The frontal sloping, frontal breadth, and parietal eminences show a small to medium amount of development, and only a small degree of fullness is found in the temporal region, see Table 92. There is a medium to pronounced degree of occipital curvature, but quite a bit of variation is noted in lambdoid flattening which ranges from none to a pronounced degree.

The face is of moderate size with a total facial height of 124.3 mm and an upper facial height of 74.9 mm. These dimensions, plus the total facial breadth of 140.5 mm, reveal a mesoprosopic face (one of medium length) with a total facial index of 88.51. The upper portion of the face is also of moderate proportions, being mesene with an upper facial index of 53.35. The orbital dimensions support the moderate tendencies of facial development with an orbital height of 34.6 mm and an orbital breadth of 44.1 mm at maxillofrontale and 41.8 mm at dacryon, yielding a mesoconch orbit with an index of 78.54 at maxillofrontale and 82.85 at dacryon. There is some variation in orbital shape with most of the population having oblong, rhomboid, or square orbits with a small to medium inclination from the horizontal axis.

The range of variation in the orbital region may be explained as the retention of some earlier Lenid traits, but Lenid tendencies are not found in the nasal region. The Anderson males display a mean nasal height of 53.7 mm and breadth of 26.8 mm, which are of moderate proportions as seen from the nasal index of 52.87. The nasal profile is slightly concavo-convex, resulting from a medium to high nasal root, a small to medium breadth, and a medium bridge height. The crania display no midfacial prognathism and only slight total facial prognathism resulting from a slight amount of prognathous development in the alveolar region. The mandible tends to be of medium to large proportions with a narrow bilateral chin form and a negative or neutral amount of chin projection, but there tends to be little eversion of the gonial angle. In general, the Anderson male population appears to be characteristic of the Ilinid physical variety while retaining a few Lenid-like tendencies, see Plate VIII A-F in Appendix F.

The Anderson females are separated into undeformed and deformed groups since occipital deformation is present and must be considered. The undeformed crania are almost longheaded with a cranial length of 176.3 mm, breadth of 132.2 mm, and height of 136.0 mm. A cranial index of 75.05, length-height index of 77.19, and a breadth-height index of 102.90 demonstrate the borderline mesocephaly and the high cranial vault (see Tables 78 and 79). The deformed crania are notably shorter in length and broader in width, i.e., 159.1 mm and 140.9 mm respectively; but cranial height is similar in both groups with 136.0 mm for undeformed and 134.6 mm for deformed crania (Tables 80 and 81). The cranial index of 88.69, a length-height index of 84.71, and a breadth-height index of 95.76 demonstrate the brachycephaly and the high, moderately broad vault of the deformed individuals. The only other cranial dimensions that differ significantly are to be found in the midfacial breadth, 90.4 mm for undeformed and 96.5 for deformed, and facial length from basion to prosthion and to alveolar point, respectively, i.e., 93.4 mm and 91.6 mm for the undeformed, and 81.8 mm and 80.1 mm for the deformed.

There is much similarity in the cranial morphology of the undeformed and deformed crania except for some divergence in regions affected by the deformation, see Table 93. For the most part, Anderson females exhibit an ovoid vault form, a trace of brow ridge development, and little robusticity. The degree of frontal sloping may vary from slight to moderate with many individuals having a bulging forehead. Most of the undeformed crania have a narrow frontal region while the deformed crania are equally divided between a narrow and moderately broad frontal breadth. There is little sagittal elevation and only a small to moderate development of parietal eminences to be found on the crania, but the temporal regions exhibit various degrees of fullness from an absence to a large amount. Most of the crania show a pronounced amount of occipital curvature although some deformed skulls have only a slight degree of curvature. As might be expected, differences between the deformed and undeformed crania appear in the degree of lambdoid flattening; however, only undeformed skulls show a pronounced amount of natural flattening. Orbital shape is highly variable with oblong, rhomboid, square, elliptical, and round shapes being found; but all tend to have a slight to moderate angle of inclination. The majority of the crania have small to moderately large zygomatic bones that show a medium or large degree of lateral projection with various degrees of anterior projection. The nasal region of the Anderson females borders on platyrrhinia, being moderately broad in height and breadth of both the nasal root and bridge. Few of the crania have midfacial prognathism, but various degrees of alveolar prognathism are found. The mandible tends to be small to medium in size with a narrow bilateral chin form and with a negative, neutral, or small amount of chin projection.

The cranial dimensions, indices, and morphology of the Anderson females reveal a predominant Ilinid physical type with some Lenid-like tendencies. Some individuals, however, appear less homogeneous as a result of the cranial deformation. Further tests must be conducted to assess the degree of homogeneity of the Anderson male and female populations and to investigate their phyletic relationships.

The Taylor mound and village component is located a short distance to the north of the Anderson site along the Little Miami River, near the mouth of Caesar's Creek. According to the field report of Moorehead (Griffin, 1943:101-04), burials were removed from the extensive village area, from a mound in the center of the village, and from gravel knolls in a section of the village that bordered the river. Some individuals buried in the gravel knolls were apparently laid in an extended position and covered with flat stones; others were merely put in prepared holes. Most of the individuals in the village were in an extended position, and some graves contained stone slabs along the sides of the grave which supported a slab cover—a burial technique similar to that found at Anderson. The Taylor village burials were commonly in the extended position and surrounded and covered with stone slabs. The village mound produced the greatest number of complete, partial, bundle, and multiple burials in various states of preservation. While many of these interments were in stone graves and were probably lying in an extended position, Moorehead (1892:102) points out that a variety of burial positions were found in the mound—fully extended, extended but lying on the side, extended with knees flexed, and fully flexed. According to Moorehead's fieldnotes, there seems to have been more than one level of occupation or period of interments in the mound, but whether the different levels represent more than one population is not known. Some burials were excavated from the base line of the mound and, while not in stone graves, they were in a well-preserved condition. Other burials, apparently at different levels above the base line, were found in a badly decayed condition, and some burials displayed evidence of being burned before being interred in the mound. Relative to the total number of individuals removed from the Taylor site, only a small percentage of them were found in association with grave goods such as arrowpoints, shell beads, and pottery. One artifact of special interest was a copper-covered wood button found with an adult buried in the mound. This seems to be the only copper item removed from a grave, although Griffin (1943:107) mentions two additional copper items being found at Taylor—a fragment of a copper ear ornament, unlike Hopewellian ear spools, and a small piece of sheet copper. Most of the pottery relates to the Anderson component with a small percentage of Madisonville wares being present.

The adult skeletal remains from the Taylor component come from the collection at the Chicago Field Museum of Natural History, the Fort Ancient Museum at Oregonia, Ohio, and from the Kercher collection at Cincinnati, Ohio. In each instance, only the catalog numbering system for the collection is known, so it is impossible to determine the precise location of the individual within the site. It is assumed that most specimens in the collection came from the mound, since the Field Museum series comprises the greatest number of individuals used in this report and, according to the field notes, those remains are from the mound. There are 25 males and 6 females in a state of preservation suitable for analysis. Only 3 individuals—2 males and 1 female—display physical traits which appear to be related to the Muskogid variety. Most of the crania exhibit Ilinid traits and, as was found in the Anderson population, a few of the Taylor crania display some morphological features of the Lenid variety, see Plate VIII G, H in Appendix F.

The male crania from the Taylor component in this study exhibit many traits found to be characteristic of the Anderson population. The skull tends to be of moderate proportions with a mean cranial length of 183.2 mm, breadth of 138.4 mm, and height of 139.9 mm. These dimensions give a cranial module of 153.8, a cranial index of 75.61, and length-height index of 76.44, which would indicate that the skull is in the lower range of mesocephaly and has a moderately high cranial vault (see Tables 82 and 83).

The vault tends to be ovoid in form with a moderate amount

of robusticity, and the frontal region displays moderate tendencies in the amount of sloping and in breadth. There is little sagittal elevation and fullness in the temporal region and only a small to medium amount of development in parietal eminences. There tends to be a pronounced degree of curvature in the occiput, but only a medium degree of lambdoid flattening in found, see Table 92.

The facial proportions of the Taylor males agree closely with those from Anderson, as is apparent in the dimensions given—total facial height, 126.0 mm; upper facial height, 75.0 mm; and total facial breadth, 140.3 mm; but there are slight differences in the total facial and midfacial indices—for Taylor 85.86 and 74.73, respectively. The predominant orbital shape is oblong with some rhomboid and ellipsoid shapes being present, but most crania display only a slight degree of inclination from the horizontal axis. In the zygomatic region, there is a tendency toward a large amount of lateral and anterior projection. The nasal structure is of moderate proportions with a mean nasal height of 53.7 mm, breadth of 27.1 mm, and an index of 50.57. The nasal root height and breadth are slightly above average in proportions, while bridge height and breadth development fall well within the medium range. The crania are homogeneous in the contours of a concavo-convex nasal profile. There is little prognathism of the face except a slight amount found in the alveolar region. The mandible tends to range from medium to large in size with an intermediate to median chin form but with almost no forward chin projection. In other words, moderate tendencies are found in the mandibular portion of the face.

The undeformed females of the Taylor site resemble the Anderson females in that they are mainly Ilinid-like in physical characteristics with some Lenid influence in the longer cranial base. Otherwise, they fall within the metrical and morphological range delineated by the Anderson population (see Tables 84, 85, and 93).

The single deformed female cranium from the Taylor site is unlike the other crania. The skull is shorter in length and broader in breadth, and the face is moderately large and broad, especially in the midfacial region (Tables 86, 87, and 93). In overall appearance, the skull is related to the Muskogid physical type rather than representing a moderately deformed Ilinid skull.

No skeletal remains are available for study from the Steel Dam and Kemp sites, northwest of the Anderson and Taylor sites, which is unfortunate since they might have provided information about the Lenid influence on the northern sites of the Anderson

Focus.

The Stokes component is located to the northeast of the Taylor-Anderson Fort Ancient complex along the upper reaches of Paint Creek in Madison County, Ohio. It is the only component of the Anderson Focus that is found outside of the Big and Little Miami River drainage system. Only three burials were found in the site; each was placed on the right side in a flexed position. Few artifactual items accompanied the burials. Two of the individuals—1 male and 1 female—are available for study from the Clark County Historical Society series at the Clark County Museum in Springfield, Ohio. Both individuals are in a fairly good state of preservation and display Lenid-Ilinid physical traits. Griffin (1943:115) notes that some of the ceramics of the Stokes site are of a form and design characteristic of Eastern Tennessee, and he assigns the site to the Anderson Focus with some reluctance. Unfortunately, the small size of the skeletal population does not contribute any information to substantiate his designation.

The single male cranium will not be fully described in this report, but an examination of Tables 88 and 89 clearly shows an individual displaying Lenid physical tendencies. He is longheaded with a high cranial vault and a medium amount of sagittal elevation, see Table 92. Less diversity is noted in the facial region and in nasal structure. Thus, the Lenid characteristics are more apparent in the cranial vault while the face displays more Ilinid tendencies.

The single female cranium from the Stokes site appears almost Lenid-like with its dolichocephaly, a high cranial vault, and a moderately long narrow face (see Tables 90, 91, and 93). The forehead is narrow and bulging; the temporal region is flat; mastoids are moderately large; and there is a pronounced amount of curvature of the occiput. The zygomatic bones are medium in size and display a medium amount of lateral and anterior projection. The skull has a high nasal root of moderate width with a medium height and breadth being found in the bridge of the nose. In other facial characteristics, the skull resembles the Anderson and Taylor crania.

In general, the Stokes crania seem to exhibit more Lenid-like traits than do the crania from Anderson and Taylor, but the examination of a single skull tends to emphasize traits that might be less apparent when working with mean values of a series. Further testing of the Anderson Focus crania may reveal more precise evidence of varietal affiliations.

THE MADISONVILLE FOCUS

The Madisonville Focus has the most extensive geographic distribution of any of the Fort Ancient foci. Components of this focus have been clearly identified in southeastern Indiana (Dearborn and Ohio Counties) and may well continue farther north in the eastern portion of the state. North central Kentucky contains numerous sites, many of which have not yet been fully investigated, but which are considered to be related to Madisonville, e.g., sites in Bourbon, Nicholas and Mason Counties (Dunnell, n.d.:171). By far the greatest concentration of Madisonville sites and population is to be found in Hamilton County, Ohio, with a northward extension into Butler County. Starr (1960:2-130) gives an extensive listing of site locations and their cultural affiliations in Hamilton County, although his method of presentation (surveying the county by township and by sections within townships, thereby lumping together Adena, Hopewell, Late Woodland, and Fort Ancient in some areas) makes it somewhat difficult to sort out pertinent information pertaining to a particular culture or a particular site.

There is no information available on the burial practices of the Sand Ridge component, located on the east bank of the Little Miami River near its junction with the Ohio River in Anderson Township, Hamilton County, Ohio. Apparently the people buried their dead in the village area since Metz (1881:293-305) found surface material of potsherds mixed with human bone, and Starr (1960:64-69) reports that the Sand Ridge site is a multiple component site with an approximate five foot stratification of Woodland Newton Focus and Fort Ancient material. Griffin (1943: 144-45) notes that the pottery from Sand Ridge appears to be of the type found in the Madisonville Focus but points out that some techniques of decoration are more closely related to material from the Anderson Focus. Starr, too, comments upon the "unusual" nature of the ceramic distribution.

The proposed relationship with the Ilinid-like population to the north is apparent in the skeletal series from the Peabody Museum collection studied in this report. All of the six adult male individuals display physical traits that are more typically associated with the Ilinid variety; no male displays cranial deformation. On the other hand, the two adult females in the series, both deformed, appear to be of the Muskogid variety. There is no record of the number of individuals removed from the site, so it is difficult to evaluate how representative this sample may be of the people living at Sand Ridge during the

Fort Ancient period of occupation. It might well be that some members of the series come from the earlier Woodland strata.

All of the Sand Ridge male crania appear to be medium in size. The vault dimensions of mean cranial length, 182.5 mm; breadth, 141.8 mm; and height, 142.8 mm, indicate that the individuals were moderately mesocephalic, cephalic index of 77.80 (see Tables 94 and 95). The cranial vault is ovoid in form and displays a moderate amount of muscularity, as seen in Table 134. The brow ridges and frontal slope show a medium amount of development with the breadth of the frontal region being rather narrow. A small degree of sagittal elevation is noted in some individuals, and all exhibit moderate development of the parietal eminences. The occiput shows a medium to pronounced amount of curvature with only a slight to medium amount of flattening of the lambdoid area. Most individuals show only a slight amount of fullness in the temporal region.

Dimensions of total facial height, 120.0 mm; upper facial height, 71.1 mm; and total facial breadth, 142.0 mm, with indices of 84.59 for the total face, 50.17 for the upper face, and 72.65 for the midfacial index, are indicative of a slightly mesoprosopic face of medium proportions. The orbits tend to be rhomboid in shape with a small to medium amount of inclination from the horizontal axis. The tendency toward a medium degree of development is apparent in the lateral and anterior projection of the zygomatic arches and in all features of the nasal structure. As might be expected, the mandible is medium in size with a medium chin form but with little eversion of the gonial angle.

In many respects, the Sand Ridge male population seems to resemble the people from the Anderson Focus who display a predominance of Ilinid physical characteristics. It will be necessary to conduct comparative tests of the two groups in order to evaluate the degree of relationship between them.

As previously noted, only two female crania are available for examination from the Sand Ridge site. Both crania display a small amount of occipital deformation and a combination of physical features more typically found in Muskogid populations. The sample size is too small to represent the total female population of the site accurately, but it demonstrates the presence of Muskogid-like people in an otherwise Ilinid-like site of the Madisonville Focus.

The females are brachycephalic, having a mean cranial length of 162.0 mm, breadth of 140.5 mm, and index of 86.72. The mean cranial height of 133.5 mm and the length of cranial base, 134.0 mm, portray an individual with a fairly high but

DESCRIPTION OF SKELETAL MATERIAL BY FOCUS 51

shortened vault, length-height index of 82.39, and a rather broad, large face (see Tables 96 and 97).

Morphologically, the crania have an ovoid vault form with only a slight amount of muscularity, see Table 135. The frontal region is rather broad and exhibits a slight degree of sloping. There is an absence of elevation in the sagittal region, but a moderate amount of fullness is found in the temporal area. A small degree of lambdoid flattening and curvature of the occiput is present. Eye shape varies, rhomboid and square, but a medium angle of inclination is found in each cranium. Zygomatic bones are small and project laterally and anteriorly to a moderate degree. The breadths of the nasal root and nasal bridge are moderate, but heights of the two regions vary between the two crania; one skull has a low root and bridge height while the other skull has a medium root and bridge height. However, both skulls display a concave nasal profile. A slight amount of midfacial prognathism and a medium amount of alveolar prognathism are found in the crania. The mandible is small to medium in size with an intermediate or a median chin form and a negative degree of forward chin projection.

The Sand Ridge females must be compared with females from other Madisonville Focus sites before definitive statements can be made about the distribution of southern Muskogid-like people in the Fort Ancient Aspect.

The Hahn's Field village site is found adjacent to, and slightly northeast of, the Sand Ridge component on Turpin Farm property. According to Starr (1960:55), the site at one time included two mounds within the village area, but there is no mention of these structures in other published accounts, so it is assumed that all burials came from the village area. The occupants of this site apparently used various methods of burying their dead. In his report of the site, Metz (1881:153) comments on finding skeletons laid out in a horizontal position, while Griffin (1943: 154) mentions the presence of flexed and bundle burials, in addition to extended ones. Some of the individuals had been placed in refuse pits, and others were found in an extended position lying upon limestone slabs. Grave articles—mainly pottery vessels—are reported to have been present with some of the burials. Griffin found that some pottery from the site was identical to vessels in the Fisher (Heally) Focus, and he surmised that they were not indigenous but had been brought or traded into the site. The physical traits of the skeletal material do not disprove the thesis that the people at Hahn's Field had contact with people to the north or northwest of them.

The skeletal remains and the artifactual material from the site were removed to the Peabody Museum, where they are available for study. While the size of the original skeletal population is unknown—Starr (1960:55) reports that "many" burials are in the collection at Peabody Museum—only 8 adults (6 males and 2 females) are in such a state of preservation that analysis of them can be made. The majority of the crania in the study series display physical characteristics of the Muskogid variety, but the variety of burial practices in the site strongly suggests that the population had some contact with the Ilinid physical variety to the northwest.

Of the six male crania representing the Hahn's Field population in this report, three display no cranial deformation; one has a medium amount of occipital flattening; and since the presence and degree of deformation of the other two is unknown, they are placed in the same category with the deformed cranium. In view of the similarity of dimensions and indices presented in Tables 98 through 101 and of the morphological homogeneity within the total group as listed in Table 134, the method used in sorting the crania into undeformed and deformed categories may have been too rigorous.

Cranial dimensions of length, 180.0 mm; breadth, 140.0 mm; height, 138.0 mm, yielding a cranial index of about 78 and a length-height index of approximately 77, portray a mesocephalic skull with a fairly high vault. The cranial vault is ovoid in form with a medium to pronounced degree of robusticity. The brow ridges are large with only a slight to medium amount of frontal sloping. The breadth of the frontal region is narrow to medium, and varying degrees of sagittal elevation are found. Most of the undeformed crania exhibit a pronounced curvature of the occiput with a medium amount of lambdoid flattening, while the deformed crania tend to have only a medium amount of occipital curvature and lambdoid flattening.

There are slight differences in facial dimensions of the two groups, with the deformed individuals exhibiting a greater width, but the differences do not appear to be significant. The two groups differ most in nasal structure; height and breadth are similar with 26 mm and approximately 56 mm, respectively; but dimensions of dacryal chord and subtense and minimum nasal breadth and subtense differ significantly. However, variations of this kind do not occur in other facial dimensions or in morphological features. Both groups tend to have orbits of an oblong shape with a medium degree of inclination. Moderate degrees of development are found in the lateral and anterior projections of the zygomatic arches and in nasal morphology. The mandible tends to be medium to large in size with a median chin form but with little eversion of the gonial angle.

Only two Hahn's Field females are available for examination, both of whom are deformed with a small amount of occipital deformation. The dangers of identifying the female members of the Hahn's Field population on the basis of two crania are apparent; hence, the following description can do no more than give a general picture of them. The two crania are homogeneous in dimensions and morphology with the exception of some variation in the midfacial region, see Tables 102, 103, and 135. They are quite brachycephalic with a broad and somewhat shortened face and an ellipsoid cranial vault displaying little robusticity. The frontal region has a slight slope and is moderate to broad in breadth. There is no sagittal elevation and only a small amount of temporal fullness, occipital curvature, and lambdoid flattening. The orbits tend to be rhomboid or square in shape and have a medium to pronounced angle of inclination. The zygomatic bones are small with little lateral or anterior projection. The nasal root and bridge tend to be moderately high though somewhat narrow, yet they still retain a slightly concavo-convex profile. Facial prognathism is present only in the alveolar region. Mandibular size, chin form, and chin projection are typically female, being small, median, and slight, respectively.

The Hahn's Field crania display many traits that suggest affiliation with the Muskogid variety, but the degree of relationship can be ascertained more precisely after comparative tests are made with larger populations.

According to the account given by Putnam (Griffin, 1943:146) of Metz's excavation of the Turpin component for the Peabody Museum, there apparently were several mounds, a habitation area, and a large cemetery present. Starr (1960:61) reports that additional excavation of the site was conducted by the Cincinnati Museum of Natural History from 1946 to 1949, and local collectors continue to collect artifacts from the site even today. He states that the area contains a concentration of Late Woodland-Fort Ancient material and doubts that the site has been fully investigated. The Fort Ancient occupation overlies the Woodland period of occupation which may account for some of the diversity found in burial practices, in physical features of the skeletal remains, and in the artifactual material.

The extended burial prevailed throughout the site although some interments were found in partially extended position, i.e., with knees flexed. Additional variations in interment practices were found in multiple, bundle, and refuse pit burials. When the burials were excavated, limestone slabs were commonly found in association, but they were not of the kind nor of the pattern associated with the Tennessee-Cumberland stone-grave arrangement. Since it appears that we are dealing with a multiple component site, it would be most advantageous to know the depth at which the burials were found. The presence of grave goods seems to have been common occurrence in the site and tends to relate to the Fort Ancient cultural period.

As with most of the skeletal remains recovered from the Madisonville Focus, the Turpin material under consideration is from the Peabody Museum collection. The sample consists of 26 adult individuals—12 males and 14 females—whose state of preservation is rather poor for obtaining complete metrical evaluations in all cases. Thus, as in other cases, morphological analyses are given greater weight. Of the total cranial sample, few individuals display physical characteristics of the Ilinid variety. As was found in the Hahn's Field component, the population seems to be mainly, though not entirely, Muskogid in physical appearance, see Plate IX A-C in Appendix F.

The male crania from the Turpin component were separated into groups of undeformed and deformed skulls. The metrical dimensions and the indices derived from them are presented in Tables 104 through 107. They demonstrate the differences in the physical appearances of the two groups. The undeformed crania tend to be mesocephalic with a cranial index of 78.30 produced from a cranial length of 178.6 mm and breadth of 139.8 mm. The vault tends to be high as is noted in the length-height index of 78.45. On the other hand, the deformed crania display a mean cranial length of 174.6 mm, a breadth of 150.5 mm, and a height of 137.8 mm which yield a cranial index of 86.19 and a length-height of 78.93. It is apparent that the occipital deformation has little effect on cranial height but does alter the width of the skull and of the face—undeformed: total facial height, 125.5 mm; upper facial height, 74.1 mm; total facial breadth, 138.0 mm, deformed: total facial height, 122.1 mm; upper facial height, 73.0 mm; total facial breadth, 143.1 mm. The differences in facial proportions of the two groups are less apparent in the dimensions than in indices, e.g., a total facial index of 90.97 (leptoprosopic) for the undeformed crania in contrast to 85.32 (mesoprosopic) for the deformed ones. There is more similarity found in the nasal structure and mandibular portion of the skulls, and a similarity is also observed in many of the morphological features.

DESCRIPTION OF SKELETAL MATERIAL BY FOCUS 55

The Turpin males tend to have an ovoid vault form and display a moderate amount of robusticity. There is some variation in slope of the frontal region, with the undeformed crania exhibiting a medium amount of sloping and a slight amount of sloping being found in the deformed group. The breadth of the frontal region is usually small in the undeformed individuals but medium to large in the deformed ones, and the latter tend to have no sagittal elevation but do have a large amount of temporal fullness. Occipital curvature is slight in the deformed crania but ranges from small to pronounced in the undeformed ones. Both groups tend to have rhomboid orbital shapes which show a small to medium amount of inclination from the horizontal axis. The zygomatic bones of both are above average in size and display a large amount of lateral projection with a moderate amount of anterior projection. The nasal features tend to be of moderate proportions in height and breadth and have a slightly concavo-convex contour in profile. The undeformed males exhibit various degrees of midfacial prognathism. Both deformed and undeformed male crania have a medium amount of alveolar prognathism. All crania have a medium to large mandible with various chin forms but with little chin projection and display little gonial angle eversion (see morphology, Table 134).

The female crania of the Turpin site were, like the males, separated into undeformed and deformed categories, with, only three individuals clearly displaying artifical cranial deformation. The undeformed group has a mesocephalic head shape resulting from a cranial length of 173.5 mm and breadth of 136.7 mm; however, the sizeable standard deviations, i.e., 6.89 and 6.05 respectively, are indicative of variation within the mesocephaly range. The length-height index of 77.13 expresses the hypsicephalic component, or high and moderately short vault; and the breadth-height index of 97.89 identifies the acrocrany, or narrow width of the skulls. The deformed series, having a cranial length of 164.0 mm, height of 137.3 mm, and breadth of 146.0 mm, are highly brachycephalic with a high and moderately broad vault (cranial index, 89.05; length-height index, 83.79; and breadth-height index, 94.08), see Tables 108 through 111. The predominant vault form of the undeformed series is an ovoid shape with only two cases of the ellipsoid or sphenoid shape (Table 135). Most of the deformed crania have a sphenoid vault form with a single individual having the ovoid shape. All Turpin females have a mere trace of brow ridge development and a small glabellar prominence. Variation is found in the slope of the frontal region within and between the female series. Most of the undeformed females have a slight to medium amount of sloping whereas the deformed group displayed a slight amount of sloping or some anterior bulging. Some of the undeformed individuals displayed evidence of median cresting accompanied by small to moderately large frontal bosses. No evidence of sagittal elevation was found among the deformed group, but a small to moderate amount of elevation was found on some of the undeformed crania. The parietal eminences of the deformed group are large, but those of the undeformed series are of a moderate size. Both groups exhibit a small to medium amount of fullness in the temporal region. Mastoids of the undeformed group are predominantly small while those of the deformed series are medium in size. The two groups display morphological differences in the occipital region with the deformed crania having a slight amount of occipital curvature while the undeformed crania range from a small to a pronounced degree of curvature. There appears to be little lambdoid flattening on the deformed skulls, but a wide variation of flattening occurs on the undeformed skulls; i.e., some lack flattening and others have a small, medium, or pronounced amount of natural flattening.

Facial dimensions of the Turpin females label the undeformed group as being mesoprosopic or moderately broad—total facial length, 112.6 mm; breadth, 129.8 mm; index, 86.80—but with a somewhat narrower upper facial region—index 53.89. The orbits of the deformed series are rhomboid in shape with a medium to pronounced angle of inclination from the horizontal axis. Orbital shape and inclination of the undeformed series are highly variable and range from oblong, rhomboid, square, to ellipsoid for the former and from an absence to a moderate amount of inclination for the latter. The deformed crania have small zygomatic bones with a moderate amount of lateral and anterior projection; the undeformed series have zygomatic bones that are small to medium in size and have mainly a moderate to pronounced amount of lateral projection with a small to medium amount of anterior projection. The nasal regions of the groups yield similar dimensions yet divergent morphological features. The nasal root height is low in the deformed skulls but ranges from a low to a pronounced height in the undeformed skulls. The nasal root is moderately broad in the deformed skulls, but the undeformed skulls display moderate to broad root breadths. Somewhat more similarity is found between the groups in the moderate proportions of the nasal bridge heights and breadths and in the slightly concavo-convex nasal profile. Each group displays a significant amount of midfacial and alveolar prognathism and shows similar mandibular features in the moderate size, narrow bilateral chin form, and negative amount of chin projection.

DESCRIPTION OF SKELETAL MATERIAL BY FOCUS 57

It has been found that the Turpin deformed and undeformed crania, both male and female series, share many common characteristics but differ in others. Whether the variability is due mainly to the effects of cranial deformation or to the intermixture of two physical populations can be evaluated more precisely after the entire Turpin population has been compared with adjacent populations.

Three components are located on the west bank of the Great Miami River in Butler County near Hamilton, Ohio. The Campbell Island site is a village site containing a number of refuse pits and 21 burials but no mounds. Most of the individuals had been interred in extended positions, being either fully or partially (knees bent) extended. There is no record of flexed burials being present even though 1 burial is reported to have been recovered from a refuse pit. Shetrone (1926) excavated the site and observed that most individuals were buried with their head toward the east, but he could identify no significant patterning of burial locations within the village. Only 1 individual was found in association with limestone slabs, and grave goods most often were found in graves of children. Of the individuals recovered from the site, only 7 adults—6 males and 1 female—are available for study in the collections at the National Museum and the Ohio State Museum. All specimens are in a good state of preservation for analysis. Only 2 members of the sample—2 males—display Ilinid physical features, which is somewhat surprising since the Kemp component of the Anderson Focus is only a short distance to the north of this component of the Madisonville Focus. Had skeletal remains from Kemp been available for comparison, they might have revealed some evidence of Ilinid influence from the Anderson Focus. Griffin (1943:158-59) noted that most of the pottery at the Campbell Island site is like that of Madisonville and Fox Farm, but that some grit-tempered sherds which are not characteristic of the Madisonville Focus are also present.

Only one of the male crania displays evidence of deformation, and it results from earth pressure rather than from cultural practices. The small amount of deformation may not be sufficient to place the individual into the deformed category, but for present purposes the distinction is made.

For the most part, the Campbell Island male population appears to be rather roundheaded with a moderately broad face and a fairly high vault (see Tables 112 through 115 and Plate IX D-G in Appendix F). The vault tends to have an ovoid shape, and only the deformed individual displays any degree of sagittal

elevation, as noted in Table 134. The frontal region is narrow
to medium in breadth with a slight to medium degree of slope.
The parietal eminences display a small to medium degree of development, and the temporal region tends to have only a small
amount of fullness. There is some degree of variability found
in the lambdoid and occipital regions, with the latter displaying
a small to pronounced amount of curvature and the former having
a small to pronounced amount of flattening. There is little homogeneity of orbital shape since the orbits of some individuals
have an oblong shape while others have a rhomboid, square, or
ellipsoid shape; the degree of orbital inclination varies, being
moderate in some crania and absent in others. The nasal root
tends to be of a medium height but varies in breadth from small
to very large. The nasal bridge height and breadth tend to be
of moderate proportions. A slight to medium amount of alveolar
prognathism is observed, which gives the impression of a similar
amount of total prognathism being present. The mandible tends
to be medium to large in size with a narrow bilateral to intermediate chin form and little forward chin projection.

Only one female cranium from the Campbell Island site is
available for examination. The individual shows no evidence of
cranial deformation but is quite brachycephalic with a cranial
length of 158.0 mm; breadth, 139.0 mm; height, 132.0 mm; and
cephalic index of 87.97 (Tables 116 and 117). According to the
length-height index of 83.54 and the breadth-height index of 94.96,
the vault is moderately broad, high, somewhat shortened, and
ovoid in form (see Table 135). The skull exhibits little robusticity, only a trace of brow ridge development, and a small glabellar prominence. The frontal region is broad and has only a
small amount of sloping, no evidence of median cresting, and
moderately developed frontal bases. The parietal bosses are
large; there is little fullness in the temporal region; and no sagittal elevation is present. A small amount of curvature is
found in the occiput, but natural flattening of the lambdoid region
is absent. The face is moderately large and broad with orbits
of a rhomboid shape displaying a medium amount of inclination
from the horizontal axis. The zygomatic bones are small in
size and exhibit a moderate amount of lateral and anterior projection. In the nasal area, the root height is low and moderately
broad; the bridge height and breadth are of moderate proportions.
There is a slight amount of prognathism in the midfacial region
and a medium amount in the alveolar area. The mandible is
small in size with an intermediate chin form (between a narrow
and wide bilateral form) and a negative amount of anterior

DESCRIPTION OF SKELETAL MATERIAL BY FOCUS

projection.

In morphology, and in most of the metrical dimensions, the Campbell Island population appears to be typical of the Madisonville people with Muskogid physical characteristics. Further comparative analyses are needed to determine to what extent the Campbell Island group may be related to neighboring peoples.

The Steel Plant site is found a short distance south of Campbell Island, slightly north of Hamilton, Ohio. No burial remains were found in the site although the type of pottery often found with burials was present. Since the pottery resembles the Madisonville wares, the occupants of Steel Plant probably displayed physical features characteristic of the Madisonville area.

The Hine mound site contributes little information regarding possible Ilinid influence from the north. This site is located approximately five miles south of Hamilton, Ohio, down river from Campbell Island and Steel Plant. It differs from the latter in that it is a mound and village, with the mound being constructed on and of village debris. Burials were found both in the living area and the mound, and all individuals seem to have been buried in extended positions. Pottery, stone, and shell grave articles were often found with burials, but only one individual was found with limestone slabs, these being placed at his feet and head.

Skeletal remains from the Hines site are unavailable for analysis or comparison with the other components in the vicinity. Although pottery from the site resembles Madisonville types, Griffin found that the shape and design of one jar was not characteristic of the type site; whether it is regarded as a trade item is not known.

On the west bank of the Little Miami River in Hamilton County, Ohio, is situated the large Madisonville site, the type site from which the focus takes its name. The site was the object of periodic organized excavation from 1879 until the 1920s, and it still produces an ample supply of artifacts and burials, to the delight of local collectors.

Metz (Hooton, 1920:3-9) began the first of a series of excavations in 1879 in the southwest section of the plateau on which the cemetery is located and exposed many burials grouped closely together.

Around 1300 burials have been systematically removed from the cemetery (1235 by actual count of burials listed in the field reports quoted in Hooton), and Starr (1960:78) reports that burials continue to be exposed and removed though in a less scientific manner. In his report on the site, Hooton devoted special attention to burial form and the depth of interments. Most graves were found in the soft leaf mould below the surface humus and above the hard yellow clay subsoil, with grave depth varying relative to the thickness of the leaf mould. Burials were found at depths of from one to two feet, but some were found in the clay subsoil at depths of up to four feet in certain parts of the cemetery. It is probable that more than one population lived in the area and used the same land for burial purposes since the topography of the region is such that few large cemeteries could be developed without intruding upon earlier burial sites. Archaeological and survey records of Hamilton County provide ample evidence of extensive occupation of the region since Paleo-Indian times.

The vast majority of the burials were found in fully extended positions, but fully flexed, disturbed and disarticulated, "sitting," and multiple burials were also excavated from the site. Most of the fully flexed and sitting burials were removed from the southern part of the cemetery, while most interments in the clay subsoil came from the north central section of the burial ground. Successive periods of occupation of the site are suggested by the manner in which some burials have been destroyed or disturbed by more recent interments and by cache pits being dug through earlier burials. Hooton proposed that the site was occupied by a population of from 450 to 500 people for approximately 100 years and that not until the current occupants had forgotten where their ancestors were buried would the earlier graves have been disturbed. He offers no explanation for this practice being found in all excavated areas of the cemetery instead of being localized in particular sections.

Some graves contained limestone slabs serving various purposes. Slabs were found under the head, lying on the body, forming a platform on which the body was placed, and lining the grave; but there is no evidence that the stone slabs were used as extensively as at the Fox Farm site in Mason County, Kentucky. Little mention is made in the literature of the use of the slabs at Madisonville, which implies that the practice was not widespread. The various investigators of the site did record and place emphasis upon the directional orientation of many burials. While most individuals seemed to have the head oriented in an eastern direction, i.e., ranging from northeast to east, southeast, and even south, a number of remains showed no particular orientation of interment.

Artifactual material was often found with burials but seemed to occur more frequently in some parts of the cemetery than in others. For example, much of the pottery and many stone implements were found in the southwestern portion of the cemetery excavated by Metz, while the northwestern section, excavated by R. E. and B. W. Merwin, contained few artifacts of any kind. There appeared to be no sex or age distinction made in the distribution of grave articles, although pipes were usually found only with adult males. Items of material culture were found not only in graves but in even greater quantity in cache pits, i.e., pottery, unio shells (often in pots), stone implements (arrow points, knives, and celts most frequently in graves but also grooved axes, spear points, chisels, and adze blades), shell objects (beads, disks, pendants, and one spoon), perforated tortoise shells, harpoons, arrow straighteners, combs, bird crania pendants, animal-teeth necklaces, and arm bands. Items of copper were found with some regularity throughout the site in graves, cache pits, and on the surface; these include flat pieces and hammered strips of copper, beads, rings and a copper cross. Some objects were found with burials that suggest historical contact with early white settlers or traders. For example, the skeleton of an adult female had what appears to be an iron sword hilt laying on the chest. Another skeleton had an iron bead-like object attached to a piece of deerskin. Additional iron pieces were found in cache pits and in the leaf mould soil. Blue glass beads were found, along with shell beads, near the head of one skeleton; all other evidence of glass beads came from a few cache pits.

The crania from the Madisonville component used in this report are from collections at the Peabody Museum at Harvard University, the American Museum of Natural History, the Cincinnati Art Museum and the Cincinnati Museum of Natural History.

The collections contain 175 undeformed and deformed male crania from which significant measurements and observations can be made. The deformed crania make up the greater portion of the sample, i.e., 115 deformed as compared to 60 undeformed male crania. Both groups contain some individuals who display Ilinid or Muskogid-like physical characteristics, but most of the deformed group appear more closely related to the Muskogid variety, see Plate IX H-O in Appendix F.

The dimensions of the different regions of the male undeformed and deformed crania listed in Tables 118 and 120 suggest a fairly homogeneous population with the exception of the length and breadth dimensions which would be altered by occipital deformation. The indices of Tables 119 and 121 reflect the dimensional similarity, but standard deviations of the four tables imply a fair amount of variation in the measurements and indices of both groups. Nevertheless, the undeformed crania appear mesocephalic with a moderately high vault of an ovoid shape, a medium to pronounced degree of frontal sloping, little or no sagittal elevation, and with only a few individuals having more than a slight amount of temporal fullness (Table 134).

The occipital region displays a medium to pronounced degree of curvature and various degrees of flattening (ranging from absent to pronounced) are noted in the lambdoid area.

The face tends to be mesoprosopic in form—total facial height, 122.9 mm; total facial breadth, 141.2 mm. Various shapes of orbits are found, ranging from oblong to rhomboid, square, and ellipsoid; but most orbits display only a small to moderate amount of inclination from the horizontal axis. The zygomatics tend to be rather large in size and display a large amount of lateral and anterior projection.

The nasal structure of the undeformed crania may be classed as hyperleptorrhine, resulting from a nasal breadth of 27.1 mm and a nasal height of 52.8 mm which yield an index of 51.50. The heights of the nasal root and the nasal bridge are medium to high in elevation. The breadth of the nasal root is also above average width, but the bridge breadth is only moderately broad. These proportions show the nose to be typically concavo-convex in profile. There is a slight amount of midfacial prognathism and a slight to medium amount of alveolar prognathism present in the undeformed crania, which makes the midfacial region appear larger than is indicated by the dimensions of this area. The mandible is medium to large in size with a few crania displaying very large jaws. Chin form is variable, but most crania have an intermediate form, i.e., a moderately bilateral chin width. However, few individuals have any anterior projection of the chin.

The deformed male crania are similar to the undeformed ones except in dimensions and morphology affected by occipital deformation. Most of the individuals have only a small amount of deformation which causes little change in the face, the nasal structure, or in the mandible. The effects of the deformation are more readily apparent in the morphological features of the skull, e.g., greater frontal breadth, less sagittal elevation, larger parietal eminences, and much greater temporal fullness. Occipital deformation would obviously cause a greater degree of lambdoid flattening and would tend to decrease the curvature of the occiput. There appears to be little change in the shape of the orbits as a result of the deformation, but it may have affected the degree of inclination of the orbits. The size and projection of the zygomatic region are equally large in the undeformed and deformed skulls, and little difference is noted in the nasal structure or in the mandibular region of the skulls.

The aforementioned collections of Madisonville material contain 216 female crania (55 undeformed and 161 deformed) from which significant metrical and morphological data can be obtained. Like the Madisonville males, the females in the deformed sample more closely resemble Muskogid-like people while the undeformed sample contains some Ilinid-like individuals.

The variation in the physical features of the deformed and undeformed groups is most apparent in the vault and facial dimensions in Tables 122 and 124. The standard deviations of the measurements of the undeformed individuals suggest some degree of homogeneity among the members, while the opposite appears true in the standard deviations for the facial dimensions of the deformed group. The indices and their standard deviations (Tables 123 and 125) show that removal of the size factor emphasizes the actual variability of the undeformed crania and de-emphasizes the degree of variation in the deformed ones.

An examination of the cranial morphology of the two groups in Table 135 will identify the source of some of the variability. The undeformed sample appears to be slightly mesocephalic with a rather high vault but having various vault shapes, i.e., ellipsoid, pentagonoid, rhomboid, sphenoid, and ovoid, which is the main vault form. The frontal region may have a narrow to broad width with a slight to pronounced amount of sloping; yet over 25 percent of the individuals display a bulging forehead. Few individuals exhibit more than a trace of brow ridge development, and all crania show only slight glabellar development. There is considerable variation in the degree of sagittal elevation, from an absence of elevation to a large amount of elevation; parietal eminences may range from small to large; fullness of the temporal region may be flat or show a small to large amount of fullness; mastoid processes tend to be small or medium in size.

Morphological variability is found at the back of the skull, where the occiput may have a small to pronounced amount of curvature and the lambdoid region may show no flattening or may have a small, medium, or large amount of flattening.

The face tends to be rather broad with a total facial height of 111.9 mm and breadth of 130.0 mm. Orbital shape is highly variable but about half of the crania exhibit a rhomboid shape while others have an ellipsoid, oblong, or round shape. Most orbits, however, display only a small to medium amount of inclination from the horizontal axis. The zygomatic bones range from small to large in size with a medium to large amount of lateral projection from the face but with a small to large amount of anterior projection. The nasal structure tends to be rather narrow or leptorrhine, as is indicated by a mean nasal breadth of 26.3 mm and mean height of 49.8 mm; but the standard deviation of the nasal index reflects the variation among the individuals. The morphological observations of the root and bridge heights and breadths verify the varied nasal forms of the crania, i.e., root heights ranging from very low to high while root breadths range from small to very broad. There is little midfacial prognathism found in the undeformed crania, but a slight to medium and in some cases pronounced amount of prognathism exists in the alveolar region. In the lower facial region, the mandible tends to be small or medium in size with a median, intermediate, or narrow bilateral chin form and a negative to small anterior amount of chin projection. Few individuals show any eversion of the gonial angle, but all mandibles show evidence of pterygoid muscle attachment, i.e., from a small to pronounced amount of stress placed upon the bone.

The female deformed crania are similar to the undeformed ones except in areas directly or indirectly affected by occipital deformation. There is considerable variation among the deformed skulls which is first apparent in the different degrees of deformation. Some individuals exhibit merely a trace of deformation, while others have a pronounced amount of flattening; most of the crania display only a small amount of deformation. The various vault forms of ellipsoid, ovoid, spheroid, pentagonoid, and birsoid result from the various degrees of deformation; yet over half of the crania retain an ovoid vault form even though the mean cranial index of 86.03 typifies a brachycephalic population. The effects of the deformation are more easily observed in the morphology of the crania—greater breadth and slope of the frontal region, less sagittal elevation, larger parietal eminences, and more fullness in the temporal region. Occipital deformation would cause some change in degree of flattening of the lambdoid region, although it is not a pronounced change in these crania, and would tend to depress the degree of curvature of the occiput. There seems to be little difference between the undeformed and deformed groups in the variation of orbital shape or in degree of orbital inclination. The nasal structure of the two groups also exhibits morphological similarity, even though a greater proportion of the deformed skulls have a moderate development of root breadth and height. The mid- and lower facial regions, i.e., zygomatics, alveolar and mandibular areas of the deformed crania are variable but only to the same extent, and in the same way, as are the undeformed female skulls.

Even when the Madisonville crania (both the male and female series) are sorted according to presence or absence of deformation, they still appear as a single physical population differing only in traits affected by the deformation. Yet from a visual inspection of the crania one finds that some individuals display a combination of traits which identify them as an Ilinid or a Muskogid physical type. Whether these traits may be typical of the parent population can only be answered by subjecting the crania to additional analyses. The Madisonville crania present a further problem in that many more of the Ilinid-like crania display evidence of deformation than have been encountered in any other site. Hence, additional subdivision of the population may be necessary to evaluate fully possible physical affiliations with adjacent or related groups.

Fox Farm is the largest component of the Madisonville Focus to be found in Kentucky. This site is located approximately 10 miles southwest of Maysville in Mason County on a small stream branching off the North Fork of the Licking River. The site covers a large area, consisting of at least 6 low mounds, a habitation section, and a large burial "field" (Smith, 1910:117; Funkhouser and Webb, 1928:101-03). The actual size of the component and number of burials cannot be established with exactness because the area has received the attention of local collectors since the region was first settled, and even now skeletal remains are exposed and destroyed each time the field is plowed. However, a sizable collection of artifactual and skeletal material has been scientifically excavated by Harlan Smith and by archaeologists from the University of Kentucky, which permits a fairly comprehensive analysis of the culture and an evaluation of the people.

The burial pattern at the site suggests that several methods were used to dispose of the dead. There are single, double, multiple, and bundle burials present with most individuals being placed in a fully extended position. Smith records the presence of flexed burials, but an examination of his burial photographs shows burials which are commonly termed as being in a partially extended position, i.e., the individual is placed on his back with the knees bent. Funkhouser and Webb (1928:101-03) found bodies placed in unusual positions which seemed to indicate that no particular method of interment was used except that of expediency. Some of the bundle burials appear to be the result of a body being forced into a small grave, while others were actually the intermixture of bones from several individuals. Partial burials were also reported by Funkhouser and Webb who accounted for this by the partial destruction of earlier burials when graves were prepared for the more recent dead. This kind of burial practice implies an extended period of time for occupation of the site, since it seems unlikely that occupants would disturb known burial locations. Burial practices at Fox Farm are similar to those used at the Madisonville type site.

Most of the burials in the field (cemetery) have limestone slabs in some kind of association and were sometimes constructed to form a well-made stone grave; other burials have limestone slab covers, slabs at the sides of the individuals or the individual is lying upon the slabs. Smith (1910: Plates LXII, LXIII) illustrates some of the differences in the utilization of stone. Funkhouser and Webb (1928:101-03) report that graves could be found wherever cultivation exposed stone slabs. Of all the components in the Madisonville Focus, the Fox Farm site most closely resembles a rudimentary "stone-grave" burial culture. This raises the question of whether this site may antedate the type site or represent southern influence.

Stone slabs are less frequently found with mound burials, although small heaps of stone are sometimes present. Individuals in the mounds were placed in burial positions similar to those in the village and cemetery, but burials in the mounds were far less numerous and less crowded. Grave articles are found with most burials in all parts of the site.

Since the cultural remains from Fox Farm have been fully described and illustrated in the publications of Smith (1910) and Griffin (1943:162-79), no attempt is made here to reiterate their findings, except for a few comments to clarify the spatial relationships of the Fox Farm people. Griffin observes that some of the shell artifacts appear much like those from the Tennessee Valley, but that some of the pipes are similar to late Woodland forms in the Northeast. Much of the pottery exhibits characteristics that are distinctive of this particular component, such as Fox Farm salt pans, Fox Farm bowls, and Fox Farm Cord-marked wares. However, the most common and most numerous type of pottery found at the site is the Madisonville Cord-marked form. The presence of this pottery would suggest close cultural ties between the two sites, and it follows that one might also expect a high degree of physical similarity between the people from the two sites. However, other ceramics like the Fox Farm Collander and Fox Farm Check-stamp wares imply that the Fox Farm people also had contact with people to the southeast of them. An examination of the physical characteristics of the skeletal population of Fox Farm may shed some light on the problem of cultural affiliations.

The skeletal material under consideration comes from collections at the American Museum of Natural History, the Blue Lick Museum (Blue Lick, Kentucky), the University of Kentucky, and from the Dodge collection at Lexington, Kentucky. The adult series consists of 38 males and 25 females who are in fair to good condition for analysis. The vast majority of the individuals of both sexes display physical traits that tend to relate them to the Muskogid variety, but a few individuals of both sexes appear to be related to the Ilinid variety. Their location within the site is not known, see Plate IX P-W in Appendix F. Unfortunately, it cannot be determined whether these Ilinid-like individuals may have been earlier occupants or even whether they were found in particular sections of the site.

The male crania from Fox Farm that are analyzed in this report have been separated into two groups according to the presence or absence of cranial deformation. The deformed group displays a greater degree of deformation than is usually found in a Fort Ancient site; this is the only population that contains a high percentage of individuals with bilatero-fronto-occipital deformation.

The small sample of undeformed males is slightly round headed with high vaults with a mean cranial length, 176.5 mm; breadth, 142.4 mm; and height, 140.0 mm, yielding a mean cranial index of 80.74 and a length-height index of 79.30 (see Tables 126 and 127). This is in sharp contrast to the hyperbrachycephaly found in the deformed crania, noted in the dimensions of: cranial length, 166.9 mm; breadth, 156.1 mm; and height, 139.0 mm, yielding a cranial index of 93.98 and a length-height index of 83.39 (Tables 128 and 129). It is readily apparent that the deformation displayed by the Fox Farm crania is more pronounced and of types not often found in other components of the Fort Ancient Aspect, but whether this is indicative of physical affiliations with populations to the South may be revealed by a more complete examination of the crania. Even with a medium to pronounced degree of deformation, the group has an ovoid vault form, as do the undeformed skulls (Table 134). Crania of both groups tend to display a slight to medium degree of frontal sloping but little evidence of sagittal elevation. Differences are noted in the breadth of the frontal region and in the size of the parietal eminences. The deformed skulls have a larger frontal diameter and display large parietal bosses, but both deformed and undeformed crania have only a small to medium amount of temporal fullness. As would be expected, the two groups differ in degree of curvature of the occiput—undeformed skulls showing a small to pronounced degree of curvature, deformed skulls having a slight amount of curvature or none at all—and in the amount of flattening of the lambdoid region—small to medium flattening in the undeformed ones, little or no flattening in the deformed ones.

A comparison of the mean facial dimensions and indices and the facial morphology of the undeformed and deformed groups reveals that the deformation is restricted to the cranial vault rather than affecting all aspects of the skull, e.g., undeformed: total facial height, 124.2 mm; upper facial height, 75.8 mm; total facial breadth, 138.5 mm; total facial index, 89.76; and upper facial index, 54.79—deformed crania: total facial height, 123.4 mm; upper facial height, 76.2 mm; total facial breadth, 140.9 mm; total facial index, 87.63; and upper facial index, 54.79. Orbital shape ranges from oblong to rhomboid to square in the undeformed group, but it is mainly rhomboid in the deformed group; orbital inclination is small to medium among the undeformed and small to pronounced in the deformed skulls. Some variation is found in size and projection of the zygomatic bones in that the undeformed display medium to very large zygomatics with a small to medium amount of lateral projection. Both groups tend to have a medium to large amount of anterior projection. Similarity is found in the nasal morphology of the two groups, with the nasal root being medium to high in elevation and medium to large in breadth and the nasal bridge being low to high in height and small to large in breadth. The nasal profile of all crania appears slightly to moderately concavo-convex in contour. There is little midfacial prognathism, but a small to medium amount of total facial prognathism is present. The undeformed crania display extensive variation in mandibular size, e.g., ranging from small to very large, while the mandibles of the deformed crania are medium to very large in size. All crania display an intermediate to median form of chin with various degrees of forward projection.

The female crania from Fox Farm are also sorted into undeformed and deformed categories, but only one female shows no evidence of cranial deformation. Like the deformed male crania, the deformed females have a significantly higher degree of deformation than is typical for Fort Ancient peoples. The females also display a higher percentage of various kinds of deformation, such as fronto-occipital, bilateral-fronto-occipital, fronto-vertico-occipital, and parieto-fronto-occipital, see Table 135.

The deformed females are hyperbrachycephalic with a mean cranial length of 157.4 mm, breadth of 149.9 mm, and height of 130.8 mm, which yield a cranial index of 94.27 and a length-height index of 83.25 (see Tables 132 and 133). The undeformed cranium is somewhat less roundheaded, but also has a high vault, see Tables 130 and 131. Facial dimensions of the deformed crania differ somewhat from the undeformed skull, although the latter does not appear to fall outside the range of variation of the former. Most of the female crania have a discernible ovoid vault form and only a trace of brow ridge development. The frontal region tends to be broad with an absence or with varying degrees of sloping. Some skulls exhibit median cresting, and frontal bosses are small to large in development. Sagittal elevation tends to be slight if present at all. Parietal eminences are moderate to large, and there are various degrees of fullness in the temporal region. Over half of the deformed skulls show no curvature of the occiput or lambdoidal flattening.

The face is moderately broad with a considerable lateral projection of the zygomatic bones. Orbits vary in shape, but most are rhomboid or square with a moderate angle of inclination. The nasal structure is moderately broad and high at the root with a moderate to broad bridge breadth and a very low to moderate bridge height. A slight to moderate amount of prognathism is noted in the midfacial and alveolar regions. Mandibular size is small with an intermediate to median chin form and little anterior chin projection. Evidence of pterygoid muscle attachment at the gonial angle is slight.

There appears to be a significant amount of variation in the physical features of the Fox Farm populations which may be the result of contact and intermixture with southern populations or with people from within the Fort Ancient Aspect. Since Fox Farm is affiliated archaeologically with the Madisonville Focus, the former might be expected to resemble the latter people most closely. Such a hypothesis can be tested by comparing the crania from the different sites within the focus to establish the degree of physical homogeneity of the people. This analysis is the next step in evaluating the physical affiliations of the people in the Fort Ancient Aspect.

IV

ANALYSES OF CRANIA WITHIN
THE FORT ANCIENT ASPECT

THERE are various methods by which skeletal remains may be examined and evaluated when they are recovered from an archaeological site. The physical traits may be described in morphological and metrical terms as was done with the cranial data in the previous chapters. The spacial distribution and the phyletic affiliation of the population can be determined by comparing the mean measurements of the crania with those of neighboring populations and with populations who are believed to have inhabited the region during earlier or more recent times.

When conducting comparative studies, the investigator tries to employ the statistical techniques that most effectively identify the significant differences or similarities between the populations under consideration. In the past decade, there has been a notable tendency to use specific multiple measurements of the cranium to express the degree of relationship or correlation between populations. While the utilization of multiple measurements is not new, the availability of computers and the statistical programs that have been adapted for use in computers are fairly new and permit the rapid processing of complex mathematical computations, enabling the investigator to evaluate large quantities of data in a relatively short period of time. But the computer reacts only upon the data that are given to it, and hence can be no more objective than the data permit.

A brief look at the literature shows that the statistical technique of the discriminant analysis is often employed to analyze the relationships between small population samples. McKern and Munro (1959:375-82) attempt to define a discriminant function that would most completely demonstrate the metrical relationships of two prehistoric skeletal populations in California. Howells (1966:3-43) relies upon a series of discriminant functions to express the degree of relationship between the prehistoric Jomon population and known Ainu and Japanese populations. Crichton

(1966:47-67) employs multiple discriminant techniques in his analysis of Negro admixture in early Egyptian crania. In testing the validity of Neumann's varietal typology, Long (1966:235-44) uses multiple discriminant analyses of specific measurements and indices to establish a metrical classification of the varietal groups. Further perusal of the literature would reveal additional studies that utilize methodologies similar to those listed, showing that skeletal populations may be tested by various statistical techniques to determine degrees of relationship and denote population distances.

In this report the metrical dimensions and indices of the crania are compared by using Student's "t" test to determine whether statistically significant differences are present (Croxton, 1959:235-44). The "t" test is most commonly used for small sample series and comparisons, which characterizes most of the component populations, but it may also be applied to large samples since the "t" distribution depends upon the degrees of freedom present in the compared populations (Yuker, 1958:64-66). The distribution is greatest for one degree of freedom and moves toward the normal distribution (resembling a normal curve) as the degrees of freedom increase toward infinity. When larger samples are subjected to the "t" test, it is found that a smaller observed difference in "t" values is necessary in order to obtain significance at a specific probability level. This statistical technique is considered to be most appropriate for present comparative purposes since the populations from different components vary in numbers. The methodology for determining the t-values and t-probabilities is given in Appendix A.

In most statistical studies where the "t" test is used, levels of significant difference are set at the 1 percent, 5 percent, or 10 percent level. This simply means that at the 1 percent level chance factors would cause the difference in the statistics compared in only 1 time out of 100 cases; similarly, at the 5 percent level, only 5 times out of 100 would the difference be due to chance. The 4 percent level of significant difference is selected for the present comparisons for two reasons. First, it is believed that the 5 percent level tends to emphasize a measure of unrelatedness in intrafocus comparisons; second, Table 4, Appendix B, illustrates the 4 percent level as it was used previously by G. Neumann (n.d.) in arriving at coefficients of relatedness on a varietal level. Although Neumann employed a slightly different statistical technique in formulating the coefficients, it is found that the 4 percent level of significant difference serves to denote comparable degrees of relatedness or population distance

ANALYSES OF CRANIA WITHIN FORT ANCIENT ASPECT 73

in the present study. Since the compared crania range from presumably homogeneous populations to unlike populations, a scale has been devised to delimit levels of relatedness. Table 5, Appendix B, demonstrates the boundaries of each class of relatedness according to the magnitude of the coefficient.

The archaeological components, foci, and physical varieties have been given in previous chapters, but an additional listing of the archaeological populations and physical groups that are involved in the comparative analyses might aid in their identification since most names will appear in the abbreviated form of Table 136, Appendix D. This table will serve as a guide for identification of specific comparative groups.

INTRAFOCUS COMPARISONS

The crania from the components of the Baum Focus are compared in order to determine whether they comprise one homogeneous population at the 4 percent level of significant difference. As noted in the preceding chapter, some of the crania display deformation, which necessitates forming two subgroups for each site—an undeformed and a deformed group. The "t" scores for the measurements and indices of the undeformed male crania of the Baum and Gartner sites are presented in Tables 137 and 138.[5] The deformed male crania of the two sites are presented in Tables 139 and 140. The "t" scores for the females of the Baum, Gartner, and Baldwin sites and the males and females from the Brush Creek site could not be calculated since the samples were too small for comparison, e.g., for the undeformed females of Baum and Gartner, N = 1 and 3, respectively; for the deformed females of Baum and Gartner, N = 4 and 1, respectively. In other words, a single individual does not represent a comparable group or series. Tables 137 through 285 contain the mean measurements and indices, the t-ratio (or t-value), the degrees of freedom (DF), and the t-probability (with 0.04 being the 4 percent level of significant difference) of the groups being compared.

An examination of the tables for Baum-Gartner males suggests that the people are closely related since the undeformed groups display significant differences in 9 of 35 measurements (H, IOB, SIOB, BOB, NB, SMN, ML, FL, and FLA) and in 5 of 22 indices (H/L + B/2, SIOB/IOB, AIB/BOB, SMN/MN, LM/BCB), yielding coefficients of 26 and 23 for the measurements and indices, respectively. These are dimensions and indices that have more than 3 degrees of freedom since, as listed in the tables, the t-probability is set to equal 1 if the degrees of freedom are

---
[5] Unless otherwise noted, all tables referred to in this chapter will be found in Appendix D beginning on page 465

equal to or less than 3. The deformed crania of the Baum-Gartner comparisons produce "t" scores in which significant differences are found in 8 of 35 measurements (CM, H, MFB, SIOB, BOB, ML, FL, FLA) and in 5 of 21 indices (UFH/MFB, SIOB/IOB, AIB/BOB, SMN/MN, LM/BCB), giving coefficients of 23 and 24, respectively. According to the "t" values, the Baum and Gartner populations apparently do not represent a single, inbreeding group, but the t-probability scores indicate that the two groups display a high degree of similarity in many dimensions and indices relating to traits that are commonly used to delineate populations.

The crania from the various components of the Feurt Focus are compared with those of the "type" site, Feurt, to see how well they represent a homogeneous population. As with the Baum crania, undeformed and deformed cranial subgroups are formed. The "t" scores for the Feurt-Fullerton Field undeformed male crania are presented in Tables 141 (measurements) and 142 (indices). A significant level of difference occurs in only 6 of 35 measurements (MFB, AIB, MN, LOBD, SH, and G/) and 3 of the 22 indices (UFH/MFB, AIB/BOB, and NB/NH). The ratios yield population distance coefficients of 17 and 14, respectively, indicating that the populations border on near identity. The "t" scores for the deformed male crania are given in Tables 143 and 144, and show degrees of relatedness similar to those found in the undeformed comparison. Only 7 of 35 measurements (CM, TP, L, H, LOBD, SH, and G/) and 3 of 22 indices (H/B, H/L + B/2, and PAH/L) show differences at the 4 percent significance level. These ratios produce coefficients of relatedness of 20 and 14, respectively. Since there are only two crania in the Fullerton Field series, the coefficients may not reflect the same degree of relationship that a larger sample would produce.

The "t" scores for measurements of the Feurt-Fullerton Field undeformed female crania cannot be calculated because of the near identity in some measurements between the two groups. The statistical variance is frequently zero, which produces a t-ratio of zero and t-probability of 1. The "t" scores for indices are presented in Table 145, which shows a significant difference in only 4 of 22 indices (UFH/MFB, MF/TFB, BA/MF, and LOH/LOBM) and a coefficient of relatedness of 18, or near identity.

The "t" scores for the Feurt-Proctorville, Gp 1 comparisons of undeformed male crania in Tables 146 and 147 show 3 of 35 measurements (H, MFB, and LOBD) and 1 of 22 indices (B/L) differing at the 4 percent level. With low coefficients of 9 and 5, respectively, the populations exhibit a high degree of homoge-

ANALYSES OF CRANIA WITHIN FORT ANCIENT ASPECT   75

neity. Corresponding levels of relatedness are found in the "t" scores of the Feurt-Proctorville, Gp 1 deformed male crania of Tables 148 and 149. In these comparisons, 4 of 35 measurements (PAH, UFH, NH, and MN) and 1 of 22 indices (SMN/MN) differ at the 4 percent level, but the differences do not relate to dimensions or indices that are primarily affected by cranial deformation. However, it must be noted that the Proctorville, Gp 1 series contains only two crania, which is hardly an ample representation of the population.

Since there are no undeformed female crania from Proctorville, "t" tests were run only on the deformed crania of Tables 150 and 151. The tests showed a significant difference in 8 of 35 measurements (B, MF, UFH, SIOB, AIB, DC, LM, and BCB) and 5 of 22 indices (UFH/TFB, UFH/MFB, TFB/B, MF/TFB, and SIOB/IOB). The coefficient of relatedness of 23 for both measurements and indices indicates less physical homogeneity among the females of the two sites than was found among the deformed males.

The cranial coefficients of the Feurt Focus fall well within the index class of "near identity" for the males, suggesting that there is little physical variability among the males. The focus females appear physically similar also, even though the deformed crania from Proctorville show some diversity.

The test for population distance among the populations of the Anderson Focus involves undeformed male series from Anderson (the type site) and from Taylor (only one male cranium and one female cranium were recovered from the Stokes site) and both undeformed and deformed female series from Anderson and Taylor. The "t" scores for the Anderson-Taylor male comparisons in Tables 152 and 153 show that the populations differ in 5 of 35 measurements (TFH, MFB, MN, LM, and BA) and in 6 of 22 indices (H/L, H/L + B/2, PAH/L, UFH/MFB, BA/MF, and BA/TFB), producing coefficients of 14 and 27, respectively.

The Anderson-Taylor undeformed female cranial comparisons in Tables 154 and 155 reveal significant differences in only 2 of 35 measurements (MB and BA) and 4 of 22 indices (H/L, H/L + B/2, AIB/BOB, and MB/ML). The coefficients of relatedness for the ratios are 6 and 18, respectively, which represents close to near identity. The deformed female crania cannot be tested since only one female is present in the Taylor series.

Since more crania from the Anderson Focus sites are involved in the "t" test, a significant difference at the 4 percent level is achieved from a smaller observed difference in the "t" values. It is apparent that the significant differences in measurements occur mainly in the face (total height and midfacial breadth of the males) and mandible (length and biangular breadth), but significant differences in indices—which eliminate the size factor—are found in the cranial vault and face. From these observations it can be concluded that the Anderson-Taylor populations are closely related but also display some physical dissimilarity.

The components of the Madisonville Focus encompass the broadest geographical distribution in the Fort Ancient Aspect, and one would expect the crania to display less physical homogeneity than other foci. With deformation being found in some crania from each site, the undeformed and deformed skulls are sorted into separate categories.

The "t" scores for the Madisonville-Turpin undeformed male crania of Tables 156 and 157 show significant differences in 4 of 35 measurements (H, TFB, LM, and RL) and in 6 of 22 indices (H/L, H/B, H/L + B/2, TFH/TFB, UFH/TFB, and MB/ML), giving coefficients of relatedness of 11 and 27, respectively. The figures signify an index of close relationship between the two populations—a relationship of near identity in terms of measurements but a moderate relatedness in terms of indices. Thus, when the size factor is removed, as occurs in the indices, the groups are less homogeneous than the measurements indicate. The "t" scores of the Madisonville-Turpin deformed male crania in Tables 158 and 159 reveal a high degree of homogeneity between the two populations since significant differences are found in only 1 of 32 measurements (MB) and 1 of 22 indices (BA/MF). The coefficients of relatedness are in the range of near identity, being 3 and 5, respectively. It is recognized that comparing samples of disproportionate magnitude may have partially obscured some physical differences, but the t-probability scores disclose a high percent of physical similarity between the two groups. Thus, there appears to be little physical heterogeneity between the groups having cranial deformation.

Comparisons of the Madisonville-Turpin female series indicate a slightly higher rate of physical heterogeneity than was found among the male series. In the comparison of undeformed crania in Tables 160 and 161, significant differences were found in 8 of 35 measurements (CM, MFB, IOB, SMN, ML, FL, FLA, and G/) and in 13 of 22 indices (H/L + B/2, PAH/L, MF/B, TFH/TFB, UFH/MFB, TFB/B, MF/TFB, BA/TFB, SIOB/IOB, AIB/BOB, DS/DC, MB/ML, and LM/BCB). The coefficients of relatedness are 24 for the measurements, indicating a close relationship, and 59 for the indices, which implies that once the size factor is removed, the two undeformed groups are unrelated.

Thus, it seems that the undeformed females display less physical similarity than was found in the undeformed males from the two sites. When the deformed female series are compared in Tables 162 and 163, they show significant differences in 6 of the 35 measurements (MF, H, PAH, MFB, FL, FLA) with a coefficient of 17, bordering on the upper range of near identity. They differ in only 2 of 22 indices (MF/B and BA/MF), producing a coefficient of relatedness of 9, which is well within the range of near identity. Hence, it appears that the deformed females from Madisonville and Turpin are much more alike physically than are the undeformed ones.

The "t" scores of the Madisonville-Fox Farm undeformed male crania (Tables 164 and 165) contain significant differences in 6 of 35 measurements (UFH, DS, ML, FL, FLA, and RL) and in 6 of 22 indices (H/L, H/L + B/2, TFH/TFB, UFH/MFB, DS/DC, and MB/ML), giving population distance coefficients of 17 and 26, respectively. This signifies only a moderate degree of relatedness between the two groups, which is to be expected in view of the spacial distance between the components. There is far greater dissimilarity in dimensional and indicial values of the deformed male members of the two sites, as can be seen in the "t" scores of Tables 166 and 167. Significant differences occur in 15 of 35 measurements (L, B, H, PAH, UFH, TFB, MFB, NH, DC, DS, MN, MB, FL, FLA, and SH) and in 11 of 22 indices (H/L, H/B, H/L + B/2, PAH/L, TFH/TFB, UFH/TFB, UFH/MFB, TFB/B, MF/TFB, DS/DC, and MB/ML). The ratios result in population distance coefficients of 46 and 55, respectively, which places them in the index class of being unrelated or even from different physical varieties. A review of the morphological characteristics of the two groups, Table 134, Appendix C, provides some clues for the lack of physical similarity.

The single undeformed Fox Farm female cannot be compared with the Madisonville undeformed group, but "t" scores for the deformed females in Tables 168 and 169 resemble those of the males. Significant differences are found in 12 of 35 measurements (CM, TP, L, B, H, LB, TFB, SIOB, MN, SMN, MB, and G/) with a coefficient of 34, indicating that only a slight to moderate degree of relationship may exist between the two groups. There are 10 of 22 indicial differences (H/L, H/B, PAH/L, TFH/TFB, UFH/TFB, UFH/MFB, TFB/B, MF/TFB, SMN/MN, and MB/ML) with a coefficient of 45. As with the deformed male groups, the deformed females exhibit cranial dissimilarity to such a degree that it can not be merely the result of various deformation practices.

The Fox Farm population displays a higher degree of cranial deformation, and more variable kinds of deformation, than is found in other Madisonville sites, which may have resulted from contact and interbreeding with more southern tribes. However, the Fox Farm crania do not strongly resemble the more southerly Historic Muskogid crania, differing significantly in one third of the measurements ("t" scores for these comparisons not listed in this report). Nevertheless, it may be concluded that the level of significant difference found in the Madisonville-Fox Farm comparisons is probably the result of different kinds of cranial deformation, as well as influence from outside populations to the south.

The "t" scores for the Madisonville-Sand Ridge undeformed male crania in Tables 170 and 171 show significant differences in 12 of 35 measurements (TFH, UFH, MFB, DS, MN, ML, FL, FLA, BCB, SH, BA and G/) and in 4 of 22 indices (H/B, H/L + B/2, BA/TFB, and LM/BCB). These ratios yield coefficients of relatedness of 34 and 18, respectively, indicating that the two groups may be unrelated in terms of dimensions but are closely related in terms of indices. The difference between the two coefficient values readily points out the dissimilar sizes of the two populations since they differ greatly in absolute dimensions but appear closely related when the size factor is eliminated. (Sand Ridge has no deformed male crania for comparison with other sites.) A similar contrast is found in the "t" scores of the undeformed male crania in the Sand Ridge-Campbell Island comparisons of Tables 172 and 173. Significant differences are found in 8 of 35 measurements (TFH, UFH, MFB, DS, MN, MB, BCB, and G/) and in 2 of 22 indices (SIOB/IOB and MB/ML), yielding values of 23 and 9, respectively, for coefficients of relatedness. The undeformed male crania of Sand Ridge and Campbell Island appear to be more closely related to each other—showing near identity in terms of indices—than they are to Madisonville. This high degree of similarity is not found in the "t" scores of the undeformed male crania in the Sand Ridge-Hahn's Field comparisons of Tables 174 and 175. In these tables, significant differences are found in 10 of 35 measurements and in 5 of 22 indices, producing coefficients of relatedness of 29 and 23, respectively. The comparisons may be somewhat less reliable since both samples are small and several of the t-ratios failed to register, even after repeated "t" score trials.

In order to enlarge the sample of Sand Ridge, Campbell Island, and Hahn's Field, the undeformed male crania from the three sites are combined and compared to the undeformed males

ANALYSES OF CRANIA WITHIN FORT ANCIENT ASPECT

from Madisonville. The "t" scores for these comparisons are given in Tables 176 and 177, with significant differences being found in a substantial number of measurements and indices. The two samples differ in 11 of 35 measurements (H, IOB, BOB, NH, DS, MN, MB, ML, FL, FLA, and $G/$) and in 9 of 22 indices (H/L, H/B, H/L + B/2, UFH/MFB, MF/TFB, BA/TFB, SMN/MN, MB/ML, and LM/BCB), which gives values of 31 and 41, respectively, for the coefficients of relatedness. According to these values, the samples are somewhat closely related in measurements but almost unrelated in indices; combining the Sand Ridge, Campbell Island, and Hahn's Field crania may have emphasized the dissimilar traits.

The Sand Ridge and Hahn's Field sites contain no undeformed female crania for comparison, and only one undeformed female skull is present at Campbell Island. A comparison is made between the deformed females of Madisonville and a combined group from Sand Ridge and Hahn's Field in Tables 178 and 179. The groups are strikingly similar in measurements and indices; a significant difference is found in only 1 of 35 measurements (MB), and no difference is found in the indices

It is apparent that the populations of the Madisonville Focus display a higher degree of heterogeneity than is displayed among the populations of the other foci. In examining the population distance between the groups, as it is summarized in Table 180, the Baum Focus coefficients are well within the index class that signifies a close relationship between the populations. There is little population distance revealed between the peoples of the Feurt Focus, especially for the males, who exhibit a high degree of physical homogeneity, with coefficients of relatedness falling mainly within the index class of near identity. A slight degree of physical variability is found in the male populations of the Anderson Focus, but on the basis of the coefficients listed, the Anderson Focus people are closely related.

According to the intrafocus comparisons, the populations of each focus—with the possible exception of the Madisonville Focus—seem to be fairly homogeneous and may be grouped into composite "focus" populations. The range of coefficients of relatedness indicates that a single physical type or variety tends to be predominant in each focus. The crania of the Madisonville Focus display a considerable degree of heterogeneity, which suggests the presence of more than one physical variety in the focus. In order to evaluate the evidence of physical homogeneity more precisely on the aspect level, it is necessary to conduct comparative studies of foci populations. Such comparisons should supply more definitive information about physical features that tend to be distinctive of a given focus.

INTERFOCI COMPARISONS

The crania of each focus are combined into a single "focus" series—maintaining undeformed and deformed categories—in order to investigate the possibility of combining all populations on an aspect level. If the populations cannot be combined, the comparisons will at least point out the degrees of relationship between the populations of specific foci.

The undeformed and deformed cranial groups (male and female) from the Baum Focus are compared with those of each of the other foci, except Anderson Focus which contains no deformed male crania. The "t" scores of the Baum-Anderson Foci undeformed male comparisons in Tables 181 and 182 show significant differences in 9 of 35 measurements (H, PAH, UFH, TFB, NB, DC, MN, LOBD, and LM) and 4 of 22 indices (PAH/L, NB/NH, LOH/LOBM, and LM/BCB), which produce coefficients of relatedness of 26 and 18, respectively. The coefficients are in the middle to low range of the index class designating close relationship, but it must be pointed out that the contrast in the values of the coefficients reflects size rather than trait differences between the two foci.

The comparison of the Baum-Anderson Foci undeformed female crania in Tables 183 and 184 shows a significant difference in 5 of 35 measurements (B, SIOB, DC, SMN, and BCB) and in 6 of 22 indices (B/L, H/B, PAH/L, SIOB/IOB, SMN/MN, and LM/BCB). The coefficient of relatedness is 14 for measurements, which falls in the upper range of near identity, but the indicial coefficient of 27 falls near the upper limit of the closely-related range. Tables 185 and 186 contain the results of the deformed female comparisons. It is noted that the crania differ significantly in 5 of the 35 measurements (H, LB, MFB, MB, and BA) and in only 1 of 22 indices (LOH/LOBD), producing coefficients of relatedness of 14 and 5, respectively. The deformed female crania of the Baum and Anderson Foci exhibit some size difference but little indicial difference and fall within the index class of near identity.

The "t" scores of the Baum-Feurt Foci undeformed male crania in Tables 187 and 188 reveal significant differences at the 4 percent level in 9 of 35 measurements (PAH, UFH, NB, DC, LOBM, LOBD, FL, FLA, and LM) and in 5 of 22 indices (PAH/L, UFH/TFB, LOH/LOBM, LOH/LOBD, and LM/BCB), with corresponding coefficients of 26 and 23, respectively. The Baum undeformed male crania exhibit the same level of relatedness—being closely related—with Feurt as they do with Anderson. However, the "t" scores for the Baum-Feurt deformed crania (Tables 189 and 190) do not exhibit such close degrees of relationship. The deformed crania differ in 12 of 35 measurements (CM, B, H, UFH, SIOB, BOB, LOH, LOBM, LOBD, FL, FLA, and LM) and in 10 of 22 indices (H/L, H/L + B/2, MF/B, UFH/TFB, UFH/MFB, SIOB/IOB, AIB/BOB, DS/DC, LOH/LOBM, and LOH/LOBD), with these ratios yielding a coefficient of 40 for the measurements and 45 for the indices. On the basis of the latter values, the deformed male crania of Baum and Feurt are unrelated. Although these values may be influenced by the kind or degree of cranial deformation, the contrasting coefficients may also indicate the presence of more than one physical variety in the comparison.

When the Baum and Feurt foci undeformed female crania are compared in Tables 191 and 192, they appear to differ in 5 of 35 measurements (DC, DS, SMN, BCB, and SH) and in 2 of 22 indices (AIB/BOB and SMN/MN). These ratios produce relatedness coefficients of 14 and 9, respectively, implying a near identity between the undeformed females of the two foci. On the other hand, the "t" scores for the deformed females in Tables 193 and 194 reveal a significant amount of dissimilarity between the two series. A sizable difference is found in 12 of 35 measurements (MF, H, PAH, LB, BOB, DS, MN, MB, FL, FLA, BCB, and BA), with a relatedness coefficient of 34, and a comparable difference is noted in 8 of 22 indices (H/L, H/B, H/L + B/2, MF/B, DS/DC, LOH/LOBM, LOH/LOBD, and MB/ML), which produces a relatedness coefficient of 36. From these figures, it appears that Baum and Feurt Foci deformed female crania, like their male counterparts, are unrelated. The two foci populations must be compared with other foci before making a definitive statement of their physical affiliations.

The "t" scores of the Baum-Madisonville Foci undeformed male crania are presented in Tables 195 and 196. Significant differences at the 4 percent level are found in 11 of 35 measurements (H, PAH, TFH, UFH, TFB, NB, NH, DC, SMN, LM, and G/) and in 11 of 22 indices (H/L, H/B, H/L + B/2, PAH/L, MF/B, UFH/MFB, TFB/B, BA/MF, NB/NH, LOH/LOBM, and LM/BCB), which results in coefficients of relatedness of 31 and 50, respectively. According to the coefficient values, the two groups are moderately related in terms of measurements but are completely unrelated in terms of indices. Before evaluating the contrast in the coefficients of the undeformed groups, an examination of the "t" scores of the deformed male groups might offer some clues as to the cause of the dissimilarities in the levels of relatedness. The "t" scores of the deformed males in Tables 197 and 198 demonstrate significant differences in 17 of 35 measurements (B, PAH, LB, TFH, UFH, TFB, BOB, NH, DC, LOH, LOBM, MB, FL, FLA, LM, RL, and G/) and in 10 of the 22 indices (H/B, MF/B, TFH/TFB, UFH/TFB, UFH/MFB, NB/NH, DS/DC, LOH/LOBM, LOH/LOBD, and MB/ML), producing coefficients of 49 and 45, respectively. The high coefficient values are more typical of unrelated populations, which suggests that the Baum-Madisonville deformed male crania may be of different physical types. The dimensions and indices that display significant differences are not concentrated in any single area of the skull but are found in all regions of the cranium. The undeformed male crania display comparable differences, with the exception of the orbital and dental arch dimensions.

In comparing the Baum and Madisonville Foci female series in Tables 199 and 200, it is found that the undeformed crania differ significantly in 6 of 35 measurements (CM, SIOB, AIB, DC, MB, and BCB) and in 9 of 22 indices (H/B, PAH/L, MF/B, TFB/B, MF/TFB, SIOB/IOB, AIB/BOB, NB/NH, and MB/ML), producing coefficients of relatedness of 17 and 41. From these figures, it appears that the two series are closely related in terms of dimensions but are unrelated when the size factor is removed. Looking at comparisons of the deformed crania in Tables 201 and 202, 12 of 35 measurements (TP, H, LB, TFH, UFH, MFB, BOB, NB, NH, DC, LOBM, and MB) and 7 of 22 indices (B/L, H/L, H/L + B/2, PAH/L, LOH/LOBM, LOH/LOBD, and MB/ML) differ significantly at the 4 percent level. The coefficients of relatedness—34 and 32, respectively—reveal a substantial degree of dissimilarity between the groups. The significant differences in dimensions and in indices of both the undeformed and deformed females suggest that comparisons may have been made between two physically different populations.

More definitive statements can be made on the physical varieties found in the Fort Ancient Aspect when additional comparisons are conducted on the remaining foci.

The "t" scores for the undeformed male crania of the Feurt-Anderson Foci are presented in Tables 203 and 204. It is apparent that the populations differ significantly in 13 of 35 measurements (CM, H, PAH, TFH, UFH, NH, DC, MN, LOBM, ML, FL, FLA, and SH) but in only 3 of 22 indices (UFH/TFB, UFH/MFB, and MB/ML). The coefficients of relatedness that result

ANALYSES OF CRANIA WITHIN FORT ANCIENT ASPECT

from these ratios—37 and 14, respectively—reveal a difference in size between the Feurt and Anderson crania, since the dimensional coefficient refers to at least a moderate degree of relationship while the indicial coefficient portrays near identity. Thus, differences are greatly reduced when the size factor is eliminated.

The Feurt-Anderson Foci undeformed females differ in 11 of 35 measurements (B, TFH, UFH, MFB, IOB, SIOB, NH, DS, LOBM, LOBD, and ML) and in 6 of 22 indices (B/L, H/B, PAH/L, TFB/B, DS/DC, and LOH/LOBM), see Tables 205 and 206. Coefficients of 31 and 27, respectively, which are derived from the dimensional and indicial ratios, represent only a moderate to close relationship between the groups. Greater physical similarity is observed in the deformed cranial comparisons of Tables 207 and 208, for significant differences are found in only 3 of 35 measurements (IOB, LOBM, and LOBD) and in 3 of 22 indices (H/B, H/L + B/2, and MF/B). The resulting coefficients of 9 and 14, respectively, imply near identity between the groups compared. The deformed female crania of Feurt and Anderson show far greater homogeneity than do the undeformed males or females. Whether the similarity may result from common cranial deformation practices or from similarity of physical affiliation can not, at this point, be determined.

The "t" scores for the Feurt-Madisonville Foci undeformed male crania in Tables 209 and 210 show that the populations differ significantly in 12 of the 35 measurements (H, PAH, TFH, UFH, NH, SMN, LOBM, LOBD, MB, FL, SH, and G/) and in 10 of the 22 indices (H/L, H/B, H/L + B/2, MF/B, TFH/TFB, UFH/TFB, UFH/MFB, TFB/B, NB/NH, and MB/ML). The coefficients obtained from these ratios—34 and 45, respectively—are of a magnitude that signifies a moderate degree of relationship in terms of the dimensions but nonrelatedness in terms of indices. In this case, population distance increases when the size factor is eliminated. The "t" scores for the deformed male crania of the Feurt-Madisonville comparisons, presented in Tables 211 and 212, produce coefficients of even greater magnitude. There are significant differences in 15 of 35 measurements (CM, H, PAH, LB, TFH, UFH, SIOB, NH, DS, LOBM, LOBD, MB, FL, SH, and G/) and in 14 of 22 indices (B/L, H/L, H/B, H/L + B/2, PAH/L, TFH/TFB, UFH/TFB, UFH/MFB, SIOB/IOB, NB/NH, LOH/LOBM, LOH/LOBD, MB/ML, and LM/BCB), resulting in coefficients of relatedness of 43 and 64, respectively. According to the magnitude of these values, the deformed male crania of the two foci are unrelated and probably are representatives of different physical varieties.

The females of Feurt and Madisonville Foci appear even more physically dissimilar than do the males. In Tables 213 and 214 the undeformed females differ in 15 of the 35 measurements, CM, H, TFH, UFH, MFB, BOB, NH, DC, DS, MN, SMN, LOBM, MB, FL, and FLA. Eighteen of the 22 indices differ at the 4 percent level of significance, but all 22 indices differ at the 12 percent level. The coefficients of relatedness of the above ratios are 43 and 82, respectively, which reflects the lack of relationship between the groups. It is noted that population distance increases greatly when the dimensional size factor is removed. Physical differences are emphasized between the deformed crania in Tables 215 and 216 if the size factor is retained; 22 of the 35 measurements differ significantly and indicate nonrelatedness—the coefficient is 63. Measurements that do not show a significant difference at the 4 percent level are TP, B, MF, and PAH of the vault; SIOB of the face; NB of the nasal structure; LOH and LOBD of the orbit; ML of the dental arch; LM, SH, and BA of the mandible; and G/, or the gonial angle. The indicial comparisons, however, show that only 7 of the 22 indices (H/L, PAH/L, TFH/TFB, UFH/TFB, DS/DC, LOH/LOBM, and MB/ML) differ significantly; according to the coefficient of relatedness, 32, the groups are moderately related. While the indicial coefficient for deformed females suggests the possibility of some physical affinity between the Feurt and Madisonville Foci, the other coefficients present rather strong evidence of different physical types in the two foci. Further comments on interfoci relationships will be presented after all comparisons have been made.

The "t" scores of the undeformed male crania from the Anderson-Madisonville Foci are given in Tables 217 and 218. Significant differences at the 4 percent level appear in 12 of 35 measurements (TP, B, H, TFH, UFH, DC, MN, LOBD, MB, ML, FLA, and G/) and in 8 of 22 indices (H/L, H/B, H/L + B/2, UFH/TFB, UFH/MFB, TFB/B, SMN/MN, MB/ML), yielding coefficients of 34 and 36, respectively. According to these values, the undeformed males display a moderate amount of relationship in both the cranial dimensions and indices, with some significant physical differences being found in all regions of the skull.

The "t" scores for the undeformed female crania of Anderson and Madisonville Foci are presented in Tables 219 and 220. Significant differences are found in 16 of 35 measurements and in 15 of 22 indices, CM, L, B, H, TFH, UFH, SIOB, AIB, DC, DS, MN, SMN, LOH, LOBD, BCB, G/, and H/B, H/L + B/2, PAH/L, MF/B, TFH/TFB, UFH/TFB, TFB/B, BA/TFB, SIOB/IOB, AIB/BOB, NB/NH, DS/DC, SMN/MN, MB/ML, and LM/BCB.

ANALYSES OF CRANIA WITHIN FORT ANCIENT ASPECT

The resulting coefficients of 46 and 68 are of the magnitude of nonrelatedness. Before discussing the source of the difference between the undeformed series, the deformed females of the foci are compared to see whether they display similar differences. From Tables 221 and 222 it is found that significant differences occur in 9 of the 35 measurements—CM, B, TFH, TFB, DC, SMN, LOH, LOBD, and G/—producing a coefficient of 26. Only 5 of the 23 indices (H/L, H/L + B/2, TFH/TFB, UFH/TFB, and UFH/MFB) differ significantly, producing a coefficient of 23. These values suggest a close relationship between the deformed females of the two foci.

In view of the discrepancy in coefficients of relatedness between the undeformed and the deformed crania of Anderson and Madisonville Foci, it appears that the undeformed skulls are from separate physical populations. On the other hand, there seems to be some physical affinity between the deformed skulls which could have resulted from intermixture, but not admixture, of the two populations. Since the foci in question are geographically adjacent to each other, contact between them is probable.

The broad range of coefficients obtained from interfoci comparisons demonstrates a major point: the total population of the Fort Ancient Aspect cannot be combined into a single group. The undeformed crania of the Baum Focus share many physical characteristics with the undeformed groups of Anderson and of Feurt, to the extent that the three foci may be classified as being closely related. This physical homogeneity may be attributed to the Ilinid-like features that prevail in most of the crania. Few skulls exhibit Muskogid-like features, e.g., one skull in each of the foci. A stronger Muskogid tendency is found among the deformed crania, and, as might be expected, it exerts some influence on the deformed group.

The Baum and Anderson Foci deformed females exhibit near identity in their physical characteristics, which may be viewed as verification of common ancestry. It is unlikely that two groups would have cranial dimensions and indices that retained a high degree of identity after the skulls had been artifically deformed unless the groups had physical characteristics and deformation practices in common. The presence of a different physical population and/or unlike deformation practices is noted in the deformed cranial comparisons of Baum and Feurt Foci, Baum and Madisonville Foci, and Feurt and Madisonville Foci. The Baum and Feurt deformed skulls display a degree of nonrelatedness sufficient to warrant placement in separate physical populations. Considering the proximity of Feurt to the Clover Focus of West

Virginia, it is probable that the Feurt people display a stronger physical affiliation with the people of the latter focus than with any group presented in this report. It is apparent from the Feurt-Madisonville "t" scores that two physically dissimilar populations are compared.

The crania of the Madisonville Focus appear to be farthest removed from the other foci in terms of population distance. All of the deformed crania display physical characteristics that are usually associated with the Muskogid physical type, which would account for many of the significant differences in the previous comparisons. The coefficients of relatedness were probably identifying the existence of more than one physical type in the comparative tests, not simply the effects of cranial deformation.

The undeformed crania of the Madisonville Focus include individuals of both Ilinid and Muskogid types. Of the 155 undeformed skulls that were used for comparative tests, over half of them (98) display physical features that characterize the Muskogid variety. The consequence of using such a heterogeneous sample is evident in the coefficients obtained from the tests. The presence of Ilinid-like individuals in the group tended to repress t-ratio differences that might have been significant, while the Muskogid individuals tended to enhance these same differences. The influence that each physical variety exerts on the other is revealed in the t-probability values signifying percent of similarity, with 1.00 (i.e., 100 percent) referring to complete homogeneity, and in the significantly different cranial distribution of the dimensions and indices.

On the basis of the results obtained from the previous comparative tests and from the above statements, the crania of the Fort Ancient Aspect are obviously not a single homogeneous population in terms of physical characteristics. Evidence of physical heterogeneity tends to be restricted mainly to the Madisonville Focus which, according to artifactual data, is the most recent focus within the aspect. The presence of more than one physical type in the aspect introduces some pertinent questions relating to the antiquity of the physical types in the aspect and to the degree of physical similarity shared with the various adjacent populations.

V

COMPARISONS ON THE VARIETAL LEVEL

THE undeformed crania of the foci are sorted into an Ilinid or a Muskogid category on the basis of distinguishable physical characteristics of each skull for purposes of investigating the presence of different physical types in the Fort Ancient Aspect. The crania of the Anderson Focus are accepted as the Fort Ancient Ilinid "type population." Smail (n.d.) compared a population from the Fisher Focus—Oakwood Mound, the "type" Ilinid variety of the report—with the population from the Anderson site of the Fort Ancient Anderson Focus and found that the two populations—both males and females—were closely related in both dimensions and indices. G. Neumann (1952:23-24) had previously used the Maple Mills Focus population, which is physically similar to the Fisher Focus and to Anderson, as the "type" series for the Lenapid (later renamed Ilinid) physical variety. Hence, there is strong evidence for building the Fort Ancient Ilinid population around the Anderson Focus series. Most of the undeformed crania from Baum, Gartner, Sand Ridge, Campbell Island, and Hahn's Field also fit in this population. In this report, combined series of undeformed Ilinid-like crania (84 males and 66 females) from the Fort Ancient sites listed are compared with a Fort Ancient Muskogid population and with series outside the Fort Ancient Aspect, especially a Shawnee series who supposedly are descendant from the archaeological Fort Ancient population.

The Fort Ancient Muskogid population consists of 50 undeformed male and 54 undeformed female Muskogid-like crania from the Madisonville, Turpin, Hahn's Field, Campbell Island, and Fox Farm components. The combined series contain crania that display strong physical resemblances to the Muskogid variety "type population" as it is defined by H. Neumann (n.d.) and presented earlier in the report. The Fort Ancient Muskogid series, like the Fort Ancient Ilinid series, will be utilized to test the degree of relationship between the major physical types in the Fort Ancient Aspect and to investigate levels of population distance to neighboring populations. Both Fort Ancient "type popu-

88   PREHISTORIC PEOPLE OF FORT ANCIENT

lations" will be compared with series of the physical varieties described in Chapter II to evaluate phyletic relationships and to reveal additional physical types that may exist in the Fort Ancient populations.

VARIETAL COMPARISONS

Before the Fort Ancient series are compared, it is advisable to examine the degrees of relationship between the physical varieties taking part in subsequent comparisons. Each of the physical types—Lenid, Iswanid, Ilinid, Muskogid, Dakotid—is contrasted with every other type to identify significant differences that occur in the measurements and indices of the crania. The comparisons follow the procedure employed in the previous chapter, i.e., use of the "t" test with a 4 percent level of significance, etc.

The "t" scores of the Lenid-Dakotid male varietal comparisons are given in Tables 224 and 225.[6] The males obviously share few traits in common, showing significant differences in 19 of 35 measurements (L, B, H, BPH, LB, UFH, TFB, MFB, NB, DC, SMN, LOH, LOBD, ML, FL, LM, BCB, RL, and G/) and in 10 of 22 indices (B/L, H/B, BPH/H, MF/B, TFB/B, MF/TFB, BA/TFB, DS/DC, MB/ML, and LM/BCB). The ratios produce coefficients of relatedness, or rather non-relatedness, of 54 and 45, respectively. Some of the varietal differences may be attributed to physical size apparent in the mean measurements of the particular trait. All regions of the skull, with the exception of the orbits, exhibit the significant differences, and the range of dissimilarity becomes even more apparent when the morphology of the group is compared.

The Lenid-Dakotid female comparisons in Tables 226 and 227 reveal a significant difference in 6 of 35 measurements (H, TFH, UFH, SIOB, DC, and RL) and in 6 of 21 indices (H/B, H/L + B/2, TFH/TFB, SIOB/IOB, SMN/MN, and LM/BCB), yielding 17 and 33, respectively, as coefficients of relatedness. According to the coefficients, the females are very closely related in size but only moderately related by indicial standards. The morphological dissimilarity of the female series is much more striking than is indicated by the metrical values.

The physical differences between the Lenid and Dakotid crania may be attributed in part to a degree of Deneid admixture in the Dakotid variety.

The "t" scores of the Lenid-Ilinid male varietal comparisons

---

[6]Unless otherwise noted, all tables referred to in this chapter may be found in Appendix E beginning on page 575

denote only slightly less physical diversity between the groups than was encountered in the Lenid-Dakotid groups. When comparing the crania in Tables 228 and 229, significant differences are found in 17 of 35 measurements, B, H, BPH, TFB, MFB, IOB, BOB, NB, DS, SMN, LOBM, LOBD, ML, LM, BCB, SH, and G/, and in 8 of 22 indices, B/L, H/L, H/L + B/2, BPH/H, DS/DC, SMN/MN, MB/ML, LM/BCB, which produces population distance values or coefficients of relatedness of 49 and 36, respectively. In dimensional terms, the populations are unrelated, and the indicial values imply only a moderate degree of relatedness. The coefficients appear to refute an earlier claim (G. Neumann, 1960) that the Middle Woodland Lenid physical type evolved into a Late Woodland and an Upper Mississippian Ilinid type in the Illinois and Middle Ohio Valleys. The morphology of the series, presented in an earlier chapter, suggests a greater physical resemblance than that proposed by the coefficients, but the metrical values seem to reflect the degree of physical diversity that can occur within ancestral lines over an extended period of time.

The females of the Lenid-Ilinid varieties appear more physically alike than the males, see Tables 230 and 231. The former differ significantly in only 5 of the 36 measurements (UFH, NB, DC, DS, and FLA) and in only 2 of the 22 indices (B/L and SMN/MN), with coefficients of relatedness of 14 and 9, respectively. Hence, the female series approach near identity in metrical values, in strong contrast to the moderate relationship found between the male series. The comparison of physical "types" from different archaeological regions and time levels tends to magnify the physical variation of the groups, and such being the case, would hardly account for the near identity of the above female groups unless there was indeed a retention of Lenid characteristics into the Ilinid time period.

The "t" scores of the Lenid-Iswanid male varietal comparisons are presented in Tables 232 and 233. The varieties exhibit a high level of significant difference in 22 of the 34 measurements—the only measurements not involved are TP, B, H, TFB, MFB, IOB, MN, LOBM, LOBD, BCB, BA, and RL—and in 13 of the 21 indices—(indices not involved are TFH/TFB, UFH/MFB, TFB/B, BA/MF, BA/TFB, NB/NH, DS/DC, and LOH/LOBD). Corresponding coefficients of relatedness are 65 and 62, respectively. The magnitude of the coefficients and of the t-probabilities below the 4 percent level demonstrates the extreme physical diversity of the two Archaic populations. An Iswanid female series is not available to test the degree of nonrelatedness between the females of the two physical varieties.

The "t" scores of the Lenid-Muskogid male varieties in Tables 234 and 235 signify that unrelated series are being compared. Significant differences are found in 18 of 35 measurements, B, H, BPH, TFH, UFH, TFB, MFB, IOB, BOB, NB, DS, MN, LOBM, LOBD, MB, BCB, SH, and G/, with a coefficient of 51, and in 10 of 22 indices, B/L, H/L, H/B, H/L + B/2, BPH/H, NB/NH, DS/DC, SMN/MN, MB/ML, and LM/BCB, with a coefficient of 45. The Lenid and Muskogid males are clearly not related. The Muskogid and Dakotid series differ from the Lenid physical type to about the same extent, but it remains to be seen whether the former have physical traits in common. Unfortunately, no Muskogid female series is available to compare with the Lenid females for substantiation of the physical diversity between the varieties.

The Iswanid-Ilinid male varietal comparisons in Tables 236 and 237 show that significant differences occur in 30 of 35 measurements (those not affected are TP, MN, BA, RL, and G/), but in only 5 of 22 indices, BA/MF, DS/DC, SMN/MN, MB/ML, and LM/BCB, yielding coefficients of relatedness of 86 and 23, respectively. It is evident that the two series differ more in size than general physical variability, as exemplified by the mean measurements of each series. According to the dimensional coefficient of 86, the males are totally unrelated, but the indicial coefficient of 23 typifies a close relationship between the Archaic Iswanid and Woodland Ilinid males. Without an Iswanid female series, the degree of similarity between the females can not be determined.

The "t" scores of the Iswanid-Muskogid male varietal comparisons are listed in Tables 238 and 239. No females from these varieties are available for comparison. Levels of significant differences are displayed that somewhat resemble those of the Iswanid-Ilinid series. Differences occur in 31 of 34 measurements, only TP, BA, and G/ are not involved, and in 7 of 21 indices (UFH/TFB, BA/MF, SIOB/IOB, AIB/BOB, NB/NH, LOH/LOBM, and LM/BCB). These ratios produce a dimensional coefficient of 91—unrelated—and an indicial coefficient of 33—moderately related. The contrasting coefficient values confirm the substantial size difference in the male crania of the two groups, but the size factor does not account for all variation between the groups. When the combined ratios of the Iswanid-Ilinid tests (35/57) and the Iswanid-Muskogid tests (38/55) are examined, the Muskogid variety appears to resemble the Iswanid type to a lesser degree than does the Ilinid variety. However, the level of physical relatedness between the Ilinid and Muskogid varieties remains to be tested.

The "t" scores of the Ilinid-Dakotid male varietal comparisons are presented in Tables 240 and 241. Significant differences are found in 11 of 35 measurements (CM, B, H, BPH, LB, UFH, BOB, DC, LOH, FL, and RL) and in 7 of 22 indices (B/L, H/L, H/B, H/L + B/2, BPH/H, MF/B, and TFB/B), with corresponding coefficients of relatedness of 31 and 32, respectively, which signifies a moderate degree of relationship between the two groups. Dimensional differences are found in all regions of the cranium, but the indicial differences are restricted mainly to the cranial vault. Consequently, difference in cranial size accounts for many variations between the male series, while the significantly differing values of the vault probably represent Deneid admixture in the Dakotid variety.

The "t" scores for the Ilinid-Dakotid female comparisons, Tables 242 and 243 show significant differences in 10 of the 35 measurements (H, TFH, UFH, SIOB, AIB, NH, ML, LM, SH, and RL) and in 8 of 21 indices (H/L, H/B, H/L + B/2, TFH/TFB, UFH/TFB, SIOB/IOB, AIB/BOB, and LM/BCB). The coefficients of 29 and 38, respectively, derived from the ratios, represent a close to moderate relationship in dimensions but only slight relatedness in indices. Hence, the females of the varieties are as physically dissimilar as the males.

The "t" scores of the Ilinid-Muskogid male comparisons in Tables 244 and 245 imply a close relationship between the two physical types. Statistically significant differences are observed in 7 of 35 measurements (H, UFH, DS, MN, SMN, MB, and ML) and in 4 of 22 indices (H/L + B/2, UFH/TFB, DS/DC, SMN/MN), which produces coefficients of relatedness of 20 and 18, respectively. Since these physical types are of somewhat comparable time levels and are represented in populations who frequently inhabited adjacent areas, it is not surprising that they display a greater physical resemblance to each other than to any of their ancestral groups. The high degree of relatedness may have resulted from some interbreeding or from similar environmental pressures, but it must be pointed out that only dimensions and indices are compared in the "t" test. Consequently, the t-values may mislead the investigator if the morphology of the two groups is ignored. Ilinid and Muskogid physical types are easily distinguishable in terms of morphological observations. The level of population distance between the Ilinid and Muskogid types will be pertinent in the comparisons of the Fort Ancient "type" populations.

The "t" scores of the Muskogid-Dakotid varietal comparisons

in Tables 246 and 247 demonstrate a substantial level of population distance between the physical types. There are significant differences in 17 of 35 measurements (CM, L, B, H, BPH, LB, IOB, BOB, DC, DS, MN, SMN, LOBM, MB, ML, FL, and SH) and in 9 of 22 indices (B/L, H/L, H/B, H/L + B/2, BPH/H, MF/B, TFB/B, DS/DC, and SMN/MN) with coefficient values of 49 for the former and 41 for the latter. Once again, size differences are noted in several regions of the cranium, and Deneid influence seems most pronounced in the cranial vault. Subsequently, if there is Dakotid influence in the Fort Ancient Aspect, it could be identified.

The population distance ratios at the varietal level of comparison are presented in Table 248. The levels of relatedness (coefficients) are not identical to those in Table 4, but the former exhibit similar magnitudinal qualities and, therefore, are acceptable as guides for the comparisons in this report.

FORT ANCIENT "VARIETAL" COMPARISONS

The Fort Ancient "derived" physical varieties, Fort Ancient Ilinid and Fort Ancient Muskogid, are tested with each other in order to determine the degree of relationship between the two proposed groups. Additional comparative tests are made with some of the known physical types previously examined to gather information pertaining to ancestral relationships that may exist in the aspect. Since it has frequently been stated that the Fort Ancient people were influenced by northern and/or southern populations, the Fort Ancient derived physical types are compared with adjacent groups to investigate the validity of the statements. And, finally, comparisons of the Fort Ancient groups and a known Shawnee series are made, which should supply some evidence about the origin of the Shawnee Indians.

The "t" scores of the Fort Ancient Ilinid-Fort Ancient Muskogid male varieties are presented in Tables 249 and 250. Significant differences at the 4 percent level are found in 16 of 35 measurements (L, B, H, PAH, UFH, AIB, NH, DC, DS, MN, LOH, LOBD, MB, FL, FLA, and G/) and in 8 of 22 indices (H/B, H/L + B/2, UFH/TFB, UFH/MFB, TFB/B, AIB/BOB, NB/NH, and MB/ML). These ratios produce coefficients of relatedness of 46 and 36, respectively. The males are unrelated in terms of dimensions and moderately related in terms of indices. The lower indicial coefficient is indicative of some difference in the size of the crania, but the combined ratio (24 significant differences in 57 items compared) is considerably higher than that found in the

COMPARISONS ON THE VARIETAL LEVEL 93

Ilinid-Muskogid "type" varietal comparisons, i.e., 11 of 57 items.

Tables 251 and 252 contain the comparisons of the Fort Ancient Ilinid and Fort Ancient Muskogid females. They differ significantly in 12 of the 35 measurements (CM, L, B, TFH, UFH, IOB, BOB, AIB, DC, DS, MN, and BCB) and in 18 of the 22 indices (only B/L, H/L, BA/MF, and LOH/LOBM are not involved). The coefficients resulting from the ratios are 37 and 82, respectively, which reflects a moderate relationship in dimensions but total nonrelatedness in indices. Hence, the females from the Fort Ancient Ilinid and the Fort Ancient Muskogid series exhibit greater physical dissimilarity than do their male counterparts.

It may be concluded that there are in fact two distinct physical types in the Fort Ancient Aspect. How unique the types are may be revealed in the results of subsequent tests.

The Fort Ancient Ilinid and Ilinid varieties are not compared since, as noted earlier, the Anderson population is nearly identical to the Oakwood Mound series, the "type" Ilinid variety. It follows that the Fort Ancient Ilinid series, of which the Anderson population comprises a sizable sample, would show practically the same measure of near identity in dimensional and indicial values.

The "t" scores of Fort Ancient Ilinid-Lenid male comparisons are given in Tables 253 and 254 and demonstrate considerable population distance between the groups. There are 20 examples of significantly differing measurements and 10 significantly differing indices in the cranium, B, H, UFH, TFB, MFB, IOB, BOB, NB, DC, DS, LOH, LOBM, LOBD, MB, ML, FL, FLA, LM, BCB, and G/; and B/L, H/L, H/L + B/2, BA/TFB, SIOB/IOB, AIB/BOB, NB/NH, LOH/LOBM, MB/ML, and LM/BCB. The coefficients of 59 for measurements and 48 for indices place the two groups into different varietal categories. The Fort Ancient Ilinid male variety look less like the Lenids than does the Ilinid "type" variety. However, when size factors are eliminated, some physical similarity is observed in the facial region, implying the retention of some ancestral Lenid traits.

The females of the Fort Ancient Ilinid and the Lenid varieties display numerous physical characteristics in common, as is apparent in the "t" scores of Tables 255 and 256. Only 4 of 35 measurements (NB, DC, DS, and MB) and 2 of 22 indices (TFH/TFB and DS/DC) diverge at the 4 percent level of significant difference. Both coefficients, 11 and 9 respectively, fall well within the index class of near identity and manifest the retention of Archaic Lenid physical features in the Upper Mississippian Fort Ancient female population.

The "t" scores of the Fort Ancient Ilinid-Iswanid male groups in Tables 257 and 258 show an extreme population distance in the measurements but a moderate relatedness in indices. The groups share only 2 of 35 measurements (TP and BA) and one of those, parietal thickness, does little to differentiate populations. However, there are significant differences in only 7 of 22 indices (UFH/TFB, BA/MF, BA/TFB, AIB/BOB, NB/NH, SMN/MN, and MB/ML), disclosing the influence of the size factor. The coefficients of relatedness, 94 for measurements and 32 for indices, are somewhat like the correlations found in the Iswanid-Ilinid comparisons. The Fort Ancient Ilinid male skulls are larger than the Iswanids but do exhibit similar vault proportions; in the absence of a female Iswanid comparative series, it may be tentatively assumed the females would display similar differences. Nevertheless, it must be remembered that these physical types are from quite different temporal levels, i.e., Archaic and Protohistoric periods.

The scores of the Fort Ancient Ilinid-Muskogid "t" test for the male crania are listed in Tables 259 and 260 and show significant differences in 13 of 34 measurements (H, LB, TFB, SIOB, DC, MN, LOBD, ML, FL, FLA, LM, BCB, and SH) and in 7 of 21 indices (H/L, H/B, H/L + B/2, TFB/ B, SIOB/IOB, MB/ML, and LM/BCB). These ratios yield coefficients of relatedness of 38 and 33, respectively, portraying a moderate degree of relatedness between the groups. The physical characteristics of the females cannot be examined due to the unavailability of a Muskogid series. There is a greater distance between the Fort Ancient Ilinids and Muskogids than was found between the Muskogid and Ilinid "type" varieties, which may be attributed to spacial and temporal differences of the former groups. The source of the variation will be investigated later in this report.

The "t" scores of the Fort Ancient Ilinid-Seneca male series are presented in Tables 261 and 262. Significant differences are observed in 19 of 34 measurements and in 10 of 21 indices, i.e., measurements: TP, L, B, LB, TFB, MFB, IOB, SIOB, BOB, LOH, LOBM, LOBD, ML, FL, FLA, LM, BCB, SH, and G/, indices: B/L, H/L, H/B, TFH/TFB, UFH/TFB, UFH/MFB, MF/TFB, BA/ TFB, SIOB/IOB, and MB/ML, giving values of 59 and 48 respectively, as the coefficients of relatedness. The magnitude of the coefficients places the two series in different varieties, meaning that if the Fort Ancient group exhibits Ilinid-like features, then the Seneca series must represent another varietal type. The most probable varietal affiliation of the Seneca would be with the Lenid physical type; and it may be recalled that in an earlier comparison, the Fort Ancient Ilinid males displayed a varietal order of difference to the Lenids. Thus, although the Seneca supposedly display Ilinid characteristics, they may retain a significant number of Lenid features, which would influence t-values. The present tables reveal contrasting metrical and indicial values in all regions of the male skull except in the nasal structure. Perhaps a comparison of the females will supply additional information of relatedness for the series.

The Fort Ancient Ilinid and Seneca females in Tables 263 and 264 reveal a significant difference in 15 of the 34 measurements (TP, L, LB, SIOB, AIB, DS, MN, LOBM, LOBD, ML, FL, FLA, LM, BCB, and G/) and in 6 of 21 indices (B/L, SIOB/IOB, AIB/BOB, LOH/LOBM, MB/ML, and LM/BCB). These ratios produce coefficients of relatedness of 43 and 29, respectively, meaning nonrelationship of dimensions but a close to moderate relationship of indices. Physically the Fort Ancient Ilinid and Seneca females exhibit a closer resemblance than do the males of the series, but they appear to be less closely related than are the Fort Ancient Ilinid and Lenid females in an earlier comparison. An additional comparison was made of the Lenid and Seneca females ("t" scores not present) to test the extent of their relatedness. The females differ significantly in 7 of 34 measurements and 6 of 21 indices, which represents close relationship in dimension values but more of a moderate relationship in indicial values, i.e., coefficients of relatedness are 21 and 29, respectively. In the final analysis, the protohistoric Seneca and Fort Ancient Ilinid females do not closely resemble one another; the latter seem to have retained more Lenid-like characteristics than the former. Thus, on the basis of the present evidence, it may be concluded that there appears to have been little physical admixture of the Seneca with the Fort Ancient peoples.

The "t" scores of the Fort Ancient Ilinid-Shawnee male comparisons are found in Tables 265 and 266. Significant differences are recorded for 4 of 34 measurements (TFH, MB, FL, and FLA) and for 2 of 22 indices (LOH/LOBM and MB/ML), which yields coefficients of 12 and 9, respectively; the coefficients fall well within the index class of "near identity." The reliability of the coefficients may be questioned, however, in view of the disproportionate samples, especially since some of the pertinent dimensions and indices failed to register by having less than three degrees of freedom. Further evaluation of this test is withheld until the Fort Ancient Muskogid-Shawnee tests are made.

Only one Shawnee female is available for study so it is not possible to make valid comparisons between the Fort Ancient

Ilinid and Shawnee females. A visual comparison of the series suggests that a close relationship exists between the groups, but that statement is true only if additional Shawnee females are like the existing one.

The "t" scores of the Fort Ancient Muskogid-Lenid groups in Tables 267 and 268 show significant differences at the 4 percent level in 16 of 34 measurements (L, TFB, MFB, IOB, SIOB, BOB, NB, DS, MN, LOBM, LOBD, ML, FL, FLA, LM, and BCB) and in 12 of 22 indices (B/L, H/B, PAH/L, MF/B, UFH/TFB, UFH/MFB, TFB/B, SIOB/IOB, NB/NH, SMN/MN, LOH/LOBM and LM/BCB), which produces coefficients of relatedness of 50 and 55, respectively. The coefficient values readily demonstrate that the male series are from different varieties, and this is substantiated by the distribution of variation found in all parts of the skull.

The females of the Fort Ancient Muskogid and Lenid series of Tables 269 and 270 vary in 9 of 35 measurements (CM, LM, B, NB, DC, DS, SMN, BCB, and SH) and in 12 of 22 indices (H/B, PAH/L, MF/B, TFH/TFB, UFH/MFB, TFB/B, MF/TFB, SIOB/IOB, AIB/BOB, NB/NH, SMN/MN, and MB/ML). According to the coefficients of relatedness, 26 and 55, respectively, the females have a fairly close dimensional relationship but exhibit no indicial relationship. Although the validity of the coefficients might be questioned on the basis of the ill-proportioned samples, it is probable that had the samples contained an equal number of crania, a significant increase in dissimilar traits would have been found.

The "t" scores of the Fort Ancient Muskogid-Iswanid male series are presented in Tables 271 and 272. In this case, significant differences are observed in 27 of 36 measurements (only TP, L, PAH, SIOB, LOBD, MB, BA, RL, and G/ are not affected) and in 9 of 21 indices (H/L, H/B, H/L + B/2, $\overline{TFB/B}$, BA/MF, BA/TFB, AIB/BOB, NB/NH, and MB/ML), resulting in coefficients of 79 and 43, respectively. The groups differ notably in cranial size and are distinctive enough to be viewed as separate physical varieties. Except for size differences, there seems to be less population distance between the Fort Ancient Muskogids and the Iswanid physical type than between the former and the Lenid type. However, the indicial coefficient of the Fort Ancient Muskogid-Iswanid test is somewhat higher than that exhibited with the Fort Ancient Ilinid series. The females are not compared due to the lack of an Iswanid series.

The "t" scores of the Fort Ancient Muskogid-Muskogid male series are presented in Tables 273 and 274. Significant differences are found in 16 of 34 measurements (CM, B, H, LB, UFH,

TFB, SIOB, NB, MB, ML, FL, FLA, LM, BCB, SH, and G/) and 12 of 21 indices (only B/L, TFH/TFB, MF/TFB, BA/MF, BA/TFB, AIB/BOB, DS/DC, SMN/MN, and LOH/LOBD are not affected), which yields coefficients of 47 and 57, respectively. According to those values, the Fort Ancient Muskogids do not belong to the same physical variety as the Muskogid "type" series, and in earlier tests the Muskogid "type" series appeared to be more closely related to the Fort Ancient Ilinid series than the Fort Ancient series are related to each other. An examination of the morphology of the three series would not convey the same implication, which emphasizes the necessity of using dimensions, indices, and morphological observations when correlating physical groups.

The "t" scores of the Fort Ancient Muskogid-Historic Muskogid male series are presented in Tables 275 and 276 in order to investigate the possibility of physical admixture with more southern tribes. Significant differences occur in 17 of 34 measurements (B, H, UFH, IOB, SIOB, BOB, AIB, NB, DC, MB, ML, FL, FLA, LM, BCB, SH, and G/) and in 9 of 21 indices (H/L, H/B, H/L + B/2, TFH/TFB, UFH/TFB, SIOB/IOB, AIB/BOB, NB/NH, and DS/DC), producing coefficient values of 50 and 43, respectively. The groups seem unrelated in both dimensions and indices, implying that little physical admixture occured between the males of the southern components of the Fort Ancient Aspect and the historic tribes to the south of Fort Ancient.

A tentative comparison of the Fort Ancient Muskogid and Historic Muskogid females is presented in Tables 277 and 278. The series differ in 4 of 27 measurements (CM, MF, H, and AIB), but several dimensions failed to register any degrees of freedom in producing the t-probability, which cut the measurement ratio still further, i.e., to 4 of 23 measurements. Coefficients of relatedness for the ratios are 15 and 19, respectively, and represent close relationship in dimensional values. Significant differences in 7 of 17 indices (H/L, H/B, H/L + B/2, MF/B, SIOB/IOB, AIB/BOB, and MB/ML), producing a coefficient of relatedness of 41, suggest nonrelationship between the groups when the size factor is removed. However, the samples contain highly unequal numbers of individuals, and with the mandibles missing from the Historic Muskogid series, fewer significant measurements could be taken. These factors undoubtedly affected the ratios produced and the coefficients derived from them, but the extent cannot be determined. There is close agreement between the male and the female indicial coefficients in that both signify nonrelatedness between the Protohistoric Fort Ancient Muskogids and the Historic

Muskogid tribe. Such a degree of difference is unexpected since both groups supposedly derive from the same basic ancestral stock. Whether the difference arises from physical changes or adjustments made by each group to its environment or from some degree of Ilinid admixture in the Fort Ancient Muskogids is difficult to say. A comparison of the Fort Ancient Muskogid and Ilinid female "type" varieties shows a significant difference in 16 of the 35 measurements and in 14 of the 22 indices, CM, TP, B, LB, UFH, MFB, AIB, NB, MN, LOBM, FL, FLA, LM, BCB, SH, and RL; H/B, H/L + B/2, PAH/L, MF/B, TFH/TFB, UFH/TFB, UFH/MFB, TFB/B, MF/TFB, SIOB/IOB, AIB/BOB, NB/NH, MB/ML, and LM/BCB (Tables 279 and 280). Coefficients of relatedness of 46 and 64, respectively, result from the metrical ratios. The Fort Ancient Muskogid females obviously did not receive physical input from the Ilinid variety; rather, they exhibit a closer degree of relationship to the Historic Muskogids than to either the Ilinid "type" variety or the Fort Ancient Ilinids. Accordingly, one may deduce that the level of differing physical characteristics of the Fort Ancient Muskogid and Historic Muskogid females resulted from a trend toward increasing homogeneity in two inbreeding populations.

The "t" scores of the Fort Ancient Muskogid-Shawnee male series are presented in Tables 281 and 282. These comparisons produced the highest degree of metrical homogeneity of any series examined, although the series were very different in the number of individuals contained in them and the degrees of freedom were insufficient for some values to register. Only 2 of the 35 measurements (MN and LOBM) and none of the 22 indices displayed significant differences. The coefficients of relatedness that resulted from these ratios were 6 and 0, respectively, indicating almost complete identity of the groups. Before definitive statements are made about the degrees of physical similarity between the Shawnee and the Fort Ancient derived series, the possible relationships between the Shawnee and the Historic Muskogid series will be examined, especially since reference is often made in the literature to the Shawnee living in the South at some earlier time.

The "t" scores of the Shawnee-Historic Muskogid male comparisons are given in Tables 283 and 284. Significant differences are observed in 6 of 34 measurements (TFH, MN, LOBM, MB, LM, and BCB) and in 1 of 21 indices (LOH/LOBM), yielding coefficients of 18 and 5, respectively; slightly larger coefficients are produced if traits having more than 3 degrees of freedom are counted, i.e., differences in 6 of 26 measurements and in 1 of 17 indices, yielding coefficients of 23 and 6, respectively.

COMPARISONS ON THE VARIETAL LEVEL 99

The coefficients indicate a close degree of relatedness, moving toward near identity in terms of measurements, and near identity in terms of indices. There is a slight difference in the cranial size of the two groups, with the mean measurement columns revealing that the male Shawnee have a slightly larger cranium.

The Shawnee-Historic Muskogid male test suffers from the same inadequacy that was found in the earlier tests involving the Shawnee, i.e., the small sample of available Shawnee crania that are used in the comparisons. Such dissimilarity of sample size has resulted in the loss of information of vital measurements, e.g., breadth, height, upper facial height, etc., and their corresponding indices. However, until a larger sample of Shawnee crania is available, the present series must serve as a tentative representation of the tribe.

The single Shawnee female is an insufficient sample for obtaining "t" score values when it is compared with the Fort Ancient Muskogid females or with the Historic Muskogid females. In a visual comparison of the dimensional and indicial values of the three groups (metrical tables of the Shawnee not in report), the Shawnee female does not resemble the Historic Muskogid group at all, and it exhibits few physical characteristics in common with the Fort Ancient Muskogid females. The Shawnee female closely resembles the Fort Ancient Ilinid females in most parts of the skull, as noted previously, but some dissimilarity in the mandibular region is still present.

Table 285 summarizes the results of the "t" tests of the Fort Ancient varietal types. The Fort Ancient Ilinid males are clearly differentiated from the Lenid and Seneca series at a varietal level of difference, but the distinction is more apparent in the metrical values than in the morphology of the groups. The Fort Ancient Ilinid females, on the other hand, exhibit metrical values along the phyletic lines of the Lenid female variety, although some morphological distinctions are noted in the facial region of the former, e.g., an shorter, broader face. Strong physical differences between the Seneca and Fort Ancient Ilinid females are inferred from the contrasting metrical values even though the cranial morphology of the females is somewhat less divergent.

The Fort Ancient Ilinid males exhibit a moderate indicial relationship with the phyletically older Iswanid series, but the dimensional coefficients and the morphological observations clearly reflect the contrasting cranial sizes. The moderate degree of relationship found in the metrical values of the Fort Ancient Ilinids and those of the Muskogid variety may reflect some measure of admixture between the Fort Ancient Ilinids and the Upper Mississippi Muskogids, but the coefficient levels resulting from the comparisons of the Fort Ancient "derived" Ilinid and Muskogid groups (46 and 36, respectively) make that theory questionable. It is more probable that the source of the physical similarity between the Fort Ancient Ilinids and the Iswanids and Muskogids is to be found elsewhere, e.g., in the close relationship of the "type" Ilinid and Muskogid varieties. In Table 248, the Ilinid and Muskogid comparative values border on "near identity;" hence, it appears that the physical similarity, as it is expressed in metrical terms, is retained in the Fort Ancient Ilinid group to some extent. It must be pointed out, however, that such close physical similarity is not found in the cranial morphology of the groups. The level of difference may be partially accounted for in terms of regional (geographic) variations that occur among populations. The moderate degree of similarity expressed in the indicial coefficient (32) of the Fort Ancient Ilinid-Iswanid test may be indicative of intermixture between pre-Fort Ancient populations. The indicial coefficient (23) of the Iswanid-Ilinid test strongly suggests that admixture was under way in the population inhabiting the Middle Ohio Valley as the Fort Ancient culture gradually developed. This theory will be pursued further in a later section.

The Fort Ancient Muskogid males are differentiated from the Lenid, Iswanid, Muskogid, and Historic Muskogid series at the varietal level; but the dissimilarity is mainly in terms of metrical values since some morphological similarity with the latter two series can be observed. The Fort Ancient Muskogid females exhibit almost as much physical distinction as their male counterparts when tested with the females of the above series. It is unfortunate that female series of the Iswanid and Muskogid cannot be acquired for comparison in order to determine more fully the extent of the physical diversity in the populations. The present metrical evidence suggests nonrelatedness of the Fort Ancient Muskogids with the Iswanids and Muskogid "type" varieties even though the protohistoric group is believed to have developed along the Iswanid and Muskogid phyletic lines, and such evidence would be highly misleading if the morphology of the skulls were ignored. An additional point to remember is that the Fort Ancient Muskogid "derived" physical type tends to be restricted to the Madisonville focus, and especially to the Madisonville site, in which case inbreeding may have contributed making the population distinct from those around it, i.e., the Fort Ancient Ilinid peoples, and from its ancestral line. This possibility will be explored further in the next section.

COMPARISONS ON THE VARIETAL LEVEL

The small Shawnee male series exhibits physical characteristics at a level of "near identity" with the Fort Ancient "derived" Ilinid and Muskogid types and with the Historic Muskogid series. The female Shawnee skull, however, displays a closer resemblance to the Fort Ancient Ilinid series than to either of the other groups. These lines of interrelationship must be investigated further to determine what contribution each has made, if any, to the evolvement of the Shawnee tribe.

VI

THE RECONSTRUCTION OF
FORT ANCIENT PHYLETIC HISTORY

THE metrical comparisons and cranial analyses of the preceding chapters serve as guides in the attempt to reconstruct the phyletic history of the Fort Ancient population. It will be recalled that the crania of each focus were found to be rather homogeneous in their physical features—except for some degree of heterogeneity in the crania of the Madisonville Focus—making it possible to delineate foci populations. Too much physical diversity existed among foci populations to warrant the grouping of all crania into a single aspect population, although metrical values indicated that there was a fairly close relationship between some foci, e.g., Baum and Anderson. In an effort to better understand the interrelationships of the Fort Ancient people with respect to their geographical distribution, a further examination of the temporal range of their culture is essential.

Since the publication of The Fort Ancient Aspect (Griffin, 1943), numerous radiocarbon dates have enabled investigators to define more precisely the antiquity of the Fort Ancient culture. As noted earlier, the Graham village site of the Baum Focus is dated at A. D. 1180 $\pm$ 145 years and A. D. 1665 $\pm$ 220 years as a result of Carbon - 14 analyses of two pieces of charcoal (McKenzie, 1967:75-77). However, the latter date is rejected since neither Madisonville traits nor historical traits are present. The shell-tempered sherds of the site bear some resemblance to the Feurt Incised wares, which introduces the possibility that Baum and Feurt coexisted in the same temporal period. Additional evidence of the antiquity of the Baum Focus comes from radiocarbon dates obtained from charcoal in the Blain village site in Ross County, Ohio, (Crane and Griffin, 1968:85). That site is dated at A. D. 1460 $\pm$ 100 years at a depth of 6 to 12 inches below the soil surface and A. D. 1190 $\pm$ 100 years at a 3-foot depth. The former date is rejected as being too recent for the Baum cultural complex, but the latter date is consistent with other dates for the Baum Focus. Rather than ignoring the A. D. 1460 ± 100 years date from the Blain site and the A. D. 1665 ± 220 years date from the Graham site, serious thought should be given to the view that the dates may give some indication of the decline of the Baum Focus.

A single radiocarbon date is known from a component of the Feurt Focus from the McCune village site in Athens, Ohio, (Crane and Griffin, 1968:78). A charcoal sample from 14 inches below the ground surface and plow zone is dated at A. D. 1320 ± 100 years; the sample comes from a level above a stratum containing Late Woodland pottery fragments. The site is viewed as being representative of the Feurt "phase" of Fort Ancient in that area, i.e., being intermediate between the Baum and Madisonville Foci.

A radiocarbon date of A. D. 1480 ± 150 years is assigned to the Pleasant Hill site (Crane and Griffin, 1959:173-98), a fortified Fort Ancient site near Troy, Ohio, a short distance north of the Steel Dam component of the Anderson Focus. The Pleasant Hill site displays a basic Woodland pattern with a Fort Ancient admixture in terms of the pottery removed from the village and grave areas. The presence of stone slabs in association with graves is reminiscent of burial practices in the Anderson Focus and, to a lesser extent, at Madisonville. The Erp site, a Fort Ancient village site located to the west of the Pleasant Hill site, is dated at A. D. 1435 ± 75 years, according to the Carbon - 14 analysis of a charcoal sample from a campfire (Crane and Griffin, 1963:230). There is some evidence of Late Woodland influence in the manufacture of the projectile points and of the pottery, but the site is believed to have been associated with the Steel Dam site of the Anderson Focus.

Few radiocarbon dates are available for dating the various components of the Madisonville Focus. European trade goods identify the recent temporal boundaries, but they supply no information about the antiquity of the focus. The Turpin component is dated at A. D. 1275 ± 150 years by radiocarbon analysis of charcoal samples (Crane and Griffin, 1961:110-11). The samples were found in association with Madisonville pottery at the bottom of a refuse pit 2 to 3 feet below ground surface. A second date comes from the Haffner-Kuntz site in Cincinnati, Ohio, (33Ha9); a date of A. D. 575 ± 150 years comes from a Carbon - 14 analysis of charcoal found at a 3 to 4 foot depth (Crane and Griffin, 1961:111). The site contained Madisonville Plain sherds, some cord-marked fragments, and a vessel resembling a long-necked water bottle. Two extended burials were recovered, one being found in a slab-lined grave. While the Carbon - 14 date is an early date for a Fort Ancient site, it should not be completely rejected unless factors such as contamination would cast doubt on its authenticity. If the date is valid, at least a portion of the Madisonville Focus would have the greatest antiquity in the Fort Ancient Aspect, but additional dates of such antiquity are needed from the focus before this can be fully accepted, especially in view of the extreme time difference between the Haffner-Kuntz date and the Turpin date. The latter date is in general agreement with the temporal period of Fort Ancient occupation.

According to the various acceptable radiocarbon dates, the Fort Ancient culture covered a temporal span from about A. D. 1100 until historic times, with the Baum Focus exhibiting slightly greater antiquity than the other foci. The Madisonville Focus appears to be nearly as old as Baum (on the basis of the Turpin date) and exhibits a temporal depth beyond the Anderson-like components of Pleasant Hill and Erp.

Earlier in the study it was stated that a detailed examination was made of the physical characteristics of the Fort Ancient crania exhibiting Ilinid- or Muskogid-like tendencies, and two Fort Ancient "type" populations were formed on the basis of these resemblances. It was later found that the Fort Ancient Muskogid "type" seemed to be restricted mainly to the Madisonville Focus but was not the predominant type in all components of that focus, e.g., the Ilinid-like Sand Ridge component. The Fort Ancient Ilinid "type" was found to be fairly widespread throughout the aspect, being the main physical type in every focus except Madisonville, where it was present but overshadowed by the Muskogid type. The "t" score results of the Fort Ancient "types" clearly demonstrate that there are two physical types in the aspect and that they exhibit no more than a moderate degree of relationship to each other. However, the Fort Ancient Muskogid series displays less of a population distance to the Fort Ancient Ilinids than to any other varietal series with which it is compared. On the other hand, there is substantial evidence that the Fort Ancient Ilinid series is nearly identical to the Ilinid physical variety; is moderately related to the Muskogid variety; and is somewhat reminiscent of the Lenid variety in a few physical characteristics.

It becomes apparent that the Fort Ancient Ilinids display temporal and spacial relatedness with several populations, both ancestrally and contemporaneously. Such evidence of relatedness is not unexpected when a group has occupied an area over a long period of time. Cultural and physical contact between adjacent populations modifies each population to some extent, but at the same time, each group will retain some traits unique to itself. These principles apply well to the Fort Ancient Ilinid people.

It is proposed that the Fort Ancient Ilinid peoples represent the original inhabitants of the Fort Ancient cultural area, having evolved from a Woodland cultural base. The diversity of the artifactual remains makes it apparent that the Fort Ancient people did not live in isolation; there was contact between the different foci and with some neighboring populations. The physical characteristics of the people reinforce the proposal in that individuals having Ilinid-like traits are found in nearly all Fort Ancient components except Fox Farm.

In most components, burial practices were mainly of two types—the extended burial often found in Upper Mississippi sites and the flexed or partially flexed burial typical of the general Woodland cultural period. In addition, many Fort Ancient sites were actually multicomponent sites in which the Fort Ancient material from the upper strata was intermixed with the Woodland material below it or both strata were present without apparent admixture. The Madisonville type site illustrates the point. If the radiocarbon date of A. D. 575 ± 150 years is accepted, the component was inhabited for a long period, going back into Woodland times. Such time depth would account for the numerous Ilinid-like individuals in the site who probably were the earlier occupants. It might also provide an explanation for the ash pits and burials, found by the archaeologists, that had been dug through earlier burials. This supposition implies that the Fort Ancient Muskogid physical type was a later arrival on the site and in the aspect, possibly coming from the immediate south. Supporting evidence for the theory is to be found in the scarcity of the Fort Ancient Muskogid physical type in other foci of the aspect—those to the north and east of Madisonville—and in the northern Madisonville Focus components like Sand Ridge. There seems to have been little interbreeding between the populations in contact since few individuals in the Aspect display an admixture of Ilinid and Muskogid physical characteristics. The high values of the coefficients of relatedness which resulted from the comparisons of the Fort Ancient Ilinid and Fort Ancient Muskogid "type" series demonstrate the small amount of physical admixture of the groups.

The question of the origin of the Fort Ancient Muskogid group then arises. In this report, the author is unable to offer conclusive evidence of the physical relationships between the Fort Ancient Muskogid and prehistoric tribes immediately to the south of the Fort Ancient culture area, i.e., the Tennessee Stone-Grave peoples. The inability to secure a Stone-Grave series for comparative testing is felt to compromise the position of the Fort Ancient Muskogids somewhat, since their phyletic affiliation to the former must, at present, rest on hypotheses or speculations or, at best, permit tentative conclusions to be drawn. This is recognized as a less than desirable position when attempting to identify clearly the ancestral lines of the Fort Ancient Muskogids, account for their appearance in the Middle Ohio Valley, and delineate their relationship to the historic Shawnee Indian Tribe.

As noted earlier, the Madisonville Focus contains the greatest number of Fort Ancient Muskogid individuals, and they are concentrated mainly in the southern components. However, there is a substantial degree of dissimilarity between the deformed Muskogid-like crania of the Madisonville site and those of the Fox Farm site in Kentucky, i.e., cranial deformation is more prevalent and more extreme among the Fox Farm people. Whether the Fox Farm people exhibit a close metrical and/or morphological relationship to people of the West Virginia Clover Focus, e.g., the population of the Buffalo site, is not presently known; but the former do not appear to be closely related to the people of the Hardin Village site, who strike one as being more like the Madisonville Muskogids. (Reconstruction of the Hardin Village population was not completed in time for its inclusion in this report.) The Fort Ancient sites in north central Kentucky contain individuals who also look like the Madisonville Muskogid group; and it is less common for a Fort Ancient Ilinid individual to be found in these sites.

The distribution of the Muskogid-like crania strongly suggests a northern movement of a Muskogid population in late prehistoric times. They met the Ilinid-like Fort Ancient people in the middle Ohio Valley and, at some sites, replaced the former inhabitants. The Muskogid penetration can be demarcated through the physical characteristics of the people and from a cultural tradition, the use of stone in burying their dead—crudely fashioned stone-lined grave, stone at head and foot, body placed on stone slab, etc. The Fort Ancient Muskogid burial practices are reminiscent of the Tennessee Stone-Grave people but do not attain the level of refinement diagnostic of the latter group. This series of events introduces the hypothesis that the Fort Ancient Muskogids originated as a northern thrust of the early Tennessee Stone-Grave culture, reaching the Middle Ohio Valley in the latter part of the Upper Mississippian period. They became the dominant physical type in the northern Kentucky sites and at Madisonville, but interaction and inbreeding with people from the Anderson or

Baum Focus had hardly begun before white contact. Given the above premises, the relationship of the Fort Ancient Muskogids to the Shawnee people needs attention.

It is recognized that the small sample of known Shawnee crania may not typify the entire tribe and, of necessity, permits only tentative conclusions to be drawn from the data. Nevertheless, the coefficients of relatedness for the comparisons of the Shawnee and the Fort Ancient "type" series suggest that an admixture of the predominant physical types in the area during protohistoric times resulted in the historic Shawnee people. Since some of the late prehistoric crania noted earlier display similar kinds of admixture, it is believed that the historic Shawnee peoples were the descendants of the Fort Ancient archaeological population and not recent comers to the Middle Ohio Valley, as is often proposed in the literature. The fact that the Shawnee crania exhibit some Muskogid characteristics is considered to be merely an indication of the admixture that was occurring in late prehistoric times, was present in early historic times, and is to be found today in the unmixed Shawnee.

Supporting evidence for this proposal is found in other fields of study. For many years linguists have recognized a Central Algonquian linguistic affiliation of the Shawnee (C. F. Voegelin, 1940:409). While Haas (1958:254) places the Shawnee into a Proto-Central Eastern Algonkian category with the Miami, Delaware, and New England languages, Pierce (n.d.) proposes that the Shawnee, Kickapoo (a southern tribe) and Sauk-Fox (a northern tribe) are members of a closely related group of speech communities. In the recent Map of North American Indian Languages compiled by C. F. and F. M. Voegelin (1964; 1965), the Shawnee language is viewed as belonging to the Algonquian language family.

Much of the ethnohistorical literature is believed to be a less than reliable source of information on Shawnee antiquity, since the early travelers encountered the historic descendants of the tribe. However, the ethnohistorical record provides indirect evidence of the social environment of the late prehistoric Shawnee and the resulting migratory pattern of life of their descendants. Marquette notes that the Iroquois traveled south to the Shawnee country for purposes of making war with the Shawnee and taking captives from them (Jesuit Relations and Allied Documents, 1900: 45). Numerous references are made in the Jesuit Relations (Vols. 47:145-49; 53:49; 54:115-17; 62:209) to hostilities between the Shawnee and other tribes. From Brinton's report (1866:1-4), it would appear that the Shawnee tribe was, by tradition, a nomadic population; but when closely examined, many of the statements are actually speculative comments which expose the bias of the speaker. E. W. Voegelin (1944:240-379) observes that obsolete Shawnee burial practices are more like the practices of northern tribes than of populations to the south, and maintains that the early Shawnee habitation region was centered to the north and east of Madisonville. While some Shawnee are known to have migrated southward into Creek territory, they do not represent the entire tribe but only various bands from the five different Shawnee divisions who went southward in more recent times. Witthoft and Hunter (1955:42-57) propose that the Shawnee tribe is indigeneous in the Ohio region and comprised at least a portion of the Fort Ancient population. Their thesis is based upon the archaeological manifestation of Madisonville, Shawnee traditions as they appear in early historical accounts, and excerpts from early French records that pertain to the Shawnee.

In view of the brief linguistic and ethnohistorical review and of the archaeological and physical evidence that has been presented in this report, the author is convinced that the Shawnee Indians are indeed the descendants of the Fort Ancient population. Moreover, it is maintained that the historic Shawnee represent a physical admixture of the Fort Ancient Ilinid and the Fort Ancient Muskogid varieties, but that the prehistoric Shawnee were more like the Fort Ancient Ilinid variety, i.e., the original Fort Ancient people. The social environment of the protohistoric Shawnee population appears to have attained stability, and not until pressure was exerted on the tribe by the Iroquois from the north and then the early white contact from the east did the later Shawnee develop the tribal mobility for which they are known.

The author does not feel that this report resolves all questions pertaining to the Shawnee Fort Ancient population; on the contrary, it is hoped that additional research may result from this analysis: perusal of the Iroquoian-Shawnee relationship, investigation of the Tennessee Stone-Grave influence on Fort Ancient, studies of the position of the Clover Focus people in the Fort Ancient Aspect. This study is viewed at present as an initial step in setting the stage for future studies of the early inhabitants of the Middle and Upper Ohio Valley.

REFERENCES

Brinton, D. G. (M.D.)
   1866   The Shawnee and their Migrations. The Historical Magazine Vol. 10, No. 1:1-4.

Crane, H. R. and James B. Griffin
   1959   University of Michigan Radiocarbon Dates IV. American Journal of Science Radiocarbon Supplement, 1:173-98.
   1961   University of Michigan Radiocarbon Dates VI. Radiocarbon 3:105-25.
   1963   University of Michigan Radiocarbon Dates VIII. Radiocarbon 5:228-53.
   1968   University of Michigan Radiocarbon Dates XII. Radiocarbon 10:61-114.

Crichton, J. M.
   1966   A Multiple Discriminant Analysis of Egyptian and African Negro Crania. Papers of the Peabody Museum of Archaeology and Ethnology, Harvard University LVII, 1:47-67.

Croxton, Frederick E.
   1959   Elementary Statistics with Applications in Medicine and the Biological Sciences. Dover Publications, Inc. Dover, New York.

Dunnell, Robert C.
   n.d.   A General Survey of Fort Ancient in the Kentucky-West Virginia Area. Unpublished manuscript on file at the Museum of Anthropology, University of Kentucky. Lexington.

Funkhouser, W. D.
   1938   A Study of the Physical Anthropology and Pathology of the Osteological Material from the Norris Basin. In: An Archaeological Survey of the Norris Basin in Eastern Tennessee, by W. S. Webb. Bureau of American Ethnology Bulletin No. 118:225-51

Funkhouser, W. D. and W. S. Webb
   1928   Ancient Life in Kentucky. The Kentucky Geological Survey Series 6, Vol. 34. Frankfort.

Griffin, James B.
   1943   The Fort Ancient Aspect. University of Michigan Press. Ann Arbor. (Reissued, 1966, as Anthropological Paper No. 28 of the University of Michigan Museum of Anthropology).

Haas, Mary R.
   1958   A New Linguistic Relationship in North America: Algonkian and the Gulf Languages. Southwestern Journal of Anthropology 14:231-64.

Hooton, E. A. and C. C. Willoughby
   1920   Indian Village Site and Cemetery near Madisonville, Ohio. Papers of the Peabody Museum of American Archaeology and Ethnology, Harvard University VIII, 1.

Howells, W. W.
   1966   Craniometry and Multivariate Analysis. Papers of the Peabody Museum of Archaeology and Ethnology, Harvard University LVII, No. 1:3-43.

Jesuit Relations and Allied Documents, The
   1896-   Travels and Explorations of the Jesuit Missionaries in New
   1901   France, 1610-1791, 73 volumes. Reuben Gold Thwaites, ed. Burrows Brothers. Cleveland.

Long, Joseph K.
   1966   A Test of Multiple-Discriminant Analysis as a Means of Determining Evolutionary Changes and Intergroup Relationships in Physical Anthropology. American Anthropologist, 68, 2, 1:444-64.

Martin, Rudolf
   1928   Lehrbuch der Anthropologie. Jena: Gustav Fischer, 2nd ed.

McKenzie, Douglas H.
   1967   The Graham Village Site: a Fort Ancient Settlement in the Hocking Valley, Ohio. In: Studies in Ohio Archaeology, Olaf Prufer and Douglas H. McKenzie, eds. Press of Western Reserve University. Cleveland.

McKern, T. W. and E. H. Munro
   1959   A Statistical Technique for Classifying Human Skeletal Remains. American Antiquity, XXIV, 4:375-82.

Metz, Charles L.
   1881   The Prehistoric Monuments of Anderson Township, Hamilton County, Ohio. The Journal of the Cincinnati Society of Natural History, 4, 4:293-305.

Mills, William C.
   1904   Explorations of the Gartner Mound and Village Site. The Ohio Archaeological and Historical Quarterly 13, 2:129-89.
   1906   Explorations of the Baum Prehistoric Village Site.. The Ohio Archaeological and Historical Quarterly 15:45-136.
   1922   The Feurt Mounds and Village Site. Ohio Archaeological and Historical Society Publications, 26:304-449.

Moorehead, Warren K.
   1892   Primitive Man in Ohio. G. P. Putnam's Sons. New York.
   1897   Report of Field Work. Ohio Archaeological and Historical Publications 5:165-275.

REFERENCES

Neumann, Georg K.
n.d. Racial Differentiation in the American Indian. Unpublished Ph. D. dissertation, University of Chicago.
1942 Types of Artificial Cranial Deformation in the Eastern United States. American Antiquity VII, 3:306-10.
1952 Archaeology and Race in the American Indian. In: Archaeology of Eastern United States. James B. Griffin, ed. University of Chicago Press. Chicago.
1960 Origins of the Indians of the Middle Mississippi Area. Proceedings of the Indiana Academy of Science 69:66-68.

Neumann, Holm W.
n.d. The Delimitation of the Walcolid Variety of Man. Unpublished Master's thesis. Indiana University.

Pierce, J. E.
n.d. A Test of the Mutual Intelligibility of the Shawnee, Kickapoo, Ojibwa, and Sauk-Fox. Unpublished Master's thesis. Indiana University.

Robbins, Louise M.
n.d. Physical and Cultural Relationships of the Late Archaic Red Ocher People of the Illinois Valley. Unpublished Master's thesis. Indiana University.

Shetrone, Henry C.
1926 Explorations of the Hopewell Group of Prehistoric Earthworks. Ohio Archaeological and Historical Quarterly Vol. 37, No. 1:1-227. Columbus.

Smail, J. Kenneth
n.d. The Use of Female Crania in Demonstrating Racial Relationships. Unpublished Master's thesis. Indiana University.

Smith, Harlan I.
1910 The Prehistoric Ethnology of a Kentucky Site. Anthropological Papers of the American Museum of Natural History VI, 2:173-233.

Snow, Charles E.
1948 Indian Knoll Skeletons. The University of Kentucky Reports in Anthropology IV, 3, II:371-555.

Starr, S. Frederick
1960 The Archaeology of Hamilton County, Ohio. The Journal of the Cincinnati Museum of Natural History 23, 1:2-130.

Thomas, Cyrus
1894 Report on the Mound Explorations of the Bureau of Ethnology. Twelfth Annual Report of the Bureau of American Ethnology.

Voegelin, C. F.
1940 Shawnee Stems and the Jacob P. Dunn Miami Dictionary, Part V. Indiana Historical Society, Prehistory Research Series, 1, 10:409-78.

Voegelin, C. F. and F. M. Voegelin
    1964   Languages of the World: Native America Fascicle One.
              Anthropological Linguistics 6, 6.
    1965   Languages of the World: Native America Fascicle Two.
              Anthropological Linguistics 7, 7.

Voegelin, Erminie Wheeler
    1944   Mortuary Customs of the Shawnee and Other Eastern Tribes.
              Indiana Historical Society, Prehistory Research Series II,
              4:240-379.

Witthoft, John and William A. Hunter
    1955   The Seventeenth-Century Origins of the Shawnee. Ethnohistory
              II, 1:42-57.

Yuker, Harold E.
    1958   A Guide to Statistical Calculations. G. P. Putnam's Sons.
              New York.

APPENDIXES

APPENDIX A

METRICAL AND MORPHOLOGICAL TERMINOLOGY
(SEE CHAPTER I)

APPENDIX A

STATISTICAL PROCEDURES

The numerical values of the metrical dimensions, indices, and morphological observations of all crania were placed on punch cards to expedite the handling of the mathematical calculations that were involved in the various statistical tests of the study. The facilities of the University of Kentucky Computing Center were made available to the author, and with the assistance of the programer, all tests were run on the IBM 0360 computer.

The morphological observation percentages were obtained by using the One Way Frequency Tables Program—ØWFTS. The program can build one way frequency tables and provide the percentage for each response of each item or question.

The means and standard deviations of all series were obtained from two programs. Means and standard deviations in Chapter III resulted from the XBAR program (mean, standard deviation and variance); means, etc., in succeeding chapters were computed as a part of the TMISS program (paired t-tests with missing data).

The TMISS program was used to gain t-scores for uncorrelated data. In uncorrelated t-tests, a test is performed to determine the homogeneity of the variance of the metrical values. The appropriate standard error of differences and the degrees of freedom are chosen accordingly. A "two-tail" hypothesis is used in the test, since it takes into consideration any deviation that occurs on either side of the mean. The computer output consists of sums, means, standard deviations, standard error, sums of deviations squared, coefficient of variation, number of observations, t-ratios and t-probabilities, and degrees of freedom.

See Statistical Method on following pages.

METHOD:

The following formulas are used in computing:

Sum: $\sum X_i$

Mean: $\dfrac{\sum X_i}{N_i}$

Variance: $\dfrac{N_i \sum X_i^2 - (\sum X_i)^2}{N_i(N_i - 1)} = S_i^2$

Standard deviation: $\sqrt{S_i^2} = SD_i$

Standard error: $\dfrac{SD_i}{\sqrt{N_i - 1}}$

Coefficient of variation: $\dfrac{SD_i}{\text{mean}_i}$

T-ratio: $\dfrac{\text{mean}_i - \text{mean}_j}{\text{standard error of difference}}$

Standard error of difference:

Correlated variables — $\dfrac{\sqrt{\text{var}_i + \text{var}_j - 2r_{ij}\sqrt{\text{var}_i \text{var}_j}}}{N_{ij}}$

Uncorrelated variables — (unequal variances) $\sqrt{\dfrac{\text{var}_i}{N_i} + \dfrac{\text{var}_j}{N_j}}$

Uncorrelated variables — (equal variances) $\sqrt{S_p^2 \left[\dfrac{1}{N_i} + \dfrac{1}{N_j} \right]}$

where $S_p^2 = \dfrac{(N_i - 1)S_i^2 + (N_j - 1)S_j^2}{N_i + N_j - 2}$

APPENDIX A

Degrees of freedom:

for correlated variables - $N_{ij} - 1$

for uncorrelated variables - $\dfrac{S_d^4}{\dfrac{(S_i^2/N_i)^2}{N_i+1} + \dfrac{(S_j^2/N_j)^2}{N_j+1}} - 1.5$
(unequal variances)

where $S_d^4 = \dfrac{S_i^2}{N_i} + \dfrac{S_j^2}{N_j}$

for uncorrelated variables - $N_i + N_j - 2$
(equal variances)

Table 1

LIST OF MEASUREMENTS AND INDICES
(According to Martin, 1928:628-678)

Measurement	Abbrev.	Measuring Points
Cranial vault		
Cranial module	CM	L+B+H/3
Mean thickness, left parietal	TP	mean of three measurements
Glabello-occipital length	L	g - op
Maximum breadth	B	eu - eu
Minimum frontal breadth	MF	ft - ft
Basion-bregma height	H	ba - b
Basion-porion height	BPH	ba - po (proj.)
Length of cranial base	LB	n - ba
Face		
Total facial height	TFH	n - gn
Upper facial height	UFH	n - alv. pt.
Total facial breadth	TFB	zy - zy
Midfacial breadth	MFB	zmi - zmi
Interior biorbital breadth	IOB	fmo - fmo
Subtense to interior biorbital arc	SIOB	n $\downarrow$ fmo - fmo
Biorbital breadth	BOB	ec - ec
Anterior interorbital breadth	AIB	mf - mf
Nasal structure		
Nasal breadth	NB	maximum aperture breadth
Nasal height	NH	n - ns
Dacryal chord	DC	d - d
Dacryal subtense to arc	DS	subtense to arc d - d
Minimum nasal breadth	MN	minimum breadth of nasals
Subtense to nasal arc	SMN	subtense to MN arc

APPENDIX A

Table 1 - continued

Orbit

Left orbital height	LOH	rt ⊥ to LOB
Left orbital breadth, maxillofrontale	LOBM	mf - ec
Left orbital breadth, dacryon	LOBD	d - ec

Dental arch and profile

Maxillo-alveolar breadth	MB	ecm - ecm
Maxillo-alveolar length	ML	pr - alv
Facial length, prosthion	FL	ba - pr
Facial length, alveolar pt.	FLA	ba - alv. pt.

Mandible

Length of mandible	LM	condylo-symphyseal length
Bicondylar breadth	BCB	cdl - cdl
Symphyseal height	SH	it - gn
Biangular breadth	BA	go - go (ang - ang)
Minimum ramus length	RL	ant. - post. of ramus
Gonial angle	G∠	gonio-osteometric measure

Table 2

CRANIAL INDICES

Cranial vault

B/L	Cranial
H/L	Length-height
H/B	Breadth-height
H/(L+B/2)	Mean height
PAH/L	Length-auricular
BPH/H	Flatness of the cranial base
MF/B	Transverse fronto-parietal

Face

TFH/TFB	Total facial
UFH/TFB	Upper facial
UFH/MFB	Midfacial
TFB/B	Transverse cranio-facial
MF/TFB	Zygo-frontal
BA/MF	Fronto-mandibular
BA/TFB	Zygo-mandibular
SIOB/IOB	Facial flatness
AIB/BOB	Anterior interorbital

Nasal structure

NB/NH	Nasal
DS/DC	Nasal root height
SMN/MN	Nasal bone height
HNB/BNB	Nasal bridge height

Orbit

LOH/LOBM	Left orbital (mf)
LOH/LOBD	Left orbital (d)

Dental arch

MB/ML	Maxillo-alveolar

Mandible

LM/BCB	Mandibular

APPENDIX A

Table 3

CRANIAL OBSERVATIONS

General

Muscularity
    Small
    Medium
    Large
    V. Large

Deformation
    None
    Occipital
    Lambdoid
    Fronto-occip.
    Pariet-front-occip.
    Bilat-front-occip.
    Pathological
    Earth Pressure

Degree of deformation
    None
    Trace
    Small
    Medium
    Pronounced

Vault form
    Ellipsoid
    Ovoid
    Spheroid
    Pentagonoid
    Rhomboid
    Sphenoid
    Birsoid

Frontal Region

Brow ridge size
    None
    Trace
    Small
    Medium
    Large
    V. Large

Glabella prominence
    Flat
    Small
    Medium
    Large
    V. Large

Frontal slope
    Bulging
    None
    Slight
    Medium
    Pronounced
    V. Pronounced

Postorbital constriction
    Small
    Medium
    Large

Frontal eminences
    Small
    Medium
    Large

Table 3 - continued

Median crest
    None
    Small
    Medium
    Large

Frontal breadth
    Small
    Medium
    Large

Parietal Region

Sagittal elevation
    None
    Small
    Medium
    Large
    V. Large

Parietal eminences
    Small
    Medium
    Large

Temporal and Occipital Region

Temporal fullness
    Flat
    Small
    Medium
    Large

Mastoids
    Small
    Medium
    Large
    V. Large

Supramastoid crest
    Small
    Medium
    Large

Sphenoid depression
    Small
    Medium
    Large

Occipital curve
    None
    Small
    Medium
    Pronounced

Lambdoid flattening
    None
    Small
    Medium
    Pronounced

Condyle elevation
    Small
    Medium
    Large

Basion
    Low
    Medium
    High

Styloid processes
    Small
    Medium
    Large

Table 3 - continued

Glenoid fossa depth
    Small
    Medium
    Large

Tympanic plate
    Thin
    Medium
    Thick
    V. Thick

Facial Region

Orbit shape
    Oblong
    Rhomboid
    Square
    Ellipse
    Round

Orbit inclination
    None
    Small
    Medium
    Pronounced

Suborbital fossa
    Absent
    Slight
    Medium
    Deep

Zygomatic size
    Small
    Medium
    Large
    V. Large

Zygomatic, lateral projection
    Small
    Medium
    Large

Zygomatic, anterior projection
    Small
    Medium
    Large

Nasal root height
    V. Low
    Low
    Medium
    High
    V. High

Nasal root breadth
    V. Small
    Small
    Medium
    Large
    V. Large

Nasal bridge height
    V. Low
    Low
    Medium
    High
    V. High

Nasal bridge breadth
    Small
    Medium
    Large

Table 3 - continued

Nasal profile
    Concave
    Straight
    Sl. Concavo-Convex
    Concavo-Convex
    V. Concavo-Convex

Nasion depression
    Absent
    Small
    Medium
    Deep

Nasal sills
    Absent
    Dull
    Medium
    Sharp

Nasal spine
    Absent
    Small
    Rt. Angle
    Large

Subnasal grooves
    Absent
    Small
    Medium
    Pronounced
    Sulci

Mid-facial prognathism
    Absent
    Slight
    Medium
    Pronounced

Alveolar prognathism
    Absent
    Slight
    Medium
    Pronounced

Total prognathism
    Absent
    Slight
    Medium
    Pronounced

Palate shape
    Parabolic
    Hyperbolic
    Elliptical
    Small "U"
    Large "U"

Palate height
    Low
    Medium
    High
    V. High

Palatine torus
    Absent
    Small Ridge
    Medium Ridge
    Large Ridge
    Small Mound
    Medium Mound
    Large Mound

APPENDIX A

Table 3 - continued

Mandible size
    Small
    Medium
    Large
    V. Large

Chin form
    Narrow Bilateral
    Wide Bilateral
    Intermediate
    Median

Chin projection
    Negative
    Netural
    Small
    Medium
    Large

Pterygoid attachment
    Small
    Medium
    Pronounced
    V. Pronounced

Gonial angle eversion
    None
    Small
    Medium
    Pronounced

APPENDIX B

METRICAL AND MORPHOLOGICAL DATA FOR MAJOR PHYSICAL VARIETIES IN EASTERN UNITED STATES

(SEE CHAPTER II)

APPENDIX B

Table 4

COEFFICIENTS OF RELATEDNESS ON A VARIETAL LEVEL
(Significantly differing 3 P.E.D.'s* on .04 level)
(% of measurements differing significantly)

	Ratio Measurements	Coeff. Measurements	Ratio Indices	Coeff. Indices	Coeff. Combined
Otamid-Ilinid	11/32	34	9/20	45	40
Otamid-Hanid	10/21	48	5/8	62	55
Iswanid-Hanid	7/22	32	5/8	62	47
Iswanid-Ilinid	23/35	66	9/22	41	54
Ilinid-Muskogid	10/35	29	6/22	27	28
Ilinid-Hanid	11/22	50	2/8	25	38
Inuitid-Ilinid	8/12	67	4/5	80	74
Muskogid-Deneid	15/25	60	12/17	71	66
Deneid-Dakotid	7/13	54	6/10	60	57

* Probable error of the difference between the means

Table 5

INDEX CLASSES OF THE COEFFICIENT OF RELATEDNESS FOR THE FORT ANCIENT POPULATION

Index Class	Coeff. Boundary	Coeff. Range
Near identity	< 15	5 - 15
Closely related	< 25	20 - 30
Moderately related	< 35	30 - 40
Unrelated, different varieties	< 50	33 - 60 +

Table 6

Mean Measurements of the Lenid Male Variety*

	Mean**	Standard Dev.
Cranial vault		
Capacity	-----	------
Cranial module	153.1	5.66
Mean thickness of left parietal	4.9	0.84
Glabello-occipital length	187.2	6.08
Maximum breadth	136.2	4.49
Minimum frontal breadth	93.9	3.99
Basion-bregma height	137.4	4.20
Porion-apex height	115.6	3.53
Basion-porion height	23.1	2.64
Length of cranial base	104.5	4.87
Face		
Total facial height	123.1	4.98
Upper facial height	73.7	3.19
Total facial breadth	137.5	4.45
Midfacial breadth	99.8	3.73
Interior biorbital breadth	97.4	3.44
Subtense to interior biorbital arc	18.6	2.27
Biorbital breadth	98.8	3.09
Anterior interorbital breadth	20.2	2.03
Nasal structure		
Nasal breadth	25.2	1.16
Nasal height	53.7	3.47
Dacryal chord	22.4	2.13
Dacryal subtense to arc	12.3	1.35
Minimum nasal breadth	8.5	1.34
Subtense to nasal arc	4.0	0.75

* N = 45

** means in millimeters (mm.) unless listed otherwise

APPENDIX B 135

Table 6 - continued

Orbit
    Left orbital height 34.0 1.52
    Left orbital breadth, maxillofrontale 42.0 2.11
    Left orbital breadth, dacryon 39.3 1.96

Dental arch and profile
    Maxillo-alveolar breadth 65.5 2.29
    Maxillo-alveolar length 56.9 2.52
    Facial length, prosthion 101.9 4.51
    Facial length, alveolar point 100.5 4.55

Mandible
    Length of mandible 110.1 4.33
    Bicondylar breadth 122.1 2.82
    Symphysial height 36.4 2.05
    Biangular breadth 104.5 7.59
    Minimum ramus length 35.2 2.85

Angles
    Facial profile angle ----- ------
    Midfacial profile angle ----- ------
    Alveolar profile angle ----- ------
    Gonial angle 120.5° 4.17

Table 7

Mean Indices of the Lenid Male Variety*

	Mean	Standard Dev.
Cranial vault		
Cranial	71.90	6.90
Length-height	72.53	5.87
Breadth-height	100.92	4.32
Mean height	84.77	2.78
Length-auricular height	59.96	9.01
Flatness of cranial base	16.80	1.75
Transverse fronto-parietal	68.96	2.75
Face		
Total facial	88.05	2.91
Upper facial	53.62	2.34
Midfacial	73.95	3.58
Transverse cranio-facial	101.05	4.29
Zygo-frontal	68.31	2.83
Fronto-mandibular	111.38	8.27
Zygo-mandibular	75.97	4.88
Facial flatness	19.15	2.24
Anterior interorbital	20.46	2.05
Nasal structure		
Nasal	47.22	3.69
Nasal root height	55.58	7.99
Nasal bone height	48.14	9.20
Orbit		
Left orbital, maxillofrontale	81.31	4.95
Left orbital, dacryon	86.36	4.68
Dental arch		
Maxillo-alveolar	115.26	5.44
Mandible		
Mandibular	90.21	2.87

* N = 45

APPENDIX B 137

Table 8

Mean Measurements of the Lenid Female Variety*

	Mean**	Standard Dev.
Cranial vault		
Capacity	-----	-----
Cranial module	150.5	4.27
Mean thickness of left parietal	4.4	0.89
Glabello-occipital length	181.2	6.72
Maximum breadth	135.2	4.76
Minimum frontal breadth	88.2	3.77
Basion-bregma height	135.0	2.12
Porion-apex height	116.0	4.00
Basion-porion height	23.2	1.64
Length of cranial base	99.0	6.71
Face		
Total facial height	113.4	2.07
Upper facial height	69.6	1.95
Total facial breadth	133.0	3.74
Midfacial breadth	95.4	2.30
Interior biorbital breadth	92.8	3.90
Subtense to interior biorbital arc	16.0	1.22
Biorbital breadth	96.2	2.59
Anterior interorbital breadth	18.6	2.19
Nasal structure		
Nasal breadth	23.2	0.84
Nasal height	49.2	3.11
Dacryal chord	23.0	0.71
Dacryal subtense to arc	12.8	0.45
Minimum nasal breadth	8.4	3.51
Subtense to nasal arc	2.8	1.10
Orbit		
Left orbital height	33.6	1.67
Left orbital breadth, maxillofrontale	41.0	2.24
Left orbital breadth, dacryon	38.8	1.92
Dental arch and profile		
Maxillo-alveolar breadth	60.6	2.88
Maxillo-alveolar length	53.0	2.55
Facial length, prosthion	98.4	4.04
Facial length, alveolar point	97.0	3.74

Table 8 - continued

Mandible
- Length of mandible — 99.6 — 5.94
- Bicondylar breadth — 121.0 — 1.00
- Symphyseal height — 34.6 — 2.19
- Biangular breadth — 97.8 — 5.72
- Minimum ramus length — 32.0 — 2.00

Angles
- Facial profile angle — ----- — -----
- Midfacial profile angle — ----- — -----
- Alveolar profile angle — ----- — -----
- Gonial angle — 124.0° — 4.95

*N = 5
**Measurements in millimeters (mm.) unless listed otherwise

APPENDIX B

Table 9

Mean Indices of the Lenid Female Variety*

	Mean	Standard Dev.
Cranial vault		
Cranial	74.63	1.23
Length-height	74.56	2.13
Breadth-height	99.92	2.60
Mean height	85.39	2.24
Length-auricular height	64.04	1.83
Flatness of cranial base	17.20	1.37
Transverse fronto-parietal	65.23	1.13
Face		
Total facial	85.33	3.31
Upper facial	52.36	1.97
Midfacial	72.96	1.32
Transverse cranio-facial	98.48	4.65
Zygo-frontal	66.35	3.30
Fronto-mandibular	110.99	6.91
Zygo-mandibular	73.62	5.47
Facial flatness	17.25	1.23
Anterior interorbital	19.34	2.29
Nasal structure		
Nasal	47.28	3.05
Nasal root height	55.73	3.39
Nasal bone height	33.79	4.20
Orbit		
Left orbital, maxillofrontale	82.12	5.61
Left orbital, dacryon	86.75	5.67
Dental arch		
Maxillo-alveolar	114.49	6.71
Mandible		
Mandibular	82.33	5.06

*N = 5

Table 10

Mean Measurements of the Ilinid Male Variety*

	Mean**	Standard Dev.
Cranial vault		
Capacity	1400.00cc.	28.92
Cranial module	154.6	2.65
Mean thickness of left parietal	4.8	0.63
Glabello-occipital length	181.7	4.75
Maximum breadth	140.1	3.63
Minimum frontal breadth	94.8	4.40
Basion-bregma height	142.0	2.46
Porion-apex height	118.8	1.28
Basion-porion height	25.1	1.77
Length of cranial base	107.1	3.57
Face		
Total facial height	124.1	3.42
Upper facial height	73.6	2.59
Total facial breadth	140.3	4.80
Midfacial breadth	102.1	3.94
Interior biorbital breadth	99.9	2.48
Subtense to interior biorbital arc	18.7	2.22
Biorbital breadth	101.0	2.64
Anterior interorbital breadth	19.7	1.85
Nasal structure		
Nasal breadth	26.4	1.46
Nasal height	53.6	2.05
Dacryal chord	21.7	2.27
Dacryal subtense to arc	13.2	1.34
Minimum nasal breadth	8.7	1.04
Subtense to nasal arc	5.0	0.79

* N = 17

** means in millimeters (mm.) unless listed otherwise

APPENDIX B

Table 10 - continued

Orbit		
Left orbital height	33.8	2.08
Left orbital breadth, maxillofrontale	43.2	1.43
Left orbital breadth, dacryon	40.3	1.22
Dental arch and profile		
Maxillo-alveolar breadth	65.3	3.65
Maxillo-alveolar length	55.8	2.97
Facial length, prosthion	101.0	4.61
Facial length, alveolar point	99.2	4.57
Mandible		
Length of mandible	106.1	3.47
Bicondylar breadth	126.7	4.14
Symphysial height	37.9	2.16
Biangular breadth	104.1	3.94
Minimum ramus length	35.0	1.90
Angles		
Facial profile angle	-----	------
Midfacial profile angle	-----	------
Alveolar profile angle	-----	------
Gonial angle	116.5°	3.98

Table 11

Mean Indices of the Ilinid Male Variety*

	Mean	Standard Dev.
Cranial vault		
Cranial	77.12	2.35
Length-height	78.20	2.21
Breadth-height	101.43	2.66
Mean height	88.29	2.04
Length-auricular height	65.40	1.66
Flatness of cranial base	17.71	1.02
Transverse fronto-parietal	67.72	3.78
Face		
Total facial	88.50	3.17
Upper facial	52.52	2.38
Midfacial	72.17	3.65
Transverse cranio-facial	100.20	3.41
Zygo-frontal	67.60	3.32
Fronto-mandibular	110.00	4.84
Zygo-mandibular	74.30	3.73
Facial flatness	18.72	2.28
Anterior interorbital	19.56	1.71
Nasal structure		
Nasal	49.31	3.44
Nasal root height	61.66	10.66
Nasal bone height	58.21	11.41
Orbit		
Left orbital, maxillofrontale	78.41	4.90
Left orbital, dacryon	84.02	5.51
Dental arch		
Maxillo-alveolar	119.53	5.13
Mandible		
Mandibular	83.78	3.59

* N = 17

APPENDIX B

Table 12

Mean Measurements of the Ilinid Female Variety*

	Mean**	Standard Dev.
Cranial vault		
Capacity	1302.1cc.	46.50
Cranial module	147.6	4.63
Mean thickness of left parietal	4.5	0.70
Glabello-occipital length	174.0	7.02
Maximum breadth	135.5	4.36
Minimum frontal breadth	91.0	4.26
Basion-bregma height	133.3	4.68
Porion-apex height	113.9	4.52
Basion-porion height	22.6	2.71
Length of cranial base	96.9	3.23
Face		
Total facial height	112.0	2.55
Upper facial height	66.7	1.66
Total facial breadth	131.7	4.75
Midfacial breadth	95.0	3.76
Interior biorbital breadth	94.8	3.79
Subtense to interior biorbital arc	15.3	2.00
Biorbital breadth	95.8	3.44
Anterior interorbital breadth	17.5	1.50
Nasal structure		
Nasal breadth	24.7	1.86
Nasal height	49.9	1.63
Dacryal chord	20.4	1.87
Dacryal subtense to arc	11.3	2.06
Minimum nasal breadth	7.8	1.83
Subtense to nasal arc	3.9	1.05
Orbit		
Left orbital height	33.0	1.75
Left orbital breadth, maxillofrontale	41.4	1.74
Left orbital breadth, dacryon	39.0	1.58
Dental arch and profile		
Maxillo-alveolar breadth	60.1	1.56
Maxillo-alveolar length	51.1	2.66
Facial length, prosthion	95.0	3.03
Facial length, alveolar point	92.9	3.35

Table 12 - continued

Mandible
    Length of mandible   99.2   2.97
    Bicondylar breadth   118.9   4.78
    Symphyseal height   34.1   1.63
    Biangular breadth   95.2   6.96
    Minimum ramus length   30.8   1.96

Angles
    Facial profile angle   -----   -----
    Midfacial profile angle   -----   -----
    Alveolar profile angle   -----   -----
    Gonial angle   123.6°   4.35

*N = 19
**Measurement in millimeters (mm.) unless listed otherwise

APPENDIX B

Table 13

Mean Indices of the Ilinid Female Variety*

	Mean	Standard Dev.
Cranial vault		
Cranial	77.93	2.78
Length-height	76.60	2.07
Breadth-height	98.37	3.18
Mean height	86.11	2.03
Length-auricular height	65.48	2.52
Flatness of cranial base	16.98	1.87
Transverse fronto-parietal	67.14	3.03
Face		
Total facial	85.15	3.39
Upper facial	50.72	2.15
Midfacial	70.29	2.70
Transverse cranio-facial	97.24	3.13
Zygo-frontal	69.07	3.09
Fronto-mandibular	104.79	8.37
Zygo-mandibular	72.23	4.58
Facial flatness	16.14	1.88
Anterior interorbital	18.26	1.61
Nasal structure		
Nasal	49.56	4.49
Nasal root height	55.60	9.86
Nasal bone height	46.50	14.85
Orbit		
Left orbital, maxillofrontale	79.76	5.17
Left orbital, dacryon	84.70	5.30
Dental arch		
Maxillo-alveolar	117.83	5.00
Mandible		
Mandibular	83.57	4.04

*N = 19

Table 14

Mean Measurements of the Iswanid Male Variety*

Cranial vault	Mean**	Standard Dev.
Capacity	1367.5cc.	80.00
Cranial module	150.2	2.68
Mean thickness of left parietal	4.9	0.63
Glabello-occipital length	176.9	4.41
Maximum breadth	134.8	3.97
Minimum frontal breadth	90.6	3.51
Basion-bregma height	138.7	3.13
Porion-apex height	115.9	2.83
Basion-porion height	-----	------
Length of cranial base	99.9	3.07
Face		
Total facial height	118.0	4.17
Upper facial height	70.8	3.37
Total facial breadth	135.8	3.97
Midfacial breadth	98.3	3.48
Interior biorbital breadth	96.0	3.08
Subtense to interior biorbital arc	17.1	1.40
Biorbital breadth	96.1	2.92
Anterior interorbital breadth	17.8	1.85
Nasal structure		
Nasal breadth	23.9	1.99
Nasal height	51.2	2.64
Dacryal chord	19.6	2.09
Dacryal subtense to arc	10.2	1.24
Minimum nasal breadth	8.1	1.37
Subtense to nasal arc	3.2	0.73

* N = 33

** means in millimeters (mm.) unless listed otherwise

APPENDIX B

Table 14 - continued

Orbit
    Left orbital height   32.6   1.67
    Left orbital breadth, maxillofrontale   42.0   1.23
    Left orbital breadth, dacryon   39.3   1.19

Dental arch and profile
    Maxillo-alveolar breadth   63.6   2.20
    Maxillo-alveolar length   51.8   2.10
    Facial length, prosthion   94.6   2.98
    Facial length, alveolar point   92.9   2.92

Mandible
    Length of mandible   99.2   4.28
    Bicondylar breadth   123.8   4.24
    Symphysial height   34.9   2.29
    Biangular breadth   103.7   5.02
    Minimum ramus length   34.5   2.26

Angles
    Facial profile angle   84.0°   2.56
    Midfacial profile angle   88.1°   2.80
    Alveolar profile angle   71.3°   4.30
    Gonial angle   117.7°   4.88

Table 15

Mean Indices of the Iswanid Male Variety*

	Mean	Standard Dev.
Cranial vault		
Cranial	76.24	2.56
Length-height	78.46	2.42
Breadth-height	102.96	3.24
Mean height	89.03	2.36
Length-auricular height	65.54	2.02
Flatness of cranial base	------	------
Transverse fronto-parietal	67.20	2.58
Face		
Total facial	86.89	2.98
Upper facial	52.16	2.03
Midfacial	72.16	4.52
Transverse cranio-facial	100.79	3.32
Zygo-frontal	66.70	2.58
Fronto-mandibular	114.66	7.34
Zygo-mandibular	76.39	4.19
Facial flatness	17.83	1.38
Anterior interorbital	18.54	1.68
Nasal structure		
Nasal	46.78	4.31
Nasal root height	52.60	8.23
Nasal bone height	39.59	8.93
Orbit		
Left orbital, maxillofrontale	77.77	4.42
Left orbital, dacryon	83.09	4.37
Dental arch		
Maxillo-alveolar	122.98	5.26
Mandible		
Mandibular	80.24	4.08

* N = 33

APPENDIX B

Table 16

Mean Measurements of the Dakotid Male Variety*

	Mean**	Standard Dev.
Cranial vault		
Capacity	1490.7cc.	61.27
Cranial module	151.7	3.91
Mean thickness of left parietal	4.6	1.00
Glabello-occipital length	178.3	6.17
Maximum breadth	145.6	6.38
Minimum frontal breadth	94.2	4.08
Basion-bregma height	131.0	6.24
Porion-apex height	116.8	1.36
Basion-porion height	19.6	3.95
Length of cranial base	101.3	4.60
Face		
Total facial height	124.9	5.75
Upper facial height	75.6	5.15
Total facial breadth	141.3	5.48
Midfacial breadth	102.8	5.03
Interior biorbital breadth	98.4	3.79
Subtense to interior biorbital arc	18.9	2.26
Biorbital breadth	99.0	4.07
Anterior interorbital breadth	19.7	1.89
Nasal structure		
Nasal breadth	26.1	2.05
Nasal height	54.0	3.61
Dacryal chord	20.3	2.01
Dacryal subtense to arc	12.5	1.42
Minimum nasal breadth	9.0	1.60
Subtense to nasal arc	4.6	1.02

* N = 58

** means in millimeters (mm.) unless listed otherwise

Table 16 - continued

Orbit		
Left orbital height	35.2	1.88
Left orbital breadth, maxillofrontale	42.4	2.03
Left orbital breadth, dacryon	40.7	1.85
Dental arch and profile		
Maxillo-alveolar breadth	65.9	3.36
Maxillo-alveolar length	54.1	2.66
Facial length, prosthion	97.5	4.33
Facial length, alveolar point	97.0	4.05
Mandible		
Length of mandible	106.8	4.78
Bicondylar breadth	125.0	5.31
Symphysial height	36.7	2.51
Biangular breadth	104.5	4.62
Minimum ramus length	36.8	2.35
Angles		
Facial profile angle	-----	------
Midfacial profile angle	-----	------
Alveolar profile angle	-----	------
Gonial angle	115.9°	5.80

APPENDIX B

Table 17

Mean Indices of the Dakotid Male Variety*

	Mean	Standard Dev.
Cranial vault		
Cranial	81.77	4.96
Length-height	73.47	2.74
Breadth-height	90.16	6.39
Mean height	80.89	3.73
Length-auricular height	64.64	1.43
Flatness of cranial base	14.94	2.80
Transverse fronto-parietal	64.80	3.29
Face		
Total facial	88.53	5.01
Upper facial	53.61	3.85
Midfacial	73.65	4.81
Transverse cranio-facial	97.11	3.82
Zygo-frontal	66.76	3.16
Fronto-mandibular	111.02	6.52
Zygo-mandibular	74.01	3.58
Facial flatness	19.28	2.23
Anterior interorbital	19.95	1.80
Nasal structure		
Nasal	48.53	5.11
Nasal root height	61.96	8.09
Nasal bone height	52.61	12.83
Orbit		
Left orbital, maxillofrontale	82.00	4.89
Left orbital, dacryon	86.09	4.07
Dental arch		
Maxillo-alveolar	121.92	6.53
Mandible		
Mandibular	85.12	4.87

* N = 58

Table 18

Mean Measurements of the Dakotid Female Variety*

	Mean**	Standard Dev.
Cranial vault		
Capacity	-----	-----
Cranial module	145.7	1.29
Mean thickness of left parietal	5.2	0.75
Glabello-occipital length	175.2	2.32
Maximum breadth	134.5	2.26
Minimum frontal breadth	92.2	2.93
Basion-bregma height	127.5	2.59
Porion-apex height	-----	-----
Basion-porion height	21.2	2.64
Length of cranial base	98.7	3.44
Face		
Total facial height	122.2	2.33
Upper facial height	74.8	2.48
Total facial breadth	132.2	5.19
Midfacial breadth	101.5	6.63
Interior biorbital breadth	94.8	3.31
Subtense to interior biorbital arc	18.0	1.41
Biorbital breadth	96.0	3.85
Anterior interorbital breadth	19.7	1.97
Nasal structure		
Nasal breadth	24.3	2.07
Nasal height	51.8	2.32
Dacryal chord	19.7	1.37
Dacryal subtense to arc	11.7	1.37
Minimum nasal breadth	8.2	0.75
Subtense to nasal arc	4.0	1.10
Orbit		
Left orbital height	33.7	1.51
Left orbital breadth, maxillofrontale	40.7	2.58
Left orbital breadth, dacryon	39.3	2.42
Dental arch and profile		
Maxillo-alveolar breadth	64.0	3.63
Maxillo-alveolar length	54.0	2.19
Facial length, prosthion	97.0	5.18
Facial length, alveolar point	95.5	4.72

APPENDIX B

Table 18 - continued

Mandible
    Length of mandible   105.7   1.86
    Bicondylar breadth   118.5   4.93
    Symphyseal height   36.5   2.43
    Biangular breadth   98.8   4.07
    Minimum ramus length   35.3   1.86

Angles
    Facial profile angle   -----   -----
    Midfacial profile angle   -----   -----
    Alveolar profile angle   -----   -----
    Gonial angle $120.8°$ 2.93

*N = 6
**Measurements in millimeters (mm.) unless listed otherwise

Table 19

Mean Indices of the Dakotid Female Variety*

	Mean	Standard Dev.
Cranial vault		
Cranial	76.80	1.95
Length-height	72.78	0.94
Breadth-height	94.83	3.14
Mean height	82.35	1.67
Length-auricular height	-----	-----
Flatness of cranial base	16.58	1.80
Transverse fronto-parietal	68.56	3.09
Face		
Total facial	92.52	2.88
Upper facial	56.69	2.78
Midfacial	73.96	4.89
Transverse cranio-facial	98.29	4.29
Zygo-frontal	69.82	3.23
Fronto-mandibular	107.39	6.90
Zygo-mandibular	74.88	4.28
Facial flatness	18.96	0.85
Anterior interorbital	20.49	1.92
Nasal structure		
Nasal	46.99	4.19
Nasal root height	59.43	6.66
Nasal bone height	48.88	11.53
Orbit		
Left orbital, maxillofrontale	82.95	4.48
Left orbital, dacryon	85.78	5.11
Dental arch		
Maxillo-alveolar	118.56	5.69
Mandible		
Mandibular	89.31	4.36

*N = 6

APPENDIX B

Table 20

Mean Measurements of the Muskogid Male Variety*

	Mean**	Standard Dev.
Cranial vault		
Capacity	-----	------
Cranial module	154.9	3.54
Mean thickness of left parietal	4.7	0.79
Glabello-occipital length	181.1	4.96
Maximum breadth	139.5	4.89
Minimum frontal breadth	94.7	4.53
Basion-bregma height	144.1	3.73
Porion-apex height	-----	------
Basion-porion height	25.8	2.45
Length of cranial base	105.8	3.68
Face		
Total facial height	125.7	4.34
Upper facial height	75.6	3.09
Total facial breadth	139.6	4.65
Midfacial breadth	103.2	4.20
Interior biorbital breadth	100.0	3.07
Subtense to interior biorbital arc	19.0	2.27
Biorbital breadth	100.8	2.93
Anterior interorbital breadth	20.1	1.97
Nasal structure		
Nasal breadth	26.2	1.61
Nasal height	53.7	2.79
Dacryal chord	22.1	2.22
Dacryal subtense to arc	11.2	1.25
Minimum nasal breadth	9.9	1.77
Subtense to nasal arc	4.1	0.80

* N = 48

** means in millimeters (mm.) unless listed otherwise

Table 20 - continued

Orbit		
Left orbital height	34.5	1.63
Left orbital breadth, maxillofrontale	43.3	1.70
Left orbital breadth, dacryon	40.7	1.66
Dental arch and profile		
Maxillo-alveolar breadth	68.6	3.27
Maxillo-alveolar length	56.7	2.90
Facial length, prosthion	101.7	2.71
Facial length, alveolar point	100.0	3.06
Mandible		
Length of mandible	108.0	5.58
Bicondylar breadth	126.4	5.12
Symphysial height	38.2	2.40
Biangular breadth	104.6	6.02
Minimum ramus length	35.9	2.81
Angles		
Facial profile angle	-----	------
Midfacial profile angle	-----	------
Alveolar profile angle	-----	------
Gonial angle	116.2°	4.61

APPENDIX B

Table 21

Mean Indices of the Muskogid Male Variety*

	Mean	Standard Dev.
Cranial vault		
Cranial	77.07	2.51
Length-height	79.61	2.56
Breadth-height	103.35	3.56
Mean height	89.92	2.57
Length-auricular height	------	------
Flatness of cranial base	17.89	1.56
Transverse fronto-parietal	67.97	3.93
Face		
Total facial	88.04	13.02
Upper facial	54.21	2.46
Midfacial	73.35	3.93
Transverse cranio-facial	100.10	3.26
Zygo-frontal	67.92	3.64
Fronto-mandibular	110.64	8.74
Zygo-mandibular	74.94	4.21
Facial flatness	19.04	2.07
Anterior interorbital	20.01	1.82
Nasal structure		
Nasal	48.84	3.38
Nasal root height	51.52	7.63
Nasal bone height	43.01	10.79
Orbit		
Left orbital, maxillofrontale	79.67	3.56
Left orbital, dacryon	84.69	4.13
Dental arch		
Maxillo-alveolar	121.01	6.98
Mandible		
Mandibular	85.59	5.37

* N = 48

Table 22

Cranial Observations of the Male Physical Varieties

Muscularity	Sm	Med	Lge	V. Lge			
Lenid (N = 45)	-----	40.0%	57.8%	2.2%			
Ilinid (N = 17)	11.8%	52.9%	35.3%	-----			
Iswanid (N = 33)	3.0%	87.9%	9.1%	-----			
Dakotid (N = 58)	-----	60.3	39.7%	-----			
Muskogid (N = 48)	4.2%	54.2%	41.7%	-----			

Deformation	None	Occ	Lambd	Fr-occ	Bil-fr-occ	Earth Press	Path
Lenid (N = 45)	95.6%	-----	-----	-----	-----	4.4%	-----
Ilinid (N = 17)	100.0%	-----	-----	-----	-----	-----	-----
Iswanid (N = 33)	100.0%	-----	-----	-----	-----	-----	-----
Dakotid (N = 58)	79.3%	15.5%	-----	-----	-----	3.4%	1.7%
Muskogid (N = 48)	75.0%	16.7%	-----	-----	-----	8.4%	-----

Degree of Deform.	None	Trace	Sm	Med	Pron
Lenid (N = 45)	95.6%	-----	2.2%	2.2%	-----
Ilinid (N = 17)	100.0%	-----	-----	-----	-----
Iswanid (N = 33)	100.0%	-----	-----	-----	-----
Dakotid (N = 58)	77.6%	6.9%	10.3%	3.4%	1.7%
Muskogid (N = 48)	75.0%	20.8%	4.2%	-----	-----

Vault Form	Ell	Ov	Spher	Pentag	Rhom	Sphen	Birs
Lenid (N = 45)	17.8%	73.3%	-----	8.9%	-----	-----	-----
Ilinid (N = 17)	11.8%	88.2%	-----	-----	-----	-----	-----
Iswanid (N = 33)	3.0%	97.0%	-----	-----	-----	-----	-----
Dakotid (N = 58)	5.2%	51.7%	3.4%	5.2%	3.4%	3.4%	27.6%
Muskogid (N = 48)	22.9%	68.8%	-----	-----	-----	2.1%	6.2%

Browridge size	None	Trace	Sm	Med	Lge	V. Lge
Lenid (N = 45)	-----	2.2%	24.4%	40.0%	28.9%	4.4%
Ilinid (N = 17)	-----	-----	17.6%	52.9%	29.4%	-----
Iswanid (N = 33)	-----	15.2%	42.4%	39.4%	3.0%	-----
Dakotid (N = 58)	-----	3.4%	34.5%	37.9%	20.0%	3.4%
Muskogid (N = 48)	-----	2.1%	22.9%	41.7%	31.3%	2.1%

Glabella prom.	Flat	Sm	Med.	Lge	V. Lge
Lenid (N = 45)	-----	42.2%	37.8%	20.0%	-----
Ilinid (N = 17)	-----	17.6%	70.6%	5.9%	5.9%
Iswanid (N = 33)	-----	75.8%	24.2%	-----	-----
Dakotid (N = 58)	-----	43.1%	37.9%	12.1%	6.9%
Muskogid (N = 48)	-----	37.5%	45.8%	14.6%	2.1%

APPENDIX B

Table 22 - continued

Frontal slope	Bulg	None	Sl	Med	Pron	V.Pron
Lenid (N = 45)	-----	-----	8.9%	91.1%	-----	-----
Ilinid (N = 17)	-----	-----	17.6%	82.4%	-----	-----
Iswanid (N = 33)	-----	-----	21.2%	69.7%	9.1%	-----
Dakotid (N = 58)	-----	-----	15.5%	75.9%	8.6%	-----
Muskogid (N = 48)		-----	27.1%	70.8%	2.1%	-----

Postorb. constr.	Sm	Med	Lge
Lenid (N = 45)	62.2%	37.8%	-----
Ilinid (N = 17)	100.0%	-----	-----
Iswanid (N = 33)	33.3%	54.5%	12.1%
Dakotid (N = 58)	17.2%	60.3%	22.4%
Muskogid (N = 48)	25.0%	54.2%	20.8%

Fron. emin.	Sm	Med	Lge
Lenid (N = 45)	75.6%	24.4%	-----
Ilinid (N = 17)	41.2%	58.8%	-----
Iswanid (N = 33)	100.0%	-----	-----
Dakotid (N = 58)	65.5%	34.5%	-----
Muskogid (N = 48)	56.3%	43.8%	-----

Fr. Median crest	None	Sm	Med	Lge
Lenid (N = 45)	35.6%	42.2%	17.8%	4.4%
Ilinid (N = 17)	70.6%	23.5%	5.9%	-----
Iswanid (N = 33)	48.5%	42.4%	9.1%	-----
Dakotid (N = 58)	77.6%	17.2%	3.4%	1.7%
Muskogid (N = 48)	58.3%	35.4%	6.2%	-----

Fron. br.	Sm	Med	Lge
Lenid (N = 45)	37.8%	62.2%	-----
Ilinid (N = 17)	5.9%	88.2%	5.9%
Iswanid (N = 33)	84.8%	15.2%	-----
Dakotid (N = 58)	17.2%	69.0%	13.8%
Muskogid (N = 48)	14.6%	75.0%	10.4%

Sag. elev.	None	Sm	Med	Lge	V.Lge
Lenid (N = 45)	15.6%	46.7%	28.9%	6.7%	2.2%
Ilinid (N = 17)=	11.8%	58.8%	11.8%	17.6%	-----
Iswanid (N = 33)	30.3%	60.6%	9.1%	-----	-----
Dakotid (N = 58)	51.7%	36.2%	8.6%	-----	3.4%
Muskogid (N = 48)	41.7%	50.0%	4.2%	4.2%	-----

Table 22 - continued

Pariet. emin.	Sm	Med	Lge	
Lenid (N = 45)	37.8%	62.2%	-----	
Ilinid (N = 17)	11.8%	88.2%	-----	
Iswanid (N = 33)	18.2%	78.8%	3.0%	
Dakotid (N = 58)	8.6%	86.2%	5.2%	
Muskogid (N = 48)	4.2%	93.8%	2.1%	

Temp. fullness	Flat	Sm	Med	Lge
Lenid (N = 45)	37.8%	53.8%	6.7%	2.2%
Ilinid (N = 17)	5.9%	35.3%	47.1%	11.8%
Iswanid (N = 33)	9.1%	84.8%	6.1%	-----
Dakotid (N = 58)	1.7%	27.6%	20.7%	50.0%
Muskogid (N = 48)	2.1%	35.4%	56.3%	6.2%

Mastoids	Sm	Med	Lge	V. Lge
Lenid (N = 45)	-----	40.0%	55.6%	4.4%
Ilinid (N = 17)	5.9%	41.2%	35.3%	17.6%
Iswanid (N = 33)	24.2%	72.7%	3.0%	-----
Dakotid (N = 58)	12.1%	58.6%	25.9%	3.4%
Muskogid (N = 48)	6.2%	37.5%	54.2%	2.1%

Supramast. crest	Sm	Med	Lge
Lenid (N = 45)	8.9%	46.7%	44.4%
Ilinid (N = 17)	100.0%	-----	-----
Iswanid (N = 33)	6.1%	42.4%	51.5%
Dakotid (N = 58)	10.3%	62.1%	27.6%
Muskogid (N = 48)	6.2%	33.3%	60.4%

Sphen. depress.	Sm	Med	Lge
Lenid (N = 45)	82.2%	17.8%	-----
Ilinid (N = 17)	100.0%	-----	-----
Iswanid (N = 33)	63.6%	33.3%	3.0%
Dakotid (N = 58)	43.1%	41.4%	15.5%
Muskogid (N = 48)	68.8%	31.3%	-----

Occip. curve	None	Sm	Med	Pron
Lenid (N = 45)	-----	-----	44.4%	55.6%
Ilinid (N = 17)	-----	11.8%	70.6%	17.6%
Iswanid (N = 33)	-----	-----	63.6%	36.4%
Dakotid (N = 58)	1.7%	44.8%	39.7%	13.8%
Muskogid (N = 48)	-----	25.0%	66.7%	8.3%

APPENDIX B

Table 22 - continued

Lambd. flat.	None	Sm	Med	Pron
Lenid (N = 45)	13.3%	26.7%	42.2%	17.8%
Ilinid (N = 17)	-----	35.3%	52.9%	11.8%
Iswanid (N = 33)	6.1%	72.7%	21.2%	-----
Dakotid (N = 58)	62.1%	25.9%	12.1%	-----
Muskogid (N = 48)	50.0%	43.8%	6.2%	-----

Cond. elev.	Sm	Med	Lge
Lenid (N = 45)	6.7%	62.2%	31.1%
Ilinid (N = 17)	100.0%	-----	-----
Iswanid (N = 33)	-----	45.5%	54.5%
Dakotid (N = 58)	24.1%	51.7%	24.1%
Muskogid (N = 48)	14.6%	52.1%	33.3%

Basion	Low	Med	High
Lenid (N = 45)	15.6%	84.4%	-----
Ilinid (N = 17)	100.0%	-----	-----
Iswanid (N = 33)	6.1%	60.6%	33.3%
Dakotid (N = 58)	37.9%	60.3%	1.7%
Muskogid (N = 48)	8.3%	85.4%	6.2%

Styl. proc.	Sm	Med	Lge
Lenid (N = 45)	57.8%	40.0%	2.2%
Ilinid (N = 17)	58.8%	35.3%	5.9%
Iswanid (N = 33)	48.5%	45.5%	6.1%
Dakotid (N = 58)	41.4%	31.0%	27.6%
Muskogid (N = 48)	35.4%	37.5%	27.1%

Glen. fos. depth	Sm	Med	Lge
Lenid (N = 45)	-----	62.2%	37.8%
Ilinid (N = 17)	-----	52.9%	47.1%
Iswanid (N = 33)	12.1%	78.8%	9.1%
Dakotid (N = 58)	3.4%	70.7%	25.9%
Muskogid (N = 48)	2.1%	68.8%	29.2%

Tymp. plate	Thin	Med	Thick	V. Thick
Lenid (N = 45)	77.8%	15.6%	6.7%	-----
Ilinid (N = 17)	82.4%	17.6%	-----	-----
Iswanid (N = 33)	81.2%	15.2%	3.0%	-----
Dakotid (N = 58)	86.2%	13.8%	-----	-----
Muskogid (N = 48)	83.3%	16.7%	-----	-----

Table 22 - continued

Orbit shape	Obl	Rhom	Sq	Ell	Rou
Lenid (N = 45)	26.7%	37.8%	35.6%	-----	-----
Ilinid (N = 17)	35.3%	17.6%	41.2%	-----	5.9%
Iswanid (N = 33)	54.5%	12.1%	27.3%	6.1%	-----
Dakotid (N = 58)	10.3%	74.1%	15.5%	-----	-----
Muskogid (N = 48)	20.8%	43.8%	35.4%	-----	-----

Orbit incl.	None	Sm	Med	Pron
Lenid (N = 45)	-----	53.3%	37.8%	8.9%
Ilinid (N = 17)	5.9%	58.8%	35.3%	-----
Iswanid (N = 33)	-----	57.6%	42.4%	-----
Dakotid (N = 58)	1.7%	36.2%	39.7%	22.4%
Muskogid (N = 48)	-----	35.4%	54.2%	10.4%

Suborb. fossa	Ab	Sl	Med	Deep
Lenid (N = 45)	-----	64.4%	35.6%	-----
Ilinid (N = 17)	-----	41.2%	41.2%	17.6%
Iswanid (N = 33)	33.3%	60.6%	6.1%	-----
Dakotid (N = 58)	5.2%	34.5%	39.7%	20.7%
Muskogid (N = 48)	16.7%	52.1%	29.2%	2.1%

Zyg. size	Sm	Med	Lge	V. Lge
Lenid (N = 45)	8.9%	62.2%	26.7%	2.2%
Ilinid (N = 17)	17.6%	70.6%	11.8%	-----
Iswanid (N = 33)	12.1%	78.8%	9.1%	-----
Dakotid (N = 58)	1.7%	44.8%	39.7%	13.8%
Muskogid (N = 48)	4.2%	39.6%	52.1%	4.2%

Zyg. lat. proj.	Sm	Med	Lge
Lenid (N = 45)	-----	53.3%	46.7%
Ilinid (N = 17)	-----	17.6%	82.4%
Iswanid (N = 33)	-----	15.2%	84.8%
Dakotid (N = 58)	-----	22.4%	77.6%
Muskogid (N = 48)	4.2%	20.8%	75.0%

Zyg. ant. proj.	Sm	Med	Lge
Lenid (N = 45)	11.1%	86.7%	2.2%
Ilinid (N = 17)	11.8%	88.2%	-----
Iswanid (N = 33)	12.1%	81.8%	6.1%
Dakotid (N = 58)	-----	51.7%	48.3%
Muskogid (N = 48)	6.2%	41.7%	52.1%

APPENDIX B

Table 22 - continued

Zyg. proc. thick.	Sm	Med.	Pron
Lenid (N = 45)	6.7%	68.9%	24.4%
Ilinid (N = 17)	100.0%	-----	-----
Iswanid (N = 33)	12.1%	72.7%	15.2%
Dakotid (N = 58)	3.4%	82.8%	13.8%
Muskogid (N = 48)	2.1%	75.0%	22.9%

Nas rt. ht.	V.Low	Low	Med	High	V.High
Lenid (N = 45)	-----	4.4%	86.7%	8.9%	-----
Ilinid (N = 17)	-----	-----	82.4%	17.6%	-----
Iswanid (N = 33)	-----	-----	51.5%	48.5%	-----
Dakotid (N = 58)	-----	-----	48.3%	44.8%	6.9%
Muskogid (N = 48)	-----	-----	91.7%	8.3%	-----

Nas. rt. br.	V.Sm	Sm	Med	Lge	V.Lge
Lenid (N = 45)	-----	28.9%	60.0%	11.1%	-----
Ilinid (N = 17)	5.9%	35.3%	58.8%	-----	-----
Iswanid (N = 33)	9.1%	36.4%	54.5%	-----	-----
Dakotid (N = 58)	1.7%	37.9%	56.9%	3.4%	-----
Muskogid (N = 48)	-----	16.7%	75.0%	8.3%	-----

Nas. bridg. ht.	V.Low	Low	Med	High	V.High
Lenid (N = 45)	-----	2.2%	84.4%	13.3%	-----
Ilinid (N = 17)	-----	-----	70.6%	29.4%	-----
Iswanid (N = 33)	-----	3.0%	69.7%	27.3%	-----
Dakotid (N = 58)	-----	-----	39.7%	36.2%	24.1%
Muskogid (N = 48)	-----	- 4.2%	72.9%	22.9%	-----

Nas. bridg. br.	Sm	Med.	Lge
Lenid (N = 45)	20.0%	80.0%	-----
Ilinid (N = 17)	5.9%	94.1%	-----
Iswanid (N = 33)	15.2%	81.8%	3.0%
Dakotid (N = 58)	27.6%	70.7%	1.7%
Muskogid (N = 48)	10.4%	77.1%	12.5%

Nas. profile	Conc	Str	Sl.Conc-Conv	Conc-Conv.	V.C-C
Lenid (N = 45)	-----	-----	97.8%	-----	2.2%
Ilinid (N = 17)	-----	-----	100.0%	-----	-----
Iswanid (N = 33)	-----	-----	100.0%	-----	-----
Dakotid (N = 58)	-----	55.2%	41.4%	3.4%	-----
Muskogid (N = 48)	-----	-----	81.3%	12.5%	6.2%

Table 22 - continued

Nas. depress.	Abs	Sm	Med	Lge	
Lenid (N = 45)	15.6%	44.4%	40.0%	-----	
Ilinid (N = 17)	11.8%	58.8%	29.4%	-----	
Iswanid (N = 33)	6.1%	63.6%	30.3%	-----	
Dakotid (N = 58)	36.2%	51.7%	12.1%	-----	
Muskogid (N = 48)	16.7%	58.3%	25.0%	-----	

Nas. sills	Abs	Dull	Med	Sharp	
Lenid (N = 45)	4.4%	44.4%	51.1%	-----	
Ilinid (N = 17)	11.8%	5.9%	58.8%	23.5%	
Iswanid (N = 33)	-----	18.2%	57.6%	24.2%	
Dakotid (N = 58)	5.2%	24.1%	58.6%	12.1%	
Muskogid (N = 48)	4.2%	27.1%	58.3%	10.4%	

Nas. spine	Abs	Sm	Med	Rt. Ang	Lge
Lenid (N = 45)	2.2%	71.1%	24.4%	-----	2.2%
Ilinid (N = 17)	-----	11.8%	76.5%	-----	11.8%
Iswanid (N = 33)	3.0%	81.8%	15.2%	-----	-----
Dakotid (N = 58)	-----	17.2%	60.3%	-----	22.4%
Muskogid (N = 48)	2.1%	52.1%	43.8%	-----	2.1%

Subnas. grooves	Abs	Sm	Med	Pron	Sulci
Lenid (N = 45)	91.1%	6.7%	2.2%	-----	-----
Ilinid (N = 17)	76.5%	17.6%	5.9%	-----	-----
Iswanid (N = 33)	78.8%	18.2%	3.0%	-----	-----
Dakotid (N = 58)	67.2%	19.0%	6.9%	5.2%	1.7%
Muskogid (N = 48)	77.1%	16.7%	4.2%	2.1%	-----

Midfac. progn.	Abs	Sl	Med	Pron	
Lenid (N = 45)	62.2%	33.3%	4.4%	-----	
Ilinid (N = 17)	64.7%	35.3%	-----	-----	
Iswanid (N = 33)	60.6%	33.3%	6.1%	-----	
Dakotid (N = 58)	50.0%	50.0%	-----	-----	
Muskogid (N = 48)	60.4%	29.2%	8.2%	2.1%	

Alveol. progn.	Abs	Sl	Med	Pron	
Lenid (N = 45)	2.2%	40.0%	55.6%	2.2%	
Ilinid (N = 17)	11.8%	82.4%	5.9%	-----	
Iswanid (N = 33)	-----	42.4%	54.0%	3.0%	
Dakotid (N = 58)	6.9%	70.7%	22.4%	-----	
Muskogid (N = 48)	4.2%	35.4%	58.3%	2.1%	

APPENDIX B

Table 22 - continued

Total progn.	Abs	Sl	Med	Pron			
Lenid (N = 45)	2.2%	71.1%	26.7%	-----			
Ilinid (N = 17)	11.8%	88.2%	-----	-----			
Iswanid (N = 33)	3.0%	36.4%	57.6%	3.0%			
Dakotid (N = 58)	5.2%	75.9%	19.0%	-----			
Muskogid (N = 48)	6.2%	39.6%	47.9%	6.2%			

Palate shape	Parab	Hyperb	Ell	Sm U	Lge U		
Lenid (N = 45)	75.6%	4.4%	13.3%	6.7%	-----		
Ilinid (N = 17)	94.1%	-----	5.9%	-----	-----		
Iswanid (N = 33)	97.0%	3.0%	-----	-----	-----		
Dakotid (N = 58)	91.4%	1.7%	3.4%	1.7%	1.7%		
Muskogid (N = 48)	81.3%	10.4%	-----	6.2%	2.1%		

Palate ht.	Low	Med	High	V.High			
Lenid (N = 45)	-----	44.4%	42.2%	13.3%			
Ilinid (N = 17)	100.0%	-----	-----	-----			
Iswanid (N = 33)	3.0%	39.4%	45.5%	12.1%			
Dakotid (N = 58)	1.7%	39.7%	44.8%	13.8%			
Muskogid (N = 48)	-----	58.3%	39.6%	2.1%			

Palat. torus	Abs	Sm Ridg	Med Ridg	Lge Ridg	SmMd	MedMd	LMd
Lenid (N = 45)	71.1%	11.1%	6.7%	-----	4.4%	6.7%	-----
Ilinid (N = 17)	100.0%	-----	-----	-----	-----	-----	-----
Iswanid (N = 33)	90.9%	6.1%	-----	-----	3.0%	-----	-----
Dakotid (N = 58)	84.5%	10.3%	-----	-----	3.4%	1.7%	-----
Muskogid (N = 48)	75.0%	22.9%	-----	-----	2.1%	-----	-----

Mand. size	Sm	Med	Lge	V.Lge			
Lenid (N = 45)	22.2%	57.8%	20.0%	-----			
Ilinid (N = 17)	5.9%	64.7%	29.4%	-----			
Iswanid (N = 33)	21.2%	78.8%	-----	-----			
Dakotid (N = 58)	1.7%	39.7%	55.2%	3.4%			
Muskogid (N = 48)	4.2%	37.5%	52.1%	6.2%			

Chin form	Nar Bilat	Wide Bilat	Inter-med	Median			
Lenid (N = 45)	22.2%	26.7%	28.9%	22.2%			
Ilinid (N = 17)	100.0%	-----	-----	-----			
Iswanid (N = 33)	24.2%	-----	54.5%	21.2%			
Dakotid (N = 58)	19.0%	48.3%	25.9%	6.9%			
Muskogid (N = 48)	54.2%	16.7%	22.9%	6.2%			

Table 22 - continued

Chin proj.	Negat	Neut	Sm	Med	Lge
Lenid (N = 45)	-----	68.9%	20.0%	6.7%	4.4%
Ilinid (N = 17)	-----	70.6%	17.6%	11.8%	-----
Iswanid (N = 33)	51.5%	36.4%	6.1%	6.1%	-----
Dakotid (N = 58)	6.9%	69.0%	8.6%	10.3%	5.2%
Muskogid (N = 48)	12.5%	60.4%	14.6%	12.5%	-----

Pteryg. attach.	Sm	Med	Pron	V. Pron
Lenid (N = 45)	2.2%	75.6%	20.0%	2.2%
Ilinid (N = 17)	100.0%	-----	-----	-----
Iswanid (N = 33)	6.1%	48.5%	36.4%	9.1%
Dakotid (N = 58)	5.2%	51.7%	36.2%	6.9%
Muskogid (N = 48)	4.2%	52.1%	29.2%	14.6%

Gonial ang. evers.	None	Sm	Med	Pron
Lenid (N = 45)	33.3%	40.0%	8.9%	17.8%
Ilinid (N = 17)	23.5%	76.5%	-----	-----
Iswanid (N = 33)	15.2%	45.5%	15.2%	24.2%
Dakotid (N = 58)	31.0%	48.3%	20.7%	-----
Muskogid (N = 48)	33.3%	45.8%	14.6%	6.2%

APPENDIX B

Table 23

Cranial Observations of the Female Physical Varieties

Muscularity	Sm	Med	Lge	V.Lge		
Lenid (N = 5)	-----	80.0%	20.0%	-----		
Ilinid (N = 19)	47.4%	52.6%	-----	-----		
Iswanid (No Series)	-----	-----	-----	-----		
Dakotid (N = 6)	100.0%	-----	-----	-----		
Muskogid (No Series)	---	-----	-----	-----		

Deformation	None	Occ	Lambd	Fr-occ	Bil-fr-occ	Earth Press
Lenid (N = 5)	100.0%	-----	-----	-----	-----	-----
Ilinid (N = 19)	73.7%	15.8%	-----	-----	-----	10.5%
Iswanid (No Series)	-----	-----	-----	-----	-----	-----
Dakotid (N = 6)	100.0%	-----	-----	-----	-----	-----
Muskogid (No Series)	---	-----	-----	-----	-----	-----

Degree of Deform.	None	Trace	Sm	Med	Pron	
Lenid (N = 5)	100.0%	-----	-----	-----	-----	
Ilinid (N = 19)	73.7%	-----	5.3%	15.8%	5.3%	
Iswanid (No Series)	-----	-----	-----	-----	-----	
Dakotid (N = 6)	100.0%	-----	-----	-----	-----	
Muskogid (No Series)	---	-----	-----	-----	-----	

Vault form	Ell	Ov	Spher	Pentag	Rhom	Sphen
Lenid (N = 5)	-----	60.0%	-----	40.0%	-----	-----
Ilinid (N = 19)	10.5%	84.2%	-----	5.3%	-----	-----
Iswanid (No Series)	-----	-----	-----	-----	-----	-----
Dakotid (N = 6)	-----	83.3%	-----	16.7%	-----	-----
Muskogid (No Series)	---	-----	-----	-----	-----	-----

Browridge size	None	Trace	Sm	Med	Lge	V.Lge
Lenid (N = 5)	-----	80.0%	20.0%	-----	-----	-----
Ilinid (N = 19)	-----	26.3%	52.6%	21.1%	-----	-----
Iswanid (No Series)	-----	-----	-----	-----	-----	-----
Dakotid (N = 6)	-----	83.3%	-----	16.7%	-----	-----
Muskogid (No Series)	---	-----	-----	-----	-----	-----

Glabella prom.	Flat	Sm	Med	Lge	V.Lge	
Lenid (N = 5)	-----	100.0%	-----	-----	-----	
Ilinid (N = 19)	-----	84.2%	15.8%	-----	-----	
Iswanid (No Series)	-----	-----	-----	-----	-----	
Dakotid (N = 6)	-----	83.3%	16.7%	-----	-----	
Muskogid (No Series)	---	-----	-----	-----	-----	

Table 23 - continued

Frontal slope	Bulg	None	Sl	Med	Pron	V.Pron
Lenid (N = 5)	40.0%	-----	60.0%	-----	-----	-----
Ilinid (N = 19)	-----	-----	73.7%	26.3%	-----	-----
Iswanid (No Series)	-----	-----	-----	-----	-----	-----
Dakotid (N = 6)	-----	-----	-----	100.0%	-----	-----
Muskogid (No Series)	-----	-----	-----	-----	-----	-----

Postorb. constr.	Sm	Med	Lge
Lenid (N = 5)	100.0%	-----	-----
Ilinid (N = 19)	15.8%	68.4%	15.8%
Iswanid (No Series)	-----	-----	-----
Dakotid (N = 6)	50.0%	50.0%	-----
Muskogid (No Series)	-----	-----	-----

Fron. emin.	Sm	Med	Lge
Lenid (N = 5)	-----	100.0%	-----
Ilinid (N = 19)	15.8%	84.2%	-----
Iswanid (No Series)	-----	-----	-----
Dakotid (N = 6)	83.3%	16.7%	-----
Muskogid (No Series)	-----	-----	-----

Fr. median crest	None	Sm	Med	Lge
Lenid (N = 5)	-----	80.0%	-----	20.0%
Ilinid (N = 19)	68.4%	26.3%	-----	5.3%
Iswanid (No Series)	-----	-----	-----	-----
Dakotid (N = 6)	83.3%	16.7%	-----	-----
Muskogid (No Series)	-----	-----	-----	-----

Fron. br.	Sm	Med	Lge
Lenid (N = 5)	60.0%	40.0%	-----
Ilinid (N = 19)	26.3%	73.7%	-----
Iswanid (No Series)	-----	-----	-----
Dakotid (N = 6)	100.0%	-----	-----
Muskogid (No Series)	-----	-----	-----

Sag. elev.	None	Sm	Med	Lge	V.Lge
Lenid (N = 5)	-----	40.0%	60.0%	-----	-----
Ilinid (N = 19)	21.1%	68.4%	10.5%	-----	-----
Iswanid (No Series)	-----	-----	-----	-----	-----
Dakotid (N = 6)	33.3%	50.0%	16.7%	-----	-----
Muskogid (No Series)	-----	-----	-----	-----	-----

APPENDIX B

Table 23 - continued

Pariet. emin.	Sm	Med	Lge	
Lenid (N = 5)	-----	100.0%	-----	
Ilinid (N = 19)	5.3%	78.9%	15.8%	
Iswanid (No Series)	-----	-----	-----	
Dakotid (N = 6)	50.0%	50.0%	-----	
Muskogid (No Series)	---	-----	-----	

Temp. fullness	Flat	Sm	Med	Lge
Lenid (N = 5)	80.0%	20.0%	-----	-----
Ilinid (N = 19)	5.3%	21.1%	57.9%	15.8%
Iswanid (No Series)	-----	-----	-----	-----
Dakotid (N = 6)	-----	50.0%	33.3%	16.7%
Muskogid (No Series)	---	-----	-----	-----

Mastoids	Sm	Med	Lge	V. Lge
Lenid (N = 5)	60.0%	40.0%	-----	-----
Ilinid (N = 19)	31.6%	63.2%	5.3%	-----
Iswanid (No Series)	-----	-----	-----	-----
Dakotid (N = 6)	83.3%	16.7%	-----	-----
Muskogid (No Series)	---	-----	-----	-----

Supramast. crest	Sm	Med	Lge
Lenid (N = 5)	20.0%	60.0%	20.0%
Ilinid (N = 19)	26.3%	68.4%	5.3%
Iswanid (No Series)	-----	-----	-----
Dakotid (N = 6)	33.3%	50.0%	16.7%
Muskogid (No Series)	---	-----	-----

Sphen. depress.	Sm	Med	Lge
Lenid (N = 5)	80.0%	20.0%	-----
Ilinid (N = 19)	42.1%	57.9%	-----
Iswanid (No Series)	-----	-----	-----
Dakotid (N = 6)	33.3%	66.7%	-----
Muskogid (No Series)	---	-----	-----

Occip. curve	None	Sm	Med	Pron
Lenid (N = 5)	-----	-----	20.0%	80.0%
Ilinid (N = 19)	-----	10.5%	57.9%	31.6%
Iswanid (No Series)	-----	-----	-----	-----
Dakotid (N = 6)	-----	-----	66.7%	33.3%
Muskogid (No Series)	---	-----	-----	-----

Table 23 - continued

Lambd. flat.	None	Sm	Med	Pron
Lenid (N = 5)	-----	-----	20.0%	80.0%
Ilinid (N = 19)	10.5%	26.3%	42.1%	21.1%
Iswanid (No Series)	-----	-----	-----	-----
Dakotid (N = 6)	16.7%	83.3%	-----	-----
Muskogid (No Series)	---	-----	-----	-----

Cond. elev.	Sm	Med	Lge
Lenid (N = 5)	-----	-----	100.0%
Ilinid (N = 19)	10.5%	36.8%	52.6%
Iswanid (No Series)	-----	-----	-----
Dakotid (N = 6)	33.3%	66.7%	-----
Muskogid (No Series)	---	-----	-----

Basion	Low	Med	High
Lenid (N = 5)	-----	100.0%	-----
Ilinid (N = 19)	-----	89.5%	10.5%
Iswanid (No Series)	-----	-----	-----
Dakotid (N = 6)	33.3%	66.7%	-----
Muskogid (No Series)	---	-----	-----

Styl. proc.	Sm	Med	Lge
Lenid (N = 5)	80.0%	20.0%	-----
Ilinid (N = 19)	73.7%	26.3%	-----
Iswanid (No Series)	-----	-----	-----
Dakotid (N = 6)	83.3%	16.7%	-----
Muskogid (No Series)	---	-----	-----

Glen. fos. depth	Sm	Med	Lge
Lenid (N = 5)	-----	100.0%	-----
Ilinid (N = 19)	5.3%	63.2%	31.6%
Iswanid (No Series)	-----	-----	-----
Dakotid (N = 6)	16.7%	83.3%	-----
Muskogid (No Series)	---	-----	-----

Tymp. plate	Thin	Med	Thick	V. Thick
Lenid (N = 5)	100.0%	-----	-----	-----
Ilinid (N = 19)	84.2%	15.8%	-----	-----
Iswanid (No Series)	-----	-----	-----	-----
Dakotid (N = 6)	100.0%	-----	-----	-----
Muskogid (No Series)	---	-----	-----	-----

APPENDIX B

Table 23 - continued

Orbit shape	Obl	Rhom	Sq	Ell	Rou
Lenid (N = 5)	-----	20.0%	80.0%	-----	-----
Ilinid (N = 19)	26.3%	36.8%	36.8%	-----	-----
Iswanid (No Series)	-----	-----	-----	-----	-----
Dakotid (N = 6)	-----	50.0%	50.0%	-----	-----
Muskogid (No Series)	---	-----	-----	-----	-----

Orbit incl.	None	Sm	Med	Pron
Lenid (N = 5)	60.0%	40.0%	-----	-----
Ilinid (N = 19)	5.3%	73.7%	15.8%	5.3%
Iswanid (No Series)	-----	-----	-----	-----
Dakotid (N = 6)	-----	66.7%	33.3%	-----
Muskogid (No Series)	---	-----	-----	-----

Suborb. fossa	Ab	Sl	Med	Deep
Lenid (N = 5)	-----	-----	100.0%	-----
Ilinid (N = 19)	-----	36.8%	36.8%	26.3%
Iswanid (No Series)	-----	-----	-----	-----
Dakotid (N = 6)	-----	50.0%	50.0%	-----
Muskogid (No Series)	---	-----	-----	-----

Zyg. size	Sm	Med	Lge	V. Lge
Lenid (N = 5)	40.0%	60.0%	-----	-----
Ilinid (N = 19)	52.6%	47.4%	-----	-----
Iswanid (No Series)	-----	-----	-----	-----
Dakotid (N = 6)	16.7%	83.3%	-----	-----
Muskogid (No Series)	---	-----	-----	-----

Zyg. lat. proj.	Sm	Med	Lge
Lenid (N = 5)	40.0%	60.0%	-----
Ilinid (N = 19)	10.5%	78.9%	10.5%
Iswanid (No Series)	-----	-----	-----
Dakotid (N = 6)	-----	83.3%	16.7%
Muskogid (No Series)	---	-----	-----

Zyg. ant. proj.	Sm	Med	Lge
Lenid (N = 5)	100.0%	-----	-----
Ilinid (N = 19)	73.7%	26.3%	-----
Iswanid (No Series)	-----	-----	-----
Dakotid (N = 6)	16.7%	50.0%	33.3%
Muskogid (No Series)	---	-----	-----

Table 23 - continued

Zyg. proc. thick.	Sm	Med	Pron		
Lenid (N = 5)	20.0%	80.0%	-----		
Ilinid (N = 19)	42.1%	57.9%	-----		
Iswanid (No Series)	-----	-----	-----		
Dakotid (N = 6)	33.3%	66.7%	-----		
Muskogid (No Series)	---	-----	-----		

Nas. rt. ht.	V. Low	Low	Med	High	V. High
Lenid (N = 5)	-----	-----	100.0%	-----	-----
Ilinid (N = 19)	-----	26.3%	68.4%	5.3%	-----
Iswanid (No Series)	-----	-----	-----	-----	-----
Dakotid (N = 6)	-----	-----	100.0%	-----	-----
Muskogid (No Series)	---	-----	-----	-----	-----

Nas. rt. br.	V. Sm	Sm	Med	Lge	V. Lge
Lenid (N = 5)	-----	20.0%	80.0%	-----	-----
Ilinid (N = 19)	-----	36.8%	63.2%	-----	-----
Iswanid (No Series)	-----	-----	-----	-----	-----
Dakotid (N = 6)	-----	66.7%	33.3%	-----	-----
Muskogid (No Series)	---	-----	-----	-----	-----

Nas. bridg. br.	V. Low	Low	Med	High	V. High
Lenid (N = 5)	-----	80.0%	20.0%	-----	-----
Ilinid (N = 19)	-----	-----	94.7%	5.3%	-----
Iswanid (No Series)	-----	-----	-----	-----	-----
Dakotid (N = 6)	-----	-----	100.0%	-----	-----
Muskogid (No Series)	---	-----	-----	-----	-----

Nas. bridg. br.	Sm	Med	Lge
Lenid (N = 5)	-----	100.0%	-----
Ilinid (N = 19)	5.3%	89.5%	5.3%
Iswanid (No Series)	-----	-----	-----
Dakotid (N = 6)	16.7%	83.3%	-----
Muskogid (No Series)	---	-----	-----

Nas. profile	Conc	Str	Sl. Conc-Conv	Conc-Conv.	V. C-C
Lenid (N = 5)	-----	-----	100.0%	-----	-----
Ilinid (N = 19)	-----	10.5%	89.5%	-----	-----
Iswanid (No Series)	-----	-----	-----	-----	-----
Dakotid (N = 6)	-----	83.3%	16.7%	-----	-----
Muskogid (No Series)	---	-----	-----	-----	-----

APPENDIX B

Table 23 - continued

Nas. depress.	Abs	Sm	Med	Lge
Lenid (N = 5)	80.0%	20.0%	-----	-----
Ilinid (N = 19)	15.8%	73.7%	10.5%	-----
Iswanid (No Series)	-----	-----	-----	-----
Dakotid (N = 6)	83.3%	16.7%	-----	-----
Muskogid (No Series)	---	-----	-----	-----

Nas. sills	Abs	Dull	Med	Sharp
Lenid (N = 5)	-----	40.0%	60.0%	-----
Ilinid (N = 19)	-----	10.5%	21.1%	68.4%
Iswanid (No Series)	-----	-----	-----	-----
Dakotid (N = 6)	-----	50.0%	33.3%	16.7%
Muskogid (No Series)	---	-----	-----	-----

Nas. spine	Abs	Sm	Med	Rt. Ang	Lge
Lenid (N = 5)	-----	100.0%	-----	-----	-----
Ilinid (N = 19)	-----	21.1%	78.9%	-----	-----
Iswanid (No Series)	-----	-----	-----	-----	-----
Dakotid (N = 6)	-----	16.7%	66.7%	-----	16.7%
Muskogid (No Series)	---	-----	-----	-----	-----

Subnas. grooves	Abs	Sm	Med	Pron	Sulci
Lenid (N = 5)	80.0%	20.0%	-----	-----	-----
Ilinid (N = 19)	84.2%	10.5%	-----	5.3%	-----
Iswanid (No Series)	-----	-----	-----	-----	-----
Dakotid (N = 6)	66.7%	16.7%	16.7%	-----	-----
Muskogid (No Series)	---	-----	-----	-----	-----

Midfac. progn.	Abs	Sl	Med	Pron
Lenid (N = 5)	40.0%	60.0%	-----	-----
Ilinid (N = 19)	78.9%	15.8%	5.3%	-----
Iswanid (No Series)	-----	-----	-----	-----
Dakotid (N = 6)	66.7%	33.3%	-----	-----
Muskogid (No Series)	---	-----	-----	-----

Alveol. progn.	Abs	Sl	Med	Pron
Lenid (N = 5)	-----	40.0%	60.0%	-----
Ilinid (N = 19)	15.8%	68.4%	10.5%	5.3%
Iswanid (No Series)	-----	-----	-----	-----
Dakotid (N = 6)	-----	50.0%	50.0%	-----
Muskogid (No Series)	---	-----	-----	-----

Table 23 - continued

Total progn.	Abs.	Sl	Med	Pron
Lenid (N = 5)	-----	60.0%	40.0%	-----
Ilinid (N = 19)	26.3%	57.9%	15.8%	-----
Iswanid (No Series)	-----	-----	-----	-----
Dakotid (N = 6)	-----	83.3%	16.7%	-----
Muskogid (No Series)	---	-----	-----	-----

Palate shape	Parab	Hyperb	Ell	Sm U	Lge U
Lenid (N = 5)	100.0%	-----	-----	-----	-----
Ilinid (N = 19)	73.7%	10.5%	5.3%	5.3%	5.3%
Iswanid (No Series)	-----	-----	-----	-----	-----
Dakotid (N = 6)	66.7%	-----	16.7%	16.7%	-----
Muskogid (No Series)	---	-----	-----	-----	-----

Palate ht.	Low	Med	High	V. High
Lenid (N = 5)	-----	60.0%	40.0%	-----
Ilinid (N = 19)	10.5%	63.2%	26.3%	-----
Iswanid (No Series)	-----	-----	-----	-----
Dakotid (N = 6)	-----	50.0%	33.3%	16.7%
Muskogid (No Series)	---	-----	-----	-----

Palat. torus	Abs	Sm Ridg	Med Ridg	Lge Ridg	SmMd	MedMd	LMd
Lenid (N = 5)	60.0%	-----	-----	-----	40.0%	-----	-----
Ilinid (N = 19)	78.9%	15.8%	-----	-----	5.3%	-----	-----
Iswanid (No Series)	-----	-----	-----	-----	-----	-----	-----
Dakotid (N = 6)	83.3%	-----	-----	-----	16.7%	-----	-----
Muskogid (No Series)	---	-----	-----	-----	-----	-----	-----

Mand. size	Sm	Med	Lge	V. Lge
Lenid (N = 5)	20.0%	80.0%	-----	-----
Ilinid (N = 19)	79.8%	15.8%	-----	5.3%
Iswanid (No Series)	-----	-----	-----	-----
Dakotid (N = 6)	100.0%	-----	-----	-----
Muskogid (No Series)	---	-----	-----	-----

Chin form	Nar Bilat	Wide Bilat	Inter-med	Median
Lenid (N = 5)	40.0%	40.0%	-----	20.0%
Ilinid (N = 19)	15.8%	-----	-----	84.2%
Iswanid (No Series)	-----	-----	-----	-----
Dakotid (N = 6)	33.3%	16.7%	-----	50.0%
Muskogid (No Series)	---	-----	-----	-----

APPENDIX B

Table 23 - continued

Chin proj.	Negat	Neut	Sm	Med	Lge
Lenid (N = 5)	20.0%	40.0%	40.0%	-----	-----
Ilinid (N = 19)	21.1%	26.3%	42.1%	5.3%	5.3%
Iswanid (No Series)	-----	-----	-----	-----	-----
Dakotid (N = 6)	33.3%	33.3%	-----	-----	33.3%
Muskogid (No Series)	---	-----	-----	-----	-----

Pteryg. attach.	Sm	Med	Pron	V. Pron
Lenid (N = 5)	-----	40.0%	40.0%	20.0%
Ilinid (N = 19)	73.7%	26.3%	-----	-----
Iswanid (No Series)	-----	-----	-----	-----
Dakotid (N = 6)	33.3%	66.7%	-----	-----
Muskogid (No Series)	---	-----	-----	-----

Gonial ang. evers.	None	Sm	Med	Pron
Lenid (N = 5)	40.0%	40.0%	20.0%	-----
Ilinid (N = 19)	47.4%	47.4%	5.3%	-----
Iswanid (No Series)	-----	-----	-----	-----
Dakotid (N = 6)	50.0%	50.0%	-----	-----
Muskogid (No Series)	---	-----	-----	-----

APPENDIX C

DESCRIPTION OF SKELETAL MATERIAL BY FOCUS
(SEE CHAPTER III)

APPENDIX C

Table 24

Mean Measurements of Baum Male Crania (Undeformed)*

	Mean**	Standard Dev.
Cranial vault		
Capacity	1480.0cc.	46.18
Cranial module	155.2	3.46
Mean thickness of left parietal	4.8	0.37
Glabello-occipital length	182.0	7.70
Maximum breadth	138.8	7.40
Minimum frontal breadth	97.2	5.21
Basion-bregma height	145.0	2.23
Porion-apex height	121.7	2.87
Basion-porion height	-----	-----
Length of cranial base	104.8	3.76
Face		
Total facial height	126.0	0.00
Upper facial height	76.0	1.15
Total facial breadth	143.1	2.91
Midfacial breadth	101.7	2.36
Interior biorbital breadth	102.7	2.42
Subtense to interior biorbital arc	19.0	1.15
Biorbital breadth	102.0	1.15
Anterior interorbital breadth	20.1	0.37
Nasal structure		
Nasal breadth	26.7	0.48
Nasal height	55.0	0.57
Dacryal chord	20.2	0.48
Dacryal subtense to arc	11.1	1.46
Minimum nasal breadth	10.2	0.75
Subtense to nasal arc	4.0	0.00

* N = 7

** means in millimeters (mm.) unless listed otherwise

Table 24 - continued

Orbit		
Left orbital height	35.2	1.25
Left orbital breadth, maxillofrontale	43.1	0.89
Left orbital breadth, dacryon	41.1	0.89
Dental arch and profile		
Maxillo-alveolar breadth	64.5	9.07
Maxillo-alveolar length	56.2	0.75
Facial length, prosthion	96.7	0.75
Facial length, alveolar point	94.7	0.75
Mandible		
Length of mandible	110.1	1.46
Bicondylar breadth	124.1	0.89
Symphysial height	36.2	2.75
Biangular breadth	102.7	2.62
Minimum ramus length	35.0	2.00
Angles		
Facial profile angle	85.0°	0.00
Midfacial profile angle	88.1°	0.89
Alveolar profile angle	73.8°	7.55
Gonial angle	116.7°	1.11

APPENDIX C

Table 25

Mean Indices of Baum Male Crania (Undeformed)*

	Mean	Standard Dev.
Cranial vault		
Cranial	76.44	5.84
Length-height	79.77	3.14
Breadth-height	104.69	6.10
Mean height	90.44	2.80
Length-auricular height	66.97	3.15
Flatness of cranial base	------	------
Transverse fronto-parietal	70.07	1.39
Face		
Total facial	88.05	1.79
Upper facial	53.10	0.96
Midfacial	74.73	0.70
Transverse cranio-facial	103.33	5.74
Zygo-frontal	67.96	3.50
Fronto-mandibular	105.82	6.03
Zygo-mandibular	71.75	1.35
Facial flatness	18.50	1.09
Anterior interorbital	19.74	0.24
Nasal structure		
Nasal	48.57	1.00
Nasal root height	54.93	6.87
Nasal bone height	39.04	2.52
Orbit		
Left orbital, maxillofrontale	81.76	1.19
Left orbital, dacryon	85.74	1.17
Dental arch		
Maxillo-alveolar	114.91	17.22
Mandible		
Mandibular	88.71	0.54

* $N = 7$

Table 26

Mean Measurements of Baum Male Crania (Deformed)*

	Mean**	Standard Dev.
Cranial vault		
Capacity	1480.0cc.	0.00
Cranial module	151.4	2.01
Mean thickness of left parietal	5.0	0.73
Glabello-occipital length	172.2	4.66
Maximum breadth	145.0	7.21
Minimum frontal breadth	95.3	5.33
Basion-bregma height	137.0	0.47
Porion-apex height	120.0	2.42
Basion-porion height	-----	------
Length of cranial base	103.6	0.67
Face		
Total facial height	126.0	0.00
Upper facial height	75.8	0.31
Total facial breadth	140.3	3.68
Midfacial breadth	102.0	0.94
Interior biorbital breadth	99.8	2.64
Subtense to interior biorbital arc	17.6	1.82
Biorbital breadth	99.7	0.63
Anterior interorbital breadth	19.7	0.63
Nasal structure		
Nasal breadth	27.0	0.47
Nasal·height	54.8	0.31
Dacryal chord	19.8	0.73
Dacryal subtense to arc	11.0	0.00
Minimum nasal breadth	9.6	0.67
Subtense to nasal arc	4.0	0.00

* N = 10

** means in millimeters (mm.) unless listed otherwise

APPENDIX C 183

Table 26 - continued

Orbit
    Left orbital height   34.8   0.73
    Left orbital breadth, maxillofrontale   43.0   0.00
    Left orbital breadth, dacryon   41.0   0.00

Dental arch and profile
    Maxillo-alveolar breadth   68.0   1.88
    Maxillo-alveolar length   55.8   1.66
    Facial length, prosthion   97.1   0.63
    Facial length, alveolar point   95.1   0.63

Mandible
    Length of mandible   103.0   1.37
    Bicondylar breadth   125.8   2.37
    Symphysial height   36.0   1.69
    Biangular breadth   104.6   1.82
    Minimum ramus length   34.7   2.09

Angles
    Facial profile angle   85.0°   0.00
    Midfacial profile angle   88.0°   0.00
    Alveolar profile angle   71.0°   0.00
    Gonial angle   115.1°   2.65

Table 27

Mean Indices of Baum Male Crania (Deformed)*

Cranial vault	Mean	Standard Dev.
Cranial	84.26	5.74
Length-height	79.56	2.17
Breadth-height	94.70	4.93
Mean height	86.37	1.55
Length-auricular height	69.74	2.21
Flatness of cranial base	------	------
Transverse fronto-parietal	65.87	3.77
Face		
Total facial	89.80	2.41
Upper facial	54.09	1.56
Midfacial	74.41	0.51
Transverse cranio-facial	97.01	4.97
Zygo-frontal	67.93	3.09
Fronto-mandibular	110.10	7.35
Zygo-mandibular	74.63	2.92
Facial flatness	17.69	1.53
Anterior interorbital	19.83	0.51
Nasal structure		
Nasal	49.17	0.67
Nasal root height	55.34	2.18
Nasal bone height	41.44	3.31
Orbit		
Left orbital, maxillofrontale	81.16	1.71
Left orbital, dacryon	85.12	1.80
Dental arch		
Maxillo-alveolar	121.65	0.51
Mandible		
Mandibular	81.93	2.56

*N = 10

APPENDIX C

Table 28

Mean Measurements of Baum Female Crania (Undeformed)*

	Mean**	Standard Dev.
Cranial vault		
Capacity	1375.0cc.	0.00
Cranial module	148.7	0.00
Mean thickness of left parietal	5.0	0.00
Glabello-occipital length	180.0	0.00
Maximum breadth	136.0	0.00
Minimum frontal breadth	92.0	0.00
Basion-bregma height	130.0	0.00
Porion-apex height	118.0	0.00
Basion-porion height	-----	----
Length of cranial base	98.0	0.00
Face		
Total facial height	118.0	0.00
Upper facial height	75.0	0.00
Total facial breadth	141.0	0.00
Midfacial breadth	103.0	0.00
Interior biorbital breadth	96.0	0.00
Subtense to interior biorbital arc	15.0	0.00
Biorbital breadth	101.0	0.00
Anterior interorbital breadth	18.0	0.00
Nasal structure		
Nasal breadth	28.0	0.00
Nasal height	54.0	0.00
Dacryal chord	19.0	0.00
Dacryal subtense to arc	10.0	0.00
Minimum nasal breadth	9.0	0.00
Subtense to nasal arc	4.0	0.00
Orbit		
Left orbital height	34.0	0.00
Left orbital breadth, maxillofrontale	44.0	0.00
Left orbital breadth, dacryon	43.0	0.00
Dental arch and profile		
Maxillo-alveolar breadth	68.0	0.00
Maxillo-alveolar length	53.0	0.00
Facial length, prosthion	97.0	0.00
Facial length, alveolar point	96.0	0.00

Table 28 - continued

Mandible
    Length of mandible   102.0   0.00
    Bicondylar breadth   125.0   0.00
    Symphyseal height   30.0   0.00
    Biangular breadth   101.0   0.00
    Minimum ramus length   32.0   0.00

Angles
    Facial profile angle $84.0°$ 0.00
    Midfacial profile angle $88.0°$ 0.00
    Alveolar profile angle $72.0°$ 0.00
    Gonial angle $126.0°$ 0.00

*N = 1
**Measurements in millimeters (mm.) unless listed otherwise

APPENDIX C

Table 29

Mean Indices of Baum Female Crania (Undeformed)*

	Mean	Standard Dev.
Cranial vault		
Cranial	75.56	0.00
Length-height	72.22	0.00
Breadth-height	95.95	0.00
Mean height	82.28	0.00
Length-auricular height	65.56	0.00
Flatness of cranial base	------	----
Transverse fronto-parietal	67.65	0.00
Face		
Total facial	83.69	0.00
Upper facial	53.19	0.00
Midfacial	72.82	0.00
Transverse cranio-facial	103.68	0.00
Zygo-frontal	65.25	0.00
Fronto-mandibular	109.78	0.00
Zygo-mandibular	71.63	0.00
Facial flatness	15.62	0.00
Anterior interorbital	17.82	0.00
Nasal structure		
Nasal	51.85	0.00
Nasal root height	52.63	0.00
Nasal bone height	44.44	0.00
Orbit		
Left orbital, maxillofrontale	77.27	0.00
Left orbital, dacryon	79.07	0.00
Dental arch		
Maxillo-alveolar	128.30	0.00
Mandible		
Mandibular	81.60	0.00

*N = 1

Table 30

Mean Measurements of Baum Female Crania (Deformed)*

	Mean**	Standard Dev.
Cranial vault		
Capacity	1381.2cc.	12.49
Cranial module	147.6	2.47
Mean thickness of left parietal	5.0	0.00
Glabello-occipital length	160.8	3.40
Maximum breadth	144.8	5.31
Minimum frontal breadth	95.8	1.89
Basion-bregma height	137.2	1.26
Porion-apex height	116.8	2.99
Basion-porion height	-----	----
Length of cranial base	100.2	0.50
Face		
Total facial height	118.0	0.00
Upper facial height	75.0	0.82
Total facial breadth	140.8	2.87
Midfacial breadth	103.0	0.82
Interior biorbital breadth	97.0	2.94
Subtense to interior biorbital arc	16.5	1.00
Biorbital breadth	100.0	0.00
Anterior interorbital breadth	18.0	0.82
Nasal structure		
Nasal breadth	27.8	1.26
Nasal height	54.2	1.26
Dacryal chord	19.0	0.82
Dacryal subtense to arc	10.2	1.26
Minimum nasal breadth	9.0	0.82
Subtense to nasal arc	4.0	0.82
Orbit		
Left orbital height	34.2	0.50
Left orbital breadth, maxillofrontale	44.2	0.50
Left orbital breadth, dacryon	43.0	0.00
Dental arch and profile		
Maxillo-alveolar breadth	68.2	0.50
Maxillo-alveolar length	53.0	2.45
Facial length, prosthion	97.0	0.00
Facial length, alveolar point	96.0	0.00

APPENDIX C

Table 30 - continued

Mandible		
Length of mandible	102.8	1.50
Bicondylar breadth	125.0	0.82
Symphyseal height	29.8	1.25
Biangular breadth	104.2	3.95
Minimum ramus length	31.8	0.50
Angles		
Facial profile angle	$84.2°$	1.26
Midfacial profile angle	$88.2°$	0.50
Alveolar profile angle	$72.2°$	5.31
Gonial angle	$126.0°$	3.27

*N = 4
**Measurements in millimeters (mm.) unless listed otherwise

Table 31

Mean Indices of Baum Female Crania (Deformed)*

	Mean	Standard Dev.
Cranial vault		
Cranial	90.04	2.54
Length-height	85.41	2.02
Breadth-height	94.93	4.15
Mean height	89.91	2.82
Length-auricular height	72.64	1.80
Flatness of cranial base	------	----
Transverse fronto-parietal	66.20	2.45
Face		
Total facial	83.86	1.72
Upper facial	53.30	1.00
Midfacial	72.82	1.37
Transverse cranio-facial	97.36	4.64
Zygo-frontal	68.06	2.19
Fronto-mandibular	108.94	5.57
Zygo-mandibular	74.06	1.82
Facial flatness	17.04	1.45
Anterior interorbital	17.82	0.81
Nasal structure		
Nasal	51.14	1.39
Nasal root height	53.82	4.31
Nasal bone height	44.38	7.99
Orbit		
Left orbital, maxillofrontale	77.40	0.26
Left orbital, dacryon	79.65	1.16
Dental arch		
Maxillo-alveolar	128.95	5.28
Mandible		
Mandibular	82.21	1.68

*N = 4

APPENDIX C

Table 32

Mean Measurements of Gartner Male Crania (Undeformed)*

	Mean**	Standard Dev.
Cranial vault		
Capacity	1485.0cc.	12.24
Cranial module	155.3	2.92
Mean thickness of the left parietal	5.1	0.98
Glabello-occipital length	181.1	5.19
Maximum breadth	143.8	6.61
Minimum frontal breadth	96.6	3.01
Basion-bregma height	141.0	2.89
Porion-apex height	124.0	3.40
Basion-porion height	-----	------
Length of cranial base	104.8	2.04
Face		
Total facial height	129.6	6.83
Upper facial height	76.5	1.22
Total facial breadth	145.3	5.53
Midfacial breadth	103.8	0.40
Interior biorbital breadth	98.1	1.94
Subtense to interior biorbital arc	16.3	0.81
Biorbital breadth	98.0	0.00
Anterior interorbital breadth	19.8	0.40
Nasal structure		
Nasal breadth	25.6	0.81
Nasal height	55.3	0.81
Dacryal chord	20.0	0.00
Dacryal subtense to arc	11.0	0.00
Minimum nasal breadth	10.1	0.98
Subtense to nasal arc	5.0	0.63

* N = 6

** means in millimeters (mm.) unless listed otherwise

Table 32 - continued

Orbit		
Left orbital height	34.5	0.54
Left orbital breadth, maxillofrontale	43.1	0.98
Left orbital breadth, dacryon	40.8	0.40
Dental arch and profile		
Maxillo-alveolar breadth	68.8	0.40
Maxillo-alveolar length	51.8	0.40
Facial length, prosthion	98.1	0.40
Facial length, alveolar point	96.1	0.40
Mandible		
Length of mandible	106.5	5.54
Bicondylar breadth	130.3	5.12
Symphysial height	38.0	3.89
Biangular breadth	101.6	7.99
Minimum ramus length	37.1	2.63
Angles		
Facial profile angle	88.8°	0.00
Midfacial profile angle	92.0°	0.00
Alveolar profile angle	77.0°	0.00
Gonial angle	114.0°	6.09

APPENDIX C

Table 33

Mean Indices of Gartner Male Crania (Undeformed)*

	Mean	Standard Dev.
Cranial vault		
Cranial	79.49	5.24
Length-height	77.87	2.38
Breadth-height	98.15	3.60
Mean height	86.76	0.69
Length-auricular height	68.49	2.78
Flatness of cranial base	------	------
Transverse fronto-parietal	67.35	4.34
Face		
Total facial	89.26	4.32
Upper facial	52.69	2.13
Midfacial	73.68	1.48
Transverse cranio-facial	101.13	3.76
Zygo-frontal	66.63	4.07
Fronto-mandibular	105.26	9.05
Zygo-mandibular	70.08	6.85
Facial flatness	16.64	0.98
Anterior interorbital	20.23	0.41
Nasal structure		
Nasal	46.40	2.10
Nasal root height	55.00	0.00
Nasal bone height	49.07	2.26
Orbit		
Left orbital, maxillofrontale	79.96	2.34
Left orbital, dacryon	84.49	1.22
Dental arch		
Maxillo-alveolar	132.79	0.28
Mandible		
Mandibular	81.69	2.23

*N = 6

Table 34

Mean Measurements of Gartner Male Crania (Deformed)*

Cranial vault	Mean**	Standard Dev.
Capacity	1480.0cc.	0.00
Cranial module	154.3	1.73
Mean thickness of left parietal	5.0	1.09
Glabello-occipital length	177.1	7.13
Maximum breadth	148.0	6.48
Minimum frontal breadth	96.1	1.16
Basion-bregma height	138.0	0.00
Porion-apex height	121.5	1.22
Basion-porion height	-----	------
Length of cranial base	103.0	2.44
Face		
Total facial height	125.6	0.81
Upper facial height	75.3	0.81
Total facial breadth	141.1	0.40
Midfacial breadth	104.3	0.81
Interior biorbital breadth	97.8	0.40
Subtense to interior biorbital arc	16.0	0.63
Biorbital breadth	98.0	0.00
Anterior interorbital breadth	20.1	0.40
Nasal structure		
Nasal breadth	26.5	1.22
Nasal height	54.8	0.40
Dacryal chord	20.0	0.00
Dacryal subtense to arc	11.0	0.00
Minimum nasal breadth	9.8	0.98
Subtense to nasal arc	4.8	0.40

* N = 6

** means in millimeters (mm.) unless listed otherwise

APPENDIX C

Table 34 - continued

Orbit		
Left orbital height	35.0	1.09
Left orbital breadth, maxillofrontale	43.1	1.32
Left orbital breadth, dacryon	41.0	0.63
Dental arch and profile		
Maxillo-alveolar breadth	69.0	2.89
Maxillo-alveolar length	52.5	0.54
Facial length, prosthion	98.0	0.00
Facial length, alveolar point	96.0	0.00
Mandible		
Length of mandible	102.8	3.97
Bicondylar breadth	131.5	5.20
Symphysial height	37.1	2.22
Biangular breadth	104.8	6.30
Minimum ramus length	36.3	1.21
Angles		
Facial profile angle	88.0°	0.00
Midfacial profile angle	92.0°	0.00
Alveolar profile angle	77.0°	0.00
Gonial angle	113.5°	2.66

Table 35

Mean Indices of Gartner Male Crania (Deformed)*

	Mean	Standard Dev.
Cranial vault		
Cranial	83.73	6.51
Length-height	77.99	3.06
Breadth-height	93.38	4.00
Mean height	84.89	1.37
Length-auricular height	68.65	2.28
Flatness of cranial base	------	------
Transverse fronto-parietal	65.07	2.84
Face		
Total facial	89.01	0.84
Upper facial	53.36	0.70
Midfacial	72.20	0.76
Transverse cranio-facial	95.52	3.88
Zygo-frontal	68.12	0.94
Fronto-mandibular	108.97	5.59
Zygo-mandibular	74.26	4.56
Facial flatness	16.35	0.70
Anterior interorbital	20.57	0.41
Nasal structure		
Nasal	48.32	2.03
Nasal root height	55.00	0.00
Nasal bone height	49.24	1.85
Orbit		
Left orbital, maxillofrontale	81.09	1.50
Left orbital, dacryon	85.35	1.64
Dental arch		
Maxillo-alveolar	131.43	5.64
Mandible		
Mandibular	78.21	1.73

*N = 6

APPENDIX C

Table 36

Mean Measurements of Gartner Female Crania (Undeformed)*

	Mean**	Standard Dev.
Cranial vault		
Capacity	1366.7cc.	14.42
Cranial module	147.0	1.53
Mean thickness of left parietal	4.7	0.58
Glabello-occipital length	169.0	2.65
Maximum breadth	136.0	2.00
Minimum frontal breadth	88.0	1.00
Basion-bregma height	136.0	4.00
Porion-apex height	114.7	2.52
Basion-porion height	-----	----
Length of cranial base	98.0	4.00
Face		
Total facial height	110.3	0.58
Upper facial height	67.0	0.00
Total facial breadth	133.3	8.33
Midfacial breadth	96.0	7.00
Interior biorbital breadth	92.7	2.52
Subtense to interior biorbital arc	15.0	0.00
Biorbital breadth	97.0	3.51
Anterior interorbital breadth	18.0	1.73
Nasal structure		
Nasal breadth	24.7	0.58
Nasal height	49.0	1.00
Dacryal chord	19.0	1.00
Dacryal subtense to arc	10.0	0.00
Minimum nasal breadth	7.7	0.58
Subtense to nasal arc	4.0	1.00
Orbit		
Left orbital height	32.7	1.53
Left orbital breadth, maxillofrontale	40.7	1.53
Left orbital breadth, dacryon	39.0	1.00
Dental arch and profile		
Maxillo-alveolar breadth	66.7	3.51
Maxillo-alveolar length	50.0	0.00
Facial length, prosthion	96.0	0.00
Facial length, alveolar point	95.0	0.00

Table 36 - continued

Mandible
- Length of mandible — 98.3 — 6.35
- Bicondylar breadth — 129.3 — 0.58
- Symphyseal height — 32.3 — 0.58
- Biangular breadth — 99.3 — 8.02
- Minimum ramus length — 32.7 — 0.58

Angles
- Facial profile angle — 85.0° — 2.00
- Midfacial profile angle — 89.3° — 2.52
- Alveolar profile angle — 69.7° — 1.15
- Gonial angle — 124.0° — 0.00

*N = 3
**Measurements in millimeters (mm.) unless listed otherwise

APPENDIX C

Table 37

Mean Indices of Gartner Female Crania (Undeformed)*

	Mean	Standard Dev.
Cranial vault		
Cranial	80.50	2.42
Length-height	80.49	2.87
Breadth-height	100.00	2.55
Mean height	89.18	2.48
Length-auricular height	67.85	0.85
Flatness of cranial base	------	----
Transverse fronto-parietal	64.71	0.22
Face		
Total facial	82.97	5.20
Upper facial	50.38	3.23
Midfacial	70.04	5.12
Transverse cranio-facial	98.00	4.78
Zygo-frontal	66.15	3.52
Fronto-mandibular	112.82	7.84
Zygo-mandibular	74.45	1.72
Facial flatness	16.20	0.44
Anterior interorbital	18.60	1.26
Nasal structure		
Nasal	50.34	0.59
Nasal root height	52.73	2.78
Nasal bone height	51.79	9.94
Orbit		
Left orbital, maxillofrontale	80.33	2.30
Left orbital, dacryon	83.75	3.00
Dental arch		
Maxillo-alveolar	133.33	7.02
Mandible		
Mandibular	76.05	5.24

*N = 3

Table 38

Mean Measurements of Gartner Female Crania (Deformed)*

	Mean**	Standard Dev.
Cranial vault		
Capacity	1375.0cc.	0.00
Cranial module	149.3	0.00
Mean thickness of left parietal	5.0	0.00
Glabello-occipital length	159.0	0.00
Maximum breadth	151.0	0.00
Minimum frontal breadth	96.0	0.00
Basion-bregma height	138.0	0.00
Porion-apex height	121.0	0.00
Basion-porion height	-----	----
Length of cranial base	98.0	0.00
Face		
Total facial height	114.0	0.00
Upper facial height	66.0	0.00
Total facial breadth	131.0	0.00
Midfacial breadth	96.0	0.00
Interior biorbital breadth	94.0	0.00
Subtense to interior biorbital arc	14.0	0.00
Biorbital breadth	97.0	0.00
Anterior interorbital breadth	19.0	0.00
Nasal structure		
Nasal breadth	25.0	0.00
Nasal height	48.0	0.00
Dacryal chord	20.0	0.00
Dacryal subtense to arc	10.0	0.00
Minimum nasal breadth	10.0	0.00
Subtense to nasal arc	4.0	0.00
Orbit		
Left orbital height	31.0	0.00
Left orbital breadth, maxillofrontale	41.0	0.00
Left orbital breadth, dacryon	39.0	0.00
Dental arch and profile		
Maxillo-alveolar breadth	67.0	0.00
Maxillo-alveolar length	50.0	0.00
Facial length, prosthion	96.0	0.00
Facial length, alveolar point	95.0	0.00

APPENDIX C

Table 38 - continued

Mandible
    Length of mandible   102.0   0.00
    Bicondylar breadth   127.0   0.00
    Symphyseal height   34.0   0.00
    Biangular breadth   101.0   0.00
    Minimum ramus length   34.0   0.00

Angles
    Facial profile angle $85.0°$ 0.00
    Midfacial profile angle $89.0°$ 0.00
    Alveolar profile angle $75.0°$ 0.00
    Gonial angle $123.0°$ 0.00

*N = 1
**Measurements in millimeters (mm.) unless listed otherwise

Table 39

Mean Indices of Gartner Female Crania (Deformed)*

	Mean	Standard Dev.
Cranial vault		
Cranial	94.97	0.00
Length-height	86.79	0.00
Breadth-height	91.39	0.00
Mean height	89.03	0.00
Length-auricular height	76.10	0.00
Flatness of cranial base	------	----
Transverse fronto-parietal	63.58	0.00
Face		
Total facial	87.02	0.00
Upper facial	50.38	0.00
Midfacial	68.75	0.00
Transverse cranio-facial	86.75	0.00
Zygo-frontal	73.28	0.00
Fronto-mandibular	105.21	0.00
Zygo-mandibular	77.10	0.00
Facial flatness	14.89	0.00
Anterior interorbital	19.59	0.00
Nasal structure		
Nasal	52.08	0.00
Nasal root height	50.00	0.00
Nasal bone height	40.00	0.00
Orbit		
Left orbital, maxillofrontale	75.61	0.00
Left orbital, dacryon	79.49	0.00
Dental arch		
Maxillo-alveolar	134.00	0.00
Mandible		
Mandibular	80.31	0.00

*N = 1

APPENDIX C

Table 40

Mean Measurements of Baldwin Female Crania (Undeformed)*

	Mean**	Standard Dev.
Cranial vault		
Capacity	1220.0cc.	0.00
Cranial module	147.7	0.00
Mean thickness of left parietal	6.0	0.00
Glabello-occipital length	175.0	0.00
Maximum breadth	133.0	0.00
Minimum frontal breadth	86.0	0.00
Basion-bregma height	135.0	0.00
Porion-apex height	110.0	0.00
Basion-porion height	-----	----
Length of cranial base	103.0	0.00
Face		
Total facial height	117.0	0.00
Upper facial height	71.0	0.00
Total facial breadth	129.0	0.00
Midfacial breadth	95.0	0.00
Interior biorbital breadth	93.0	0.00
Subtense to interior biorbital arc	15.0	0.00
Biorbital breadth	95.0	0.00
Anterior interorbital breadth	16.0	0.00
Nasal structure		
Nasal breadth	24.0	0.00
Nasal height	50.0	0.00
Dacryal chord	18.0	0.00
Dacryal subtense to arc	12.0	0.00
Minimum nasal breadth	10.0	0.00
Subtense to nasal arc	5.0	0.00
Orbit		
Left orbital height	36.0	0.00
Left orbital breadth, maxillofrontale	42.0	0.00
Left orbital breadth, dacryon	39.0	0.00
Dental arch and profile		
Maxillo-alveolar breadth	62.0	0.00
Maxillo-alveolar length	54.0	0.00
Facial length, prosthion	99.0	0.00
Facial length, alveolar point	97.0	0.00

Table 40 - continued

Mandible		
Length of mandible	103.0	0.00
Bicondylar breadth	124.0	0.00
Symphyseal height	33.0	0.00
Biangular breadth	92.0	0.00
Minimum ramus length	30.0	0.00
Angles		
Facial profile angle	$83.0°$	0.00
Midfacial profile angle	$88.0°$	0.00
Alveolar profile angle	$71.0°$	0.00
Gonial angle	$112.0°$	0.00

*N = 1
**Measurements in millimeters (mm.) unless listed otherwise

APPENDIX C

Table 41

Mean Indices of Baldwin Female Crania (Undeformed)*

	Mean	Standard Dev.
Cranial vault		
Cranial	76.00	0.00
Length-height	77.14	0.00
Breadth-height	101.50	0.00
Mean height	87.66	0.00
Length-auricular height	62.86	0.00
Flatness of cranial base	------	----
Transverse fronto-parietal	64.66	0.00
Face		
Total facial	90.70	0.00
Upper facial	55.04	0.00
Midfacial	74.74	0.00
Transverse cranio-facial	96.99	0.00
Zygo-frontal	66.67	0.00
Fronto-mandibular	106.98	0.00
Zygo-mandibular	71.32	0.00
Facial flatness	16.13	0.00
Anterior interorbital	16.84	0.00
Nasal structure		
Nasal	48.00	0.00
Nasal root height	66.67	0.00
Nasal bone height	50.00	0.00
Orbit		
Left orbital, maxillofrontale	85.71	0.00
Left orbital, dacryon	92.31	0.00
Dental arch		
Maxillo-alveolar	114.81	0.00
Mandible		
Mandibular	83.06	0.00

*N = 1

Table 42

Mean Measurements of Brush Creek Male Crania (Undeformed)*

	Mean**	Standard Dev.
Cranial vault		
Capacity	1460.0cc.	0.00
Cranial module	153.3	0.00
Mean thickness of left parietal	6.0	0.00
Glabello-occipital length	179.0	0.00
Maximum breadth	143.0	0.00
Minimum frontal breadth	100.0	0.00
Basion-bregma height	138.0	0.00
Porion-apex height	116.0	0.00
Basion-porion height	-----	------
Length of cranial base	103.0	0.00
Face		
Total facial height	122.0	0.00
Upper facial height	75.0	0.00
Total facial breadth	140.0	0.00
Midfacial breadth	99.0	0.00
Interior biorbital breadth	101.0	0.00
Subtense to interior biorbital arc	19.0	0.00
Biorbital breadth	101.0	0.00
Anterior interorbital breadth	19.0	0.00
Nasal structure		
Nasal breadth	26.0	0.00
Nasal height	48.0	0.00
Dacryal chord	21.0	0.00
Dacryal subtense to arc	10.0	0.00
Minimum nasal breadth	7.0	0.00
Subtense to nasal arc	4.0	0.00

* N = 1

** means in millimeters (mm.) unless listed otherwise

Table 42 - continued

Orbit
Left orbital height	33.0	0.00
Left orbital breadth, maxillofrontale	44.0	0.00
Left orbital breadth, dacryon	41.0	0.00

Dental arch and profile
Maxillo-alveolar breadth	63.0	0.00
Maxillo-alveolar length	57.0	0.00
Facial length, prosthion	104.0	0.00
Facial length, alveolar point	103.0	0.00

Mandible
Length of mandible	105.0	0.00
Bicondylar breadth	131.0	0.00
Symphysial height	38.0	0.00
Biangular breadth	107.0	0.00
Minimum ramus length	38.0	0.00

Angles
Facial profile angle	$80.0°$	0.00
Midfacial profile angle	$86.0°$	0.00
Alveolar profile angle	$67.0°$	0.00
Gonial angle	$114.0°$	0.00

Table 43

Mean Indices of Brush Creek Male Crania (Undeformed)*

	Mean	Standard Dev.
Cranial vault		
Cranial	79.89	0.00
Length-height	77.09	0.00
Breadth-height	96.50	0.00
Mean height	85.71	0.00
Length-auricular height	64.80	0.00
Flatness of cranial base	------	------
Transverse fronto-parietal	69.93	0.00
Face		
Total facial	87.14	0.00
Upper facial	53.57	0.00
Midfacial	75.76	0.00
Transverse cranio-facial	97.90	0.00
Zygo-frontal	71.43	0.00
Fronto-mandibular	107.00	0.00
Zygo-mandibular	76.43	0.00
Facial flatness	18.81	0.00
Anterior interorbital	18.81	0.00
Nasal structure		
Nasal	54.17	0.00
Nasal root height	47.62	0.00
Nasal bone height	57.14	0.00
Orbit		
Left orbital, maxillofrontale	75.00	0.00
Left orbital, dacryon	80.49	0.00
Dental arch		
Maxillo-alveolar	110.53	0.00
Mandible		
Mandibular	80.15	0.00

*N = 1

APPENDIX C

Table 44

Mean Measurements of Brush Creek Female Crania (Undeformed)*

	Mean**	Standard Dev.
Cranial vault		
Capacity	1410.0cc.	0.00
Cranial module	151.0	0.00
Mean thickness of left parietal	6.0	0.00
Glabello-occipital length	172.0	0.00
Maximum breadth	140.0	0.00
Minimum frontal breadth	94.0	0.00
Basion-bregma height	141.0	0.00
Porion-apex height	120.0	0.00
Basion-porion height	-----	----
Length of cranial base	101.0	0.00
Face		
Total facial height	118.0	0.00
Upper facial height	67.0	0.00
Total facial breadth	136.0	0.00
Midfacial breadth	98.0	0.00
Interior biorbital breadth	102.0	0.00
Subtense to interior biorbital arc	13.0	0.00
Biorbital breadth	103.0	0.00
Anterior interorbital breadth	18.0	0.00
Nasal structure		
Nasal breadth	25.0	0.00
Nasal height	47.0	0.00
Dacryal chord	19.0	0.00
Dacryal subtense to arc	10.0	0.00
Minimum nasal breadth	8.0	0.00
Subtense to nasal arc	4.0	0.00
Orbit		
Left orbital height	32.0	0.00
Left orbital breadth, maxillofrontale	45.0	0.00
Left orbital breadth, dacryon	42.0	0.00
Dental arch and profile		
Maxillo-alveolar breadth	67.0	0.00
Maxillo-alveolar length	56.0	0.00
Facial length, prosthion	104.0	0.00
Facial length, alveolar point	102.0	0.00

Table 44 - continued

Mandible
- Length of mandible — 101.0 — 0.00
- Bicondylar breadth — 128.0 — 0.00
- Symphyseal height — 31.0 — 0.00
- Biangular breadth — 98.0 — 0.00
- Minimum ramus length — 32.0 — 0.00

Angles
- Facial profile angle — 77.0° — 0.00
- Midfacial profile angle — 86.0° — 0.00
- Alveolar profile angle — 55.0° — 0.00
- Gonial angle — 121.0° — 0.00

*N = 1
**Measurements in millimeters (mm.) unless listed otherwise

Table 45

Mean Indices of Brush Creek Female Crania (Undeformed)*

	Mean	Standard Dev.
Cranial vault		
Cranial	81.40	0.00
Length-height	81.98	0.00
Breadth-height	100.71	0.00
Mean height	90.38	0.00
Length-auricular height	69.77	0.00
Flatness of cranial base	------	----
Transverse fronto-parietal	67.14	0.00
Face		
Total facial	86.76	0.00
Upper facial	49.26	0.00
Midfacial	68.37	0.00
Transverse cranio-facial	97.14	0.00
Zygo-frontal	69.12	0.00
Fronto-mandibular	104.26	0.00
Zygo-mandibular	72.06	0.00
Facial flatness	12.75	0.00
Anterior interorbital	17.48	0.00
Nasal structure		
Nasal	53.19	0.00
Nasal root height	52.63	0.00
Nasal bone height	50.00	0.00
Orbit		
Left orbital, maxillofrontale	71.11	0.00
Left orbital, dacryon	76.19	0.00
Dental arch		
Maxillo-alveolar	119.64	0.00
Mandible		
Mandibular	78.91	0.00

*N = 1

Table 46

Cranial Observations of the Baum Focus (Males)

Muscularity	Sm	Med	Lge	V.Lge			
Baum (U) N = 7	----	42.9%	57.1%	----			
Baum (D) N = 10	10.0%	60.0%	30.0%	----			
Gartner (U) N = 6	16.7%	83.3%	----	----			
Gartner (D) N = 6	----	83.3%	16.7%	----			
Brush Creek (U) N = 1	----	100.0%	----	----			

Deformation	None	Occ	Lambd	Fr-occ	Bil-fr-occ	Path	Earth Press
Baum (U) N = 7	100.0%	----	----	----	----	----	----
Baum (D) N = 10	----	60.0%	----	----	----	10.0%	30.0%
Gartner (U) N = 6	100.0%	----	----	----	----	----	----
Gartner (D) N = 6	----	33.3%	----	----	----	----	66.7%
Brush Creek (U) N = 1	100.0%	----	----	----	----	----	----

Degree of deform.	None	Trace	Sm	Med	Pron		
Baum (U) N = 7	100.0%	----	----	----	----		
Baum (D) N = 10	----	40.0%	50.0%	10.0%	----		
Gartner (U) N = 6	100.0%	----	----	----	----		
Gartner (D) N = 6	----	50.0%	16.7%	33.3%	----		
Brush Creek (U) N = 1	100.0%	----	----	----	----		

Vault form	Ell	Ov	Spher	Pentag	Rhom	Sphen	
Baum (U) N = 7	28.6%	71.4%	----	----	----	----	
Baum (D) N = 10	----	90.0%	10.0%	----	----	----	
Gartner (U) N = 6	----	83.3%	----	----	16.7%	----	
Gartner (D) N = 6	----	100.0%	----	----	----	----	
Brush Creek (U) N = 1	----	100.0%	----	----	----	----	

Table 46 - continued

	None	Trace	Sm	Med	Lge	V.Lge
Brow ridge size						
Baum (U) N = 7	-----	14.3%	57.1%	14.3%	14.3%	-----
Baum (D) N = 10	-----	-----	30.0%	40.0%	30.0%	-----
Gartner (U) N = 6	-----	33.3%	-----	66.7%	-----	-----
Gartner (D) N = 6	-----	-----	83.3%	16.7%	-----	-----
Brush Creek (U) N = 1	-----	-----	-----	-----	100.0%	-----

	Flat	Sm	Med	Lge	V.Lge	
Glabella prom.						
Baum (U) N = 7	-----	85.7%	14.3%	-----	-----	
Baum (D) N = 10	-----	70.0%	30.0%	-----	-----	
Gartner (U) N = 6	-----	66.7%	16.7%	-----	16.7%	
Gartner (D) N = 6	-----	100.0%	-----	-----	-----	
Brush Creek (U) N = 1	-----	-----	100.0%	-----	-----	

	Bulg	None	Sl	Med	Pron	V.Pron
Frontal slope						
Baum (U) N = 7	-----	-----	14.3%	85.7%	-----	-----
Baum (D) N = 10	-----	-----	-----	100.0%	-----	-----
Gartner (U) N = 6	16.7%	16.7%	-----	66.7%	-----	-----
Gartner (D) N = 6	-----	-----	50.0%	50.0%	-----	-----
Brush Creek (U) N = 1	-----	-----	-----	100.0%	-----	-----

	Sm	Med	Lge			
Postorb. constr.						
Baum (U) N = 7	42.9%	57.1%	-----			
Baum (D) N = 10	30.0%	50.0%	20.0%			
Gartner (U) N = 6	50.0%	50.0%	-----			
Gartner (D) N = 6	16.7%	66.7%	16.7%			
Brush Creek (U) N = 1	-----	100.0%	-----			

Table 46 - continued

	Sm	Med	Lge	V.Lge
Fron. emin.				
Baum (U) N = 7	100.0%	-----	-----	
Baum (D) N = 10	80.0%	-----	-----	
Gartner (U) N = 6	66.7%	20.0%	16.7%	
Gartner (D) N = 6	83.3%	16.7%	-----	
Brush Creek (U) N = 1	100.0%	16.7%	-----	
Fr. median crest	None	Sm	Med	Lge
Baum (U) N = 7	28.6%	28.6%	28.6%	14.3%
Baum (D) N = 10	40.0%	60.0%	-----	-----
Gartner (U) N = 6	50.0%	33.3%	16.7%	-----
Gartner (D) N = 6	83.3%	-----	-----	-----
Brush Creek (U) N = 1	-----	100.0%	-----	16.7%
Fron. br.	Sm	Med	Lge	
Baum (U) N = 7	42.9%	42.9%	14.3%	
Baum (D) N = 10	30.0%	20.0%	50.0%	
Gartner (U) N = 6	33.3%	66.7%	-----	
Gartner (D) N = 6	33.3%	16.7%	50.0%	
Brush Creek (U) N = 1	-----	100.0%	-----	
Sag. elev.	None	Sm	Med	Lge
Baum (U) N = 7	28.6%	57.1%	-----	14.3%
Baum (D) N = 10	60.0%	40.0%	-----	-----
Gartner (U) N = 6	16.7%	66.7%	16.7%	-----
Gartner (D) N = 6	83.3%	-----	16.7%	-----
Brush Creek (U) N = 1	100.0%	-----	-----	-----

Table 46 - continued

Pariet. emin.	Sm	Med	Lge	
Baum (U) N = 7	28.6%	71.4%	-----	
Baum (D) N = 10	10.0%	50.0%	40.0%	
Gartner (U) N = 6	50.0%	50.0%	-----	
Gartner (D) N = 6	16.7%	66.7%	16.7%	
Brush Creek (U) N = 1	-----	-----	100.0%	

Temp. fullness	Flat	Sm	Med	Lge
Baum (U) N = 7	14.3%	71.4%	14.3%	-----
Baum (D) N = 10	20.0%	30.0%	40.0%	10.0%
Gartner (U) N = 6	-----	83.3%	16.7%	-----
Gartner (D) N = 6	33.3%	33.3%	33.3%	-----
Brush Creek (U) N = 1	-----	-----	100.0%	-----

Mastoids	Sm	Med	Lge	V. Lge
Baum (U) N = 7	14.3%	71.4%	14.3%	-----
Baum (D) N = 10	10.0%	70.0%	20.0%	-----
Gartner (U) N = 6	33.3%	50.0%	16.7%	-----
Gartner (D) N = 6	-----	100.0%	-----	-----
Brush Creek (U) N = 1	-----	100.0%	-----	-----

Supramast. crest	Sm	Med	Lge	
Baum (U) N = 7	-----	42.9%	57.1%	
Baum (D) N = 10	10.0%	30.0%	60.0%	
Gartner (U) N = 6	16.7%	50.0%	33.3%	
Gartner (D) N = 6	-----	50.0%	50.0%	
Brush Creek (U) N = 1	-----	100.0%	-----	

Table 46 - continued

Sphen. depress.	Sm	Med	Lge	Pron
Baum (U) N = 7	85.7%	14.3%	-----	-----
Baum (D) N = 10	90.0%	10.0%	-----	-----
Gartner (U) N = 6	66.7%	33.3%	-----	-----
Gartner (D) N = 6	100.0%	-----	-----	-----
Brush Creek (U) N = 1	-----	100.0%	-----	-----

Occip. curve	None	Sm	Med	Pron
Baum (U) N = 7	-----	28.6%	14.3%	57.1%
Baum (D) N = 10	10.0%	60.0%	10.0%	20.0%
Gartner (U) N = 6	-----	66.7%	16.7%	16.7%
Gartner (D) N = 6	16.7%	16.7%	50.0%	16.7%
Brush Creek (U) N = 1	-----	-----	100.0%	-----

Lambd. flat.	None	Sm	Med	Pron
Baum (U) N = 7	14.3%	14.3%	71.4%	-----
Baum (D) N = 10	30.0%	40.0%	10.0%	20.0%
Gartner (U) N = 6	50.0%	16.7%	33.3%	-----
Gartner (D) N = 6	-----	100.0%	-----	-----
Brush Creek (U) N = 1	-----	100.0%	-----	-----

Cond. elev.	Sm	Med	Lge	
Baum (U) N = 7	14.3%	14.3%	71.4%	
Baum (D) N = 10	-----	40.0%	60.0%	
Gartner (U) N = 6	-----	83.3%	16.7%	
Gartner (D) N = 6	100.0%	-----	-----	
Brush Creek (U) N = 1	-----	100.0%	-----	

Table 46 - continued

Basion	Low	Med	High	
Baum (U) N = 7	28.6%	57.1%	14.3%	
Baum (D) N = 10	10.0%	80.0%	10.0%	
Gartner (U) N = 6	16.7%	83.3%	-----	
Gartner (D) N = 6	83.3%	16.7%	-----	
Brush Creek (U) N = 1	-----	100.0%	-----	

Styl. proc.	Sm	Med	Lge	
Baum (U) N = 7	71.4%	14.3%	14.3%	
Baum (D) N = 10	80.0%	-----	20.0%	
Gartner (U) N = 6	83.3%	16.7%	-----	
Gartner (D) N = 6	83.3%	16.7%	-----	
Brush Creek (U) N = 1	100.0%	-----	-----	

Glen. fos. depth	Sm	Med	Lge	
Baum (U) N = 7	-----	71.4%	28.6%	
Baum (D) N = 10	10.0%	80.0%	10.0%	
Gartner (U) N = 6	-----	50.0%	50.0%	
Gartner (D) N = 6	16.7%	33.3%	50.0%	
Brush Creek (U) N = 1	-----	100.0%	-----	

Tymp. plate	Thin	Med	Thick	V. Thick
Baum (U) N = 7	71.4%	28.6%	-----	-----
Baum (D) N = 10	80.0%	10.0%	10.0%	-----
Gartner (U) N = 6	100.0%	-----	-----	-----
Gartner (D) N = 6	83.3%	16.7%	-----	-----
Brush Creek (U) N = 1	100.0%	-----	-----	-----

Table 46 - continued

	Obl	Rhom	Sq	Ell	Rou
Orbit shape					
Baum (U) N = 7	28.6%	----	71.4%	----	----
Baum (D) N = 10	10.0%	10.0%	80.0%	----	----
Gartner (U) N = 6	16.7%	----	83.3%	----	----
Gartner (D) N = 6	----	----	83.3%	16.7%	----
Brush Creek (U) N = 1	----	100.0%	----	----	----

	None	Sm	Med	Pron	
Orbit incl.					
Baum (U) N = 7	----	71.4%	28.6%	----	
Baum (D) N = 10	----	100.0%	----	----	
Gartner (U) N = 6	----	16.7%	83.3%	----	
Gartner (D) N = 6	----	66.7%	33.3%	----	
Brush Creek (U) N = 1	----	100.0%	----	----	

	Abs	Sl	Med	Deep	
Suborb. fossa					
Baum (U) N = 7	----	85.7%	----	14.3%	
Baum (D) N = 10	20.0%	80.0%	----	----	
Gartner (U) N = 6	----	100.0%	----	----	
Gartner (D) N = 6	16.7%	66.7%	16.7%	----	
Brush Creek (U) N = 1	----	100.0%	----	----	

	Sm	Med	Lge	V. Lge	
Zyg. size					
Baum (U) N = 7	14.3%	71.4%	14.3%	----	
Baum (D) N = 10	----	40.0%	60.0%	----	
Gartner (U) N = 6	----	16.7%	66.7%	----	
Gartner (D) N = 6	----	66.7%	33.3%	16.7%	
Brush Creek (U) N = 1	----	----	100.0%	----	

APPENDIX C 219

Table 46 - continued

	Sm	Med	Lge
Zyg. lat. proj.			
Baum (U) N = 7	14.3%	-----	85.7%
Baum (D) N = 10	-----	10.0%	90.0%
Gartner (U) N = 6	-----	-----	100.0%
Gartner (D) N = 6	-----	33.3%	66.7%
Brush Creek (U) N = 1	-----	-----	100.0%
Zyg. ant. proj.	Sm	Med	Lge
Baum (U) N = 7	28.6%	71.4%	-----
Baum (D) N = 10	10.0%	80.0%	10.0%
Gartner (U) N = 6	16.7%	66.7%	16.7%
Gartner (D) N = 6	-----	83.3%	16.7%
Brush Creek (U) N = 1	-----	100.0%	-----
Zyg. proc. thick.	Sm	Med	Pron
Baum (U) N = 7	14.3%	85.7%	-----
Baum (D) N = 10	10.0%	80.0%	10.0%
Gartner (U) N = 6	16.7%	33.3%	50.0%
Gartner (D) N = 6	16.7%	83.3%	-----
Brush Creek (U) N = 1	-----	100.0%	-----

	V.Low	Low	Med	High	V.High
Nas. rt. ht.					
Baum (U) N = 7	-----	-----	71.4%	28.6%	-----
Baum (D) N = 10	-----	-----	80.0%	20.0%	-----
Gartner (U) N = 6	-----	-----	83.3%	16.7%	-----
Gartner (D) N = 6	-----	-----	83.3%	16.7%	-----
Brush Creek (U) N = 1	-----	-----	100.0%	-----	-----

Table 46 - continued

	V.Sm	Sm	Med	Lge	V.Lge
Nas. rt. br.					
Baum (U) N = 7	-----	-----	85.7%	14.3%	-----
Baum (D) N = 10	-----	10.0%	70.0%	20.0%	-----
Gartner (U) N = 6	16.7%	-----	83.3%	-----	-----
Gartner (D) N = 6	-----	-----	100.0%	-----	-----
Brush Creek (U) N = 1	-----	-----	100.0%	-----	-----

	V.Low	Low	Med	High	V.High
Nas. bridg. ht.					
Baum (U) N = 7	-----	-----	71.4%	28.6%	-----
Baum (D) N = 10	-----	-----	40.0%	60.0%	-----
Gartner (U) N = 6	-----	-----	-----	100.0%	-----
Gartner (D) N = 6	-----	-----	-----	100.0%	-----
Brush Creek (U) N = 1	-----	-----	100.0%	-----	-----

	Sm	Med	Lge		
Nas. bridg. br.					
Baum (U) N = 7	-----	100.0%	-----		
Baum (D) N = 10	-----	100.0%	-----		
Gartner (U) N = 6	100.0%	-----	-----		
Gartner (D) N = 6	83.3%	16.7%	-----		
Brush Creek (U) N = 1	-----	100.0%	-----		

	Conc	Str	Sl. Conc-Conv	Conc-Conv	V.C-C
Nas. profile					
Baum (U) N = 7	-----	-----	100.0%	-----	-----
Baum (D) N = 10	-----	-----	90.0%	10.0%	-----
Gartner (U) N = 6	-----	100.0%	-----	-----	-----
Gartner (D) N = 6	-----	-----	-----	100.0%	-----
Brush Creek (U) N = 1	-----	-----	-----	-----	100.0%

APPENDIX C 221

Table 46 - continued

Nas. depress.	Abs	Sm	Med	Lge
Baum (U) N = 7	14.3%	71.4%	14.3%	-----
Baum (D) N = 10	-----	50.0%	50.0%	-----
Gartner (U) N = 6	-----	83.3%	16.7%	-----
Gartner (D) N = 6	-----	100.0%	-----	-----
Brush Creek (U) N = 1	-----	-----	100.0%	-----

Nas. sills	Abs	Dull	Med	Sharp
Baum (U) N = 7	-----	14.3%	71.4%	14.3%
Baum (D) N = 10	-----	10.0%	70.0%	20.0%
Gartner (U) N = 6	-----	-----	100.0%	-----
Gartner (D) N = 6	-----	16.7%	16.7%	66.7%
Brush Creek (U) N = 1	-----	100.0%	-----	-----

Nas. spine	Abs	Sm	Med	Rt. Ang	Lge
Baum (U) N = 7	-----	100.0%	-----	-----	-----
Baum (D) N = 10	-----	100.0%	-----	-----	-----
Gartner (U) N = 6	-----	100.0%	-----	-----	-----
Gartner (D) N = 6	-----	83.3%	-----	-----	16.7%
Brush Creek (U) N = 1	-----	100.0%	-----	-----	-----

Subnas. grooves	Abs	Sm	Med	Pron	Sulci
Baum (U) N = 7	85.7%	14.3%	-----	-----	-----
Baum (D) N = 10	90.0%	10.0%	-----	-----	-----
Gartner (U) N = 6	16.7%	83.3%	-----	-----	-----
Gartner (D) N = 6	100.0%	-----	-----	-----	-----
Brush Creek (U) N = 1	100.0%	-----	-----	-----	-----

Table 46 - continued

	Abs	Sl	Med	Pron
Midfac. progn.				
Baum (U) N = 7	14.3%	85.7%	----	----
Baum (D) N = 10	10.0%	90.0%	----	----
Gartner (U) N = 6	83.3%	16.7%	----	----
Gartner (D) N = 6	100.0%	----	----	----
Brush Creek (U) N = 1	----	100.0%	----	----
Alveol. progn.				
Baum (U) N = 7	----	85.7%	14.3%	----
Baum (D) N = 10	----	10.0%	90.0%	----
Gartner (U) N = 6	----	83.3%	16.7%	----
Gartner (D) N = 6	----	83.3%	16.7%	----
Brush Creek (U) N = 1	----	----	----	100.0%
Total progn.				
Baum (U) N = 7	14.3%	85.7%	----	----
Baum (D) N = 10	----	80.0%	20.0%	----
Gartner (U) N = 6	----	16.7%	83.3%	----
Gartner (D) N = 6	----	83.3%	16.7%	----
Brush Creek (U) N = 1	----	----	100.0%	----

	Parab	Hyperb	Ell	Sm U	Lge U
Palate shape					
Baum (U) N = 7	85.7%	14.3%	----	----	----
Baum (D) N = 10	100.0%	----	----	----	----
Gartner (U) N = 6	100.0%	----	----	----	----
Gartner (D) N = 6	100.0%	----	----	----	----
Brush Creek (U) N = 1	100.0%	----	----	----	----

Table 46 - continued

Palate ht.

	Low	Med	High	V.High
Baum (U) N = 7	14.3%	42.9%	42.9%	-----
Baum (D) N = 10	-----	50.0%	50.0%	-----
Gartner (U) N = 6	16.7%	-----	83.3%	-----
Gartner (D) N = 6	-----	66.7%	33.3%	-----
Brush Creek (U) N = 1	-----	100.0%	-----	-----

Palat. torus

	Abs	SmRidg	MedRidg	LgeRidg	SmMd	MedMd	LMd
Baum (U) N = 7	100.0%	-----	-----	-----	-----	-----	-----
Baum (D) N = 10	90.0%	10.0%	-----	-----	-----	-----	-----
Gartner (U) N = 6	83.3%	16.7%	-----	-----	-----	-----	-----
Gartner (D) N = 6	100.0%	-----	-----	-----	-----	-----	-----
Brush Creek (U) N = 1	100.0%	-----	-----	-----	-----	-----	-----

Mand. size

	Sm	Med	Lge	V.Lge
Baum (U) N = 7	14.3%	71.4%	-----	14.3%
Baum (D) N = 10	-----	80.0%	20.0%	-----
Gartner (U) N = 6	16.7%	66.7%	16.7%	-----
Gartner (D) N = 6	16.7%	66.7%	16.7%	-----
Brush Creek (U) N = 1	-----	100.0%	-----	-----

Chin form

	Nar Bilat.	Wide Bilat.	Inter-med	Median
Baum (U) N = 7	14.3%	-----	14.3%	71.4%
Baum (D) N = 10	20.0%	-----	70.0%	10.0%
Gartner (U) N = 6	-----	-----	33.3%	66.7%
Gartner (D) N = 6	16.7%	-----	33.3%	50.0%
Brush Creek (U) N = 1	-----	-----	-----	100.0%

Table 46 - continued

	Negat	Neut	Sm	Med	Lge
Chin proj.					
Baum (U) N = 7	71.4%	14.3%	----	14.3%	----
Baum (D) N = 10	20.0%	70.0%	10.0%	----	----
Gartner (U) N = 6	66.7%	33.3%	----	----	----
Gartner (D) N = 6	16.7%	83.3%	----	----	----
Brush Creek (U) N = 1	100.0%	----	----	----	----

	Sm	Med	Pron	V. Pron	
Pteryg. attach.					
Baum (U) N = 7	14.3%	85.7%	----	----	
Baum (D) N = 10	20.0%	70.0%	10.0%	----	
Gartner (U) N = 6	33.3%	66.7%	----	----	
Gartner (D) N = 6	16.7%	83.3%	----	----	
Brush Creek (U) N = 1	----	100.0%	----	----	

	None	Sm	Med	Pron	
Gonial ang. evers.					
Baum (U) N = 7	85.7%	14.3%	----	----	
Baum (D) N = 10	10.0%	90.0%	----	----	
Gartner (U) N = 6	83.3%	16.7%	----	----	
Gartner (D) N = 6	83.3%	16.7%	----	----	
Brush Creek (U) N = 1	----	----	100.0%	----	

Table 47

Cranial Observations of the Baum Focus (Females)

Muscularity	Sm	Med	Lge	V.Lge		
Baum (U) N = 1	100.0%	-----	-----	-----		
Baum (D) N = 4	75.0%	25.0%	-----	-----		
Gartner (U) N = 3	100.0%	-----	-----	-----		
Gartner (D) N = 1	100.0%	-----	-----	-----		
Brush Creek (U) N = 1	100.0%	-----	-----	-----		
Baldwin (U) N = 1	100.0%	-----	-----	-----		

Deformation	None	Occ	Lambd	Fr-occ	Bil-fr-occ	
Baum (U) N = 1	100.0%	-----	-----	-----	-----	
Baum (D) N = 4	-----	100.0%	-----	-----	-----	
Gartner (U) N = 3	100.0%	-----	-----	-----	-----	
Gartner (D) N = 1	-----	100.0%	-----	-----	-----	
Brush Creek (U) N = 1	100.0%	-----	-----	-----	-----	
Baldwin (U) N = 1	100.0%	-----	-----	-----	-----	

Degree of deform.	None	Trace	Sm	Med	Pron	
Baum (U) N = 1	100.0%	-----	-----	-----	-----	
Baum (D) N = 4	-----	-----	-----	100.0%	-----	
Gartner (U) N = 3	100.0%	-----	-----	-----	-----	
Gartner (D) N = 1	-----	-----	-----	100.0%	-----	
Brush Creek (U) N = 1	100.0%	-----	-----	-----	-----	
Baldwin (U) N = 1	100.0%	-----	-----	-----	-----	

Vault form	Ell	Ov	Spher	Pentag	Rhom	Sphen
Baum (U) N = 1	-----	100.0%	-----	-----	-----	-----
Baum (D) N = 4	-----	100.0%	-----	-----	-----	-----
Gartner (U) N = 3	-----	66.7%	-----	-----	33.3%	-----
Gartner (D) N = 1	-----	100.0%	-----	-----	-----	-----
Brush Creek (U) N = 1	-----	100.0%	-----	-----	-----	-----
Baldwin (U) N = 1	-----	100.0%	-----	-----	-----	-----

Table 47 - continued

Browridge size

	None	Trace	Sm	Med	Lge	V.Lge
Baum (U) N = 1	-----	100.0%	-----	-----	-----	-----
Baum (D) N = 4	-----	100.0%	-----	-----	-----	-----
Gartner (U) N = 3	-----	100.0%	-----	-----	-----	-----
Gartner (D) N = 1	-----	100.0%	-----	-----	-----	-----
Brush Creek (U) N = 1	-----	100.0%	-----	-----	-----	-----
Baldwin (U) N = 1	-----	100.0%	-----	-----	-----	-----

Glabella prom.

	Flat	Sm	Med	Lge	V.Lge	
Baum (U) N = 1	-----	100.0%	-----	-----	-----	
Baum (D) N = 4	-----	100.0%	-----	-----	-----	
Gartner (U) N = 3	-----	100.0%	-----	-----	-----	
Gartner (D) N = 1	-----	100.0%	-----	-----	-----	
Brush Creek (U) N = 1	-----	100.0%	-----	-----	-----	
Baldwin (U) N = 1	-----	100.0%	-----	-----	-----	

Frontal slope

	Bulg	None	Sl	Med	Pron	V.Pron
Baum (U) N = 1	100.0%	-----	-----	-----	-----	-----
Baum (D) N = 4	25.0%	-----	75.0%	-----	-----	-----
Gartner (U) N = 3	33.3%	-----	33.3%	33.3%	-----	-----
Gartner (D) N = 1	100.0%	-----	-----	-----	-----	-----
Brush Creek (U) N = 1	-----	-----	100.0%	-----	-----	-----
Baldwin (U) N = 1	-----	-----	100.0%	-----	-----	-----

Postorb. constr.

	Sm	Med	Lge			
Baum (U) N = 1	-----	100.0%	-----			
Baum (D) N = 4	75.0%	25.0%	-----			
Gartner (U) N = 3	33.3%	33.3%	33.3%			
Gartner (D) N = 1	100.0%	-----	-----			
Brush Creek (U) N = 1	-----	100.0%	-----			
Baldwin (U) N = 1	-----	100.0%	-----			

Table 47 - continued

Fron. emin.	Sm	Med	Lge
Baum (U) N = 1	-----	100.0%	-----
Baum (D) N = 4	-----	100.0%	-----
Gartner (U) N = 3	33.3%	66.7%	-----
Gartner (D) N = 1	-----	-----	100.0%
Brush Creek (U) N = 1	100.0%	-----	-----
Baldwin (U) N = 1	-----	100.0%	-----

Fr. median crest	None	Sm	Med	Lge
Baum (U) N = 1	100.0%	-----	-----	-----
Baum (D) N = 4	75.0%	25.0%	-----	-----
Gartner (U) N = 3	33.3%	66.7%	-----	-----
Gartner (D) N = 1	100.0%	-----	-----	-----
Brush Creek (U) N = 1	-----	100.0%	-----	-----
Baldwin (U) N = 1	-----	100.0%	-----	-----

Fron. br.	Sm	Med	Lge
Baum (U) N = 1	100.0%	-----	-----
Baum (D) N = 4	25.0%	50.0%	25.0%
Gartner (U) N = 3	66.7%	-----	33.3%
Gartner (D) N = 1	-----	-----	100.0%
Brush Creek (U) N = 1	-----	-----	100.0%
Baldwin (U) N = 1	100.0%	-----	-----

Sag. elev.	None	Sm	Med	Lge	V.Lge
Baum (U) N = 1	-----	100.0%	-----	-----	-----
Baum (D) N = 4	50.0%	50.0%	-----	-----	-----
Gartner (U) N = 3	66.7%	33.3%	-----	-----	-----
Gartner (D) N = 1	100.0%	-----	-----	-----	-----
Brush Creek (U) N = 1	-----	100.0%	-----	-----	-----
Baldwin (U) N = 1	-----	100.0%	-----	-----	-----

Table 47 - continued

Pariet. emin.	Sm	Med	Lge
Baum (U) N = 1	-----	100.0%	-----
Baum (D) N = 4	25.0%	75.0%	-----
Gartner (U) N = 3	33.3%	66.7%	-----
Gartner (D) N = 1	-----	-----	100.0%
Brush Creek (U) N = 1	-----	-----	100.0%
Baldwin (U) N = 1	100.0%	-----	-----

Temp. fullness	Flat	Sm	Med
Baum (U) N = 1	-----	100.0%	-----
Baum (D) N = 4	100.0%	-----	-----
Gartner (U) N = 3	-----	100.0%	-----
Gartner (D) N = 1	-----	-----	100.0%
Brush Creek (U) N = 1	-----	-----	100.0%
Baldwin (U) N = 1	-----	100.0%	-----

Mastoids	Sm	Med	Lge	V.Lge
Baum (U) N = 1	100.0%	-----	-----	-----
Baum (D) N = 4	-----	-----	-----	-----
Gartner (U) N = 3	100.0%	-----	-----	-----
Gartner (D) N = 1	100.0%	-----	-----	-----
Brush Creek (U) N = 1	100.0%	-----	100.0%	-----
Baldwin (U) N = 1	100.0%	-----	-----	-----

Supramast. crest	Sm	Med	Lge
Baum (U) N = 1	-----	100.0%	-----
Baum (D) N = 4	-----	50.0%	50.0%
Gartner (U) N = 3	66.7%	33.3%	-----
Gartner (D) N = 1	100.0%	-----	-----
Brush Creek (U) N = 1	-----	100.0%	-----
Baldwin (U) N = 1	100.0%	-----	-----

Table 47 - continued

Sphen. depress.	Sm	Med	Lge	
Baum (U) N = 1	100.0%	----	----	
Baum (D) N = 4	75.0%	----	25.0%	
Gartner (U) N = 3	100.0%	----	----	
Gartner (D) N = 1	100.0%	----	----	
Brush Creek (U) N = 1	100.0%	----	----	
Baldwin (U) N = 1	----	100.0%	----	

Occip. curve	None	Sm	Med	Pron
Baum (U) N = 1	----	----	----	100.0%
Baum (D) N = 4	75.0%	25.0%	----	----
Gartner (U) N = 3	----	66.7%	----	33.3%
Gartner (D) N = 1	100.0%	----	----	----
Brush Creek (U) N = 1	----	100.0%	----	----
Baldwin (U) N = 1	----	----	----	100.0%

Lambd. flat.	None	Sm	Med	Pron
Baum (U) N = 1	----	100.0%	----	----
Baum (D) N = 4	100.0%	----	----	----
Gartner (U) N = 3	----	66.7%	33.3%	----
Gartner (D) N = 1	----	----	100.0%	----
Brush Creek (U) N = 1	100.0%	----	----	----
Baldwin (U) N = 1	----	----	100.0%	----

Cond. elev.	Sm	Med	Lge	
Baum (U) N = 1	100.0%	----	----	
Baum (D) N = 4	----	----	100.0%	
Gartner (U) N = 3	66.7%	33.3%	----	
Gartner (D) N = 1	100.0%	----	----	
Brush Creek (U) N = 1	----	100.0%	----	
Baldwin (U) N = 1	----	100.0%	----	

Table 47 - continued

Basion	Low	Med	High
Baum (U) N = 1	100.0%	-----	-----
Baum (D) N = 4	-----	100.0%	-----
Gartner (U) N = 3	66.7%	33.3%	-----
Gartner (D) N = 1	100.0%	-----	-----
Brush Creek (U) N = 1	100.0%	-----	-----
Baldwin (U) N = 1	-----	100.0%	-----

Styl. proc.	Sm	Med	Lge
Baum (U) N = 1	100.0%	-----	-----
Baum (D) N = 4	75.0%	25.0%	-----
Gartner (U) N = 3	100.0%	-----	-----
Gartner (D) N = 1	100.0%	-----	-----
Brush Creek (U) N = 1	100.0%	-----	-----
Baldwin (U) N = 1	100.0%	-----	-----

Glen. fos. depth	Sm	Med	Lge
Baum (U) N = 1	-----	100.0%	-----
Baum (D) N = 4	50.0%	50.0%	-----
Gartner (U) N = 3	-----	66.7%	33.3%
Gartner (D) N = 1	-----	100.0%	-----
Brush Creek (U) N = 1	-----	-----	100.0%
Baldwin (U) N = 1	-----	100.0%	-----

Tymp. plate	Thin	Med	Thick	V. Thick
Baum (U) N = 1	100.0%	-----	-----	-----
Baum (D) N = 4	100.0%	-----	-----	-----
Gartner (U) N = 3	100.0%	-----	-----	-----
Gartner (D) N - 1	100.0%	-----	-----	-----
Brush Creek (U) N = 1	-----	100.0%	-----	-----
Baldwin (U) N = 1	100.0%	-----	-----	-----

Table 47 - continued

	Obl	Rhom	Sq	Ell	Rou
Orbit shape					
Baum (U) N = 1	-----	-----	100.0%	-----	-----
Baum (D) N = 4	-----	-----	50.0%	25.0%	25.0%
Gartner (U) N = 3	-----	66.7%	33.3%	-----	-----
Gartner (D) N = 1	-----	100.0%	-----	-----	-----
Brush Creek (U) N = 1	-----	100.0%	-----	-----	-----
Baldwin (U) N = 1	-----	-----	100.0%	-----	-----

	None	Sm	Med	Pron	
Orbit. incl.					
Baum (U) N = 1	-----	100.0%	-----	-----	
Baum (D) N = 4	-----	100.0%	-----	-----	
Gartner (U) N = 3	-----	-----	33.3%	66.7%	
Gartner (D) N = 1	-----	-----	100.0%	-----	
Brush Creek (U) N = 1	-----	-----	100.0%	-----	
Baldwin (U) N = 1	-----	-----	100.0%	-----	

	Abs	Sl	Med	Deep	
Suborb. fossa					
Baum (U) N = 1	-----	100.0%	-----	-----	
Baum (D) N = 4	25.0%	75.0%	-----	-----	
Gartner (U) N = 3	-----	-----	100.0%	-----	
Gartner (D) N = 1	-----	100.0%	-----	-----	
Brush Creek (U) N = 1	100.0%	-----	-----	-----	
Baldwin (U) N = 1	-----	-----	100.0%	-----	

	Sm	Med	Lge	V.Lge	
Zyg. size					
Baum (U) N = 1	-----	100.0%	-----	-----	
Baum (D) N = 4	25.0%	50.0%	25.0%	-----	
Gartner (U) N = 3	33.3%	66.7%	-----	-----	
Gartner (D) N = 1	-----	100.0%	-----	-----	
Brush Creek (U) N = 1	100.0%	-----	-----	-----	
Baldwin (U) N = 1	100.0%	-----	-----	-----	

Table 47 - continued

Zyg. lat. proj.	Sm	Med	Lge
Baum (U) N = 1	-----	-----	100.0%
Baum (D) N = 4	-----	-----	100.0%
Gartner (U) N = 3	33.3%	66.7%	-----
Gartner (D) N = 1	-----	100.0%	-----
Brush Creek (U) N = 1	-----	100.0%	-----
Baldwin (U) N = 1	-----	100.0%	-----

Zyg. ant. proj.	Sm	Med	Lge
Baum (U) N = 1	-----	100.0%	-----
Baum (D) N = 4	-----	75.0%	25.0%
Gartner (U) N = 3	33.3%	33.3%	33.3%
Gartner (D) N = 1	-----	100.0%	-----
Brush Creek (U) N = 1	-----	100.0%	-----
Baldwin (U) N = 1	-----	100.0%	-----

Zyg. proc. thick.	Sm	Med	Pron
Baum (U) N = 1	-----	100.0%	-----
Baum (D) N = 4	50.0%	50.0%	-----
Gartner (U) N = 3	100.0%	-----	-----
Gartner (D) N = 1	-----	100.0%	-----
Brush Creek (U) N = 1	-----	100.0%	-----
Baldwin (U) N = 1	100.0%	-----	-----

Nas. rt. ht.	V.Low	Low	Med	High	V.High
Baum (U) N = 1	-----	-----	-----	100.0%	-----
Baum (D) N = 4	-----	-----	75.0%	25.0%	-----
Gartner (U) N = 3	-----	-----	66.7%	33.3%	-----
Gartner (D) N = 1	-----	100.0%	-----	-----	-----
Brush Creek (U) N = 1	-----	-----	-----	100.0%	-----
Baldwin (U) N = 1	-----	-----	-----	100.0%	-----

Table 47 - continued

Nas. rt. br.	V.Sm	Sm	Med	Lge	V.Lge
Baum (U) N = 1	-----	-----	-----	100.0%	-----
Baum (D) N = 4	-----	25.0%	75.0%	-----	-----
Gartner (U) N = 3	-----	66.7%	-----	33.3%	-----
Gartner (D) N = 1	-----	100.0%	-----	-----	-----
Brush Creek (U) N = 1	-----	-----	100.0%	-----	-----
Baldwin (U) N = 1	-----	100.0%	-----	-----	-----

Nas. bridg. ht.	V.Low	Low	Med	High	V.High
Baum (U) N = 1	-----	-----	-----	100.0%	-----
Baum (D) N = 4	-----	25.0%	-----	75.0%	-----
Gartner (U) N = 3	-----	-----	100.0%	-----	-----
Gartner (D) N = 1	-----	-----	100.0%	-----	-----
Brush Creek (U) N = 1	-----	-----	100.0%	-----	-----
Baldwin (U) N = 1	-----	-----	100.0%	-----	-----

Nas. bridg. br.	Sm	Med	Lge
Baum (U) N = 1	-----	100.0%	-----
Baum (D) N = 4	-----	100.0%	-----
Gartner (U) N = 3	-----	33.3%	66.7%
Gartner (D) N = 1	-----	-----	100.0%
Brush Creek (U) N = 1	-----	100.0%	-----
Baldwin (U) N = 1	-----	100.0%	-----

Nas. profile	Conc	Str	Sl.Conc-Conv	Conc-Conv.	V.C-C
Baum (U) N = 1	-----	-----	100.0%	-----	-----
Baum (D) N = 4	-----	50.0%	50.0%	-----	-----
Gartner (U) N = 3	-----	66.7%	-----	33.3%	-----
Gartner (D) N = 1	-----	-----	-----	100.0%	-----
Brush Creek (U) N = 1	-----	-----	100.0%	-----	-----
Baldwin (U) N = 1	100.0%	-----	-----	-----	-----

Table 47 - continued

	Abs	Sm	Med	Lge
Nas. depress.				
Baum (U) N = 1	100.0%	----	----	----
Baum (D) N = 4	50.0%	50.0%	----	----
Gartner (U) N = 3	33.3%	66.7%	----	----
Gartner (D) N = 1	----	----	100.0%	----
Brush Creek (U) N = 1	----	100.0%	----	----
Baldwin (U) N = 1	100.0%	----	----	----

	Abs	Dull	Med	Sharp
Nas. sills				
Baum (U) N = 1	----	----	----	100.0%
Baum (D) N = 4	----	25.0%	25.0%	50.0%
Gartner (U) N = 3	----	----	66.7%	33.3%
Gartner (D) N = 1	----	----	100.0%	----
Brush Creek (U) N = 1	----	100.0%	----	----
Baldwin (U) N = 1	----	----	100.0%	----

	Abs	Sm	Med	Rt. Ang	Lge
Nas. spine					
Baum (U) N = 1	----	100.0%	----	----	----
Baum (D) N = 4	----	75.0%	25.0%	----	----
Gartner (U) N = 3	----	100.0%	----	----	----
Gartner (D) N = 1	----	100.0%	----	----	----
Brush Creek (U) N = 1	----	100.0%	----	----	----
Baldwin (U) N = 1	----	100.0%	----	----	----

	Abs	Sm	Med	Pron	Sulci
Subnas. grooves					
Baum (U) N = 1	100.0%	----	----	----	----
Baum (D) N = 4	75.0%	----	----	25.0%	----
Gartner (U) N = 3	100.0%	----	----	----	----
Gartner (D) N = 1	----	100.0%	----	----	----
Brush Creek (U) N = 1	100.0%	----	----	----	----
Baldwin (U) N = 1	100.0%	----	----	----	----

Table 47 - continued

Midfac. progn.	Abs	Sl	Med	Pron
Baum (U) N = 1	100.0%	-----	-----	-----
Baum (D) N = 4	100.0%	-----	-----	-----
Gartner (U) N = 3	100.0%	-----	-----	-----
Gartner (D) N = 1	100.0%	-----	-----	-----
Brush Creek (U) N = 1	100.0%	-----	-----	-----
Baldwin (U) N = 1	100.0%	-----	-----	-----

Alveol. progn.	Abs	Sl	Med	Pron
Baum (U) N = 1	-----	-----	100.0%	-----
Baum (D) N = 4	-----	50.0%	50.0%	-----
Gartner (U) N = 3	-----	100.0%	-----	-----
Gartner (D) N = 1	-----	-----	100.0%	-----
Brush Creek (U) N = 1	-----	-----	-----	100.0%
Baldwin (U) N = 1	-----	100.0%	-----	-----

Total progn.	Abs	Sl	Med	Pron
Baum (U) N = 1	-----	100.0%	-----	-----
Baum (D) N = 4	-----	75.0%	25.0%	-----
Gartner (U) N = 3	-----	100.0%	-----	-----
Gartner (D) N = 1	-----	100.0%	-----	-----
Brush Creek (U) N = 1	-----	-----	-----	100.0%
Baldwin (U) N = 1	-----	100.0%	-----	-----

Palate shape	Parab	Hyperb	Ell	Sm U	Lge U
Baum (U) N = 1	100.0%	-----	-----	-----	-----
Baum (D) N = 4	50.0%	50.0%	-----	-----	-----
Gartner (U) N = 3	100.0%	-----	-----	-----	-----
Gartner (D) N = 1	100.0%	-----	-----	-----	-----
Brush Creek (U) N = 1	100.0%	-----	-----	-----	-----
Baldwin (U) N = 1	100.0%	-----	-----	-----	-----

Table 47 - continued

Palate ht.

	Low	Med	High	V.High
Baum (U) N = 1	-----	100.0%	-----	-----
Baum (D) N = 4	25.0%	75.0%	-----	-----
Gartner (U) N = 3	-----	100.0%	-----	-----
Gartner (D) N = 1	-----	-----	100.0%	-----
Brush Creek (U) N = 1	-----	100.0%	-----	-----
Baldwin (U) N = 1	-----	100.0%	-----	-----

Palat. torus

	Abs	SmRidg	MedRidg	LgeRidg
Baum (U) N = 1	100.0%	-----	-----	-----
Baum (D) N = 4	100.0%	-----	-----	-----
Gartner (U) N = 3	100.0%	-----	-----	-----
Gartner (D) N = 1	100.0%	-----	-----	-----
Brush Creek (U) N = 1	100.0%	-----	-----	-----
Baldwin (U) N = 1	100.0%	-----	-----	-----

Mand. size

	Sm	Med	Lge	V.Lge	SmMd	MedMd	LMd
Baum (U) N = 1	-----	100.0%	-----	-----	-----	-----	-----
Baum (D) N = 4	25.0%	75.0%	-----	-----	-----	-----	-----
Gartner (U) N = 3	100.0%	-----	-----	-----	-----	-----	-----
Gartner (D) N = 1	100.0%	-----	-----	-----	-----	-----	-----
Brush Creek (U) N = 1	-----	100.0%	-----	-----	-----	-----	-----
Baldwin (U) N = 1	100.0%	-----	-----	-----	-----	-----	-----

Chin form

	NarBilat	WideBilat	Intermed	Median
Baum (U) N = 1	-----	-----	100.0%	-----
Baum (D) N = 4	-----	-----	50.0%	50.0%
Gartner (U) N = 3	-----	-----	33.3%	66.7%
Gartner (D) N = 1	-----	-----	-----	100.0%
Brush Creek (U) N = 1	100.0%	-----	-----	-----
Baldwin (U) N = 1	-----	-----	-----	100.0%

Table 47 - continued

Chin proj.	Negat	Neut	Sm	Med	Lge
Baum (U) N = 1	100.0%	-----	-----	-----	-----
Baum (D) N = 4	100.0%	-----	-----	-----	-----
Gartner (U) N = 3	100.0%	-----	-----	-----	-----
Gartner (D) N - 1	100.0%	-----	-----	-----	-----
Brush Creek (U) N = 1	-----	100.0%	-----	-----	-----
Baldwin (U) N = 1	-----	100.0%	-----	-----	-----

Pteryg. attach.	Sm	Med	Pron	V.Pron	
Baum (U) N = 1	-----	100.0%	-----	-----	
Baum (D) N = 4	-----	75.0%	25.0%	-----	
Gartner (U) N = 3	33.3%	66.7%	-----	-----	
Gartner (D) N = 1	-----	100.0%	-----	-----	
Brush Creek (U) N = 1	-----	100.0%	-----	-----	
Baldwin (U) N = 1	-----	100.0%	-----	-----	

Gonial ang. evers.	None	Sm	Med	Pron	
Baum (U) N = 1	100.0%	-----	-----	-----	
Baum (D) N = 4	25.0%	75.0%	-----	-----	
Gartner (U) N = 3	66.7%	-----	33.3%	-----	
Gartner (D) N = 1	100.0%	-----	-----	-----	
Brush Creek (U) N = 1	-----	-----	100.0%	-----	
Baldwin (U) N = 1	100.0%	-----	-----	-----	

Table 48

Mean Measurements of Feurt Male Crania (Undeformed)*

	Mean**	Standard Dev.
Cranial vault		
Capacity	1460.0cc.	55.65
Cranial module	155.2	3.01
Mean thickness of left parietal	4.9	0.65
Glabello-occipital length	182.4	7.32
Maximum breadth	141.0	6.80
Minimum frontal breadth	96.5	3.35
Basion-bregma height	142.9	2.01
Porion-apex height	119.0	2.39
Basion-porion height	-----	------
Length of cranial base	105.6	3.04
Face		
Total facial height	126.7	1.71
Upper facial height	77.4	1.76
Total facial breadth	141.8	3.77
Midfacial breadth	104.5	2.40
Interior biorbital breadth	100.7	3.86
Subtense to interior biorbital arc	18.2	2.35
Biorbital breadth	101.6	1.53
Anterior interorbital breadth	20.1	1.66
Nasal structure		
Nasal breadth	27.5	1.32
Nasal height	55.4	1.46
Dacryal chord	22.0	1.17
Dacryal subtense to arc	11.4	0.87
Minimum nasal breadth	10.0	1.27
Subtense to nasal arc	4.2	0.91

* N = 17

** means in millimeters (mm.) unless listed otherwise

Table 48 - continued

Orbit
  Left orbital height   34.1   1.77
  Left orbital breadth, maxillofrontale   44.6   0.99
  Left orbital breadth, dacryon   41.8   0.48

Dental arch and profile
  Maxillo-alveolar breadth   69.1   1.83
  Maxillo-alveolar length   55.2   1.43
  Facial length, prosthion   100.3   1.49
  Facial length, alveolar point   98.4   1.69

Mandible
  Length of mandible   105.1   2.94
  Bicondylar breadth   128.7   4.35
  Symphysial height   37.1   1.59
  Biangular breadth   103.7   4.05
  Minimum ramus length   34.7   1.64

Angles
  Facial profile angle   84.8°   2.36
  Midfacial profile angle   88.9°   2.30
  Alveolar profile angle   72.1°   2.89
  Gonial angle   114.4°   3.44

Table 49

Mean Indices of Feurt Male Crania (Undeformed)*

	Mean	Standard Dev.
Cranial vault		
Cranial	76.42	4.36
Length-height	78.13	2.40
Breadth-height	102.42	4.24
Mean height	88.57	2.04
Length-auricular height	65.04	2.23
Flatness of cranial base	------	------
Transverse fronto-parietal	69.31	3.08
Face		
Total facial	89.19	2.00
Upper facial	54.54	1.92
Midfacial	74.20	2.77
Transverse cranio-facial	101.84	4.92
Zygo-frontal	68.11	2.38
Fronto-mandibular	107.77	3.58
Zygo-mandibular	73.34	1.66
Facial flatness	18.01	2.13
Anterior interorbital	19.96	1.55
Nasal structure		
Nasal	49.85	2.38
Nasal root height	51.52	5.01
Nasal bone height	43.33	9.37
Orbit		
Left orbital, maxillofrontale	76.67	3.41
Left orbital, dacryon	81.74	4.25
Dental arch		
Maxillo-alveolar	126.00	3.85
Mandible		
Mandibular	81.71	3.18

*N = 17

APPENDIX C

Table 50

Mean Measurements of Feurt Male Crania (Deformed)*

	Mean**	Standard Dev.
Cranial vault		
Capacity	1487.1cc.	39.47
Cranial module	155.5	1.78
Mean thickness of left parietal	5.6	0.49
Glabello-occipital length	172.4	4.41
Maximum breadth	150.7	5.95
Minimum frontal breadth	95.5	4.21
Basion-bregma height	143.5	3.39
Porion-apex height	121.9	4.19
Basion-porion height	-----	------
Length of cranial base	104.5	1.74
Face		
Total facial height	127.3	2.84
Upper facial height	79.0	1.59
Total facial breadth	141.9	4.35
Midfacial breadth	102.6	3.38
Interior biorbital breadth	100.2	2.61
Subtense to interior biorbital arc	18.7	1.57
Biorbital breadth	101.5	1.65
Anterior interorbital breadth	19.5	1.22
Nasal structure		
Nasal breadth	27.0	1.63
Nasal height	56.2	1.06
Dacryal chord	21.4	1.28
Dacryal subtense to arc	11.1	0.53
Minimum nasal breadth	9.6	0.74
Subtense to nasal arc	4.2	0.80

* N = 15

** means in millimeters (mm.) unless listed otherwise

Table 50 - continued

Orbit
    Left orbital height   33.8   1.09
    Left orbital breadth, maxillofrontale   45.0   0.73
    Left orbital breadth, dacryon   42.0   0.78

Dental arch and profile
    Maxillo-alveolar breadth   68.9   0.73
    Maxillo-alveolar length   55.2   2.54
    Facial length, prosthion   99.7   3.16
    Facial length, alveolar point   97.7   3.35

Mandible
    Length of mandible   106.1   2.79
    Bicondylar breadth   129.5   1.28
    Symphysial height   36.7   1.71
    Biangular breadth   104.2   3.74
    Minimum ramus length   35.5   1.65

Angles
    Facial profile angle $85.0°$ 2.84
    Midfacial profile angle $89.3°$ 2.56
    Alveolar profile angle $71.8°$ 4.24
    Gonial angle $118.0°$ 4.13

APPENDIX C

Table 51

Mean Indices of Feurt Male Crania (Deformed)*

Cranial vault	Mean	Standard Dev.
Cranial	87.90	5.28
Length-height	83.46	2.56
Breadth-height	95.16	4.58
Mean height	88.85	2.34
Length-auricular height	70.77	2.61
Flatness of cranial base	------	------
Transverse fronto-parietal	63.08	2.26
Face		
Total facial	89.93	2.60
Upper facial	55.74	1.47
Midfacial	76.90	2.98
Transverse cranio-facial	93.85	3.16
Zygo-frontal	67.25	2.31
Fronto-mandibular	108.92	6.33
Zygo-mandibular	73.13	2.37
Facial flatness	18.80	1.78
Anterior interorbital	19.29	1.06
Nasal structure		
Nasal	47.86	2.50
Nasal root height	52.16	5.87
Nasal bone height	43.29	6.37
Orbit		
Left orbital, maxillofrontale	75.00	2.10
Left orbital, dacryon	80.47	2.07
Dental arch		
Maxillo-alveolar	124.59	5.26
Mandible		
Mandibular	81.97	1.83

* N = 15

Table 52

Mean Measurements of Feurt Female Crania (Undeformed)*

	Mean**	Standard Dev.
Cranial vault		
Capacity	1350.0cc.	24.49
Cranial module	148.4	2.87
Mean thickness of left parietal	5.5	1.05
Glabello-occipital length	173.7	4.08
Maximum breadth	137.3	5.39
Minimum frontal breadth	91.0	1.55
Basion-bregma height	134.2	0.98
Porion-apex height	113.2	2.40
Basion-porion height	-----	----
Length of cranial base	99.0	4.49
Face		
Total facial height	116.0	0.00
Upper facial height	71.8	0.41
Total facial breadth	130.2	4.49
Midfacial breadth	99.3	0.82
Interior biorbital breadth	93.0	1.67
Subtense to interior biorbital arc	15.3	2.88
Biorbital breadth	95.7	0.82
Anterior interorbital breadth	19.2	0.98
Nasal structure		
Nasal breadth	26.2	0.41
Nasal height	51.0	0.00
Dacryal chord	20.2	0.41
Dacryal subtense to arc	9.0	0.00
Minimum nasal breadth	7.3	1.03
Subtense to nasal arc	2.7	0.52
Orbit		
Left orbital height	33.2	0.98
Left orbital breadth, maxillofrontale	40.7	0.52
Left orbital breadth, dacryon	38.8	0.41
Dental arch and profile		
Maxillo-alveolar breadth	64.7	0.82
Maxillo-alveolar length	52.0	0.00
Facial length, prosthion	94.8	0.42
Facial length, alveolar point	93.0	0.00

Table 52 - continued

Mandible		
Length of mandible	101.0	0.00
Bicondylar breadth	121.0	2.45
Symphyseal height	33.3	0.82
Biangular breadth	96.8	0.41
Minimum ramus length	32.0	0.63
Angles		
Facial profile angle	82.2°	0.41
Midfacial profile angle	88.3°	0.82
Alveolar profile angle	67.2°	2.04
Gonial angle	125.8°	2.04

*N = 6
**Measurements in millimeters (mm.) unless listed otherwise

Table 53

Mean Indices of Feurt Female Crania (Undeformed)*

	Mean	Standard Dev.
Cranial vault		
Cranial	79.08	2.67
Length-height	77.28	1.65
Breadth-height	97.82	3.97
Mean height	86.33	2.27
Length-auricular height	65.18	1.74
Flatness of cranial base	------	----
Transverse fronto-parietal	66.31	1.58
Face		
Total facial	89.21	3.26
Upper facial	55.25	2.10
Midfacial	72.32	0.99
Transverse cranio-facial	94.81	1.96
Zygo-frontal	69.95	1.41
Fronto-mandibular	106.44	2.04
Zygo-mandibular	74.47	2.81
Facial flatness	16.45	2.86
Anterior interorbital	20.04	1.20
Nasal structure		
Nasal	51.31	0.80
Nasal root height	44.64	0.87
Nasal bone height	37.63	11.24
Orbit		
Left orbital, maxillofrontale	81.58	2.91
Left orbital, dacryon	85.44	3.52
Dental arch		
Maxillo-alveolar	124.36	1.57
Mandible		
Mandibular	83.50	1.75

*N = 6

APPENDIX C 247

Table 54

Mean Measurements of Feurt Female Crania (Deformed)*

Cranial vault	Mean**	Standard Dev.
Capacity	1332.2 cc.	19.86
Cranial module	146.3	42.23
Mean thickness of left parietal	5.2	0.83
Glabello-occipital length	159.1	4.40
Maximum breadth	148.1	4.08
Minimum frontal breadth	92.9	2.93
Basion-bregma height	131.8	2.86
Porion-apex height	114.0	1.12
Basion-porion height	-----	-----
Lenght of cranial base	96.9	0.78
Face		
Total facial height	116.0	0.00
Upper facial height	72.1	1.27
Total facial breadth	132.6	1.13
Midfacial breadth	98.8	0.67
Interior biorbital breadth	94.8	1.99
Subtense to interior biorbital arc	16.6	1.42
Biorbital breadth	96.3	1.00
Anterior interorbital breadth	19.1	0.33
Nasal structure		
Nasal breadth	26.2	0.44
Nasal height	50.8	0.67
Dacryal chord	20.0	0.00
Dacryal subtense to arc	9.2	0.67
Minimum nasal breadth	7.0	0.00
Subtense to nasal arc	3.0	0.00
Orbit		
Left orbital height	33.1	0.78
Left orbital breadth, maxillofrontale	41.2	0.44
Left orbital breadth, dacryon	39.2	0.44
Dental arch and profile		
Maxillo-alveolar breadth	64.8	0.67
Maxillo-alveolar length	52.8	1.56
Facial length, prosthion	95.2	2.05
Facial length, alveolar point	93.3	2.35

Table 54 - continued

Mandible
- Length of mandible — 100.7 — 1.00
- Bicondylar breadth — 121.7 — 1.00
- Symphyseal height — 30.7 — 2.65
- Biangular breadth — 97.2 — 5.21
- Minimum ramus length — 30.6 — 1.88

Angles
- Facial profile angle — 81.9° — 1.27
- Midfacial profile angle — 87.8° — 1.09
- Alveolar profile angle — 68.4° — 2.19
- Gonial angle — 124.4° — 2.88

*N = 9
**Measurements in millimeters (mm.) unless listed otherwise

APPENDIX C

Table 55

Mean Indices of Feurt Female Crania (Deformed)*

	Mean	Standard Dev.
Cranial vault		
Cranial	82.10	29.18
Length-height	82.89	3.41
Breadth-height	89.02	2.59
Mean height	85.79	1.92
Length-auricular height	71.70	2.23
Flatness of cranial base	------	----
Transverse fronto-parietal	62.76	2.57
Face		
Total facial	87.52	0.74
Upper facial	54.41	0.88
Midfacial	73.00	1.05
Transverse cranio-facial	89.55	2.12
Zygo-frontal	70.08	2.23
Fronto-mandibular	104.74	6.31
Zygo-mandibular	73.35	3.98
Facial flatness	17.47	1.42
Anterior interorbital	19.84	0.14
Nasal structure		
Nasal	51.65	1.00
Nasal root height	46.11	3.33
Nasal bone height	42.86	0.05
Orbit		
Left orbital, maxillofrontale	80.33	1.81
Left orbital, dacryon	84.43	1.92
Dental arch		
Maxillo-alveolar	122.85	4.29
Mandible		
Mandibular	82.74	0.20

*N = 9

Table 56

Mean Measurements of Fullerton Field Male Crania (Undeformed)*

	Mean**	Standard Dev.
Cranial vault		
Capacity	1480.0cc.	24.49
Cranial module	156.0	2.58
Mean thickness of left parietal	5.0	0.00
Glabello-occipital length	184.1	5.30
Maximum breadth	141.0	2.44
Minimum frontal breadth	94.5	2.34
Basion-bregma height	143.0	0.00
Porion-apex height	119.0	0.00
Basion-porion height	-----	------
Length of cranial base	105.0	0.00
Face		
Total facial height	126.0	0.00
Upper facial height	78.0	0.00
Total facial breadth	142.0	0.00
Midfacial breadth	102.0	0.00
Interior biorbital breadth	100.0	0.00
Subtense to interior biorbital arc	18.0	0.00
Biorbital breadth	102.0	0.00
Anterior interorbital breadth	19.0	0.00
Nasal structure		
Nasal breadth	27.0	0.00
Nasal height	56.3	0.81
Dacryal chord	21.6	0.81
Dacryal subtense to arc	11.0	0.00
Minimum nasal breadth	9.0	0.00
Subtense to nasal arc	4.1	0.40

* N = 6

** means in millimeters (mm.) unless listed otherwise

Table 56 - continued

Orbit		
Left orbital height	34.0	0.00
Left orbital breadth, maxillofrontale	44.8	0.40
Left orbital breadth, dacryon	42.8	0.40
Dental arch and profile		
Maxillo-alveolar breadth	68.1	2.04
Maxillo-alveolar length	55.0	0.00
Facial length, prosthion	100.0	0.00
Facial length, alveolar point	98.0	0.00
Mandible		
Length of mandible	103.1	2.99
Bicondylar breadth	132.1	5.15
Symphysial height	38.8	1.32
Biangular breadth	104.8	1.60
Minimum ramus length	35.0	3.28
Angles		
Facial profile angle	-----	------
Midfacial profile angle	91.0°	0.00
Alveolar profile angle	-----	------
Gonial angle	108.1°	0.40

Table 57

Mean Indices of Fullerton Field Male Crania (Undeformed)*

Cranial vault	Mean	Standard Dev.
Cranial	76.57	0.83
Length-height	77.69	2.13
Breadth-height	101.44	1.71
Mean height	87.99	2.02
Length-auricular height	64.65	1.77
Flatness of cranial base	------	------
Transverse fronto-parietal	67.04	2.43
Face		
Total facial	88.73	0.00
Upper facial	54.93	0.00
Midfacial	76.47	0.00
Transverse cranio-facial	100.73	1.70
Zygo-frontal	66.55	1.65
Fronto-mandibular	110.88	3.33
Zygo-mandibular	73.82	1.12
Facial flatness	18.00	0.00
Anterior interorbital	18.63	0.00
Nasal structure		
Nasal	47.93	0.67
Nasal root height	50.83	2.04
Nasal bone height	46.29	4.53
Orbit		
Left orbital, maxillofrontale	75.84	0.69
Left orbital, dacryon	79.38	0.76
Dental arch		
Maxillo-alveolar	123.90	3.71
Mandible		
Mandibular	78.22	5.14

* N = 6

APPENDIX C

Table 58

Mean Measurements of Fullerton Field Male Crania (Deformed)*

Cranial vault	Mean**	Standard Dev.
Capacity	1500.0cc.	42.42
Cranial module	160.0	0.00
Mean thickness of left parietal	4.5	0.70
Glabello-occipital length	181.0	0.00
Maximum breadth	146.0	0.00
Minimum frontal breadth	93.5	0.70
Basion-bregma height	153.0	0.00
Porion-apex height	123.5	0.70
Basion-porion height	-----	------
Length of cranial base	107.5	3.53
Face		
Total facial height	126.0	0.00
Upper facial height	78.0	0.00
Total facial breadth	139.0	0.00
Midfacial breadth	102.0	0.00
Interior biorbital breath	101.0	1.41
Subtense to interior biorbital arc	20.5	3.53
Biorbital breadth	102.0	0.00
Anterior interorbital breadth	18.0	1.41
Nasal structure		
Nasal breadth	27.0	1.41
Nasal height	54.5	1.62
Dacryal chord	19.5	3.53
Dacryal subtense to arc	10.5	0.70
Minimum nasal breadth	9.0	0.00
Subtense to nasal arc	3.5	0.70

* N = 2

* means in millimeters (mm.) unless listed otherwise

Table 58 - continued

Orbit		
Left orbital height	34.0	0.00
Left orbital breadth, maxillofrontale	45.5	0.70
Left orbital breadth, dacryon	44.0	1.41
Dental arch and profile		
Maxillo-alveolar breadth	69.0	0.00
Maxillo-alveolar length	55.0	0.00
Facial length, prosthion	100.0	0.00
Facial length, alveolar point	98.0	0.00
Mandible		
Length of mandible	106.0	1.41
Bicondylar breadth	126.5	3.53
Symphysial height	40.0	2.82
Biangular breadth	104.0	0.00
Minimum ramus length	33.0	1.41
Angles		
Facial profile angle	-----	------
Midfacial profile angle	91.0°	0.00
Alveolar profile angle	-----	------
Gonial angle	108.0°	0.00

APPENDIX C

Table 59

Mean Indices of Fullerton Field Male Crania (Deformed)*

	Mean	Standard Dev.
Cranial vault		
Cranial	80.66	0.00
Length-height	84.53	0.00
Breadth-height	104.79	0.00
Mean height	93.58	0.00
Length-auricular height	68.23	0.38
Flatness of cranial base	------	------
Transverse fronto-parietal	64.04	0.48
Face		
Total facial	90.65	0.00
Upper facial	56.12	0.00
Midfacial	76.47	0.00
Transverse cranio-facial	95.21	0.00
Zygo-frontal	67.27	0.50
Fronto-mandibular	111.23	0.84
Zygo-mandibular	74.82	0.00
Facial flatness	20.27	3.21
Anterior interorbital	17.65	1.38
Nasal structure		
Nasal	51.42	0.50
Nasal root height	54.41	6.23
Nasal bone height	38.88	7.85
Orbit		
Left orbital, maxillofrontale	74.73	1.16
Left orbital, dacryon	77.31	2.48
Dental arch		
Maxillo-alveolar	125.45	0.00
Mandible		
Mandibular	83.84	3.45

* N = 2

Table 60

Mean Measurements of Fullerton Field Female Crania (Undeformed)*

	Mean**	Standard Dev.
Cranial vault		
Capacity	1408.3cc.	57.74
Cranial module	152.0	0.00
Mean thickness of left parietal	4.3	0.58
Glabello-occipital length	176.0	0.00
Maximum breadth	140.0	0.00
Minimum frontal breadth	88.7	4.04
Basion-bregma height	140.0	0.00
Porion-apex height	119.0	0.00
Basion-porion height	-----	----
Length of cranial base	97.7	1.15
Face		
Total facial height	106.0	0.00
Upper facial height	70.0	0.00
Total facial breadth	134.0	0.00
Midfacial breadth	99.0	0.00
Interior biorbital breadth	93.0	3.00
Subtense to interior biorbital arc	13.0	3.61
Biorbital breadth	97.3	0.58
Anterior interorbital breadth	18.0	0.00
Nasal structure		
Nasal breadth	25.0	1.73
Nasal height	52.0	1.73
Dacryal chord	20.0	0.00
Dacryal subtense to arc	9.0	0.00
Minimum nasal breadth	8.3	0.58
Subtense to nasal arc	3.0	0.00
Orbit		
Left orbital height	35.3	0.58
Left orbital breadth, maxillofrontale	41.0	0.00
Left orbital breadth, dacryon	39.3	0.58
Dental arch and profile		
Maxillo-alveolar breadth	65.7	1.15
Maxillo-alveolar length	51.7	0.58
Facial length, prosthion	94.3	1.15
Facial length, alveolar point	92.7	0.58

APPENDIX C

Table 60 - continued

Mandible
- Length of mandible   99.3   3.06
- Bicondylar breadth   124.3   9.02
- Symphyseal height   32.7   1.15
- Biangular breadth   99.7   1.53
- Minimum ramus length   32.0   2.00

Angles
- Facial profile angle $85.0°$ 0.00
- Midfacial profile angle $89.0°$ 0.00
- Alveolar profile angle $68.0°$ 0.00
- Gonial angle $118.3°$ 2.31

*N = 3
**Measurements in millimeters (mm.) unless listed otherwise

Table 61

Mean Indices of Fullerton Field Female Crania (Undeformed)*

	Mean	Standard Dev.
Cranial vault		
Cranial	79.55	0.00
Length-height	79.55	0.00
Breadth-height	100.00	0.00
Mean height	88.61	0.00
Length-auricular height	67.61	0.00
Flatness of cranial base	------	----
Transverse fronto-parietal	63.33	2.89
Face		
Total facial	86.57	0.00
Upper facial	52.24	0.00
Midfacial	70.71	0.00
Transverse cranio-facial	95.71	0.00
Zygo-frontal	66.17	3.01
Fronto-mandibular	112.52	3.64
Zygo-mandibular	74.38	1.14
Facial flatness	13.96	3.80
Anterior interorbital	18.50	0.11
Nasal structure		
Nasal	48.08	2.94
Nasal root height	45.00	0.00
Nasal bone height	36.11	2.41
Orbit		
Left orbital, maxillofrontale	86.18	1.40
Left orbital, dacryon	89.83	0.15
Dental arch		
Maxillo-alveolar	127.12	3.68
Mandible		
Mandibular	80.15	5.90

*N = 3

APPENDIX C

Table 62

Mean Measurements of Fullerton Field Female Crania (Deformed)*

	Mean**	Standard Dev.
Cranial vault		
Capacity	1375.0cc.	0.00
Cranial module	151.3	0.00
Mean thickness of left parietal	5.0	0.00
Glabello-occipital length	165.0	0.00
Maximum breadth	150.0	0.00
Minimum frontal breadth	91.0	0.00
Basion-bregma height	139.0	0.00
Porion-apex height	120.0	0.00
Basion-porion height	-----	----
Length of cranial base	97.0	0.00
Face		
Total facial height	116.0	0.00
Upper facial height	70.0	0.00
Total facial breadth	134.0	0.00
Midfacial breadth	99.0	0.00
Interior biorbital breadth	93.0	0.00
Subtense to interior biorbital arc	17.0	0.00
Biorbital breadth	97.0	0.00
Anterior interorbital breadth	18.0	0.00
Nasal structure		
Nasal breadth	24.0	0.00
Nasal height	51.0	0.00
Dacryal chord	20.0	0.00
Dacryal subtense to arc	9.0	0.00
Minimum nasal breadth	8.0	0.00
Subtense to nasal arc	3.0	0.00
Orbit		
Left orbital height	35.0	0.00
Left orbital breadth, maxillofrontale	41.0	0.00
Left orbital breadth, dacryon	39.0	0.00
Dental arch and profile		
Maxillo-alveolar breadth	61.0	0.00
Maxillo-alveolar length	47.0	0.00
Facial length, prosthion	95.0	0.00
Facial length, alveolar point	93.0	0.00

Table 62 - continued

Mandible		
Length of mandible	91.0	0.00
Bicondylar breadth	120.0	0.00
Symphyseal height	31.0	0.00
Biangular breadth	92.0	0.00
Minimum ramus length	32.0	0.00
Angles		
Facial profile angle	85.0°	0.00
Midfacial profile angle	89.0°	0.00
Alveolar profile angle	68.0°	0.00
Gonial angle	113.0°	0.00

*N = 1
**Measurements in millimeters (mm.) unless listed otherwise

APPENDIX C

Table 63

Mean Indices of Fullerton Field Female Crania (Deformed)*

Cranial vault	Mean	Standard Dev.
Cranial	90.91	0.00
Length-height	84.24	0.00
Breadth-height	92.67	0.00
Mean height	88.25	0.00
Length-auricular height	72.73	0.00
Flatness of cranial base	------	----
Transverse fronto-parietal	60.67	0.00
Face		
Total facial	86.57	0.00
Upper facial	52.24	0.00
Midfacial	70.71	0.00
Transverse cranio-facial	89.33	0.00
Zygo-frontal	67.91	0.00
Fronto-mandibular	101.10	0.00
Zygo-mandibular	68.66	0.00
Facial flatness	18.28	0.00
Anterior interorbital	18.56	0.00
Nasal structure		
Nasal	47.06	0.00
Nasal root height	45.00	0.00
Nasal bone height	37.50	0.00
Orbit		
Left orbital, maxillofrontale	85.37	0.00
Left orbital, dacryon	89.74	0.00
Dental arch		
Maxillo-alveolar	129.79	0.00
Mandible		
Mandibular	75.83	0.00

*N = 1

Table 64

Mean Measurements of Proctorville Male Crania (Undeformed)*

	Mean**	Standard Dev.
Cranial vault		
Capacity	1300.0cc.	0.00
Cranial module	147.0	0.94
Mean thickness of left parietal	5.0	0.00
Glabello-occipital length	168.0	0.00
Maximum breadth	136.0	0.00
Minimum frontal breadth	94.5	0.70
Basion-bregma height	137.0	2.82
Porion-apex height	115.0	0.00
Basion-porion height	-----	------
Length of cranial base	100.0	0.00
Face		
Total facial height	126.0	0.00
Upper facial height	75.5	0.70
Total facial breadth	136.0	0.00
Midfacial breadth	98.0	0.00
Interior biorbital breadth	101.0	0.00
Subtense to interior biorbital arc	19.5	0.70
Biorbital breadth	100.0	0.00
Anterior interorbital breadth	21.0	1.41
Nasal structure		
Nasal breadth	27.5	2.12
Nasal height	54.5	0.70
Dacryal chord	22.5	0.70
Dacryal subtense to arc	11.5	0.70
Minimum nasal breadth	11.5	0.70
Subtense to nasal arc	4.5	0.70

* N = 2

** means in millimeters (mm.) unless listed otherwise

APPENDIX C 263

Table 64 - continued

Orbit
- Left orbital height .... 35.0 .... 0.00
- Left orbital breadth, maxillofrontale ... 44.0 ... 0.00
- Left orbital breadth, dacryon .... 40.5 .... 0.70

Dental arch and profile
- Maxillo-alveolar breadth .... 70.0 .... 1.41
- Maxillo-alveolar length .... 57.0 .... 0.00
- Facial length, prosthion .... 98.0 .... 0.00
- Facial length, alveolar point ... 96.0 .... 0.00

Mandible
- Length of mandible .... 105.0 ... 0.00
- Bicondylar breadth .... 127.0 ... 0.00
- Symphysial height .... 37.5 .... 0.70
- Biangular breadth .... 104.0 ... 0.00
- Minimum ramus length .... 31.5 .... 0.70

Angles
- Facial profile angle .... 80.0° ... 0.00
- Midfacial profile angle .... 84.0° ... 0.00
- Alveolar profile angle .... 73.0° ... 0.00
- Gonial angle .... 110.0° .. 0.00

Table 65

Mean Indices of Proctorville Male Crania (Undeformed)*

	Mean	Standard Dev.
Cranial vault		
Cranial	80.95	0.00
Length-height	81.55	1.68
Breadth-height	100.73	2.08
Mean height	90.13	1.85
Length-auricular height	68.45	0.00
Flatness of cranial base	------	------
Transverse fronto-parietal	69.48	0.51
Face		
Total facial	92.65	0.00
Upper facial	55.51	0.51
Midfacial	77.04	0.72
Transverse cranio-facial	100.00	0.00
Zygo-frontal	69.48	0.51
Fronto-mandibular	110.05	0.82
Zygo-mandibular	76.47	0.00
Facial flatness	19.30	0.70
Anterior interorbital	21.00	1.41
Nasal structure		
Nasal	50.44	3.23
Nasal root height	51.19	4.75
Nasal bone height	39.39	8.57
Orbit		
Left orbital, maxillofrontale	79.55	0.00
Left orbital, dacryon	86.43	1.50
Dental arch		
Maxillo-alveolar	122.80	2.48
Mandible		
Mandibular	82.68	0.00

*N = 2

APPENDIX C

Table 66

Mean Measurements of Proctorville Male Crania (Deformed)*

	Mean**	Standard Dev.
Cranial vault		
Capacity	1330.0cc.	0.00
Cranial module	153.0	0.00
Mean thickness of left parietal	5.0	0.00
Glabello-occipital length	170.0	0.00
Maximum breadth	150.0	0.00
Minimum frontal breadth	94.0	0.00
Basion-bregma height	139.0	0.00
Porion-apex height	118.0	0.00
Basion-porion height	-----	------
Length of cranial base	100.0	0.00
Face		
Total facial height	126.0	0.00
Upper facial height	76.0	0.00
Total facial breadth	136.0	0.00
Midfacial breadth	98.0	0.00
Interior biorbital breadth	101.0	0.00
Subtense to interior biorbital arc	19.0	0.00
Biorbital breadth	100.0	0.00
Anterior interorbital breadth	20.0	0.00
Nasal structure		
Nasal breadth	28.0	0.00
Nasal height	54.0	0.00
Dacryal chord	22.0	0.00
Dacryal subtense to arc	11.0	0.00
Minimum nasal breadth	12.0	0.00
Subtense to nasal arc	4.0	0.00

* N = 1

** means in millimeters (mm.) unless listed otherwise

Table 66 - continued

Orbit
    Left orbital height   35.0   0.00
    Left orbital breadth, maxillofrontale   44.0   0.00
    Left orbital breadth, dacryon   41.0   0.00

Dental arch and profile
    Maxillo-alveolar breadth   69.0   0.00
    Maxillo-alveolar length   55.0   0.00
    Facial length, prosthion   100.0   0.00
    Facial length, alveolar point   98.0   0.00

Mandible
    Length of mandible   105.0   0.00
    Bicondylar breadth   129.0   0.00
    Symphysial height   37.0   0.00
    Biangular breadth   104.0   0.00
    Minimum ramus length   32.0   0.00

Angles
    Facial profile angle $80.0°$ 0.00
    Midfacial profile angle $84.0°$ 0.00
    Alveolar profile angle $73.0°$ 0.00
    Gonial angle $110.0°$ 0.00

APPENDIX C

Table 67

Mean Indices of Proctorville Male Crania (Deformed)*

	Mean	Standard Dev.
Cranial vault		
Cranial	88.24	0.00
Length-height	81.76	0.00
Breadth-height	92.67	0.00
Mean height	86.87	0.00
Length-auricular height	69.41	0.00
Flatness of cranial base	------	------
Transverse fronto-parietal	62.67	0.00
Face		
Total facial	92.65	0.00
Upper facial	55.88	0.00
Midfacial	77.55	0.00
Transverse cranio-facial	90.67	0.00
Zygo-frontal	69.12	0.00
Fronto-mandibular	110.64	0.00
Zygo-mandibular	76.47	0.00
Facial flatness	18.81	0.00
Anterior interorbital	20.00	0.00
Nasal structure		
Nasal	51.85	0.00
Nasal root height	50.00	0.00
Nasal bone height	33.33	0.00
Orbit		
Left orbital, maxillofrontale	79.55	0.00
Left orbital, dacryon	85.37	0.00
Dental arch		
Maxillo-alveolar	125.45	0.00
Mandible		
Mandibular	81.40	0.00

* N = 1

Table 68

Mean Measurements of Proctorville Female Crania (Deformed)*

Cranial vault	Mean**	Standard Dev.
Capacity	1345.0cc.	36.74
Cranial module	144.8	2.68
Mean thickness of left parietal	4.8	0.75
Glabello-occipital length	163.0	6.16
Maximum breadth	141.7	3.88
Minimum frontal breadth	88.2	1.47
Basion-bregma height	129.8	2.99
Porion-apex height	114.2	2.23
Basion-porion height	-----	----
Length of cranial base	94.2	2.99
Face		
Total facial height	116.0	0.00
Upper facial height	69.0	1.26
Total facial breadth	133.0	0.00
Midfacial breadth	100.2	3.49
Interior biorbital breadth	93.2	2.56
Subtense to interior biorbital arc	13.2	0.75
Biorbital breadth	97.0	1.90
Anterior interorbital breadth	16.8	0.98
Nasal structure		
Nasal breadth	26.2	1.60
Nasal height	51.2	2.23
Dacryal chord	18.0	0.63
Dacryal subtense to arc	8.8	0.98
Minimum nasal breadth	7.5	1.22
Subtense to nasal arc	3.0	0.63
Orbit		
Left orbital height	32.8	0.75
Left orbital breadth, maxillofrontale	41.2	0.98
Left orbital breadth, dacryon	38.7	1.37
Dental arch and profile		
Maxillo-alveolar breadth	65.8	1.60
Maxillo-alveolar length	52.2	0.98
Facial length, prosthion	94.8	0.41
Facial length, alveolar point	93.5	1.22

APPENDIX C

Table 68 - continued

Mandible		
Length of mandible	104.2	0.75
Bicondylar breadth	124.0	0.63
Symphyseal height	32.8	1.94
Biangular breadth	97.7	2.16
Minimum ramus length	31.7	1.21
Angles		
Facial profile angle	81.0°	0.00
Midfacial profile angle	85.0°	0.00
Alveolar profile angle	69.0°	0.00
Gonial angle	101.3°	49.77

*N = 6
**Measurements in millimeters (mm.) unless listed otherwise

Table 69

Mean Indices of Proctorville Female Crania (Deformed)*

	Mean	Standard Dev.
Cranial vault		
Cranial	87.06	5.17
Length-height	79.70	1.69
Breadth-height	91.71	3.61
Mean height	85.23	1.02
Length-auricular height	70.11	2.53
Flatness of cranial base	------	----
Transverse fronto-parietal	62.27	1.79
Face		
Total facial	87.22	0.00
Upper facial	51.88	0.95
Midfacial	68.94	2.35
Transverse cranio-facial	93.94	2.61
Zygo-frontal	66.29	1.11
Fronto-mandibular	110.81	3.56
Zygo-mandibular	73.43	1.62
Facial flatness	14.13	0.71
Anterior interorbital	17.35	0.70
Nasal structure		
Nasal	51.15	2.38
Nasal root height	48.97	3.96
Nasal bone height	40.00	5.00
Orbit		
Left orbital, maxillofrontale	79.76	1.01
Left orbital, dacryon	85.00	3.53
Dental arch		
Maxillo-alveolar	126.24	4.26
Mandible		
Mandibular	84.01	0.99

*N = 6

APPENDIX C

Table 70

Mean Measurements of Gp 1 Male Crania (Undeformed)*

	Mean**	Standard Dev.
Cranial vault		
Capacity	1485.0cc.	63.63
Cranial module	156.2	6.59
Mean thickness of left parietal	5.5	2.12
Glabello-occipital length	183.0	11.31
Maximum breadth	145.5	4.94
Minimum frontal breadth	96.0	4.24
Basion-bregma height	140.5	3.53
Porion-apex height	120.0	0.00
Basion-porion height	-----	------
Length of cranial base	104.5	0.70
Face		
Total facial height	126.0	0.00
Upper facial height	76.0	1.41
Total facial breadth	141.0	1.41
Midfacial breadth	103.0	0.00
Interior biorbital breadth	100.0	0.00
Subtense to interior biorbital arc	16.0	2.82
Biorbital breadth	101.0	1.41
Anterior interorbital breadth	18.5	3.53
Nasal structure		
Nasal breadth	25.5	4.94
Nasal height	54.0	1.41
Dacryal chord	20.5	2.12
Dacryal subtense to arc	11.0	0.00
Minimum nasal breadth	9.0	1.41
Subtense to nasal arc	3.5	0.70

* N = 2

** means in millimeters (mm.) unless listed otherwise

Table 70 - continued

Orbit		
Left orbital height	34.0	1.41
Left orbital breadth, maxillofrontale	44.0	1.41
Left orbital breadth, dacryon	40.5	0.70
Dental arch and profile		
Maxillo-alveolar breadth	68.0	1.41
Maxillo-alveolar length	55.5	0.70
Facial length, prosthion	101.5	2.12
Facial length, alveolar point	100.0	2.82
Mandible		
Length of mandible	104.5	2.12
Bicondylar breadth	127.5	2.12
Symphysial height	38.0	0.00
Biangular breadth	103.0	1.41
Minimum ramus length	32.5	6.36
Angles		
Facial profile angle	$84.0°$	0.00
Midfacial profile angle	$88.0°$	0.00
Alveolar profile angle	$72.0°$	1.41
Gonial angle	$119.0°$	5.65

APPENDIX C

Table 71

Mean Indices of Gp 1 Male Crania (Undeformed)*

Cranial vault	Mean	Standard Dev.
Cranial	79.57	2.21
Length-height	76.86	2.82
Breadth-height	96.57	0.85
Mean height	85.59	2.08
Length-auricular height	65.70	4.05
Flatness of cranial base	------	------
Transverse fronto-parietal	66.07	5.16
Face		
Total facial	89.36	0.89
Upper facial	53.91	1.54
Midfacial	73.79	1.37
Transverse cranio-facial	96.94	2.32
Zygo-frontal	68.10	3.69
Fronto-mandibular	107.43	6.22
Zygo-mandibular	73.05	0.26
Facial flatness	16.00	2.82
Anterior interorbital	18.34	3.75
Nasal structure		
Nasal	47.12	7.93
Nasal root height	53.94	5.57
Nasal bone height	38.75	1.76
Orbit		
Left orbital, maxillofrontale	77.36	5.70
Left orbital, dacryon	83.99	4.95
Dental arch		
Maxillo-alveolar	122.54	4.10
Mandible		
Mandibular	81.96	0.29

* N = 2

Table 72

Mean Measurements of Gp 1 Male Crania (Deformed)*

Cranial vault	Mean**	Standard Dev.
Capacity	1450.0cc.	0.00
Cranial module	154.6	0.00
Mean thickness of left parietal	5.0	0.00
Glabello-occipital length	165.0	0.00
Maximum breadth	157.0	0.00
Minimum frontal breadth	102.0	0.00
Basion-bregma height	142.0	0.00
Porion-apex height	119.0	0.00
Basion-porion height	-----	------
Length of cranial base	104.0	0.00
Face		
Total facial height	125.0	0.00
Upper facial height	76.0	0.00
Total facial breadth	151.0	0.00
Midfacial breadth	104.0	0.00
Interior biorbital breadth	106.0	0.00
Subtense to interior biorbital arc	19.0	0.00
Biorbital breadth	108.0	0.00
Anterior interorbital breadth	24.0	0.00
Nasal structure		
Nasal breadth	28.0	0.00
Nasal height	54.0	0.00
Dacryal chord	26.0	0.00
Dacryal subtense to arc	12.0	0.00
Minimum nasal breadth	13.0	0.00
Subtense to nasal arc	4.0	0.00

* N = 1

** means in millimeters (mm.) unless listed otherwise

APPENDIX C

Table 72 - continued

Orbit		
Left orbital height	35.0	0.00
Left orbital breadth, maxillofrontale	46.0	0.00
Left orbital breadth, dacryon	43.0	0.00
Dental arch and profile		
Maxillo-alveolar breadth	73.0	0.00
Maxillo-alveolar length	60.0	0.00
Facial length, prosthion	103.0	0.00
Facial length, alveolar point	103.0	0.00
Mandible		
Length of mandible	108.0	0.00
Bicondylar breadth	137.0	0.00
Symphysial height	38.0	0.00
Biangular breadth	114.0	0.00
Minimum ramus length	37.0	0.00
Angles		
Facial profile angle	$82.0°$	0.00
Midfacial profile angle	$86.0°$	0.00
Alveolar profile angle	$71.0°$	0.00
Gonial angle	$123.0°$	0.00

Table 73

Mean Indices of Gp 1 Male Crania (Deformed)*

	Mean	Standard Dev.
Cranial vault		
Cranial	81.14	0.00
Length-height	78.86	0.00
Breadth-height	97.18	0.00
Mean height	87.07	0.00
Length-auricular height	68.57	0.00
Flatness of cranial base	------	------
Transverse fronto-parietal	69.72	0.00
Face		
Total facial	90.00	0.00
Upper facial	55.00	0.00
Midfacial	74.76	0.00
Transverse cranio-facial	98.59	0.00
Zygo-frontal	70.71	0.00
Fronto-mandibular	103.03	0.00
Zygo-mandibular	72.86	0.00
Facial flatness	18.00	0.00
Anterior interorbital	21.00	0.00
Nasal structure		
Nasal	52.73	0.00
Nasal root height	50.00	0.00
Nasal bone height	37.50	0.00
Orbit		
Left orbital, maxillofrontale	81.40	0.00
Left orbital, dacryon	87.50	0.00
Dental arch		
Maxillo-alveolar	119.64	0.00
Mandible		
Mandibular	81.75	0.00

* N = 1

Table 74

Cranial Observations of the Feurt Focus (Males)

Muscularity	Sm	Med	Lge	V.Lge		
Feurt (U) N = 17	-----	52.9%	47.1%	-----		
Feurt (D) N = 15	-----	60.0%	40.0%	-----		
Ful. Field (U) N = 6	-----	50.0%	50.0%	-----		
Ful. Field (D) N = 2	-----	-----	100.0%	-----		
P'ville (U) N = 2	-----	50.0%	50.0%	-----		
P'ville (D) N = 1	-----	100.0%	-----	-----		
Gp 1 (U) N = 2	-----	50.0%	50.0%	-----		
Gp 1 (D) N = 1	-----	100.0%	-----	-----		

Deformation	None	Occ	Lambd	Fr-occ	Bil-fr-occ	Path.
Feurt (U) N = 17	100.0%	-----	-----	-----	-----	-----
Feurt (D) N = 15	-----	93.3%	-----	-----	-----	6.7%
Ful. Field (U) N = 6	100.0%	-----	-----	-----	-----	-----
Ful. Field (D) N = 2	-----	100.0%	-----	-----	-----	-----
P'ville (U) N = 2	100.0%	-----	-----	-----	-----	-----
P'ville (D) N = 1	-----	100.0%	-----	-----	-----	-----
Gp 1 (U) N = 2	100.0%	-----	-----	-----	-----	-----
Gp 1 (D) N = 1	-----	100.0%	-----	-----	-----	-----

Degree of deform.	None	Trace	Sm	Med	Pron	
Feurt (U) N = 17	94.1%	-----	5.9%	-----	-----	
Feurt (D) N = 15	-----	13.3%	13.3%	46.7%	26.7%	
Ful. Field (U) N = 6	100.0%	-----	-----	-----	-----	
Ful. Field (D) N = 2	-----	-----	100.0%	-----	-----	
P'ville (U) N = 2	100.0%	-----	-----	-----	-----	
P'ville (D) N = 1	-----	-----	-----	100.0%	-----	
Gp 1 (U) N = 2	100.0%	-----	-----	-----	-----	
Gp 1 (D) N = 1	-----	-----	100.0%	-----	-----	

APPENDIX C

278 PREHISTORIC PEOPLE OF FORT ANCIENT

Table 74 - continued

Vault form	Ell	Ov	Spher	Pentag	Rhom	Sphen
Feurt (U) N = 17	17.6%	76.5%	----	----	----	5.9%
Feurt (D) N = 15	----	93.3%	----	6.7%	----	----
Ful. Field (U) N = 6	----	100.0%	----	----	----	----
Ful. Field (D) N = 2	----	100.0%	----	----	----	----
P'ville (U) N = 2	----	100.0%	----	----	----	----
P'ville (D) N = 1	----	100.0%	----	----	----	----
Gp 1 (U) N = 2	----	100.0%	----	----	----	----
Gp 1 (D) N = 1	----	100.0%	----	----	----	----

Brow ridge size	None	Trace	Sm	Med	Lge	V.Lge
Feurt (U) N = 17	----	5.9%	23.5%	47.1%	23.5%	----
Feurt (D) N = 15	----	----	33.3%	40.0%	26.7%	----
Ful. Field (U) N = 6	----	----	16.7%	83.3%	----	----
Ful. Field (D) N = 2	----	----	----	50.0%	50.0%	----
P'ville (U) N = 2	----	----	50.0%	50.0%	----	----
P'ville (D) N = 1	----	----	100.0%	----	----	----
Gp 1 (U) N = 2	----	----	50.0%	50.0%	----	----
Gp 1 (D) N = 1	----	----	100.0%	----	----	----

Glabella prom.	Flat	Sm	Med	Lge	V.Lge
Feurt (U) N = 17	----	64.7%	35.3%	----	----
Feurt (D) N = 15	----	40.0%	46.7%	13.3%	----
Ful. Field (U) N = 6	----	83.3%	16.7%	----	----
Ful. Field (D) N = 2	----	50.0%	----	50.0%	----
P'ville (U) N = 2	----	50.0%	50.0%	----	----
P'ville (D) N = 1	----	100.0%	----	----	----
Gp 1 (U) N = 2	----	100.0%	----	----	----
Gp 1 (D) N = 1	----	100.0%	----	----	----

APPENDIX C 279

Table 74 - continued

Frontal slope	Bulg	None	Sl	Med	Pron	V.Pron
Feurt (U) N = 17	-----	-----	23.5%	76.5%	-----	-----
Feurt (D) N = 15	-----	-----	20.0%	73.3%	6.7%	-----
Ful. Field (U) N = 6	-----	-----	-----	100.0%	-----	-----
Ful. Field (D) N = 2	-----	-----	50.0%	-----	50.0%	-----
P'ville (U) N = 2	-----	-----	-----	100.0%	-----	-----
P'ville (D) N = 1	-----	-----	100.0%	-----	-----	-----
Gp 1 (U) N = 2	-----	-----	100.0%	-----	-----	-----
Gp 1 (D) N = 1	-----	-----	100.0%	-----	-----	-----

Postorb. constr.	Sm	Med	Lge
Feurt (U) N = 17	47.1%	52.9%	-----
Feurt (D) N = 15	6.7%	60.0%	33.3%
Ful. Field (U) N = 6	-----	83.3%	16.7%
Ful. Field (D) N = 2	50.0%	50.0%	-----
P'ville (U) N = 2	50.0%	50.0%	-----
P'ville (D) N = 1	-----	100.0%	-----
Gp 1 (U) N = 2	-----	50.0%	50.0%
Gp 1 (D) N = 1	100.0%	-----	-----

Fron. emin.	Sm	Med	Lge
Feurt (U) N = 17	82.4%	17.6%	-----
Feurt (D) N = 15	93.3%	6.7%	-----
Ful. Field (U) N = 6	100.0%	-----	-----
Ful. Field (D) N = 2	50.0%	50.0%	-----
P'ville (U) N = 2	100.0%	-----	-----
P'ville (D) N = 1	100.0%	-----	-----
Gp 1 (U) N = 2	100.0%	-----	-----
Gp 1 (D) N = 1	-----	100.0%	-----

Table 74 - continued

Fr. median crest	None	Sm	Med	Lge
Feurt (U) N = 17	94.1%	5.9%	----	----
Feurt (D) N = 15	73.3%	20.0%	----	6.7%
Ful. Field (U) N = 6	----	83.3%	16.7%	----
Ful. Field (D) N = 2	50.0%	50.0%	----	----
P'ville (U) N = 2	100.0%	----	----	----
P'ville (D) N = 1	----	100.0%	----	----
Gp 1 (U) N = 2	50.0%	----	----	50.0%
Gp 1 (D) N = 1	----	100.0%	----	----

Fron. br.		Sm	Med	Lge
Feurt (U) N = 17		70.6%	23.5%	5.9%
Feurt (D) N = 15		20.0%	20.0%	60.0%
Ful. Field (U) N = 6		100.0%	----	----
Ful. Field (D) N = 2		50.0%	----	50.0%
P'ville (U) N = 2		50.0%	50.0%	----
P'ville (D) N = 1		----	100.0%	----
Gp 1 (U) N = 2		50.0%	50.0%	----
Gp 1 (D) N = 1		----	100.0%	----

Sag. elev.	None	Sm	Med	Lge	V. Lge
Feurt (U) N = 17	47.1%	52.9%	----	----	----
Feurt (D) N = 15	33.3%	66.7%	----	----	----
Ful. Field (U) N = 6	16.7%	83.3%	----	----	----
Ful. Field (D) N = 2	----	100.0%	----	----	----
P'ville (U) N = 2	100.0%	----	----	----	----
P'ville (D) N = 1	100.0%	----	----	----	----
Gp 1 (U) N = 2	----	100.0%	----	----	----
Gp 1 (D) N = 1	----	100.0%	----	----	----

APPENDIX C 281

Table 74 - continued

Pariet. emin.	Sm	Med	Lge	
Feurt (U) N = 17	58.8%	41.2%	----	
Feurt (D) N = 15	----	46.7%	53.3%	
Ful. Field (U) N = 6	----	100.0%	----	
Ful. Field (D) N = 2	50.0%	----	50.0%	
P'ville (U) N = 2	50.0%	50.0%	----	
P'ville (D) N = 1	----	100.0%	----	
Gp 1 (U) N = 2	50.0%	50.0%	----	
Gp 1 (D) N = 1	----	----	100.0%	

Temp. fullness	Flat	Sm	Med	Lge
Feurt (U) N = 17	23.5%	52.9%	17.6%	5.9%
Feurt (D) N = 15	6.7%	26.7%	33.3%	33.3%
Ful. Field (U) N = 6	16.7%	83.3%	----	----
Ful. Field (D) N = 2	----	100.0%	----	----
P'ville (U) N = 2	----	50.0%	50.0%	----
P'ville (D) N = 1	----	----	100.0%	----
Gp 1 (U) N = 2	----	100.0%	----	----
Gp 1 (D) N = 1	----	----	----	100.0%

Mastoids	Sm	Med	Lge	V.Lge
Feurt (U) N = 17	11.8%	64.7%	23.5%	----
Feurt (D) N = 15	20.0%	60.0%	20.0%	----
Ful. Field (U) N = 6	----	66.7%	33.3%	----
Ful. Field (D) N = 2	----	100.0%	----	----
P'ville (U) N = 2	50.0%	50.0%	----	----
P'ville (D) N = 1	----	----	100.0%	----
Gp 1 (U) N = 2	50.0%	50.0%	----	----
Gp 1 (D) N = 1	100.0%	----	----	----

Table 74 - continued

Supramast. crest	Sm	Med	Lge
Feurt (U) N = 17	11.8%	23.5%	64.7%
Feurt (D) N = 15	20.0%	46.7%	33.3%
Ful. Field (U) N = 6	-----	100.0%	-----
Ful. Field (D) N = 2	-----	100.0%	-----
P'ville (U) N = 2	50.0%	-----	50.0%
P'ville (D) N = 1	100.0%	-----	-----
Gp 1 (U) N = 2	-----	50.0%	50.0%
Gp 1 (D) N = 1	-----	100.0%	-----

Sphen. depress.	Sm	Med	Lge
Feurt (U) N = 17	76.5%	23.5%	-----
Feurt (D) N = 15	86.7%	6.7%	6.7%
Ful. Field (U) N = 6	100.0%	-----	-----
Ful. Field (D) N = 2	100.0%	-----	-----
P'ville (U) N = 2	100.0%	-----	-----
P'ville (D) N = 1	100.0%	-----	-----
Gp 1 (U) N = 2	100.0%	-----	-----
Gp 1 (D) N = 1	-----	100.0%	-----

Occip. curve	None	Sm	Med	Pron
Feurt (U) N = 17	-----	17.6%	29.4%	52.9%
Feurt (D) N = 15	40.0%	46.7%	13.3%	-----
Ful. Field (U) N = 6	-----	33.3%	-----	66.7%
Ful. Field (D) N = 2	-----	100.0%	-----	-----
P'ville (U) N = 2	-----	100.0%	-----	-----
P'ville (D) N = 1	-----	100.0%	-----	-----
Gp 1 (U) N = 2	-----	-----	50.0%	50.0%
Gp 1 (D) N = 1	-----	100.0%	-----	-----

Table 74 - continued

Lambd. flat.	None	Sm	Med	Pron
Feurt (U) N = 17	17.6%	41.2%	29.4%	11.8%
Feurt (D) N = 15	26.7%	73.3%	-----	-----
Ful. Field (U) N = 6	33.3%	33.3%	-----	33.3%
Ful. Field (D) N = 2	50.0%	50.0%	-----	-----
P'ville (U) N = 2	100.0%	-----	-----	-----
P'ville (D) N = 1	100.0%	-----	-----	-----
Gp 1 (U) N = 2	-----	50.0%	-----	50.0%
Gp 1 (D) N = 1	-----	100.0%	-----	-----

Cond. elev.	Sm	Med	Lge
Feurt (U) N = 17	11.8%	58.8%	29.4%
Feurt (D) N = 15	13.3%	60.0%	26.7%
Ful. Field (U) N = 6	-----	-----	100.0%
Ful. Field (D) N = 2	-----	50.0%	50.0%
P'ville (U) N = 2	-----	50.0%	50.0%
P'ville (D) N = 1	-----	100.0%	-----
Gp 1 (U) N = 2	50.0%	50.0%	-----
Gp 1 (D) N = 1	-----	-----	100.0%

Basion	Low	Med	High
Feurt (U) N = 17	11.8%	70.6%	17.6%
Feurt (D) N = 15	6.7%	80.0%	13.3%
Ful. Field (U) N = 6	-----	100.0%	-----
Ful. Field (D) N = 2	-----	100.0%	-----
P'ville (U) N = 2	-----	100.0%	-----
P'ville (D) N = 1	-----	100.0%	-----
Gp 1 (U) N = 2	-----	100.0%	-----
Gp 1 (D) N = 1	-----	100.0%	-----

Table 74 - continued

Styl. proc.	Sm	Med	Lge
Feurt (U) N = 17	47.1%	29.4%	23.5%
Feurt (D) N = 15	26.7%	33.3%	40.0%
Ful. Field (U) N = 6	16.7%	83.3%	-----
Ful. Field (D) N = 2	50.0%	50.0%	-----
P'ville (U) N = 2	50.0%	50.0%	-----
P'ville (D) N = 1	-----	100.0%	-----
Gp 1 (U) N = 2	50.0%	-----	50.0%
Gp 1 (D) N = 1	100.0%	-----	-----

Glen. fos. depth	Sm	Med	Lge
Feurt (U) N = 17	11.8%	52.9%	35.3%
Feurt (D) N = 15	6.7%	73.3%	20.0%
Ful. Field (U) N = 6	-----	83.3%	16.7%
Ful. Field (D) N = 2	-----	100.0%	-----
P'ville (U) N = 2	-----	100.0%	-----
P'ville (D) N = 1	-----	-----	100.0%
Gp 1 (U) N = 2	-----	50.0%	50.0%
Gp 1 (D) N = 1	-----	100.0%	-----

Tymp. plate	Thin	Med	Thick	V.Thick
Feurt (U) N = 17	94.1%	5.9%	-----	-----
Feurt (D) N = 15	73.3%	26.7%	-----	-----
Ful. Field (U) N = 6	100.0%	-----	-----	-----
Ful. Field (D) N = 2	100.0%	-----	-----	-----
P'ville (U) N = 2	100.0%	-----	-----	-----
P'ville (D) N = 1	100.0%	-----	-----	-----
Gp 1 (U) N = 2	50.0%	-----	50.0%	-----
Gp 1 (D) N = 1	100.0%	-----	-----	-----

Table 74 - continued

Orbit shape	Obl	Rhom	Sq	Ell	Rou
Feurt (U) N = 17	70.6%	17.6%	11.8%	-----	-----
Feurt (D) N = 15	20.0%	73.3%	6.7%	-----	-----
Ful. Field (U) N = 6	-----	-----	100.0%	-----	-----
Ful. Field (D) N = 2	-----	-----	100.0%	-----	-----
P'ville (U) N = 2	-----	100.0%	-----	-----	-----
P'ville (D) N = 1	-----	100.0%	-----	-----	-----
Gp 1 (U) N = 2	50.0%	-----	-----	50.0%	-----
Gp 1 (D) N = 1	-----	-----	-----	100.0%	-----

Orbit incl.	None	Sm	Med	Pron	
Feurt (U) N = 17	-----	64.7%	23.5%	11.8%	
Feurt (D) N = 15	-----	-----	80.0%	20.0%	
Ful. Field (U) N = 6	-----	100.0%	-----	-----	
Ful. Field (D) N = 2	-----	50.0%	50.0%	-----	
P'ville (U) N = 2	-----	-----	-----	100.0%	
P'ville (D) N = 1	-----	-----	-----	100.0%	
Gp 1 (U) N = 2	-----	100.0%	-----	-----	
Gp 1 (D) N = 1	-----	-----	100.0%	-----	

Suborb. fossa	Abs	Sl	Med	Deep	
Feurt (U) N = 17	-----	88.2%	11.8%	-----	
Feurt (D) N = 15	-----	66.7%	26.7%	6.7%	
Ful. Field (U) N = 6	-----	33.3%	66.7%	-----	
Ful. Field (D) N = 2	-----	100.0%	-----	-----	
P'ville (U) N = 2	-----	100.0%	-----	-----	
P'ville (D) N = 1	-----	100.0%	-----	-----	
Gp 1 (U) N = 2	50.0%	50.0%	-----	-----	
Gp 1 (D) N = 1	-----	100.0%	-----	-----	

Table 74 - continued

	Sm	Med	Lge	V.Lge
Zyg. size				
Feurt (U) N = 17	11.8%	58.8%	23.5%	5.9%
Feurt (D) N = 15	-----	80.0%	20.0%	-----
Ful. Field (U) N = 6	16.7%	83.3%	-----	-----
Ful. Field (D) N = 2	-----	50.0%	50.0%	-----
P'ville (U) N = 2	-----	50.0%	50.0%	-----
P'ville (D) N = 1	-----	100.0%	-----	-----
Gp 1 (U) N = 2	50.0%	-----	50.0%	-----
Gp 1 (D) N = 1	-----	100.0%	-----	-----

	Sm	Med	Lge
Zyg. lat. proj.			
Feurt (U) N = 17	-----	5.9%	94.1%
Feurt (D) N = 15	-----	13.3%	86.7%
Ful. Field (U) N = 6	-----	-----	100.0%
Ful. Field (D) N = 2	-----	-----	100.0%
P'ville (U) N = 2	-----	-----	100.0%
P'ville (D) N = 1	-----	-----	100.0%
Gp 1 (U) N = 2	-----	50.0%	50.0%
Gp 1 (D) N = 1	-----	-----	100.0%

	Sm	Med	Lge
Zyg. ant. proj.			
Feurt (U) N = 17	5.9%	82.4%	11.8%
Feurt (D) N = 15	13.3%	60.0%	26.7%
Ful. Field (U) N = 6	-----	100.0%	-----
Ful. Field (D) N = 2	-----	100.0%	-----
P'ville (U) N = 2	-----	100.0%	-----
P'ville (D) N = 1	-----	100.0%	-----
Gp 1 (U) N = 2	50.0%	50.0%	-----
Gp 1 (D) N = 1	-----	100.0%	-----

APPENDIX C   287

Table 74 - continued

Zyg. proc. thick.	Sm	Med	Pron	High	V.High
Feurt (U) N = 17	23.5%	70.6%	5.9%		
Feurt (D) N = 15	20.0%	66.7%	13.3%		
Ful. Field (U) N = 6	16.7%	83.3%	-----		
Ful. Field (D) N = 2	-----	50.0%	50.0%		
P'ville (U) N = 2	-----	100.0%	-----		
P'ville (D) N = 1	-----	100.0%	-----		
Gp 1 (U) N = 2	-----	100.0%	-----		
Gp 1 (D) N = 1	-----	100.0%	-----		

Nas. rt. ht.	V.Low	Low	Med	High	V.High
Feurt (U) N = 17	-----	-----	23.5%	76.5%	-----
Feurt (D) N = 15	-----	-----	26.7%	73.3%	-----
Ful. Field (U) N = 6	-----	-----	83.3%	16.7%	-----
Ful. Field (D) N = 2	-----	-----	50.0%	50.0%	-----
P'ville (U) N = 2	-----	-----	50.0%	50.0%	-----
P'ville (D) N = 1	-----	-----	100.0%	-----	-----
Gp 1 (U) N = 2	-----	-----	100.0%	-----	-----
Gp 1 (D) N = 1	-----	-----	-----	100.0%	-----

Nas. rt. br.	V.Sm	Sm	Med	Lge	V.Lge
Feurt (U) N = 17	-----	5.9%	82.4%	11.8%	-----
Feurt (D) N = 15	-----	6.7%	80.0%	13.3%	-----
Ful. Field (U) N = 6	-----	83.3%	-----	16.7%	-----
Ful. Field (D) N = 2	-----	50.0%	50.0%	-----	-----
P'ville (U) N = 2	-----	-----	100.0%	-----	-----
P'ville (D) N = 1	-----	-----	100.0%	-----	-----
Gp 1 (U) N = 2	-----	50.0%	50.0%	-----	-----
Gp 1 (D) N = 1	-----	-----	-----	100.0%	-----

Table 74 - continued

Nas. bridg. ht.	V. Low	Low	Med	High	V. High
Feurt (U) N = 17	5.9%	----	88.2%	5.9%	----
Feurt (D) N = 15	----	----	80.0%	13.3%	6.7%
Ful. Field (U) N = 6	----	----	100.0%	----	----
Ful. Field (D) N = 2	----	----	100.0%	----	----
P'ville (U) N = 2	----	----	100.0%	----	----
P'ville (D) N = 1	----	----	100.0%	----	----
Gp 1 (U) N = 2	----	----	50.0%	50.0%	----
Gp 1 (D) N = 1	----	----	100.0%	----	----

Nas. bridg. br.	Sm	Med	Lge
Feurt (U) N = 17	----	94.1%	5.9%
Feurt (D) N = 15	13.3%	86.7%	----
Ful. Field (U) N = 6	----	100.0%	----
Ful. Field (D) N = 2	----	100.0%	----
P'ville (U) N = 2	----	50.0%	50.0%
P'ville (D) N = 1	----	100.0%	----
Gp 1 (U) N = 2	50.0%	50.0%	----
Gp 1 (D) N = 1	----	----	100.0%

Nas. profile	Conc	Str	Sl. Conc-Conv	Conc-Conv	V.C-C
Feurt (U) N = 17	----	5.9%	82.4%	5.9%	5.9%
Feurt (D) N = 15	----	13.3%	73.3%	13.3%	----
Ful. Field (U) N = 6	100.0%	----	----	----	----
Ful. Field (D) N = 2	50.0%	50.0%	----	50.0%	----
P'ville (U) N = 2	----	----	----	50.0%	----
P'ville (D) N = 1	----	----	----	100.0%	----
Gp 1 (U) N = 2	----	----	----	----	100.0%
Gp 1 (D) N = 1	----	----	----	----	100.0%

APPENDIX C 289

Table 74 - continued

Nas. depress.	Abs	Sm	Med	Lge
Feurt (U) N = 17	5.9%	35.3%	58.8%	-----
Feurt (D) N = 15	6.7%	66.7%	26.7%	-----
Ful. Field (U) N = 6	16.7%	-----	83.3%	-----
Ful. Field (D) N = 2	-----	-----	100.0%	-----
P'ville (U) N = 2	-----	50.0%	50.0%	-----
P'ville (D) N = 1	-----	100.0%	-----	-----
Gp 1 (U) N = 2	-----	100.0%	-----	-----
Gp 1 (D) N = 1	-----	100.0%	-----	-----

Nas. sills	Abs	Dull	Med	Sharp
Feurt (U) N = 17	-----	17.6%	17.6%	64.7%
Feurt (D) N = 15	-----	6.7%	13.3%	80.0%
Ful. Field (U) N = 6	-----	-----	-----	100.0%
Ful. Field (D) N = 2	-----	-----	50.0%	50.0%
P'ville (U) N = 2	-----	50.0%	50.0%	-----
P'ville (D) N = 1	-----	-----	100.0%	-----
Gp 1 (U) N = 2	50.0%	-----	-----	50.0%
Gp 1 (D) N = 1	100.0%	-----	-----	-----

Nas. spine	Abs	Sm	Med	Rt. Ang	Lge
Feurt (U) N = 17	-----	94.1%	5.9%	-----	-----
Feurt (D) N = 15	-----	80.0%	20.0%	-----	-----
Ful. Field (U) N = 6	-----	100.0%	-----	-----	-----
Ful. Field (D) N = 2	-----	100.0%	-----	-----	-----
P'ville (U) N = 2	-----	100.0%	-----	-----	-----
P'ville (D) N = 1	-----	100.0%	-----	-----	-----
Gp 1 (U) N = 2	-----	50.0%	50.0%	-----	-----
Gp 1 (D) N = 1	-----	100.0%	-----	-----	-----

Table 74 - continued

Subnas. grooves	Abs	Sm	Med	Pron	Sulci
Feurt (U) N = 17	88.2%	5.9%	-----	5.9%	-----
Feurt (D) N = 15	86.7%	-----	13.3%	-----	-----
Ful. Field (U) N = 6	100.0%	-----	-----	-----	-----
Ful. Field (D) N = 2	50.0%	50.0%	-----	50.0%	-----
P'ville (U) N = 2	-----	50.0%	-----	-----	-----
P'ville (D) N = 1	-----	100.0%	-----	-----	-----
Gp 1 (U) N = 2	-----	-----	100.0%	-----	-----
Gp 1 (D) N = 1	-----	-----	100.0%	-----	-----

Midfac. progn.	Abs	Sl	Med	Pron	
Feurt (U) N = 17	70.6%	29.4%	-----	-----	
Feurt (D) N = 15	73.3%	13.3%	13.3%	-----	
Ful. Field (U) N = 6	100.0%	-----	-----	-----	
Ful. Field (D) N = 2	100.0%	-----	-----	-----	
P'ville (U) N = 2	50.0%	50.0%	-----	-----	
P'ville (D) N = 1	100.0%	-----	-----	-----	
Gp 1 (U) N = 2	100.0%	-----	-----	-----	
Gp 1 (D) N = 1	-----	100.0%	-----	-----	

Alveol. progn.	Abs	Sl	Med	Pron	
Feurt (U) N = 17	11.8%	17.6%	70.6%	-----	
Feurt (D) N = 15	-----	26.7%	60.0%	13.3%	
Ful. Field (U) N = 6	-----	33.3%	66.7%	-----	
Ful. Field (D) N = 2	-----	100.0%	-----	-----	
P'ville (U) N = 2	-----	-----	100.0%	-----	
P'ville (D) N = 1	-----	-----	100.0%	-----	
Gp 1 (U) N = 2	-----	50.0%	50.0%	-----	
Gp 1 (D) N = 1	-----	-----	100.0%	-----	

APPENDIX C   291

Table 74 - continued

Total progn.	Abs	Sl	Med	Pron	
Feurt (U) N = 17	11.8%	70.6%	17.6%	-----	
Feurt (D) N = 15	13.3%	13.3%	60.0%	13.3%	
Ful. Field (U) N = 6	-----	66.7%	33.3%	-----	
Ful. Field (D) N = 2	-----	50.0%	50.0%	-----	
P'ville (U) N = 2	-----	-----	100.0%	-----	
P'ville (D) N = 1	-----	-----	100.0%	-----	
Gp 1 (U) N = 2	-----	100.0%	-----	-----	
Gp 1 (D) N = 1	-----	-----	100.0%	-----	

Palate shape	Parab	Hyperb	Ell	Sm U	Lge U
Feurt (U) N = 17	94.1%	5.9%	-----	-----	-----
Feurt (D) N = 15	80.0%	20.0%	-----	-----	-----
Ful. Field (U) N = 6	100.0%	-----	-----	-----	-----
Ful. Field (D) N = 2	100.0%	-----	-----	-----	-----
P'ville (U) N = 2	100.0%	-----	-----	-----	-----
P'ville (D) N = 1	100.0%	-----	-----	-----	-----
Gp 1 (U) N = 2	100.0%	-----	-----	-----	-----
Gp 1 (D) N = 1	100.0%	-----	-----	-----	-----

Palate ht.	Low	Med	High	V. High	
Feurt (U) N = 17	-----	23.5%	70.6%	5.9%	
Feurt (D) N = 15	-----	33.3%	60.0%	6.7%	
Ful. Field (U) N = 6	-----	83.3%	16.7%	-----	
Ful. Field (D) N = 2	-----	100.0%	-----	-----	
P'ville (U) N = 2	-----	50.0%	50.0%	-----	
P'ville (D) N = 1	-----	100.0%	-----	-----	
Gp 1 (U) N = 2	-----	100.0%	-----	-----	
Gp 1 (D) N = 1	-----	-----	100.0%	-----	

Table 74 - continued

Palat. torus	Abs	SmRidg	MedRidg	LgeRidg	SmMd	MedMd	LMd
Feurt (U) N = 17	100.0%	----	----	----	----	----	----
Feurt (D) N = 15	100.0%	----	----	----	----	----	----
Ful. Field (U) N = 6	100.0%	----	----	----	----	----	----
Ful. Field (D) N = 2	100.0%	----	----	----	----	----	----
P'ville (U) N = 2	100.0%	----	----	----	----	----	----
P'ville (D) N = 1	100.0%	----	----	----	----	----	----
Gp 1 (U) N = 2	50.0%	----	----	----	----	50.0%	----
Gp 1 (D) N = 1	100.0%	----	----	----	----	----	----

Mand. size	Sm	Med	Lge	V. Lge
Feurt (U) N = 17	5.9%	35.3%	58.8%	----
Feurt (D) N = 15	6.7%	73.3%	20.0%	----
Ful. Field (U) N = 6	----	----	83.3%	16.7%
Ful. Field (D) N = 1	----	----	100.0%	----
P'ville (U) N = 2	----	100.0%	----	----
P'ville (D) N = 1	----	100.0%	----	----
Gp 1 (U) N = 2	----	100.0%	----	----
Gp 1 (D) N = 1	----	100.0%	----	----

Chin form	Nar Bilat	Wide Bilat	Inter-med	Median
Feurt (U) N = 17	5.9%	----	82.4%	11.8%
Feurt (D) N = 15	20.0%	----	73.3%	6.7%
Ful. Field (U) N = 6	16.7%	----	83.3%	----
Ful. Field (D) N = 2	50.0%	----	50.0%	----
P'ville (U) N = 2	----	----	100.0%	----
P'ville (D) N = 1	----	----	----	----
Gp 1 (U) N = 2	50.0%	----	----	100.0%
Gp 1 (D) N = 1	100.0%	----	----	50.0%

APPENDIX C 293

Table 74 - continued

Chin proj.		Negat	Neut	Sm	Med	Lge
Feurt (U)	N = 17	17.6%	76.5%	-----	5.9%	-----
Feurt (D)	N = 15	66.7%	33.3%	-----	-----	-----
Ful. Field (U)	N = 6	33.3%	66.7%	-----	-----	-----
Ful. Field (D)	N = 2	50.0%	50.0%	-----	-----	-----
P'ville (U)	N = 2	-----	100.0%	-----	-----	-----
P'ville (D)	N = 1	100.0%	-----	-----	-----	-----
Gp 1 (U)	N = 2	50.0%	50.0%	-----	-----	-----
Gp 1 (D)	N = 1	100.0%	-----	-----	-----	-----

Pteryg. attach.		Sm	Med	Pron	V.Pron	
Feurt (U)	N = 17	11.8%	82.4%	5.9%	-----	
Feurt (D)	N = 15	6.7%	26.7%	66.7%	-----	
Ful. Field (U)	N = 6	-----	83.3%	16.7%	-----	
Ful. Field (D)	N = 2	-----	50.0%	50.0%	-----	
P'ville (U)	N = 2	-----	100.0%	-----	-----	
P'ville (D)	N = 1	100.0%	-----	-----	-----	
Gp 1 (U)	N = 2	-----	100.0%	-----	-----	
Gp 1 (D)	N = 1	100.0%	-----	-----	-----	

Gonial ang. evers.		None	Sm	Med	Pron	
Feurt (U)	N = 17	17.6%	82.4%	-----	-----	
Feurt (D)	N = 15	26.7%	66.7%	6.7%	-----	
Ful. Field (U)	N = 6	33.3%	66.7%	-----	-----	
Ful. Field (D)	N = 2	-----	-----	100.0%	-----	
P'ville (U)	N = 2	50.0%	50.0%	-----	-----	
P'ville (D)	N = 1	-----	100.0%	-----	-----	
Gp 1 (U)	N = 2	-----	100.0%	-----	-----	
Gp 1 (D)	N = 1	-----	100.0%	-----	-----	

Table 75

Cranial Observations of the Feurt Focus (Females)

Muscularity	Sm	Med	Lge	V.Lge		
Feurt (U) N = 6	100.0%	-----	-----	-----		
Feurt (D) N = 9	88.9%	11.1%	-----	-----		
Ful. Field (U) N = 3	100.0%	-----	-----	-----		
Ful. Field (D) N = 1	100.0%	-----	-----	-----		
P'ville (D) N = 6	100.0%	-----	-----	-----		

Deformation	None	Occ	Lambd	Fr-occ	Bil-fr-occ	Earth Press
Feurt (U) N = 6	100.0%	-----	-----	-----	-----	-----
Feurt (D) N = 9	-----	88.9%	-----	-----	-----	11.1%
Ful. Field (U) N = 3	33.3%	-----	-----	-----	-----	66.7%
Ful. Field (D) N = 1	-----	100.0%	-----	-----	-----	-----
P'ville (D) N = 6	-----	66.7%	-----	-----	-----	33.3%

Degree of deform.	None	Trace	Sm	Med	Pron	
Feurt (U) N = 6	100.0%	-----	-----	-----	-----	
Feurt (D) N = 9	-----	-----	22.2%	55.6%	22.2%	
Ful. Field (U) N = 3	100.0%	-----	-----	-----	-----	
Ful. Field (D) N = 1	-----	-----	-----	100.0%	-----	
P'ville (D) N = 6	-----	-----	16.7%	66.7%	16.7%	

Vault form	Ell	O.	Spher	Pentag	Rhom	Sphen
Feurt (U) N = 6	-----	83.3%	-----	-----	-----	16.7%
Feurt (D) N = 9	-----	88.9%	11.1%	-----	-----	-----
Ful. Field (U) N = 3	-----	100.0%	-----	-----	-----	-----
Ful. Field (D) N = 1	-----	100.0%	-----	-----	-----	-----
P'ville (D) N = 6	-----	83.3%	-----	16.7%	-----	-----

Table 75 - continued

Browridge size

	None	Trace	Sm	Med	Lge	V Lge
Feurt (U) N = 6	-----	100.0%	-----	-----	-----	-----
Feurt (D) N = 9	-----	88.9%	11.1%	-----	-----	-----
Ful. Field (U) N = 3	-----	100.0%	-----	-----	-----	-----
Ful. Field (D) N = 1	-----	100.0%	-----	-----	-----	-----
P'ville (D) N = 6	-----	66.7%	33.3%	-----	-----	-----

Glabella prom.

	Flat	Sm	Med	Lge	V.Lge	
Feurt (U) N = 6	-----	100.0%	-----	-----	-----	
Feurt (D) N = 9	-----	100.0%	-----	-----	-----	
Ful. Field (U) N = 3	-----	100.0%	-----	-----	-----	
Ful. Field (D) N - 1	-----	100.0%	-----	-----	-----	
P'ville (D) N = 6	-----	100.0%	-----	-----	-----	

Frontal slope

	Bulg	None	Sl	Med	Pron	V.Pron
Feurt (U) N = 6	50.0%	-----	33.3%	16.7%	-----	-----
Feurt (D) N = 9	33.3%	-----	44.4%	22.2%	-----	-----
Ful. Field (U) N = 3	33.3%	-----	66.7%	-----	-----	-----
Ful. Field (D) N = 1	-----	-----	-----	100.0%	-----	-----
P'ville (D) N = 6	-----	-----	66.7%	33.3%	-----	-----

Postorb. constr.

	Sm	Med	Lge			
Feurt (U) N = 6	83.3%	16.7%	-----			
Feurt (D) N = 9	11.1%	88.9%	-----			
Ful. Field (U) N = 3	-----	100.0%	-----			
Ful. Field (D) N = 1	-----	100.0%	-----			
P'ville (D) N = 6	50.0%	33.3%	16.7%			

Table 75 - continued

	None	Sm	Med	Lge	V.Lge
Fron. emin.					
Feurt (U) N = 6		33.3%	50.0%	16.7%	
Feurt (D) N = 9		22.2%	55.6%	22.2%	
Ful. Field (U) N = 3		66.7%	33.3%	-----	
Ful. Field (D) N = 1		100.0%	-----	-----	
P'ville (D) N = 6		100.0%	-----	-----	
Fr. median crest					
Feurt (U) N = 6	83.3%	16.7%	-----	-----	
Feurt (D) N = 9	77.8%	22.2%	-----	-----	
Ful. Field (U) N = 3	66.7%	33.3%	-----	-----	
Ful. Field (D) N = 1	100.0%	-----	-----	-----	
P'ville (D) N = 6	100.0%	-----	-----	-----	
Fron. br.					
Feurt (U) N = 6		83.3%	16.7%	-----	
Feurt (D) N = 9		11.1%	22.2%	66.7%	
Ful. Field (U) N = 3		66.7%	33.3%	-----	
Ful. Field (D) N = 1		-----	-----	100.0%	
P'ville (D) N = 6		16.7%	66.7%	16.7%	
Sag. elev.					
Feurt (U) N = 6	66.7%	33.3%	-----	-----	-----
Feurt (D) N = 9	88.9%	11.1%	-----	-----	-----
Ful. Field (U) N = 3	-----	100.0%	-----	-----	-----
Ful. Field (D) N = 1	100.0%	-----	-----	-----	-----
P'ville (D) N = 6	100.0%	-----	-----	-----	-----

APPENDIX C

Table 75 - continued

Pariet. emin.	Sm	Med	Lge	
Feurt (U) N = 6	16.7%	83.3%	-----	
Feurt (D) N = 9	-----	33.3%	66.7%	
Ful. Field (U) N = 3	66.7%	33.3%	-----	
Ful. Field (D) N = 1	-----	-----	100.0%	
P'ville (D) N = 6	-----	66.7%	33.3%	

Temp. fullness	Flat	Sm	Med	
Feurt (U) N = 6	16.7%	83.3%	-----	
Feurt (D) N = 9	11.1%	22.2%	22.2%	
Ful. Field (U) N = 3	-----	66.7%	33.3%	
Ful. Field (D) N = 1	-----	-----	-----	
P'ville (D) N = 6	-----	33.3%	50.0%	

Mastoids	Sm	Med	Lge	V.Lge
Feurt (U) N = 6	83.3%	16.7%	-----	-----
Feurt (D) N - 9	88.9%	11.1%	-----	-----
Ful. Field (U) N = 3	100.0%	-----	-----	-----
Ful. Field (D) N - 1	100.0%	-----	-----	-----
P'ville (D) N = 6	83.3%	16.7%	-----	-----

Supramast. crest	Sm	Med	Lge	
Feurt (U) N = 6	83.3%	16.7%	-----	
Feurt (D) N = 9	66.7%	33.3%	-----	
Ful. Field (U) N = 3	66.7%	33.3%	-----	
Ful. Field (D) N = 1	-----	100.0%	-----	
P'ville (D) N = 6	83.3%	-----	16.7%	

Table 75 - continued

	Sm	Med	Lge	Pron
Sphen. depress.				
Feurt (U) N = 6	66.7%	33.3%	----	----
Feurt (D) N = 9	66.7%	33.3%	----	----
Ful. Field (U) N = 3	100.0%	----	----	----
Ful. Field (D) N = 1	100.0%	----	----	----
P'ville (D) N = 6	66.7%	33.3%	----	----

	None	Sm	Med	Pron
Occip. curve				
Feurt (U) N = 6	----	16.7%	33.3%	50.0%
Feurt (D) N = 9	44.4%	55.6%	----	----
Ful. Field (U) N = 3	----	----	100.0%	----
Ful. Field (D) N = 1	100.0%	----	----	----
P'ville (D) N = 6	16.7%	83.3%	----	----

	None	Sm	Med	Pron
Lambd. flat.				
Feurt (U) N = 6	16.7%	66.7%	16.7%	----
Feurt (D) N = 9	77.8%	22.2%	----	----
Ful. Field (U) N = 3	----	33.3%	66.7%	----
Ful. Field (D) N = 1	----	----	100.0%	----
P'ville (D) N = 6	16.7%	83.3%	----	----

	Sm	Med	Lge	Pron
Cond. elev.				
Feurt (U) N = 6	----	100.0%	----	----
Feurt (D) N = 9	77.8%	----	22.2%	----
Ful. Field (U) N = 3	66.7%	33.3%	----	----
Ful. Field (D) N = 1	100.0%	----	----	----
P'ville (D) N = 6	16.7%	66.7%	16.7%	----

APPENDIX C

Table 75 - continued

Basion	Low	Med	High
Feurt (U) N = 6	-----	100.0%	-----
Feurt (D) N = 9	11.1%	88.9%	-----
Ful. Field (U) N = 3	-----	100.0%	-----
Ful. Field (D) N = 1	-----	-----	100.0%
P'ville (D) N = 6	-----	83.3%	16.7%

Styl. proc.	Sm	Med	Lge
Feurt (U) N = 6	83.3%	16.7%	-----
Feurt (D) N = 9	88.9%	11.1%	-----
Ful. Field (U) N = 3	100.0%	-----	-----
Ful. Field (D) N = 1	-----	100.0%	-----
P'ville (D) N = 6	83.3%	16.7%	-----

Glen. fos. depth	Sm	Med	Lge
Feurt (U) N = 6	16.7%	66.7%	16.7%
Feurt (D) N = 9	11.1%	88.9%	-----
Ful. Field (U) N = 3	-----	100.0%	-----
Ful. Field (D) N = 1	-----	100.0%	-----
P'ville (D) N = 6	16.7%	50.0%	33.3%

Tymp. plate	Thin	Med	Thick	V. Thick
Feurt (U) N = 6	100.0%	-----	-----	-----
Feurt (D) N = 9	88.9%	11.1%	-----	-----
Ful. Field (U) N = 3	66.7%	33.3%	-----	-----
Ful. Field (D) N = 1	100.0%	-----	-----	-----
P'ville (D) N = 6	100.0%	-----	-----	-----

Table 75 - continued

	Obl	Rhom	Sq	Ell	Rou
Orbit shape					
Feurt (U) N = 6	16.7%	66.7%	-----	-----	16.7%
Feurt (D) N = 9	11.1%	88.9%	-----	-----	-----
Ful. Field (U) N = 3	-----	66.7%	33.3%	-----	-----
Ful. Field (D) N = 1	-----	100.0%	-----	-----	-----
P'ville (D) N = 6	50.0%	-----	16.7%	16.7%	16.7%

	None	Sm	Med	Pron	
Orbit. incl.					
Feurt (U) N = 6	-----	66.7%	33.3%	-----	
Feurt (D) N = 9	-----	88.9%	-----	11.1%	
Ful. Field (U) N = 3	-----	66.7%	33.3%	-----	
Ful. Field (D) N = 1	-----	100.0%	-----	-----	
P'ville (D) N = 6	-----	100.0%	-----	-----	

	Ab	Sl	Med	Deep	
Suborb. fossa					
Feurt (U) N = 6	11.1%	100.0%	-----	-----	
Feurt (D) N = 9	11.1%	55.6%	22.2%	11.1%	
Ful. Field (U) N = 3	-----	-----	-----	100.0%	
Ful. Field (D) N = 1	-----	100.0%	-----	-----	
P'ville (D) N = 6	-----	100.0%	-----	-----	

	Sm	Med	Lge	V.Lge	
Zyg. size					
Feurt (U) N = 6	83.3%	16.7%	-----	-----	
Feurt (D) N = 9	88.9%	11.1%	-----	-----	
Ful. Field (U) N = 3	100.0%	-----	-----	-----	
Ful. Field (D) N = 1	100.0%	-----	-----	-----	
P'ville (D) N = 6	100.0%	-----	-----	-----	

APPENDIX C 301

Table 75 - continued

	Sm	Med	Lge
Zyg. lat. proj.			
Feurt (U) N = 6	16.7%	16.7%	66.7%
Feurt (D) N = 9	-----	11.1%	88.9%
Ful. Field (U) N = 3	-----	-----	100.0%
Ful. Field (D) N = 1	-----	100.0%	-----
P'ville (D) N = 6	-----	66.7%	33.3%
Zyg. ant. proj.	Sm	Med	Lge
Feurt (U) N = 6	83.3%	16.7%	-----
Feurt (D) N = 9	88.9%	11.1%	-----
Ful. Field (U) N = 3	33.3%	66.7%	-----
Ful. Field (D) N = 1	-----	100.0%	-----
P'ville (D) N = 6	16.7%	83.3%	-----
Zyg. proc. thick.	Sm	Med	Pron
Feurt (U) N = 6	100.0%	-----	-----
Feurt (D) N = 9	44.4%	55.6%	-----
Ful. Field (U) N = 3	100.0%	-----	-----
Ful. Field (D) N = 1	100.0%	-----	-----
P'ville (D) N = 6	100.0%	-----	-----

	V.Low	Low	Med	High	V.High
Nas. rt. ht.					
Feurt (U) N = 6	-----	16.7%	66.7%	16.7%	-----
Feurt (D) N = 9	-----	33.3%	55.6%	11.1%	-----
Ful. Field (U) N = 3	-----	-----	100.0%	-----	-----
Ful. Field (D) N = 1	-----	-----	100.0%	-----	-----
P'ville (D) N = 6	-----	16.7%	83.3%	-----	-----

Table 75 - continued

	V.Sm	Sm	Med	Lge	V.Lge
Nas. rt. br.					
Feurt (U) N = 6	-----	50.0%	50.0%	-----	-----
Feurt (D) N = 9	-----	11.1%	77.8%	11.1%	-----
Ful. Field (U) N = 3	-----	33.3%	66.7%	-----	-----
Ful. Field (D) N = 1	-----	-----	100.0%	-----	-----
P'ville (D) N = 6	16.7%	50.0%	33.3%	-----	-----

	V.Low	Low	Med	High	V.High
Nas. bridg. ht.					
Feurt (U) N = 6	-----	100.0%	-----	-----	-----
Feurt (D) N = 9	-----	-----	88.9%	11.1%	-----
Ful. Field (U) N = 3	-----	-----	100.0%	-----	-----
Ful. Field (D) N = 1	-----	-----	100.0%	-----	-----
P'ville (D) N = 6	-----	-----	100.0%	-----	-----

	Sm	Med	Lge		
Nas. bridg. br.					
Feurt (U) N = 6	-----	100.0%	-----		
Feurt (D) N = 9	-----	100.0%	-----		
Ful. Field (U) N = 3	-----	100.0%	-----		
Ful. Field (D) N = 1	-----	100.0%	-----		
P'ville (D) N = 6	-----	100.0%	-----		

	Conc	Str	Sl. Conc-Conv	Conc-Conv.	V.C-C
Nas. profile					
Feurt (U) N = 6	-----	16.7%	-----	83.3%	-----
Feurt (D) N = 9	-----	33.3%	11.1%	55.6%	-----
Ful. Field (U) N = 3	100.0%	-----	-----	-----	-----
Ful. Field (D) N = 1	100.0%	-----	-----	-----	-----
P'ville (D) N = 6	-----	-----	100.0%	-----	-----

Table 75 - continued

Nas. depress.	Abs	Sm	Med	Lge
Feurt (U) N = 6	16.7%	83.3%	-----	-----
Feurt (D) N = 9	66.7%	33.3%	-----	-----
Ful. Field (U) N = 3	-----	100.0%	-----	-----
Ful. Field (D) N = 1	-----	100.0%	-----	-----
P'ville (D) N = 6	16.7%	83.3%	-----	-----

Nas. sills	Abs	Dull	Med	Sharp
Feurt (U) N = 6	-----	-----	100.0%	-----
Feurt (D) N = 9	-----	11.1%	66.7%	22.2%
Ful. Field (U) N = 3	-----	-----	66.7%	33.3%
Ful. Field (D) N = 1	-----	-----	-----	100.0%
P'ville (D) N = 6	-----	16.7%	50.0%	33.3%

Nas. spine	Abs	Sm	Med	Rt. Ang	Lge
Feurt (U) N = 6	-----	100.0%	-----	-----	-----
Feurt (D) N = 9	-----	100.0%	-----	-----	-----
Ful. Field (U) N = 3	-----	100.0%	-----	-----	-----
Ful. Field (D) N = 1	-----	100.0%	-----	-----	-----
P'ville (D) N = 6	-----	100.0%	-----	-----	-----

Subnas. grooves	Abs	Sm	Med	Pron	Sulci
Fuert (U) N = 6	100.0%	-----	-----	-----	-----
Fuert (D) N = 9	100.0%	-----	-----	-----	-----
Ful. Field (U) N = 3	100.0%	-----	-----	-----	-----
Ful. Field (D) N = 1	100.0%	-----	-----	-----	-----
P'ville (D) N = 6	100.0%	-----	-----	-----	-----

Table 75 - continued

		Abs	Sl	Med	Pron
Midfac. progn.					
	Feurt (U) N = 6	100.0%	----	----	----
	Feurt (D) N = 9	100.0%	----	----	----
	Ful. Field (U) N = 3	100.0%	----	----	----
	Ful. Field (D) N = 1	100.0%	----	----	----
	P'ville (D) N = 6	16.7%	83.3%	----	----
Alveol. progn.					
	Feurt (U) N = 6	----	33.3%	66.7%	----
	Feurt (D) N = 9	----	----	100.0%	----
	Ful. Field (U) N = 3	----	66.7%	33.3%	----
	Ful. Field (D) N = 1	----	100.0%	----	----
	P'ville (D) N = 6	----	50.0%	50.0%	----
Total progn.					
	Feurt (U) N = 6	----	66.7%	33.3%	----
	Feurt (D) N = 9	----	11.1%	88.9%	----
	Ful. Field (U) N = 3	----	100.0%	----	----
	Ful. Field (D) N = 1	----	100.0%	----	----
	P'ville (D) N = 6	----	16.7%	83.3%	----

		Parab	Hyperb	Ell	Sm U	Lge U
Palate shape						
	Feurt (U) N = 6	100.0%	----	----	----	----
	Feurt (D) N = 9	88.9%	11.1%	----	----	----
	Ful. Field (U) N = 3	100.0%	----	----	----	----
	Ful. Field (D) N = 1	100.0%	----	----	----	----
	P'ville (D) N = 6	100.0%	----	----	----	----

Table 75 - continued

Palate ht.	Low	Med	High	V.High
Feurt (U) N = 6	-----	100.0%	-----	-----
Feurt (D) N = 9	11.1%	55.6%	11.1%	22.2%
Ful. Field (U) N = 3	33.3%	66.7%	-----	-----
Ful. Field (D) N = 1	-----	100.0%	-----	-----
P'ville (D) N = 6	-----	83.3%	16.7%	-----

Palat. torus	Abs	SmRidg	MedRidg	LgeRidg	SmMd	MedMd	LMd
Feurt (U) N = 6	100.0%	-----	-----	-----	-----	-----	-----
Feurt (D) N = 9	100.0%	-----	-----	-----	-----	-----	-----
Ful. Field (U) N = 3	100.0%	-----	-----	-----	-----	-----	-----
Ful. Field (D) N = 1	100.0%	-----	-----	-----	-----	-----	-----
P'ville (D) N = 6	100.0%	-----	-----	-----	-----	-----	-----

Mand. size	Sm	Med	Lge	V.Lge
Feurt (U) N = 6	100.0%	-----	-----	-----
Feurt (D) N = 9	88.9%	11.1%	-----	-----
Ful. Field (U) N = 3	66.7%	33.3%	-----	-----
Ful. Field (D) N = 1	100.0%	-----	-----	-----
P'ville (D) N = 6	100.0%	-----	-----	-----

Chin form	NarBilat	WideBilat	Intermed	Median
Feurt (U) N = 6	-----	-----	-----	100.%
Feurt (D) N = 9	-----	-----	-----	100.0%
Ful. Field (U) N = 3	66.7%	-----	-----	33.3%
Ful. Field (D) N = 1	-----	-----	-----	100.0%
P'ville (D) N = 6	16.7%	-----	-----	83.3%

Table 75 - continued

	Negat	Neut	Sm	Med	Lge
Chin proj.					
Feurt (U) N = 6	83.3%	-----	16.7%	-----	-----
Feurt (D) N = 9	100.0%	-----	-----	-----	-----
Ful. Field (U) N = 3	100.0%	-----	-----	-----	-----
Ful. Field (D) N = 1	-----	100.0%	-----	-----	-----
P'ville (D) N = 6	66.7%	16.7%	16.7%	-----	-----

	Sm	Med	Pron	V.Pron	
Ptergy. attach.					
Feurt (U) N = 6	83.3%	16.7%	-----	-----	
Feurt (D) N = 9	77.8%	11.1%	11.1%	-----	
Ful. Field (U) N = 3	66.7%	33.3%	-----	-----	
Ful. Field (D) N = 1	100.0%	-----	-----	-----	
P'ville (D) N = 6	50.0%	33.3%	-----	16.7%	

	None	Sm	Med	Pron	
Gonial ang. evers.					
Feurt (U) N = 6	100.0%	-----	-----	-----	
Feurt (D) N = 9	88.9%	11.1%	-----	-----	
Ful. Field (U) N = 3	66.7%	33.3%	-----	-----	
Ful. Field (D) N = 1	100.0%	-----	-----	-----	
P'ville (D) N = 6	100.0%	-----	-----	-----	

APPENDIX C

Table 76

Mean Measurements of Anderson Male Crania*

	Mean**	Standard Dev.
Cranial vault		
Capacity	1450.2cc.	78.82
Cranial module	152.8	3.06
Mean thickness of left parietal	4.8	0.70
Glabello-occipital length	179.7	7.74
Maximum breadth	138.1	5.97
Minimum frontal breadth	92.7	13.24
Basion-bregma height	140.6	3.43
Porion-apex height	117.7	5.39
Basion-porion height	-----	------
Length of cranial base	104.2	3.16
Face		
Total facial height	124.3	4.71
Upper facial height	74.9	3.90
Total facial breadth	140.5	3.74
Midfacial breadth	103.1	3.78
Interior biorbital breadth	100.1	3.55
Subtense to interior biorbital arc	18.1	1.63
Biorbital breadth	100.9	3.23
Anterior interorbital breadth	19.7	1.86
Nasal structure		
Nasal breadth	26.8	1.62
Nasal height	53.7	2.30
Dacryal chord	20.8	1.59
Dacryal subtense to arc	10.9	1.04
Minimum nasal breadth	8.7	1.05
Subtense to nasal arc	3.9	0.69

* N = 46, all undeformed

** means in millimeters (mm.) unless listed otherwise

Table 76 - continued

Orbit		
Left orbital height	34.6	1.61
Left orbital breadth, maxillofrontale	44.1	1.62
Left orbital breadth, dacryon	41.8	1.62
Dental arch and profile		
Maxillo-alveolar breadth	69.2	2.92
Maxillo-alveolar length	54.3	1.86
Facial length, prosthion	97.9	3.57
Facial length, alveolar point	96.0	3.73
Mandible		
Length of mandible	105.3	4.62
Bicondylar breadth	129.2	5.34
Symphysial height	36.2	2.01
Biangular breadth	104.8	5.68
Minimum ramus length	35.2	2.57
Angles		
Facial profile angle	-----	------
Midfacial profile angle	-----	------
Alveolar profile angle	-----	------
Gonial angle	114.1°	6.16

APPENDIX C

Table 77

Mean Indices of Anderson Male Crania*

	Mean	Standard Dev.
Cranial vault		
Cranial	77.07	5.85
Length-height	78.36	3.52
Breadth-height	101.93	4.12
Mean height	88.49	1.98
Length-auricular height	65.64	4.27
Flatness of cranial base	------	------
Transverse fronto-parietal	67.14	9.58
Face		
Total facial	88.51	3.88
Upper facial	53.35	3.01
Midfacial	72.67	3.50
Transverse cranio-facial	101.85	3.84
Zygo-frontal	66.04	9.56
Fronto-mandibular	111.19	7.31
Zygo-mandibular	74.67	4.45
Facial flatness	18.14	1.54
Anterior interorbital	19.53	1.84
Nasal structure		
Nasal	49.97	3.61
Nasal root height	52.87	6.70
Nasal bone height	45.46	8.48
Orbit		
Left orbital, maxillofrontale	78.54	4.29
Left orbital, dacryon	82.85	4.81
Dental arch		
Maxillo-alveolar	127.41	4.91
Mandible		
Mandibular	81.63	4.88

* N = 46, all undeformed

Table 78

Mean Measurements of Anderson Female Crania (Undeformed)*

	Mean**	Standard Dev.
Cranial vault		
Capacity	1296.2 cc.	36.28
Cranial module	148.2	2.41
Mean thickness of left parietal	4.6	0.88
Glabello-occipital length	176.3	4.23
Maximum breadth	132.2	2.92
Minimum frontal breadth	88.4	16.32
Basion-bregma height	136.0	3.08
Porion-apex height	113.6	1.85
Basion-porion height	-----	----
Length of cranial base	93.3	25.09
Face		
Total facial height	115.2	2.45
Upper facial height	69.8	1.72
Total facial breadth	129.9	2.21
Midfacial breadth	90.4	22.72
Interior biorbital breadth	94.9	2.45
Subtense to interior biorbital arc	17.3	0.90
Biorbital breadth	97.0	1.58
Anterior interorbital breadth	18.3	1.50
Nasal structure		
Nasal breadth	25.8	1.21
Nasal height	50.0	1.46
Dacryal chord	20.1	1.87
Dacryal subtense to arc	10.1	0.73
Minimum nasal breadth	8.1	1.35
Subtense to nasal arc	3.1	0.62
Orbit		
Left orbital height	33.7	1.40
Left orbital breadth, maxillofrontale	42.1	0.85
Left orbital breadth, dacryon	39.8	0.96
Dental arch and profile		
Maxillo-alveolar breadth	65.2	1.61
Maxillo-alveolar length	53.0	1.35
Facial length, prosthion	93.4	16.28
Facial length, alveolar point	91.6	16.30

APPENDIX C

Table 78 - continued

Mandible		
Length of mandible	102.0	2.80
Bicondylar breadth	120.4	4.39
Symphyseal height	33.4	1.85
Biangular breadth	96.6	5.28
Minimum ramus length	33.1	2.64
Angles		
Facial profile angle	-----	----
Midfacial profile angle	-----	----
Alveolar profile angle	-----	----
Gonial angle	121.3°	4.28

*N = 31
**Measurements in millimeters (mm.) unless listed otherwise

Table 79

Mean Indices of Anderson Female Crania (Undeformed)*

	Mean	Standard Dev.
Cranial vault		
Cranial	75.05	2.17
Length-height	77.19	2.06
Breadth-height	102.90	3.15
Mean height	88.19	2.17
Length-auricular height	64.51	1.69
Flatness of cranial base	------	----
Transverse fronto-parietal	66.85	12.30
Face		
Total facial	88.68	2.47
Upper facial	53.75	1.57
Midfacial	70.72	10.47
Transverse cranio-facial	98.28	2.26
Zygo-frontal	68.05	12.55
Fronto-mandibular	122.08	88.96
Zygo-mandibular	74.38	4.10
Facial flatness	18.21	0.83
Anterior interorbital	18.83	1.51
Nasal structure		
Nasal	51.72	2.97
Nasal root height	50.59	7.06
Nasal bone height	39.19	7.73
Orbit		
Left orbital, maxillofrontale	80.04	3.58
Left orbital, dacryon	84.80	4.08
Dental arch		
Maxillo-alveolar	123.19	3.32
Mandible		
Mandibular	84.83	3.68

*N = 31

APPENDIX C 313

Table 80

Mean Measurements of Anderson Female Crania (Deformed)*

	Mean**	Standard Dev.
Cranial vault		
Capacity	1275.0 cc.	31.69
Cranial module	144.9	3.22
Mean thickness of left parietal	5.2	0.89
Glabello-occipital length	159.1	6.73
Maximum breadth	140.9	6.71
Minimum frontal breadth	92.6	3.38
Basion-bregma height	134.6	1.77
Porion-apex height	115.0	2.73
Basion-porion height	-----	----
Length of cranial base	96.8	3.45
Face		
Total facial height	114.5	3.46
Upper facial height	70.4	1.92
Total facial breadth	130.8	2.76
Midfacial breadth	96.5	2.73
Interior biorbital breadth	96.6	3.02
Subtense to interior biorbital arc	16.6	3.20
Biorbital breadth	98.2	2.66
Anterior interorbital breadth	18.5	2.00
Nasal structure		
Nasal breadth	26.4	1.51
Nasal height	50.8	1.28
Dacryal chord	20.0	1.77
Dacryal subtense to arc	8.6	3.66
Minimum nasal breadth	7.9	3.91
Subtense to nasal arc	3.2	0.71
Orbit		
Left orbital height	34.0	1.20
Left orbital breadth, maxillofrontale	42.6	1.30
Left orbital breadth, dacryon	40.5	1.07
Dental arch and profile		
Maxillo-alveolar breadth	64.6	2.20
Maxillo-alveolar length	52.6	1.69
Facial length, prosthion	71.8	42.26
Facial length, alveolar point	80.1	31.22

Table 80 - continued

Mandible
    Length of mandible   100.8   3.06
    Bicondylar breadth   122.9   4.55
    Symphyseal height   33.0   1.93
    Biangular breadth   99.0   2.93
    Minimum ramus length   32.4   3.02

Angles
    Facial profile angle   -----   ----
    Midfacial profile angle   -----   ----
    Alveolar profile angle   -----   ----
    Gonial angle $121.6°$ 3.78

*N = 8
**Measurements in millimeters (mm.) unless listed otherwise

APPENDIX C

Table 81

Mean Indices of Anderson Female Crania (Deformed)*

	Mean	Standard Dev.
Cranial vault		
Cranial	88.69	5.89
Length-height	84.71	3.13
Breadth-height	95.76	5.03
Mean height	89.80	2.32
Length-auricular height	72.40	3.81
Flatness of cranial base	------	----
Transverse fronto-parietal	65.84	2.91
Face		
Total facial	87.61	3.31
Upper facial	53.86	2.12
Midfacial	72.97	2.61
Transverse cranio-facial	92.98	4.44
Zygo-frontal	70.87	2.97
Fronto-mandibular	107.04	5.72
Zygo-mandibular	75.72	1.80
Facial flatness	17.25	3.55
Anterior interorbital	18.82	1.81
Nasal structure		
Nasal	52.00	3.14
Nasal root height	42.44	17.37
Nasal bone height	32.29	13.56
Orbit		
Left orbital, maxillofrontale	79.80	2.72
Left orbital, dacryon	83.96	2.52
Dental arch		
Maxillo-alveolar	122.94	6.46
Mandible		
Mandibular	82.09	3.87

*N = 8

Table 82

Mean Measurements of Taylor Male Crania*

Measurement	Mean**	Standard Dev.
Cranial vault		
Capacity	1470.3cc.	93.75
Cranial module	153.8	3.26
Mean thickness of left parietal	4.6	0.63
Glabello-occipital length	183.2	5.91
Maximum breadth	138.4	4.78
Minimum frontal breadth	95.5	3.21
Basion-bregma height	139.9	2.82
Porion-apex height	115.7	3.92
Basion-porion height	-----	------
Length of cranial base	103.6	3.74
Face		
Total facial height	126.0	1.83
Upper facial height	75.0	2.43
Total facial breadth	140.3	4.04
Midfacial breadth	100.4	3.85
Interior biorbital breadth	99.9	2.92
Subtense to interior biorbital arc	17.7	1.76
Biorbital breadth	101.0	2.74
Anterior interorbital breadth	19.9	1.56
Nasal structure		
Nasal breadth	27.1	1.49
Nasal height	53.7	2.21
Dacryal chord	21.0	1.52
Dacryal subtense to arc	11.2	1.30
Minimum nasal breadth	8.1	1.21
Subtense to nasal arc	3.9	0.81

* N = 25, all undeformed

** means in millimeters (mm.) unless listed otherwise

APPENDIX C

Table 82 - continued

Orbit		
Left orbital height	34.7	2.31
Left orbital breadth, maxillofrontale	43.1	2.81
Left orbital breadth, dacryon	41.1	1.41
Dental arch and profile		
Maxillo-alveolar breadth	68.8	3.81
Maxillo-alveolar length	53.9	2.24
Facial length, prosthion	97.5	3.16
Facial length, alveolar point	95.6	3.09
Mandible		
Length of mandible	102.8	3.29
Bicondylar breadth	128.5	5.85
Symphysial height	36.9	1.82
Biangular breadth	100.9	2.42
Minimum ramus length	35.7	2.35
Angles		
Facial profile angle	85.8°	1.90
Midfacial profile angle	89.9°	2.49
Alveolar profile angle	71.9°	2.96
Gonial angle	115.0°	4.96

Table 83

Mean Indices of Taylor Male Crania*

	Mean	Standard Dev.
Cranial vault		
Cranial	75.61	3.45
Length-height	76.44	2.53
Breadth-height	101.17	2.84
Mean height	87.04	1.85
Length-auricular height	63.20	2.29
Flatness of cranial base	------	------
Transverse fronto-parietal	69.08	2.94
Face		
Total facial	85.86	17.97
Upper facial	53.47	2.28
Midfacial	74.73	3.56
Transverse cranio-facial	101.42	2.24
Zygo-frontal	68.10	2.22
Fronto-mandibular	105.75	4.19
Zygo-mandibular	71.97	2.36
Facial flatness	17.70	1.45
Anterior interorbital	19.74	1.34
Nasal structure		
Nasal	50.57	3.67
Nasal root height	54.06	8.02
Nasal bone height	48.53	10.22
Orbit		
Left orbital, maxillofrontale	77.20	9.00
Left orbital, dacryon	80.30	16.67
Dental arch		
Maxillo-alveolar	127.72	6.41
Mandible		
Mandibular	80.14	4.20

* N = 25, all undeformed

APPENDIX C

Table 84

Mean Measurements of Taylor Female Crania (Undeformed)*

	Mean**	Standard Dev.
Cranial vault		
Capacity	1372.0 cc.	94.18
Cranial module	147.9	5.13
Mean thickness of left parietal	4.8	0.84
Glabello-occipital length	178.8	7.89
Maximum breadth	132.0	3.67
Minimum frontal breadth	92.0	3.00
Basion-bregma height	133.0	5.66
Porion-apex height	112.4	4.98
Basion-porion height	-----	----
Length of cranial base	100.8	4.97
Face		
Total facial height	115.2	1.64
Upper facial height	70.4	3.36
Total facial breadth	128.2	5.07
Midfacial breadth	95.2	3.96
Interior biorbital breadth	95.6	2.79
Subtense to interior biorbital arc	17.8	1.30
Biorbital breadth	96.2	3.11
Anterior interorbital breadth	19.2	0.84
Nasal structure		
Nasal breadth	26.2	0.84
Nasal height	51.0	1.41
Dacryal chord	20.2	0.84
Dacryal subtense to arc	9.6	0.89
Minimum nasal breadth	8.2	1.30
Subtense to nasal arc	3.4	0.55
Orbit		
Left orbital height	33.8	1.80
Left orbital breadth, maxillofrontale	42.2	1.79
Left orbital breadth, dacryon	40.0	1.22
Dental arch and profile		
Maxillo-alveolar breadth	63.0	1.87
Maxillo-alveolar length	53.0	2.12
Facial length, prosthion	97.6	2.88
Facial length, alveolar point	95.6	2.70

Table 84 - continued

Mandible		
Length of mandible	100.0	2.74
Bicondylar breadth	119.6	1.95
Symphyseal height	32.0	1.41
Biangular breadth	92.2	1.30
Minimum ramus length	32.2	1.48
Angles		
Facial profile angle	86.2°	0.84
Midfacial profile angle	92.2°	1.79
Alveolar profile angle	69.0°	4.30
Gonial angle	122.0°	8.46

*N = 5
**Measurements in millimeters (mm.) unless listed otherwise

APPENDIX C

Table 85

Mean Indices of Taylor Female Crania (Undeformed)*

	Mean	Standard Dev.
Cranial vault		
Cranial	73.90	2.80
Length-height	74.43	2.85
Breadth-height	100.73	1.74
Mean height	85.58	2.12
Length-auricular height	62.87	1.18
Flatness of cranial base	------	----
Transverse fronto-parietal	69.72	2.23
Face		
Total facial	89.96	3.30
Upper facial	54.93	2.11
Midfacial	74.02	3.93
Transverse cranio-facial	97.18	4.62
Zygo-frontal	71.81	2.50
Fronto-mandibular	100.29	3.17
Zygo-mandibular	71.98	2.22
Facial flatness	18.65	1.70
Anterior interorbital	19.96	0.48
Nasal structure		
Nasal	51.42	2.61
Nasal root height	47.57	4.58
Nasal bone height	41.53	2.77
Orbit		
Left orbital, maxillofrontale	80.13	3.54
Left orbital, dacryon	84.56	5.08
Dental arch		
Maxillo-alveolar	118.98	4.77
Mandible		
Mandibular	83.62	2.31

*N = 5

Table 86

Mean Measurements of Taylor Female Crania (Deformed)*

Cranial vault	Mean**	Standard Dev.
Capacity	1370.0cc.	0.00
Cranial module	145.0	0.00
Mean thickness of left parietal	5.0	0.00
Glabello-occipital length	165.0	0.00
Maximum breadth	141.0	0.00
Minimum frontal breadth	92.0	0.00
Basion-bregma height	129.0	0.00
Porion-apex height	109.0	0.00
Basion-porion height	-----	----
Length of cranial base	95.0	0.00
Face		
Total facial height	119.0	0.00
Upper facial height	74.0	0.00
Total facial breadth	130.0	0.00
Midfacial breadth	102.0	0.00
Interior biorbital breadth	99.0	0.00
Subtense to interior biorbital arc	15.0	0.00
Biorbital breadth	101.0	0.00
Anterior interorbital breadth	19.0	0.00
Nasal structure		
Nasal breadth	26.0	0.00
Nasal height	51.0	0.00
Dacryal chord	20.0	0.00
Dacryal subtense to arc	8.0	0.00
Minimum nasal breadth	9.0	0.00
Subtense to nasal arc	3.0	0.00
Orbit		
Left orbital height	33.0	0.00
Left orbital breadth, maxillofrontale	43.0	0.00
Left orbital breadth, dacryon	41.0	0.00
Dental arch and profile		
Maxillo-alveolar breadth	67.0	0.00
Maxillo-alveolar length	55.0	0.00
Facial length, prosthion	98.0	0.00
Facial length, alveolar point	96.0	0.00

APPENDIX C

Table 86 - continued

Mandible		
Length of mandible	106.0	0.00
Bicondylar breadth	124.0	0.00
Symphyseal height	33.0	0.00
Biangular breadth	92.0	0.00
Minimum ramus length	31.0	0.00
Angles		
Facial profile angle	81.0°	0.00
Midfacial profile angle	86.0°	0.00
Alveolar profile angle	68.0°	0.00
Gonial angle	126.0°	0.00

*N = 1
**Measurements in millimeters (mm.) unless listed otherwise

Table 87

Mean Indices of Taylor Female Crania (Deformed)*

	Mean	Standard Dev.
Cranial vault		
Cranial	85.45	0.00
Length-height	78.18	0.00
Breadth-height	91.49	0.00
Mean height	84.31	0.00
Length-auricular height	66.06	0.00
Flatness of cranial base	------	----
Transverse fronto-parietal	65.25	0.00
Face		
Total facial	91.54	0.00
Upper facial	56.92	0.00
Midfacial	72.55	0.00
Transverse cranio-facial	92.20	0.00
Zygo-frontal	70.77	0.00
Fronto-mandibular	100.00	0.00
Zygo-mandibular	70.77	0.00
Facial flatness	15.15	0.00
Anterior interorbital	18.81	0.00
Nasal structure		
Nasal	50.98	0.00
Nasal root height	40.00	0.00
Nasal bone height	33.33	0.00
Orbit		
Left orbital, maxillofrontale	76.74	0.00
Left orbital, dacryon	80.49	0.00
Dental arch		
Maxillo-alveolar	121.82	0.00
Mandible		
Mandibular	85.48	0.00

*N = 1

APPENDIX C

Table 88

Mean Measurements of Stokes Male Crania (Undeformed)*

	Mean**	Standard Dev.
Cranial vault		
Capacity	1480.0cc.	0.00
Cranial module	159.6	0.00
Mean thickness of left parietal	6.0	0.00
Glabello-occipital length	192.0	0.00
Maximum breadth	138.0	0.00
Minimum frontal breadth	100.0	0.00
Basion-bregma height	149.0	0.00
Porion-apex height	118.0	0.00
Basion-porion height	-----	------
Length of cranial base	113.0	0.00
Face		
Total facial height	126.0	0.00
Upper facial height	75.0	0.00
Total facial breadth	140.0	0.00
Midfacial breadth	101.0	0.00
Interior biorbital breadth	106.0	0.00
Subtense to interior biorbital arc	21.0	0.00
Biorbital breadth	101.0	0.00
Anterior interorbital breadth	23.0	0.00
Nasal structure		
Nasal breadth	27.0	0.00
Nasal height	54.0	0.00
Dacryal chord	26.0	0.00
Dacryal subtense to arc	13.0	0.00
Minimum nasal breadth	12.0	0.00
Subtense to nasal arc	6.0	0.00

* N = 1

** means in millimeters (mm.) unless listed otherwise

Table 88 - continued

Orbit
    Left orbital height   38.0   0.00
    Left orbital breadth, maxillofrontale   45.0   0.00
    Left orbital breadth, dacryon   42.0   0.00

Dental arch and profile
    Maxillo-alveolar breadth   69.0   0.00
    Maxillo-alveolar length   54.0   0.00
    Facial length, prosthion   96.0   0.00
    Facial length, alveolar point   94.0   0.00

Mandible
    Length of mandible   104.0   0.00
    Bicondylar breadth   131.0   0.00
    Symphysial height   37.0   0.00
    Biangular breadth   114.0   0.00
    Minimum ramus length   40.0   0.00

Angles
    Facial profile angle   86.0°   0.00
    Midfacial profile angle   90.0°   0.00
    Alveolar profile angle   72.0°   0.00
    Gonial angle   108.0°   0.00

APPENDIX C

Table 89

Mean Indices of Stokes Male Crania (Undeformed)*

Cranial vault	Mean	Standard Dev.
Cranial	71.88	0.00
Length-height	77.60	0.00
Breadth-height	107.97	0.00
Mean height	90.30	0.00
Length-auricular height	61.46	0.00
Flatness of cranial base	0.00	0.00
Transverse fronto-parietal	72.46	0.00
Face		
Total facial	90.00	0.00
Upper facial	53.57	0.00
Midfacial	74.26	0.00
Transverse cranio-facial	101.45	0.00
Zygo-frontal	71.43	0.00
Fronto-mandibular	114.00	0.00
Zygo-mandibular	81.43	0.00
Facial flatness	19.81	0.00
Anterior interorbital	22.77	0.00
Nasal structure		
Nasal	50.00	0.00
Nasal root height	50.00	0.00
Nasal bone height	50.00	0.00
Orbit		
Left orbital, maxillofrontale	84.44	0.00
Left orbital, dacryon	90.48	0.00
Dental arch		
Maxillo-alveolar	127.78	0.00
Mandible		
Mandibular	79.39	0.00

* N = 1

Table 90

Mean Measurements of Stokes Female Crania (Undeformed)*

	Mean**	Standard Dev.
Cranial vault		
Capacity	1370.0cc.	0.00
Cranial module	151.7	0.00
Mean thickness of left parietal	8.0	0.00
Glabello-occipital length	184.0	0.00
Maximum breadth	134.0	0.00
Minimum frontal breadth	93.0	0.00
Basion-bregma height	137.0	0.00
Porion-apex height	121.0	0.00
Basion-porion height	-----	----
Length of cranial base	99.0	0.00
Face		
Total facial height	116.0	0.00
Upper facial height	71.0	0.00
Total facial breadth	130.0	0.00
Midfacial breadth	96.0	0.00
Interior biorbital breadth	91.0	0.00
Subtense to interior biorbital arc	17.0	0.00
Biorbital breadth	97.0	0.00
Anterior interorbital breadth	19.0	0.00
Nasal structure		
Nasal breadth	26.0	0.00
Nasal height	51.0	0.00
Dacryal chord	20.0	0.00
Dacryal subtense to arc	9.0	0.00
Minimum nasal breadth	8.0	0.00
Subtense to nasal arc	3.0	0.00
Orbit		
Left orbital height	33.0	0.00
Left orbital breadth, maxillofrontale	42.0	0.00
Left orbital breadth, dacryon	40.0	0.00
Dental arch and profile		
Maxillo-alveolar breadth	63.0	0.00
Maxillo-alveolar length	53.0	0.00
Facial length, prosthion	98.0	0.00
Facial length, alveolar point	96.0	0.00

APPENDIX C

Table 90 - continued

Mandible		
Length of mandible	99.0	0.00
Bicondylar breadth	119.0	0.00
Symphyseal height	38.0	0.00
Biangular breadth	97.0	0.00
Minimum ramus length	36.0	0.00
Angles		
Facial profile angle	$85.0°$	0.00
Midfacial profile angle	$91.0°$	0.00
Alveolar profile angle	$69.0°$	0.00
Gonial angle	$118.0°$	0.00

*N = 1
**Measurements in millimeters (mm.) unless listed otherwise

Table 91

Mean Indices of Stokes Female Crania (Undeformed)*

Cranial vault	Mean	Standard Dev.
Cranial	72.83	0.00
Length-height	74.46	0.00
Breadth-height	102.24	0.00
Mean height	86.16	0.00
Length-auricular height	65.76	0.00
Flatness of cranial base	------	----
Transverse fronto-parietal	69.40	0.00
Face		
Total facial	89.23	0.00
Upper facial	54.62	0.00
Midfacial	73.96	0.00
Transverse cranio-facial	97.01	0.00
Zygo-frontal	71.54	0.00
Fronto-mandibular	104.30	0.00
Zygo-mandibular	74.62	0.00
Facial flatness	18.68	0.00
Anterior interorbital	19.59	0.00
Nasal structure		
Nasal	50.98	0.00
Nasal root height	45.00	0.00
Nasal bone height	37.50	0.00
Orbit		
Left orbital, maxillofrontale	78.57	0.00
Left orbital, dacryon	82.50	0.00
Dental arch		
Maxillo-alveolar	118.87	0.00
Mandible		
Mandibular	83.19	0.00

*N = 1

Table 92

Cranial Observations of the Anderson Focus (Males)*

Muscularity	Sm	Med	Lge	V.Lge		
Anderson (N = 46)	2.2%	37.0%	60.9%	-----		
Taylor (N = 25)	-----	64.0%	36.0%	-----		
Stokes (N = 1)	-----	-----	100.0%	-----		

Deformation	None	Occ	Lambd	Fr-occ	Bil-fr-occ	Earth Press
Anderson (N = 46)	100.0%	-----	-----	-----	-----	-----
Taylor (N = 25)	72.0%	8.0%	-----	-----	-----	20.0%
Stokes (N = 1)	100.0%	-----	-----	-----	-----	-----

Degree of deform.	None	Trace	Sm	Med	Pron	
Anderson (N = 46)	100.0%	-----	-----	-----	-----	
Taylor (N = 25)	80.0%	4.0%	8.0%	8.0%	-----	
Stokes (N = 1)	100.0%	-----	-----	-----	-----	

Vault form	Ell	Ov	Spher	Pentag	Rhom	Sphen
Anderson (N = 46)	6.5%	89.1%	2.2%	2.2%	-----	-----
Taylor (N = 25)	16.0%	84.0%	-----	-----	-----	-----
Stokes (N = 1)	-----	100.0%	-----	-----	-----	-----

Brow ridge size	None	Trace	Sm	Med	Lge	V.Lge
Anderson (N = 46)	-----	2.2%	39.1%	41.3%	17.4%	-----
Taylor (N = 25)	-----	-----	28.0%	48.0%	20.0%	4.0%
Stokes (N = 1)	-----	-----	-----	100.0%	-----	-----

* All Anderson Focus male crania are undeformed.

Table 92 - continued

	Flat	Sm	Med	Lge	V. Lge	V.Pron
Glabella prom.						
Anderson (N = 46)	-----	58.7%	32.6%	8.7%	-----	-----
Taylor (N = 25)	-----	32.0%	52.0%	16.0%	-----	-----
Stokes (N = 1)	-----	100.0%	-----	-----	-----	-----

	Bulg	None	Sl	Med	Pron	
Frontal slope						
Anderson (N = 46)	-----	-----	19.6%	67.4%	13.0%	
Taylor (N = 25)	-----	-----	12.0%	88.0%	-----	
Stokes (N = 1)	-----	-----	-----	100.0%	-----	

	Sm	Med	Lge			
Postorb. constr.						
Anderson (N = 46)	100.0%	-----	-----			
Taylor (N = 25)	36.0%	60.0%	4.0%			
Stokes (N = 1)	-----	100.0%	-----			

	Sm	Med	Lge			
Fron. emin.						
Anderson (N = 46)	76.1%	19.6%	4.3%			
Taylor (N = 25)	88.0%	12.0%	-----			
Stokes (N = 1)	100.0%	-----	-----			

	None	Sm	Med	Lge		
Fr. median crest						
Anderson (N = 46)	39.1%	39.1%	17.4%	4.3%		
Taylor (N = 25)	52.0%	28.0%	8.0%	12.0%		
Stokes (N = 1)	-----	-----	-----	100.0%		

	Sm	Med	Lge			
Fron. br.						
Anderson (N = 46)	28.3%	65.2%	6.5%			
Taylor (N = 25)	12.0%	68.0%	20.0%			
Stokes (N = 1)	100.0%	-----	-----			

APPENDIX C 333

Table 92 - continued

Sag. elev.	None	Sm	Med	Lge	V.Lge
Anderson (N = 46)	15.2%	76.1%	2.2%	6.5%	-----
Taylor (N = 25)	20.0%	76.0%	4.0%	-----	-----
Stokes (N = 1)	-----	-----	100.0%	-----	-----
Pariet. emin.	Sm	Med	Lge		
Anderson (N = 46)	39.1%	60.9%	-----		
Taylor (N = 25)	28.0%	68.0%	4.0%		
Stokes (N = 1)	100.0%	-----	-----		
Temp. fullness	Flat	Sm	Med	Lge	
Anderson (N = 46)	26.1%	65.2%	6.5%	2.2%	
Taylor (N = 25)	24.0%	60.0%	8.0%	8.0%	
Stokes (N = 1)	100.0%	-----	-----	-----	
Mastoids	Sm	Med	Lge	V.Lge	
Anderson (N = 46)	-----	67.4%	30.4%	2.2%	
Taylor (N = 25)	16.0%	60.0%	24.0%	-----	
Stokes (N = 1)	-----	100.0%	-----	-----	
Supramast. crest	Sm	Med	Lge		
Anderson (N = 46)	100.0%	-----	-----		
Taylor (N = 25)	24.0%	52.0%	24.0%		
Stokes (N = 1)	-----	-----	100.0%		
Sphen. depress.	Sm	Med	Lge		
Anderson (N = 46)	100.0%	-----	-----		
Taylor (N = 25)	44.0%	52.0%	4.0%		
Stokes (N = 1)	100.0%	-----	-----		

Table 92 - continued

	None	Sm	Med	Pron
Occip. curve				
Anderson (N = 46)	-----	10.9%	43.5%	45.7%
Taylor (N = 25)	-----	4.0%	24.0%	72.0%
Stokes (N = 1)	-----	-----	-----	100.0%

	None	Sm	Med	Pron
Lambd. flat.				
Anderson (N = 46)	10.9%	23.9%	10.9%	54.3%
Taylor (N = 25)	4.0%	4.0%	72.0%	20.0%
Stokes (N = 1)	-----	-----	-----	100.0%

	Sm	Med	Lge
Cond. elev.			
Anderson (N = 46)	100.0%	-----	-----
Taylor (N = 25)	4.0%	72.0%	24.0%
Stokes (N = 1)	-----	-----	100.0%

	Low	Med	High
Basion			
Anderson (N = 46)	100.0%	-----	-----
Taylor (N = 25)	-----	88.0%	12.0%
Stokes (N = 1)	-----	-----	100.0%

	Sm	Med	Lge
Styl. proc.			
Anderson (N = 46)	60.9%	32.6%	6.5%
Taylor (N = 25)	60.0%	36.0%	4.0%
Stokes (N = 1)	-----	100.0%	-----

	Sm	Med	Lge
Glen. fos. depth			
Anderson (N = 46)	-----	76.1%	23.9%
Taylor (N = 25)	20.0%	72.0%	8.0%
Stokes (N = 1)	-----	-----	100.0%

Table 92 - continued

	Thin	Med	Thick	V. Thick	
Tymp. plate					
Anderson (N = 46)	89.1%	8.7%	2.2%	----	
Taylor (N = 25)	96.0%	4.0%	----	----	
Stokes (N = 1)	100.0%	----	----	----	

	Obl	Rhom	Sq	Ell	Rou
Orbit shape					
Anderson (N = 46)	28.3%	28.3%	30.4%	10.9%	2.2%
Taylor (N = 25)	56.0%	20.0%	8.0%	16.0%	----
Stokes (N = 1)	----	----	100.0%	----	----

	None	Sm	Med	Pron	
Orbit incl.					
Anderson (N = 46)	4.3%	60.9%	32.6%	2.2%	
Taylor (N = 25)	----	84.0%	16.0%	----	
Stokes (N = 1)	----	100.0%	----	----	

	Abs	Sl	Med	Deep	
Suborb. fossa					
Anderson (N = 46)	23.9%	47.8%	21.7%	6.5%	
Taylor (N = 25)	20.0%	60.0%	20.0%	----	
Stokes (N = 1)	----	100.0%	----	----	

	Sm	Med	Lge	V. Lge	
Zyg. size					
Anderson (N = 46)	4.3%	39.1%	41.3%	15.2%	
Taylor (N = 25)	----	60.0%	32.0%	8.0%	
Stokes (N = 1)	----	100.0%	----	----	

	Sm	Med	Lge		
Zyg. lat. proj.					
Anderson (N = 46)	----	8.7%	91.3%		
Taylor (N = 25)	----	4.0%	96.0%		
Stokes (N = 1)	----	100.0%	----		

Table 92 - continued

	V.Sm	Sm	Med	Lge	V.Lge
Zyg. ant. proj.					
Anderson (N = 46)		4.3%	43.5%	52.2%	----
Taylor (N = 25)		8.0%	28.0%	64.0%	----
Stokes (N = 1)		----	100.0%	----	----

		Sm	Med	Pron	
Zyg. proc. thick.					
Anderson (N = 46)		100.0%	----	----	
Taylor (N = 25)		4.0%	84.0%	12.0%	
Stokes (N = 1)		----	100.0%	----	

	V.Low	Low	Med	High	V.High
Nas. rt. ht.					
Anderson (N = 46)	----	2.2%	52.2%	45.7%	----
Taylor (N = 25)	----	----	72.0%	24.0%	4.0%
Stokes (N = 1)	----	----	----	----	100.0%

	V.Sm	Sm	Med	Lge	V.Lge
Nas. rt. br.					
Anderson (N = 46)	----	21.7%	71.7%	4.3%	2.2%
Taylor (N = 25)	----	8.0%	72.0%	20.0%	----
Stokes (N = 1)	----	----	100.0%	----	----

	V.Low	Low	Med	High	V.High
Nas. bridg. ht.					
Anderson (N = 46)	----	4.3%	80.4%	13.0%	2.2%
Taylor (N = 25)	----	4.0%	76.0%	16.0%	4.0%
Stokes (N = 1)	----	----	100.0%	----	----

		Sm	Med	Lge	
Nas. bridg. br.					
Anderson (N = 46)		17.4%	80.4%	2.2%	
Taylor (N = 25)		8.0%	92.0%	----	
Stokes (N = 1)		----	100.0%	----	

APPENDIX C   337

Table 92 - continued

	Conc	Str	Sl. Conc-Conv	Conc-Conv	V.C-C
Nas. profile					
Anderson (N = 46)	-----	13.0%	87.0%	-----	-----
Taylor (N = 25)	-----	-----	-----	100.0%	-----
Stokes (N = 1)	-----	-----	-----	100.0%	
Nas. depress.	Abs	Sm	Med	Lge	
Anderson (N = 46)	13.0%	54.3%	32.6%	-----	
Taylor (N = 25)	-----	44.0%	52.0%	4.0%	
Stokes (N = 1)	-----	100.0%	-----	-----	
Nas. sills	Abs	Dull	Med	Sharp	
Anderson (N = 46)	10.9%	17.4%	37.0%	34.8%	
Taylor (N = 25)	4.0%	20.0%	16.0%	60.0%	
Stokes (N = 1)	-----	-----	-----	100.0%	
Nas. spine	Abs	Sm	Med	Rt. Ang	Lge
Anderson (N = 46)	-----	80.4%	19.6%	-----	-----
Taylor (N = 25)	4.0%	76.0%	20.0%	-----	-----
Stokes (N = 1)	-----	100.0%	-----	-----	-----
Subnas. grooves	Abs	Sm	Med	Pron	Sulci
Anderson (N = 46)	71.7%	23.9%	2.2%	2.2%	-----
Taylor (N = 25)	84.0%	16.0%	-----	-----	-----
Stokes (N = 1)	100.0%	-----	-----	-----	-----
Midfac. progn.	Abs	Sl	Med	Pron	
Anderson (N = 46)	84.8%	13.0%	2.2%	-----	
Taylor (N = 25)	88.0%	12.0%	-----	-----	
Stokes (N = 1)	100.0%	-----	-----	-----	

Table 92 - continued

Alveol. progn.	Abs	Sl	Med	Pron	
Anderson (N = 46)	13.0%	56.5%	28.3%	2.2%	
Taylor (N = 25)	8.0%	68.0%	20.0%	4.0%	
Stokes (N = 1)	-----	100.0%	-----	-----	
Total progn.	Abs	Sl	Med	Pron	
Anderson (N = 46)	10.9%	73.9%	15.2%	-----	
Taylor (N = 25)	8.0%	80.0%	12.0%	-----	
Stokes (N = 1)	-----	100.0%	-----	-----	
Palate shape	Parab	Hyperb	Ell	Sm U	Lge U
Anderson (N = 46)	80.4%	8.7%	2.2%	8.7%	-----
Taylor (N = 25)	92.0%	4.0%	4.0%	-----	-----
Stokes (N = 1)	100.0%	-----	-----	-----	-----
Palate ht.	Low	Med	High	V. High	
Anderson (N = 46)	100.0%	-----	-----	-----	
Taylor (N = 25)	12.0%	64.0%	24.0%	-----	
Stokes (N = 1)	-----	100.0%	-----	-----	
Palat. torus	Abs	SmRidg	MedRidg	LgeRidg	SmMd	MedMd	LMd
Anderson (N = 46)	100.0%	-----	-----	-----	-----	-----	-----
Taylor (N = 25)	88.0%	8.0%	-----	-----	4.0%	-----	-----
Stokes (N = 1)	100.0%	-----	-----	-----	-----	-----	-----
Mand. size	Sm	Med	Lge	V. Lge			
Anderson (N = 46)	-----	60.9%	34.8%	4.3%			
Taylor (N = 25)	4.0%	76.0%	16.0%	4.0%			
Stokes (N = 1)	-----	-----	100.0%	-----			

Table 92 - continued

Chin form	Nar Bilat	Wide Bilat	Inter-med	Median	Lge
Anderson (N = 46)	100.0%	-----	-----	-----	-----
Taylor (N = 25)	20.0%	-----	56.0%	24.0%	-----
Stokes (N = 1)	-----	-----	100.0%	-----	-----
Chin proj.	Negat	Neut	Sm	Med	
Anderson (N = 46)	58.7%	26.1%	8.7%	6.5%	
Taylor (N = 25)	36.0%	56.0%	8.0%	-----	
Stokes (N = 1)	-----	100.0%	-----	-----	
Pteryg. attach.	Sm	Med	Pron	V. Pron	
Anderson (N = 46)	100.0%	-----	-----	-----	
Taylor (N = 25)	12.0%	72.0%	16.0%	-----	
Stokes (N = 1)	-----	-----	100.0%	-----	
Gonial ang. evers.	None	Sm	Med	Pron	
Anderson (N = 46)	26.1%	52.2%	13.0%	8.7%	
Taylor (N = 25)	80.0%	8.0%	12.0%	-----	
Stokes (N = 1)	-----	-----	-----	100.0%	

340 PREHISTORIC PEOPLE OF FORT ANCIENT

Table 93

Cranial Observations of the Anderson Focus (Females)

Muscularity	Sm	Med	Lge	V.Lge		
Anderson (U) N = 31	74.2%	25.8%	-----	-----		
Anderson (D) N = 8	75.0%	25.0%	-----	-----		
Taylor (U) N = 5	80.0%	20.0%	-----	-----		
Taylor (D) N = 1	-----	100.0%	-----	-----		
Stokes (U) N = 1	100.0%	-----	-----	-----		

Deformation	None	Occ	Lambd	Fr-occ	Bil-fr-occ	
Anderson (U) N = 31	100.0%	-----	-----	-----	-----	
Anderson (D) N = 8	-----	100.0%	-----	-----	-----	
Taylor (U) N = 5	100.0%	-----	-----	-----	-----	
Taylor (D) N = 1	-----	100.0%	-----	-----	-----	
Stokes (U) N = 1	100.0%	-----	-----	-----	-----	

Degree of deform.	None	Trace	Sm	Med	Pron	
Anderson (U) N = 31	100.0%	-----	-----	-----	-----	
Anderson (D) N = 8	-----	-----	100.0%	-----	-----	
Taylor (U) N = 5	100.0%	-----	-----	-----	-----	
Taylor (D) N = 1	-----	-----	-----	100.0%	-----	
Stokes (U) N = 1	100.0%	-----	-----	-----	-----	

Vault form	Ell	Ov	Spher	Pentag	Rhom	Sphen
Anderson (U) N = 31	6.5%	90.3%	-----	3.2%	-----	-----
Anderson (D) N = 8	-----	100.0%	-----	-----	-----	-----
Taylor (U) N = 5	-----	100.0%	-----	-----	-----	-----
Taylor (D) N = 1	-----	100.0%	-----	-----	-----	-----
Stokes (U) N = 1	-----	100.0%	-----	-----	-----	-----

Table 93 - continued.

	None	Trace	Sm	Med	Lge	V.Lge
Browridge size						
Anderson (U) N = 31	-----	90.3%	9.7%	-----	-----	-----
Anderson (D) N = 8	-----	100.0%	-----	-----	-----	-----
Taylor (U) N = 5	-----	100.0%	-----	-----	-----	-----
Taylor (D) N = 1	-----	100.0%	-----	-----	-----	-----
Stokes (U) N = 1	-----	100.0%	-----	-----	-----	-----

	Flat	Sm	Med	Lge	V.Lge	
Glabella prom.						
Anderson (U) N = 31	-----	100.0%	-----	-----	-----	
Anderson (D) N = 8	-----	100.0%	-----	-----	-----	
Taylor (U) N = 5	-----	100.0%	-----	-----	-----	
Taylor (D) N = 1	-----	100.0%	-----	-----	-----	
Stokes (U) N = 1	-----	100.0%	-----	-----	-----	

	Bulg	None	Sl	Med	Pron	V.Pron
Frontal slope						
Anderson (U) N = 31	51.6%	3.2%	22.6%	22.6%	-----	-----
Anderson (D) N = 8	37.5%	-----	50.0%	12.5%	-----	-----
Taylor (U) N = 5	60.0%	-----	20.0%	20.0%	-----	-----
Taylor (D) N = 1	-----	-----	-----	-----	-----	-----
Stokes (U) N = 1	100.0%	-----	100.0%	-----	-----	-----

	Sm	Med	Lge			
Postorb. constr.						
Anderson (U) N = 31	100.0%	-----	-----			
Anderson (D) N = 8	100.0%	-----	-----			
Taylor (U) N = 5	20.0%	80.0%	-----			
Taylor (D) N = 1	100.0%	-----	-----			
Stokes (U) N = 1	-----	100.0%	-----			

Table 93 - continued

	Sm	Med	Lge	V.Lge
Fron. emin.				
Anderson (U) N = 31	29.0%	51.6%	19.4%	
Anderson (D) N = 8	25.0%	75.0%	-----	
Taylor (U) N = 5	20.0%	80.0%	-----	
Taylor (D) N = 1	100.0%	-----	-----	
Stokes (U) N = 1	-----	-----	100.0%	

	None	Sm	Med	Lge
Fr. median crest				
Anderson (U) N = 31	25.8%	51.6%	12.9%	9.7%
Anderson (D) N = 8	37.5%	62.5%	-----	-----
Taylor (U) N = 5	40.0%	40.0%	20.0%	-----
Taylor (D) N = 1	100.0%	-----	-----	-----
Stokes (U) N = 1	-----	-----	100.0%	-----

	Sm	Med	Lge	
Fron. br.				
Anderson (U) N = 31	83.9%	16.1%	-----	
Anderson (D) N = 8	50.0%	50.0%	-----	
Taylor (U) N = 5	60.0%	40.0%	-----	
Taylor (D) N = 1	-----	-----	-----	
Stokes (U) N = 1	100.0%	-----	100.0%	

	None	Sm	Med	Lge	V.Lge
Sag. elev.					
Anderson (U) N = 31	19.4%	71.0%	9.7%	-----	-----
Anderson (D) N = 8	37.5%	62.5%	-----	-----	-----
Taylor (U) N = 5	20.0%	60.0%	-----	20.0%	-----
Taylor (D) N = 1	100.0%	-----	-----	-----	-----
Stokes (U) N = 1	-----	100.0%	-----	-----	-----

Table 93 - continued

	Sm	Med	Lge	
Pariet. emin.				
Anderson (U) N = 31	64.5%	335.5%	-----	
Anderson (D) N = 8	100.0%	-----	-----	
Taylor (U) N = 5	60.0%	40.0%	-----	
Taylor (D) N = 1	-----	100.0%	-----	
Stokes (U) N = 1	100.0%	-----	-----	

	Flat	Sm	Med	Lge
Temp. fullness				
Anderson (U) N = 31	12.9%	71.0%	12.9%	3.2%
Anderson (D) N = 8	25.0%	37.5%	25.0%	12.5%
Taylor (U) N = 5	40.0%	60.0%	-----	-----
Taylor (D) N = 1	-----	100.0%	-----	-----
Stokes (U) N = 1	100.0%	-----	-----	-----

	Sm	Med	Lge	V.Lge
Mastoids				
Anderson (U) N = 31	87.1%	12.9%	-----	-----
Anderson (D) N = 8	87.5%	12.5%	-----	-----
Taylor (U) N = 5	20.0%	80.0%	-----	-----
Taylor (D) N = 1	100.0%	-----	-----	-----
Stokes (U) N = 1	-----	100.0%	-----	-----

	Sm	Med	Lge	
Supramast. crest				
Anderson (U) N = 31	100.0%	-----	-----	
Anderson (D) N = 8	100.0%	-----	-----	
Taylor (U) N = 5	80.0%	20.0%	-----	
Taylor (D) N = 1	-----	100.0%	-----	
Stokes (U) N = 1	-----	100.0%	-----	

Table 93 - continued

Sphen. depress.	Sm	Med	Lge	
Anderson (U) N = 31	100.0%	-----	-----	
Anderson (D) N = 8	100.0%	-----	-----	
Taylor (U) N = 5	60.0%	-----	40.0%	
Taylor (D) N = 1	100.0%	-----	-----	
Stokes (U) N = 1	100.0%	-----	-----	

Occip. curve	None	Sm	Med	Pron
Anderson (U) N = 31	-----	-----	29.0%	71.0%
Anderson (D) N = 8	-----	12.5%	-----	87.5%
Taylor (U) N = 5	-----	-----	-----	100.0%
Taylor (D) N = 1	-----	100.0%	-----	-----
Stokes (U) N = 1	-----	-----	-----	100.0%

Lambd. flat.	None	Sm	Med	Pron
Anderson (U) N = 31	3.2%	35.5%	38.7%	22.6%
Anderson (D) N = 8	-----	37.5%	62.5%	-----
Taylor (U) N = 5	-----	20.0%	60.0%	20.0%
Taylor (D) N = 1	-----	100.0%	-----	-----
Stokes (U) N = 1	-----	-----	100.0%	-----

Cond. elev.	Sm	Med	Lge	
Anderson (U) N = 31	100.0%	-----	-----	
Anderson (D) N = 8	100.0%	-----	-----	
Taylor (U) N = 5	40.0%	60.0%	-----	
Taylor (D) N = 1	-----	100.0%	-----	
Stokes (U) N = 1	-----	100.0%	-----	

Table 93 - continued

Basion		Low	Med	High	
	Anderson (U) N = 31	100.0%	-----	-----	
	Anderson (D) N = 8	100.0%	-----	-----	
	Taylor (U) N = 5	80.0%	20.0%	-----	
	Taylor (D) N = 1	100.0%	-----	-----	
	Stokes (U) N = 1	-----	100.0%	-----	

Styl. proc.		Sm	Med	Lge	
	Anderson (U) N = 31	90.3%	9.7%	-----	
	Anderson (D) N = 8	87.5%	12.5%	-----	
	Taylor (U) N = 5	100.0%	-----	-----	
	Taylor (D) N = 1	100.0%	-----	-----	
	Stokes (U) N = 1	100.0%	-----	-----	

Glen. fos. depth		Sm	Med	Lge	
	Anderson (U) N = 31	3.2%	80.6%	16.1%	
	Anderson (D) N = 8	25.0%	62.5%	12.5%	
	Taylor (U) N = 5	20.0%	80.0%	-----	
	Taylor (D) N = 1	-----	100.0%	-----	
	Stokes (U) N = 1	-----	100.0%	-----	

Tymp. plate		Thin	Med	Thick	V. Thick
	Anderson (U) N = 31	87.1%	12.9%	-----	-----
	Anderson (D) N = 8	87.5%	12.5%	-----	-----
	Taylor (U) N = 5	80.0%	20.0%	-----	-----
	Taylor (D) N = 1	100.0%	-----	-----	-----
	Stokes (U) N = 1	100.0%	-----	-----	-----

Table 93 - continued

	Obl	Rhom	Sq	Ell	Rou
Orbit shape					
Anderson (U) N = 31	16.1%	32.3%	32.3%	12.9%	6.5%
Anderson (D) N = 8	12.5%	50.0%	25.0%	----	12.5%
Taylor (U) N = 5	----	40.0%	----	40.0%	20.0%
Taylor (D) N = 1	----	100.0%	----	----	----
Stokes (U) N = 1	----	100.0%	----	----	----

	None	Sm	Med	Pron	
Orbit. incl.					
Anderson (U) N = 31	----	80.6%	19.4%	----	
Anderson (D) N = 8	----	50.0%	37.5%	12.5%	
Taylor (U) N = 5	----	80.0%	20.0%	----	
Taylor (D) N = 1	----	100.0%	----	----	
Stokes (U) N = 1	----	100.0%	----	----	

	Ab	Sl	Med	Deep	
Suborb. fossa					
Anderson (U) N = 31	25.8%	64.5%	6.5%	3.2%	
Anderson (D) N = 8	37.5%	37.5%	25.0%	----	
Taylor (U) N = 5	----	60.0%	40.0%	----	
Taylor (D) N = 1	----	----	100.0%	----	
Stokes (U) N = 1	----	100.0%	----	----	

	Sm	Med	Lge	V.Lge	
Zyg. size					
Anderson (U) N = 31	54.8%	41.9%	3.2%	----	
Anderson (D) N = 8	37.5%	62.5%	----	----	
Taylor (U) N = 5	20.0%	80.0%	----	----	
Taylor (D) N = 1	100.0%	----	----	----	
Stokes (U) N = 1	----	100.0%	----	----	

Table 93 - continued

Zyg. lat. prog.

	Sm	Med	Lge
Anderson (U) N = 31	6.5%	25.8%	67.7%
Anderson (D) N = 8	-----	25.0%	75.0%
Taylor (U) N = 5	-----	60.0%	40.0%
Taylor (D) N = 1	-----	-----	100.0%
Stokes (U) N = 1	-----	100.0%	-----

Zyg. ant. proj.

	Sm	Med	Lge
Anderson (U) N = 31	19.4%	71.0%	9.7%
Anderson (D) N = 8	12.5%	75.0%	12.5%
Taylor (U) N = 5	-----	100.0%	-----
Taylor (D) N = 1	-----	-----	100.0%
Stokes (U) N = 1	-----	100.0%	-----

Zyg. proc. thick.

	Sm	Med	Pron
Anderson (U) N = 31	100.0%	-----	-----
Anderson (D) N = 8	100.0%	-----	-----
Taylor (U) N = 5	20.0%	80.0%	-----
Taylor (D) N = 1	-----	100.0%	-----
Stokes (U) N = 1	-----	100.0%	-----

Nas. rt. ht.

	V.Low	Low	Med	High	V.High
Anderson (U) N = 31	3.2%	6.5%	77.4%	9.7%	3.2%
Anderson (D) N = 8	-----	12.5%	75.0%	12.5%	-----
Taylor (U) N = 5	-----	20.0%	60.0%	20.0%	-----
Taylor (D) N = 1	-----	-----	100.0%	-----	-----
Stokes (U) N = 1	-----	-----	-----	100.0%	-----

Table 93 - continued

Nas. rt. br.	V.Sm	Sm	Med	Lge	V.Lge
Anderson (U) N = 31	-----	32.3%	61.3%	6.5%	-----
Anderson (D) N = 8	-----	12.5%	75.0%	12.5%	-----
Taylor (U) N = 5	-----	40.0%	60.0%	-----	-----
Taylor (D) N = 1	-----	-----	100.0%	-----	-----
Stokes (U) N = 1	-----	-----	100.0%	-----	-----

Nas. bridg. ht.	V.Low	Low	Med	High	V.High
Anderson (U) N = 31	-----	9.7%	80.6%	9.7%	-----
Anderson (D) N = 8	-----	25.0%	75.0%	-----	-----
Taylor (U) N = 5	-----	-----	80.0%	20.0%	-----
Taylor (D) N = 1	-----	-----	100.0%	-----	-----
Stokes (U) N = 1	-----	-----	100.0%	-----	-----

Nas. bridg. br.	Sm	Med	Lge		
Anderson (U) N = 31	6.5%	87.1%	6.5%		
Anderson (D) N = 8	12.5%	87.5%	-----		
Taylor (U) N = 5	20.0%	80.0%	-----		
Taylor (D) N = 1	-----	100.0%	-----		
Stokes (U) N = 1	-----	100.0%	-----		

Nas. profile	Conc	Str	Sl.Conc-Conv	Conc-Conv.	V.C-C
Anderson (U) N = 31	3.2%	12.9%	83.9%	-----	-----
Anderson (D) N = 8	-----	12.5%	87.5%	-----	-----
Taylor (U) N = 5	-----	20.0%	-----	80.0%	-----
Taylor (D) N = 1	-----	-----	-----	-----	100.0%
Stokes (U) N = 1	-----	-----	-----	100.0%	-----

Table 93 - continued

Nas. depress.	Abs	Sm	Med	Lge
Anderson (U) N = 31	67.7%	29.0%	3.2%	-----
Anderson (D) N = 8	62.5%	37.5%	-----	-----
Taylor (U) N = 5	40.0%	60.0%	-----	-----
Taylor (D) N = 1	100.0%	-----	-----	-----
Stokes (U) N = 1	100.0%	-----	-----	-----

Nas. sills	Abs	Dull	Med	Sharp
Anderson (U) N = 31	6.5%	12.9%	51.6%	29.0%
Anderson (D) N = 8	-----	-----	62.5%	37.5%
Taylor (U) N = 5	-----	20.0%	40.0%	40.0%
Taylor (D) N = 1	-----	-----	100.0%	-----
Stokes (U) N = 1	-----	-----	100.0%	-----

Nas. spine	Abs	Sm	Med	Rt.Ang	Lge
Anderson (U) N = 31	3.2%	96.8%	-----	-----	-----
Anderson (D) N = 8	-----	100.0%	-----	-----	-----
Taylor (U) N = 5	-----	100.0%	-----	-----	-----
Taylor (D) N = 1	-----	100.0%	-----	-----	-----
Stokes (U) N = 1	-----	100.0%	-----	-----	-----

Subnas. grooves	Abs	Sm	Med	Pron	Sulci
Anderson (U) N = 31	80.6%	12.9%	6.5%	-----	-----
Anderson (D) N = 8	100.0%	-----	-----	-----	-----
Taylor (U) N = 5	80.0%	20.0%	-----	-----	-----
Taylor (D) N = 1	100.0%	-----	-----	-----	-----
Stokes (U) N = 1	100.0%	-----	-----	-----	-----

APPENDIX C

Table 93 - continued

Midfac. progn.	Abs	Sl	Med	Pron	
Anderson (U) N = 31	77.4%	22.6%	----	----	
Anderson (D) N = 8	87.5%	12.5%	----	----	
Taylor (U) N = 5	100.0%	----	----	----	
Taylor (D) N = 1	----	100.0%	----	----	
Stokes (U) N = 1	100.0%	----	----	----	

Alveol. progn.	Abs	Sl	Med	Pron	
Anderson (U) N = 31	----	35.5%	61.3%	3.2%	
Anderson (D) N = 8	25.0%	25.0%	25.0%	25.0%	
Taylor (U) N = 5	20.0%	20.0%	60.0%	----	
Taylor (D) N = 1	----	----	100.0%	----	
Stokes (U) N = 1	----	----	100.0%	----	

Total progn.	Abs	Sl	Med	Pron	
Anderson (U) N = 31	3.2%	58.1%	38.7%	----	
Anderson (D) N = 8	25.0%	25.0%	50.0%	----	
Taylor (U) N = 5	20.0%	40.0%	40.0%	----	
Taylor (D) N = 1	----	----	100.0%	----	
Stokes (U) N = 1	----	----	100.0%	----	

Palate shape	Parab	Hyperb	Ell	Sm U	Lge U
Anderson (U) N = 31	93.5%	6.5%	----	----	----
Anderson (D) N = 8	87.5%	12.5%	----	----	----
Taylor (U) N = 5	60.0%	----	20.0%	20.0%	----
Taylor (D) N = 1	100.0%	----	----	----	----
Stokes (U) N = 1	100.0%	----	----	----	----

Table 93 - continued

Palate ht.

	Low	Med	High	V.High
Anderson (U) N = 31	100.0%	-----	-----	-----
Anderson (D) N = 8	100.0%	-----	-----	-----
Taylor (U) N = 5	20.0%	60.0%	20.0%	-----
Taylor (D) N = 1	-----	-----	100.0%	-----
Stokes (U) N = 1	-----	100.0%	-----	-----

Palat. torus

	Abs	SmRidg	MedRidg	LgeRidg	SmMd	MedMd	LMd
Anderson (U) N = 31	100.0%	-----	-----	-----	-----	-----	-----
Anderson (D) N = 8	100.0%	-----	-----	-----	-----	-----	-----
Taylor (U) N = 5	40.0%	60.0%	-----	-----	-----	-----	-----
Taylor (D) N = 1	-----	100.0%	-----	-----	-----	-----	-----
Stokes (U) N = 1	100.0%	-----	-----	-----	-----	-----	-----

Mand. size

	Sm	Med	Lge	V.Lge
Anderson (U) N = 31	58.1%	41.9%	-----	-----
Anderson (D) N = 8	75.0%	25.0%	-----	-----
Taylor (U) N = 5	80.0%	20.0%	-----	-----
Taylor (D) N = 1	-----	100.0%	-----	-----
Stokes (U) N = 1	-----	100.0%	-----	-----

Chin form

	NarBilat	WideBilat	Intermed	Median
Anderson (U) N = 31	100.0%	-----	-----	-----
Anderson (D) N = 8	100.0%	-----	-----	-----
Taylor (U) N = 5	-----	-----	-----	100.0%
Taylor (D) N = 1	-----	-----	-----	100.0%
Stokes (U) N = 1	100.0%	-----	-----	-----

Table 93 - continued

	Negat	Neut	Sm	Med	Lge
Chin proj.					
Anderson (U) N = 31	64.5%	22.6%	9.7%	3.2%	-----
Anderson (D) N = 8	62.5%	25.0%	12.5%	-----	-----
Taylor (U) N = 5	100.0%	-----	-----	-----	-----
Taylor (D) N = 1	100.0%	-----	-----	-----	-----
Stokes (U) N = 1	-----	100.0%	-----	-----	-----

	Sm	Med	Pron	V.Pron	
Ptergy. attach.					
Anderson (U) N = 31	100.0%	-----	-----	-----	
Anderson (D) N = 8	100.0%	-----	-----	-----	
Taylor (U) N = 5	20.0%	80.0%	-----	-----	
Taylor (D) N = 1	100.0%	-----	-----	-----	
Stokes (U) N = 1	100.0%	-----	-----	-----	

	None	Sm	Med	Pron	
Gonial ang. evers.					
Anderson (U) N = 31	74.2%	22.6%	-----	3.2%	
Anderson (D) N = 8	75.0%	25.0%	-----	-----	
Taylor (U) N = 5	80.0%	20.0%	-----	-----	
Taylor (D) N = 1	100.0%	-----	-----	-----	
Stokes (U) N = 1	100.0%	-----	-----	-----	

APPENDIX C

Table 94

Mean Measurements of Sand Ridge Male Crania*

	Mean**	Standard Dev.
Cranial vault		
Capacity	1471.6cc.	113.91
Cranial module	155.7	4.45
Mean thickness of left parietal	5.6	1.36
Glabello-occipital length	182.5	7.42
Maximum breadth	141.8	4.21
Minimum frontal breadth	91.8	4.70
Basion-bregma height	142.8	6.91
Porion-apex height	119.1	5.26
Basion-porion height	-----	------
Length of cranial base	102.6	6.94
Face		
Total facial height	120.0	0.00
Upper facial height	71.1	0.98
Total facial breadth	142.0	5.09
Midfacial breadth	98.0	2.28
Interior biorbital breadth	97.5	3.72
Subtense to interior biorbital arc	16.3	2.16
Biorbital breadth	100.1	3.48
Anterior interorbital breadth	20.1	0.98
Nasal structure		
Nasal breadth	27.0	2.28
Nasal height	53.0	1.09
Dacryal chord	19.6	4.88
Dacryal subtense to arc	9.8	0.40
Minimum nasal breadth	7.0	0.63
Subtense to nasal arc	3.0	0.00

* N = 6, all undeformed

** means in millimeters (mm.) unless listed otherwise

Table 94 — continued

Orbit		
Left orbital height	33.8	2.31
Left orbital breadth, maxillofrontale	42.1	2.04
Left orbital breadth, dacryon	40.0	1.78
Dental arch and profile		
Maxillo-alveolar breadth	64.1	2.22
Maxillo-alveolar length	54.0	0.00
Facial length, prosthion	95.0	1.67
Facial length, alveolar point	93.1	1.83
Mandible		
Length of mandible	105.0	0.00
Bicondylar breadth	128.0	0.00
Symphysial height	35.0	0.00
Biangular breadth	100.0	4.42
Minimum ramus length	35.8	0.40
Angles		
Facial profile angle	83.0°	1.67
Midfacial profile angle	89.8°	1.60
Alveolar profile angle	64.8°	1.32
Gonial angle	114.1°	1.60

APPENDIX C

Table 95

Mean Indices of Sand Ridge Male Crania*

	Mean	Standard Dev.
Cranial vault		
Cranial	77.80	3.52
Length-height	78.35	4.60
Breadth-height	100.70	3.86
Mean height	88.09	4.02
Length-auricular height	65.37	3.68
Flatness of cranial base	------	------
Transverse fronto-parietal	64.76	3.25
Face		
Total facial	84.59	3.07
Upper facial	50.17	2.19
Midfacial	72.65	2.33
Transverse cranio-facial	100.15	3.49
Zygo-frontal	64.67	2.50
Fronto-mandibular	108.97	3.65
Zygo-mandibular	70.43	2.36
Facial flatness	16.72	1.87
Anterior interorbital	20.15	1.20
Nasal structure		
Nasal	50.89	3.46
Nasal root height	53.69	17.94
Nasal bone height	43.15	3.97
Orbit		
Left orbital, maxillofrontale	80.21	3.30
Left orbital, dacryon	84.53	3.19
Dental arch		
Maxillo-alveolar	118.82	4.13
Mandible		
Mandibular	82.02	0.12

* N = 6 all undeformed

Table 96

Mean Measurements of Sand Ridge Female Crania (Deformed)*

	Mean**	Standard Dev.
Cranial vault		
Capacity	1295.0cc.	49.50
Cranial module	145.3	4.72
Mean thickness of left parietal	4.5	0.71
Glabello-occipital length	162.0	1.41
Maximum breadth	140.5	4.95
Minimum frontal breadth	89.5	7.78
Basion-bregma height	133.5	7.78
Porion-apex height	113.5	6.36
Basion-porion height	-----	----
Length of cranial base	134.0	1.41
Face		
Total facial height	117.0	8.49
Upper facial height	71.5	3.54
Total facial breadth	134.0	1.41
Midfacial breadth	101.0	0.00
Interior biorbital breadth	97.0	4.24
Subtense to interior biorbital arc	14.5	2.12
Biorbital breadth	98.5	2.12
Anterior interorbital breadth	19.0	1.14
Nasal structure		
Nasal breadth	28.0	2.83
Nasal height	50.5	0.71
Dacryal chord	20.0	0.00
Dacryal subtense to arc	10.5	2.12
Minimum nasal breadth	9.0	0.00
Subtense to nasal arc	4.5	0.71
Orbit		
Left orbital height	34.0	0.00
Left orbital breadth, maxillofrontale	41.5	0.71
Left orbital breadth, dacryon	39.0	1.41
Dental arch and profile		
Maxillo-alveolar breadth	68.0	2.83
Maxillo-alveolar length	53.5	3.54
Facial length, prosthion	95.0	4.24
Facial length, alveolar point	97.0	0.00

APPENDIX C

Table 96 - continued

Mandible		
Length of mandible	100.0	0.00
Bicondylar breadth	122.0	0.00
Symphyseal height	34.5	4.95
Biangular breadth	100.5	4.95
Minimum ramus length	31.0	1.41
Angles		
Facial profile angle	82.0°	1.41
Midfacial profile angle	86.5°	2.12
Alveolar profile angle	67.5°	0.71
Gonial angle	124.0°	0.00

*N = 2
**Measurements in millimeters (mm.) unless listed otherwise

PREHISTORIC PEOPLE OF FORT ANCIENT

Table 97

Mean Indices of Sand Ridge Female Crania (Deformed)*

	Mean	Standard Dev.
Cranial vault		
Cranial	86.72	2.30
Length-height	82.39	4.09
Breadth-height	94.98	2.19
Mean height	88.23	3.28
Length-auricular height	70.04	3.32
Flatness of cranial base	------	----
Transverse fronto-parietal	63.64	3.30
Face		
Total facial	87.35	7.25
Upper facial	53.38	3.20
Midfacial	70.80	3.50
Transverse cranio-facial	95.45	4.37
Zygo-frontal	66.82	6.51
Fronto-mandibular	112.48	4.25
Zygo-mandibular	75.02	4.49
Facial flatness	14.92	1.53
Anterior interorbital	19.28	1.02
Nasal structure		
Nasal	55.41	4.82
Nasal root height	52.50	10.61
Nasal bone height	50.00	7.86
Orbit		
Left orbital, maxillofrontale	81.94	1.40
Left orbital, dacryon	87.24	3.16
Dental arch		
Maxillo-alveolar	127.20	3.12
Mandible		
Mandibular	81.97	0.00

*N = 2

APPENDIX C

Table 98

Mean Measurements of Hahn's Field Male Crania (Undeformed)*

Cranial vault	Mean**	Standard Dev.
Capacity	-----	------
Cranial module	152.5	1.50
Mean thickness of left parietal	5.0	1.00
Glabello-occipital length	179.6	0.57
Maximum breadth	140.0	5.00
Minimum frontal breadth	93.6	7.02
Basion-bregma height	138.0	0.00
Porion-apex height	117.0	0.00
Basion-porion height	-----	------
Length of cranial base	96.0	1.73
Face		
Total facial height	124.0	0.00
Upper facial height	78.3	0.57
Total facial breadth	141.0	0.00
Midfacial breadth	104.3	0.57
Interior biorbital breadth	95.6	2.51
Subtense to interior biorbital arc	17.0	1.00
Biorbital breadth	97.0	0.00
Anterior interorbital breadth	18.0	1.73
Nasal structure		
Nasal breadth	26.0	0.00
Nasal height	56.6	1.15
Dacryal chord	21.0	0.00
Dacryal subtense to arc	11.0	0.00
Minimum nasal breadth	7.6	2.51
Subtense to nasal arc	4.0	1.00

* N = 3

** means in millimeters (mm.) unless listed otherwise

Table 98 - continued

Orbit
    Left orbital height   37.0   0.00
    Left orbital breadth, maxillofrontale 45.0   0.00
    Left orbital breadth, dacryon   43.0   0.00

Dental arch and profile
    Maxillo-alveolar breadth   66.3   0.57
    Maxillo-alveolar length   55.6   0.57
    Facial length, prosthion   100.0   0.00
    Facial length, alveolar point   99.0   0.00

Mandible
    Length of mandible   113.0   0.00
    Bicondylar breadth   140.0   0.00
    Symphysial height   36.3   0.57
    Biangular breadth   106.0   0.00
    Minimum ramus length   36.3   4.04

Angles
    Facial profile angle   -----   ------
    Midfacial profile angle   -----   ------
    Alveolar profile angle   -----   ------
    Gonial angle   117.6°   4.04

APPENDIX C

Table 99

Mean Indices of Hahn's Field Male Crania (Undeformed)*

	Mean	Standard Dev.
Cranial vault		
Cranial	77.93	3.00
Length-height	76.81	0.24
Breadth-height	98.65	3.52
Mean height	86.35	1.21
Length-auricular height	65.12	0.20
Flatness of cranial base	------	------
Transverse fronto-parietal	66.89	4.13
Face		
Total facial	87.94	0.00
Upper facial	55.55	0.40
Midfacial	75.08	0.13
Transverse cranio-facial	100.79	3.60
Zygo-frontal	66.43	4.98
Fronto-mandibular	133.59	8.45
Zygo-mandibular	75.18	0.00
Facial flatness	17.79	1.51
Anterior interorbital	18.55	1.78
Nasal structure		
Nasal	45.89	0.92
Nasal root height	52.38	0.00
Nasal bone height	53.33	5.77
Orbit		
Left orbital, maxillofrontale	82.22	0.00
Left orbital, dacryon	86.05	0.00
Dental arch		
Maxillo-alveolar	119.18	2.28
Mandible		
Mandibular	80.71	0.00

* N = 3

Table 100

Mean Measurements of Hahn's Field Male Crania (Deformed)*

	Mean**	Standard Dev.
Cranial vault		
Capacity	-----	------
Cranial module	152.6	0.00
Mean thickness of left parietal	3.6	0.57
Glabello-occipital length	180.0	0.00
Maximum breadth	140.0	0.00
Minimum frontal breadth	92.0	1.73
Basion-bregma height	138.0	0.00
Porion-apex height	118.0	0.00
Basion-porion height	-----	------
Length of cranial base	95.0	0.00
Face		
Total facial height	124.0	0.00
Upper facial height	77.6	0.57
Total facial breadth	143.0	0.00
Midfacial breadth	104.0	0.00
Interior biorbital breadth	96.3	0.57
Subtense to interior biorbital arc	17.0	0.00
Biorbital breadth	97.0	0.00
Anterior interorbital breadth	19.6	0.57
Nasal structure		
Nasal breadth	26.0	0.00
Nasal height	55.3	1.15
Dacryal chord	26.0	0.00
Dacryal subtense to arc	21.3	1.15
Minimum nasal breadth	10.6	1.52
Subtense to nasal arc	8.0	3.46

* N = 3

** means in millimeters (mm.) unless listed otherwise

APPENDIX C

Table 100- continued

Orbit		
Left orbital height	37.0	0.00
Left orbital breadth, maxillofrontale	45.0	0.00
Left orbital breadth, dacryon	43.0	0.00
Dental arch and profile		
Maxillo-alveolar breadth	65.3	1.15
Maxillo-alveolar length	56.6	1.15
Facial length, prosthion	100.0	0.00
Facial length, alveolar point	99.0	0.00
Mandible		
Length of mandible	113.0	0.00
Bicondylar breadth	140.0	0.00
Symphysial height	35.6	0.57
Biangular breadth	106.0	4.00
Minimum ramus length	32.3	2.08
Angles		
Facial profile angle	-----	------
Midfacial profile angle	-----	------
Alveolar profile angle	-----	------
Gonial angle	122.3°	6.80

Table 101

Mean Indices of Hahn's Field Male Crania (Deformed)*

	Mean	Standard Dev.
Cranial vault		
Cranial	77.78	0.00
Length-height	76.67	0.00
Breadth-height	98.57	0.00
Mean height	86.25	0.00
Length-auricular height	65.56	0.00
Flatness of cranial base	------	------
Transverse fronto-parietal	65.71	1.23
Face		
Total facial	86.71	0.00
Upper facial	54.31	0.40
Midfacial	74.68	0.55
Transverse cranio-facial	102.14	0.00
Zygo-frontal	64.33	1.20
Fronto-mandibular	155.24	4.82
Zygo-mandibular	74.12	2.79
Facial flatness	17.65	0.10
Anterior interorbital	20.27	0.59
Nasal structure		
Nasal	47.00	0.99
Nasal root height	50.15	8.00
Nasal bone height	47.22	4.80
Orbit		
Left orbital, maxillofrontale	82.22	0.00
Left orbital, dacryon	86.05	0.00
Dental arch		
Maxillo-alveolar	115.35	4.34
Mandible		
Mandibular	80.71	0.00

* N = 3

APPENDIX C

Table 102

Mean Measurements of Hahn's Field Female Crania (Deformed)*

	Mean**	Standard Dev.
Cranial vault		
Capacity	0.0	0.00
Cranial module	147.3	0.00
Mean thickness of left parietal	7.0	2.83
Glabello-occipital length	167.0	0.00
Maximum breadth	147.0	0.00
Minimum frontal breadth	91.0	0.00
Basion-bregma height	128.0	0.00
Porion-apex height	114.0	0.00
Basion-porion height	-----	----
Length of cranial base	104.0	0.00
Face		
Total facial height	112.0	0.00
Upper facial height	70.0	0.00
Total facial breadth	134.0	0.00
Midfacial breadth	94.0	0.00
Interior biorbital breadth	95.0	0.00
Subtense to interior biorbital arc	18.0	0.00
Biorbital breadth	94.0	0.00
Anterior interorbital breadth	18.0	0.00
Nasal structure		
Nasal breadth	26.0	0.00
Nasal height	50.5	0.71
Dacryal chord	22.0	0.00
Dacryal subtense to arc	11.0	0.00
Minimum nasal breadth	10.0	0.00
Subtense to nasal arc	4.0	0.00
Orbit		
Left orbital height	33.0	0.00
Left orbital breadth, maxillofrontale	43.0	0.00
Left orbital breadth, dacryon	40.0	0.00
Dental arch and profile		
Maxillo-alveolar breadth	64.0	0.00
Maxillo-alveolar length	54.0	0.00
Facial length, prosthion	94.0	0.00
Facial length, alveolar point	92.0	0.00

Table 102 - continued

Mandible
- Length of mandible   105.0   0.00
- Bicondylar breadth   130.0   0.00
- Symphyseal height   30.0   0.00
- Biangular breadth   98.0   0.00
- Minimum ramus length   32.0   0.00

Angles
- Facial profile angle   -----   ----
- Midfacial profile angle -----   ----
- Alveolar profile angle   -----   ----
- Gonial angle   128.0°   0.00

*N = 2
**Measurements in millimeters (mm.) unless listed otherwise

APPENDIX C

Table 103

Mean Indices of Hahn's Field Female Crania (Deformed)*

Cranial vault	Mean	Standard Dev.
Cranial	88.02	0.00
Length-height	76.65	0.00
Breadth-height	78.07	0.00
Mean height	81.53	0.00
Length-auricular height	68.26	0.00
Flatness of cranial base	------	----
Transverse fronto-parietal	61.90	0.00
Face		
Total facial	83.58	0.00
Upper facial	52.24	0.00
Midfacial	74.47	0.00
Transverse cranio-facial	91.16	0.00
Zygo-frontal	67.91	0.00
Fronto-mandibular	107.69	0.00
Zygo-mandibular	73.13	0.00
Facial flatness	18.95	0.00
Anterior interorbital	19.15	0.00
Nasal structure		
Nasal	51.49	0.72
Nasal root height	50.00	0.00
Nasal bone height	40.00	0.00
Orbit		
Left orbital, maxillofrontale	76.74	0.00
Left orbital, dacryon	82.50	0.00
Dental arch		
Maxillo-alveolar	118.52	0.00
Mandible		
Mandibular	80.77	0.00

*N = 2

Table 104

Mean Measurements of Turpin Male Crania (Undeformed)*

	Mean**	Standard Dev.
Cranial vault		
Capacity	1440.0cc.	0.00
Cranial module	152.8	3.51
Mean thickness of left parietal	4.5	0.54
Glabello-occipital length	178.6	4.84
Maximum breadth	139.8	4.87
Minimum frontal breadth	92.6	4.50
Basion-bregma height	140.1	4.79
Porion-apex height	117.0	2.00
Basion-porion height	-----	------
Length of cranial base	104.1	2.71
Face		
Total facial height	125.5	3.98
Upper facial height	74.1	4.49
Total facial breadth	138.0	3.46
Midfacial breadth	100.8	1.83
Interior biorbital breadth	98.0	2.89
Subtense to interior biorbital arc	16.6	1.36
Biorbital breadth	100.0	1.26
Anterior interorbital breadth	19.1	0.98
Nasal structure		
Nasal breadth	25.6	3.01
Nasal height	53.5	2.07
Dacryal chord	21.5	1.51
Dacryal subtense to arc	11.8	0.40
Minimum nasal breadth	8.8	0.98
Subtense to nasal arc	3.8	0.40

* N = 6

** means in millimeters (mm.) unless listed otherwise

APPENDIX C

Table 104 - continued

Orbit		
Left orbital height	34.0	1.26
Left orbital breadth, maxillofrontale	43.8	0.98
Left orbital breadth, dacryon	40.5	0.83
Dental arch and profile		
Maxillo-alveolar breadth	67.1	4.40
Maxillo-alveolar length	55.5	3.20
Facial length, prosthion	99.1	2.85
Facial length, alveolar point	97.8	2.85
Mandible		
Length of mandible	108.8	4.07
Bicondylar breadth	124.0	5.93
Symphysial height	36.5	2.73
Biangular breadth	101.3	6.65
Minimum ramus length	33.3	2.50
Angles		
Facial profile angle	$80.8°$	1.60
Midfacial profile angle	$85.6°$	1.63
Alveolar profile angle	$67.0°$	2.28
Gonial angle	$123.1°$	7.88

Table 105

Mean Indices of Turpin Male Crania (Undeformed)*

	Mean	Standard Dev.
Cranial vault		
Cranial	78.30	3.34
Length-height	78.45	1.83
Breadth-height	100.32	4.68
Mean height	88.02	2.47
Length-auricular height	65.50	1.21
Flatness of cranial base	------	------
Transverse fronto-parietal	66.38	4.86
Face		
Total facial	90.97	3.24
Upper facial	53.74	3.02
Midfacial	73.55	4.36
Transverse cranio-facial	98.76	3.59
Zygo-frontal	67.15	3.03
Fronto-mandibular	109.41	6.32
Zygo-mandibular	73.44	4.83
Facial flatness	17.00	1.33
Anterior interorbital	19.16	1.01
Nasal structure		
Nasal	48.02	5.74
Nasal root height	55.20	3.30
Nasal bone height	43.43	1.79
Orbit		
Left orbital, maxillofrontale	77.58	2.86
Left orbital, dacryon	83.98	3.55
Dental arch		
Maxillo-alveolar	120.98	2.04
Mandible		
Mandibular	71.32	35.05

*N = 6

APPENDIX C

Table 106

Mean Measurements of Turpin Male Crania (Deformed)*

	Mean**	Standard Dev.
Cranial vault		
Capacity	1440.0cc.	25.29
Cranial module	154.3	1.86
Mean thickness of left parietal	5.1	0.40
Glabello-occipital length	174.6	3.01
Maximum breadth	150.5	2.81
Minimum frontal breadth	97.8	3.81
Basion-bregma height	137.8	2.78
Porion-apex height	119.0	1.26
Basion-porion height	-----	------
Length of cranial base	103.3	0.81
Face		
Total facial height	122.1	2.04
Upper facial height	73.0	0.00
Total facial breadth	143.1	0.98
Midfacial breadth	102.0	0.00
Interior biorbital breadth	100.5	1.37
Subtense to interior biorbital arc	16.3	1.50
Biorbital breadth	101.0	0.00
Anterior interorbital breadth	19.8	0.98
Nasal structure		
Nasal breadth	27.3	0.51
Nasal height	52.5	1.22
Dacryal chord	21.5	0.83
Dacryal subtense to arc	11.5	1.22
Minimum nasal breadth	9.1	0.75
Subtense to nasal arc	4.1	0.40

* N = 6

** means in millimeters (mm.) unless listed otherwise

Table 106--continued

Orbit
- Left orbital height .... 33.5 .... 1.22
- Left orbital breadth, maxillofrontale .... 43.8 .... 0.98
- Left orbital breadth, dacryon .... 41.1 .... 0.40

Dental arch and profile
- Maxillo-alveolar breadth .... 66.0 .... 0.00
- Maxillo-alveolar length .... 55.1 .... 0.40
- Facial length, prosthion .... 100.5 .... 3.67
- Facial length, alveolar point .... 99.5 .... 3.67

Mandible
- Length of mandible .... 105.5 .... 1.22
- Bicondylar breadth .... 130.1 .... 0.40
- Symphysial height .... 37.0 .... 3.46
- Biangular breadth .... 102.6 .... 3.66
- Minimum ramus length .... 34.8 .... 1.72

Angles
- Facial profile angle .... 81.1° 0.40
- Midfacial profile angle .... 86.3° 0.81
- Alveolar profile angle .... 67.1° 0.40
- Gonial angle .... 121.1° 2.04

APPENDIX C

Table 107

Mean Indices of Turpin Male Crania (Deformed)*

	Mean	Standard Dev.
Cranial vault		
Cranial	86.19	2.56
Length-height	78.93	2.13
Breadth-height	91.58	0.98
Mean height	84.77	1.26
Length-auricular height	68.14	1.37
Flatness of cranial base	------	------
Transverse fronto-parietal	65.01	2.63
Face		
Total facial	85.32	1.19
Upper facial	50.99	0.35
Midfacial	71.56	0.11
Transverse cranio-facial	95.14	1.12
Zygo-frontal	68.33	2.58
Fronto-mandibular	105.00	3.76
Zygo-mandibular	71.71	2.65
Facial flatness	16.25	1.57
Anterior interorbital	19.63	0.97
Nasal structure		
Nasal	52.09	2.05
Nasal root height	53.50	5.65
Nasal bone height	45.55	3.85
Orbit		
Left orbital, maxillofrontale	76.40	1.44
Left orbital, dacryon	81.37	2.93
Dental arch		
Maxillo-alveolar	119.64	0.87
Mandible		
Mandibular	81.04	0.69

* N = 6

Table 108

Mean Measurements of Turpin Female Crania (Undeformed)*

	Mean**	Standard Dev.
Cranial vault		
Capacity	1323.4 cc.	70.42
Cranial moduel	147.9	3.66
Mean thickness of left parietal	4.7	0.90
Glabello-occipital length	173.5	6.89
Maximum breadth	136.7	6.05
Minimum frontal breadth	91.1	3.45
Basion-bregma height	133.6	3.04
Porion-apex height	114.2	2.44
Basion-porion height	-----	----
Length of cranial base	99.1	1.81
Face		
Total facial height	112.6	5.41
Upper facial height	69.9	3.83
Total facial breadth	129.8	3.49
Midfacial breadth	94.6	2.91
Interior biorbital breadth	93.1	1.70
Subtense to interior biorbital arc	16.0	1.26
Biorbital breadth	96.9	2.12
Anterior interorbital breadth	18.9	0.83
Nasal structure		
Nasal breadth	25.9	1.04
Nasal height	49.6	2.25
Dacryal chord	21.1	1.04
Dacryal subtense to arc	11.0	0.45
Minimum nasal breadth	8.9	0.54
Subtense to nasal arc	3.9	0.30
Orbit		
Left orbital height	32.4	1.29
Left orbital breadth, maxillofrontale	41.7	1.01
Left orbital breadth, dacryon	38.8	1.17
Dental arch and profile		
Maxillo-alveolar breadth	64.1	1.76
Maxillo-alveolar length	54.4	1.21
Facial length, prosthion	94.1	0.94
Facial length, alveolar point	92.3	1.27

Table 108 - continued

Mandible		
Length of mandible	104.0	5.27
Bicondylar breadth	122.4	5.18
Symphyseal height	34.4	2.38
Biangular breadth	97.4	3.80
Minimum ramus length	32.4	1.75
Angles		
Facial profile angle	82.2°	0.98
Midfacial profile angle	86.8°	2.09
Alveolar profile angle	70.6°	3.01
Gonial angle	127.6°	5.13

*N = 11
**Measurements in millimeters (mm.) unless listed otherwise

Table 109

Mean Indices of Turpin Female Crania (Undeformed)*

Measurement	Mean	Standard Dev.
Cranial vault		
Cranial	78.93	4.48
Length-height	77.13	2.97
Breadth-height	97.89	4.25
Mean height	86.22	2.57
Length-auricular height	65.89	2.01
Flatness of cranial base	------	----
Transverse fronto-parietal	66.70	3.00
Face		
Total facial	86.80	4.31
Upper facial	53.89	3.18
Midfacial	74.00	5.81
Transverse cranio-facial	95.04	3.21
Zygo-frontal	70.17	2.12
Fronto-mandibular	107.15	6.46
Zygo-mandibular	75.11	3.28
Facial flatness	17.17	1.18
Anterior interorbital	19.53	1.09
Nasal structure		
Nasal	52.36	2.62
Nasal root height	52.25	3.01
Nasal bone height	43.91	3.09
Orbit		
Left orbital, maxillofrontale	77.80	3.20
Left orbital, dacryon	83.65	3.50
Dental arch		
Maxillo-alveolar	117.73	3.34
Mandible		
Mandibular	85.15	5.92

*N = 11

APPENDIX C

Table 110

Mean Measurements of Turpin Female Crania (Deformed)*

Cranial vault	Mean**	Standard Dev.
Capacity	1333.0 cc.	0.00
Cranial module	149.1	0.84
Mean thickness of left parietal	5.0	0.00
Glabello-occipital length	164.0	3.61
Maximum breadth	146.0	1.00
Minimum frontal breadth	97.0	1.00
Basion-bregma height	137.3	4.51
Porion-apex height	118.0	3.61
Basion-porion height	-----	----
Length of cranial base	98.3	2.08
Face		
Total facial height	113.7	4.73
Upper facial height	70.3	3.51
Total facial breadth	133.0	1.00
Midfacial breadth	92.7	1.53
Interior biorbital breadth	96.3	1.53
Subtense to interior biorbital arc	17.0	2.65
Biorbital breadth	98.3	1.53
Anterior interorbital breadth	20.7	1.53
Nasal structure		
Nasal breadth	25.3	1.15
Nasal height	50.7	0.58
Dacryal chord	21.0	1.00
Dacryal subtense to arc	11.0	0.00
Minimum nasal breadth	9.0	0.00
Subtense to nasal arc	4.0	0.00
Orbit		
Left orbital height	33.3	0.58
Left orbital breadth, maxillofrontale	41.7	2.08
Left orbital breadth, dacryon	39.7	1.15
Dental arch and profile		
Maxillo-alveolar breadth	62.7	4.16
Maxillo-alveolar length	53.3	2.08
Facial length, prosthion	93.0	1.00
Facial length, alveolar point	91.3	1.15

Table 110 - continued

Mandible		
Length of mandible	101.7	1.53
Bicondylar breadth	122.7	4.04
Symphyseal height	33.7	3.06
Biangular breadth	96.0	1.73
Minimum ramus length	32.0	1.00
Angles		
Facial profile angle	85.0°	3.00
Midfacial profile angle	91.0°	4.58
Alveolar profile angle	69.0°	1.00
Gonial angle	125.7°	1.53

*N = 3
**Measurements in millimeters (mm.) unless listed otherwise

APPENDIX C

Table 111

Mean Indices of Turpin Female Crania (Deformed)*

	Mean	Standard Dev.
Cranial vault		
Cranial	89.05	2.20
Length-height	83.79	4.13
Breadth-height	94.08	3.50
Mean height	88.63	3.76
Length-auricular height	72.00	3.59
Flatness of cranial base	------	----
Transverse fronto-parietal	66.44	0.61
Face		
Total facial	85.88	4.18
Upper facial	52.90	3.04
Midfacial	75.89	3.46
Transverse cranio-facial	91.10	0.65
Zygo-frontal	72.93	1.12
Fronto-mandibular	98.97	1.03
Zygo-mandibular	72.18	1.40
Facial flatness	17.62	2.45
Anterior interorbital	21.03	1.81
Nasal structure		
Nasal	49.99	1.72
Nasal root height	52.46	2.50
Nasal bone height	44.44	0.00
Orbit		
Left orbital, maxillofrontale	80.16	5.01
Left orbital, dacryon	84.10	3.38
Dental arch		
Maxillo-alveolar	117.42	3.28
Mandible		
Mandibular	82.96	3.83

*N = 3

Table 112

Mean Measurements of Campbell Island Male Crania (Undeformed)*

	Mean**	Standard Dev.
Cranial vault		
Capacity	1392.0cc.	44.23
Cranial module	154.3	2.54
Mean thickness of left parietal	4.7	0.83
Glabello-occipital length	179.1	7.56
Maximum breadth	142.5	3.13
Minimum frontal breadth	93.0	1.87
Basion-bregma height	141.1	2.86
Porion-apex height	116.3	2.50
Basion-porion height	-----	------
Length of cranial base	104.0	1.58
Face		
Total facial height	123.0	1.41
Upper facial height	74.5	1.94
Total facial breadth	143.7	2.38
Midfacial breadth	103.1	4.08
Interior biorbital breadth	99.1	0.83
Subtense to interior biorbital arc	18.7	0.83
Biorbital breadth	100.3	1.67
Anterior interorbital breadth	19.7	1.30
Nasal structure		
Nasal breadth	27.5	1.14
Nasal height	54.5	1.51
Dacryal chord	23.0	1.73
Dacryal subtense to arc	10.7	0.44
Minimum nasal breadth	8.5	0.89
Subtense to nasal arc	4.0	0.00

* N = 5

** means in millimeters (mm.) unless listed otherwise

Table 112- continued

Orbit		
Left orbital height	34.1	1.78
Left orbital breadth, maxillofrontale	43.1	1.09
Left orbital breadth, dacryon	40.7	1.30
Dental arch and profile		
Maxillo-alveolar breadth	69.0	2.12
Maxillo-alveolar length	54.0	1.87
Facial length, prosthion	97.1	1.92
Facial length, alveolar point	95.3	2.30
Mandible		
Length of mandible	107.1	6.37
Bicondylar breadth	126.0	1.87
Symphysial height	36.0	2.00
Biangular breadth	105.1	2.94
Minimum ramus length	36.5	1.67
Angles		
Facial profile angle	84.3°	1.51
Midfacial profile angle	88.3°	3.36
Alveolar profile angle	72.5°	6.02
Gonial angle	118.3°	3.04

Table 113

Mean Indices of Campbell Island Male Crania (Undeformed)*

	Mean	Standard Dev.
Cranial vault		
Cranial	79.73	4.94
Length-height	78.87	2.58
Breadth-height	99.07	3.56
Mean height	87.76	1.44
Length-auricular height	65.08	4.04
Flatness of cranial base	------	------
Transverse fronto-parietal	65.25	2.26
Face		
Total facial	85.54	1.16
Upper facial	51.87	0.78
Midfacial	72.42	4.52
Transverse cranio-facial	100.88	3.09
Zygo-frontal	64.68	1.33
Fronto-mandibular	113.16	4.15
Zygo-mandibular	73.15	1.55
Facial flatness	18.95	0.90
Anterior interorbital	19.71	1.17
Nasal structure		
Nasal	50.57	2.47
Nasal root height	47.06	1.85
Nasal bone height	46.88	4.54
Orbit		
Left orbital, maxillofrontale	79.15	3.29
Left orbital, dacryon	83.89	5.35
Dental arch		
Maxillo-alveolar	127.91	6.23
Mandible		
Mandibular	85.13	6.08

* N = 5

APPENDIX C

Table 114

Mean Measurements of Campbell Island Male Crania (Deformed)*

	Mean**	Standard Dev.
Cranial vault		
Capacity	1230.0cc.	0.00
Cranial module	146.3	0.00
Mean thickness of left parietal	6.0	0.00
Glabello-occipital length	168.0	0.00
Maximum breadth	135.0	0.00
Minimum frontal breadth	90.0	0.00
Basion-bregma height	136.0	0.00
Porion-apex height	111.0	0.00
Basion-porion height	-----	------
Length of cranial base	100.0	0.00
Face		
Total facial height	115.0	0.00
Upper facial height	71.0	0.00
Total facial breadth	140.0	0.00
Midfacial breadth	96.0	0.00
Interior biorbital breadth	96.0	0.00
Subtense to interior biorbital arc	16.0	0.00
Biorbital breadth	97.0	0.00
Anterior interorbital breadth	26.0	0.00
Nasal structure		
Nasal breadth	29.0	0.00
Nasal height	52.0	0.00
Dacryal chord	27.0	0.00
Dacryal subtense to arc	12.0	0.00
Minimum nasal breadth	10.0	0.00
Subtense to nasal arc	4.0	0.00

* N = 1

** means in millimeters (mm.) unless listed otherwise

Table 114- continued

Orbit
    Left orbital height   33.0   0.00
    Left orbital breadth, maxillofrontale   38.0   0.00
    Left orbital breadth, dacryon   35.0   0.00

Dental arch and profile
    Maxillo-alveolar breadth   69.0   0.00
    Maxillo-alveolar length   52.0   0.00
    Facial length, prosthion   95.0   0.00
    Facial length, alveolar point   93.0   0.00

Mandible
    Length of mandible   107.0   0.00
    Bicondylar breadth   130.0   0.00
    Symphysial height   34.0   0.00
    Biangular breadth   104.0   0.00
    Minimum ramus length   40.0   0.00

Angles
    Facial profile angle   82.0°   0.00
    Midfacial profile angle   87.0°   0.00
    Alveolar profile angle   68.0°   0.00
    Gonial angle   118.0°   0.00

APPENDIX C

Table 115

Mean Indices of Campbell Island Male Crania (Deformed)*

	Mean	Standard Dev.
Cranial vault		
Cranial	80.36	0.00
Length-height	80.95	0.00
Breadth-height	100.74	0.00
Mean height	89.77	0.00
Length-auricular height	66.07	0.00
Flatness of cranial base	------	------
Transverse fronto-parietal	66.67	0.00
Face		
Total facial	82.14	0.00
Upper facial	50.71	0.00
Midfacial	73.96	0.00
Transverse cranio-facial	103.70	0.00
Zygo-frontal	64.29	0.00
Fronto-mandibular	115.56	0.00
Zygo-mandibular	74.29	0.00
Facial flatness	16.67	0.00
Anterior interorbital	26.80	0.00
Nasal structure		
Nasal	55.77	0.00
Nasal root height	44.44	0.00
Nasal bone height	40.00	0.00
Orbit		
Left orbital, maxillofrontale	86.84	0.00
Left orbital, dacryon	94.29	0.00
Dental arch		
Maxillo-alveolar	132.69	0.00
Mandible		
Mandibular	82.31	0.00

* N = 1

Table 116

Mean Measurements of Campbell Island Female Crania (Undeformed)*

	Mean**	Standard Dev.
Cranial vault		
Capacity	1270.0cc.	0.00
Cranial module	143.0	0.00
Mean thickness of left parietal	5.0	0.00
Glabello-occipital length	158.0	0.00
Maximum breadth	139.0	0.00
Minimum frontal breadth	87.0	0.00
Basion-bregma height	132.0	0.00
Porion-apex height	114.0	0.00
Basion-porion height	-----	----
Length of cranial base	90.0	0.00
Face		
Total facial height	110.0	0.00
Upper facial height	66.0	0.00
Total facial breadth	127.0	0.00
Midfacial breadth	98.0	0.00
Interior biorbital breadth	93.0	0.00
Subtense to interior biorbital arc	12.0	0.00
Biorbital breadth	94.0	0.00
Anterior interorbital breadth	17.0	0.00
Nasal structure		
Nasal breadth	25.0	0.00
Nasal height	49.0	0.00
Dacryal chord	18.0	0.00
Dacryal subtense to arc	8.0	0.00
Minimum nasal breadth	8.0	0.00
Subtense to nasal arc	3.0	0.00
Orbit		
Left orbital height	33.0	0.00
Left orbital breadth, maxillofrontale	40.0	0.00
Left orbital breadth, dacryon	39.0	0.00
Dental arch and profile		
Maxillo-alveolar breadth	64.0	0.00
Maxillo-alveolar length	54.0	0.00
Facial length, prosthion	88.0	0.00
Facial length, alveolar point	87.0	0.00

APPENDIX C

Table 116 - continued

Mandible		
Length of mandible	93.0	0.00
Bicondylar breadth	119.0	0.00
Symphyseal height	33.0	0.00
Biangular breadth	92.0	0.00
Minimum ramus length	33.0	0.00
Angles		
Facial profile angle	82.0°	0.00
Midfacial profile angle	87.0°	0.00
Alveolar profile angle	66.0°	0.00
Gonial angle	116.0°	0.00

*N = 1
**Measurements in millimeters (mm.) unless listed otherwise

Table 117

Mean Indices of Campbell Island Female Crania (Deformed)*

	Mean	Standard Dev.
Cranial vault		
Cranial	87.97	0.00
Length-height	83.54	0.00
Breadth-height	94.96	0.00
Mean height	88.89	0.00
Length-auricular height	72.15	0.00
Flatness of cranial base	------	----
Transverse fronto-parietal	62.59	0.00
Face		
Total facial	86.61	0.00
Upper facial	51.97	0.00
Midfacial	67.35	0.00
Transverse cranio-facial	91.37	0.00
Zygo-frontal	68.50	0.00
Fronto-mandibular	105.75	0.00
Zygo-mandibular	72.44	0.00
Facial flatness	12.90	0.00
Anterior interorbital	18.09	0.00
Nasal structure		
Nasal	51.02	0.00
Nasal root height	44.44	0.00
Nasal bone height	37.50	0.00
Orbit		
Left orbital, maxillofrontale	82.50	0.00
Left orbital, dacryon	84.62	0.00
Dental arch		
Maxillo-alveolar	118.52	0.00
Mandible		
Mandibular	78.15	0.00

*N = 1

APPENDIX C

Table 118

Mean Measurements of Madisonville Male Crania (Undeformed)*

	Mean**	Standard Dev.
Cranial vault		
Capacity	1438.1cc.	67.80
Cranial module	153.1	3.96
Mean thickness of left parietal	5.0	0.99
Glabello-occipital length	180.2	9.16
Maximum breadth	143.0	5.31
Minimum frontal breadth	95.3	4.76
Basion-bregma height	136.0	4.41
Porion-apex height	116.7	3.38
Basion-porion height	-----	------
Length of cranial base	104.3	4.80
Face		
Total facial height	122.9	7.70
Upper facial height	72.7	3.05
Total facial breadth	141.2	3.44
Midfacial breadth	102.7	3.44
Interior biorbital breadth	100.2	3.05
Subtense to interior biorbital arc	17.5	2.27
Biorbital breadth	101.3	2.21
Anterior interorbital breadth	20.5	1.87
Nasal structure		
Nasal breadth	27.1	1.47
Nasal height	52.8	2.28
Dacryal chord	22.3	1.82
Dacryal subtense to arc	11.6	1.09
Minimum nasal breadth	9.7	1.51
Subtense to nasal arc	3.9	0.80

* N = 60

** means in millimeters (mm.) unless listed otherwise

Table 118- continued

Orbit
    Left orbital height   34.0   1.72
    Left orbital breadth, maxillofrontale   43.6   1.12
    Left orbital breadth, dacryon   40.8   1.17

Dental arch and profile
    Maxillo-alveolar breadth   63.8   5.24
    Maxillo-alveolar length   55.2   1.93
    Facial length, prosthion   99.4   2.72
    Facial length, alveolar point   98.1   2.67

Mandible
    Length of mandible   104.6   3.01
    Bicondylar breadth   129.7   2.84
    Symphysial height   35.9   2.35
    Biangular breadth   105.2   3.89
    Minimum ramus length   35.6   2.32

Angles
    Facial profile angle   84.4°   2.36
    Midfacial profile angle   88.6°   2.63
    Alveolar profile angle   71.2°   4.23
    Gonial angle   119.4°   5.03

APPENDIX C

Table 119

Mean Indices of Madisonville Male Crania (Undeformed)*

Cranial vault	Mean	Standard Dev.
Cranial	77.95	9.02
Length-height	74.05	9.36
Breadth-height	95.25	4.85
Mean height	84.27	3.93
Length-auricular height	64.94	4.25
Flatness of cranial base	------	------
Transverse fronto-parietal	66.68	3.52
Face		
Total facial	85.39	8.82
Upper facial	51.51	2.17
Midfacial	70.87	3.54
Transverse cranio-facial	98.82	3.75
Zygo-frontal	67.51	3.31
Fronto-mandibular	110.67	6.67
Zygo-mandibular	74.55	2.86
Facial flatness	17.49	2.04
Anterior interorbital	20.26	1.62
Nasal structure		
Nasal	51.50	3.51
Nasal root height	52.69	6.53
Nasal bone height	41.16	8.14
Orbit		
Left orbital, maxillofrontale	77.96	3.93
Left orbital, dacryon	83.26	4.50
Dental arch		
Maxillo-alveolar	115.48	9.32
Mandible		
Mandibular	80.72	3.03

* N = 60

Table 120

Mean Measurements of Madisonville Male Crania (Deformed)*

	Mean**	Standard Dev.
Cranial vault		
Capacity	1445.0cc.	72.07
Cranial module	153.6	2.47
Mean thickness of left parietal	5.2	0.69
Glabello-occipital length	174.0	3.82
Maximum breadth	150.0	4.02
Minimum frontal breadth	95.2	3.11
Basion-bregma height	136.8	3.30
Porion-apex height	117.8	3.01
Basion-porion height	-----	------
Length of cranial base	103.1	2.22
Face		
Total facial height	122.3	3.22
Upper facial height	72.8	2.29
Total facial breadth	143.0	2.46
Midfacial breadth	101.9	2.48
Interior biorbital breadth	99.4	2.71
Subtense to interior biorbital arc	17.3	5.79
Biorbital breadth	101.2	1.88
Anterior interorbital breadth	20.0	1.19
Nasal structure		
Nasal breadth	26.9	1.30
Nasal height	52.8	1.87
Dacryal chord	21.7	1.18
Dacryal subtense to arc	12.0	0.88
Minimum nasal breadth	9.8	1.57
Subtense to nasal arc	4.1	0.77

* N = 115

** means in millimeters (mm.) unless listed otherwise

APPENDIX C

Table 120 - continued

Orbit		
Left orbital height	33.9	0.96
Left orbital breadth, maxillofrontale	43.8	1.06
Left orbital breadth, dacryon	41.0	1.00
Dental arch and profile		
Maxillo-alveolar breadth	65.1	2.92
Maxillo-alveolar length	54.8	1.67
Facial length, prosthion	99.0	1.99
Facial length, alveolar point	97.9	1.98
Mandible		
Length of mandible	104.4	3.96
Bicondylar breadth	129.9	3.79
Symphysial height	35.6	2.23
Biangular breadth	104.9	4.03
Minimum ramus length	35.0	2.40
Angles		
Facial profile angle	85.1°	1.75
Midfacial profile angle	89.2°	2.01
Alveolar profile angle	72.1°	4.08
Gonial angle	119.9°	4.96

Table 121

Mean Indices of Madisonville Male Crania (Deformed)*

Cranial vault	Mean	Standard Dev.
Cranial	86.22	2.82
Length-height	78.67	2.36
Breadth-height	91.28	2.96
Mean height	84.48	2.24
Length-auricular height	67.73	1.91
Flatness of cranial base	------	------
Transverse fronto-parietal	63.49	2.20
Face		
Total facial	85.58	2.33
Upper facial	50.93	1.44
Midfacial	71.50	2.48
Transverse cranio-facial	95.37	2.69
Zygo-frontal	66.59	2.27
Fronto-mandibular	110.37	5.37
Zygo-mandibular	73.43	2.97
Facial flatness	17.43	5.53
Anterior interorbital	19.82	1.12
Nasal structure		
Nasal	50.95	3.10
Nasal root height	55.46	4.42
Nasal bone height	42.69	8.09
Orbit		
Left orbital, maxillofrontale	77.33	2.60
Left orbital, dacryon	82.67	2.87
Dental arch		
Maxillo-alveolar	118.93	5.83
Mandible		
Mandibular	80.45	3.68

* N = 115

APPENDIX C

Table 122

Mean Measurements of Madisonville Female Crania (Undeformed)*

	Mean**	Standard Dev.
Cranial vault		
Capacity	1326.2cc.	61.76
Cranial module	139.4	22.08
Mean thickness of left parietal	5.1	0.86
Glabello-occipital length	173.1	4.99
Maximum breadth	138.9	4.73
Minimum frontal breadth	91.7	3.56
Basion-bregma height	132.1	6.58
Porion-apex height	113.0	3.94
Basion-porion height	-----	----
Length of cranial base	100.1	2.81
Face		
Total facial height	111.9	2.24
Upper facial height	68.2	2.38
Total facial breadth	130.0	3.65
Midfacial breadth	98.0	2.64
Interior biorbital breadth	95.2	2.60
Subtense to interior biorbital arc	16.3	1.47
Biorbital breadth	97.5	2.04
Anterior interorbital breadth	19.3	1.65
Nasal structure		
Nasal breadth	26.3	1.28
Nasal height	49.8	1.77
Dacryal chord	20.9	1.64
Dacryal subtense to arc	11.0	1.13
Minimum nasal breadth	8.8	1.75
Subtense to nasal arc	3.6	0.81
Orbit		
Left orbital height	33.1	1.27
Left orbital breadth, maxillofrontale	42.2	1.38
Left orbital breadth, dacryon	39.2	1.08
Dental arch and profile		
Maxillo-alveolar breadth	63.6	2.43
Maxillo-alveolar length	53.4	2.01
Facial length, prosthion	97.1	2.47
Facial length, alveolar point	96.0	2.33

Table 122 - continued

Mandible
    Length of mandible   101.5   2.72
    Bicondylar breadth   125.0   2.72
    Symphyseal height   32.8   1.53
    Biangular breadth   97.7   2.99
    Minimum ramus length   33.3   1.62

Angles
    Facial profile angle $82.5°$ 1.48
    Midfacial profile angle $87.8°$ 2.09
    Alveolar profile angle $69.1°$ 2.99
    Gonial angle $123.3°$ 3.26

*N = 55
**Measurements in millimeters (mm.) unless listed otherwise

APPENDIX C

Table 123

Mean Indices of Madisonville Female Crania (Undeformed)*

	Mean	Standard Dev.
Cranial vault		
Cranial	76.18	10.42
Length-height	75.10	4.56
Breadth-height	94.81	5.43
Mean height	82.33	6.77
Length-auricular height	57.01	20.23
Flatness of cranial base	------	----
Transverse fronto-parietal	58.86	17.73
Face		
Total facial	76.40	23.65
Upper facial	52.64	2.47
Midfacial	67.27	7.10
Transverse cranio-facial	86.08	18.59
Zygo-frontal	72.16	4.87
Fronto-mandibular	103.10	9.36
Zygo-mandibular	67.03	19.79
Facial flatness	26.58	23.04
Anterior interorbital	23.74	9.90
Nasal structure		
Nasal	56.02	13.75
Nasal root height	56.38	11.19
Nasal bone height	48.44	19.23
Orbit		
Left orbital, maxillofrontale	79.05	3.98
Left orbital, dacryon	82.22	6.64
Dental arch		
Maxillo-alveolar	101.79	42.59
Mandible		
Mandibular	78.44	7.01

*N = 55

Table 124

Mean Measurements of Madisonville Female Crania (Deformed)*

	Mean**	Standard Dev.
Cranial vault		
Capacity	1335.8cc.	56.20
Cranial module	148.9	2.60
Mean thickness of left parietal	5.1	0.81
Glabello-occipital length	167.8	3.82
Maximum breadth	145.9	4.26
Minimum frontal breadth	91.8	7.93
Basion-bregma height	133.0	2.99
Porion-apex height	114.1	2.29
Basion-porion height	-----	----
Length of cranial base	104.1	64.18
Face		
Total facial height	112.8	12.75
Upper facial height	68.2	5.19
Total facial breadth	135.8	21.80
Midfacial breadth	102.1	56.28
Interior biorbital breadth	99.2	41.05
Subtense to interior biorbital arc	16.0	1.50
Biorbital breadth	102.4	56.85
Anterior interorbital breadth	19.3	2.21
Nasal structure		
Nasal breadth	25.9	3.11
Nasal height	49.4	4.60
Dacryal chord	21.0	1.17
Dacryal subtense to arc	10.9	0.74
Minimum nasal breadth	9.1	1.11
Subtense to nasal arc	3.9	0.57
Orbit		
Left orbital height	33.2	1.64
Left orbital breadth, maxillofrontale	42.0	1.15
Left orbital breadth, dacryon	39.2	1.13
Dental arch and profile		
Maxillo-alveolar breadth	63.8	1.86
Maxillo-alveolar length	53.6	1.79
Facial length, prosthion	97.1	1.37
Facial length, alveolar point	96.0	1.39

APPENDIX C

Table 124 - continued

Mandible
    Length of mandible   101.5   2.74
    Bicondylar breadth   128.4   3.60
    Symphyseal height   32.8   1.88
    Biangular breadth   98.1   3.24
    Minimum ramus length   32.8   2.15

Angles
    Facial profile angle   82.0°   1.08
    Midfacial profile angle   87.0°   1.38
    Alveolar profile angle   68.6°   2.04
    Gonial angle   124.5°   4.10

*N = 161
**Measurements in millimeters (mm.) unless listed otherwise

Table 125

Mean Indices of Madisonville Female Crania (Deformed)*

Cranial vault	Mean	Standard Dev.
Cranial	86.03	6.78
Length-height	79.24	2.16
Breadth-height	91.53	3.02
Mean height	84.91	1.92
Length-auricular height	67.92	1.79
Flatness of cranial base	------	----
Transverse fronto-parietal	63.13	5.61
Face		
Total facial	83.30	2.64
Upper facial	50.85	4.20
Midfacial	69.82	6.07
Transverse cranio-facial	93.14	15.07
Zygo-frontal	68.18	6.91
Fronto-mandibular	111.26	62.75
Zygo-mandibular	72.84	4.50
Facial flatness	16.66	1.87
Anterior interorbital	19.47	1.69
Nasal structure		
Nasal	52.03	6.48
Nasal root height	51.97	4.07
Nasal bone height	42.49	5.83
Orbit		
Left orbital, maxillofrontale	78.46	4.82
Left orbital, dacryon	84.25	4.06
Dental arch		
Maxillo-alveolar	119.17	4.44
Mandible		
Mandibular	81.63	2.68

*N = 161

Table 126

Mean Measurements of Fox Farm Male Crania (Undeformed)*

	Mean**	Standard Dev.
Cranial vault		
Capacity	1447.1cc.	138.16
Cranial module	153.1	3.52
Mean thickness of left parietal	5.5	1.13
Glabello-occipital length	176.5	6.34
Maximum breadth	142.4	8.14
Minimum frontal breadth	95.8	4.37
Basion-bregma height	140.0	7.41
Porion-apex height	115.4	4.03
Basion-porion height	-----	------
Length of cranial base	101.4	3.59
Face		
Total facial height	124.2	4.99
Upper facial height	75.8	4.45
Total facial breadth	138.5	5.79
Midfacial breadth	101.7	4.23
Interior biorbital breadth	99.1	3.89
Subtense to interior biorbital arc	17.2	1.25
Biorbital breadth	101.0	2.30
Anterior interorbital breadth	20.0	1.52
Nasal structure		
Nasal breadth	26.5	1.71
Nasal height	52.5	3.30
Dacryal chord	22.5	1.51
Dacryal subtense to arc	9.7	1.27
Minimum nasal breadth	8.7	1.49
Subtense to nasal arc	3.2	0.95

* N = 7

** means in millimeters (mm.) unless listed otherwise

Table 126 - continued

Orbit
    Left orbital height   33.7   1.49
    Left orbital breadth, maxillofrontale   43.2   1.11
    Left orbital breadth, dacryon   40.4   1.13

Dental arch and profile
    Maxillo-alveolar breadth   66.8   3.38
    Maxillo-alveolar length   53.7   0.75
    Facial length, prosthion   95.1   3.28
    Facial length, alveolar point   93.8   3.67

Mandible
    Length of mandible   104.2   5.15
    Bicondylar breadth   128.7   2.92
    Symphysial height   35.8   1.34
    Biangular breadth   105.2   8.82
    Minimum ramus length   33.2   2.87

Angles
    Facial profile angle   84.7°   2.05
    Midfacial profile angle   89.0°   2.88
    Alveolar profile angle   73.4°   2.99
    Gonial angle   119.8°   7.49

APPENDIX C

Table 127

Mean Indices of Fox Farm Male Crania (Undeformed)*

	Mean	Standard Dev.
Cranial vault		
Cranial	80.74	5.30
Length-height	79.30	3.56
Breadth-height	98.59	8.11
Mean height	87.82	4.77
Length-auricular height	65.44	3.40
Flatness of cranial base	------	------
Transverse fronto-parietal	67.41	3.53
Face		
Total facial	89.76	3.90
Upper facial	54.79	3.43
Midfacial	74.62	4.20
Transverse cranio-facial	97.46	5.09
Zygo-frontal	69.18	1.63
Fronto-mandibular	109.82	7.94
Zygo-mandibular	75.91	4.53
Facial flatness	17.45	1.35
Anterior interorbital	19.79	1.30
Nasal structure		
Nasal	50.68	4.37
Nasal root height	42.30	4.15
Nasal bone height	37.70	8.51
Orbit		
Left orbital, maxillofrontale	77.88	2.59
Left orbital, dacryon	83.43	4.17
Dental arch		
Maxillo-alveolar	124.44	5.37
Mandible		
Mandibular	81.00	3.01

* N = 7

Table 128

Mean Measurements of Fox Farm Male Crania (Deformed)*

Measurement	Mean**	Standard Dev.
Cranial vault		
Capacity	1512.2cc.	35.55
Cranial module	154.0	3.11
Mean thickness of left parietal	5.3	0.79
Glabello-occipital length	166.9	7.99
Maximum breadth	156.1	5.14
Minimum frontal breadth	96.0	4.59
Basion-bregma height	139.0	4.71
Porion-apex height	119.0	2.71
Basion-porion height	-----	-----
Length of cranial base	99.6	4.49
Face		
Total facial height	123.4	3.48
Upper facial height	76.2	2.32
Total facial breadth	140.9	3.57
Midfacial breadth	103.0	2.56
Interior biorbital breadth	99.9	3.56
Subtense to interior biorbital arc	17.0	1.91
Biorbital breadth	101.4	2.26
Anterior interorbital breadth	19.9	1.42
Nasal structure		
Nasal breadth	26.7	1.67
Nasal height	53.7	2.01
Dacryal chord	22.7	1.28
Dacryal subtense to arc	10.0	0.70
Minimum nasal breadth	8.7	2.14
Subtense to nasal arc	3.9	0.78

* N = 31

** means in millimeters (mm.) unless listed otherwise

APPENDIX C

Table 128- continued

Orbit		
Left orbital height	34.2	1.29
Left orbital breadth, maxillofrontale	43.9	1.18
Left orbital breadth, dacryon	40.9	1.30
Dental arch and profile		
Maxillo-alveolar breadth	67.9	2.50
Maxillo-alveolar length	54.2	2.17
Facial length, prosthion	96.3	2.67
Facial length, alveolar point	95.1	2.49
Mandible		
Length of mandible	104.0	4.55
Bicondylar breadth	130.7	5.55
Symphysial height	36.6	2.54
Biangular breadth	105.0	5.55
Minimum ramus length	34.6	2.16
Angles		
Facial profile angle	$84.5°$	2.60
Midfacial profile angle	$88.0°$	3.09
Alveolar profile angle	$73.5°$	4.06
Gonial angle	$117.7°$	7.18

Table 129

Mean Indices of the Fox Farm Crania (Deformed)*

	Mean	Standard Dev.
Cranial vault		
Cranial	77.72	32.17
Length-height	93.39	3.95
Breadth-height	89.11	4.72
Mean height	86.05	3.03
Length-auricular height	71.49	3.64
Flatness of cranial base	------	------
Transverse fronto-parietal	61.53	3.34
Face		
Total facial	87.63	3.11
Upper facial	54.17	2.15
Midfacial	74.09	2.30
Transverse cranio-facial	90.29	3.36
Zygo-frontal	68.17	3.17
Fronto-mandibular	109.64	7.92
Zygo-mandibular	74.57	3.59
Facial flatness	17.08	1.83
Anterior interorbital	19.67	1.30
Nasal structure		
Nasal	49.84	3.85
Nasal root height	44.12	3.33
Nasal bone height	41.76	10.22
Orbit		
Left orbital, maxillofrontale	78.08	3.19
Left orbital, dacryon	83.88	3.53
Dental arch		
Maxillo-alveolar	125.39	4.94
Mandible		
Mandibular	79.73	4.81

* N = 31

APPENDIX C

Table 130

Mean Measurements of Fox Farm Female Crania (Undeformed)*

	Mean**	Standard Dev.
Cranial vault		
Capacity	1380.0cc.	0.00
Cranial module	150.0	0.00
Mean thickness of left parietal	6.0	0.00
Glabello-occipital length	171.0	0.00
Maximum breadth	145.0	0.00
Minimum frontal breadth	97.0	0.00
Basion-bregma height	134.0	0.00
Porion-apex height	109.0	0.00
Basion-porion height	-----	----
Length of cranial base	102.0	0.00
Face		
Total facial height	116.0	0.00
Upper facial height	73.0	0.00
Total facial breadth	140.0	0.00
Midfacial breadth	104.0	0.00
Interior biorbital breadth	102.0	0.00
Subtense to interior biorbital arc	18.0	0.00
Biorbital breadth	103.0	0.00
Anterior interorbital breadth	19.0	0.00
Nasal structure		
Nasal breadth	28.0	0.00
Nasal height	52.0	0.00
Dacryal chord	25.0	0.00
Dacryal subtense to arc	11.0	0.00
Minimum nasal breadth	9.0	0.00
Subtense to nasal arc	2.0	0.00
Orbit		
Left orbital height	36.0	0.00
Left orbital breadth, maxillofrontale	45.0	0.00
Left orbital breadth, dacryon	40.0	0.00
Dental arch and profile		
Maxillo-alveolar breadth	64.0	0.00
Maxillo-alveolar length	56.0	0.00
Facial length, prosthion	98.0	0.00
Facial length, alveolar point	96.0	0.00

Table 130 - continued

Mandible
- Length of mandible — 100.0 — 0.00
- Bicondylar breadth — 135.0 — 0.00
- Symphyseal height — 33.0 — 0.00
- Biangular breadth — 99.0 — 0.00
- Minimum ramus length — 38.0 — 0.00

Angles
- Facial profile angle — 80.0° — 0.00
- Midfacial profile angle — 85.0° — 0.00
- Alveolar profile angle — 63.0° — 0.00
- Gonial angle — 113.0° — 0.00

*N = 1
**Measurements in millimeters (mm.) unless listed otherwise

APPENDIX C

Table 131

Mean Indices of Fox Farm Female Crania (Undeformed)*

	Mean	Standard Dev.
Cranial vault		
Cranial	84.80	0.00
Length-height	78.36	0.00
Breadth-height	92.41	0.00
Mean height	84.81	0.00
Length-auricular height	63.74	0.00
Flatness of cranial base	------	----
Transverse fronto-parietal	66.90	0.00
Face		
Total facial	82.86	0.00
Upper facial	54.14	0.00
Midfacial	70.19	0.00
Transverse cranio-facial	96.55	0.00
Zygo-frontal	69.29	0.00
Fronto-mandibular	102.06	0.00
Zygo-mandibular	70.71	0.00
Facial flatness	17.65	0.00
Anterior interorbital	18.45	0.00
Nasal structure		
Nasal	53.85	0.00
Nasal root height	44.00	0.00
Nasal bone height	22.22	0.00
Orbit		
Left orbital, maxillofrontale	80.00	0.00
Left orbital, dacryon	90.00	0.00
Dental arch		
Maxillo-alveolar	114.29	0.00
Mandible		
Mandibular	74.07	0.00

*N = 1

Table 132

Mean Measurements of Fox Farm Female Crania (Deformed)*

Cranial vault	Mean**	Standard Dev.
Capacity	1354.2cc.	33.96
Cranial module	146.0	2.11
Mean thickness of left parietal	5.5	0.93
Glabello-occipital length	157.4	6.14
Maximum breadth	149.9	6.61
Minimum frontal breadth	93.0	4.01
Basion-bregma height	130.8	2.57
Porion-apex height	113.8	3.18
Basion-porion height	-----	----
Length of cranial base	96.9	2.78
Face		
Total facial height	111.7	4.12
Upper facial height	70.3	3.79
Total facial breadth	132.0	2.92
Midfacial breadth	98.2	3.20
Interior biorbital breadth	96.4	2.57
Subtense to interior biorbital arc	16.8	1.61
Biorbital breadth	97.5	2.13
Anterior interorbital breadth	19.8	2.03
Nasal structure		
Nasal breadth	25.9	1.69
Nasal height	49.9	2.54
Dacryal chord	21.5	1.96
Dacryal subtense to arc	10.6	1.44
Minimum nasal breadth	10.0	1.41
Subtense to nasal arc	3.3	0.55
Orbit		
Left orbital height	33.2	1.42
Left orbital breadth, maxillofrontale	41.8	1.09
Left orbital breadth, dacryon	39.2	1.10
Dental arch and profile		
Maxillo-alveolar breadth	64.8	1.18
Maxillo-alveolar length	52.9	2.23
Facial length, prosthion	96.0	2.51
Facial length, alveolar point	95.0	2.68

Table 132 - continued

Mandible		
Length of mandible	100.0	4.10
Bicondylar breadth	124.0	3.42
Symphyseal height	33.2	2.83
Biangular breadth	97.2	2.99
Minimum ramus length	32.6	2.26
Angles		
Facial profile angle	81.9°	2.66
Midfacial profile angle	86.2°	2.83
Alveolar profile angle	69.2°	3.60
Gonial angle	122.0°	4.05

*N = 24
**Measurements in millimeters (mm.) unless listed otherwise

Table 133

Mean Indices of Fox Farm Female Crania (Deformed)*

	Mean	Standard Dev.
Cranial vault		
Cranial	94.27	36.72
Length-height	83.25	3.64
Breadth-height	87.43	4.24
Mean height	85.18	2.32
Length-auricular height	72.43	3.94
Flatness of cranial base	------	----
Transverse fronto-parietal	62.16	3.53
Face		
Total facial	84.66	3.32
Upper facial	53.28	3.10
Midfacial	71.66	4.14
Transverse cranio-facial	88.19	3.88
Zygo-frontal	70.54	3.90
Fronto-mandibular	104.64	5.96
Zygo-mandibular	73.63	2.28
Facial flatness	17.42	1.57
Anterior interorbital	20.25	2.06
Nasal structure		
Nasal	52.17	5.18
Nasal root height	49.81	8.60
Nasal bone height	33.52	7.40
Orbit		
Left orbital, maxillofrontale	79.52	3.80
Left orbital, dacryon	84.86	4.07
Dental arch		
Maxillo-alveolar	122.72	5.02
Mandible		
Mandibular	80.71	3.61

*N = 24

APPENDIX C   413

Table 134

Cranial Observations of the Madisonville Focus (Males)

Muscularity	Sm	Med	Lge	V.Lge
M'ville (U) N = 60	3.3%	36.7%	60.0%	----
M'ville (D) N = 115	3.5%	51.3%	45.2%	----
Sand Ridge (All undeformed) (N = 6)	16.7%	66.7%	16.7%	----
Turpin (U) N = 6	----	100.0%	----	----
Turpin (D) N = 6	----	83.3%	16.7%	----
Hahn's Field (U) N = 3	----	66.7%	33.3%	----
Hahn's Field (D) N = 3	----	66.7%	33.3%	----
Campbell Is (U) N = 5	----	40.0%	60.0%	----
Campbell Is (D) N = 1	----	100.0%	----	----
Fox Farm (U) N = 7	----	57.1%	42.9%	----
Fox Farm (D) N = 31	----	58.1%	41.9%	----

Deformation	None	Occ	Lambd	Fr-occ	Bil-fr-occ	Earth Press
M'ville (U) N = 60	100.0%	----	----	----	----	----
M'ville (D) N = 115	----	81.7%	5.2%	1.7%	----	11.3%
Sand Ridge N = 6	100.0%	----	----	----	----	----
Turpin (U) N = 6	100.0%	----	----	----	----	----
Turpin (D) N = 6	----	83.3%	----	----	----	16.7%
Hahn's Field (U) N = 3	100.0%	----	----	----	----	----
Hahn's Field (D) N = 3	66.7%	33.3%	----	----	----	----
Campbell Is (U) N = 5	100.0%	----	----	----	----	----
Campbell Is (D) N = 1	----	----	----	----	----	100.0%
Fox Farm (U) N = 7	100.0%	----	----	----	----	----
Fox Farm (D) N = 31	3.2%	38.7%	----	----	58.1%	----

Table 134- continued

Degree of deform.	None	Trace	Sm	Med	Pron
M'ville (U) N = 60	100.0%	----	----	----	----
M'ville (D) N = 115	1.7%	13.0%	50.4%	20.9%	13.9%
Sand Ridge N = 6	100.0%	----	----	----	----
Turpin (U) N = 6	100.0%	----	----	----	----
Turpin (D) N = 6	16.7%	16.7%	33.3%	16.7%	16.7%
Hahn's Field (U) N = 3	100.0%	----	----	----	----
Hahn's Field (D) N = 3	66.7%	----	----	33.3%	----
Campbell Is (U) N = 5	100.0%	----	----	----	----
Campbell Is (D) N = 1	----	100.0%	----	----	----
Fox Farm (U) N = 7	100.0%	----	----	----	----
Fox Farm (D) N = 31	3.2%	----	12.9%	48.4%	35.5%

Vault form	Ell	Ov	Spher	Pentag	Rhom	Sphen
M'ville (U) N = 60	18.3%	71.7%	----	6.7%	----	3.3%
M'ville (D) N = 115	0.9%	94.8%	0.9%	0.9%	----	2.6%
Sand Ridge N = 6	16.7%	83.3%	----	----	----	----
Turpin (U) N = 6	16.7%	66.7%	----	16.7%	----	----
Turpin (D) N = 6	16.7%	66.7%	----	----	----	16.7%
Hahn's Field (U) N = 3	----	100.0%	----	----	----	----
Hahn's Field (D) N = 3	----	100.0%	----	----	----	----
Campbell Is (U) N = 5	----	60.0%	20.0%	20.0%	----	----
Campbell Is (D) N = 1	----	100.0%	----	----	----	----
Fox Farm (U) N = 7	----	57.1%	----	14.3%	----	28.6%
Fox Farm (D) N = 31	----	93.5%	----	----	----	6.4%

Table 134 - continued

Brow ridge size	None	Trace	Sm	Med	Lge	V. Lge
M'ville (U) N = 60	----	6.7%	18.3%	40.0%	26.7%	8.3%
M'ville (D) N = 115	----	3.5%	17.4%	56.5%	20.9%	1.7%
Sand Ridge N = 6	----	----	50.0%	33.3%	16.7%	----
Turpin (U) N = 6	----	16.7%	50.0%	16.7%	16.7%	----
Turpin (D) N = 6	----	----	33.3%	50.0%	----	16.7%
Hahn's Field (U) N = 3	----	----	----	----	66.7%	----
Hahn's Field (D) N = 3	----	----	33.3%	----	66.7%	33.3%
Campbell Is (U) N = 5	----	----	60.0%	40.0%	----	----
Campbell Is (D) N = 1	----	----	100.0%	----	----	----
Fox Farm (U) N = 7	----	----	28.6%	42.9%	28.6%	----
Fox Farm (D) N = 31	----	6.5%	45.2%	35.5%	3.2%	9.7%

Glabella prom.	Flat	Sm	Med	Lge	V. Lge	
M'ville (U) N = 60	----	41.7%	38.3%	15.0%	5.0%	
M'ville (D) N = 115	----	25.2%	64.3%	9.6%	0.9%	
Sand Ridge N = 6	----	100.0%	----	----	----	
Turpin (U) N = 6	----	83.3%	16.7%	----	----	
Turpin (D) N = 6	----	50.0%	33.3%	16.7%	----	
Hahn's Field (U) N = 3	----	33.3%	----	66.7%	----	
Hahn's Field (D) N = 3	----	33.3%	33.3%	----	33.3%	
Campbell Is (U) N = 5	----	60.0%	40.0%	----	----	
Campbell Is (D) N = 1	----	100.0%	----	----	----	
Fox Farm (U) N = 7	----	57.1%	28.6%	14.3%	----	
Fox Farm (D) N = 31	----	51.6%	35.5%	6.5%	6.5%	

Table 134 - continued

Fron. emin.	Sm	Med	Lge
M'ville (U) N = 60	78.3%	20.0%	1.7%
M'ville (D) N = 115	83.5%	13.9%	2.6%
Sand Ridge N = 6	100.0%	-----	-----
Turpin (U) N = 6	83.3%	16.7%	-----
Turpin (D) N = 6	66.7%	33.3%	-----
Hahn's Field (U) N = 3	100.0%	-----	-----
Hahn's Field (D) N = 3	100.0%	-----	-----
Campbell Is (U) N = 5	80.0%	20.0%	-----
Campbell Is (D) N = 1	100.0%	-----	-----
Fox Farm (U) N = 7	85.7%	14.3%	-----
Fox Farm (D) N = 31	96.8%	3.2%	-----

Fr. median crest	None	Sm	Med	Lge
M'ville (U) N = 60	16.7%	36.7%	33.3%	13.3%
M'ville (D) N = 115	65.2%	19.1%	12.2%	3.5%
Sand Ridge N = 6	16.7%	83.3%	-----	-----
Turpin (U) N = 6	66.7%	33.3%	-----	-----
Turpin (D) N = 6	83.3%	16.7%	-----	-----
Hahn's Field (U) N = 3	66.7%	-----	-----	33.3%
Hahn's Field (D) N = 3	66.7%	-----	33.3%	-----
Campbell Is (U) N = 5	80.0%	20.0%	-----	-----
Campbell Is (D) N = 1	-----	-----	-----	100.0%
Fox Farm (U) N = 7	57.1%	42.9%	-----	-----
Fox Farm (D) N = 31	93.5%	3.2%	3.2%	-----

Table 134- continued

Fron. br.

	Sm	Med	Lge
M'ville (U) N = 60	20.0%	66.7%	13.3%
M'ville (D) N = 115	5.2%	65.2%	29.6%
Sand Ridge N = 6	66.7%	33.3%	-----
Turpin (U) N = 6	66.7%	-----	33.3%
Turpin (D) N = 6	-----	33.3%	66.7%
Hahn's Field (U) N = 3	66.7%	33.3%	-----
Hahn's Field (D) N = 3	-----	100.0%	-----
Campbell Is (U) N = 5	40.0%	60.0%	-----
Campbell Is (D) N = 1	100.0%	-----	-----
Fox Farm (U) N = 7	42.9%	28.6%	28.6%
Fox Farm (D) N = 31	3.2%	12.9%	83.9%

Sag. elev.

	None	Sm	Med	Lge	V.Lge
M'ville (U) N = 60	25.0%	50.0%	11.7%	11.7%	1.7%
M'ville (D) N = 115	23.5%	66.1%	9.6%	-----	0.9%
Sand Ridge N = 6	50.0%	50.0%	-----	-----	-----
Turpin (U) N = 6	33.3%	66.7%	-----	-----	-----
Turpin (D) N = 6	83.3%	16.7%	-----	-----	-----
Hahn's Field (U) N = 3	33.3%	33.3%	33.3%	-----	-----
Hahn's Field (D) N = 3	100.0%	-----	-----	-----	-----
Campbell Is (U) N = 5	20.0%	80.0%	-----	-----	-----
Campbell Is (D) N = 1	-----	-----	100.0%	-----	-----
Fox Farm (U) N = 7	57.1%	42.9%	-----	-----	-----
Fox Farm (D) N = 31	74.2%	25.8%	-----	-----	-----

Table 134- continued

Pariet. emin.	Sm	Med	Lge
M'ville (U) N = 60	26.7%	70.0%	3.3%
M'ville (D) N = 115	3.5%	67.8%	28.7%
Sand Ridge N = 6	-----	100.0%	-----
Turpin (U) N = 6	-----	50.0%	50.0%
Turpin (D) N = 6	-----	100.0%	-----
Hahn's Field (U) N = 3	66.7%	33.3%	-----
Hahn's Field (D) N = 3	100.0%	-----	-----
Campbell Is (U) N = 5	40.0%	60.0%	-----
Campbell Is (D) N = 1	-----	100.0%	-----
Fox Farm (U) N = 7	28.6%	57.1%	14.3%
Fox Farm (D) N = 31	-----	12.9%	87.1%

Temp. fullness	Flat	Sm	Med	Lge
M'ville (U) N = 60	16.7%	50.0%	16.7%	16.7%
M'ville (D) N = 115	2.6%	11.3%	31.3%	54.8%
Sand Ridge N = 6	16.7%	83.3%	-----	-----
Turpin (U) N = 6	-----	16.7%	66.7%	16.7%
Turpin (D) N = 6	-----	-----	16.7%	83.3%
Hahn's Field (U) N = 3	-----	-----	100.0%	-----
Hahn's Field (D) N = 3	-----	33.3%	66.7%	-----
Campbell Is (U) N = 5	-----	80.0%	20.0%	-----
Campbell Is (D) N = 1	100.0%	-----	-----	-----
Fox Farm (U) N = 7	14.3%	28.6%	42.9%	14.3%
Fox Farm (D) N = 31	-----	25.8%	54.8%	19.4%

Table 134 - continued

Mastoids	Sm	Med	Lge	V. Lge
M'ville (U) N = 60	8.3%	61.7%	30.0%	-----
M'ville (D) N = 115	12.2%	75.7%	12.2%	-----
Sand Ridge N = 6	-----	50.0%	50.0%	-----
Turpin (U) N = 6	-----	50.0%	50.0%	-----
Turpin (D) N = 6	-----	50.0%	50.0%	-----
Hahn's Field (U) N = 3	-----	100.0%	-----	-----
Hahn's Field (D) N = 3	-----	66.7%	33.3%	-----
Campbell Is (U) N = 5	40.0%	40.0%	20.0%	-----
Campbell Is (D) N = 1	100.0%	-----	-----	-----
Fox Farm (U) N = 7	28.6%	42.9%	28.6%	-----
Fox Farm (D) N = 31	3.2%	67.7%	29.0%	-----

Supramast. crest	Sm	Med	Lge
M'ville (U) N = 60	25.0%	53.3%	21.7%
M'ville (D) N = 115	18.3%	68.7%	13.0%
Sand Ridge N = 6	16.7%	66.7%	16.7%
Turpin (U) N = 6	16.7%	50.0%	33.3%
Turpin (D) N = 6	33.3%	50.0%	16.7%
Hahn's Field (U) N = 3	-----	-----	100.0%
Hahn's Field (D) N = 3	-----	33.3%	66.7%
Campbell Is (U) N = 5	20.0%	40.0%	40.0%
Campbell Is (D) N = 1	-----	100.0%	-----
Fox Farm (U) N = 7	14.3%	14.3%	71.4%
Fox Farm (D) N = 31	12.9%	41.9%	45.2%

Table 134- continued

Sphen. depress.	Sm	Med	Lge	
M'ville (U) N = 60	28.3%	58.3%	13.3%	
M'ville (D) N = 115	24.3%	66.1%	9.6%	
Sand Ridge N = 6	100.0%	-----	-----	
Turpin (U) N = 6	100.0%	-----	-----	
Turpin (D) N = 6	50.0%	33.3%	16.7%	
Hahn's Field (U) N = 3	-----	-----	100.0%	
Hahn's Field (D) N = 3	-----	-----	100.0%	
Campbell Is (U) N = 5	100.0%	-----	-----	
Campbell Is (D) N = 1	-----	100.0%	-----	
Fox Farm (U) N = 7	57.1%	28.6%	14.3%	
Fox Farm (D) N = 31	83.9%	12.9%	3.2%	

Occip. curve	None	Sm	Med	Pron
M'ville (U) N = 60	-----	10.0%	65.0%	25.0%
M'ville (D) N = 115	7.0%	25.2%	66.1%	1.7%
Sand Ridge N = 6	-----	-----	83.3%	16.7%
Turpin (U) N = 6	-----	16.7%	66.7%	16.7%
Turpin (D) N = 6	-----	100.0%	-----	-----
Hahn's Field (U) N = 3	-----	-----	33.3%	66.7%
Hahn's Field (D) N = 3	-----	-----	66.7%	33.3%
Campbell Is (U) N = 5	-----	40.0%	20.0%	40.0%
Campbell Is (D) N = 3	-----	100.0%	-----	-----
Fox Farm (U) N = 7	-----	14.3%	71.4%	14.3%
Fox Farm (D) N = 31	58.1%	35.5%	6.5%	-----

APPENDIX C

Table 134- continued

Lambd. flat.	None	Sm	Med	Pron
M'ville (U) N = 60	3.3%	31.7%	40.0%	25.0%
M'ville (D) N = 115	6.1%	12.2%	77.4%	4.3%
Sand Ridge N = 6	-----	66.7%	33.3%	-----
Turpin (U) N = 6	33.3%	33.3%	33.3%	-----
Turpin (D) N = 6	50.0%	16.7%	33.3%	-----
Hahn's Field (U) N = 3	-----	-----	100.0%	-----
Hahn's Field (D) N = 3	33.3%	-----	66.7%	-----
Campbell Is (U) N = 5	-----	60.0%	20.0%	20.0%
Campbell Is (D) N = 1	-----	100.0%	-----	-----
Fox Farm (U) N = 7	-----	85.7%	14.3%	-----
Fox Farm (D) N = 31	41.9%	54.8%	3.2%	-----

Cond. elev.	Sm	Med	Lge
M'ville (U) N = 60	3.3%	71.7%	25.0%
M'ville (D) N = 115	4.3%	80.9%	14.8%
Sand Ridge N = 6	16.7%	16.7%	66.7%
Turpin (U) N = 6	-----	50.0%	50.0%
Turpin (D) N = 6	-----	83.3%	16.7%
Hahn's Field (U) N = 3	-----	-----	100.0%
Hahn's Field (D) N = 3	-----	-----	100.0%
Campbell Is (U) N = 5	-----	60.0%	40.0%
Campbell Is (D) N = 1	-----	100.0%	-----
Fox Farm (U) N = 7	14.3%	57.1%	28.6%
Fox Farm (D) N = 31	12.9%	61.3%	25.8%

Table 134- continued

Basion	Low	Med	High
M'ville (U) N = 60	13.3%	73.3%	13.3%
M'ville (D) N = 115	4.3%	81.7%	13.9%
Sand Ridge N = 6	33.3%	16.7%	50.0%
Turpin (U) N = 6	-----	66.7%	33.3%
Turpin (D) N = 6	-----	100.0%	-----
Hahn's Field (U) N = 3	-----	100.0%	-----
Hahn's Field (D) N = 3	-----	100.0%	-----
Campbell Is (U) N = 5	-----	60.0%	40.0%
Campbell Is (D) N = 1	-----	100.0%	-----
Fox Farm (U) N = 7	28.6%	57.1%	14.3%
Fox Farm (D) N = 31	9.7%	80.6%	9.7%

Styl. proc.	Sm	Med	Lge
M'ville (U) N = 60	65.0%	28.3%	6.7%
M'ville (D) N = 115	67.0%	29.6%	3.5%
Sand Ridge N = 6	50.0%	50.0%	-----
Turpin (U) N = 6	50.0%	50.0%	-----
Turpin (D) N = 6	50.0%	50.0%	-----
Hahn's Field (U) N = 3	33.3%	-----	16.7%
Hahn's Field (D) N = 3	66.7%	-----	33.3%
Campbell Is (U) N = 5	100.0%	-----	-----
Campbell Is (D) N = 1	20.0%	60.0%	20.0%
Fox Farm (U) N = 7	100.0%	-----	-----
Fox Farm (D) N = 31	42.9%	57.1%	-----
	32.3%	48.4%	19.4%

APPENDIX C 423

Table 134- continued

Glen. fos. depth	Sm	Med	Lge
M'ville (U) N = 60	6.7%	78.3%	15.0%
M'ville (D) N = 115	6.1%	80.0%	13.9%
Sand Ridge N = 6	-----	50.0%	50.0%
Turpin (U) N = 6	16.7%	50.0%	33.3%
Turpin (D) N = 6	-----	50.0%	50.0%
Hahn's Field (U) N = 3	33.3%	66.7%	-----
Hahn's Field (D) N = 3	33.3%	66.7%	-----
Campbell Is (U) N = 5	20.0%	60.0%	20.0%
Campbell Is (D) N = 1	100.0%	-----	-----
Fox Farm (U) N = 7	-----	57.1%	42.9%
Fox Farm (D) N = 31	3.2%	71.0%	25.8%

Tymp. plate	Thin	Med	Thick	V. Thick
M'ville (U) N = 60	70.0%	28.3%	1.7%	-----
M'ville (D) N = 115	79.1%	18.3%	2.6%	-----
Sand Ridge N = 6	83.3%	16.7%	-----	-----
Turpin (U) N = 6	100.0%	-----	-----	-----
Turpin (D) N = 6	100.0%	-----	-----	-----
Hahn's Field (U) N = 3	100.0%	-----	-----	-----
Hahn's Field (D) N = 3	100.0%	-----	-----	-----
Campbell Is (U) N = 5	100.0%	-----	-----	-----
Campbell Is (D) N = 1	100.0%	-----	-----	-----
Fox Farm (U) N = 7	100.0%	-----	-----	-----
Fox Farm (D) N = 31	80.6%	19.4%	-----	-----

Table 134- continued

Orbit shape	Obl	Rhom	Sq	Ell	Rou
M'ville (U) N = 60	41.7%	30.0%	11.7%	15.0%	1.7%
M'ville (D) N = 115	48.7%	24.3%	7.0%	19.1%	0.9%
Sand Ridge N = 6	16.7%	66.7%	16.7%	-----	-----
Turpin (U) N = 6	-----	16.7%	66.7%	16.7%	-----
Turpin (D) N = 6	16.7%	16.7%	50.0%	16.7%	-----
Hahn's Field (U) N = 3	100.0%	-----	-----	-----	-----
Hahn's Field (D) N = 3	66.7%	-----	33.3%	-----	-----
Campbell Is (U) N = 5	60.0%	20.0%	-----	20.0%	-----
Campbell Is (D) N = 1	-----	-----	100.0%	-----	-----
Fox Farm (U) N = 7	57.1%	28.6%	14.3%	-----	-----
Fox Farm (D) N = 31	6.5%	74.2%	16.1%	-----	3.2%

Orbit incl.	None	Sm	Med	Pron	
M'ville (U) N = 60	5.0%	65.0%	26.7%	3.3%	
M'ville (D) N = 115	1.7%	81.7%	14.8%	1.7%	
Sand Ridge N = 6	-----	33.3%	50.0%	16.7%	
Turpin (U) N = 6	-----	16.7%	66.7%	16.7%	
Turpin (D) N = 6	-----	33.3%	50.0%	16.7%	
Hahn's Field (U) N = 3	-----	33.3%	66.7%	-----	
Hahn's Field (D) N = 3	-----	-----	100.0%	-----	
Campbell Is (U) N = 5	-----	80.0%	20.0%	-----	
Campbell Is (D) N = 1	100.0%	-----	-----	-----	
Fox Farm (U) N = 7	-----	57.1%	42.9%	-----	
Fox Farm (D) N = 31	-----	29.0%	58.1%	12.9%	

Table 134- continued

Suborb. fossa	Ab	Sl	Med	Deep
M'ville (U) N = 60	21.7%	31.7%	43.3%	3.3%
M'ville (D) N = 115	16.5%	31.3%	46.1%	6.1%
Sand Ridge N = 6	16.7%	50.0%	16.7%	16.7%
Turpin (U) N = 6	16.7%	16.7%	50.0%	16.7%
Turpin (D) N = 6	-----	16.7%	83.3%	-----
Hahn's Field (U) N = 3	-----	66.7%	33.3%	-----
Hahn's Field (D) N = 3	-----	33.3%	66.7%	-----
Campbell Is (U) N = 5	-----	60.0%	40.0%	-----
Campbell Is (D) N = 1	100.0%	-----	-----	-----
Fox Farm (U) N = 7	28.6%	57.1%	14.3%	-----
Fox Farm (D) N = 31	16.1%	58.1%	19.4%	6.5%

Zyg. size	Sm	Med	Lge	V. Lge
M'ville (U) N = 60	1.7%	36.7%	51.7%	10.0%
M'ville (D) N = 115	6.1%	23.5%	65.2%	2.5%
Sand Ridge N = 6	16.7%	66.7%	16.7%	-----
Turpin (U) N = 6	-----	83.3%	16.7%	-----
Turpin (D) N = 6	-----	83.3%	16.7%	-----
Hahn's Field (U) N = 3	-----	-----	100.0%	-----
Hahn's Field (D) N = 3	-----	33.3%	66.7%	-----
Campbell Is (U) N = 5	-----	100.0%	-----	-----
Campbell Is (D) N = 1	100.0%	-----	-----	-----
Fox Farm (U) N = 7	-----	85.7%	-----	14.3%
Fox Farm (D) N = 31	6.5%	61.3%	32.3%	-----

Table 134- continued

Zyg. lat. proj.	Sm	Med	Lge
M'ville (U) N = 60	-----	1.7%	98.3%
M'ville (D) N = 115	-----	1.7%	98.3%
Sand Ridge N = 6	-----	33.3%	66.7%
Turpin (U) N = 6	-----	-----	100.0%
Turpin (D) N = 6	16.7%	-----	83.3%
Hahn's Field (U) N = 3	-----	-----	100.0%
Hahn's Field (D) N = 3	-----	-----	100.0%
Campbell Is (U) N = 5	-----	-----	100.0%
Campbell Is (D) N = 1	-----	-----	100.0%
Fox Farm (U) N = 7	14.3%	85.7%	-----
Fox Farm (D) N = 31	3.2%	3.2%	93.5%

Zgy. ant. proj.	Sm	Med	Lge
M'ville (U) N = 60	-----	30.0%	70.0%
M'ville (D) N = 115	1.7%	23.5%	74.8%
Sand Ridge N = 6	16.7%	66.7%	16.7%
Turpin (U) N = 6	16.7%	83.3%	-----
Turpin (D) N = 6	-----	83.3%	16.7%
Hahn's Field (U) N = 3	-----	66.7%	33.3%
Hahn's Field (D) N = 3	-----	100.0%	-----
Campbell Is (U) N = 5	-----	100.0%	-----
Campbell Is (D) N = 1	-----	100.0%	-----
Fox Farm (U) N = 7	-----	71.4%	28.6%
Fox Farm (D) N = 31	3.2%	58.1%	38.7%

APPENDIX C   427

Table 134 - continued

Zyg. proc. thick.	Sm	Med	Pron	High	V.High
M'ville (U) N = 60	11.7%	70.0%	18.3%		
M'ville (D) N = 115	7.0%	83.5%	9.6%		
Sand Ridge N = 6	16.7%	50.0%	33.3%		
Turpin (U) N = 6	16.7%	66.7%	16.7%		
Turpin (D) N = 6	16.7%	66.7%	16.7%		
Hahn's Field (U) N = 3	-----	100.0%	-----		
Hahn's Field (D) N = 3	-----	100.0%	-----		
Campbell Is (U) N = 5	-----	100.0%	-----		
Campbell Is (D) N = 1	100.0%	-----	-----		
Fox Farm (U) N = 7	-----	85.7%	14.3%		
Fox Farm (D) N = 31	25.8%	54.8%	19.4%		

Nas. rt. ht.	V.Low	Low	Med	High	V.High
M'ville (U) N = 60	-----	1.7%	70.0%	28.3%	-----
M'ville (D) N = 115	-----	2.6%	78.3%	18.3%	-----
Sand Ridge N = 6	-----	16.7%	66.7%	16.7%	-----
Turpin (U) N = 6	-----	-----	66.7%	33.3%	-----
Turpin (D) N = 6	-----	-----	83.3%	16.7%	-----
Hahn's Field (U) N = 3	-----	-----	100.0%	-----	-----
Hahn's Field (D) N = 3	-----	-----	66.7%	33.3%	-----
Campbell Is (U) N = 5	-----	-----	80.0%	20.0%	-----
Campbell Is (D) N = 1	-----	-----	100.0%	-----	-----
Fox Farm (U) N = 7	-----	-----	42.9%	57.1%	-----
Fox Farm (D) N = 31	-----	3.2%	64.5%	32.3%	-----

Table 134- continued

Nas. rt. br.	V.Sm	Sm	Med	Lge	V.Lge
M'ville (U) N = 60	-----	8.3%	68.3%	23.3%	-----
M'ville (D) N = 115	-----	7.0%	84.3%	7.8%	0.9%
Sand Ridge N = 6	-----	-----	83.3%	16.7%	-----
Turpin (U) N = 6	-----	16.7%	83.3%	-----	-----
Turpin (D) N = 6	-----	-----	83.3%	16.7%	-----
Hahn's Field (U) N = 3	33.3%	-----	66.7%	-----	-----
Hahn's Field (D) N = 3	-----	33.3%	66.7%	-----	-----
Campbell Is (U) N = 5	-----	40.0%	60.0%	-----	-----
Campbell Is (D) N = 1	-----	-----	-----	-----	100.0%
Fox Farm (U) N = 7	-----	-----	85.7%	14.3%	-----
Fox Farm (D) N = 31	-----	-----	61.3%	38.7%	-----

Nas. bridg. ht.	V.Low	Low	Med	High	V.High
M'ville (U) N = 60	-----	5.0%	71.7%	20.0%	3.3%
M'ville (D) N = 115	-----	3.5%	87.0%	7.0%	2.6%
Sand Ridge N = 6	-----	16.7%	83.3%	-----	-----
Turpin (U) N = 6	-----	-----	100.0%	-----	-----
Turpin (D) N = 6	-----	-----	83.3%	16.7%	-----
Hahn's Field (U) N = 3	-----	-----	66.7%	33.3%	-----
Hahn's Field (D) N = 3	-----	-----	100.0%	-----	-----
Campbell Is (U) N = 5	-----	-----	100.0%	-----	-----
Campbell Is (D) N = 1	-----	100.0%	-----	-----	-----
Fox Farm (U) N = 7	-----	14.3%	42.9%	42.9%	-----
Fox Farm (D) N = 31	-----	6.5%	87.1%	3.2%	3.2%

APPENDIX C 429

Table 134 - continued

Nas. bridg. br.

	Sm	Med	Lge
M'ville (U) N = 60	10.0%	80.0%	10.0%
M'ville (D) N = 115	12.2%	85.2%	2.6%
Sand Ridge N = 6	-----	100.0%	-----
Turpin (U) N = 6	-----	100.0%	-----
Turpin (D) N = 6	-----	83.3%	16.7%
Hahn's Field (U) N = 3	-----	100.0%	-----
Hahn's Field (D) N = 3	-----	100.0%	-----
Campbell Is (U) N = 5	-----	100.0%	-----
Campbell Is (D) N = 1	-----	100.0%	-----
Fox Farm (U) N = 7	14.3%	71.4%	14.3%
Fox Farm (D) N = 31	9.7%	80.6%	9.7%

Nas. profile

	Conc	Str	Sl. Conc-Conv	Conc-Conv	V. C-C
M'ville (U) N = 60	1.7%	3.3%	1.7%	93.3%	-----
M'ville (D) N = 115	-----	3.5%	0.9%	95.7%	-----
Sand Ridge N = 6	-----	16.7%	83.3%	-----	-----
Turpin (U) N = 6	-----	-----	100.0%	-----	-----
Turpin (D) N = 6	-----	-----	100.0%	-----	-----
Hahn's Field (U) N = 3	-----	-----	100.0%	-----	-----
Hahn's Field (D) N = 3	-----	-----	100.0%	-----	-----
Campbell Is (U) N = 5	-----	-----	100.0%	-----	-----
Campbell Is (D) N = 1	-----	100.0%	-----	-----	-----
Fox Farm (U) N = 7	-----	-----	28.6%	71.4%	-----
Fox Farm (D) N = 31	-----	3.2%	19.4%	77.4%	-----

Table 134- continued

Nas. depress.	Abs	Sm	Med	Lge
M'ville (U) N = 60	18.3%	58.3%	21.7%	1.7%
M'ville (D) N = 115	12.2%	73.9%	13.9%	--
Sand Ridge N = 6	16.7%	50.0%	33.3%	--
Turpin (U) N = 6	16.7%	16.7%	66.7%	--
Turpin (D) N = 6	--	33.3%	50.0%	16.7%
Hahn's Field (U) N = 3	--	100.0%	--	--
Hahn's Field (D) N = 3	--	33.3%	66.7%	--
Campbell Is (U) N = 5	--	100.0%	--	--
Campbell Is (D) N = 1	--	100.0%	--	--
Fox Farm (U) N = 7	--	14.3%	85.7%	--
Fox Farm (D) N = 31	19.4%	67.7%	12.9%	--

Nas. sills	Abs	Dull	Med	Sharp
M'ville (U) N = 60	15.0%	25.0%	50.0%	10.0%
M'ville (D) N = 115	10.4%	17.4%	59.1%	13.0%
Sand Ridge N = 6	--	--	83.3%	16.7%
Turpin (U) N = 6	--	--	66.7%	33.3%
Turpin (D) N = 6	--	--	83.3%	16.7%
Hahn's Field (U) N = 3	--	--	66.7%	33.3%
Hahn's Field (D) N = 3	--	33.3%	66.7%	--
Campbell Is (U) N = 5	--	40.0%	60.0%	--
Campbell Is (D) N = 1	--	100.0%	--	--
Fox Farm (U) N = 7	14.3%	--	57.1%	28.6%
Fox Farm (D) N = 31	--	3.2%	22.6%	74.2%

APPENDIX C 431

Table 134- continued

Nas. spine	Abs	Sm	Med	Rt. Ang	Lge
M'ville (U) N = 60	-----	88.3%	11.7%	-----	-----
M'ville (D) N = 115	0.9%	91.3%	7.0%	-----	0.9%
Sand Ridge N = 6	-----	100.0%	-----	-----	-----
Turpin (U) N = 6	-----	100.0%	-----	-----	-----
Turpin (D) N = 6	-----	100.0%	-----	-----	-----
Hahn's Field (U) N = 3	-----	100.0%	-----	-----	-----
Hahn's Field (D) N = 3	-----	100.0%	-----	-----	-----
Campbell Is (U) N = 5	-----	100.0%	-----	-----	-----
Campbell Is (D) N = 1	-----	100.0%	-----	-----	-----
Fox Farm (U) N = 7	-----	100.0%	-----	-----	-----
Fox Farm (D) N = 31	3.2%	77.4%	16.1%	-----	3.2%

Subnas. grooves	Abs	Sm	Med	Pron	Sulci
M'ville (U) N = 60	36.7%	41.7%	13.3%	8.3%	-----
M'ville (D) N = 115	29.6%	57.4%	6.1%	7.0%	-----
Sand Ridge N = 6	100.0%	-----	-----	-----	-----
Turpin (U) N = 6	100.0%	-----	-----	-----	-----
Turpin (D) N = 6	100.0%	-----	-----	-----	-----
Hahn's Field (U) N = 3	33.3%	66.7%	-----	-----	-----
Hahn's Field (D) N = 3	66.7%	33.3%	-----	-----	-----
Campbell Is (U) N = 5	100.0%	-----	-----	-----	-----
Campbell Is (D) N = 1	-----	-----	100.0%	-----	-----
Fox Farm (U) N = 7	71.4%	14.3%	14.3%	-----	-----
Fox Farm (D) N = 31	100.0%	-----	-----	-----	-----

Table 134- continued

	Abs	Sl	Med	Pron
Midfac. progn.				
M'ville (U) N = 60	75.0%	21.7%	3.3%	----
M'ville (D) N = 115	81.7%	17.4%	0.9%	----
Sand Ridge N = 6	83.3%	16.7%	----	----
Turpin (U) N = 6	66.7%	16.7%	----	16.7%
Turpin (D) N = 6	100.0%	----	----	----
Hahn's Field (U) N = 3	100.0%	----	----	----
Hahn's Field (D) N = 3	100.0%	----	----	----
Campbell Is (U) N = 5	60.0%	40.0%	----	----
Campbell Is (D) N = 1	100.0%	----	----	----
Fox Farm (U) N = 7	71.4%	14.3%	14.3%	----
Fox Farm (D) N = 31	64.5%	32.3%	3.2%	----
Alveol. progn.	Abs	Sl	Med	Pron
M'ville (U) N = 60	8.3%	61.7%	25.0%	5.0%
M'ville (D) N = 115	10.4%	63.5%	20.9%	5.2%
Sand Ridge N = 6	----	33.3%	66.7%	----
Turpin (U) N = 6	----	16.7%	66.7%	16.7%
Turpin (D) N = 6	16.7%	----	83.3%	----
Hahn's Field (U) N = 3	33.3%	----	66.7%	----
Hahn's Field (D) N = 3	66.7%	----	33.3%	----
Campbell Is (U) N = 5	----	20.0%	80.0%	----
Campbell Is (D) N = 1	----	100.0%	----	----
Fox Farm (U) N = 7	----	57.1%	42.9%	----
Fox Farm (D) N = 31	6.5%	22.6%	67.7%	3.2%

Table 134- continued

Total progn.	Abs	Sl	Med	Pron
M'ville (U) N = 60	11.7%	60.0%	28.3%	----
M'ville (D) N = 115	9.6%	65.2%	21.7%	3.5%
Sand Ridge N = 6	----	83.3%	16.7%	----
Turpin (U) N = 6	----	16.7%	66.7%	16.7%
Turpin (D) N = 6	16.7%	----	83.3%	----
Hahn's Field (U) N = 3	33.3%	33.3%	33.3%	----
Hahn's Field (D) N = 3	66.7%	----	33.3%	----
Campbell Is (U) N = 5	----	20.0%	80.0%	----
Campbell Is (D) N = 1	----	100.0%	----	----
Fox Farm (U) N = 7	----	42.9%	57.1%	----
Fox Farm (D) N = 31	6.5%	25.8%	64.5%	3.2%

Palate shape	Parab	Hyperb	Ell	Sm U	Lge U
M'ville (U) N = 60	83.3%	1.7%	10.0%	3.3%	1.7%
M'ville (D) N = 115	89.6%	2.6%	4.3%	2.6%	0.9%
Sand Ridge N = 6	66.7%	----	16.7%	16.7%	----
Turpin (U) N = 6	83.3%	16.7%	----	----	----
Turpin (D) N = 6	83.3%	----	16.7%	----	----
Hahn's Field (U) N = 3	100.0%	----	----	----	----
Hahn's Field (D) N = 3	100.0%	----	----	----	----
Campbell Is (U) N = 5	100.0%	----	----	----	----
Campbell Is (D) N = 1	----	----	----	100.0%	----
Fox Farm (U) N = 7	100.0%	----	----	----	----
Fox Farm (D) N = 31	96.8%	----	3.2%	----	----

Table 134- continued

Palate ht.	Low	Med	High	V. High		
M'ville (U) N = 60	13.3%	65.0%	20.0%	1.7%		
M'ville (D) N = 115	8.7%	65.2%	23.5%	2.6%		
Sand Ridge N = 6	-----	83.3%	16.7%	-----		
Turpin (U) N = 6	16.7%	16.7%	50.0%	16.7%		
Turpin (D) N = 6	-----	16.7%	66.7%	16.7%		
Hahn's Field (U) N = 3	-----	100.0%	-----	-----		
Hahn's Field (D) N = 3	-----	66.7%	33.3%	-----		
Campbell Is (U) N = 5	-----	60.0%	40.0%	-----		
Campbell Is (D) N = 1	-----	100.0%	-----	-----		
Fox Farm (U) N = 7	14.3%	42.9%	28.6%	14.3%		
Fox Farm (D) N = 31	3.2%	58.1%	29.0%	9.7%		

Palat. torus	Abs	SmRidg	MedRidg	LgeRidg	SmMd	MedMd	LMd
M'ville (U) N = 60	86.7%	5.0%	1.7%	-----	6.7%	-----	-----
M'ville (D) N = 115	93.9%	5.2%	-----	-----	0.9%	-----	-----
Sand Ridge N = 6	66.7%	33.3%	-----	-----	-----	-----	-----
Turpin (U) N = 6	100.0%	-----	-----	-----	-----	-----	-----
Turpin (D) N = 6	83.3%	-----	-----	-----	-----	-----	-----
Hahn's Field (U) N = 3	66.3%	33.3%	-----	-----	16.7%	-----	-----
Hahn's Field (D) N = 3	100.0%	-----	-----	-----	-----	-----	-----
Campbell Is (U) N = 5	100.0%	-----	-----	-----	-----	-----	-----
Campbell Is (D) N = 1	100.0%	-----	-----	-----	-----	-----	-----
Fox Farm (U) N = 7	85.7%	14.3%	-----	-----	-----	-----	-----
Fox Farm (D) N = 31	87.1%	12.9%	-----	-----	-----	-----	-----

Table 134- continued

Mand. size	Sm	Med	Lge	V.Lge
M'ville (U) N = 60	1.7%	75.0%	18.3%	5.0%
M'ville (D) N = 115	3.5%	65.2%	27.0%	4.3%
Sand Ridge N = 6	-----	100.0%	-----	-----
Turpin (U) N = 6	-----	66.7%	33.3%	-----
Turpin (D) N = 6	-----	33.3%	66.7%	-----
Hahn's Field (U) N =3	-----	66.7%	33.3%	-----
Hahn's Field (D) N = 3	-----	33.3%	66.7%	-----
Campbell Is (U) N = 5	-----	40.0%	60.0%	-----
Campbell Is (D) N = 1	100.0%	-----	-----	-----
Fox Farm (U) N = 7	28.6%	28.6%	14.3%	28.6%
Fox Farm (D) N = 31	-----	58.1%	25.8%	16.1%

Chin form	Nar Bilat	Wide Bilat	Inter- med	Median
M'ville (U) N = 60	16.7%	-----	68.3%	15.0%
M'ville (D) N = 115	21.7%	-----	62.6%	15.7%
Sand Ridge N = 6	-----	-----	-----	100.0%
Turpin (U) N = 6	33.3%	-----	33.3%	33.3%
Turpin (D) N = 6	16.7%	-----	66.7%	16.7%
Hahn's Field (U) N = 3	33.3%	-----	-----	66.7%
Hahn's Field (D) N = 3	-----	-----	-----	100.0%
Campbell Is (U) N = 5	20.0%	-----	80.0%	-----
Campbell Is (D) N = 1	-----	-----	-----	100.0%
Fox Farm (U) N = 7	-----	-----	57.1%	42.9%
Fox Farm (D) N = 31	16.1%	-----	58.1%	25.8%

Table 134 - continued

Chin proj.	Negat	Neut	Sm	Med	Lge
M'ville (U) N = 60	11.7%	73.3%	10.0%	5.0%	----
M'ville (D) N = 115	12.2%	68.7%	11.3%	7.8%	----
Sand Ridge N = 6	50.0%	----	----	50.0%	----
Turpin (U) N = 6	33.3%	33.3%	33.3%	----	----
Turpin (D) N = 6	66.7%	33.3%	----	----	----
Hahn's Field (U) N = 3	33.3%	66.7%	----	----	----
Hahn's Field (D) N = 3	66.7%	33.3%	----	----	----
Campbell Is (U) N = 5	60.0%	20.0%	20.0%	----	----
Campbell Is (D) N = 1	----	----	----	100.0%	----
Fox Farm (U) N = 7	14.3%	71.4%	14.3%	----	----
Fox Farm (D) N = 31	38.7%	41.9%	12.9%	6.5%	----

Pteryg. attach.	Sm	Med	Pron	V.Pron
M'ville (U) N = 60	35.0%	53.3%	8.3%	3.3%
M'ville (D) N = 115	38.3%	44.3%	13.9%	3.5%
Sand Ridge N = 6	50.0%	----	50.0%	----
Turpin (U) N = 6	16.7%	66.7%	16.7%	----
Turpin (D) N = 6	----	66.7%	33.3%	----
Hahn's Field (U) N = 3	----	66.7%	33.3%	----
Hahn's Field (D) N = 3	33.3%	66.7%	----	----
Campbell Is (U) N = 5	----	80.0%	20.0%	----
Campbell Is (D) N = 1	----	100.0%	----	----
Fox Farm (U) N = 7	14.3%	57.1%	14.3%	14.3%
Fox Farm (D) N = 31	12.9%	67.7%	19.4%	----

Table 134 - continued

Gonial ang. evers.	None	Sm	Med	Pron
M'ville (U) N = 60	13.3%	70.0%	10.0%	6.7%
M'ville (D) N = 115	29.6%	53.9%	14.8%	1.7%
Sand Ridge N = 6	50.0%	50.0%	-----	-----
Turpin (U) N = 6	66.7%	33.3%	-----	-----
Turpin (D) N = 6	66.7%	16.7%	16.7%	-----
Hahn's Field (U) N = 3	33.3%	33.3%	-----	33.3%
Hahn's Field (D) N = 3	66.7%	33.3%	-----	-----
Campbell Is (U) N = 5	20.0%	80.0%	-----	-----
Campbell Is (D) N = 1	100.0%	-----	-----	-----
Fox Farm (U) N = 7	42.9%	28.6%	14.3%	14.3%
Fox Farm (D) N = 31	58.1%	35.5%	6.5%	-----

Table 135

Cranial Observations of the Madisonville Focus (Females)

Muscularity	Sm	Med	Lge	V.Lge
M'ville (U) N = 55	69.1%	29.1%	1.8%	-----
M'ville (D) N = 161	63.4%	36.6%	-----	-----
Sand Ridge (D) N = 2	100.0%	-----	-----	-----
Turpin (U) N = 11	90.9%	9.1%	-----	-----
Turpin (D) N = 3	100.0%	-----	-----	-----
Hahn's Field (D) N = 2	100.0%	-----	-----	-----
Campbell Is (U) N = 1	100.0%	-----	-----	-----
Fox Farm (U) N = 1	-----	100.0%	-----	-----
Fox Farm (D) N = 24	87.5%	12.5%	-----	-----

Deformation	None	Occ	Lambd	Fr-occ	Bil-fr-occ	Fr. Vert. Occ.	Par. Fr. Occ.	Earth Press
M'ville (U) N = 55	100.0%	-----	-----	-----	-----	-----	-----	-----
M'ville (D) N = 161	-----	89.5%	1.9%	-----	-----	-----	-----	8.7%
Sand Ridge (D) N = 2	-----	100.0%	-----	-----	-----	-----	-----	-----
Turpin (U) N = 11	100.0%	-----	-----	-----	-----	-----	-----	-----
Turpin (D) N = 3	-----	100.0%	-----	-----	-----	-----	-----	-----
Hahn's Field (D) N = 2	-----	100.0%	-----	-----	-----	-----	-----	-----
Campbell Is (U) N = 1	100.0%	-----	-----	-----	-----	-----	-----	-----
Fox Farm (U) N = 1	100.0%	-----	-----	-----	-----	-----	-----	-----
Fox Farm (D) N = 24	4.2%	16.7%	-----	8.3%	62.5%	4.2%	-----	4.2%

Table 135 - continued

Degree of deform.	None	Trace	Sm	Med	Pron
M'ville (U) N = 55	98.2%	----	1.8%	----	----
M'ville (D) N = 161	0.6%	10.6%	60.9%	16.1%	11.8%
Sand Ridge (D) N = 2	----	----	100.0%	----	----
Turpin (U) N = 11	100.0%	----	----	----	----
Turpin (D) N = 3	----	----	66.7%	----	33.3%
Hahn's Field (D) N = 2	----	----	100.0%	----	----
Campbell Is (U) N = 1	100.0%	----	----	----	----
Fox Farm (U) N = 1	100.0%	----	----	----	----
Fox Farm (D) N = 24	4.2%	----	20.8%	33.3%	41.7%

Vault form	Ell	Ov	Spher	Pentag	Rhom	Sphen	Birs
M'ville (U) N = 55	9.1%	74.5%	----	3.6%	3.6%	9.1%	----
M'ville (D) N = 161	0.6%	96.9%	1.2%	0.6%	----	----	0.6%
Sand Ridge (D) N = 2	----	100.0%	----	----	----	----	----
Turpin (U) N = 11	9.1%	81.8%	----	----	----	9.1%	----
Turpin (D) N = 3	----	33.3%	----	----	----	66.7%	----
Hahn's Field (D) N = 2	100.0%	----	----	----	----	----	----
Campbell Is (U) N = 1	----	----	----	----	----	100.0%	----
Fox Farm (U) N = 1	----	100.0%	----	----	----	----	----
Fox Farm (D) N = 24	----	95.8%	----	----	----	4.2%	----

Table 135 - continued

Browridge size	None	Trace	Sm	Med	Lge	V.Lge
M'ville (U) N = 55	----	83.6%	16.4%	----	----	----
M'ville (D) N = 161	0.6%	77.6%	21.7%	----	----	----
Sand Ridge (D) N = 2	----	100.0%	----	----	----	----
Turpin (U) N = 11	----	100.0%	----	----	----	----
Turpin (D) N = 3	----	100.0%	----	----	----	----
Hahn's Field (D) N = 2	----	100.0%	----	----	----	----
Campbell Is (U) N = 1	----	100.0%	----	----	----	----
Fox Farm (U) N = 1	----	100.0%	----	----	----	----
Fox Farm (D) N = 24	----	100.0%	----	----	----	----

Glabella prom.	Flat	Sm	Med	Lge	V.Lge	
M'ville (U) N = 55	----	100.0%	----	----	----	
M'ville (D) N = 161	----	97.5%	2.5%	----	----	
Sand Ridge (D) N = 2	----	100.0%	----	----	----	
Turpin (U) N = 11	----	100.0%	----	----	----	
Turpin (D) N = 3	----	100.0%	----	----	----	
Hahn's Field (D) N = 2	----	100.0%	----	----	----	
Campbell Is (U) N = 1	----	100.0%	----	----	----	
Fox Farm (D) N = 1	----	100.0%	----	----	----	
Fox Farm (U) N = 24	----	91.7%	8.3%	----	----	

Table 135 - continued

Frontal slope	Bulg	None	Sl	Med	Pron	V.Pron
M'ville (U) N = 55	27.3%	-----	30.9%	40.0%	1.8%	-----
M'ville (D) N = 161	9.9%	-----	29.2%	60.2%	0.6%	-----
Sand Ridge (D) N = 2	-----	-----	100.0%	-----	-----	-----
Turpin (U) N = 11	-----	9.1%	72.7%	18.2%	-----	-----
Turpin (D) N = 3	33.3%	-----	66.7%	-----	-----	-----
Hahn's Field (D) N = 2	-----	-----	100.0%	-----	-----	-----
Campbell Is (U) N = 1	-----	-----	100.0%	-----	-----	-----
Fox Farm (U) N = 1	100.0%	-----	-----	-----	-----	-----
Fox Farm (D) N = 24	8.3%	-----	41.7%	45.8%	4.2%	-----

Postorb. constr.	Sm	Med	Lge
M'ville (U) N = 55	49.1%	49.1%	1.8%
M'ville (D) N = 161	27.3%	68.9%	3.7%
Sand Ridge (D) N = 2	50.0%	50.0%	-----
Turpin (U) N = 11	45.5%	54.5%	-----
Turpin (D) N = 3	33.3%	66.7%	-----
Hahn's Field (D) N = 2	50.0%	50.0%	-----
Campbell Is (U) N = 1	-----	100.0%	-----
Fox Farm (U) N = 1	100.0%	-----	-----
Fox Farm (D) N = 24	4.2%	62.5%	33.3%

Table 135 - continued

Fron. emin.	Sm	Med	Lge
M'ville (U) N = 55	36.4%	43.6%	20.0%
M'ville (D) N = 161	29.2%	66.5%	4.3%
Sand Ridge (D) N = 2	50.0%	-----	50.0%
Turpin (U) N = 11	18.2%	81.8%	-----
Turpin (D) N = 3	-----	66.7%	33.3%
Hahn's Field (D) N = 2	-----	100.0%	-----
Campbell Is (U) N = 1	-----	100.0%	-----
Fox Farm (U) N = 1	-----	-----	100.0%
Fox Farm (D) N = 24	70.8%	25.0%	4.2%

Fr. median crest	None	Sm	Med	Lge
M'ville (U) N = 55	45.5%	41.8%	12.7%	-----
M'ville (D) N = 161	52.8%	42.2%	4.3%	0.6%
Sand Ridge (D) N = 2	100.0%	-----	-----	-----
Turpin (U) N = 11	63.6%	27.3%	9.1%	-----
Turpin (D) N = 3	100.0%	-----	-----	-----
Hahn's Field (D) N = 2	100.0%	-----	-----	-----
Campbell Is (U) N = 1	100.0%	-----	-----	-----
Fox Farm (U) N = 1	100.0%	-----	-----	-----
Fox Farm (D) N = 24	83.3%	4.2%	8.3%	4.2%

Table 135 - continued

Fron. br.

	Sm	Med	Lge
M'ville (U) N = 55	49.1%	36.4%	14.5%
M'ville (D) N = 161	13.0%	64.6%	22.4%
Sand Ridge (D) N = 2	-----	50.0%	50.0%
Turpin (U) N = 11	45.5%	36.4%	18.2%
Turpin (D) N = 3	-----	-----	100.0%
Hahn's Field (D) N = 2	-----	50.0%	50.0%
Campbell Is (U) N = 1	-----	-----	100.0%
Fox Farm (U) N = 1	-----	-----	100.0%
Fox Farm (D) N = 24	4.2%	25.0%	70.8%

Sag. elev.

	None	Sm	Med	Lge	V.Lge
M'ville (U) N = 55	54.5%	40.0%	3.6%	1.8%	-----
M'ville (D) N = 161	75.2%	23.0%	1.9%	-----	-----
Sand Ridge (D) N = 2	100.0%	-----	-----	-----	-----
Turpin (U) N = 11	81.8%	9.1%	9.1%	-----	-----
Turpin (D) N = 3	100.0%	-----	-----	-----	-----
Hahn's Field (D) N = 2	100.0%	-----	-----	-----	-----
Campbell Is (U) N = 1	100.0%	-----	-----	-----	-----
Fox Farm (U) N = 1	-----	100.0%	-----	-----	-----
Fox Farm (D) N = 24	83.3%	16.7%	-----	-----	-----

Table 135 - continued

Pariet. emin.	Sm	Med	Lge
M'ville (U) N = 55	21.8%	70.9%	7.3%
M'ville (D) N = 161	5.0%	72.0%	23.0%
Sand Ridge (D) N = 2	-----	50.0%	50.0%
Turpin (U) N = 11	-----	90.9%	9.1%
Turpin (D) N = 3	-----	-----	100.0%
Hahn's Field (D) N = 2	-----	100.0%	-----
Campbell Is (U) N = 1	-----	-----	100.0%
Fox Farm (U) N = 1	-----	100.0%	-----
Fox Farm (D) N = 24	-----	16.7%	83.3%

Temp. fullness	Flat	Sm	Med	Lge
M'ville (U) N = 55	10.9%	47.3%	25.5%	16.4%
M'ville (D) N = 161	0.6%	18.6%	62.7%	18.0%
Sand Ridge (D) N = 2	-----	-----	100.0%	-----
Turpin (U) N = 11	9.1%	54.5%	36.4%	-----
Turpin (D) N = 3	-----	33.3%	66.7%	-----
Hahn's Field (D) N = 2	-----	100.0%	-----	-----
Campbell Is (U) N = 1	-----	100.0%	-----	-----
Fox Farm (U) N = 1	-----	100.0%	-----	-----
Fox Farm (D) N = 24	4.2%	12.5%	54.2%	29.2%

Table 135 - continued

Mastoids	Sm	Med	Lge	V.Lge
M'ville (U) N = 55	89.1%	10.9%	-----	-----
M'ville (D) N = 161	88.8%	11.2%	-----	-----
Sand Ridge (D) N = 2	100.0%	-----	-----	-----
Turpin (U) N = 11	81.8%	18.2%	-----	-----
Turpin (D) N = 3	33.3%	66.7%	-----	-----
Hahn's Field (D) N = 2	100.0%	-----	-----	-----
Campbell Is (U) N = 1	100.0%	-----	-----	-----
Fox Farm (U) N = 1	100.0%	-----	-----	-----
Fox Farm (D) N = 24	91.7%	8.3%	-----	-----

Supramast. crest	Sm	Med	Lge	
M'ville (U) N = 55	56.4%	40.0%	3.6%	
M'ville (D) N = 161	66.5%	31.1%	2.5%	
Sand Ridge (D) N = 2	-----	100.0%	-----	
Turpin (U) N = 11	36.4%	63.6%	-----	
Turpin (D) N = 3	66.7%	33.3%	-----	
Hahn's Field (D) N = 2	100.0%	-----	-----	
Campbell Is (U) N = 1	100.0%	-----	-----	
Fox Farm (U) N = 1	-----	-----	100.0%	
Fox Farm (D) N = 24	33.3%	62.5%	4.2%	

Table 135 - continued

Sphen. depress.	Sm	Med	Lge
M'ville (U) N = 55	54.5%	38.2%	7.3%
M'ville (D) N = 161	26.7%	60.9%	12.4%
Sand Ridge (D) N = 2	50.0%	50.0%	-----
Turpin (U) N = 11	18.2%	72.7%	9.1%
Turpin (D) N = 3	-----	100.0%	-----
Hahn's Field (D) N = 2	100.0%	-----	-----
Campbell Is (U) N = 1	100.0%	-----	-----
Fox Farm (U) N = 1	-----	100.0%	-----
Fox Farm (D) N = 24	79.2%	20.8%	-----

Occip. curve	None	Sm	Med	Pron
M'ville (U) N = 55	-----	20.0%	50.9%	29.1%
M'ville (D) N = 161	5.0%	23.6%	68.9%	2.5%
Sand Ridge (D) N = 2	-----	100.0%	-----	-----
Turpin (U) N = 11	-----	9.1%	63.6%	27.3%
Turpin (D) N = 3	-----	100.0%	-----	-----
Hahn's Field (D) N = 2	-----	100.0%	-----	-----
Campbell Is (U) N = 1	-----	100.0%	-----	-----
Fox Farm (U) N = 1	-----	-----	100.0%	-----
Fox Farm (D) N = 24	62.5%	33.3%	4.2%	-----

Table 135 - continued

Lambd. flat.	None	Sm	Med	Pron
M'ville (U) N = 55	12.7%	29.1%	38.2%	20.0%
M'ville (D) N = 161	6.2%	72.0%	16.8%	5.0%
Sand Ridge (D) N = 2	-----	100.0%	-----	-----
Turpin (U) N = 11	18.2%	45.5%	18.2%	18.2%
Turpin (D) N = 3	66.7%	33.3%	-----	-----
Hahn's Field (D) N = 2	-----	100.0%	-----	-----
Campbell Is (U) N = 1	100.0%	-----	-----	-----
Fox Farm (U) N = 1	-----	100.0%	-----	-----
Fox Farm (D) N = 24	79.2%	20.8%	-----	-----

Cond. elev.	Sm	Med	Lge	
M'ville (U) N = 55	10.9%	69.1%	20.0%	
M'ville (D) N = 161	10.6%	78.9%	10.6%	
Sand Ridge (D) N = 2	50.0%	50.0%	-----	
Turpin (U) N = 11	9.1%	54.5%	36.4%	
Turpin (D) N = 3	-----	100.0%	-----	
Hahn's Field (D) N = 2	-----	100.0%	-----	
Campbell Is (U) N = 1	-----	100.0%	-----	
Fox Farm (U) N = 1	-----	-----	100.0%	
Fox Farm (D) N = 24	25.0%	75.0%	-----	

Table 135 - continued

Basion	Low	Med	High
M'ville (U) N = 55	3.6%	74.5%	21.8%
M'ville (D) N = 161	6.2%	77.0%	16.8%
Sand Ridge (D) N = 2	----	100.0%	----
Turpin (U) N = 11	9.1%	90.9%	----
Turpin (D) N = 3	----	100.0%	----
Hahn's Field (D) N = 2	100.0%	----	----
Campbell Is (U) N = 1	----	100.0%	----
Fox Farm (U) N = 1	----	100.0%	----
Fox Farm (D) N = 24	66.7%	33.3%	----

Styl. proc.	Sm	Med	Lge
M'ville (U) N = 55	87.3%	12.7%	----
M'ville (D) N = 161	87.6%	12.4%	----
Sand Ridge (D) N = 2	100.0%	----	----
Turpin (U) N = 11	63.6%	36.4%	----
Turpin (D) N = 3	100.0%	----	----
Hahn's Field (D) N = 2	100.0%	----	----
Campbell Is (U) N = 1	100.0%	----	----
Fox Farm (U) N = 1	100.0%	----	----
Fox Farm (D) N = 24	83.3%	12.5%	4.2%

Table 135 - continued

Glen. fos. depth	Sm	Med	Lge
M'ville (U) N = 55	7.3%	87.3%	5.5%
M'ville (D) N = 161	12.4%	83.2%	4.3%
Sand Ridge (D) N = 2	-----	100.0%	-----
Turpin (U) N = 11	-----	54.5%	45.5%
Turpin (D) N = 3	-----	100.0%	-----
Hahn's Field (D) N = 2	-----	100.0%	-----
Campbell Is (U) N = 1	-----	100.0%	-----
Fox Farm (U) N = 1	-----	100.0%	-----
Fox Farm (D) N = 24	4.2%	87.5%	8.3%

Tymp. plate	Thin	Med	Thick	V. Thick
M'ville (U) N = 55	83.6%	16.4%	-----	-----
M'ville (D) N = 161	83.2%	16.1%	0.6%	-----
Sand Ridge (D) N = 2	100.0%	-----	-----	-----
Turpin (U) N = 11	90.9%	-----	9.1%	-----
Turpin (D) N = 3	100.0%	-----	-----	-----
Hahn's Field (D) N = 2	100.0%	-----	-----	-----
Campbell Is (U) N = 1	-----	100.0%	-----	-----
Fox Farm (U) N = 1	-----	-----	100.0%	-----
Fox Farm (D) N = 24	75.0%	25.0%	-----	-----

Table 135 - continued

Orbit shape	Obl	Rhom	Sq	Ell	Rou
M'ville (U) N = 55	9.1%	52.7%	9.1%	23.6%	5.5%
M'ville (D) N = 161	8.7%	66.5%	11.2%	11.8%	1.9%
Sand Ridge (D) N = 2	-----	50.0%	50.0%	-----	-----
Turpin (U) N = 11	27.3%	36.4%	18.2%	18.2%	-----
Turpin (D) N = 3	-----	100.0%	-----	-----	-----
Hahn's Field (D) N = 2	-----	50.0%	50.0%	-----	-----
Campbell Is (U) N = 1	-----	100.0%	-----	-----	-----
Fox Farm (U) N = 1	-----	-----	100.0%	-----	-----
Fox Farm (D) N = 24	12.5%	54.2%	16.7%	8.3%	8.3%

Orbit incl.	None	Sm	Med	Pron	
M'ville (U) N = 55	1.8%	81.8%	16.4%	-----	
M'ville (D) N = 161	1.9%	87.0%	9.9%	1.2%	
Sand Ridge (D) N = 2	-----	-----	100.0%	-----	
Turpin (U) N = 11	9.1%	18.2%	72.7%	-----	
Turpin (D) N = 3	-----	-----	33.3%	66.7%	
Hahn's Field (D) N = 2	-----	-----	50.0%	50.0%	
Campbell Is (U) N = 1	-----	-----	100.0%	-----	
Fox Farm (U) N = 1	-----	100.0%	-----	-----	
Fox Farm (D) N = 24	-----	16.7%	66.7%	16.7%	

Table 135 - continued

Suborb. fossa	Ab	Sl	Med	Deep
M'ville (U) N = 55	20.0%	65.5%	9.1%	5.5%
M'ville (D) N = 161	14.3%	50.3%	32.3%	3.1%
Sand Ridge (D) N = 2	50.0%	50.0%	-----	-----
Turpin (U) N = 11	18.2%	63.6%	9.1%	9.1%
Turpin (D) N = 3	33.3%	33.3%	-----	33.3%
Hahn's Field (D) N = 2	-----	50.0%	50.0%	-----
Campbell Is (U) N = 1	100.0%	-----	-----	-----
Fox Farm (U) N = 1	-----	-----	100.0%	-----
Fox Farm (D) N = 24	4.2%	58.3%	29.2%	8.3%

Zyg. size	Sm	Med	Lge	V.Lge
M'ville (U) N = 55	36.4%	58.2%	5.5%	-----
M'ville (D) N = 161	43.5%	54.7%	1.9%	-----
Sand Ridge (D) N = 2	100.0%	-----	-----	-----
Turpin (U) N = 11	81.8%	18.2%	-----	-----
Turpin (D) N = 3	100.0%	-----	-----	-----
Hahn's Field (D) N = 2	100.0%	-----	-----	-----
Campbell Is (U) N = 1	100.0%	-----	-----	-----
Fox Farm (U) N = 1	-----	100.0%	-----	-----
Fox Farm (D) N = 24	62.5%	37.5%	-----	-----

Table 135 - continued

	Sm	Med	Lge
Zyg. lat. proj.			
M'ville (U) N = 55	----	20.0%	80.0%
M'ville (D) N = 161	0.6%	15.5%	83.9%
Sand Ridge (D) N = 2	----	100.0%	----
Turpin (U) N = 11	9.1%	54.5%	36.4%
Turpin (D) N = 3	----	100.0%	----
Hahn's Field (D) N = 2	100.0%	----	----
Campbell Is (U) N = 1	----	100.0%	----
Fox Farm (U) N = 1	----	----	100.0%
Fox Farm (D) N = 24	4.2%	12.5%	83.3%

	Sm	Med	Lge
Zyg. ant. proj.			
M'ville (U) N = 55	10.9%	81.8%	7.3%
M'ville (D) N = 161	9.9%	82.6%	7.5%
Sand Ridge (D) N = 2	----	100.0%	----
Turpin (U) N = 11	36.4%	54.5%	9.1%
Turpin (D) N = 3	33.3%	66.7%	----
Hahn's Field (D) N = 2	100.0%	----	----
Campbell Is (U) N = 1	----	100.0%	----
Fox Farm (U) N = 1	----	100.0%	----
Fox Farm (D) N = 24	16.7%	83.3%	----

Table 135 - continued

Zyg. proc. thick.	Sm	Med	Pron
M'ville (U) N = 55	45.5%	54.5%	-----
M'ville (D) N = 161	36.9%	62.1%	-----
Sand Ridge (D) N = 2	100.0%	-----	-----
Turpin (U) N = 11	72.7%	27.3%	-----
Turpin (D) N = 3	100.0%	-----	-----
Hahn's Field (D) N = 2	100.0%	-----	-----
Campbell Is (U) N = 1	-----	100.0%	-----
Fox Farm (U) N = 1	100.0%	-----	-----
Fox Farm (D) N = 24	75.0%	25.0%	-----

Nas. rt. ht.	V. Low	Low	Med	High	V. High
M'ville (U) N = 55	1.8%	9.1%	69.1%	20.0%	-----
M'ville (D) N = 161	0.6%	7.5%	80.7%	11.2%	-----
Sand Ridge (D) N = 2	-----	50.0%	50.0%	-----	-----
Turpin (U) N = 11	-----	36.4%	54.5%	9.1%	-----
Turpin (D) N = 3	-----	100.0%	-----	-----	-----
Hahn's Field (D) N = 2	-----	-----	100.0%	-----	-----
Campbell Is (U) N = 1	-----	100.0%	-----	-----	-----
Fox Farm (U) N = 1	-----	-----	-----	100.0%	-----
Fox Farm (D) N = 24	-----	12.5%	62.5%	25.0%	-----

Table 135 - continued

Nas. rt. br.	V.Sm	Sm	Med	Lge	V.Lge
M'ville (U) N = 55	-----	23.6%	61.8%	12.7%	1.8%
M'ville (D) N = 161	1.2%	7.5%	82.6%	8.7%	-----
Sand Ridge (D) N = 2	-----	-----	100.0%	-----	-----
Turpin (U) N = 11	-----	9.1%	72.7%	18.2%	-----
Turpin (D) N = 3	-----	-----	100.0%	-----	-----
Hahn's Field (D) N = 2	-----	100.0%	-----	-----	-----
Campbell Is (U) N = 1	-----	-----	100.0%	-----	-----
Fox Farm (U) N = 1	-----	-----	-----	100.0%	-----
Fox Farm (D) N = 24	4.2%	4.2%	58.3%	29.2%	4.2%

Nas. bridg. ht.	V.Low	Low	Med	High	V.High
M'ville (U) N = 55	3.6%	7.3%	81.8%	7.3%	-----
M'ville (D) N = 161	0.6%	7.5%	87.6%	4.3%	-----
Sand Ridge (D) N = 2	-----	50.0%	50.0%	-----	-----
Turpin (U) N = 11	-----	18.2%	81.8%	-----	-----
Turpin (D) N = 3	-----	-----	100.0%	-----	-----
Hahn's Field (D) N = 2	-----	-----	100.0%	-----	-----
Campbell Is (U) N = 1	-----	-----	100.0%	-----	-----
Fox Farm (U) N = 1	-----	100.0%	-----	-----	-----
Fox Farm (D) N = 24	16.7%	16.7%	62.5%	4.2%	-----

APPENDIX C

Table 135 - continued

Nas. bridge br.	Sm	Med	Lge
M'ville (U) N = 55	10.9%	81.8%	7.3%
M'ville (D) N = 161	10.6%	87.0%	2.5%
Sand Ridge (D) N = 2	----	100.0%	----
Turpin (U) N = 11	9.1%	81.8%	9.1%
Turpin (D) N = 3	----	100.0%	----
Hahn's Field (D) N = 2	100.0%	----	----
Campbell Is (U) N = 1	----	100.0%	----
Fox Farm (U) N = 1	----	100.0%	----
Fox Farm (D) N = 24	4.2%	62.5%	33.3%

Nas. profile	Conc	Str	Sl. Conc-Conv	Conc-Conv	V.C-C
M'ville (U) N = 55	----	----	3.6%	96.4%	----
M'ville (D) N = 161	0.6%	3.1%	1.2%	95.0%	----
Sand Ridge (D) N = 2	100.0%	----	----	----	----
Turpin (U) N = 11	9.1%	----	81.8%	9.1%	----
Turpin (D) N = 3	----	----	100.0%	----	----
Hahn's Field (D) N = 2	----	----	100.0%	----	----
Campbell Is (U) N = 1	----	----	100.0%	----	----
Fox Farm (U) N = 1	----	----	100.0%	----	----
Fox Farm (D) N = 24	4.2%	----	20.8%	75.0%	----

Table 135 - continued

Nas. depress	Ab	Sm	Med	Lge
M'ville (U) N = 55	45.5%	54.5%	-----	-----
M'ville (D) N = 161	28.6%	70.2%	1.2%	-----
Sand Ridge (D) N = 2	50.0%	50.0%	-----	-----
Turpin (U) N = 11	36.4%	63.6%	-----	-----
Turpin (D) N = 3	33.3%	66.7%	-----	-----
Hahn's Field (D) N = 2	100.0%	-----	-----	-----
Campbell Is (U) N = 1	100.0%	-----	-----	-----
Fox Farm (U) N = 1	100.0%	-----	-----	-----
Fox Farm (D) N = 24	62.5%	37.5%	-----	-----

Nas. sills	Abs	Dull	Med	Sharp
M'ville (U) N = 55	7.3%	14.5%	70.9%	7.3%
M'ville (D) N = 161	2.5%	22.4%	62.1%	13.0%
Sand Ridge (D) N = 2	-----	-----	100.0%	-----
Turpin (U) N = 11	-----	-----	36.4%	63.6%
Turpin (D) N = 3	-----	-----	66.7%	33.3%
Hahn's Field (D) N = 2	-----	-----	100.0%	-----
Campbell Is (U) N = 1	-----	-----	100.0%	-----
Fox Farm (U) N = 1	-----	-----	100.0%	-----
Fox Farm (D) N = 24	-----	-----	33.3%	66.7%

Table 135 - continued

Nas. spine	Abs	Sm	Med	Rt.Ang	Lge
M'ville (U) N = 55	1.8%	90.9%	7.3%	----	----
M'ville (D) N = 161	0.6%	97.5%	1.9%	----	----
Sand Ridge (D) N = 2	----	100.0%	----	----	----
Turpin (U) N = 11	----	100.0%	----	----	----
Turpin (D) N = 3	----	100.0%	----	----	----
Hahn's Field (D) N = 2	----	100.0%	----	----	----
Campbell Is (U) N = 1	----	100.0%	----	----	----
Fox Farm (U) N = 1	----	100.0%	----	----	----
Fox Farm (D) N = 24	----	87.5%	12.5%	----	----

Subnas. grooves	Abs	Sm	Med	Pron	Sulci
M'ville (U) N = 55	80.0%	16.4%	1.8%	1.8%	----
M'ville (D) N = 161	83.9%	11.8%	3.1%	1.2%	----
Sand Ridge (D) N = 2	100.0%	----	----	----	----
Turpin (U) N = 11	100.0%	----	----	----	----
Turpin (D) N = 3	100.0%	----	----	----	----
Hahn's Field (D) N = 2	100.0%	----	----	----	----
Campbell Is (U) N = 1	100.0%	----	----	----	----
Fox Farm (U) N = 1	100.0%	----	----	----	----
Fox Farm (D) N = 24	100.0%	----	----	----	----

Table 135 - continued

Midfac. progn.	Abs	Sl	Med	Pron
M'ville (U) N = 55	78.2%	16.4%	5.5%	-----
M'ville (D) N = 161	78.9%	16.8%	4.3%	-----
Sand Ridge (D) N = 2	-----	100.0%	-----	-----
Turpin (U) N = 11	54.5%	36.4%	9.1%	-----
Turpin (D) N = 3	66.7%	33.3%	-----	-----
Hahn's Field (D) N = 2	100.0%	-----	-----	-----
Campbell Is (U) N = 1	-----	100.0%	-----	-----
Fox Farm (U) N = 1	-----	100.0%	-----	-----
Fox Farm (D) N = 24	29.2%	58.3%	12.5%	-----

Alveol. progn.	Abs	Sl	Med	Pron
M'ville (U) N = 55	9.1%	21.8%	60.0%	9.1%
M'ville (D) N = 161	1.9%	24.2%	67.1%	6.8%
Sand Ridge (D) N = 2	-----	-----	100.0%	-----
Turpin (U) N = 11	-----	9.1%	72.7%	18.2%
Turpin (D) N = 3	-----	33.3%	33.3%	33.3%
Hahn's Field (D) N = 2	-----	100.0%	-----	-----
Campbell Is (U) N = 1	-----	-----	100.0%	-----
Fox Farm (U) N = 1	-----	-----	100.0%	-----
Fox Farm (D) N = 24	-----	8.3%	75.0%	16.7%

Table 135 - continued

Total progn.	Abs	Sl	Med	Pron
M'ville (U) N = 55	9.1%	40.0%	49.1%	1.8%
M'ville (D) N = 161	0.6%	41.0%	54.7%	3.7%
Sand Ridge (D) N = 2	-----	-----	100.0%	-----
Turpin (U) N = 11	-----	18.2%	63.6%	18.2%
Turpin (D) N = 3	-----	-----	66.7%	33.3%
Hahn's Field (D) N = 2	-----	100.0%	-----	-----
Campbell Is (U) N = 1	-----	-----	100.0%	-----
Fox Farm (U) N = 1	-----	-----	100.0%	-----
Fox Farm (D) N = 24	-----	12.5%	75.0%	12.5%

Palate shape	Parab	Hyperb	Ell	Sm U	Lge U
M'ville (U) N = 55	83.6%	3.6%	7.3%	-----	5.5%
M'ville (D) N = 161	85.1%	3.7%	6.8%	3.7%	0.6%
Sand Ridge (D) N = 2	50.0%	50.0%	-----	-----	-----
Turpin (U) N = 11	81.8%	-----	9.1%	-----	9.1%
Turpin (D) N = 3	66.7%	33.3%	-----	-----	-----
Hahn's Field (D) N = 1	-----	-----	100.0%	-----	-----
Campbell Is (U) N = 1	100.0%	-----	-----	-----	-----
Fox Farm (U) N = 1	100.0%	-----	-----	-----	-----
Fox Farm (D) N = 24	91.7%	-----	4.2%	4.2%	-----

Table 135 - continued

Palate ht.	Low	Med	High	V.High
M'ville (U) N = 55	12.7%	78.2%	9.1%	----
M'ville (D) N = 161	14.9%	69.6%	13.7%	1.9%
Sand Ridge (D) N = 2	----	100.0%	----	----
Turpin (U) N = 11	90.9%	9.1%	----	----
Turpin (D) N = 3	33.3%	33.3%	----	33.3%
Hahn's Field (D) N = 2	100.0%	----	----	----
Campbell Is (U) N = 1	----	100.0%	----	----
Fox Farm (U) N = 1	----	100.0%	----	----
Fox Farm (D) N = 24	12.5%	66.7%	20.8%	----

Palat. torus	Abs	SmRidg	MedRidg	LgeRidg	SmMd	MedMd	LMd
M'ville (U) N = 55	87.3%	7.3%	----	----	5.5%	----	----
M'ville (D) N = 161	91.3%	6.2%	----	----	2.5%	----	----
Sand Ridge (D) N = 2	100.0%	----	----	----	----	----	----
Turpin (U) N = 11	90.9%	9.1%	----	----	----	----	----
Turpin (D) N = 3	100.0%	----	----	----	----	----	----
Hahn's Field (D) N = 2	100.0%	----	----	----	----	----	----
Campbell Is (U) N = 1	100.0%	----	----	----	----	----	----
Fox Farm (U) N = 1	100.0%	----	----	----	----	----	----
Fox Farm (D) N = 24	100.0%	----	----	----	----	----	----

Table 135 - continued

Mand. size	Sm	Med	Lge	V.Lge
M'ville (U) N = 55	45.5%	54.5%	-----	-----
M'ville (D) N = 161	42.2%	56.5%	1.2%	-----
Sand Ridge (D) N = 2	50.0%	50.0%	-----	-----
Turpin (U) N = 11	27.3%	72.7%	-----	-----
Turpin (D) N = 3	33.3%	66.7%	-----	-----
Hahr's Field (D) N = 2	100.0%	-----	-----	-----
Campbell Is (U) N = 1	100.0%	-----	-----	-----
Fox Farm (U) N = 1	-----	100.0%	-----	-----
Fox Farm (D) N = 24	70.8%	29.2%	-----	-----

Chin form	Nar Bilat	Wide Bilat	Inter-med	Median
M'ville (U) N = 55	7.3%	-----	5.5%	87.3%
M'ville (D) N = 161	16.1%	-----	9.3%	74.5%
Sand Ridge (D) N = 2	-----	-----	50.0%	50.0%
Turpin (U) N = 11	72.7%	-----	9.1%	18.2%
Turpin (D) N = 3	66.7%	-----	-----	33.3%
Hahr's Field (D) N = 2	-----	-----	-----	100.0%
Campbell Is (U) N = 1	100.0%	-----	100.0%	-----
Fox Farm (U) N = 1	100.0%	-----	-----	-----
Fox Farm (D) N = 24	4.2%	-----	12.5%	83.3%

Table 135 - continued

Chin proj.	Negat	Neut	Sm	Med	Lge
M'ville (U) N = 55	80.0%	12.7%	7.3%	----	----
M'ville (D) N = 161	64.6%	24.8%	7.5%	1.9%	1.2%
Sand Ridge (D) N = 2	100.0%	----	----	----	----
Turpin (U) N = 11	72.7%	27.3%	----	----	----
Turpin (D) N = 3	100.0%	----	----	----	----
Hahn's Field (D) N = 2	----	----	100.0%	----	----
Campbell Is (U) N = 1	100.0%	100.0%	----	----	----
Fox Farm (U) N = 1	----	----	----	----	----
Fox Farm (D) N = 24	75.0%	25.0%	4.2%	----	----

Pteryg. attach.	Sm	Med	Pron	V.Pron
M'ville (U) N = 55	80.0%	18.2%	1.8%	----
M'ville (D) N = 161	78.3%	17.4%	4.3%	----
Sand Ridge (D) N = 2	100.0%	----	----	----
Turpin (U) N = 11	36.4%	63.6%	----	----
Turpin (D) N = 3	66.7%	33.3%	----	----
Hahn's Field (D) N = 2	----	100.0%	----	----
Campbell Is (U) N = 1	----	100.0%	----	----
Fox Farm (U) N = 1	----	----	100.0%	----
Fox Farm (D) N = 24	66.7%	29.2%	4.2%	----

Table 135 - continued

Gonial ang. evers.	None	Sm	Med	Pron
M'ville (U) N = 55	94.5%	5.5%	----	----
M'ville (D) N = 161	88.8%	9.3%	1.9%	----
Sand Ridge (D) N = 2	----	100.0%	----	----
Turpin (U) N = 11	72.7%	27.3%	----	----
Turpin (D) N = 3	100.0%	----	----	----
Hahn's Field (D) N = 2	100.0%	----	----	----
Campbell Is (U) N = 1	100.0%	----	----	----
Fox Farm (U) N = 1	100.0%	----	----	----
Fox Farm (D) N = 24	91.7%	8.3%	----	----

APPENDIX D

ANALYSIS OF CRANIA IN THE FORT ANCIENT ASPECT
(SEE CHAPTER IV)

APPENDIX D

Table 136

IDENTIFICATION OF CRANIAL SERIES IN COMPARATIVE ANALYSES

POPULATION IDENTIFICATION	ABBREVIATION
FORT ANCIENT COMPONENTS	
Baum Focus	BF
Baum Site	Ba
Gartner Site	Ga
Feurt Focus	FF
Feurt Site	Fe
Fullerton Field Site	Fu
Proctorville Site	Pr
Gp 1 Site	Gp
Anderson Focus	AF
Anderson Site	An
Taylor Site	Ta
Stokes Site	St
Madisonville Focus	MF
Madisonville Site	Ma
Sand Ridge Site	Sa
Turpin Site	Tu
Hahn's Field Site	Ha
Campbell Island Site	Ca
Fox Farm Site	Fo
PHYSICAL TYPES	
Varietal	
Lenid	Len
Iswanid	Isw
Ilinid	Ili
Muskogid	Mus
Dakotid	Dak
Fort Ancient Ilinid	FAI
Fort Ancient Muskogid	FAM

Table 136 - continued

COMPARATIVE HISTORICAL SERIES

    Seneca   Sen
    Shawnee   Sha
    Historic Muskogid Series   HMS

APPENDIX D

Table 137

"t" SCORES FOR MEASUREMENTS OF:
BAUM-GARTNER UNDEFORMED MALE CRANIA

(N = Baum 7; Gartner 6)

	$\bar{X}_{Ba}$	$\bar{X}_{Ga}$	t-ratio	DF**	t-prob.	Sig. diff.
Cranial vault						
CM	155.29	155.39	- 0.026	3	1.000	
TP	4.86	5.17	- 0.726	4	0.508	
L	182.00	181.17	0.224	11	0.827	
B	138.86	143.83	- 1.268	11	0.231	
MF	97.29	96.67	0.225	11	0.803	
H	145.00	141.00	2.810	11	0.017	*
PAH	121.71	124.00	- 1.315	11	0.215	
BPH	------	------	-------	---	-----	
LB	104.86	104.83	0.014	11	0.989	
Face						
TFH	126.00	129.67	- 1.314	3	1.000	
UFH	76.00	76.50	- 0.757	11	0.465	
TFB	143.14	145.33	- 0.914	11	0.380	
MFB	101.71	103.83	- 2.334	4	0.080	
IOB	102.71	98.17	3.680	11	0.004	*
SIOB	19.00	16.33	4.722	11	0.001	*
BOB	102.00	98.00	9.165	4	0.000	*
AIB	20.14	19.83	1.419	11	0.184	
Nasal structure						
NB	26.71	25.66	2.862	11	0.015	*
NH	55.00	55.33	- 0.860	11	0.408	
DC	20.29	20.00	1.549	4	0.196	
DS	11.14	11.00	0.258	4	0.809	
MN	10.29	10.17	0.247	11	0.810	
SMN	4.00	5.00	- 4.215	11	0.001	*
Orbit						
LOH	35.29	34.50	1.500	6	0.184	
LOBM	43.14	43.17	- 0.046	11	0.964	
LOBD	41.14	40.83	0.817	7	0.440	
Dental arch						
MB	64.57	68.83	- 1.241	4	0.282	
ML	56.29	51.83	12.851	11	0.000	*
FL	96.71	98.17	- 4.192	11	0.002	*
FLA	94.71	96.17	- 4.192	11	0.002	*
Mandible						
LM	110.14	106.50	1.564	4	0.193	
BCB	124.14	130.33	- 2.920	3	1.000	
SH	36.29	38.00	- 0.927	11	0.374	
BA	102.71	101.67	0.307	4	0.774	
RL	35.00	37.17	- 1.684	11	0.120	
Facial angles						
G∠	116.71	114.00	1.075	3	1.000	

** DF ≤ 3, t-prob. = 1

Table 138

"t" SCORES FOR INDICES OF: BAUM-GARTNER UNDEFORMED MALE CRANIA

(N = Baum 7; Gartner 6)

	$\bar{X}_{Ba}$	$\bar{X}_{Ga}$	t-ratio	DF**	t-prob.	Sig. diff.
Cranial vault						
B/L	76.44	79.49	- 0.983	11	0.347	
H/L	79.78	77.87	1.213	11	0.251	
H/B	104.69	98.16	2.294	11	0.042	
H/L+B/2	90.45	86.77	3.353	5	0.020	*
PAH/L	66.97	68.49	- 0.913	11	0.381	
BPH/H	------	------	-------	---	-----	
MF/B	70.07	67.35	1.468	4	0.216	
Face						
TFH/TFB	88.05	89.26	- 0.638	4	0.558	
UFH/TFB	53.11	52.70	0.430	5	0.685	
UFH/MFB	74.73	73.68	1.588	5	0.173	
TFB/B	103.33	101.13	0.800	11	0.441	
MF/TFB	67.97	66.63	0.636	11	0.538	
BA/MF	105.82	105.27	0.132	11	0.898	
BA/TFB	71.76	70.09	0.588	3	1.000	
SOIB/IOB	18.50	16.65	3.186	11	0.009	*
AIB/BOB	19.75	20.24	- 2.652	11	0.022	*
Nasal structure						
NB/NH	48.58	46.41	2.302	5	0.070	
DS/DC	54.93	55.00	- 0.026	4	0.981	
SMN/MN	39.05	49.07	- 7.476	11	0.000	*
Orbit						
LOH/LOBM	81.77	79.96	1.796	11	0.100	
LOH/LOBD	85.75	84.49	1.880	11	0.087	
Dental arch						
MB/ML	114.92	132.80	- 2.746	4	0.052	
Mandible						
LM/BCB	88.72	81.70	7.500	4	0.000	*

** DF $\leq$ 3, t-prob. = 1

APPENDIX D

Table 139

"t" SCORES FOR MEASUREMENTS OF:
BAUM-GARTNER DEFORMED MALE CRANIA

(N = Baum 10; Gartner 6)

	$\bar{X}_{Ba}$	$\bar{X}_{Ga}$	t-ratio	DF**	t-prob.	Sig. diff.
Cranial vault						
CM	151.43	154.39	- 2.973	14	0.010	*
TP	5.10	5.00	0.219	14	0.829	
L	172.30	177.17	- 1.660	14	0.119	
B	145.00	148.00	- 0.835	14	0.418	
MF	95.40	96.17	- 0.437	8	0.674	
H	137.00	138.00	- 6.708	7	0.000	*
PAH	120.10	121.50	- 1.305	14	0.213	
BPH	------	------	-------	---	-----	
LB	103.70	103.00	0.684	3	1.000	
Face						
TFH	126.00	125.67	1.315	14	0.210	
UFH	75.90	75.33	1.628	4	0.179	
TFB	140.40	141.17	- 0.650	7	0.536	
MFB	102.00	104.33	- 5.021	14	0.000	*
IOB	99.90	97.83	2.424	8	0.042	
SIOB	17.70	16.00	2.684	10	0.023	*
BOB	99.80	98.00	8.969	7	0.000	*
AIB	19.80	20.17	- 1.262	14	0.228	
Nasal structure						
NB	27.00	26.50	0.958	4	0.392	
NH	54.90	54.83	0.366	14	0.720	
DC	19.90	20.00	- 0.429	7	0.681	
DS	11.00	11.00	0.000	- 1	1.000	
MN	9.70	9.83	- 0.323	14	0.751	
SMN	4.00	4.83	- 4.999	3	1.000	
Orbit						
LOH	34.90	35.00	- 0.219	14	0.829	
LOBM	43.00	43.17	- 0.406	14	0.691	
LOBD	41.00	41.00	0.000	14	1.000	
Dental arch						
MB	68.00	69.00	- 0.842	14	0.414	
ML	55.90	52.50	5.949	10	0.000	*
FL	97.20	98.00	- 3.986	7	0.005	*
FLA	95.20	96.00	- 3.986	7	0.005	*
Mandible						
LM	103.10	102.83	0.159	4	0.881	
BCB	125.90	131.50	- 2.484	4	0.068	
SH	36.00	37.17	- 1.186	14	0.256	
BA	104.70	104.83	- 0.051	4	0.962	
RL	34.79	36.33	- 1.622	14	0.127	
Facial angles						
G∠	115.20	113.50	1.237	14	0.236	

** DF ≤ 3, t-prob. = 1

Table 140

"t" SCORES FOR INDICES OF:
BAUM-GARTNER DEFORMED MALE CRANIA

(N = Baum 10; Gartner 6)

	$\bar{x}_{Ba}$	$\bar{x}_{Ga}$	t-ratio	DF**	t-prob.	Sig. diff.
Cranial vault						
B/L	84.27	83.74	0.171	14	0.866	
H/L	79.57	78.00	1.202	14	0.249	
H/B	94.70	93.39	0.550	14	0.591	
H/L+B/2	86.38	84.89	1.923	14	0.075	
PAH/L	69.75	86.65	0.944	14	0.361	
BPH/H	------	------	-------	---	-----	
MF/B	65.87	65.08	0.445	14	0.663	
Face						
TFH/TFB	89.80	89.02	0.932	10	0.373	
UFH/TFB	54.10	53.36	1.278	11	0.227	
UFH/MFB	74.42	72.21	6.909	14	0.000	*
TFB/B	97.02	95.52	0.626	14	0.541	
MF/TFB	67.94	68.12	- 0.178	10	0.862	
BA/MF	110.10	108.97	0.323	14	0.751	
BA/TFB	74.64	74.27	0.198	14	0.846	
SIOB/IOB	17.70	16.36	2.371	11	0.037	*
AIB/BOB	19.84	20.58	- 2.983	14	0.010	*
Nasal structure						
NB/NH	49.18	48.32	0.996	4	0.376	
DS/DC	55.35	55.00	0.505	7	0.629	
SMN/MN	41.44	49.24	- 5.243	14	0.000	*
Orbit						
LOH/LOBM	81.17	81.09	0.083	14	0.935	
LOH/LOBD	85.12	85.36	- 0.256	14	0.801	
Dental arch						
MB/ML	121.65	131.44	- 4.238	3	1.000	
Mandible						
LM/BCB	81.94	78.22	3.126	14	0.007	*

** DF ≤ 3, t-prob. = 1

APPENDIX D 473

Table 141

"t" SCORES FOR MEASUREMENTS OF:
FEURT-FULLERTON FIELD UNDEFORMED MALE CRANIA

(N = Feurt 17; Fullerton Field 6)

	$\bar{X}_{Fe}$	$\bar{X}_{Fu}$	t-ratio	DF**	t-prob.	Sig. diff.
Cranial vault						
CM	155.27	156.05	- 0.564	21	0.579	
TP	4.88	5.00	- 0.696	14	0.498	
L	182.12	184.17	- 0.364	21	0.719	
B	139.76	141.00	- 0.715	18	0.484	
MF	96.76	94.50	1.600	21	0.125	
H	142.94	143.00	- 0.120	14	0.906	
PAH	119.00	119.00	0.0	14	1.000	
BPH	------	------	-------	---	-----	
LB	105.65	105.00	- 0.120	14	0.906	
Face						
TFH	126.71	126.00	1.688	14	0.114	
UFH	77.47	78.00	- 1.232	14	0.238	
TFB	142.12	142.00	0.133	14	0.896	
MFB	104.47	102.00	4.197	14	0.001	*
IOB	100.82	100.00	0.891	14	0.388	
SIOB	18.18	18.00	0.309	14	0.762	
BOB	101.59	102.00	- 1.100	14	0.290	
AIB	20.29	19.00	3.096	14	0.008	*
Nasal structure						
NB	27.59	27.00	1.898	14	0.078	
NH	55.35	56.33	- 1.693	21	0.105	
DC	22.23	21.67	0.863	21	0.398	
DS	11.41	11.00	1.951	14	0.071	
MN	10.00	9.00	3.234	14	0.006	*
SMN	4.29	4.17	0.458	7	0.653	
Orbit						
LOH	34.24	34.00	0.554	14	0.588	
LOBM	44.65	44.83	- 0.634	18	0.534	
LOBD	41.88	42.83	- 4.278	21	0.000	*
Dental arch						
MB	69.41	68.17	1.592	21	0.126	
ML	55.12	55.00	0.316	14	0.757	
FL	100.35	100.00	0.971	14	0.348	
FLA	98.47	98.00	1.141	14	0.272	
Mandible						
LM	105.41	103.17	1.687	21	0.106	
BCB	129.12	132.17	- 1.492	21	0.150	
SH	37.18	38.83	- 2.277	21	0.033	*
BA	104.24	104.83	- 0.570	17	0.576	
RL	34.82	35.00	- 0.126	15	0.906	
Facial angles						
G∠	114.65	108.17	7.676	15	0.000	*

** DF ≤ 3, t-prob. = 1

Table 142

"t" SCORES FOR INDICES OF: FEURT-FULLERTON FIELD UNDEFORMED MALE CRANIA

(N = Feurt 17; Fullerton Field 6)

	$\bar{X}_{Fe}$	$\bar{X}_{Fu}$	t-ratio	DF	t-prob.	Sig. diff.
Cranial vault						
B/L	76.42	76.58	-0.141	17	0.889	
H/L	78.13	77.70	0.389	21	0.701	
H/B	102.43	101.44	0.793	18	0.438	
H/L+B/2	88.58	87.99	0.602	21	0.554	
PAH/L	65.05	64.65	0.385	21	0.704	
BPH/H	------	------	-------	---	-----	
MF/B	69.32	67.05	1.625	21	0.119	
Face						
TFH/TFB	89.19	88.72	0.953	14	0.357	
UFH/TFB	54.55	54.93	-0.819	14	0.426	
UFH/MFB	74.21	76.47	-3.369	14	0.005	*
TFB/B	101.85	100.73	0.805	19	0.431	
MF/TFB	68.11	66.55	1.473	21	0.155	
BA/MF	107.78	110.99	-1.919	21	0.069	
BA/TFB	73.35	73.83	-0.647	15	0.525	
SIOB/IOB	18.02	18.00	0.034	14	0.973	
AIB/BOB	19.97	18.63	3.551	14	0.003	*
Nasal structure						
NB/NH	49.85	47.93	2.993	19	0.007	*
DS/DC	51.52	50.83	0.469	18	0.645	
SMN/MN	43.33	46.29	-1.010	16	0.328	
Orbit						
LOH/LOBM	76.68	75.84	0.952	17	0.355	
LOH/LOBD	81.75	79.38	2.192	17	0.043	
Dental arch						
MB/ML	126.01	123.93	1.141	21	0.267	
Mandible						
LM/BCB	81.71	78.23	1.961	21	0.063	

APPENDIX D

Table 143
"t" SCORES FOR MEASUREMENTS OF:
FEURT-FULLERTON FIELD DEFORMED MALE CRANIA

(N = Feurt 15; Fullerton Field 2)

	$\bar{X}_{Fe}$	$\bar{X}_{Fu}$	t-ratio	DF**	t-prob.	Sig. diff.
Cranial vault						
CM	155.56	160.00	- 3.414	15	0.004	*
TP	5.60	4.50	2.795	15	0.014	*
L	172.07	181.00	- 2.742	15	0.015	*
B	151.07	146.00	1.181	15	0.256	
MF	95.27	93.50	1.489	11	0.164	
H	143.53	153.00	- 3.980	15	0.001	*
PAH	121.73	123.50	- 1.505	10	0.163	
BPH	------	------	-------	---	-----	
LB	104.53	107.50	- 1.169	0	1.000	
Face						
TFH	127.33	126.00	0.668	15	0.514	
UFH	78.93	78.00	0.790	15	0.442	
TFB	141.67	139.00	0.849	15	0.409	
MFB	102.73	102.00	0.307	15	0.763	
IOB	100.13	101.00	- 0.456	15	0.655	
SIOB	18.80	20.50	- 0.672	0	1.000	
BOB	101.53	102.00	- 0.402	15	0.694	
AIB	19.60	18.00	1.771	15	0.097	
Nasal structure						
NB	27.00	27.00	0.0	15	1.000	
NH	56.40	54.50	2.079	15	0.055	
DC	21.47	19.50	0.780	0	1.000	
DS	11.13	10.50	1.584	15	0.134	
MN	9.67	9.00	1.267	15	0.225	
SMN	4.20	3.50	1.207	15	0.246	
Orbit						
LOH	33.80	34.00	- 0.254	15	0.803	
LOBM	45.07	45.50	- 0.818	15	0.426	
LOBD	42.00	44.00	- 3.254	15	0.005	*
Dental arch						
MB	68.67	69.00	- 0.371	15	0.716	
ML	55.20	55.00	0.112	15	0.912	
FL	99.80	100.00	- 0.090	15	0.929	
FLA	97.80	98.00	- 0.085	15	0.933	
Mandible						
LM	105.80	106.00	- 0.091	15	0.929	
BCB	129.07	126.50	1.412	15	0.178	
SH	36.73	40.00	- 2.453	15	0.027	*
BA	103.60	104.00	- 0.127	15	0.900	
RL	35.33	33.00	1.824	15	0.088	
Facial angles						
G∠	117.60	108.00	3.089	15	0.007	*

** DF ≤ 3, t-prob. = 1

Table 144

"t" SCORES FOR INDICES OF:
FEURT-FULLERTON FIELD DEFORMED MALE CRANIA

(N = Feurt 15; Fullerton Field 2)

	$\bar{x}_{Fe}$	$\bar{x}_{Fu}$	t-ratio	DF**	t-prob.	Sig. diff.
Cranial vault						
B/L	87.91	80.66	1.885	15	0.079	
H/L	83.46	84.53	- 0.573	15	0.575	
H/B	95.16	104.78	- 2.886	15	0.011	*
H/L+B/2	88.85	93.58	- 2.774	15	0.014	*
PAH/L	70.78	68.23	3.488	12	0.004	*
BPH/H	-----	-----	-------	---	-----	
MF/B	63.09	64.04	- 1.403	8	0.198	
Face						
TFH/TFB	89.94	90.65	- 0.377	15	0.712	
UFH/TFB	55.75	56.12	- 0.347	15	0.734	
UFH/MFB	76.91	76.47	0.201	15	0.843	
TFB/B	93.85	95.21	- 0.589	15	0.565	
MF/TFB	67.26	67.27	- 0.018	7	0.986	
BA/MF	108.92	111.23	- 1.330	12	0.208	
BA/TFB	73.14	74.82	- 0.972	15	0.347	
SIOB/IOB	18.80	20.27	- 1.024	15	0.322	
AIB/BOB	19.30	17.65	2.011	15	0.063	
Nasal structure						
NB/NH	47.86	65.64	- 0.925	0	1.000	
DS/DC	52.16	54.41	- 0.506	15	0.620	
SMN/MN	43.30	38.88	0.903	15	0.381	
Orbit						
LOH/LOBM	75.00	74.73	0.173	15	0.865	
LOH/LOBD	80.47	77.31	1.990	15	0.065	
Dental arch						
MB/ML	124.59	125.45	- 0.224	15	0.826	
Mandible						
LM/BCB	81.98	83.84	- 1.249	15	0.231	

** DF $\leq$ 3, t-prob. = 1

APPENDIX D

Table 145
"t" SCORES FOR INDICES OF: FEURT-FULLERTON FIELD
UNDEFORMED FEMALE CRANIA

(N = Feurt 6; Fullerton Field 3)

	$\bar{X}_{Fe}$	$\bar{X}_{Fu}$	t-ratio	DF*	t-prob.	Sig. diff.
Cranial vault						
B/L	79.08	79.55	- 0.428	3	1.000	
H/L	77.28	79.55	- 3.355	3	1.000	
H/B	97.82	100.00	- 0.917	7	0.390	
H/L+B/2	86.33	88.61	- 2.458	3	1.000	
PAH/L	65.18	67.61	- 2.324	7	0.053	
BPH/H	------	------	-------	--	-----	
MF/B	66.31	63.33	2.063	7	0.078	
Face						
TFH/TFB	89.21	86.57	1.982	3	1.000	
UFH/TFB	55.25	52.24	2.390	7	0.048	
UFH/MFB	72.32	70.71	2.717	7	0.030	*
TFB/B	94.81	95.71	- 1.115	3	1.000	
MF/TFB	69.95	66.17	2.667	7	0.032	*
BA/MF	106.44	112.52	- 3.302	7	0.013	*
BA/TFB	74.47	74.38	0.054	7	0.959	
SIOB/IOB	16.45	13.96	1.114	7	0.302	
AIB/BOB	20.04	18.50	3.127	3	1.000	
Nasal structure						
NB/NH	51.31	48.08	1.868	0	1.000	
DS/DC	44.64	45.00	- 0.682	7	0.517	
SMN/MN	37.63	36.11	0.318	4	0.767	
Orbit						
LOH/LOBM	81.58	86.18	- 2.532	7	0.039	*
LOH/LOBD	85.44	89.83	- 3.127	3	1.000	
Dental arch						
MB/ML	124.36	127.12	- 1.245	0	1.000	
Mandible						
LM/BCB	83.50	80.15	0.964	0	1.000	

*DF $\leq$ 3, t-prob. = 1

Table 146

"t" SCORES FOR MEASUREMENTS OF: FEURT-PROCTORVILLE, Gp 1 UNDEFORMED MALE CRANIA

(N = Feurt 17; Proctorville, Gp 1, 4)

	$\bar{X}_{Fe}$	$\bar{X}_{Gp}^{Pr}$	t-ratio	DF**	t-prob.	Sig. diff.
Cranial vault						
CM	155.27	151.67	1.063	1	1.000	
TP	4.88	5.25	- 0.564	1	1.000	
L	183.12	175.50	1.352	1	1.000	
B	139.76	140.75	- 0.302	19	0.766	
MF	96.76	95.25	0.886	19	0.387	
H	142.94	138.75	3.325	19	0.004	*
PAH	119.00	117.50	1.088	19	0.290	
BPH	------	------	-------	---	-----	
LB	105.65	102.25	2.052	19	0.054	
Face						
TFH	126.71	126.00	0.803	19	0.432	
UFH	77.47	75.75	1.854	19	0.079	
TFB	142.12	138.50	1.836	19	0.082	
MFB	104.47	100.50	2.852	19	0.010	*
IOB	100.82	100.50	0.334	16	0.743	
SIOB	18.18	17.75	0.320	19	0.752	
BOB	101.59	100.50	1.331	19	0.199	
AIB	20.29	19.75	0.516	19	0.611	
Nasal structure						
NB	27.59	26.50	0.645	1	1.000	
NH	55.35	54.25	1.563	19	0.135	
DC	22.24	21.50	0.850	19	0.406	
DS	11.41	11.25	0.354	19	0.727	
MN	10.00	10.25	- 0.333	19	0.743	
SMN	4.29	4.00	0.585	19	0.565	
Orbit						
LOH	34.24	34.50	- 0.288	19	0.777	
LOBM	44.65	44.00	1.200	19	0.245	
LOBD	41.88	40.50	4.967	19	0.000	*
Dental arch						
MB	69.41	69.00	0.486	19	0.632	
ML	55.12	56.25	- 1.395	19	0.179	
FL	100.35	99.75	0.652	19	0.522	
FLA	98.47	98.00	0.440	19	0.665	
Mandible						
LM	105.41	104.75	0.464	19	0.648	
BCB	129.12	127.25	1.616	15	0.127	
SH	37.18	37.75	- 1.248	15	0.231	
BA	104.24	103.50	0.765	15	0.456	
RL	34.82	32.00	1.478	1	1.000	
Facial angles						
G∠	114.65	114.50	0.046	1	1.000	

** DF $\leq$ 3, t-prob. = 1

APPENDIX D

Table 147

"t" SCORES FOR INDICES OF:
FEURT-PROCTORVILLE, Gp 1 UNDEFORMED MALE CRANIA

(N = Feurt 17; Proctorville, Gp 1 4)

	$\bar{X}_{Fe}$	$\bar{X}_{Gp}^{Pr}$	t-ratio	DF**	t-prob.	Sig. diff.
Cranial vault						
B/L	76.42	80.26	- 2.957	13	0.011	*
H/L	78.13	79.21	- 0.754	19	0.460	
H/B	102.43	98.65	1.678	19	0.110	
H/L+B/2	88.58	87.86	0.573	19	0.573	
PAH/L	65.05	67.07	- 1.558	19	0.136	
BPH/H	-----	-----	-----	---	-----	
MF/B	69.32	67.78	0.875	19	0.392	
Face						
TFH/TFB	89.19	91.01	- 1.629	19	0.120	
UFH/TFB	54.55	54.71	- 0.161	19	0.874	
UFH/MFB	74.21	75.41	- 0.814	19	0.426	
TFB/B	101.85	98.47	1.319	19	0.203	
MF/TFB	68.11	68.79	- 0.515	19	0.612	
BA/MF	107.78	108.74	- 0.476	19	0.639	
BA/TFB	73.35	74.76	- 1.478	19	0.156	
SIOB/IOB	18.02	17.65	0.298	19	0.769	
AIB/BOB	19.97	19.67	0.205	1	1.000	
Nasal structure						
NB/NH	49.85	48.78	0.396	1	1.000	
DS/DC	51.52	52.57	- 0.380	19	0.708	
SMN/MN	43.33	39.07	0.868	19	0.396	
Orbit						
LOH/LOBM	76.68	78.46	- 0.932	19	0.363	
LOH/LOBD	81.75	85.21	- 1.513	19	0.147	
Dental arch						
MB/ML	126.01	122.67	1.617	19	0.122	
Mandible						
LM/BCB	81.71	82.32	- 0.753	16	0.462	

** DF ≤ 3, t-prob. = 1

Table 148

"t" SCORES FOR MEASUREMENTS OF:
FEURT-PROCTORVILLE, Gp 1 DEFORMED MALE CRANIA

(N = Feurt 15; Proctorville, Gp 1 2)

	$\bar{X}_{Fe}$	$\bar{X}^{Pr}_{Gp}$	t-ratio	DF**	t-prob.	Sig. diff.
Cranial vault						
CM	155.56	153.83	1.301	15	0.213	
TP	5.60	5.00	1.627	15	0.125	
L	172.00	167.50	1.372	15	0.190	
B	151.07	153.50	- 0.554	15	0.588	
MF	95.27	98.00	- 0.848	15	0.410	
H	143.53	140.50	1.257	15	0.228	
PAH	121.73	118.50	2.754	10	0.020	*
BPH	-----	-----	-----	---	-----	
LB	104.53	102.00	1.886	15	0.079	
Face						
TFH	127.33	125.50	0.917	15	0.374	
UFH	78.93	76.00	2.483	15	0.025	*
TFB	141.67	143.50	- 0.242	0	1.000	
MFB	120.73	101.00	0.686	15	0.503	
IOB	100.13	103.50	- 1.680	15	0.114	
SIOB	18.80	19.00	- 0.181	15	0.859	
BOB	101.53	104.00	- 0.613	0	1.000	
AIB	19.60	22.00	- 1.186	0	1.000	
Nasal structure						
NB	27.00	28.00	- 0.857	15	0.405	
NH	56.40	54.00	2.943	15	0.010	*
DC	21.47	24.00	- 1.251	0	1.000	
DS	11.13	11.50	- 0.917	15	0.374	
MN	9.67	12.50	- 5.208	15	0.000	*
SMN	4.20	4.00	0.355	15	0.728	
Orbit						
LOH	33.80	35.00	- 1.524	15	0.148	
LOBM	45.07	45.00	0.066	0	1.000	
LOBD	42.00	42.00	0.0	0	1.000	
Dental arch						
MB	68.67	71.00	- 1.152	0	1.000	
ML	55.20	57.50	- 1.202	15	0.248	
FL	99.80	101.50	- 0.753	15	0.463	
FLA	97.80	100.50	- 1.102	15	0.288	
Mandible						
LM	105.80	106.50	- 0.315	15	0.757	
BCB	129.07	133.00	- 0.973	0	1.000	
SH	36.73	37.60	- 0.628	15	0.539	
BA	103.60	109.00	- 1.574	15	0.136	
RL	35.33	34.50	0.328	0	1.000	
Facial angles						
G∠	117.60	116.50	0.167	0	1.000	

** DF ≤ 3, t-prob. = 1

APPENDIX D

Table 149
"t" SCORES FOR INDICES OF:
FEURT-PROCTORVILLE, Gp 1 DEFORMED MALE CRANIA

(N = Feurt 15; Proctorville, Gp 1 2)

	$\overline{X}_{Fe}$	$\overline{X}^{Pr}_{Gp}$	t-ratio	DF**	t-prob.	Sig. diff.
Cranial vault						
B/L	87.91	91.69	- 0.956	15	0.354	
H/L	83.46	83.91	- 0.229	15	0.822	
H/B	95.16	91.56	1.075	15	0.299	
H/L+B/2	88.85	87.53	0.769	15	0.454	
PAH/L	70.77	70.76	0.006	15	0.995	
BPH/H	------	------	------	---	-----	
MF/B	63.09	63.82	- 0.434	15	0.670	
Face						
TFH/TFB	89.94	87.72	0.446	0	1.000	
UFH/TFB	55.75	53.10	0.944	0	1.000	
UFH/MFB	76.91	75.31	0.706	15	0.491	
TFB/B	83.85	93.42	0.177	15	0.862	
MF/TFB	67.26	68.33	- 0.634	15	0.536	
BA/MF	108.92	111.20	- 1.318	13	0.210	
BA/TFB	73.14	75.98	- 1.640	15	0.121	
SIOB/IOB	18.80	18.36	0.336	15	0.741	
AIB/BOB	19.30	21.11	- 2.174	15	0.046	
Nasal structure						
NB/NH	47.86	51.85	- 2.193	15	0.044	
DS/DC	52.16	48.08	0.949	15	0.358	
SMN/MN	43.30	32.05	2.418	15	0.029	*
Orbit						
LOH/LOBM	75.00	77.82	- 1.759	15	0.099	
LOH/LOBD	80.47	83.38	- 1.811	15	0.090	
Dental arch						
MB/ML	124.59	123.56	0.267	15	0.793	
Mandible						
LM/BCB	81.98	80.11	1.348	15	0.198	

** DF ≤ 3, t-prob. = 1

482   PREHISTORIC PEOPLE OF FORT ANCIENT

Table 150

"t" SCORES FOR MEASUREMENTS OF: FEURT-PROCTORVILLE
DEFORMED FEMALE CRANIA

(N = Feurt 9; Proctorville 6)

	$\bar{X}_{Fe}$	$\bar{X}_{Pr}$	t-ratio	DF*	t-prob.	Sig. diff.
Cranial vault						
CM	146.33	144.83	1.295	4	0.265	
TP	5.22	4.83	0.919	13	0.375	
L	159.11	163.00	- 1.432	13	0.176	
B	148.11	141.67	3.055	13	0.009	*
MF	92.89	88.17	3.617	13	0.003	*
H	131.78	129.83	1.266	13	0.228	
PAH	114.00	114.16	- 0.169	5	0.872	
BPH	------	------	------	--	-----	
LB	96.89	94.17	2.177	3	1.000	
Face						
TFH	116.00	116.00	0.0	- 1	1.000	
UFH	72.11	69.00	4.657	13	0.000	*
TFB	132.56	133.00	- 1.178	6	0.283	
MFB	98.78	100.17	- 0.964	3	1.000	
IOB	94.78	93.17	1.373	13	0.193	
SIOB	16.56	13.17	5.311	13	0.000	*
BOB	93.33	97.00	- 0.791	5	0.465	
AIB	19.11	16.83	5.469	4	0.005	*
Nasal structure						
NB	26.22	26.17	0.083	4	0.938	
NH	50.78	51.17	- 0.415	4	0.699	
DC	20.00	18.00	9.675	13	0.0	*
DS	9.22	8.83	0.919	13	0.375	
MN	7.00	7.50	- 1.249	13	0.234	
SMN	3.00	3.00	0.0	13	1.000	
Orbit						
LOH	33.11	32.83	0.684	13	0.506	
LOBM	41.22	41.17	0.130	4	0.903	
LOBD	39.22	38.67	0.963	4	0.390	

APPENDIX D

Table 150 - continued

Dental arch						
MB	64.78	65.83	- 1.528	4	0.201	
ML	52.78	52.17	0.846	13	0.413	
FL	95.22	94.83	0.553	7	0.597	
FLA	93.33	93.50	- 0.159	13	0.876	
Mandible						
LM	100.67	104.17	- 7.274	13	0.0	*
BCB	121.67	124.00	- 5.048	13	0.000	*
SH	30.67	32.83	0.659	13	0.521	
BA	97.22	97.67	- 0.228	9	0.825	
RL	30.56	31.67	- 1.275	13	0.225	
Facial angles						
G∠	124.44°	101.33°	1.136	3	1.000	

*DF $\leq$ 3, t-prob. = 1

Table 151

"t" SCORES FOR INDICES OF: FEURT-PROCTORVILLE

DEFORMED FEMALE CRANIA

(N = Feurt 9; Proctorville 6)

	$\overline{X}_{Fe}$	$\overline{X}_{Pr}$	t-ratio	DF	t-prob.	Sig. diff.
Cranial vault						
B/L	82.10	87.06	- 0.499	7	0.633	
H/L	82.89	79.70	2.110	13	0.055	
H/B	89.02	91.72	- 1.694	13	0.114	
H/L+B/2	85.79	85.23	0.648	13	0.528	
PAH/L	71.70	70.11	1.284	13	0.221	
BPH/H	------	------	-------	--	-----	
MF/B	62.76	62.27	0.403	13	0.694	
Face						
TFH/TFB	87.52	87.22	1.197	6	0.277	
UFH/TFB	54.41	51.88	5.268	13	0.000	*
UFH/MFB	73.00	68.94	3.971	4	0.017	*
TFB/B	89.55	93.94	- 3.595	13	0.003	*
MF/TFB	70.08	66.29	3.821	13	0.002	*
BA/MF	104.74	110.81	- 2.124	13	0.053	
BA/TFB	73.35	73.43	- 0.058	9	0.955	
SIOB/IOB	17.47	14.13	5.265	13	0.000	*
AIB/BOB	19.84	17.35	8.542	3	1.000	
Nasal structure						
NB/NH	51.65	51.15	0.483	4	0.655	
DS/DC	46.11	48.97	- 1.511	13	0.155	
SMN/MN	42.86	40.00	1.401	3	1.000	
Orbit						
LOH/LOBM	80.33	79.76	0.687	13	0.504	
LOH/LOBD	84.43	85.00	- 0.365	5	0.730	
Dental arch						
MB/ML	122.85	126.24	- 1.506	13	0.156	
Mandible						
LM/BCB	82.74	84.01	- 3.075	3	1.000	

APPENDIX D

Table 152
"t" SCORES FOR MEASUREMENTS OF:
ANDERSON-TAYLOR MALE CRANIA

(N = Anderson 46; Taylor 25)

	$\bar{X}_{An}$	$\bar{X}_{Ta}$	t-ratio	DF	t-prob.	Sig. diff.
Cranial vault						
CM	152.86	153.88	- 1.302	69	0.197	
TP	4.83	4.64	1.093	69	0.278	
L	179.76	183.24	- 1.955	69	0.055	
B	138.17	138.44	- 0.191	69	0.849	
MF	92.72	95.56	- 1.383	52	0.173	
H	140.65	139.96	0.861	69	0.392	
PAH	117.78	115.76	1.809	61	0.075	
BPH	------	------	-------	---	-----	
LB	104.28	103.64	0.766	69	0.447	
Face						
TFH	124.35	126.04	- 2.150	62	0.035	*
UFH	74.96	75.00	- 0.057	66	0.954	
TFB	140.57	140.36	0.214	69	0.831	
MFB	103.20	100.48	2.871	69	0.005	*
IOB	100.20	99.96	0.283	69	0.778	
SIOB	18.17	17.72	1.085	69	0.282	
BOB	100.99	101.04	- 0.081	69	0.936	
AIB	19.72	19.96	- 0.551	69	0.583	
Nasal structure						
NB	26.83	27.16	- 0.851	69	0.398	
NH	53.76	53.80	- 0.069	69	0.945	
DC	20.89	21.00	- 0.278	69	0.782	
DS	10.98	11.28	- 1.063	69	0.291	
MN	8.78	8.16	2.255	69	0.027	*
SMN	3.96	3.92	0.199	69	0.843	
Orbit						
LOH	34.61	34.72	- 0.214	35	0.832	
LOBM	44.11	43.12	1.615	31	0.117	
LOBD	41.83	41.20	1.621	69	0.109	
Dental arch						
MB	69.22	68.88	0.417	69	0.678	
ML	54.35	53.96	0.778	69	0.439	
FL	97.96	97.56	0.464	69	0.644	
FLA	96.07	95.64	0.486	69	0.629	
Mandible						
LM	105.37	102.88	2.625	62	0.011	*
BCB	129.28	128.60	0.497	69	0.621	
SH	36.26	36.92	- 1.359	69	0.178	
BA	104.89	100.96	4.060	64	0.000	*
RL	35.28	35.76	- 0.768	69	0.445	
Facial angles						
G/	114.13	115.00	- 0.605	69	0.547	

Table 153

"t" SCORES FOR INDICES OF:
ANDERSON-TAYLOR MALE CRANIA

(N = Anderson 46; Taylor 25)

	$\bar{x}_{An}$	$\bar{x}_{Ta}$	t-ratio	DF	t-prob.	Sig. diff.
Cranial vault						
B/L	77.08	75.62	1.320	66	0.191	
H/L	78.37	76.44	2.650	62	0.010	*
H/B	101.94	101.17	0.916	63	0.363	
H/L+B/2	88.49	87.04	3.003	69	0.004	*
PAH/L	65.65	63.21	3.127	67	0.003	*
BPH/H	------	------	-------	---	-----	
MF/B	67.14	69.09	- 1.272	57	0.209	
Face						
TFH/TFB	88.51	85.87	0.728	23	0.474	
UFH/TFB	53.35	53.47	- 0.173	69	0.863	
UFH/MFB	72.67	74.74	- 2.363	69	0.021	*
TFB/B	101.86	101.43	0.594	67	0.554	
MF/TFB	66.05	68.11	- 1.391	51	0.170	
BA/MF	111.20	105.76	3.980	67	0.000	*
BA/TFB	74.67	71.97	3.333	67	0.001	*
SIOB/IOB	18.14	17.71	1.153	69	0.253	
AIB/BOB	19.54	19.45	- 0.553	61	0.582	
Nasal structure						
NB/NH	49.98	50.58	- 0.665	69	0.508	
DS/DC	52.87	54.06	- 0.666	69	0.508	
SMN/MN	45.47	48.53	- 1.352	69	0.181	
Orbit						
LOH/LOBM	78.55	77.20	0.704	28	0.487	
LOH/LOBD	82.85	80.31	0.746	24	0.463	
Dental arch						
MB/ML	127.41	127.73	- 0.229	69	0.819	
Mandible						
LM/BCB	81.64	80.14	1.290	69	0.201	

APPENDIX D

Table 154

"t" SCORES FOR MEASUREMENTS OF: ANDERSON-TAYLOR

UNDEFORMED FEMALE CRANIA

(N = Anderson 31; Taylor 5)

	$\overline{X}_{An}$	$\overline{X}_{Ta}$	t-ratio	DF*	t-prob.	Sig. diff.
Cranial vault						
CM	148.16	147.93	0.097	2	1.000	
TP	4.61	4.80	- 0.443	34	0.661	
L	176.26	178.80	- 0.704	2	1.000	
B	132.23	132.00	0.155	34	0.878	
MF	88.39	92.00	- 1.121	31	0.271	
H	136.00	133.00	1.159	2	1.000	
PAH	113.65	112.40	0.553	2	1.000	
BPH	------	------	-------	--	-----	
LB	93.29	100.80	- 1.495	30	0.145	
Face						
TFH	115.16	115.20	- 0.034	34	0.973	
UFH	69.81	70.40	- 0.387	2	1.000	
TFB	129.90	128.20	0.740	2	1.000	
MFB	90.39	95.20	- 1.082	31	0.288	
IOB	94.94	95.60	- 0.553	34	0.584	
SIOB	17.29	17.80	- 1.104	34	0.277	
BOB	96.97	96.20	0.540	2	1.000	
AIB	18.26	19.20	- 1.355	34	0.184	
Nasal structure						
NB	25.84	26.20	- 0.638	34	0.528	
NH	50.00	51.00	- 1.426	34	0.163	
DC	20.10	20.20	- 0.205	10	0.841	
DS	10.06	9.60	1.287	34	0.207	
MN	8.10	8.20	- 0.159	34	0.874	
SMN	3.13	3.40	- 0.921	34	0.364	
Orbit						
LOH	33.71	33.80	- 0.130	34	0.898	
LOBM	42.13	42.20	- 0.087	2	1.000	
LOBD	39.77	40.00	- 0.473	34	0.640	

Table 154 - continued

Dental arch						
MB	65.23	63.00	2.816	34	0.008	*
ML	52.96	53.00	- 0.046	34	0.964	
FL	93.42	97.60	- 1.309	31	0.200	
FLA	91.55	95.60	- 1.279	32	0.210	
Mandible						
LM	102.00	100.00	1.484	34	0.147	
BCB	120.39	119.60	0.669	10	0.519	
SH	33.35	32.00	1.555	34	0.129	
BA	96.61	92.20	3.962	26	0.001	*
RL	33.13	32.20	0.761	34	0.452	
Facial angles						
G∠	121.32°	122.00°	- 0.176	2	1.000	

*DF ≤ 3, t-prob. = 1

Table 155

"t" SCORES FOR INDICES OF: ANDERSON-TAYLOR

UNDEFORMED FEMALE CRANIA

(N = Anderson 31; Taylor 5)

	$\bar{X}_{An}$	$\bar{X}_{Ta}$	t-ratio	DF*	t-prob.	Sig. diff.
Cranial vault						
B/L	75.05	73.90	1.060	34	0.296	
H/L	77.19	74.43	2.634	34	0.013	*
H/B	102.90	100.73	1.492	34	0.145	
H/L+B/2	88.19	85.58	2.503	34	0.017	*
PAH/L	64.51	62.87	2.063	34	0.047	
BPH/H	------	------	-------	--	-----	
MF/B	66.85	69.72	- 1.182	31	0.246	
Face						
TFH/TFB	88.68	89.96	- 1.029	34	0.311	
UFH/TFB	53.75	54.93	- 1.485	34	0.147	
UFH/MFB	70.72	74.02	- 1.282	14	0.221	
TFB/B	98.28	97.18	0.519	2	1.000	
MF/TFB	68.05	71.81	- 1.495	30	0.145	
BA/MF	122.08	100.29	1.358	28	0.185	
BA/TFB	74.38	71.98	1.269	34	0.213	
SIOB/IOB	18.21	18.65	- 0.562	2	1.000	
AIB/BOB	18.83	19.96	- 3.254	18	0.004	*
Nasal structure						
NB/NH	51.72	51.42	0.215	34	0.831	
DS/DC	50.59	47.57	0.919	34	0.364	
SMN/MN	39.19	41.53	- 1.260	15	0.227	
Orbit						
LOH/LOBM	80.04	80.13	- 0.051	34	0.960	
LOH/LOBD	84.80	84.56	0.118	34	0.906	
Dental arch						
MB/ML	123.19	118.98	2.478	34	0.018	*
Mandible						
LM/BCB	84.83	83.62	0.706	34	0.485	

*DF $\leq$ 3, t-prob. = 1

Table 156

"t" SCORES FOR MEASUREMENTS OF: MADISONVILLE-TURPIN UNDEFORMED MALE CRANIA

(N = Madisonville 60; Turpin 6)

	$\bar{X}_{Ma}$	$\bar{X}_{Tu}$	t-ratio	DF**	t-prob.	Sig. diff.
Cranial vault						
CM	153.11	152.89	0.132	64	0.896	
TP	5.08	4.50	1.406	64	0.165	
L	180.22	178.67	0.406	64	0.686	
B	143.05	139.83	1.422	64	0.160	
MF	95.32	92.67	1.306	64	0.196	
H	136.07	140.17	-2.154	64	0.035	*
PAH	116.72	117.00	-0.201	64	0.842	
BPH	------	------	-------	----	-----	
LB	104.35	104.17	0.092	64	0.927	
Face						
TFH	122.92	125.50	-0.807	64	0.423	
UFH	72.73	74.17	-1.050	64	0.298	
TFB	141.22	138.00	2.176	64	0.033	*
MFB	102.72	100.83	1.312	64	0.194	
IOB	100.22	98.00	1.682	64	0.097	
SIOB	17.55	16.67	0.931	64	0.355	
BOB	101.32	100.00	1.427	64	0.158	
AIB	20.55	19.17	1.776	64	0.080	
Nasal structure						
NB	27.20	25.67	1.233	3	1.000	
NH	52.90	53.50	-0.616	64	0.540	
DC	22.35	21.50	1.103	64	0.274	
DS	11.70	11.82	-0.610	12	0.553	
MN	9.73	8.83	1.418	64	0.161	
SMN	3.97	3.83	0.680	7	0.519	
Orbit						
LOH	34.03	34.00	0.046	64	0.963	
LOBM	43.67	43.83	-0.348	64	0.729	
LOBD	40.90	40.50	0.811	64	0.420	
Dental arch						
MB	63.82	67.17	-1.510	64 /	0.136	
ML	55.28	55.50	-0.162	3	1.000	
FL	99.43	99.17	0.228	64	0.820	
FLA	98.20	97.83	0.319	64	0.751	
Mandible						
LM	104.68	108.83	-3.114	64	0.003	*
BCB	129.75	124.00	2.347	64	1.000	
SH	35.95	36.50	-0.538	64	0.592	
BA	105.25	101.33	1.418	3	1.000	
RL	35.67	33.33	2.328	64	0.023	*
Facial angles						
G∠	119.45	123.17	-1.131	3	1.000	

** DF ≤ 3, t-prob. = 1

APPENDIX D

Table 157

"t" SCORES FOR INDICES OF: MADISONVILLE-TURPIN UNDEFORMED MALE CRANIA

(N = Madisonville 60; Turpin 6)

	$\bar{X}_{Ma}$	$\bar{X}_{Tu}$	t-ratio	DF**	t-prob.	Sig. diff.
Cranial vault						
B/L	77.95	78.31	- 0.200	12	0.845	
H/L	74.06	78.45	- 3.091	39	0.004	*
H/B	95.25	100.33	- 2.452	64	0.017	*
H/L+B/2	84.27	88.02	- 2.278	64	0.026	*
PAH/L	64.95	65.51	- 0.760	20	0.456	
BPH/H	------	------	-------	---	-----	
MF/B	66.69	66.38	0.192	64	0.848	
Face						
TFH/TFB	85.39	90.97	- 3.194	12	0.008	*
UFH/TFB	51.52	53.75	- 2.304	64	0.024	*
UFH/MFB	70.87	73.56	- 1.737	64	0.087	
TFB/B	98.82	98.76	0.037	64	0.970	
MF/TFB	67.51	67.16	0.251	64	0.803	
BA/MF	110.68	109.42	0.443	64	0.659	
BA/TFB	74.56	73.45	0.552	3	1.000	
SIOB/IOB	17.49	17.01	0.568	64	0.572	
AIB/BOB	20.27	19.17	1.623	64	0.109	
Nasal structure						
NB/NH	51.51	48.03	1.455	3	1.000	
DS/DC	52.70	55.21	- 1.574	8	0.154	
SMN/MN	41.17	43.44	- 1.769	32	0.086	
Orbit						
LOH/LOBM	77.96	77.58	0.230	64	0.819	
LOH/LOBD	83.26	83.98	- 0.379	64	0.706	
Dental arch						
MB/ML	115.49	120.99	- 3.753	33	0.001	*
Mandible						
LM/BCB	80.73	71.33	0.656	3	1.000	

** DF $\leq$ 3, t-prob. = 1

Table 158

"t" SCORES FOR MEASUREMENTS OF: MADISONVILLE-TURPIN DEFORMED MALE CRANIA

(N = Madisonville 115; Turpin 6)

	$\bar{X}_{Ma}$	$\bar{X}_{Tu}$	t-ratio	DF**	t-prob.	Sig. diff.
Cranial vault						
CM	153.65	154.33	- 0.661	119	0.510	
TP	5.24	5.17	0.267	119	0.790	
L	174.05	174.67	- 0.387	119	0.699	
B	150.02	150.50	- 0.289	119	0.773	
MF	95.21	97.83	- 1.994	119	0.048	
H	136.87	137.83	- 0.699	119	0.486	
PAH	117.85	119.00	- 1.952	6	0.099	
BPH	------	------	--------	---	-----	
LB	103.14	103.33	- 0.494	8	0.634	
Face						
TFH	122.37	122.17	0.155	119	0.877	
UFH	72.83	73.00	- 0.771	112	0.442	
TFB	143.00	143.17	- 0.359	7	0.730	
MFB	101.90	102.00	- 0.413	112	0.681	
IOB	99.49	100.50	- 1.642	5	0.162	
SIOB	17.37	16.33	1.272	13	0.226	
BOB	101.23	101.00	1.336	112	0.184	
AIB	20.07	19.83	0.477	119	0.634	
Nasal structure						
NB	26.91	27.33	- 1.726	7	0.128	
NH	52.89	52.50	0.500	119	0.618	
DC	21.76	21.50	0.524	119	0.601	
DS	12.04	11.50	1.443	119	0.152	
MN	9.83	9.17	1.962	6	0.097	
SMN	4.16	4.17	- 0.032	119	0.975	
Orbit						
LOH	33.93	33.50	1.055	119	0.294	
LOBM	43.90	43.83	0.140	119	0.889	
LOBD	41.06	41.17	- 0.553	7	0.598	
Dental arch						
MB	65.17	66.00	- 3.063	112	0.003	*
ML	54.83	55.17	- 1.491	15	0.157	
FL	99.03	100.50	- 0.975	3	1.000	
FLA	97.91	99.50	- 1.050	3	1.000	
Mandible						
LM	104.43	105.50	- 1.712	10	0.118	
BCB	129.90	130.17	- 0.668	75	0.506	
SH	35.63	37.00	- 0.961	3	1.000	
BA	104.98	102.67	1.376	119	0.171	
RL	35.01	34.83	0.176	119	0.860	
Facial angles						
G∠	119.95	121.17	- 1.277	7	0.242	

** DF ≤ 3, t-prob. = 1

APPENDIX D

Table 159
"t" SCORES FOR INDICES OF:
MADISONVILLE-TURPIN DEFORMED MALE CRANIA

(N = Madisonville 115; Turpin 6)

	$\bar{X}_{Ma}$	$\bar{X}_{Tu}$	t-ratio	DF	t-prob.	Sig. diff.
Cranial vault						
B/L	86.23	86.20	0.025	119	0.980	
H/L	78.67	78.93	- 0.266	119	0.791	
H/B	91.29	91.58	- 0.610	9	0.557	
H/L+B/2	84.49	84.77	- 0.303	119	0.763	
PAH/L	67.73	68.15	- 0.509	119	0.617	
BPH/H	------	------	-------	---	-----	
MF/B	63.49	65.02	- 1.631	119	0.106	
Face						
TFH/TFB	85.59	85.33	0.481	5	0.651	
UFH/TFB	50.94	50.99	- 0.279	15	0.784	
UFH/MFB	71.50	71.57	- 0.284	117	0.777	
TFB/B	95.38	95.14	0.447	7	0.669	
MF/TFB	66.59	68.33	- 1.809	119	0.073	
BA/MF	110.37	105.00	2.404	119	0.018	*
BA/TFB	73.43	71.72	1.377	119	0.171	
SIOB/IOB	17.43	16.26	1.420	11	0.183	
AIB/BOB	19.82	19.63	0.402	119	0.689	
Nasal structure						
NB/NH	50.95	52.10	- 0.891	119	0.374	
DS/DC	55.46	53.51	1.036	119	0.302	
SMN/MN	42.69	45.55	- 1.639	6	0.152	
Orbit						
LOH/LOBM	77.33	73.41	0.855	119	0.394	
LOH/LOBD	82.68	81.38	1.070	119	0.287	
Dental arch						
MB/ML	118.94	119.64	- 1.088	43	0.283	
Mandible						
LM/BCB	80.45	81.05	- 1.332	26	0.194	

Table 160

"t" SCORES FOR MEASUREMENTS OF: MADISONVILLE-TURPIN

UNDEFORMED FEMALE CRANIA

(N = Madisonville 55; Turpin 11)

	$\bar{X}_{Ma}$	$\bar{X}_{Tu}$	t-ratio	DF	t-prob.	Sig. diff.
Cranial vault						
CM	139.43	147.94	- 2.678	61	0.010	*
TP	5.13	4.73	1.390	63	0.170	
L	173.04	173.45	- 0.236	63	0.814	
B	138.93	136.73	1.329	63	0.189	
MF	91.72	91.09	0.534	63	0.595	
H	132.13	133.64	- 1.170	31	0.251	
PAH	113.06	114.18	- 1.232	20	0.232	
BPH	------	------	-------	--	-----	
LB	100.09	99.09	1.121	63	0.267	
Face						
TFH	111.87	112.64	- 0.462	9	0.655	
UFH	68.15	69.91	- 1.466	10	0.173	
TFB	129.94	129.82	0.104	63	0.917	
MFB	98.00	94.64	3.761	63	0.000	*
IOB	95.15	93.09	2.487	63	0.016	*
SIOB	16.28	16.00	0.578	63	0.565	
BOB	97.46	96.91	0.811	63	0.420	
AIB	19.30	18.91	1.145	27	0.262	
Nasal structure						
NB	26.33	25.91	1.024	63	0.310	
NH	49.83	49.55	0.465	63	0.643	
DC	20.91	21.09	- 0.474	20	0.640	
DS	10.94	11.00	- 0.270	39	0.788	
MN	8.81	8.91	- 0.324	51	0.747	
SMN	3.59	3.91	- 2.210	42	0.033	*
Orbit						
LOH	33.07	32.45	1.455	63	0.151	
LOBM	42.20	41.73	1.075	63	0.286	
LOBD	39.15	38.82	0.905	63	0.369	

Table 160 - continued

Dental arch						
MB	63.63	64.09	-0.592	63	0.556	
ML	53.39	54.45	-2.327	21	0.030	*
FL	97.13	94.09	6.864	40	0.0	*
FLA	96.06	92.27	7.573	24	0.0	*
Mandible						
LM	101.54	104.00	-1.509	9	0.165	
BCB	125.02	122.36	1.654	9	0.132	
SH	32.80	34.45	-2.223	10	0.050	
BA	97.78	97.45	0.316	63	0.753	
RL	33.26	32.45	1.476	63	0.145	
Facial angles						
G∠	123.46°	127.55°	-2.552	9	0.031	*

Table 161

"t" SCORES FOR INDICES OF: MADISONVILLE-TURPIN

UNDEFORMED FEMALE CRANIA

(N = Madisonville 55; Turpin 11)

	$\bar{X}_{Ma}$	$\bar{X}_{Tu}$	t-ratio	DF	t-prob.	Sig. diff.
Cranial vault						
B/L	76.18	78.93	- 1.407	34	0.168	
H/L	75.10	77.13	- 1.416	64	0.161	
H/B	94.81	97.89	- 1.766	64	0.082	
H/L+B/2	82.33	86.22	- 3.250	40	0.002	*
PAH/L	57.01	65.89	- 3.178	57	0.002	*
BPH/H	------	------	-------	--	-----	
MF/B	58.86	66.70	- 3.068	62	0.003	*
Face						
TFH/TFB	76.40	86.80	- 3.020	62	0.004	*
UFH/TFB	52.64	53.89	- 1.454	64	0.151	
UFH/MFB	67.27	74.00	- 2.946	64	0.004	*
TFB/B	86.08	95.04	- 3.337	62	0.001	*
MF/TFB	72.16	70.17	2.168	33	0.037	*
BA/MF	103.10	107.15	- 1.366	64	0.177	
BA/TFB	67.03	75.11	- 2.838	61	0.006	*
SIOB/IOB	26.58	17.17	3.007	53	0.004	*
AIB/BOB	23.74	19.53	3.063	58	0.003	*
Nasal structure						
NB/NH	56.02	52.36	1.816	62	0.074	
DS/DC	56.38	52.25	2.341	57	0.023	*
SMN/MN	48.44	43.91	1.642	61	0.106	
Orbit						
LOH/LOBM	79.05	77.80	0.975	64	0.333	
LOH/LOBD	82.22	83.65	- 1.034	25	0.311	
Dental arch						
MB/ML	101.79	117.73	- 2.734	55	0.008	*
Mandible						
LM/BCB	78.44	85.15	- 2.967	64	0.004	*

APPENDIX D

Table 162

"t" SCORES FOR MEASUREMENTS OF: MADISONVILLE-TURPIN

DEFORMED FEMALE CRANIA

(N = Madisonville 161; Turpin 3)

	$\bar{X}_{Ma}$	$\bar{X}_{Tu}$	t-ratio	DF*	t-prob.	Sig. diff.
Cranial vault						
CM	148.86	149.11	- 0.462	1	1.000	
TP	5.11	5.00	0.237	162	0.813	
L	167.81	164.00	1.712	162	0.089	
B	145.89	146.00	- 0.158	2	1.000	
MF	91.79	97.00	- 6.115	7	0.0	*
H	133.02	137.33	- 2.457	162	0.015	*
PAH	114.11	118.00	- 2.881	162	0.005	*
BPH	------	------	-------	---	-----	
LB	99.08	98.33	0.619	162	0.537	
Face						
TFH	111.83	113.67	- 1.028	162	0.306	
UFH	68.59	70.33	- 1.340	162	0.182	
TFB	134.09	133.00	0.789	162	0.431	
MFB	97.69	92.67	3.299	162	0.001	*
IOB	95.99	96.33	- 0.250	162	0.803	
SIOB	16.08	17.00	- 0.600	0	1.000	
BOB	97.98	98.33	- 0.341	162	0.734	
AIB	19.16	20.67	- 2.014	162	0.046	
Nasal structure						
NB	26.23	25.33	1.387	162	0.167	
NH	49.84	50.67	- 0.900	162	0.369	
DC	20.99	21.00	- 0.018	162	0.985	
DS	10.88	11.00	- 0.274	162	0.785	
MN	9.12	9.00	0.184	162	0.854	
SMN	3.86	4.00	- 0.434	162	0.665	
Orbit						
LOH	33.11	33.33	- 0.399	162	0.690	
LOBM	42.06	41.67	0.323	0	1.000	
LOBD	39.23	39.67	- 0.738	162	0.462	

Table 162 - continued

Dental arch					
MB	63.82	62.67	0.479	0	1.000
ML	53.60	53.33	0.251	162	0.802
FL	97.10	93.00	5.127	162	0.000 *
FLA	96.02	91.33	5.797	162	0.000 *
Mandible					
LM	101.53	101.67	- 0.087	162	0.931
BCB	124.45	122.67	0.851	162	0.396
SH	32.78	33.67	- 0.798	162	0.426
BA	98.07	96.00	1.104	162	0.271
RL	32.78	32.00	0.623	162	0.534
Facial angles					
G$\angle$	124.48°	125.67°	- 0.500	162	0.618

*DF $\leq$ 3, t-prob. = 1

APPENDIX D

Table 163

"t" SCORES FOR INDICES OF: MADISONVILLE-TURPIN

DEFORMED FEMALE CRANIA

(N = Madisonville 161; Turpin 3)

	$\bar{X}_{Ma}$	$\bar{X}_{Tu}$	t-ratio	DF*	t-prob.	Sig. diff.
Cranial vault						
B/L	86.03	85.39	0.162	162	0.871	
H/L	79.24	83.79	- 1.904	0	1.000	
H/B	91.53	94.08	- 1.431	162	0.154	
H/L+B/2	84.91	88.63	- 1.708	0	1.000	
PAH/L	67.92	72.00	- 1.967	0	1.000	
BPH/H	------	------	-------	---	-----	
MF/B	63.13	66.44	- 5.858	11	0.000	*
Face						
TFH/TFB	83.30	85.48	- 1.393	162	0.166	
UFH/TFB	50.85	52.90	- 0.837	162	0.404	
UFH/MFB	69.82	75.89	- 1.719	162	0.088	
TFB/B	93.14	91.10	1.636	101	0.105	
MF/TFB	68.18	72.93	- 5.607	4	0.005	
BA/MF	111.26	98.97	2.467	160	0.015	*
BA/TFB	72.84	72.18	0.740	1	1.000	
SIOB/IOB	16.61	17.62	- 0.880	162	0.380	
AIB/BOB	19.47	21.03	- 1.583	162	0.115	
Nasal structure						
NB/NH	52.03	49.99	1.833	1	1.000	
DS/DC	51.97	52.46	- 0.206	162	0.837	
SMN/MN	42.49	44.44	- 0.579	162	0.564	
Orbit						
LOH/LOBM	78.46	80.16	- 0.604	162	0.547	
LOH/LOBD	84.25	84.10	0.065	162	0.948	
Dental arch						
MB/ML	119.17	117.42	0.683	162	0.496	
Mandible						
LM/BCB	81.63	82.96	- 0.839	162	0.403	

*DF $\leq$ 3, t-prob. = 1

Table 164

"t" SCORES FOR MEASUREMENTS OF:
MADISONVILLE-FOX FARM UNDEFORMED MALE CRANIA

(N = Madisonville 60; Fox Farm 7)

	$\bar{X}_{Ma}$	$\bar{X}_{Fo}$	t-ratio	DF	t-prob.	Sig. diff.
Cranial vault						
CM	153.11	153.00	0.067	65	0 947	
TP	5.08	5.57	- 1 210	65	0 231	
L	180.22	176.57	1.020	65	0 311	
B	143.05	142.43	0.197	5	0.851	
MF	95.32	95.86	- 0.286	65	0 776	
H	136.07	140.00	- 1.375	5	0.228	
PAH	116.72	115.43	0.935	65	0.353	
BPH	------	------	-------	---	-----	
LB	104.35	101.43	1.554	65	0 125	
Face						
TFH	122.92	124.29	- 0.457	65	0.649	
UFH	72.73	75.86	- 2.439	65	0.017	*
TFB	141.22	138.57	1 183	5	0.290	
MFB	102.72	101.71	0.711	65	0.480	
IOB	100.22	99.14	0.847	65	0.400	
SIOB	17.55	17.29	0.301	65	0 764	
BOB	101.32	101.00	0.357	65	0 722	
AIB	20.55	20 00	0.747	65	0.458	
Nasal structure						
NB	27.20	26.57	1.053	65	0.296	
NH	52.90	52.57	0.342	65	0.733	
DC	22.35	22.57	- 0.309	65	0.758	
DS	11.70	9.57	4.794	65	0 000	*
MN	9.73	8.71	1.684	65	0 097	
SMN	3 97	3 29	2.087	65	0 041	
Orbit						
LOH	34.03	33.71	0.468	65	0.641	
LOBM	43.67	43.29	0.845	65	0.401	
LOBD	40.90	40.43	1.008	65	0.317	
Dental arch						
MB	63.82	66.86	- 1.493	65	0 140	
ML	55.28	53.71	4.137	16	0.001	*
FL	99.43	95.14	3.867	65	0.000	*
FLA	98.20	93.86	3.911	65	0.000	*
Mandible						
LM	104.68	104.29	0.200	4	0.851	
BCB	129 75	128.71	0.907	65	0 367	
SH	35.95	35 86	0.102	65	0.919	
BA	105.25	105.29	- 0.011	4	0.992	
RL	35.67	33.29	2.503	65	0.015	*
Facial angles						
G/	119.45	119.86	- 0.140	5	0.894	

APPENDIX D

Table 165

"t" SCORES FOR INDICES OF:
MADISONVILLE-FOX FARM UNDEFORMED MALE CRANIA

(N = Madisonville 60; Fox Farm 7)

	$\bar{X}_{Ma}$	$\bar{X}_{Fo}$	t-ratio	DF	t-prob.	Sig. diff.
Cranial vault						
B/L	77.95	80.75	- 0.800	65	0.426	
H/L	74.06	79.31	- 2.899	16	0.010	*
H/B	95.25	98.60	- 1.069	5	0.334	
H/L+B/2	84.27	87.82	- 2.209	65	0 031	*
PAH/L	64.95	65.45	- 0.300	65	0.765	
BPH/H	------	------	--------	---	-----	
MF/B	66.69	67.41	- 0 516	65	0.608	
Face						
TFH/TFB	85.39	89.77	- 2.347	13	0.035	*
UFH/TFB	51.52	54.80	- 2.465	5	0.057	
UFH/MFB	70.87	74.63	- 2.607	65	0.011	*
TFB/B	98.82	87.46	0.874	65	0.385	
MF/TFB	67.51	69.18	- 2.223	11	0.048	
BA/MF	110.68	109.82	0.315	65	0.754	
BA/TFB	74.56	75.91	- 0.774	5	0.474	
SIOB/IOB	17.49	17.45	0.049	65	0.961	
AIB/BOB	20.27	19.79	0.745	65	0.459	
Nasal structure						
NB/NH	51.51	50.69	0.567	65	0.573	
DS/DC	52.70	42.31	4.097	65	0.000	*
SMN/MN	41.17	37.71	1.058	65	0.294	
Orbit						
LOH/LOBM	77.96	77.88	0.052	65	0.959	
LOH/LOBD	83.26	83.44	- 0.100	65	0.921	
Dental arch						
MB/ML	115.49	124.44	- 2.483	65	0.016	*
Mandible						
LM/BCB	80.73	81.00	- 0.229	65	0.820	

Table 166

"t" SCORES FOR MEASUREMENTS OF: MADISONVILLE-FOX FARM DEFORMED MALE CRANIA

(N = Madisonville 115; Fox Farm 31)

	$\bar{X}_{Ma}$	$\bar{X}_{Fo}$	t-ratio	DF	t-prob.	Sig. diff.
Cranial vault						
CM	153.65	154.04	- 0.653	39	0.518	
TP	5.24	5.35	- 0.766	144	0.445	
L	174.05	166.94	4.812	32	0.000	*
B	150.02	156.19	- 6.188	38	0.000	*
MF	95.21	96.03	- 0.942	36	0.353	
H	136.87	139.00	- 2.365	36	0.024	*
PAH	117.85	119.10	- 2.082	144	0.039	*
BPH	------	------	-------	---	-----	
LB	103.14	99.61	4.226	32	0.000	*
Face						
TFH	122.37	123.42	- 1.574	144	0.118	
UFH	72.83	76.29	- 7.412	144	0.000	*
TFB	143.00	140.90	3.077	36	0.004	*
MFB	101.90	103.00	- 2.163	144	0.032	*
IOB	99.49	99.90	- 0.605	38	0.549	
SIOB	17.37	17.06	0.483	137	0.630	
BOB	101.23	101.45	- 0.544	144	0.587	
AIB	20.07	19.97	0.405	144	0.686	
Nasal structure						
NB	26.91	26.74	0.528	38	0.601	
NH	52.89	53.74	- 2.220	144	0.028	*
DC	21.76	22.77	- 4.178	144	0.000	*
DS	12.04	10.03	11.708	144	0.000	*
MN	9.83	8.77	2.577	37	0.014	*
SMN	4.16	3.90	1.602	144	0.111	
Orbit						
LOH	33.93	34.29	- 1.443	37	0.158	
LOBM	43.90	43.94	- 0.181	144	0.857	
LOBD	41.06	40.90	0.627	38	0.535	
Dental arch						
MB	65.17	67.94	- 4.819	144	0.000	*
ML	54.83	54.23	1.429	38	0.161	
FL	99.03	96.32	5.259	37	0.000	*
FLA	97.91	95.19	5.609	39	0.000	*
Mandible						
LM	104.43	104.06	0.446	144	0.656	
BCB	129.90	130.74	- 0.791	36	0.434	
SH	35.62	36.68	- 2.256	144	0.026	*
BA	104.98	105.06	- 0.077	37	0.939	
RL	35.01	34.68	0.695	144	0.488	
Facial angles						
G∠	119.95	117.71	1.632	36	0.111	

APPENDIX D

Table 167
"t" SCORES FOR INDICES OF:
MADISONVILLE-FOX FARM DEFORMED MALE CRANIA

(N = Madisonville 115; Fox Farm 31)

	$\bar{x}_{Ma}$	$\bar{x}_{Fo}$	t-ratio	DF	t-prob.	Sig. diff.
Cranial vault						
B/L	86.23	77.72	1.470	28	0.153	
H/L	78.67	83.40	- 6.350	34	0.000	*
H/B	91.29	89.11	2.433	35	0.020	*
H/L+B/2	84.49	86.06	- 2.678	38	0.011	*
PAH/L	67.73	71.49	- 5.526	33	0.000	*
BPH/H	------	------	-------	---	-----	
MF/B	63.49	61.53	3.081	35	0.004	*
Face						
TFH/TFB	85.59	87.64	- 3.404	38	0.002	*
UFH/TFB	50.98	54.18	- 7.886	36	0.000	*
UFH/MFB	71.50	74.09	- 5.154	144	0.000	*
TFB/B	95.38	90.29	8.761	144	0.000	*
MF/TFB	66.59	68.17	- 2.600	37	0.013	*
BA/MF	110.37	109.65	0.478	36	0.635	
BA/TFB	73.43	74.57	- 1.804	144	0.073	
SIOB/IOB	17.43	17.09	0.561	137	0.575	
AIB/BOB	19.82	19.68	0.611	144	0.542	
Nasal structure						
NB/NH	50.95	49.85	1.622	144	0.099	
DS/DC	55.46	44.13	15.554	60	0.000	*
SMN/MN	42.69	41.76	0.470	39	0.641	
Orbit						
LOH/LOBM	77.33	78.08	- 1.353	144	0.178	
LOH/LOBD	82.68	83.89	- 1.975	144	0.050	
Dental arch						
MB/ML	118.94	125.39	- 5.632	144	0.000	*
Mandible						
LM/BCB	80.45	79.73	0.774	38	0.444	

Table 168

"t" SCORES FOR MEASUREMENTS OF: MADISONVILLE-FOX FARM
DEFORMED FEMALE CRANIA

(N = Madisonville 161; Fox Farm 24)

	$\bar{X}_{Ma}$	$\bar{X}_{Fo}$	t-ratio	DF	t-prob.	Sig. diff.
Cranial vault						
CM	148.86	146.04	5.045	183	0.000	*
TP	5.11	5.54	-2.368	183	0.019	*
L	167.81	157.38	8.095	24	0.0	*
B	145.89	149.92	-2.891	24	0.008	*
MF	91.79	93.04	-1.211	53	0.231	
H	133.02	130.83	3.410	183	0.001	*
PAH	114.11	113.79	0.476	25	0.638	
BPH	------	------	-------	---	-----	
LB	99.08	96.92	3.664	25	0.001	*
Face						
TFH	111.83	111.71	0.142	25	0.888	
UFH	68.59	70.29	-2.144	23	0.043	
TFB	134.09	132.00	3.884	183	0.000	*
MFB	97.69	98.17	-0.807	183	0.421	
IOB	95.99	96.38	-0.734	183	0.464	
SIOB	16.08	16.79	-2.291	183	0.023	*
BOB	97.98	97.54	1.071	183	0.286	
AIB	19.16	19.75	-1.382	24	0.180	
Nasal structure						
NB	26.23	25.92	0.879	24	0.388	
NH	49.84	49.88	-0.057	24	0.955	
DC	20.99	21.46	-1.149	23	0.262	
DS	10.88	10.58	0.995	23	0.330	
MN	9.12	10.00	-2.924	25	0.007	*
SMN	3.86	3.29	4.564	183	0.000	*
Orbit						
LOH	33.11	33.25	-0.461	24	0.649	
LOBM	42.03	41.83	0.907	183	0.365	
LOBD	39.23	39.21	0.096	183	0.924	

Table 168 - continued

Dental arch						
MB	63.82	64.79	-3.447	40	0.001	*
ML	53.60	52.88	1.777	183	0.077	
FL	97.10	96.04	2.019	23	0.055	
FLA	96.02	94.96	1.902	23	0.070	

Mandible						
LM	101.53	100.00	1.769	24	0.090	
BCB	124.45	123.96	0.633	183	0.528	
SH	32.78	33.25	-0.783	24	0.441	
BA	98.07	97.17	1.293	183	0.198	
RL	32.78	32.62	0.320	183	0.750	

Facial angles						
G$\angle$	124.48°	122.04°	2.721	183	0.007	*

Table 169

"t" SCORES FOR INDICES OF: MADISONVILLE-FOX FARM DEFORMED FEMALE CRANIA

(N = Madisonville 161; Fox Farm 24)

	$\bar{X}_{Ma}$	$\bar{X}_{Fo}$	t-ratio	DF	t-prob.	Sig. diff.
Cranial vault						
B/L	86.03	74.66	1.512	21	0.145	
H/L	79.24	83.25	- 5.258	24	0.000	*
H/B	91.53	87.43	4.562	25	0.000	*
H/L+B/2	84.91	85.18	- 0.619	183	0.537	
PAH/L	67.92	72.43	- 5.535	22	0.000	*
BPH/H	------	------	-------	---	-----	
MF/B	63.13	62.16	1.143	41	0.260	
Face						
TFH/TFB	83.30	84.66	- 2.247	183	0.026	*
UFH/TFB	50.85	53.28	- 3.390	35	0.002	*
UFH/MFB	69.82	71.66	- 1.892	38	0.066	*
TFB/B	93.14	88.19	3.466	139	0.000	*
MF/TFB	68.18	70.54	- 2.453	46	0.018	*
BA/MF	111.26	104.64	1.300	173	0.195	
BA/TFB	72.84	73.63	- 1.350	53	0.183	
SIOB/IOB	16.66	17.42	- 1.901	183	0.059	
AIB/BOB	19.47	20.25	- 2.044	183	0.042	
Nasal structure						
NB/NH	52.03	52.17	- 0.104	183	0.917	
DS/DC	51.97	49.81	1.214	23	0.237	
SMN/MN	42.49	33.52	5.678	25	0.000	*
Orbit						
LOH/LOBM	78.46	79.52	- 1.030	183	0.304	
LOH/LOBD	84.25	84.86	- 0.678	183	0.499	
Dental arch						
MB/ML	119.17	122.72	- 3.607	183	0.000	*
Mandible						
LM/BCB	81.63	80.71	1.187	25	0.246	

APPENDIX D

Table 170

"t" SCORES FOR MEASUREMENTS OF:
MADISONVILLE-SAND RIDGE UNDEFORMED MALE CRANIA

(N = Madisonville 60; Sand Ridge 6)

	$\bar{X}_{Ma}$	$\bar{X}_{Sa}$	t-ratio	DF**	t-prob.	Sig. diff.
Cranial vault						
CM	153.11	155.72	- 1.523	64	0.133	
TP	5.08	5.67	- 1.323	64	0.191	
L	180.22	182.50	- 0.590	64	0.558	
B	143.05	141.83	0.542	64	0.589	
MF	95.32	91.83	1.710	64	0.092	
H	136.07	142.83	- 2.350	3	1.000	
PAH	116.72	119.17	- 1.116	3	1.000	
BPH	------	------	-------	---	-----	
LB	104.35	102.67	0.786	64	0.435	
Face						
TFH	122.92	120.00	2.933	57	0.005	*
UFH	72.73	71.17	2.785	16	0.013	*
TFB	141.22	142.00	- 0.507	64	0.614	
MFB	102.72	98.00	3.265	64	0.002	*
IOB	100.22	97.50	2.016	64	0.048	
SIOB	17.55	16.33	1.255	64	0.214	
BOB	101.32	100.17	0.792	3	1.000	
AIB	20.55	20.17	0.492	64	0.624	
Nasal structure						
NB	27.20	27.00	0.210	3	1.000	
NH	52.90	53.00	- 0.187	8	0.857	
DC	22.35	19.67	1.336	3	1.000	
DS	11.70	9.83	8.544	12	0.000	*
MN	9.73	7.00	8.435	10	0.000	*
SMN	3.97	3.00	0.262	64	0.794	
Orbit						
LOH	34.03	33.83	0.262	64	0.794	
LOBM	43.67	42.17	1.773	3	1.000	
LOBD	40.90	40.00	1.207	3	1.000	
Dental arch						
MB	63.82	64.17	- 0.309	10	0.764	
ML	55.28	54.00	5.146	57	0.000	*
FL	99.43	95.00	3.901	64	0.000	*
FLA	98.20	93.17	4.491	64	0.000	*
Mandible						
LM	104.68	105.00	- 0.813	57	0.420	
BCB	129.74	128.00	4.756	57	0.000	*
SH	35.95	35.00	3.126	57	0.003	*
BA	105.25	100.00	3.109	64	0.003	*
RL	35.67	35.83	- 0.485	46	0.630	
Facial angles						
G$\angle$	119.45	114.17	5.722	16	0.000	*

** DF $\leq$ 3, t-prob. = 1

Table 171

"t" SCORES FOR INDICES OF:
MADISONVILLE-SAND RIDGE UNDEFORMED MALE CRANIA

(N = Madisonville 60; Sand Ridge 6)

	$\bar{X}_{Ma}$	$\bar{X}_{Sa}$	t-ratio	DF**	t-prob.	Sig. diff.
Cranial vault						
B/L	77.95	77.81	0.076	11	0.941	
H/L	74.06	78.35	- 1.922	8	0.091	
H/B	95.25	100.70	- 2.665	64	0.001	*
H/L+B/2	84.27	88.10	- 2.265	64	0.027	*
PAH/L	64.95	65.37	- 0.238	64	0.813	
BPH/H	------	------	-------	---	-----	
MF/B	66.69	64.76	1.280	64	0.205	
Face						
TFH/TFB	85.39	84.60	0.469	14	0.646	
UFH/TFB	51.52	50.18	1.436	64	0.156	
UFH/MFB	70.84	72.66	- 1.205	64	0.233	
TFB/B	98.82	100.15	- 0.830	64	0.410	
MF/TFB	67.51	64.67	2.035	64	0.046	
BA/MF	110.68	108.98	0.613	64	0.542	
BA/TFB	74.56	70.43	3.407	64	0.001	*
SIOB/IOB	17.49	16.73	0.877	64	0.384	
AIB/BOB	20.27	20.15	0.170	64	0.866	
Nasal structure						
NB/NH	51.51	50.89	0.406	64	0.686	
DS/DC	52.70	53.69	- 0.135	3	1.000	
SMN/MN	41.17	43.16	- 1.028	8	0.334	
Orbit						
LOH/LOBM	77.96	80.21	- 1.352	64	0.181	
LOH/LOBD	83.26	84.54	- 0.674	64	0.502	
Dental arch						
MB/ML	115.49	118.83	- 1.613	9	0.141	
Mandible						
LM/BCB	80.73	82.03	- 3.295	59	0.002	*

** DF $\leq$ 3, t-prob. = 1

APPENDIX D

Table 172
"t" SCORES FOR MEASUREMENTS OF:
SAND RIDGE-CAMPBELL ISLAND UNDEFORMED MALE CRANIA

(N = Sand Ridge 6; Campbell Island 5)

	$\bar{X}_{Sa}$	$\bar{X}_{Ca}$	t-ratio	DF**	t-prob.	Sig. diff.
Cranial vault						
CM	155.72	154.33	0.615	9	0.553	
TP	5.67	4.80	1.233	9	0.249	
L	182.50	179.20	0.728	9	0.485	
B	141.83	142.60	- 0.336	9	0.745	
MF	91.83	93.00	- 0.557	5	0.602	
H	142.83	141.20	0.527	5	0.621	
PAH	119.17	116.40	1.070	9	0.313	
BPH	------	------	-------	---	-----	
LB	102.67	104.00	- 0.456	4	0.672	
Face						
TFH	120.00	123.00	- 5.255	9	0.001	*
UFH	71.17	74.60	- 3.800	9	0.004	*
TFB	142.00	143.80	- 0.721	9	0.489	
MFB	98.00	103.20	- 2.674	9	0.025	*
IOB	97.50	99.20	- 1.085	4	0.339	
SIOB	16.33	18.80	- 2.575	5	0.050	
BOB	100.17	100.40	- 0.136	9	0.895	
AIB	20.17	19.80	0.533	9	0.607	
Nasal structure						
NB	27.00	27.60	- 0.532	9	0.607	
NH	53.00	54.60	- 2.033	9	0.073	
DC	19.67	23.00	- 1.558	4	0.194	
DS	9.83	10.80	- 3.747	9	0.005	*
MN	7.00	8.60	- 3.476	9	0.007	*
SMN	3.00	4.00	0.000	1	1.000	
Orbit						
LOH	33.83	34.20	- 0.289	9	0.779	
LOBM	42.17	43.20	- 1.011	9	0.338	
LOBD	40.00	40.80	- 0.830	9	0.428	
Dental arch						
MB	64.17	69.00	- 3.659	9	0.005	*
ML	54.00	54.00	0.000	9	1.000	
FL	95.00	97.20	- 2.031	9	0.073	
FLA	93.17	95.40	- 1.794	9	0.106	
Mandible						
LM	105.00	107.20	- 0.771	2	1.000	
BCB	128.00	126.00	2.648	9	0.027	*
SH	35.00	36.00	- 1.239	9	0.247	
BA	100.00	105.20	- 2.236	9	0.052	
RL	35.83	36.60	- 0.999	2	1.000	
Facial angles						
G$\angle$	114.17	118.40	- 2.962	9	0.016	*

** DF $\leq$ 3, t-prob. = 1

Table 173

"t" SCORES FOR INDICES OF:
SAND RIDGE-CAMPBELL ISLAND UNDEFORMED MALE CRANIA

(N = Sand Ridge 6; Campbell Island 5)

	$\bar{x}_{Sa}$	$\bar{x}_{Ca}$	t-ratio	DF**	t-prob.	Sig. diff.
Cranial vault						
B/L	77.81	79.74	- 0.755	9	0.470	
H/L	78.35	78.87	- 0.222	9	0.829	
H/B	100.70	99.07	0.722	9	0.489	
H/L+B/2	88.10	87.76	0.190	4	0.859	
PAH/L	65.37	65.08	0.122	9	0.905	
BPH/H	------	------	-------	---	-----	
MF/B	64.76	65.25	- 0.282	9	0.784	
Face						
TFH/TFB	84.60	85.55	- 0.697	5	0.517	
UFH/TFB	50.18	51.87	- 1.761	4	0.153	
UFH/MFB	72.66	72.43	0.111	9	0.914	
TFB/B	100.15	100.89	- 0.366	9	0.722	
MF/TFB	64.67	64.68	- 0.007	9	0.995	
BA/MF	108.98	113.16	- 1.779	9	0.109	
BA/TFB	70.43	73.16	- 2.196	9	0.056	
SIOB/IOB	16.73	18.95	- 2.415	9	0.039	*
AIB/BOB	20.15	19.72	0.606	9	0.559	
Nasal structure						
NB/NH	50.89	50.58	0.172	9	0.867	
DS/DC	53.69	47.06	0.899	3	1.000	
SMN/MN	43.16	46.89	- 1.454	9	0.180	
Orbit						
LOH/LOBM	80.21	79.15	0.529	9	0.609	
LOH/LOBD	84.54	83.90	0.245	9	0.812	
Dental arch						
MB/ML	118.83	127.92	- 2.902	9	0.018	*
Mandible						
LM/BCB	82.03	85.14	- 1.142	2	1.000	

** DF $\leq$ 3, t-prob. = 1

APPENDIX D

Table 174

"t" SCORES FOR MEASUREMENTS OF:
SAND RIDGE-HAHN'S FIELD UNDEFORMED MALE CRANIA

(N = Sand Ridge 6; Hahn's Field 3)

	$\bar{X}_{Sa}$	$\bar{X}_{Ha}$	t-ratio	DF**	t-prob.	Sig. diff.
Cranial vault						
CM	155.72	152.56	1.163	7	0.283	
TP	5.67	5.00	0.741	7	0.483	
L	182.50	179.67	0.929	3	1.000	
B	141.83	140.00	0.582	7	0.579	
MF	91.83	93.67	-0.474	7	0.650	
H	142.83	138.00	1.170	7	0.280	
PAH	119.17	117.00	0.688	7	0.514	
BPH	------	------	--------	---	-----	
LB	102.67	96.00	2.217	4	0.091	
Face						
TFH	120.00	124.00	0.000	7	1.000	
UFH	71.17	78.33	-11.430	7	0.000	*
TFB	142.00	141.00	0.328	7	0.752	
MFB	98.00	104.33	-6.404	4	0.000	*
IOB	97.50	95.67	0.757	7	0.474	
SIOB	16.33	17.00	-0.496	7	0.635	
BOB	100.17	97.00	1.519	7	0.173	
AIB	20.17	18.00	2.463	7	0.043	
Nasal structure						
NB	27.00	26.00	0.734	7	0.487	
NH	53.00	56.67	-4.660	7	0.002	*
DC	19.67	21.00	-0.457	7	0.662	
DS	9.83	11.00	-4.781	7	0.002	*
MN	7.00	7.67	-0.452	0	1.000	
SMN	3.00	4.00	-2.646	7	0.033	*
Orbit						
LOH	35.83	37.00	-2.287	7	0.056	
LOBM	42.16	45.00	-2.323	7	0.053	
LOBD	40.00	43.00	-2.806	7	0.026	*
Dental arch						
MB	64.17	66.33	-2.236	4	0.089	
ML	54.00	56.67	-7.630	7	0.000	*
FL	95.00	100.00	-5.000	7	0.002	*
FLA	93.17	99.00	-5.319	7	0.001	*
Mandible						
LM	105.00	113.00	0.000	7	1.000	
BCB	128.00	140.00	0.000	7	1.000	
SH	35.00	36.00	-6.110	7	0.000	*
BA	100.00	106.00	-2.268	7	0.058	
RL	35.83	36.33	-0.214	0	1.000	
Facial angles						
G∠	114.17	117.67	-1.444	0	1.000	

** DF ≤ 3, t-prob. = 1

Table 175

"t" SCORES FOR INDICES OF:
SAND RIDGE-HAHN'S FIELD UNDEFORMED MALE CRANIA

(N = Sand Ridge 6; Hahn's Field 3)

	$\bar{X}_{Sa}$	$\bar{X}_{Ha}$	t-ratio	DF**	t-prob.	Sig. diff.
Cranial vault						
B/L	77.81	77.93	- 0.050	7	0.961	
H/L	78.35	76.81	0.819	3	1.000	
H/B	100.70	98.65	0.770	7	0.467	
H/L+B/2	88.10	86.35	0.975	4	0.385	
PAH/L	65.37	65.12	0.169	3	1.000	
BPH/H	-----	-----	-------	---	-----	
MF/B	64.76	66.90	- 0.854	7	0.421	
Face						
TFH/TFB	84.60	87.94	- 2.659	3	1.000	
UFH/TFB	50.18	55.56	- 5.807	4	0.004	*
UFH/MFB	72.66	75.08	- 2.533	3	1.000	
TFB/B	100.15	100.80	- 0.259	7	0.803	
MF/TFB	64.67	66.43	- 0.731	7	0.489	
BA/MF	108.98	113.59	- 0.904	0	1.000	
BA/TFB	70.43	75.18	- 3.354	7	0.012	*
SIOB/IOB	16.73	17.80	- 0.849	7	0.424	
AIB/BOB	20.15	18.56	1.617	7	0.150	
Nasal structure						
NB/NH	50.89	45.90	3.310	4	0.030	*
DS/DC	53.69	52.38	0.122	7	0.906	
SMN/MN	43.16	53.33	- 3.153	7	0.016	*
Orbit						
LOH/LOBM	80.21	82.22	- 1.018	7	0.342	
LOH/LOBD	84.54	86.05	- 1.158	3	1.000	
Dental arch						
MB/ML	118.83	119.18	- 0.134	7	0.897	
Mandible						
LM/BCB	82.03	80.17	17.243	7	0.000	*

** DF ≤ 3, t-prob. = 1

APPENDIX D

Table 176
"t" SCORES FOR MEASUREMENTS OF:
MADISONVILLE-SAND RIDGE, CAMPBELL ISLAND, AND HAHN'S FIELD UNDEFORMED MALE CRANIA

(N = Madisonville 60; Sand Ridge, Campbell Island, Hahn's Field 14)

	$\bar{X}_{Ma}$	$\bar{X}_{Ca}^{Sa}$ $_{Ha}$	t-ratio	DF	t-prob.	Sig. diff.
Cranial vault						
CM	153.11	154.55	- 1.252	72	0.214	
TP	5.08	5.21	- 0.432	72	0.667	
L	180.22	180.71	- 0.192	72	0.848	
B	143.05	141.71	0.886	72	0.379	
MF	95.32	92.64	1.930	72	0.058	
H	136.07	141.21	- 3.840	72	0.000	*
PAH	116.72	117.71	- 0.971	72	0.335	
BPH	------	------	--------	---	-----	
LB	104.35	101.71	1.802	72	0.076	
Face						
TFH	122.92	121.93	0.881	69	0.381	
UFH	72.73	73.93	- 1.314	72	0.193	
TFB	141.22	142.43	- 1.173	72	0.245	
MFB	102.72	101.21	1.426	72	0.158	
IOB	100.22	97.71	2.757	72	0.007	*
SIOB	17.55	17.36	0.295	72	0.769	
BOB	101.32	99.57	2.538	72	0.013	*
AIB	20.55	19.57	1.828	72	0.072	
Nasal structure						
NB	27.20	27.00	0.447	72	0.656	
NH	52.90	54.36	- 2.212	72	0.030	*
DC	22.35	21.14	1.243	13	0.236	
DS	11.70	10.43	5.699	31	0.000	*
MN	9.73	7.71	4.555	72	0.000	*
SMN	3.97	3.57	1.716	72	0.090	
Orbit						
LOH	34.03	34.64	- 1.132	72	0.262	
LOBM	43.67	43.14	1.047	13	0.314	
LOBD	40.90	40.93	- 0.057	14	0.955	
Dental arch						
MB	63.82	66.36	- 2.483	34	0.018	*
ML	55.28	54.36	2.191	27	0.037	*
FL	99.43	96.86	3.240	72	0.002	*
FLA	98.20	95.21	3.715	72	0.000	*
Mandible						
LM	104.68	107.50	- 2.127	14	0.052	
BCB	129.75	129.86	- 0.069	13	0.946	
SH	35.95	35.64	0.672	35	0.506	
BA	105.25	103.14	1.788	72	0.078	
RL	35.67	36.21	- 0.819	72	0.416	
Facial angles						
G∠	119.45	116.43	2.783	28	0.010	*

514   PREHISTORIC PEOPLE OF FORT ANCIENT

Table 177

"t" SCORES FOR INDICES OF:
MADISONVILLE-SAND RIDGE, CAMPBELL ISLAND,
HAHN'S FIELD UNDEFORMED MALE CRANIA

(N = Madisonville 60; Sand Ridge, Campbell Island, Hahn's Field 14)

	$\bar{X}_{Ma}$	$\bar{X}_{Ca}^{Sa}$ Ha	t-ratio	DF	t-prob.	Sig. diff.
Cranial vault						
B/L	77.95	78.52	- 0.370	48	0.713	
H/L	74.06	78.21	- 2.775	59	0.007	*
H/B	95.25	99.68	- 3.219	72	0.002	*
H/L+B/2	84.27	87.60	- 2.992	72	0.004	*
PAH/L	64.95	65.22	- 0.225	72	0.823	
BPH/H	------	------	-------	---	-----	
MF/B	66.69	65.39	1.264	72	0.210	
Face						
TFH/TFB	85.39	85.65	- 0.198	68	0.844	
UFH/TFB	51.51	51.94	- 0.622	72	0.536	
UFH/MFB	70.87	73.09	- 2.160	72	0.034	*
TFB/B	98.82	100.55	- 1.595	72	0.115	
MF/TFB	67.51	65.05	2.579	72	0.012	*
BA/MF	110.68	111.46	- 0.410	72	0.683	
BA/TFB	74.56	72.42	2.554	72	0.013	*
SIOB/IOB	17.49	17.75	- 0.438	72	0.663	
AIB/BOB	20.27	19.65	1.310	72	0.194	
Nasal structure						
NB/NH	51.51	49.71	1.740	72	0.086	
DS/DC	52.70	51.04	0.515	13	0.615	
SMN/MN	41.17	46.67	- 2.385	72	0.020	*
Orbit						
LOH/LOBM	77.96	80.27	2.053	72	0.044	
LOH/LOBD	83.26	84.63	- 1.059	72	0.293	
Dental arch						
MB/ML	115.49	122.15	- 2.537	72	0.013	*
Mandible						
LM/BCB	80.73	82.86	- 2.245	72	0.028	*

APPENDIX D

Table 178

"t" SCORES FOR MEASUREMENTS OF: MADISONVILLE-SAND RIDGE,
AND HAHN'S FIELD

DEFORMED FEMALE CRANIA

(N = Madisonville 161; Sand Ridge, Hahn's Field 4)

	$\overline{X}_{Ma}$	$\overline{X}_{Sa, Ha}$	t-ratio	DF*	t-prob.	Sig. diff.
Cranial vault						
CM	148.86	146.33	1.908	163	0.058	
TP	5.11	5.75	- 0.575	1	1.00	
L	167.81	164.50	1.717	163	0.088	
B	145.89	143.75	0.992	163	0.323	
MF	91.79	90.25	0.387	163	0.699	
H	133.02	130.75	0.824	1	1.000	
PAH	114.11	113.75	0.195	1	1.000	
BPH	------	------	-------	--	-----	
LB	99.08	100.00	- 0.351	1	1.000	
Face						
TFH	111.83	114.50	- 0.935	1	1.000	
UFH	68.59	70.75	- 1.929	163	0.055	
TFB	134.09	134.00	0.207	2	1.000	
MFB	97.69	97.50	0.141	163	0.888	
IOB	95.99	96.00	- 0.005	163	0.996	
SIOB	16.08	16.25	- 0.143	1	1.000	
BOB	97.98	96.25	1.195	1	1.000	
AIB	19.16	18.50	1.025	163	0.307	
Nasal structure						
NB	26.23	27.00	- 0.767	1	1.000	
NH	49.84	50.50	- 2.085	2	1.000	
DC	20.99	21.00	- 0.021	163	0.983	
DS	10.88	10.75	0.209	1	1.000	
MN	9.12	9.50	- 0.685	163	0.494	
SMN	3.86	4.25	- 1.368	163	0.173	
Orbit						
LOH	33.11	33.50	- 0.807	163	0.421	
LOBM	42.06	42.25	- 0.342	163	0.733	
LOBD	39.23	39.50	- 0.527	163	0.599	

Table 178 - continued

Dental arch						
MB	63.82	66.00	- 2.287	163	0.023	*
ML	53.60	53.75	- 0.169	163	0.866	
FL	97.10	94.50	2.058	1	1.000	
FLA	96.02	94.50	1.049	1	1.000	
Mandible						
LM	101.53	102.50	- 0.701	163	0.484	
BCB	124.45	126.00	- 0.846	163	0.396	
SH	32.78	32.25	0.275	1	1.000	
BA	98.07	99.25	- 0.717	163	0.474	
RL	32.78	31.50	1.811	163	0.239	
Facial angles						
G/	124.48	126.00	- 0.738	163	0.462	

*DF $\leq$ 3, t-prob. = 1

APPENDIX D

Table 179

"t" SCORES FOR INDICES OF: MADISONVILLE-SAND RIDGE, AND HAHN'S FIELD

DEFORMED FEMALE CRANIA

(N = Madisonville 161; Sand Ridge, Hahn's Field 4)

	$\bar{X}_{Ma}$	$\bar{X}_{Sa, Ha}$	t-ratio	DF*	t-prob.	Sig. diff.
Cranial vault						
B/L	86.03	87.37	-1.435	5	0.211	
H/L	79.24	79.52	-0.137	1	1.000	
H/B	91.53	91.02	0.322	163	0.748	
H/L+B/2	84.91	84.88	0.012	1	1.000	
PAH/L	67.92	69.15	-1.349	163	0.179	
BPH/H	------	------	-------	---	-----	
MF/B	63.13	62.77	0.309	2	1.000	
Face						
TFH/TFB	83.30	85.46	-0.914	1	1.000	
UFH/TFB	50.85	52.81	-0.926	163	0.356	
UFH/MFB	69.82	72.63	-0.919	163	0.359	
TFB/B	93.14	93.30	-0.077	4	0.943	
MF/TFB	68.18	67.37	0.232	163	0.817	
BA/MF	111.26	110.08	0.222	100	0.824	
BA/TFB	72.84	74.08	-0.546	163	0.586	
SIOB/IOB	16.66	16.93	-0.285	163	0.776	
AIB/BOB	19.47	19.22	0.785	2	1.000	
Nasal structure						
NB/NH	52.03	53.45	-0.435	163	0.664	
DS/DC	51.97	51.25	0.345	163	0.730	
SMN/MN	42.49	45.00	-0.847	163	0.398	
Orbit						
LOH/LOBM	78.46	79.34	-0.361	163	0.718	
LOH/LOBD	84.25	84.87	-0.299	163	0.765	
Dental arch						
MB/ML	119.17	122.86	-1.647	163	0.101	
Mandible						
LM/BCB	81.63	81.37	0.621	4	0.568	

*DF $\leq$ 3, t-prob. = 1

Table 180

POPULATION DISTANCE RATIOS, FORT ANCIENT SERIES
(Significantly differing t-probabilities on 0.04 (4%) level)

Intra-Focus Comparisons*	Ratio Measurements	Coeff. Measurements	Ratio Indices	Coeff. Indices	Ratios Combined
Ba-Ga (U) - M	9/35	26	5/22	23	14/57
Ba-Ga (D) - M	8/35	23	5/22	23	13/57
Fe-Fu (U) - M	6/35	17	3/22	14	9/57
Fe-Fu (D) - M	7/35	20	3/22	14	10/57
Fe-Fu (U) - F	-----	--	4/22	18	-----
Fe-Pr, Gp (U) - M	3/35	9	1/22	5	4/57
Fe-Pr, Gp (D) - M	4/35	11	1/22	5	5/57
Fe-Pr (D) - F	8/35	23	5/22	23	13/57
An-Ta (U) - M	5/35	14	6/22	27	11/57
An-Ta (U) - F	2/35	6	4/22	18	6/57
Ma-Tu (U) - M	4/35	11	6/22	27	10/57
Ma-Tu (D) - M	1/35	3	1/22	5	2/57
Ma-Tu (U) - F	8/35	24	13/22	59	21/57
Ma-Tu (D) - F	6/35	17	2/22	9	8/57
Ma-Fo (U) - M	6/35	17	6/22	27	12/57
Ma-Fo (D) - M	16/35	46	12/22	55	28/57
Ma-Fo (D) - F	12/35	34	10/22	45	22/57
Ma-Sa (U) - M	12/35	34	4/22	18	16/57
Sa-Ca (U) - M	8/35	23	2/22	9	10/57
Sa-Ha (U) - M	10/35	29	5/22	23	15/57
Ma-Sa, Ca, Ha (U) - M	11/35	31	9/22	41	20/57
Ma-Sa, Ha (D) - F	1/34	3	0/22	0	1/57

*Only components with sufficient crania for comparison are presented.
(M = Male Series; F = Female Series)

APPENDIX D

Table 181

"t" SCORES FOR MEASUREMENTS OF:
BAUM-ANDERSON FOCI UNDEFORMED MALE CRANIA

(N = Baum 14; Anderson 72)

	$\bar{X}_{BF}$	$\bar{X}_{AF}$	t-ratio	DF	t-prob.	Sig. diff
Cranial vault						
CM	155.17	153.31	1.985	84	0.050	
TP	5.07	4.78	- 1.432	64	0.156	
L	181.43	181.14	- 0.138	84	0.891	
B	141.29	138.26	- 1.794	84	0.076	
MF	97.21	93.81	- 2.028	52	0.048	
H	142.79	140.53	- 2.298	84	0.024	*
PAH	122.29	117.08	- 3.733	84	0.000	
BPH	------	------	-------	---	-----	
LB	104.71	104.18	- 0.535	84	0.594	
Face						
TFH	127.29	124.96	- 1.926	84	0.058	
UFH	76.14	74.97	- 2.296	59	0.025	*
TFB	143.86	140.49	- 2.979	84	0.004	*
MFB	102.43	102.22	- 0.461	84	0.646	
IOB	100.64	100.19	0.399	84	0.691	
SIOB	17.86	18.06	0.924	84	0.358	
BOB	100.21	101.00	- 0.331	75	0.742	
AIB	19.93	19.85	1.621	46	0.112	
Nasal structure						
NB	26.21	26.94	2.583	34	0.014	*
NH	54.64	53.78	- 1.341	84	0.184	
DC	20.21	21.00	3.469	76	0.001	
DS	11.00	11.11	0.334	84	0.739	
MN	10.00	8.61	- 3.960	84	0.000	
SMN	4.43	3.97	- 2.080	84	0.041	
Orbit						
LOH	34.79	34.69	- 0.244	28	0.809	
LOBM	43.21	43.78	1.621	42	0.112	
LOBD	41.00	41.61	2.364	43	0.023	
Dental arch						
MB	66.29	69.10	1.560	12	0.145	
ML	54.43	54.21	- 0.367	84	0.715	
FL	97.86	97.79	- 0.098	28	0.923	
FLA	95.93	95.89	- 0.055	25	0.957	
Mandible						
LM	108.21	104.49	- 2.977	81	0.003	
BCB	127.29	129.07	1.144	84	0.256	
SH	37.14	36.50	- 0.730	13	0.479	
BA	102.57	103.65	0.701	84	0.485	
RL	36.14	35.51	- 0.854	84	0.395	
Facial angles						
G∠	115.36	114.35	- 0.624	54	0.535	

Table 182

"t" SCORES FOR INDICES OF:

BAUM-ANDERSON FOCI UNDEFORMED MALE CRANIA

(N = Baum 14; Anderson 72)

	$\bar{X}_{BF}$	$\bar{X}_{AF}$	t-ratio	DF	t-prob.	Sig. diff.
Cranial vault						
B/L	78.00	76.50	0.987	84	0.326	
H/L	78.77	77.69	1.140	84	0.257	
H/B	101.31	101.76	- 0.274	13	0.788	
H/L+B/2	88.53	88.02	0.800	84	0.426	
PAH/L	67.47	64.74	2.501	84	0.014	*
BPH/H	------	------	-------	---	-----	
MF/B	68.90	67.89	0.798	48	0.429	
Face						
TFH/TFB	88.51	87.61	0.584	73	0.561	
UFH/TFB	52.97	53.40	- 0.841	31	0.407	
UFH/MFB	74.36	73.41	1.756	60	0.084	
TFB/B	102.00	101.70	0.221	14	0.828	
MF/TFB	67.64	66.84	0.597	38	0.554	
BA/MF	105.67	109.35	- 1.831	84	0.071	
BA/TFB	71.38	73.83	- 1.992	84	0.050	
SIOB/IOB	17.73	18.01	- 0.649	84	0.518	
AIB/BOB	19.89	19.65	0.988	69	0.326	
Nasal structure						
NB/NH	48.05	50.19	- 2.123	84	0.037	*
DS/DC	54.44	53.25	0.596	84	0.553	
SMN/MN	44.64	46.59	- 0.764	84	0.447	
Orbit						
LOH/LOBM	80.51	78.16	2.357	50	0.022	*
LOH/LOBD	84.83	82.08	2.072	82	0.041	
Dental arch						
MB/ML	122.27	127.53	1.288	12	0.222	
Mandible						
LM/BCB	85.10	81.09	3.005	84	0.004	*

APPENDIX D

Table 183

"t" SCORES FOR MEASUREMENTS OF: BAUM-ANDERSON FOCI

UNDEFORMED FEMALE CRANIA

(N = Baum 6; Anderson 37)

	$\bar{X}_{BF}$	$\bar{X}_{AF}$	t-ratio	DF*	t-prob.	Sig. diff.
Cranial vault						
CM	148.06	148.22	0.137	41	0.892	
TP	5.17	4.73	- 1.003	41	0.322	
L	172.33	176.81	2.079	41	0.044	
B	136.17	132.24	- 3.069	41	0.004	*
MF	89.33	89.00	- 0.120	36	0.905	
H	135.67	135.62	- 0.028	41	0.978	
PAH	115.33	113.68	- 1.316	41	0.195	
BPH	------	------	-------	--	-----	
LB	99.33	94.46	- 1.207	39	0.235	
Face						
TFH	114.00	115.19	0.701	4	0.522	
UFH	69.00	69.92	0.655	4	0.548	
TFB	134.33	129.68	- 1.707	3	1.000	
MFB	97.33	91.19	- 1.514	31	0.140	
IOB	94.83	94.92	0.050	4	0.963	
SIOB	14.67	17.35	6.531	41	0.0	*
BOB	98.17	96.86	- 0.821	3	1.000	
AIB	17.67	18.41	1.171	41	0.248	
Nasal structure						
NB	25.17	25.89	1.381	41	0.175	
NH	49.67	50.16	0.487	4	0.652	
DC	18.83	20.11	3.045	14	0.009	*
DS	10.33	9.97	- 1.063	41	0.294	
MN	8.33	8.11	- 0.401	41	0.691	
SMN	4.17	3.16	- 3.670	41	0.001	*
Orbit						
LOH	33.33	33.70	0.576	41	0.568	
LOBM	42.17	43.14	- 0.036	3	1.000	
LOBD	40.17	39.81	- 0.440	3	1.000	

Table 183 - continued

Dental arch					
MB	66.17	64.86	- 1.014	4	0.368
ML	52.17	52.97	0.752	4	0.494
FL	98.00	94.11	- 1.400	36	0.170
FLA	96.17	92.22	- 1.645	38	0.108
Mandible					
LM	100.17	101.65	0.776	4	0.481
BCB	127.50	120.24	- 4.212	41	0.000 *
SH	31.83	33.30	1.747	41	0.088
BA	98.17	96.03	- 0.935	41	0.355
RL	32.00	33.08	1.770	14	0.099
Facial angles					
G/	121.83°	121.32°	- 0.237	41	0.814

*DF $\leq$ 3, t-prob. = 1

APPENDIX D

Table 184

"t" SCORES FOR INDICES OF: BAUM-ANDERSON FOCI

UNDEFORMED FEMALE CRANIA

(N = Baum 6; Anderson 37)

	$\overline{X}_{BF}$	$\overline{X}_{AF}$	t-ratio	DF	t-prob.	Sig. diff.
Cranial vault						
B/L	79.07	74.84	- 4.091	41	0.000	*
H/L	78.80	76.74	- 1.219	4	0.290	
H/B	99.63	102.59	2.253	41	0.030	*
H/L+B/2	87.97	87.78	- 0.177	41	0.860	
PAH/L	66.95	64.32	- 3.291	41	0.002	*
BPH/H	------	------	-------	--	-----	
MF/B	65.60	67.31	0.879	39	0.385	
Face						
TFH/TFB	85.01	88.87	2.022	4	0.113	
UFH/TFB	51.44	53.94	1.988	4	0.118	
UFH/MFB	71.01	71.25	0.108	15	0.915	
TFB/B	98.63	98.09	- 0.437	41	0.664	
MF/TFB	66.58	68.65	0.952	35	0.348	
BA/MF	109.91	118.65	0.640	36	0.526	
BA/TFB	73.06	74.07	1.006	11	0.336	
SIOB/IOB	15.51	18.28	6.144	41	0.0	*
AIB/BOB	17.99	19.00	1.634	41	0.110	
Nasal structure						
NB/NH	50.68	50.82	0.113	25	0.911	
DS/DC	55.02	50.03	- 1.700	41	0.097	
SMN/MN	49.97	39.46	- 3.343	41	0.002	*
Orbit						
LOH/LOBM	79.18	80.01	0.511	41	0.611	
LOH/LOBD	83.14	84.71	0.820	41	0.417	
Dental arch						
MB/ML	127.12	122.50	- 1.214	3	1.000	
Mandible						
LM/BCB	78.62	84.62	3.764	41	0.001	*

*DF $\leq$ 3, t-prob. = 1

Table 185

"t" SCORES FOR MEASUREMENTS OF: BAUM-ANDERSON FOCI

DEFORMED FEMALE CRANIA

(N = Baum 5; Anderson 9)

	$\overline{X}_{BF}$	$\overline{X}_{AF}$	t-ratio	DF*	t-prob.	Sig. diff.
Cranial vault						
CM	147.93	144.89	- 1.952	12	0.075	
TP	5.00	5.22	0.800	6	0.454	
L	160.40	159.78	- 0.197	12	0.847	
B	146.00	140.89	- 1.529	12	0.152	
MF	95.80	92.56	- 2.112	12	0.056	
H	137.40	134.00	- 2.841	12	0.015	*
PAH	117.60	114.33	- 1.813	12	0.095	
BPH	-----	------	-------	--	-----	
LB	99.80	96.56	- 2.706	9	0.024	*
Face						
TFH	117.20	115.00	- 1.275	12	0.226	
UFH	73.20	70.78	- 1.233	3	1.000	
TFB	138.80	130.67	- 3.380	3	1.000	
MFB	101.60	97.11	- 2.543	12	0.026	*
IOB	96.40	96.89	0.300	12	0.769	
SIOB	16.00	16.44	0.304	12	0.766	
BOB	100.20	98.56	- 1.229	12	0.243	
AIB	18.20	18.56	0.487	10	0.636	
Nasal structure						
NB	27.20	26.33	- 1.040	12	0.319	
NH	53.00	50.78	- 1.587	3	1.000	
DC	19.20	20.00	0.998	12	0.338	
DS	10.20	8.56	- 1.321	8	0.223	
MN	9.20	8.00	- 0.937	7	0.380	
SMN	4.00	3.22	- 2.049	12	0.063	
Orbit						
LOH	33.60	33.89	0.400	12	0.696	
LOBM	43.60	42.67	- 1.259	12	0.232	
LOBD	42.20	40.56	- 2.227	12	0.046	

APPENDIX D

Table 185 - continued

Dental arch						
MB	68.00	64.89	- 3.888	9	0.004	*
ML	52.40	52.89	0.429	12	0.676	
FL	96.80	74.67	- 1.640	6	0.152	
FLA	95.80	81.89	- 1.406	6	0.209	
Mandible						
LM	102.60	101.33	- 0.998	9	0.344	
BCB	125.40	123.00	- 1.586	8	0.151	
SH	30.60	33.00	2.217	12	0.047	
BA	103.60	98.22	- 2.651	12	0.021	*
RL	32.20	32.22	0.021	9	0.984	
Facial angles						
G$\angle$	125.40°	122.11°	- 1.634	12	0.128	

*DF $\leq$ 3, t-prob. = 1

Table 186

"t" SCORES FOR INDICES OF: BAUM-ANDERSON FOCI
DEFORMED FEMALE CRANIA

(N = Baum 5; Anderson 9)

	$\bar{X}_{BA}$	$\bar{X}_{AF}$	t-ratio	DF	t-prob.	Sig. diff.
Cranial vault						
B/L	91.03	88.33	- 0.983	12	0.345	
H/L	85.69	83.99	- 0.963	12	0.355	
H/B	94.22	95.29	0.414	12	0.686	
H/L+B/2	89.73	89.19	- 0.355	12	0.729	
PAH/L	73.33	71.69	- 0.813	12	0.432	
BPH/H	------	------	-------	--	-----	
MF/B	65.68	65.77	0.062	12	0.952	
Face						
TFH/TFB	84.49	88.05	2.127	12	0.055	
UFH/TFB	52.71	54.20	1.305	12	0.216	
UFH/MFB	72.01	72.92	0.694	12	0.501	
TFB/B	95.24	92.90	- 0.849	12	0.413	
MF/TFB	69.10	70.86	1.102	12	0.292	
BA/MF	108.19	106.26	- 0.620	12	0.547	
BA/TFB	74.66	75.17	0.401	12	0.696	
SIOB/IOB	16.61	17.02	0.251	12	0.806	
AIB/BOB	18.17	18.82	0.770	12	0.456	
Nasal structure						
NB/NH	51.33	51.88	0.488	10	0.636	
DS/DC	53.05	42.16	- 1.902	8	0.094	
SMN/MN	43.50	32.41	- 1.782	12	0.100	
Orbit						
LOH/LOBM	77.04	79.46	2.451	8	0.040	
LOH/LOBD	79.62	83.58	4.013	9	0.003	*
Dental arch						
MB/ML	129.96	122.82	- 2.226	12	0.046	
Mandible						
LM/BCB	81.83	82.47	0.434	10	0.673	

APPENDIX D 527

Table 187

"t" SCORES FOR MEASUREMENTS OF:
BAUM-FEURT FOCI UNDEFORMED MALE CRANIA

(N = Baum 14; Feurt 27)

	$\bar{X}_{BF}$	$\bar{X}_{FF}$	t-ratio	DF	t-prob.	Sig. diff.
Cranial vault						
CM	155.17	154.91	0.219	39	0.828	
TP	5.07	4.96	0.461	39	0.647	
L	181.43	182.22	- 0.351	39	0.728	
B	141.29	140.19	0.574	39	0.569	
MF	97.21	96.04	1.051	39	0.300	
H	142.79	142.33	0.490	39	0.627	
PAH	122.29	118.78	3.353	16	0.004	*
BPH	------	------	-------	---	-----	
LB	140.71	105.00	- 0.305	39	0.762	
Face						
TFH	127.29	126.44	0.634	12	0.538	
UFH	76.14	77.33	- 2.467	39	0.018	*
TFB	143.86	141.56	1.917	39	0.063	
MFB	102.43	103.33	- 1.095	39	0.280	
IOB	100.64	100.59	0.050	39	0.960	
SIOB	17.86	18.07	- 0.341	39	0.735	
BOB	100.21	101.52	- 2.066	16	0.055	
AIB	19.93	19.93	0.007	31	0.994	
Nasal structure						
NB	26.21	27.30	- 2.928	37	0.006	*
NH	54.64	55.41	- 1.282	17	0.217	
DC	20.21	22.00	- 6.053	32	0.000	*
DS	11.00	11.30	- 1.069	39	0.292	
MN	10.00	9.81	0.461	39	0.648	
SMN	4.43	4.22	0.832	39	0.410	
Orbit						
LOH	34.79	34.22	1.286	39	0.206	
LOBM	43.21	44.59	- 4.703	39	0.000	*
LOBD	41.00	41.89	- 3.394	39	0.002	*
Dental arch						
MB	66.29	69.07	- 1.557	12	0.145	
ML	54.43	55.26	- 1.200	15	0.249	
FL	97.86	100.19	- 4.290	39	0.000	*
FLA	95.93	98.30	- 3.841	39	0.000	*
Mandible						
LM	108.21	104.81	2.790	17	0.013	*
BCB	127.29	129.52	- 1.563	39	0.126	
SH	37.14	37.63	- 0.540	14	0.598	
BA	102.57	104.26	- 1.088	15	0.294	
RL	36.14	34.44	2.069	39	0.045	
Facial angles						
G∠	115.36	113.19	1.542	39	0.131	

Table 188

"t" SCORES FOR INDICES OF:
BAUM-FEURT FOCI UNDEFORMED MALE CRANIA

(N = Baum 14; Feurt 27)

	$\bar{X}_{BF}$	$\bar{X}_{FF}$	t-ratio	DF	t-prob.	Sig diff.
Cranial vault						
B/L	78.00	77.03	0.678	39	0.502	
H/L	78.77	78.19	0.681	39	0.500	
H/B	101.31	101.65	- 0.198	17	0.845	
H/L+B/2	88.53	88.34	0.240	39	0.812	
PAH/L	67.47	65.26	2.652	39	0.012	*
BPH/H	------	------	-------	---	-----	
MF/B	68.90	68.59	0.304	39	0.762	
Face						
TFH/TFB	88.51	89.36	- 0.963	16	0.350	
UFH/TFB	52.97	54.66	- 3.301	39	0.002	*
UFH/MFB	74.36	74.89	- 0.918	37	0.364	
TFB/B	102.00	101.10	0.620	39	0.539	
MF/TFB	67.64	67.87	- 0.206	16	0.840	
BA/MF	105.67	108.64	- 1.487	15	0.158	
BA/TFB	71.38	73.66	- 1.781	13	0.098	
SIOB/IOB	17.73	17.96	- 0.403	39	0.689	
AIB/BOB	19.89	19.63	0.777	32	0.443	
Nasal structure						
NB/NH	48.05	49.27	- 1.385	39	0.174	
DS/DC	54.44	51.53	1.924	39	0.062	
SMN/MN	44.64	43.36	0.509	39	0.614	
Orbit						
LOH/LOBM	80.51	76.76	3.966	39	0.000	*
LOH/LOBD	84.83	81.74	3.451	37	0.001	*
Dental arch						
MB/ML	122.27	125.05	- 0.679	12	0.510	
Mandible						
LM/BCB	85.10	81.03	3.237	39	0.002	*

APPENDIX D

Table 189
"t" SCORES FOR MEASUREMENTS OF:
BAUM-FEURT FOCI DEFORMED MALE CRANIA

(N = Baum 16; Feurt 19)

	$\bar{x}_{BF}$	$\bar{x}_{FF}$	t-ratio	DF	t-prob.	Sig. diff.
Cranial vault						
CM	152.54	155.84	- 4.231	33	0.000	*
TP	5.06	5.42	- 1.448	33	0.157	
L	174.12	172.53	0.843	33	0.405	
B	146.12	150.79	- 2.203	33	0.035	*
MF	95.69	95.37	0.228	33	0.821	
H	137.38	144.21	- 6.744	17	0.000	*
PAH	120.62	121.58	- 0.928	27	0.362	
BPH	------	------	-------	---	-----	
LB	103.44	104.58	- 1.717	33	0.095	
Face						
TFH	125.88	127.00	- 1.904	18	0.073	
UFH	75.69	78.53	- 6.750	21	0.000	*
TFB	140.69	141.58	- 0.688	28	0.498	
MFB	102.88	102.47	0.500	24	0.621	
IOB	99.12	100.58	- 1.705	33	0.098	
SIOB	17.06	19.00	- 3.403	33	0.002	*
BOB	99.12	101.84	- 4.999	25	0.000	*
AIB	19.94	19.68	0.643	21	0.527	
Nasal structure						
NB	26.81	27.11	- 0.732	27	0.470	
NH	54.88	55.95	- 3.158	18	0.005	*
DC	19.94	21.53	- 3.518	20	0.002	*
DS	11.00	11.11	- 0.809	16	0.430	
MN	9.75	9.89	- 0.428	33	0.671	
SMN	4.31	4.11	0.999	29	0.326	
Orbit						
LOH	34.94	33.95	3.066	33	0.004	*
LOBM	43.06	45.11	- 7.991	33	0.000	*
LOBD	41.00	42.21	- 4.772	21	0.000	*
Dental arch						
MB	68.38	68.95	- 0.865	23	0.396	
ML	54.62	55.42	- 1.015	33	0.318	
FL	97.50	100.00	- 3.793	18	0.001	*
FLA	95.50	98.11	- 3.587	18	0.002	*
Mandible						
LM	103.00	105.89	- 3.233	33	0.003	*
BCB	128.00	129.21	- 0.917	23	0.369	
SH	36.44	37.16	- 1.102	33	0.278	
BA	104.75	104.21	0.375	33	0.710	
RL	35.38	35.00	0.575	33	0.569	
Facial angles						
G∠	114.56	116.47	- 1.376	26	0.180	

Table 190

"t" SCORES FOR INDICES OF:
BAUM-FEURT FOCI DEFORMED MALE CRANIA

(N = Baum 16; Feurt 19)

	$\bar{X}_{BF}$	$\bar{X}_{FF}$	t-ratio	DF	t-prob.	Sig. diff.
Cranial vault						
B/L	84.07	87.54	- 1.810	33	0.079	
H/L	78.98	83.62	- 5.532	33	0.000	*
H/B	94.21	95.80	- 0.947	33	0.351	
H/L+B/2	85.82	89.21	- 4.676	29	0.000	*
PAH/L	69.34	70.51	- 1.452	33	0.156	
BPH/H	------	------	-------	---	-----	
MF/B	65.58	63.27	2.384	22	0.026	*
Face						
TFH/TFB	89.51	89.78	- 0.313	33	0.756	
UFH/TFB	53.82	55.51	- 3.082	33	0.004	*
UFH/MFB	73.58	76.69	- 4.369	24	0.000	*
TFB/B	96.46	93.95	1.899	23	0.070	
MF/TFB	68.01	67.37	0.826	33	0.415	
BA/MF	109.68	109.40	0.133	33	0.895	
BA/TFB	74.50	73.62	0.866	23	0.396	
SIOB/IOB	17.20	18.91	- 3.062	33	0.004	*
AIB/BOB	20.12	19.32	2.342	24	0.028	*
Nasal structure						
NB/NH	48.86	50.15	- 0.634	17	0.535	
DS/DC	55.22	51.97	2.385	20	0.027	*
SMN/MN	44.37	41.65	1.319	33	0.196	
Orbit						
LOH/LOBM	81.14	75.27	8.998	33	0.000	*
LOH/LOBD	85.21	80.45	6.492	33	0.000	*
Dental arch						
MB/ML	125.32	124.57	0.420	33	0.678	
Mandible						
LM/BCB	80.54	81.98	- 1.708	33	0.097	

APPENDIX D

Table 191

"t" SCORES FOR MEASUREMENTS OF: BAUM-FEURT FOCI
UNDEFORMED FEMALE CRANIA
(N = Baum 6; Feurt 9)

	$\bar{X}_{BF}$	$\bar{X}_{FF}$	t-ratio	DF*	t-prob.	Sig. diff.
Cranial vault						
CM	148.06	149.59	- 1.142	13	0.274	
TP	5.17	5.11	- 0.111	13	0.913	
L	172.33	174.44	1.002	13	0.334	
B	136.17	138.22	1.014	13	0.329	
MF	89.33	90.22	0.599	13	0.559	
H	135.67	136.11	0.236	13	0.817	
PAH	115.33	115.11	- 0.117	13	0.909	
BPH	------	------	-------	--	-----	
LB	99.33	98.56	- 0.421	13	0.680	
Face						
TFH	114.00	116.00	1.210	3	1.000	
UFH	69.00	71.22	1.583	4	0.189	
TFB	134.33	131.44	- 1.060	13	0.308	
MFB	97.33	99.22	0.866	3	1.000	
IOB	94.83	93.00	- 1.024	5	0.353	
SIOB	14.67	14.56	- 0.102	8	0.922	
BOB	98.17	96.22	- 1.215	4	0.291	
AIB	17.67	18.78	1.850	13	0.087	
Nasal structure						
NB	25.17	25.78	0.926	13	0.371	
NII	49.67	51.33	1.597	4	0.185	
DC	18.83	20.11	3.910	4	0.017	*
DS	10.33	9.00	- 4.996	13	0.000	*
MN	8.33	7.67	- 1.249	13	0.234	
SMN	4.17	2.78	- 4.535	13	0.001	*
Orbit						
LOH	33.33	33.89	0.691	13	0.502	
LOBM	42.17	40.78	- 1.570	3	1.000	
LOBD	40.17	39.00	- 1.441	3	1.000	

Table 191- continued

Dental arch						
MB	66.17	65.00	- 0.902	4	0.418	
ML	52.17	51.89	- 0.264	3	1.000	
FL	98.00	94.67	- 2.540	3	1.000	
FLA	96.67	92.89	- 3.369	3	1.000	
Mandible						
LM	100.17	100.44	0.143	4	0.893	
BCB	127.50	122.11	- 2.705	10	0.022	*
SH	31.83	33.11	2.359	13	0.035	*
BA	98.17	97.78	- 0.155	4	0.884	
RL	32.00	32.00	0.0	13	1.000	
Facial angles						
G/	121.83°	123.33°	0.621	13	0.545	

*DF ≤ 3, t-prob. = 1

APPENDIX D

Table 192

"t" SCORES FOR INDICES OF: BAUM-FEURT FOCI
UNDEFORMED FEMALE CRANIA

(N = Baum 6; Feurt 9)

	$\bar{X}_{BF}$	$\bar{X}_{FF}$	t-ratio	DF*	t-prob.	Sig. diff.
Cranial vault						
B/L	79.07	79.24	- 0.124	13	0.903	
H/L	78.80	78.04	0.437	4	0.685	
H/B	99.63	98.55	0.669	13	0.515	
H/L+B/2	87.97	87.09	0.634	13	0.537	
PAH/L	66.95	65.99	0.867	13	0.402	
BPH/H	------	------	-------	--	-----	
MF/B	65.60	65.32	0.251	13	0.806	
Face						
TFH/TFB	85.01	88.33	- 1.737	13	0.106	
UFH/TFB	51.44	54.25	- 2.078	13	0.058	
UFH/MFB	71.01	71.79	- 0.466	4	0.665	
TFB/B	98.63	95.11	2.079	4	0.106	
MF/TFB	66.58	68.69	- 1.519	13	0.153	
BA/MF	109.91	108.46	0.563	13	0.583	
BA/TFB	73.06	74.44	- 1.219	13	0.245	
SIOB/IOB	15.51	15.62	- 0.087	10	0.933	
AIB/BOB	17.99	19.53	- 2.479	13	0.028	*
Nasal structure						
NB/NH	50.68	50.23	0.404	13	0.693	
DS/DC	55.02	44.76	4.187	3	1.000	
SMN/MN	49.97	37.13	2.951	13	0.011	*
Orbit						
LOH/LOBM	79.18	83.11	- 1.835	13	0.089	
LOH/LOBD	83.14	86.90	- 1.580	13	0.138	
Dental arch						
MB/ML	127.12	125.28	0.478	4	0.657	
Mandible						
LM/BCB	78.62	82.39	- 1.775	13	0.099	

*DF $\leq$ 3, t-prob. = 1

Table 193

"t" SCORES FOR MEASUREMENTS OF: BAUM-FEURT FOCI

DEFORMED FEMALE CRANIA

(N = Baum 5; Feurt 16)

	$\bar{X}_{BF}$	$\bar{X}_{FF}$	t-ratio	DF*	t-prob.	Sig. diff.
Cranial vault						
CM	147.93	146.08	- 1.543	19	0.139	
TP	5.00	5.06	0.324	13	0.751	
L	160.40	160.94	0.215	19	0.832	
B	146.00	145.81	- 0.072	19	0.943	
MF	95.80	91.00	- 3.125	19	0.006	*
H	137.40	131.50	- 5.816	17	0.000	*
PAH	117.60	114.44	- 2.575	19	0.019	*
BPH	------	------	------	--	-----	
LB	99.80	95.88	- 3.675	19	0.001	*
Face						
TFH	117.20	116.00	- 1.499	2	1.000	
UFH	73.20	70.81	- 1.263	3	1.000	
TFB	138.80	132.81	- 2.653	2	1.000	
MFB	101.60	99.31	- 1.834	19	0.082	
IOB	96.40	94.06	- 1.912	19	0.071	
SIOB	16.00	15.31	- 0.692	19	0.497	
BOB	100.20	96.62	- 4.776	19	0.000	*
AIB	18.20	18.19	- 0.020	19	0.984	
Nasal structure						
NB	27.20	26.06	- 1.775	19	0.092	
NH	53.00	50.94	- 1.488	3	1.000	
DC	19.20	19.25	0.096	19	0.925	
DS	10.20	9.06	- 2.611	19	0.017	*
MN	9.20	7.25	- 4.830	19	0.000	*
SMN	4.00	3.00	- 3.038	3	1.000	
Orbit						
LOH	33.60	33.12	- 0.666	3	1.000	
LOBM	43.60	41.19	- 3.457	2	1.000	
LOBD	42.20	39.00	- 3.852	3	1.000	

APPENDIX D

Table 193 - continued

Dental arch						
MB	68.00	64.94	- 6.078	14	0.0	*
ML	52.40	52.19	- 0.203	19	0.842	
FL	96.80	95.06	- 4.033	17	0.001	*
FLA	95.80	93.38	- 4.796	17	0.000	*
Mandible						
LM	102.60	101.38	- 1.186	15	0.254	
BCB	125.40	122.44	- 3.927	19	0.001	*
SH	30.60	33.19	2.184	19	0.042	
BA	103.60	97.06	- 3.089	19	0.006	*
RL	32.20	31.06	- 1.431	19	0.169	
Facial angles						
G/	125.40°	115.06°	- 1.314	14	0.210	

*DF $\leq$ 3, t-prob. = 1

Table 194

"t" SCORES FOR INDICES OF: BAUM-FEURT FOCI

DEFORMED FEMALE CRANIA

(N = Baum 5; Feurt 16)

	$\bar{x}_{BF}$	$\bar{x}_{FF}$	t-ratio	DF*	t-prob.	Sig. diff.
Cranial vault						
B/L	91.03	84.51	- 1.163	15	0.263	
H/L	85.69	81.78	- 2.593	19	0.018	*
H/B	94.22	90.26	- 2.313	19	0.032	*
H/L+B/2	89.73	85.73	- 4.015	19	0.001	*
PAH/L	73.33	71.17	- 1.814	19	0.085	
BPH/H	------	------	-------	--	-----	
MF/B	65.68	62.44	- 2.801	19	0.011	*
Face						
TFH/TFB	84.49	87.35	3.063	2	1.000	
UFH/TFB	52.71	53.32	0.774	19	0.449	
UFH/MFB	72.01	71.34	- 0.533	19	0.601	
TFB/B	95.24	91.18	- 1.404	3	1.000	
MF/TFB	69.10	68.52	- 0.423	19	0.677	
BA/MF	108.19	106.79	- 0.467	19	0.646	
BA/TFB	74.66	73.08	- 1.007	19	0.323	
SIOB/IOB	16.61	16.27	- 0.338	19	0.739	
AIB/BOB	18.17	18.82	1.016	19	0.322	
Nasal structure						
NB/NH	51.33	51.17	- 0.165	19	0.871	
DS/DC	53.05	47.11	- 3.082	19	0.006	*
SMN/MN	43.50	41.45	- 0.616	3	1.000	
Orbit						
LOH/LOBM	77.04	80.43	5.484	15	0.000	*
LOH/LOBD	79.62	84.97	6.432	16	0.0	*
Dental arch						
MB/ML	129.96	124.55	- 2.264	19	0.035	
Mandible						
LM/BCB	81.83	82.78	0.947	19	0.355	

*DF $\leq$ 3, t-prob. = 1

APPENDIX D 537

Table 195

"t" SCORES FOR MEASUREMENTS OF:
BAUM-MADISONVILLE FOCI UNDEFORMED MALE CRANIA

(N = Baum 14; Madisonville 87)

	$\bar{X}_{BF}$	$\bar{X}_{MF}$	t-ratio	DF	t-prob.	Sig. diff.
Cranial vault						
CM	155.17	153.32	1.692	99	0.094	
TP	5.07	5.10	- 0.114	99	0.910	
L	181.43	179.90	0.659	99	0.512	
B	141.29	142.56	- 0.796	99	0.428	
MF	97.21	94.75	1.852	99	0.067	
H	142.79	137.49	4.989	22	0.000	*
PAH	122.29	116.79	5.539	99	0.000	*
BPH	------	------	-------	---	-----	
LB	104.71	103.68	1.115	24	0.276	
Face						
TFH	127.29	123.05	2.274	99	0.025	*
UFH	76.14	73.28	6.013	54	0.000	*
TFB	143.86	140.98	2.573	99	0.012	*
MFB	102.43	102.26	0.237	24	0.815	
IOB	100.64	99.57	1.158	99	0.250	
SIOB	17.86	17.44	0.718	99	0.474	
BOB	100.21	100.92	- 1.062	99	0.291	
AIB	19.93	20.25	- 1.415	76	0.161	
Nasal structure						
NB	26.21	27.01	- 2.852	33	0.007	*
NH	54.64	53.15	2.258	99	0.026	*
DC	20.21	22.11	- 7.353	94	0.000	*
DS	11.00	11.33	- 0.962	99	0.338	
MN	10.00	9.26	1.618	99	0.109	
SMN	4.43	3.84	2.648	99	0.009	*
Orbit						
LOH	34.79	34.10	1.928	23	0.066	
LOBM	43.21	43.56	- 1.005	99	0.317	
LOBD	41.00	40.84	0.712	28	0.482	
Dental arch						
MB	66.29	64.70	0.862	13	0.404	
ML	54.43	55.02	- 1.033	99	0.304	
FL	97.86	98.66	- 1.278	22	0.215	
FLA	95.93	97.34	- 1.623	99	0.108	
Mandible						
LM	108.21	105.39	2.551	99	0.012	*
BCB	127.29	129.29	- 1.736	99	0.086	
SH	37.14	35.93	1.375	13	0.192	
BA	102.57	104.64	- 1.483	99	0.141	
RL	36.14	35.40	1.049	99	0.297	
Facial angles						
G∠	115.36	119.25	- 2.585	99	0.011	*

Table 196
"t" SCORES FOR INDICES OF:
BAUM-MADISONVILLE FOCI UNDEFORMED MALE CRANIA

(N = Baum 14; Madisonville 87)

	$\bar{x}_{BF}$	$\bar{x}_{MF}$	t-ratio	DF	t-prob.	Sig. diff.
Cranial vault						
B/L	78.00	78.29	- 0.135	99	0.892	
H/L	78.76	75.45	2.868	55	0.006	*
H/B	101.31	96.58	3.046	99	0.003	*
H/L+B/2	88.53	85.35	2.822	99	0.006	*
PAH/L	67.47	65.07	2.216	99	0.029	*
BPH/H	-----	-----	-------	---	-----	
MF/B	68.70	66.51	2.369	99	0.019	*
Face						
TFH/TFB	88.51	86.17	2.019	44	0.050	
UFH/TFB	52.96	52.00	1.973	25	0.060	
UFH/MFB	74.36	71.72	5.068	59	0.000	*
TFB/B	102.00	98.99	2.649	99	0.009	*
MF/TFB	67.64	67.23	0.437	99	0.663	
BA/MF	105.67	110.65	- 2.649	99	0.009	*
BA/TFB	71.38	74.25	- 2.218	13	0.045	
SIOB/IOB	17.73	17.50	0.439	99	0.662	
AIB/BOB	19.89	20.06	- 0.770	59	0.445	
Nasal structure						
NB/NH	48.05	50.91	- 3.616	22	0.002	*
DS/DC	54.44	51.77	1.680	22	0.107	
SMN/MN	44.64	41.93	1.222	99	0.224	
Orbit						
LOH/LOBM	80.51	78.30	2.873	22	0.009	*
LOH/LOBD	84.83	83.55	1.953	41	0.058	
Dental arch						
MB/ML	122.27	117.66	1.112	12	0.288	
Mandible						
LM/BCB	85.10	80.44	3.159	39	0.003	*

APPENDIX D 539

Table 197

"t" SCORES FOR MEASUREMENTS OF:
BAUM-MADISONVILLE FOCI DEFORMED MALE CRANIA

(N = Baum 16; Madisonville 156)

	$\bar{x}_{BF}$	$\bar{x}_{MF}$	t-ratio	DF	t-prob.	Sig. diff.
Cranial vault						
CM	152.54	153.69	-1.660	170	0.099	
TP	5.06	5.24	-0.889	170	0.375	
L	174.12	172.74	0.920	170	0.359	
B	146.12	150.97	-2.736	15	0.015	*
MF	95.69	95.38	0.328	170	0.743	
H	137.38	137.35	0.087	138	0.931	
PAH	120.62	118.10	3.319	170	0.001	*
BPH	------	------	-------	---	-----	
LB	103.44	102.27	2.502	29	0.018	*
Face						
TFH	125.88	122.56	11.416	150	0.000	*
UFH	75.69	73.61	7.926	97	0.000	*
TFB	140.69	142.57	-2.573	170	0.011	*
MFB	102.88	102.13	1.796	23	0.086	
IOB	99.12	99.53	-0.539	170	0.591	
SIOB	17.06	17.26	-0.331	49	0.742	
BOB	99.12	101.16	-6.719	27	0.000	*
AIB	19.94	20.07	-0.749	32	0.459	
Nasal structure						
NB	26.81	26.89	-0.334	22	0.742	
NH	54.88	53.08	10.212	131	0.000	*
DC	19.94	21.97	-11.448	33	0.000	*
DS	11.00	11.60	-2.007	170	0.046	
MN	9.75	9.56	0.776	32	0.444	
SMN	4.31	4.10	1.604	22	0.123	
Orbit						
LOH	34.94	34.04	3.106	170	0.002	*
LOBM	43.06	43.88	-3.829	21	0.000	*
LOBD	41.00	41.03	-0.244	56	0.808	
Dental arch						
MB	68.38	65.78	3.401	170	0.000	*
ML	54.62	54.74	-0.235	170	0.815	
FL	97.50	98.54	-4.108	77	0.000	*
FLA	95.50	97.42	-7.616	77	0.000	*
Mandible						
LM	103.00	104.58	-2.217	22	0.037	*
BCB	128.00	130.28	-2.006	170	0.046	
SH	36.44	35.88	0.917	170	0.361	
BA	104.75	104.92	-0.153	170	0.878	
RL	35.38	34.92	0.748	22	0.037	*
Facial angles						
G/	114.56	119.58	-6.227	28	0.000	*

Table 198

"t" SCORES FOR INDICES OF:
BAUM-MADISONVILLE FOCI DEFORMED MALE CRANIA

(N = Baum 16; Madisonville 156)

	$\overline{x}_{BF}$	$\overline{x}_{MF}$	t-ratio	DF	t-prob.	Sig. diff.
Cranial vault						
B/L	84.07	84.34	- 0.141	38	0.888	
H/L	78.98	79.60	- 0.718	170	0.474	
H/B	94.21	91.07	3.192	170	0.002	*
H/L+B/2	85.82	84.88	2.087	21	0.049	
PAH/L	69.34	68.44	1.227	170	0.221	
BPH/H	-----	-----	------	---	-----	
MF/B	65.58	63.22	3.297	170	0.001	*
Face						
TFH/TFB	89.51	85.98	5.191	170	0.000	*
UFH/TFB	53.82	51.65	5.840	21	0.000	*
UFH/MFB	73.59	72.10	3.944	29	0.000	*
TFB/B	96.46	94.54	1.949	170	0.053	
MF/TFB	68.01	66.91	1.615	170	0.108	
BA/MF	109.68	110.15	- 0.294	170	0.769	
BA/TFB	74.50	73.61	1.069	170	0.287	
SIOB/IOB	17.20	17.32	- 0.232	61	0.817	
AIB/BOB	20.12	19.84	1.518	30	0.140	
Nasal structure						
NB/NH	48.86	50.73	- 4.347	35	0.000	*
DS/DC	55.22	52.96	3.429	70	0.001	*
SMN/MN	44.37	42.69	1.224	24	0.233	
Orbit						
LOH/LOBM	81.14	77.60	7.706	24	0.000	*
LOH/LOBD	85.21	83.01	4.462	26	0.000	*
Dental arch						
MB/ML	125.32	120.26	3.134	170	0.002	*
Mandible						
LM/BCB	80.54	80.35	0.194	170	0.846	

APPENDIX D

Table 199

"t" SCORES FOR MEASUREMENTS OF: BAUM-MADISONVILLE FOCI
UNDEFORMED FEMALE CRANIA
(N = Baum 6; Madisonville 68)

	$\bar{X}_{BF}$	$\bar{X}_{MF}$	t-ratio	DF*	t-prob.	Sig. diff.
Cranial vault						
CM	148.06	141.02	- 2.751	70	0.008	*
TP	5.17	5.13	- 0.100	58	0.921	
L	172.33	173.04	0.328	58	0.744	
B	136.17	138.93	1.385	58	0.171	
MF	89.33	91.72	1.562	58	0.124	
H	135.67	132.13	- 1.270	58	0.209	
PAH	115.33	113.06	- 1.336	58	0.187	
BPH	------	------	-------	--	-----	
LB	99.33	100.09	0.612	58	0.543	
Face						
TFH	114.00	111.87	- 1.266	3	1.000	
UFH	69.00	68.15	- 0.794	58	0.431	
TFB	134.33	129.94	- 1.603	3	1.000	
MFB	97.33	98.00	0.303	3	1.000	
IOB	94.83	95.15	0.185	3	1.000	
SIOB	14.67	16.28	2.601	58	0.012	*
BOB	98.17	97.46	- 0.445	3	1.000	
AIB	17.67	19.30	2.305	58	0.025	*
Nasal structure						
NB	25.17	26.33	2.077	58	0.042	
NH	49.67	49.83	0.209	58	0.835	
DC	18.83	20.91	5.448	9	0.000	*
DS	10.33	10.94	1.273	58	0.208	
MN	8.33	8.81	0.651	58	0.518	
SMN	4.17	3.59	- 1.651	58	0.104	
Orbit						
LOH	33.33	33.07	- 0.452	58	0.653	
LOBM	42.17	42.20	0.041	3	1.000	
LOBD	40.17	39.15	- 1.263	3	1.000	

Table 199 - continued

Dental arch						
MB	66.17	63.63	- 2.349	58	0.022	*
ML	52.17	53.39	1.369	58	0.176	
FL	98.00	97.13	- 0.792	58	0.432	
FLA	96.67	96.06	- 0.595	58	0.554	
Mandible						
LM	100.17	101.54	0.726	3	1.000	
BCB	127.50	125.02	- 2.157	58	0.035	*
SH	31.83	32.80	1.533	58	0.131	
BA	98.17	97.78	- 0.157	58	0.071	
RL	32.00	33.26	1.842	58	0.071	
Facial angles						
G/	121.83°	123.46°	0.771	3	1.000	

*DF $\leq$ 3, t-prob. = 1

APPENDIX D

Table 200

"t" SCORES FOR INDICES OF: BAUM-MADISONVILLE FOCI

UNDEFORMED FEMALE CRANIA

(N = Baum 6; Madisonville 68)

	$\bar{X}_{BF}$	$\bar{X}_{MF}$	t-ratio	DF	t-prob.	Sig. diff.
Cranial vault						
B/L	79.07	76.93	- 1.263	15	0.226	
H/L	78.80	75.60	- 1.701	72	0.093	
H/B	99.63	95.28	- 3.489	7	0.010	*
H/L+B/2	87.97	83.09	- 1.847	72	0.069	
PAH/L	66.95	58.77	- 3.321	61	0.002	*
BPH/H	------	------	-------	--	-----	
MF/B	65.60	60.30	- 2.581	70	0.012	*
Face						
TFH/TFB	85.01	78.33	- 2.074	33	0.046	
UFH/TFB	51.44	52.83	1.247	72	0.217	
UFH/MFB	71.01	68.41	- 0.869	72	0.388	
TFB/B	98.63	87.77	- 4.144	27	0.000	*
MF/TFB	66.58	71.74	2.736	72	0.008	*
BA/MF	109.91	103.78	- 1.647	72	0.104	
BA/TFB	73.06	68.47	- 1.975	68	0.052	
SIOB/IOB	15.51	24.73	3.522	69	0.001	*
AIB/BOB	17.99	22.90	4.133	65	0.000	*
Nasal structure						
NB/NH	50.68	55.32	2.768	57	0.008	*
DS/DC	55.02	55.35	0.076	72	0.939	
SMN/MN	49.97	47.16	- 0.793	10	0.446	
Orbit						
LOH/LOBM	79.18	78.91	- 0.160	72	0.874	
LOH/LOBD	83.14	82.60	- 0.204	72	0.839	
Dental arch						
MB/ML	127.12	103.05	- 3.878	28	0.001	*
Mandible						
LM/BCB	78.62	79.45	0.280	72	0.781	

Table 201

"t" SCORES FOR MEASUREMENTS OF: BAUM-MADISONVILLE FOCI

DEFORMED FEMALE CRANIA

(N = Baum 5; Madisonville 192)

	$\bar{X}_{BF}$	$\bar{X}_{MF}$	t-ratio	DF*	t-prob.	Sig. diff.
Cranial vault						
CM	147.93	148.46	0.432	195	0.666	
TP	5.00	5.18	2.807	189	0.006	*
L	160.40	166.38	0.962	195	0.337	
B	146.00	146.35	1.272	195	0.205	
MF	95.80	92.00	-2.545	4	0.064	
H	137.40	132.77	-2.415	195	0.017	*
PAH	117.60	114.12	-1.649	195	0.101	
BPH	------	------	-------	---	-----	
LB	99.80	98.82	-3.293	5	0.022	*
Face						
TFH	117.20	111.90	-3.315	195	0.001	*
UFH	73.20	68.88	-4.267	195	0.000	*
TFB	138.80	133.81	-1.972	2	1.000	
MFB	101.60	97.67	-3.457	195	0.001	*
IOB	96.40	96.05	-0.704	195	0.482	
SIOB	16.00	16.19	-0.322	195	0.748	
BOB	100.20	97.89	-2.968	195	0.003	*
AIB	18.20	19.24	1.647	195	0.101	
Nasal structure						
NB	27.20	26.19	-2.181	195	0.030	*
NH	53.00	49.88	-4.551	195	0.000	*
DC	19.20	21.05	2.830	195	0.005	*
DS	10.20	10.84	1.122	195	0.263	
MN	9.20	9.23	0.446	195	0.656	
SMN	4.00	3.80	-0.753	195	0.452	
Orbit						
LOH	33.60	33.14	-1.886	195	0.061	
LOBM	43.60	42.03	-3.474	195	0.001	*
LOBD	42.20	39.24	-3.685	2	1.000	

Table 201 - continued

Dental arch						
MB	68.00	63.97	- 3.995	195	0.000	*
ML	52.40	53.51	0.361	195	0.719	
FL	96.80	96.85	- 1.220	189	0.224	
FLA	95.80	95.78	- 1.719	189	0.087	
Mandible						
LM	102.60	101.36	- 0.330	195	0.742	
BCB	125.40	124.40	0.121	195	0.904	
SH	30.60	32.84	1.939	195	0.054	
BA	103.60	97.95	- 1.482	2	1.000	
RL	32.20	32.72	0.540	195	0.590	
Facial angles						
G$\underline{/}$	125.40°	124.22°	0.331	195	0.741	

*DF $\leq$ 3, t-prob. = 1

Table 202

"t" SCORES FOR INDICES OF: BAUM-MADISONVILLE FOCI

DEFORMED FEMALE CRANIA

(N = Baum 5; Madisonville 192)

	$\overline{X}_{BF}$	$\overline{X}_{MF}$	t-ratio	DF*	t-prob.	Sig. diff.
Cranial vault						
B/L	91.03	84.62	- 3.662	8	0.006	*
H/L	85.69	79.82	- 4.575	195	0.000	*
H/B	94.22	91.05	- 1.987	195	0.048	
H/L+B/2	89.73	85.00	- 4.881	195	0.000	*
PAH/L	73.33	68.57	- 3.916	195	0.000	*
BPH/H	------	------	-------	---	-----	-
MF/B	65.68	63.05	- 2.284	3	1.000	
Face						
TFH/TFB	84.49	83.55	- 0.736	195	0.463	
UFH/TFB	52.71	51.23	- 1.952	4	0.123	
UFH/MFB	72.01	70.20	- 1.702	4	0.164	
TFB/B	95.24	92.49	- 0.927	3	1.000	
MF/TFB	69.10	68.53	- 0.400	3	1.000	
BA/MF	108.19	110.21	0.426	58	0.672	
BA/TFB	74.66	72.95	- 0.900	195	0.369	
SIOB/IOB	16.61	16.78	0.202	195	0.840	
AIB/BOB	18.17	19.59	1.797	195	0.074	
Nasal structure						
NB/NH	51.33	52.05	0.996	8	0.348	
DS/DC	53.05	51.69	- 0.613	195	0.540	
SMN/MN	43.50	41.45	- 0.673	195	0.502	
Orbit						
LOH/LOBM	77.04	78.64	3.172	11	0.009	*
LOH/LOBD	79.62	84.34	8.752	6	0.0	*
Dental arch						
MB/ML	129.96	119.66	- 4.886	195	0.000	*
Mandible						
LM/BCB	81.83	81.53	- 0.236	195	0.814	

*DF ≤ 3, t-prob. = 1

APPENDIX D

Table 203
"t" SCORES FOR MEASUREMENTS OF:
FEURT-ANDERSON FOCI UNDEFORMED MALE CRANIA

(N = Feurt 27; Anderson 72)

	$\bar{x}_{FF}$	$\bar{x}_{AF}$	t-ratio	DF	t-prob.	Sig. diff.
Cranial vault						
CM	154.91	153.31	2.104	97	0.038	*
TP	4.96	4.78	1.174	97	0.243	
L	182.22	181.14	0.656	97	0.513	
B	140.19	138.26	1.570	97	0.120	
MF	96.04	93.81	1.195	90	0.114	
H	142.33	140.53	2.921	62	0.005	*
PAH	118.78	117.08	2.352	92	0.021	*
BPH	------	------	-------	---	-----	
LB	105.00	104.18	1.089	97	0.279	
Face						
TFH	126.44	124.96	2.743	95	0.007	*
UFH	77.33	74.97	4.663	90	0.000	*
TFB	141.55	140.49	1.291	97	0.200	
MFB	103.33	102.22	1.602	68	0.114	
IOB	100.59	100.19	0.537	97	0.592	
SIOB	18.07	18.06	0.045	97	0.964	
BOB	101.52	101.00	1.177	92	0.242	
AIB	19.93	19.85	0.197	97	0.844	
Nasal structure						
NB	27.30	26.94	0.997	97	0.321	
NH	55.41	53.78	4.465	77	0.000	*
DC	22.00	21.00	2.771	97	0.007	*
DS	11.30	11.11	0.950	73	0.345	
MN	9.81	8.61	4.390	97	0.000	*
SMN	4.22	3.97	1.425	97	0.157	
Orbit						
LOH	34.22	34.69	- 1.334	60	0.187	
LOBM	44.59	43.78	2.670	94	0.009	*
LOBD	41.89	41.61	1.130	82	0.262	
Dental arch						
MB	69.07	69.10	- 0.047	85	0.963	
ML	55.26	54.21	3.045	68	0.003	*
FL	100.19	97.79	4.907	93	0.000	*
FLA	98.30	95.89	4.625	89	0.000	*
Mandible						
LM	104.81	104.49	0.450	72	0.654	
BCB	129.52	129.07	0.386	97	0.700	
SH	37.63	36.50	2.704	97	0.008	*
BA	104.26	103.65	0.740	83	0.461	
RL	34.44	35.51	- 1.873	97	0.064	
Facial angles						
G∠	113.19	114.35	- 0.950	97	0.345	

Table 204

"t" SCORES FOR INDICES OF:
FEURT-ANDERSON FOCI UNDEFORMED MALE CRANIA

(N = Feurt 27; Anderson 72)

	$\overline{x}_{FF}$	$\overline{x}_{AF}$	t-ratio	DF	t-prob.	Sig. diff.
Cranial vault						
B/L	77.02	76.49	0.557	62	0.579	
H/L	78.19	77.69	0.827	61	0.412	
H/B	101.65	101.76	- 0.123	97	0.902	
H/L+B/2	88.34	88.02	0.694	97	0.490	
PAH/L	65.26	64.74	0.817	76	0.416	
BPH/H	------	------	-------	---	-----	
MF/B	68.59	67.89	0.629	95	0.531	
Face						
TFH/TFB	89.36	87.61	1.300	79	0.197	
UFH/TFB	54.66	53.40	2.834	78	0.006	*
UFH/MFB	74.89	73.40	2.308	66	0.024	*
TFB/B	101.10	101.70	- 0.742	97	0.460	
MF/TFB	67.87	66.84	1.010	92	0.315	
BA/MF	108.64	109.35	- 0.662	83	0.510	
BA/TFB	73.66	73.83	- 0.284	95	0.777	
SIOB/IOB	17.96	18.01	- 0.148	97	0.882	
AIB/BOB	19.63	19.65	- 0.071	97	0.943	
Nasal structure						
NB/NH	49.27	50.19	- 1.204	97	0.232	
DS/DC	51.53	53.25	- 1.453	74	0.151	
SMN/MN	43.36	46.59	- 1.617	97	0.109	
Orbit						
LOH/LOBM	76.76	78.16	- 1.478	89	0.143	
LOH/LOBD	81.74	82.08	- 0.233	95	0.816	
Dental arch						
MB/ML	125.05	127.53	- 2.548	65	0.013	*
Mandible						
LM/BCB	81.03	81.09	- 0.060	97	0.952	

APPENDIX D

Table 205

"t" SCORES FOR MEASUREMENTS OF: FEURT-ANDERSON FOCI
UNDEFORMED FEMALE CRANIA
(N = Feurt 9; Anderson 37)

	$\overline{X}_{FF}$	$\overline{X}_{AF}$	t-ratio	DF	t-prob.	Sig. diff.
Cranial vault						
CM	149.59	148.22	-1.282	44	0.207	
TP	5.11	4.73	1.002	44	0.322	
L	174.44	176.81	-1.361	44	0.180	
B	138.22	132.24	3.819	8	0.005	*
MF	90.22	89.00	0.467	41	0.643	
H	136.11	135.62	0.381	44	0.705	
PAH	115.11	113.68	1.348	44	0.185	
BPH	------	------	-------	--	-----	
LB	98.56	94.46	1.027	40	0.310	
Face						
TFH	116.00	115.19	2.137	34	0.039	*
UFH	71.22	62.92	2.860	24	0.009	*
TFB	131.44	129.68	1.249	8	0.247	
MFB	99.22	91.19	2.337	34	0.025	*
IOB	93.00	94.92	-2.121	44	0.039	*
SIOB	14.56	17.35	-2.652	6	0.038	*
BOB	96.22	96.86	-1.022	44	0.312	
AIB	18.78	18.41	0.732	44	0.468	
Nasal structure						
NB	25.78	25.89	-0.269	44	0.789	
NH	51.33	50.16	2.266	44	0.028	*
DC	20.11	20.11	0.010	41	0.992	
DS	9.00	9.97	-3.791	44	0.000	*
MN	7.67	8.11	-0.945	44	0.350	
SMN	2.78	3.16	-1.796	44	0.079	
Orbit						
LOH	33.89	33.70	0.357	44	0.723	
LOBM	40.78	43.14	-6.231	27	0.0	*
LOBD	39.00	39.81	-3.520	23	0.002	*

Table 205 - continued

Dental arch						
MB	65.00	64.86	0.303	20	0.765	
ML	51.89	52.97	- 4.183	42	0.000	*
FL	94.67	94.11	0.226	35	0.823	
FLA	92.89	92.22	0.273	34	0.787	
Mandible						
LM	100.44	101.65	- 1.212	44	0.232	
BCB	122.11	120.24	1.169	44	0.249	
SH	33.11	33.30	- 0.414	26	0.682	
BA	97.78	96.03	1.753	38	0.088	
RL	32.00	33.08	- 1.935	28	0.063	
Facial angles						
G/	123.33°	121.32°	1.137	44	0.262	

APPENDIX D

Table 206

"t" SCORES FOR INDICES OF: FEURT-ANDERSON FOCI

UNDEFORMED FEMALE CRANIA

(N = Feurt 9; Anderson 37)

	$\bar{X}_{FF}$	$\bar{X}_{AF}$	t-ratio	DF	t-prob.	Sig. diff.
Cranial vault						
B/L	79.24	74.84	- 5.318	44	0.000	*
H/L	78.04	76.74	- 1.554	44	0.127	
H/B	98.55	102.59	3.526	44	0.001	*
H/L+B/2	87.09	87.79	0.822	44	0.416	
PAH/L	65.99	64.32	- 2.597	44	0.013	*
BPH/H	------	------	-------	--	-----	
MF/B	65.32	67.31	0.981	42	0.332	
Face						
TFH/TFB	88.33	88.87	0.550	44	0.585	
UFH/TFB	54.25	53.94	- 0.469	44	0.642	
UFH/MFB	71.79	71.25	- 0.324	38	0.748	
TFB/B	95.11	98.09	3.265	44	0.002	*
MF/TFB	68.69	68.65	- 0.018	42	0.985	
BA/MF	108.46	118.65	0.756	35	0.455	
BA/TFB	74.44	74.07	- 0.370	19	0.715	
SIOB/IOB	15.62	18.28	2.467	6	0.049	
AIB/BOB	19.53	19.00	- 1.005	44	0.321	
Nasal structure						
NB/NH	50.23	50.82	0.471	33	0.641	
DS/DC	44.76	50.03	4.634	37	0.000	*
SMN/MN	37.13	39.46	0.833	44	0.409	
Orbit						
LOH/LOBM	83.11	80.01	- 2.410	44	0.020	*
LOH/LOBD	86.90	84.71	- 1.475	44	0.147	
Dental arch						
MB/ML	125.28	122.50	- 2.077	44	0.044	
Mandible						
LM/BCB	83.39	84.62	1.714	44	0.094	

Table 207

"t" SCORES FOR MEASUREMENTS OF: FEURT-ANDERSON FOCI DEFORMED FEMALE CRANIA

(N = Feurt 16; Anderson 9)

	$\bar{X}_{FF}$	$\bar{X}_{AF}$	t-ratio	DF	t-prob.	Sig. diff.
Cranial vault						
CM	146.08	144.89	- 1.099	23	0.283	
TP	5.06	5.22	- 0.483	23	0.634	
L	160.94	159.78	0.483	23	0.634	
B	145.81	140.89	2.155	23	0.042	
MF	91.00	92.56	- 1.155	23	0.260	
H	131.50	134.00	- 1.881	23	0.073	
PAH	114.44	114.33	0.097	23	0.923	
BPH	------	------	-------	--	-----	
LB	95.88	96.56	- 0.612	23	0.547	
Face						
TFH	116.00	115.00	0.840	6	0.433	
UFH	70.81	70.78	0.041	23	0.967	
TFB	132.81	130.67	2.396	7	0.048	
MFB	99.31	97.11	2.066	23	0.050	
IOB	94.06	96.89	- 2.712	23	0.012	*
SIOB	15.31	16.44	- 1.110	23	0.278	
BOB	96.62	98.56	- 2.039	8	0.076	
AIB	18.19	18.56	- 0.584	23	0.565	
Nasal structure						
NB	26.06	26.33	- 0.527	23	0.603	
NH	50.94	50.78	0.289	23	0.775	
DC	19.25	20.00	- 1.382	23	0.180	
DS	9.06	8.56	0.437	6	0.677	
MN	7.25	8.00	- 0.605	6	0.567	
SMN	3.00	3.22	- 0.925	9	0.379	
Orbit						
LOH	33.12	33.89	- 1.848	23	0.078	
LOBM	41.19	42.67	- 3.363	9	0.008	*
LOBD	39.00	40.56	- 3.981	23	0.001	*

Table 207 - continued

Dental arch					
MB	64.94	64.89	0.064	23	0.949
ML	52.19	52.89	- 0.906	23	0.374
FL	95.06	74.67	1.511	6	0.182
FLA	93.38	81.89	1.160	6	0.290
Mandible					
LM	101.38	101.33	0.030	23	0.977
BCB	122.44	123.00	- 0.381	7	0.714
SH	33.19	33.00	0.207	23	0.838
BA	97.06	98.22	- 0.692	23	0.496
RL	31.06	32.22	- 1.115	9	0.294
Facial angles					
G/	115.06°	122.11°	- 0.899	14	0.384

Table 208

"t" SCORES FOR INDICES OF: FEURT-ANDERSON FOCI

DEFORMED FEMALE CRANIA

(N = Feurt 16; Anderson 9)

	$\overline{X}_{FF}$	$\overline{X}_{AF}$	t-ratio	DF	t-prob.	Sig. diff.
Cranial vault						
B/L	84.51	88.33	0.665	16	0.516	
H/L	81.78	83.99	1.584	23	0.127	
H/B	90.26	95.29	3.120	23	0.005	*
H/L+B/2	85.73	89.19	3.336	9	0.009	*
PAH/L	71.17	71.69	0.348	9	0.736	
BPH/H	------	------	------	--	-----	
MF/B	62.44	65.77	3.325	23	0.003	*
Face						
TFH/TFB	87.35	88.05	0.617	6	0.560	
UFH/TFB	53.32	54.20	1.161	23	0.258	
UFH/MFB	71.34	72.92	1.520	23	0.142	
TFB/B	91.18	92.90	1.175	23	0.252	
MF/TFB	68.52	70.86	2.124	23	0.045	
BA/MF	106.79	106.26	- 0.215	23	0.831	
BA/TFB	73.08	75.17	1.677	23	0.107	
SIOB/IOB	16.27	17.02	0.602	9	0.562	
AIB/BOB	18.82	18.82	0.001	23	0.999	
Nasal structure						
NB/NH	51.17	51.88	0.728	23	0.474	
DS/DC	47.11	42.16	- 0.900	6	0.403	
SMN/MN	41.45	32.41	- 2.097	7	0.074	
Orbit						
LOH/LOBM	80.43	79.46	- 1.031	23	0.313	
LOH/LOBD	84.97	83.58	- 1.225	23	0.233	
Dental arch						
MB/ML	124.55	122.82	- 0.815	23	0.424	
Mandible						
LM/BCB	82.78	82.47	- 0.234	9	0.821	

APPENDIX D

Table 209
"t" SCORES FOR MEASUREMENTS OF:
FEURT-MADISONVILLE FOCI UNDEFORMED MALE CRANIA

(N = Feurt 27; Madisonville 87)

	$\bar{X}_{FF}$	$\bar{X}_{MF}$	t-ratio	DF	t-prob.	Sig. diff.
Cranial vault						
CM	154.91	153.32	1.875	112	0.063	
TP	4.96	5.10	- 0.808	60	0.422	
L	182.22	179.90	1.307	112	0.194	
B	140.19	142.56	- 2.040	112	0.044	
MF	96.04	94.75	1.685	67	0.097	
H	142.33	137.49	6.618	91	0.000	*
PAH	118.78	116.79	3.552	66	0.001	*
BPH	------	------	-------	---	-----	
LB	105.00	103.68	1.769	74	0.081	
Face						
TFH	126.44	123.05	4.440	103	0.000	*
UFH	77.33	73.28	8.576	91	0.000	*
TFB	141.56	140.98	0.708	112	0.481	
MFB	103.33	102.26	1.679	55	0.099	
IOB	100.59	99.57	1.453	112	0.149	
SIOB	18.07	17.44	1.393	112	0.166	
BOB	101.52	100.92	1.668	75	0.099	
AIB	19.93	20.25	- 0.842	112	0.402	
Nasal structure						
NB	27.30	27.01	0.784	112	0.435	
NH	55.41	53.15	6.357	77	0.000	*
DC	22.00	22.11	- 0.321	65	0.749	
DS	11.30	11.33	- 0.193	73	0.847	
MN	9.81	9.26	1.612	112	0.110	
SMN	4.22	3.84	2.193	112	0.030	*
Orbit						
LOH	34.22	34.10	0.321	112	0.749	
LOBM	44.59	43.56	4.745	59	0.000	*
LOBD	41.89	40.84	4.963	63	0.000	*
Dental arch						
MB	69.07	64.70	7.130	109	0.000	*
ML	55.26	55.02	0.722	62	0.473	
FL	100.19	98.66	3.577	91	0.001	*
FLA	98.30	97.34	2.052	82	0.043	
Mandible						
LM	104.81	105.39	- 0.869	58	0.389	
BCB	129.52	129.29	0.264	112	0.792	
SH	37.63	35.93	4.505	58	0.000	*
BA	104.26	104.64	- 0.519	73	0.606	
RL	34.44	35.40	- 1.763	112	0.081	
Facial angles						
G∠	113.19	119.25	- 5.333	112	0.000	*

Table 210

"t" SCORES FOR INDICES OF:
FEURT-MADISONVILLE FOCI UNDEFORMED MALE CRANIA

(N = Feurt 27; Madisonville 87)

	$\bar{x}_{FF}$	$\bar{x}_{MF}$	t-ratio	DF	t-prob.	Sig. diff.
Cranial vault						
B/L	77.02	78.29	-1.146	91	0.255	
H/L	78.19	75.45	2.751	110	0.007	*
H/B	101.65	96.58	5.486	59	0.000	*
H/L+B/2	88.34	85.35	5.002	83	0.000	*
PAH/L	65.26	65.07	0.316	73	0.753	
BPH/H	------	------	-------	---	-----	
MF/B	68.59	66.52	2.735	112	0.007	*
Face						
TFH/TFB	89.36	86.17	3.547	107	0.000	*
UFH/TFB	54.66	52.00	6.459	70	0.000	*
UFH/MFB	74.89	71.72	5.072	64	0.000	*
TFB/B	101.10	98.99	2.464	112	0.015	*
MF/TFB	67.87	67.23	1.142	60	0.258	
BA/MF	108.64	110.65	-2.031	76	0.046	
BA/TFB	73.66	74.25	-1.246	86	0.216	
SIOB/IOB	17.96	17.50	1.107	112	0.271	
AIB/BOB	19.63	20.06	-1.246	112	0.216	
Nasal structure						
NB/NH	49.27	50.91	-2.465	58	0.017	*
DS/DC	51.53	51.77	-0.207	77	0.836	
SMN/MN	43.36	41.93	0.819	112	0.415	
Orbit						
LOH/LOBM	76.76	78.30	-1.964	112	0.052	
LOH/LOBD	81.74	83.55	-1.955	112	0.053	
Dental arch						
MB/ML	125.05	117.66	6.158	99	0.000	*
Mandible						
LM/BCB	81.03	80.44	0.476	104	0.635	

APPENDIX D

Table 211

"t" SCORES FOR MEASUREMENTS OF:
FEURT-MADISONVILLE FOCI DEFORMED MALE CRANIA

(N = Feurt 19; Madisonville 156)

	$\bar{x}_{FF}$	$\bar{x}_{MF}$	t-ratio	DF	t-prob.	Sig. diff.
Cranial vault						
CM	155.35	153.69	3.445	22	0.002	*
TP	5.42	5.24	1.044	173	0.298	
L	172.53	172.74	- 0.153	173	0.879	
B	150.79	150.97	- 1.144	173	0.886	
MF	95.37	95.38	- 0.011	173	0.991	
H	144.21	137.35	7.562	173	0.000	*
PAH	121.58	118.10	3.816	19	0.001	*
BPH	------	------	-------	---	-----	
LB	104.58	102.27	3.999	26	0.000	*
Face						
TFH	127.00	122.56	5.703	173	0.000	*
UFH	78.53	73.61	10.986	28	0.000	*
TFB	141.58	142.57	- 0.904	18	0.378	
MFB	102.47	102.13	0.550	173	0.583	
IOB	100.58	99.53	1.517	173	0.131	
SIOB	19.00	17.26	3.133	69	0.003	*
BOB	101.84	101.16	1.385	173	0.168	
AIB	19.68	20.07	- 1.187	173	0.237	
Nasal structure						
NB	27.11	26.89	0.641	173	0.522	
NH	54.95	53.08	6.304	173	0.000	*
DC	21.53	21.97	- 1.016	18	0.323	
DS	11.11	11.60	- 3.049	39	0.004	*
MN	9.89	9.56	1.105	28	0.279	
SMN	4.11	4.10	0.049	173	0.961	
Orbit						
LOH	33.95	34.04	- 0.336	173	0.737	
LOBM	45.11	43.88	6.305	29	0.000	*
LOBD	42.21	41.03	4.170	173	0.000	*
Dental arch						
MB	68.95	65.78	7.683	37	0.000	*
ML	55.42	54.74	1.187	18	0.251	
FL	100.00	98.54	2.406	173	0.017	*
FLA	98.11	97.42	1.109	173	0.269	
Mandible						
LM	105.89	104.58	1.852	27	0.075	
BCB	129.21	130.28	- 1.380	26	0.179	
SH	37.16	35.88	2.272	173	0.024	*
BA	104.21	104.92	- 0.674	173	0.501	
RL	35.00	34.92	0.147	173	0.883	
Facial angles						
G∠	116.47	119.58	- 2.347	173	0.020	*

Table 212

"t" SCORES FOR INDICES OF:
FEURT-MADISONVILLE FOCI DEFORMED MALE CRANIA

(N = Feurt 17; Madisonville 156)

	$\bar{X}_{FF}$	$\bar{X}_{MF}$	t-ratio	DF	t-prob.	Sig. diff.
Cranial vault						
B/L	88.35	84.34	2.311	50	0.025	*
H/L	83.51	79.60	4.686	171	0.000	*
H/B	94.74	91.07	3.835	171	0.000	*
H/L+B/2	88.70	84.88	5.981	171	0.000	*
PAH/L	70.78	68.44	3.266	171	0.001	*
BPH/H	------	------	-------	---	-----	
MF/B	63.18	63.22	- 0.073	171	0.942	
Face						
TFH/TFB	89.67	85.98	5.386	171	0.000	*
UFH/TFB	55.44	51.65	7.172	171	0.000	*
UFH/MFB	76.72	72.10	6.755	171	0.000	*
TFB/B	93.80	94.54	- 0.797	171	0.426	
MF/TFB	67.38	66.91	0.719	171	0.473	
BA/MF	109.19	110.15	- 0.625	171	0.533	
BA/TFB	73.47	73.61	- 0.176	171	0.861	
SIOB/IOB	18.75	17.32	2.553	51	0.014	*
AIB/BOB	19.51	19.84	- 1.013	171	0.313	
Nasal structure						
NB/NH	48.33	50.73	- 2.892	171	0.004	*
DS/DC	51.68	52.96	- 0.804	171	0.423	
SMN/MN	41.97	42.69	- 0.339	171	0.735	
Orbit						
LOH/LOBM	75.33	77.60	- 3.147	171	0.002	*
LOH/LOBD	80.82	83.01	- 2.748	171	0.007	*
Dental arch						
MB/ML	124.47	120.26	2.712	171	0.007	*
Mandible						
LM/BCB	81.76	80.35	2.559	31	0.016	*

APPENDIX D

Table 213

"t" SCORES FOR MEASUREMENTS OF: FEURT-MADISONVILLE FOCI

UNDEFORMED FEMALE CRANIA

(N = Feurt 9; Madisonville 68)

	$\bar{X}_{FF}$	$\bar{X}_{MF}$	t-ratio	DF	t-prob.	Sig. diff.
Cranial vault						
CM	149.59	141.02	- 3.262	72	0.002	*
TP	5.11	5.13	- 0.115	74	0.909	
L	174.44	173.04	- 0.837	74	0.405	
B	138.22	138.93	0.247	74	0.806	
MF	90.22	91.72	1.126	74	0.264	
H	136.11	132.13	- 2.962	16	0.009	*
PAH	115.11	113.06	- 1.451	74	0.151	
BPH	------	------	-------	--	-----	
LB	98.56	100.09	1.166	74	0.247	
Face						
TFH	116.00	111.87	-10.869	64	0.0	*
UFH	71.22	68.15	- 5.857	29	0.000	*
TFB	131.44	129.94	- 1.043	74	0.300	
MFB	99.22	98.00	- 3.900	57	0.000	*
IOB	93.00	95.15	1.999	74	0.049	
SIOB	14.56	16.28	1.547	7	0.166	
BOB	96.22	97.46	2.615	16	0.019	*
AIB	18.78	19.30	0.778	74	0.439	
Nasal structure						
NB	25.78	26.33	1.110	74	0.270	
NH	51.33	49.83	- 3.791	15	0.002	*
DC	20.11	20.91	3.658	62	0.001	*
DS	9.00	10.94	14.251	64	0.0	*
MN	7.67	8.81	2.097	74	0.039	*
SMN	2.78	3.59	4.766	14	0.000	*
Orbit						
LOH	33.89	33.07	- 1.844	74	0.069	
LOBM	40.78	42.20	6.034	34	0.0	*
LOBD	39.00	39.15	0.490	18	0.630	

Table 213 - continued

Dental arch						
MB	65.00	63.63	- 2.140	72	0.036	*
ML	51.89	53.39	1.089	66	0.280	
FL	94.67	97.13	4.492	47	0.000	*
FLA	92.89	96.06	6.725	72	0.0	*
Mandible						
LM	100.44	101.54	1.870	16	0.080	
BCB	122.11	125.02	1.419	7	0.199	
SH	33.11	32.80	- 0.097	15	0.924	
BA	97.78	97.78	- 0.182	15	0.858	
RL	32.00	33.26	1.994	74	0.050	
Facial angles						
G/	123.33°	123.46°	0.368	74	0.714	

APPENDIX D

Table 214

"t" SCORES FOR INDICES OF: FEURT-MADISONVILLE FOCI UNDEFORMED FEMALE CRANIA

(N = Feurt 9; Madisonville 68)

	$\overline{X}_{FF}$	$\overline{X}_{MF}$	t-ratio	DF*	t-prob.	Sig. diff.
Cranial vault						
B/L	79.24	76.93	- 1.681	57	0.098	
H/L	78.04	75.60	- 3.088	24	0.005	*
H/B	98.55	95.28	- 1.802	75	0.076	
H/L+B/2	87.09	83.09	- 3.815	31	0.001	*
PAH/L	65.99	58.77	- 3.099	72	0.003	*
BPH/H	-----	-----	-------	--	-----	
MF/B	65.32	60.30	- 2.358	72	0.021	*
Face						
TFH/TFB	88.33	78.33	- 3.571	73	0.001	*
UFH/TFB	54.25	52.83	- 1.574	75	0.120	
UFH/MFB	71.79	68.41	- 3.553	71	0.001	*
TFB/B	95.11	87.77	- 3.429	72	0.001	*
MF/TFB	68.69	71.74	2.921	13	0.012	*
BA/MF	108.46	103.78	- 2.773	20	0.012	*
BA/TFB	74.44	68.47	- 2.570	73	0.012	*
SIOB/IOB	15.62	24.73	3.292	72	0.002	*
AIB/BOB	19.53	22.90	2.872	73	0.005	*
Nasal structure						
NB/NH	50.23	55.32	3.011	67	0.004	*
DS/DC	44.76	55.35	8.244	69	0.0	*
SMN/MN	37.13	47.16	2.719	16	0.015	*
Orbit						
LOH/LOBM	83.11	78.91	- 3.117	75	0.003	*
LOH/LOBD	86.90	82.60	- 3.105	14	0.008	*
Dental arch						
MB/ML	125.28	103.05	- 4.429	69	0.000	*
Mandible						
LM/BCB	82.39	79.45	- 1.954	16	0.068	

*DF ≤ 3, t-prob. = 1

Table 215

"t" SCORES FOR MEASUREMENTS OF: FEURT-MADISONVILLE FOCI

DEFORMED FEMALE CRANIA

(N = Feurt 16; Madisonville 192)

	$\bar{X}_{FF}$	$\bar{X}_{MF}$	t-ratio	DF	t-prob.	Sig. diff.
Cranial vault						
CM	146.08	148.46	3.394	206	0.001	*
TP	5.06	5.18	0.508	206	0.612	
L	160.94	166.38	3.282	206	0.001	*
B	145.81	146.35	0.984	206	0.326	
MF	91.00	92.00	0.957	28	0.347	
H	131.50	132.77	2.100	206	0.037	*
PAH	114.44	114.12	0.293	20	0.773	
BPH	------	------	-------	---	-----	
LB	95.88	98.82	4.593	206	0.000	*
Face						
TFH	116.00	111.90	-11.191	49	0.0	*
UFH	70.81	68.88	- 2.875	206	0.004	*
TFB	132.81	133.81	3.809	29	0.000	*
MFB	99.31	97.67	- 2.223	206	0.027	*
IOB	94.06	96.05	2.938	206	0.004	*
SIOB	15.31	16.19	1.820	14	0.090	
BOB	96.62	97.89	2.506	206	0.013	*
AIB	18.19	19.24	2.728	206	0.007	*
Nasal structure						
NB	26.06	26.19	0.017	206	0.987	
NH	50.94	49.88	- 2.289	206	0.023	*
DC	19.25	21.05	5.218	206	0.000	*
DS	9.06	10.84	7.320	206	0.0	*
MN	7.25	9.23	6.429	206	0.0	*
SMN	3.00	3.80	4.841	206	0.000	*
Orbit						
LOH	33.12	33.14	0.544	206	0.587	
LOBM	41.19	42.03	4.102	20	0.001	*
LOBD	39.00	39.24	0.910	206	0.364	

Table 215 - continued

Dental arch						
MB	64.94	63.97	- 3.497	20	0.002	*
ML	52.19	53.51	1.849	206	0.066	
FL	95.06	96.85	3.740	206	0.000	*
FLA	93.38	95.78	4.793	206	0.000	*
Mandible						
LM	101.38	101.36	- 0.599	206	0.550	
BCB	122.44	124.40	4.235	31	0.000	*
SH	33.19	32.84	- 1.202	206	0.231	
BA	97.06	97.95	0.971	206	0.333	
RL	31.06	32.72	2.786	206	0.006	*
Facial angles						
G$\underline{/}$	115.06°	124.22°	1.175	13	0.261	

Table 216

"t" SCORES FOR INDICES OF: FEURT-MADISONVILLE FOCI

DEFORMED FEMALE CRANIA

(N = Feurt 16; Madisonville 192)

	$\bar{X}_{FF}$	$\bar{X}_{MF}$	t-ratio	DF	t-prob.	Sig. diff.
Cranial vault						
B/L	84.51	84.62	0.021	14	0.984	
H/L	81.78	79.82	- 2.623	206	0.009	*
H/B	90.26	91.05	0.866	206	0.387	
H/L+B/2	85.73	85.00	- 1.340	206	0.182	
PAH/L	71.17	68.57	- 3.740	206	0.000	*
BPH/H	------	------	-------	---	-----	
MF/B	62.44	63.05	0.908	30	0.371	
Face						
TFH/TFB	87.35	83.55	-14.952	97	0.0	*
UFH/TFB	53.32	51.23	- 4.335	36	0.000	*
UFH/MFB	71.34	70.20	- 1.490	29	0.147	
TFB/B	91.18	92.49	1.033	87	0.304	
MF/TFB	68.52	68.53	0.007	33	0.994	
BA/MF	106.79	110.21	0.774	198	0.440	
BA/TFB	73.08	72.95	- 0.123	206	0.903	
SIOB/IOB	16.27	16.78	1.045	206	0.297	
AIB/BOB	18.82	19.59	1.710	206	0.089	
Nasal structure						
NB/NH	51.17	52.05	1.330	48	0.190	
DS/DC	47.11	51.69	3.648	206	0.000	*
SMN/MN	41.45	41.45	- 0.004	24	0.997	
Orbit						
LOH/LOBM	80.43	78.64	- 2.999	30	0.005	*
LOH/LOBD	84.97	84.34	- 0.842	19	0.410	
Dental arch						
MB/ML	124.55	119.66	- 4.057	206	0.000	*
Mandible						
LM/BCB	82.78	81.53	- 1.737	206	0.084	

APPENDIX D 565

Table 217

"t" SCORES FOR MEASUREMENTS OF:
ANDERSON-MADISONVILLE FOCI UNDEFORMED MALE CRANIA

(N = Anderson 72; Madisonville 87)

	$\bar{X}_{AF}$	$\bar{X}_{MF}$	t-ratio	DF	t-prob.	Sig. diff.
Cranial vault						
CM	153.31	153.32	- 0.014	157	0.989	
TP	4.78	5.10	- 2.394	150	0.018	*
L	181.14	179.90	0.986	157	0.326	
B	138.26	142.56	- 4.983	157	0.000	*
MF	93.81	94.75	- 0.687	91	0.494	
H	140.53	137.49	4.442	147	0.000	*
PAH	117.08	116.79	0.421	120	0.675	
BPH	------	------	-------	---	-----	
LB	104.18	103.68	0.761	153	0.448	
Face						
TFH	124.96	123.05	2.231	142	0.027	*
UFH	74.97	73.28	3.143	157	0.002	*
TFB	140.49	140.98	- 0.808	157	0.420	
MFB	102.22	102.26	- 0.071	157	0.944	
IOB	100.19	99.57	1.180	157	0.240	
SIOB	18.06	17.44	2.056	155	0.041	
BOB	101.00	100.92	0.185	129	0.854	
AIB	19.85	20.25	- 1.427	157	0.156	
Nasal structure						
NB	26.94	27.01	- 0.259	157	0.796	
NH	53.78	53.15	1.720	157	0.087	
DC	21.00	22.11	- 3.672	154	0.000	*
DS	11.11	11.33	- 1.167	157	0.245	
MN	8.61	9.26	- 2.899	153	0.004	*
SMN	3.97	3.84	1.070	157	0.286	
Orbit						
LOH	34.69	34.10	2.035	157	0.043	
LOBM	43.78	43.56	0.751	107	0.455	
LOBD	41.61	40.84	3.385	133	0.001	*
Dental arch						
MB	69.10	64.70	6.804	148	0.000	*
ML	54.21	55.02	- 2.616	157	0.010	*
FL	97.79	98.66	- 1.691	157	0.093	
FLA	95.89	97.34	- 2.771	157	0.006	*
Mandible						
LM	104.49	105.39	- 1.404	157	0.162	
BCB	129.07	129.29	- 0.284	123	0.777	
SH	36.50	35.93	1.729	157	0.086	
BA	103.65	104.64	- 1.248	157	0.214	
RL	35.51	35.40	0.281	157	0.779	
Facial angles						
G/	114.35	119.25	- 5.539	157	0.000	*

Table 218

"t" SCORES FOR INDICES OF:
ANDERSON-MADISONVILLE FOCI UNDEFORMED MALE CRANIA

(N = Anderson 72; Madisonville 87)

	$\bar{X}_{AF}$	$\bar{X}_{MF}$	t-ratio	DF	t-prob.	Sig. diff.
Cranial vault						
B/L	76.50	78.29	- 1.729	148	0.086	
H/L	77.69	75.45	2.325	116	0.022	*
H/B	101.76	96.58	7.160	152	0.000	*
H/L+B/2	88.02	85.35	5.338	131	0.000	*
PAH/L	64.72	65.07	- 0.530	157	0.597	
BPH/H	------	------	------	---	-----	
MF/B	67.89	66.51	1.371	92	0.174	
Face						
TFH/TFB	87.61	86.17	0.940	122	0.349	
UFH/TFB	53.40	52.00	3.305	157	0.001	*
UFH/MFB	73.41	71.72	2.870	157	0.005	*
TFB/B	101.70	98.99	4.728	157	0.000	*
MF/TFB	66.84	67.23	- 0.396	89	0.693	
BA/MF	109.35	110.65	- 1.230	157	0.221	
BA/TFB	73.83	74.25	- 0.698	131	0.486	
SIOB/IOB	18.01	17.50	1.905	155	0.059	
AIB/BOB	19.65	20.06	- 1.561	157	0.120	
Nasal structure						
NB/NH	50.19	50.91	- 1.224	157	0.223	
DS/DC	53.25	51.77	1.239	157	0.217	
SMN/MN	46.59	41.93	3.464	157	0.001	*
Orbit						
LOH/LOBM	78.16	78.30	- 0.162	108	0.872	
LOH/LOBD	82.08	83.55	- 1.109	88	0.270	
Dental arch						
MB/ML	127.53	117.66	8.604	143	0.000	*
Mandible						
LM/BCB	81.09	80.44	0.565	129	0.573	

APPENDIX D

Table 219

"t" SCORES FOR MEASUREMENTS OF: ANDERSON-MADISONVILLE FOCI

UNDEFORMED FEMALE CRANIA

(N = Anderson 37; Madisonville 68)

	$\bar{X}_{AF}$	$\bar{X}_{MF}$	t-ratio	DF	t-prob.	Sig. diff.
Cranial vault						
CM	148.22	141.02	-2.895	70	0.005	*
TP	4.73	5.13	-1.814	102	0.073	
L	176.81	173.04	3.625	102	0.000	*
B	132.24	138.93	-8.206	100	0.0	*
MF	89.00	91.72	-1.049	36	0.301	
H	135.62	132.13	3.403	100	0.001	*
PAH	113.68	113.06	0.754	93	0.453	
BPH	------	------	-------	---	-----	
LB	94.46	100.09	-1.400	35	0.170	
Face						
TFH	115.19	111.87	5.998	89	0.000	*
UFH	62.92	68.15	3.092	94	0.003	*
TFB	129.68	129.94	-0.552	93	0.582	
MFB	91.19	98.00	-1.840	35	0.074	
IOB	94.92	95.15	0.071	102	0.944	
SIOB	17.35	16.28	4.753	99	0.000	*
BOB	96.86	97.46	-1.279	102	0.204	
AIB	18.41	19.30	-2.534	102	0.013	*
Nasal structure						
NB	25.89	26.33	-1.503	102	0.136	
NH	50.16	49.83	1.008	102	0.316	
DC	20.11	20.91	-2.459	102	0.016	*
DS	9.97	10.94	-5.106	95	0.000	*
MN	8.11	8.81	-2.310	102	0.023	*
SMN	3.16	3.59	-3.280	89	0.001	*
Orbit						
LOH	33.70	33.07	2.469	102	0.015	*
LOBM	43.14	42.20	0.003	94	0.997	
LOBC	39.81	39.15	3.291	102	0.001	*

Table 219 - continued

Dental arch						
MB	64.86	63.63	2.033	75	0.046	
ML	52.97	53.39	0.193	74	0.848	
FL	94.11	97.13	- 0.966	35	0.341	
FLA	92.22	96.06	- 1.239	35	0.224	
Mandible						
LM	101.65	101.54	- 0.212	102	0.832	
BCB	120.24	125.02	- 5.683	102	0.000	*
SH	33.30	32.80	0.595	102	0.553	
BA	96.03	97.78	- 1.776	49	0.082	
RL	33.08	33.26	- 0.242	53	0.810	
Facial angles						
G/	121.32°	123.46°	- 2.848	102	0.005	*

APPENDIX D

Table 220

"t" SCORES FOR INDICES OF: ANDERSON-MADISONVILLE FOCI

UNDEFORMED FEMALE CRANIA

(N = Anderson 37; Madisonville 68)

	$\bar{X}_{AF}$	$\bar{X}_{MF}$	t-ratio	DF	t-prob.	Sig. diff.
Cranial vault						
B/L	74.84	76.93	1.693	77	0.095	
H/L	76.74	75.60	- 1.724	101	0.088	
H/B	102.59	95.28	- 9.004	101	0.0	*
H/L+B/2	87.78	83.09	- 5.454	91	0.000	*
PAH/L	64.32	58.77	- 2.450	67	0.017	*
BPH/H	------	------	-------	---	-----	
MF/B	67.31	60.30	- 2.588	95	0.011	*
Face						
TFH/TFB	88.87	78.33	- 3.959	68	0.000	*
UFH/TFB	53.94	52.83	- 2.681	98	0.009	*
UFH/MFB	71.25	68.41	- 1.563	56	0.124	
TFB/B	98.09	87.77	- 4.878	71	0.000	*
MF/TFB	68.65	71.74	1.561	40	0.127	
BA/MF	118.65	103.78	- 1.105	34	0.277	
BA/TFB	74.07	68.47	- 2.450	76	0.017	*
SIOB/IOB	18.28	24.73	2.520	66	0.014	*
AIB/BOB	19.00	22.90	3.461	71	0.001	*
Nasal structure						
NB/NH	50.82	55.32	2.497	100	0.014	*
DS/DC	50.03	55.35	3.163	98	0.002	*
SMN/MN	39.46	47.16	3.143	95	0.002	*
Orbit						
LOH/LOBM	80.01	78.91	- 1.448	103	0.151	
LOH/LOBD	84.71	82.60	- 2.083	97	0.040	
Dental arch						
MB/ML	122.50	103.05	- 3.905	67	0.000	*
Mandible						
LM/BCB	84.62	79.45	- 4.963	100	0.000	*

Table 221

"t" SCORES FOR MEASUREMENTS OF: ANDERSON-MADISONVILLE FOCI

DEFORMED FEMALE CRANIA

(N = Anderson 9; Madisonville 192)

	$\bar{X}_{AF}$	$\bar{X}_{MF}$	t-ratio	DF	t-prob.	Sig. diff.
Cranial vault						
CM	144.89	148.48	3.901	198	0.000	*
TP	5.22	5.18	- 0.152	199	0.880	
L	159.78	166.38	1.807	6	0.121	
B	140.89	146.35	3.445	199	0.001	*
MF	92.56	92.00	- 0.469	11	0.648	
H	134.00	132.77	- 2.354	8	0.046	
PAH	114.33	114.12	- 0.765	199	0.445	
BPH	------	------	-------	---	-----	
LB	96.56	98.82	1.625	6	0.155	
Face						
TFH	115.00	111.90	- 2.078	199	0.039	*
UFH	70.78	68.88	- 1.568	199	0.118	
TFB	130.67	133.81	3.663	199	0.000	*
MFB	97.11	97.67	1.059	199	0.291	
IOB	96.89	96.05	- 0.627	199	0.531	
SIOB	16.44	16.19	- 0.356	6	0.727	
BOB	98.56	97.89	- 0.511	199	0.610	
AIB	18.56	19.24	1.411	199	0.160	
Nasal structure						
NB	26.33	26.19	- 0.336	199	0.737	
NH	50.78	49.88	- 1.380	199	0.169	
DC	20.00	21.05	2.101	199	0.037	*
DS	8.56	10.84	1.666	6	0.147	
MN	8.00	9.23	1.001	6	0.353	
SMN	3.22	3.80	2.274	199	0.024	*
Orbit						
LOH	33.89	33.14	- 2.156	199	0.032	*
LOBM	42.67	42.03	- 1.371	199	0.172	
LOBD	40.56	39.24	- 3.129	199	0.002	*

APPENDIX D

Table 221 - continued

Dental arch						
MB	64.89	63.97	- 0.904	199	0.367	
ML	52.89	53.51	1.151	199	0.251	
FL	74.67	96.85	1.655	6	0.149	
FLA	81.89	95.78	1.404	6	0.210	
Mandible						
LM	101.33	101.36	0.907	199	0.366	
BCB	123.00	124.40	1.401	199	0.163	
SH	33.00	32.84	- 0.692	199	0.490	
BA	98.22	97.95	- 0.348	199	0.729	
RL	32.22	32.72	0.221	199	0.826	
Facial angles						
G/	122.11°	124.22°	2.452	199	0.015	*

Table 222

"t" SCORES FOR INDICES OF: ANDERSON-MADISONVILLE FOCI

DEFORMED FEMALE CRANIA

(N = Anderson 9; Madisonville 192)

	$\bar{X}_{AF}$	$\bar{X}_{MF}$	t-ratio	DF	t-prob.	Sig. diff.
Cranial vault						
B/L	88.34	84.62	- 1.728	12	0.110	
H/L	83.73	79.84	- 2.786	6	0.032	*
H/B	94.98	91.06	- 2.215	6	0.069	
H/L+B/2	88.92	85.01	- 3.373	6	0.015	*
PAH/L	71.65	68.58	- 2.159	6	0.074	
BPH/H	------	------	-------	---	-----	
MF/B	65.41	63.06	- 2.182	9	0.057	
Face						
TFH/TFB	87.30	83.54	- 3.833	198	0.000	*
UFH/TFB	54.02	51.21	- 3.785	9	0.004	*
UFH/MFB	73.14	70.18	- 3.169	11	0.009	*
TFB/B	92.98	92.49	- 0.284	17	0.780	
MF/TFB	70.40	68.54	- 1.631	10	0.134	
BA/MF	106.76	110.24	0.766	144	0.445	
BA/TFB	75.05	72.97	- 1.460	198	0.146	
SIOB/IOB	17.36	16.77	- 0.530	6	0.615	
AIB/BOB	18.77	19.59	1.374	198	0.171	
Nasal structure						
NB/NH	52.00	52.05	0.049	10	0.962	
DS/DC	42.98	51.72	1.601	6	0.161	
SMN/MN	32.04	41.51	2.221	6	0.068	
Orbit						
LOH/LOBM	79.66	78.64	- 1.108	9	0.297	
LOH/LOBD	84.04	84.34	0.355	8	0.732	
Dental arch						
MB/ML	122.91	119.64	- 2.029	198	0.044	
Mandible						
LM/BCB	82.06	81.53	- 0.545	198	0.587	

APPENDIX D

Table 223

POPULATION DISTANCE RATIOS, FORT ANCIENT SERIES
(Significantly differing t-probabilities on 0.04 (4%) level)

Inter-Focus Comparisons	Ratio Measurements	Coeff. Measurements	Ratio Indices	Coeff. Indices	Ratios Combined
BF-AF (U) - M	9/35	26	4/22	18	13/57
BF-AF (U) - F	5/35	14	6/22	27	11/57
BF-AF (D) - F	5/35	14	1/22	5	6/57
BF-FF (U) - M	9/35	26	5/22	23	14/57
BF-FF (D) - M	14/35	40	10/22	45	24/57
BF-FF (U) - F	5/35	14	2/22	9	7/57
BF-FF (D) - F	12/35	34	8/22	36	20/57
BF-MF (U) - M	11/35	31	11/22	50	22/57
BF-MF (D) - M	17/35	49	10/22	45	27/57
BF-MF (U) - F	6/35	17	9/22	41	15/57
BF-MF (D) - F	12/35	34	7/22	32	19/57
FF-AF (U) - M	13/35	37	3/22	14	16/57
FF-AF (U) - F	11/35	31	6/22	27	17/57
FF-AF (D) - F	3/35	9	3/22	14	6/57
FF-MF (U) - M	12/35	34	10/22	45	22/57
FF-MF (D) - M	15/35	43	14/22	64	29/57
FF-MF (U) - F	15/35	43	18/22	82	33/57
FF-MF (D) - F	22/35	63	7/22	32	29/57
AF-MF (U) - M	12/35	34	8/22	36	20/57
AF-MF (U) - F	16/35	46	15/22	68	31/57
AF-MF (D) - F	9/35	26	5/22	23	14/57

APPENDIX E

COMPARISONS ON THE VARIETAL LEVEL
(SEE CHAPTER V)

APPENDIX E

Table 224
"t" SCORES FOR MEASUREMENTS OF:
LENID-DAKOTID MALE VARIETIES

(N = Lenid 45; Dakotid 58)

	$\bar{X}_{Len}$	$\bar{X}_{Dak}$	t-ratio	DF	t-prob.	Sig. diff.
Cranial vault						
CM	153.11	151.71	1.421	73	0.160	
TP	4.91	4.62	1.555	101	0.123	
L	185.62	178.40	3.113	54	0.003	*
B	136.29	145.67	- 8.741	98	0.000	*
MF	93.96	94.28	- 0.398	101	0.691	
H	137.42	131.05	6.172	97	0.000	*
PAH	------	------	--------	---	-----	
BPH	23.11	19.62	5.355	97	0.000	*
LB	104.60	101.31	3.507	101	0.001	*
Face						
TFH	123.13	124.97	- 1.698	101	0.093	
UFH	73.76	75.69	- 2.337	95	0.022	*
TFB	137.60	141.33	- 3.707	101	0.000	*
MFB	99.82	102.86	- 3.515	99	0.001	*
IOB	97.44	98.48	- 1.433	101	0.155	
SIOB	18.67	18.98	- 0.701	101	0.485	
BOB	98.89	99.07	- 0.255	99	0.799	
AIB	20.22	19.76	1.193	101	0.236	
Nasal structure						
NB	25.29	26.10	- 2.539	91	0.013	*
NH	53.76	54.03	- 0.395	101	0.694	
DC	22.47	20.36	5.119	101	0.000	*
DS	12.38	12.53	- 0.565	101	0.573	
MN	8.56	9.00	- 1.499	101	0.137	
SMN	4.07	4.64	- 3.271	99	0.001	*
Orbit						
LOH	34.04	35.21	- 3.365	101	0.001	*
LOBM	42.00	42.47	- 1.132	101	0.260	
LOBD	39.36	40.74	- 3.667	101	0.000	*
Dental arch						
MB	65.58	65.97	- 0.695	97	0.489	
ML	56.98	54.17	5.413	101	0.000	*
FL	101.97	97.52	5.087	101	0.000	*
FLA	100.56	101.24	- 0.132	57	0.895	
Mandible						
LM	110.16	106.83	3.646	101	0.000	*
BCB	122.11	125.09	- 3.649	88	0.000	*
SH	36.44	36.74	- 0.643	101	0.522	
BA	104.56	104.50	0.043	67	0.966	
RL	35.22	36.81	- 3.098	101	0.003	*
Facial angles						
G∠	120.60	115.97	4.707	98	0.000	*

Table 225

"t" SCORES FOR INDICES OF:
LENID-DAKOTID MALE VARIETIES

(N = Lenid 45: Dakotid 58)

	$\bar{x}_{Len}$	$\bar{x}_{Dak}$	t-ratio	DF	t-prob.	Sig. diff.
Cranial vault						
B/L	71.91	81.78	- 8.099	75	0.000	*
H/L	72.53	73.47	- 0.994	57	0.324	
H/B	100.93	90.17	10.166	97	0.000	*
H/L+B/2	83.39	80.90	1.555	51	0.126	
PAH/L	38.65	------	-------	---	-----	
BPH/H	16.81	14.94	4.126	95	0.000	*
MF/B	68.97	64.80	6.822	101	0.000	*
Face						
TFH/TFB	87.32	88.54	- 0.572	51	0.570	
UFH/TFB	53.63	53.61	0.031	94	0.975	
UFH/MFB	73.95	73.66	0.359	99	0.720	
TFB/B	101.05	97.11	4.920	101	0.000	*
MF/TFB	68.31	66.77	2.570	101	0.012	*
BA/MF	111.39	111.03	0.239	80	0.812	
BA/TFB	75.98	74.01	2.269	76	0.026	*
SIOB/IOB	19.15	19.29	- 0.297	101	0.767	
AIB/BOB	20.46	19.95	1.337	101	0.184	
Nasal structure						
NB/NH	47.23	48.53	- 1.513	98	0.133	
DS/DC	55.58	61.97	- 3.990	101	0.000	*
SMN/MN	48.41	52.61	- 1.793	101	0.076	
Orbit						
LOH/LOBM	81.21	81.34	- 0.073	76	0.942	
LOH/LOBD	84.44	84.80	- 0.139	101	0.890	
Dental arch						
MB/ML	115.26	121.93	- 5.516	101	0.000	*
Mandible						
LM/BCB	90.21	83.82	3.874	63	0.000	*

APPENDIX E

Table 226

"t" SCORES FOR MEASUREMENTS OF: LENID-DAKOTID

FEMALE VARIETIES

(N = Lenid 5; Dakotid 6)

	$\bar{X}_{Len}$	$\bar{X}_{Dak}$	t-ratio	DF*	t-prob.	Sig. diff.
Cranial vault						
CM	150.47	145.72	2.391	3	1.000	
TP	4.40	5.17	- 1.546	9	0.156	
L	181.20	175.17	1.914	3	1.000	
B	135.20	134.50	0.301	3	1.000	
MF	88.20	92.17	- 1.969	9	0.080	
H	135.00	127.50	5.178	9	0.001	*
PAH	116.00	------	------	--	-----	
BPH	23.20	21.17	1.491	9	0.170	
LB	99.00	98.67	0.107	9	0.917	
Face						
TFH	113.40	122.17	- 6.542	9	0.0	*
UFH	69.60	74.83	- 3.821	9	0.004	*
TFB	133.00	132.17	0.299	9	0.772	
MFB	95.40	101.50	- 2.108	4	0.103	
IOB	92.80	94.83	- 0.937	9	0.373	
SIOB	16.00	18.00	- 2.477	9	0.035	*
BOB	96.20	96.00	0.099	9	0.924	
AIB	18.60	19.67	- 0.851	9	0.417	
Nasal structure						
NB	23.20	24.33	- 1.228	5	0.274	
NH	49.20	51.83	- 1.610	9	0.142	
DC	23.00	19.67	4.906	9	0.000	*
DS	12.80	11.67	1.913	4	0.128	
MN	8.40	8.17	0.146	2	1.000	
SMN	2.80	4.00	- 1.809	9	0.104	
Orbit						
LOH	33.60	33.67	- 0.070	9	0.946	
LOBM	41.00	40.67	- 0.226	9	0.826	
LOBD	38.80	39.33	- 0.398	9	0.700	

Table 226 - continued

Dental arch					
MB	60.60	64.00	- 1.691	9	0.125
ML	53.00	54.00	- 0.701	9	0.501
FL	98.40	97.00	0.491	9	0.635
FLA	97.00	95.50	0.574	9	0.580
Mandible					
LM	99.60	105.67	- 2.195	3	1.000
BCB	121.00	118.50	1.213	3	1.000
SH	34.60	36.50	- 1.349	9	0.210
BA	97.80	98.83	- 0.350	9	0.734
RL	32.00	35.33	- 2.860	9	0.019 *
Facial angles					
G/	124.00°	120.83°	1.322	9	0.219

*DF $\leq$ 3, t-prob. = 1

APPENDIX E

Table 227

"t" SCORES FOR INDICES OF: LENID-DAKOTID

FEMALE VARIETIES

(N = Lenid 5; Dakotid 6)

	$\bar{X}_{Len}$	$\bar{X}_{Dak}$	t-ratio	DF*	t-prob.	Sig. diff.
Cranial vault						
B/L	74.63	76.80	-2.154	9	0.060	
H/L	74.56	72.78	1.729	3	1.000	
H/B	99.92	94.83	2.887	9	0.018	*
H/L+B/2	85.39	82.35	2.580	9	0.030	*
PAH/L	64.04	------	-------	--	-----	
BPH/H	------	------	-------	--	-----	
MF/B	65.23	68.56	-2.452	5	0.058	
Face						
TFH/TFB	85.33	92.51	-3.846	9	0.004	*
UFH/TFB	52.36	56.69	-2.908	9	0.017	*
UFH/MFB	72.96	73.96	-0.480	4	0.656	
TFB/B	98.48	98.29	0.070	9	0.946	
MF/TFB	66.35	69.81	-1.753	9	0.113	
BA/MF	110.99	107.39	0.861	9	0.411	
BA/TFB	73.62	74.88	-0.428	9	0.678	
SIOB/IOB	17.25	18.96	-2.720	9	0.024	*
AIB/BOB	19.34	20.49	-0.908	9	0.388	
Nasal structure						
NB/NH	47.28	46.99	0.129	9	0.900	
DS/DC	55.73	59.43	-1.121	9	0.291	
SMN/MN	33.79	48.87	-2.978	5	0.031	*
Orbit						
LOH/LOBM	82.12	82.95	-0.275	9	0.790	
LOH/LOBD	86.75	85.78	0.298	9	0.773	
Dental arch						
MB/ML	114.49	118.55	-1.089	9	0.304	
Mandible						
LM/BCB	82.33	89.31	-2.462	9	0.036	*

*DF $\leq$ 3, t-prob. = 1

Table 228
"t" SCORES FOR MEASUREMENTS OF: LENID-ILINID MALE VARIETIES

(N = Lenid 45: Ilinid 17)

	$\bar{X}_{Len}$	$\bar{X}_{Ili}$	t-ratio	DF	t-prob.	Sig. diff.
Cranial vault						
CM	153.11	154.65	- 1.447	55	0.154	
TP	4.91	4.82	0.386	60	0.701	
L	185.62	181.76	1.567	57	0.123	
B	136.29	140.12	- 3.139	60	0.003	*
MF	93.96	94.82	- 0.742	60	0.461	
H	137.42	142.06	- 5.354	47	0.000	*
PAH	------	118.82	--------	---	-----	
BPH	23.11	25.18	- 3.535	41	0.001	*
LB	104.60	107.18	- 1.983	60	0.052	
Face						
TFH	123.13	124.12	- 0.883	40	0.383	
UFH	73.76	73.65	0.125	60	0.901	
TFB	137.60	140.35	- 2.123	60	0.038	*
MFB	99.82	102.18	- 2.180	60	0.033	*
IOB	97.44	99.94	- 2.728	60	0.008	*
SIOB	18.67	18.71	- 0.061	60	0.952	
BOB	98.89	101.00	- 2.484	60	0.016	*
AIB	20.22	19.76	0.809	60	0.422	
Nasal structure						
NB	25.29	26.41	- 3.162	60	0.002	*
NH	53.76	53.65	0.151	47	0.881	
DC	22.47	21.76	1.133	60	0.262	
DS	12.38	13.24	- 2.228	60	0.030	*
MN	8.56	8.71	- 0.416	60	0.679	
SMN	4.07	5.00	- 4.305	60	0.000	*
Orbit						
LOH	34.04	33.88	0.292	21	0.773	
LOBM	42.00	43.24	- 2.630	40	0.012	*
LOBD	39.36	40.35	- 2.392	44	0.021	*
Dental arch						
MB	65.58	66.06	- 0.694	60	0.491	
ML	56.98	55.29	2.505	60	0.015	*
FL	101.97	101.06	0.711	60	0.480	
FLA	100.56	99.24	1.017	60	0.313	
Mandible						
LM	110.16	106.12	3.437	60	0.001	*
BCB	122.11	126.76	- 4.269	20	0.000	*
SH	36.44	37.94	- 2.525	60	0.014	*
BA	104.56	104.18	0.256	52	0.799	
RL	35.22	35.00	0.354	41	0.725	
Facial angles						
G∠	120.60	116.53	3.466	60	0.000	*

APPENDIX E

Table 229

"t" SCORES FOR INDICES OF: LENID-ILINID MALE VARIETIES

(N = Lenid 45; Ilinid 17)

	$\bar{X}_{Len}$	$\bar{X}_{Ili}$	t-ratio	DF	t-prob.	Sig. diff.
Cranial vault						
B/L	71.91	77.12	- 4.432	58	0.000	*
H/L	72.53	78.20	- 5.515	58	0.000	*
H/B	100.93	101.44	- 0.558	45	0.580	
H/L+B/2	83.39	88.30	- 3.064	50	0.004	*
PAH/L	------	65.41	-------	---	-----	
BPH/H	16.81	17.71	- 2.508	47	0.016	*
MF/B	68.97	67.73	1.234	21	0.231	
Face						
TFH/TFB	87.32	88.50	- 0.546	52	0.587	
UFH/TFB	53.63	52.52	1.652	60	0.104	
UFH/MFB	73.95	72.17	1.736	60	0.088	
TFB/B	101.05	100.20	0.735	60	0.465	
MF/TFB	68.31	67.61	0.832	60	0.409	
BA/MF	111.39	110.00	0.814	47	0.420	
BA/TFB	75.98	74.30	1.277	60	0.207	
SIOB/IOB	19.15	18.73	0.662	60	0.511	
AIB/BOB	20.46	19.56	1.604	60	0.114	
Nasal structure						
NB/NH	47.23	49.31	- 2.043	60	0.045	
DS/DC	55.59	61.66	- 2.431	60	0.018	*
SMN/MN	48.41	58.21	- 3.245	60	0.002	*
Orbit						
LOH/LOBM	81.21	78.41	2.056	60	0.044	
LOH/LOBD	84.45	84.03	0.171	58	0.865	
Dental arch						
MB/ML	115.26	119.54	- 2.799	60	0.007	*
Mandible						
LM/BCB	90.21	83.78	7.320	60	0.000	*

Table 230

"t" SCORES FOR MEASUREMENTS OF: LENID-ILINID

FEMALE VARIETIES

(N = Lenid 5; Ilinid 19)

	$\overline{X}_{Len}$	$\overline{X}_{Ili}$	t-ratio	DF*	t-prob.	Sig. diff.
Cranial vault						
CM	150.47	147.61	1.244	22	0.227	
TP	4.40	4.47	0.199	22	0.844	
L	181.20	174.05	- 2.041	22	0.053	
B	135.20	135.53	0.146	22	0.885	
MF	88.20	90.95	1.309	22	0.204	
H	135.00	133.26	- 1.213	13	0.247	
PAH	116.00	113.89	- 0.945	22	0.355	
BPH	23.20	22.63	- 0.443	22	0.662	
LB	99.00	96.89	- 0.681	2	1.000	
Face						
TFH	113.40	112.05	- 1.085	22	0.290	
UFH	69.60	66.74	- 3.317	22	0.003	*
TFB	133.00	131.74	- 0.549	22	0.589	
MFB	95.40	95.05	- 0.195	22	0.847	
IOB	92.80	94.79	1.038	22	0.311	
SIOB	16.00	15.32	- 0.722	22	0.478	
BOB	96.20	95.79	- 0.247	22	0.807	
AIB	18.60	17.47	- 1.358	22	0.188	
Nasal structure						
NB	23.20	24.68	2.617	13	0.021	*
NH	49.20	49.89	0.482	3	1.000	
DC	23.00	20.42	- 4.847	16	0.000	*
DS	12.80	11.32	- 2.897	20	0.009	*
MN	8.40	7.84	- 0.343	3	1.000	
SMN	2.80	3.89	2.060	22	0.051	
Orbit						
LOH	33.60	32.95	- 0.749	22	0.462	
LOBM	41.00	41.37	0.399	22	0.694	
LOBD	38.80	38.95	0.178	22	0.860	

APPENDIX E

Table 230 - continued

Dental arch						
MB	60.60	60.11	- 0.370	3	1.000	
ML	53.00	51.11	- 1.426	22	0.168	
FL	98.40	94.95	- 2.124	22	0.045	
FLA	97.00	92.89	- 2.386	22	0.026	*
Mandible						
LM	99.60	99.21	- 0.142	3	1.000	
BCB	121.00	118.89	- 1.777	20	0.091	
SH	34.60	34.11	- 0.564	22	0.578	
BA	97.80	95.16	- 0.778	22	0.445	
RL	32.00	30.79	- 1.224	22	0.234	
Facial angles						
G/	124.00°	123.63°	- 0.164	22	0.871	

*DF ≤ 3, t-prob. = 1

Table 231

"t" SCORES FOR INDICES OF: LENID-ILINID

FEMALE VARIETIES

(N = Lenid 5; Ilinid 19)

	$\bar{X}_{Len}$	$\bar{X}_{Ili}$	t-ratio	DF	t-prob.	Sig. diff.
Cranial vault						
B/L	74.63	77.93	- 3.922	14	0.002	*
H/L	74.56	76.60	- 1.950	22	0.064	
H/B	99.92	98.37	1.002	22	0.327	
H/L+B/2	85.39	86.11	- 0.687	22	0.499	
PAH/L	64.04	65.48	- 1.188	22	0.247	
BPH/H	------	------	-------	--	-----	
MF/B	65.23	67.14	- 2.213	17	0.041	
Face						
TFH/TFB	85.33	85.15	- 0.107	22	0.916	
UFH/TFB	52.36	50.72	1.543	22	0.137	
UFH/MFB	72.96	70.29	2.119	22	0.046	
TFB/B	98.48	97.24	0.712	22	0.484	
MF/TFB	66.35	69.07	- 1.728	22	0.098	
BA/MF	110.99	104.79	1.519	22	0.143	
BA/TFB	73.62	72.23	0.581	22	0.567	
SIOB/IOB	17.25	16.14	1.235	22	0.230	
AIB/BOB	19.34	18.26	1.229	22	0.232	
Nasal structure						
NB/NH	47.28	49.56	- 1.060	22	0.300	
DS/DC	55.73	55.60	0.047	18	0.963	
SMN/MN	33.79	46.50	- 3.270	20	0.004	*
Orbit						
LOH/LOBM	82.12	79.76	0.893	22	0.382	
LOH/LOBD	86.75	84.71	0.757	22	0.457	
Dental arch						
MB/ML	114.49	117.83	- 1.241	22	0.228	
Mandible						
LM/BCB	82.33	83.57	- 0.581	22	0.567	

APPENDIX E

Table 232
"t" SCORES FOR MEASUREMENTS OF: LENID-ISWANID MALE VARIETIES

(N = Lenid 45; Iswanid 33)

	$\bar{X}_{Len}$	$\bar{X}_{Isw}$	t-ratio	DF	t-prob.	Sig. diff.
Cranial vault						
CM	153.11	150.21	3.001	65	0.004	*
TP	4.91	4.97	- 0.348	74	0.728	
L	185.62	176.97	3.751	52	0.000	*
B	136.29	134.88	1.436	76	0.155	
MF	93.96	90.61	3.845	76	0.000	*
H	137.42	138.79	- 1.641	74	0.105	
PAH	------	115.94	-------	---	-----	
BPH	23.11	------	-------	---	-----	
LB	104.60	99.97	5.130	73	0.000	*
Face						
TFH	123.13	118.03	4.772	76	0.000	*
UFH	73.76	70.88	3.840	76	0.000	*
TFB	137.60	135.88	1.762	76	0.082	
MFB	99.82	98.36	1.751	76	0.084	
IOB	97.44	96.00	1.913	76	0.060	
SIOB	18.67	17.12	3.691	72	0.000	*
BOB	98.89	96.18	3.905	76	0.000	*
AIB	20.22	17.85	5.284	76	0.000	*
Nasal structure						
NB	25.29	23.91	3.563	46	0.001	*
NH	53.75	51.21	3.519	76	0.001	*
DC	22.47	19.61	5.892	76	0.000	*
DS	12.38	10.21	7.222	76	0.000	*
MN	8.56	8.18	1.201	76	0.233	
SMN	4.07	3.21	4.997	76	0.000	*
Orbit						
LOH	34.04	32.67	3.790	76	0.000	*
LOBM	42.00	42.03	- 0.079	71	0.937	
LOBD	39.36	39.33	0.062	72	0.951	
Dental arch						
MB	65.58	63.70	3.641	76	0.000	*
ML	56.98	51.85	9.484	76	0.000	*
FL	101.98	94.61	8.664	73	0.000	*
FLA	100.56	92.94	8.971	73	0.000	*
Mandible						
LM	110.16	99.27	11.006	76	0.000	*
BCB	122.11	123.82	- 2.007	50	0.050	
SH	36.44	34.91	3.105	76	0.003	*
BA	104.56	103.73	0.579	73	0.564	
RL	35.22	34.52	1.177	76	0.243	
Facial angles						
G∠	120.60	117.73	2.792	76	0.007	*

Table 233

"t" SCORES FOR INDICES OF:
LENID-ISWANID MALE VARIETIES

(N = Lenid 45; Iswanid 33)

	$\bar{X}_{Len}$	$\bar{X}_{Isw}$	t-ratio	DF	t-prob.	Sig. diff.
Cranial vault						
B/L	71.91	76.25	- 3.871	57	0.000	*
H/L	72.53	78.47	- 6.103	60	0.000	*
H/B	100.93	102.96	- 2.376	74	0.020	*
H/L+B/2	83.39	89.04	- 3.580	48	0.001	*
PAH/L	------	65.55	-------	---	-----	
BPH/H	16.81	------	-------	---	-----	
MF/B	68.97	67.20	2.864	76	0.005	*
Face						
TFH/TFB	87.32	86.90	0.200	48	0.842	
UFH/TFB	53.63	52.17	2.875	76	0.005	*
UFH/MFB	73.95	72.16	1.952	76	0.051	
TFB/B	101.05	100.80	0.288	76	0.774	
MF/TFB	68.31	66.71	2.561	76	0.012	*
BA/MF	111.39	114.66	- 1.809	76	0.074	
BA/TFB	75.98	76.39	- 0.394	76	0.695	
SIOB/IOB	19.15	17.84	3.197	72	0.002	*
AIB/BOB	20.46	18.54	4.398	76	0.000	*
Nasal structure						
NB/NH	47.23	46.78	0.491	76	0.621	
DS/DC	55.59	52.60	1.606	76	0.112	
SMN/MN	48.41	39.59	3.945	76	0.000	*
Orbit						
LOH/LOBM	81.21	77.78	3.255	76	0.002	*
LOH/LOBD	84.45	83.09	0.622	54	0.537	
Dental arch						
MB/ML	115.26	122.99	- 6.279	76	0.000	*
Mandible						
LM/BCB	90.21	80.25	11.991	52	0.000	*

APPENDIX E 589

Table 234
"t" SCORES FOR MEASUREMENTS OF:
LENID-MUSKOGID MALE VARIETIES

(N = Lenid 45: Muskogid 48)

	$\bar{X}_{Len}$	$\bar{X}_{Mus}$	t-ratio	DF	t-prob.	Sig. diff.
Cranial vault						
CM	153.11	154.96	- 1.870	71	0.066	
TP	4.91	4.73	1.070	91	0.287	
L	185.62	181.15	1.954	51	0.056	
B	136.29	139.58	- 3.374	91	0.001	*
MF	93.96	94.77	- 0.918	91	0.361	
H	137.42	144.15	- 8.160	91	0.000	*
PAH	------	------	------	---	-----	
BPH	23.11	25.81	- 5.105	91	0.000	*
LB	104.60	105.83	- 1.370	80	0.174	
Face						
TFH	123.13	125.77	- 2.724	91	0.008	*
UFH	73.76	75.65	- 2.898	91	0.005	*
TFB	137.60	139.65	- 2.161	91	0.033	*
MFB	99.82	103.27	- 4.169	91	0.000	*
IOB	97.44	100.04	- 3.843	91	0.000	*
SIOB	18.67	19.06	- 0.839	91	0.404	
BOB	98.89	100.85	- 3.143	91	0.002	*
AIB	20.22	20.19	0.835	91	0.934	
Nasal structure						
NB	25.29	26.23	- 3.240	83	0.002	*
NH	53.76	53.79	- 0.055	91	0.956	
DC	22.47	22.12	0.754	91	0.453	
DS	12.38	11.29	4.017	91	0.000	*
MN	8.55	9.96	- 4.318	85	0.000	*
SMN	4.07	4.17	- 0.617	91	0.539	
Orbit						
LOH	34.04	34.52	- 1.451	91	0.150	
LOBM	42.00	43.35	- 3.412	91	0.001	*
LOBD	39.36	40.79	- 3.810	91	0.000	*
Dental arch						
MB	65.58	68.60	- 5.185	82	0.000	*
ML	56.98	56.79	0.329	91	0.743	
FL	101.97	101.71	0.346	69	0.730	
FLA	100.55	100.00	0.685	74	0.495	
Mandible						
LM	110.16	108.08	2.006	86	0.048	
BCB	122.11	126.46	- 5.109	72	0.000	*
SH	36.44	38.21	- 3.793	91	0.000	*
BA	104.56	104.60	- 0.034	91	0.973	
RL	35.22	35.96	- 1.253	91	0.213	
Facial angles						
G∠	120.60	116.25	4.753	91	0.000	*

Table 235

"t" SCORES FOR INDICES OF: LENID-MUSKOGID MALE VARIETIES

(N = Lenid 45; Muskogid 48)

	$\bar{X}_{Len}$	$\bar{X}_{Mus}$	t-ratio	DF	t-prob.	Sig. diff.
Cranial vault						
B/L	71.91	77.08	- 4.739	53	0.000	*
H/L	72.53	79.62	- 7.453	57	0.000	*
H/B	100.93	103.36	- 2.966	91	0.004	*
H/L+B/2	83.39	89.92	- 4.168	47	0.000	*
PAH/L	------	------	-------	---	-----	
BPH/H	16.81	17.90	- 3.179	91	0.002	*
MF/B	68.97	67.97	1.421	82	0.159	
Face						
TFH/TFB	87.32	88.05	- 0.265	91	0.791	
UFH/TFB	53.63	54.21	- 1.163	91	0.248	
UFH/MFB	73.95	73.35	0.765	91	0.446	
TFB/B	101.05	100.10	1.198	80	0.234	
MF/TFB	68.31	67.92	0.579	86	0.564	
BA/MF	111.39	110.65	0.419	91	0.676	
BA/TFB	75.98	74.94	1.099	91	0.275	
SIOB/IOB	19.15	19.04	0.249	91	0.804	
AIB/BOB	20.46	20.01	1.116	91	0.267	
Nasal structure						
NB/NH	47.23	48.85	- 2.227	91	0.028	*
DS/DC	55.59	51.52	2.506	91	0.014	*
SMN/MN	48.41	43.01	2.461	91	0.016	*
Orbit						
LOH/LOBM	81.21	79.67	1.762	80	0.082	
LOH/LOBD	84.45	84.70	- 0.119	50	0.905	
Dental arch						
MB/ML	115.26	121.02	- 4.448	86	0.000	*
Mandible						
LM/BCB	90.21	85.59	5.204	71	0.000	*

APPENDIX E 591

Table 236

"t" SCORES FOR MEASUREMENTS OF: ISWANID-ILINID MALE VARIETIES

(N = Iswanid 33; Ilinid 17)

	$\bar{X}_{Isw}$	$\bar{X}_{Ili}$	t-ratio	DF	t-prob.	Sig. diff.
Cranial vault						
CM	150.21	154.65	- 5.551	48	0.000	*
TP	4.97	4.82	- 0.769	48	0.445	
L	176.97	181.76	3.547	48	0.001	*
B	134.88	140.12	4.538	48	0.000	*
MF	90.61	94.82	3.682	48	0.001	*
H	138.79	142.06	3.737	48	0.000	*
PAH	115.94	118.82	4.934	46	0.000	*
BPH	------	25.18	-------	---	-----	
LB	99.97	107.18	7.424	48	0.000	*
Face						
TFH	118.03	124.12	5.169	48	0.000	*
UFH	70.88	73.65	2.959	48	0.005	*
TFB	135.88	140.35	3.509	48	0.001	*
MFB	98.36	102.18	3.503	48	0.001	*
IOB	96.00	99.94	4.556	48	0.000	*
SIOB	17.12	18.71	2.669	21	0.014	*
BOB	96.18	101.00	5.700	48	0.000	*
AIB	17.85	19.76	3.459	48	0.001	*
Nasal structure						
NB	23.91	26.41	4.579	48	0.000	*
NH	51.21	53.65	3.310	48	0.002	*
DC	19.61	21.76	3.355	48	0.002	*
DS	10.21	13.24	7.915	48	0.000	*
MN	8.18	8.71	1.373	48	0.176	
SMN	3.21	5.00	7.910	48	0.000	*
Orbit						
LOH	32.67	33.88	2.237	48	0.030	*
LOBM	42.03	43.24	3.087	48	0.003	*
LOBD	39.33	40.35	2.844	48	0.007	*
Dental arch						
MB	63.70	66.06	3.276	48	0.002	*
ML	51.85	55.29	5.715	48	0.000	*
FL	94.61	101.06	5.226	21	0.000	*
FLA	92.94	99.24	5.156	21	0.000	*
Mandible						
LM	99.27	106.12	5.687	48	0.000	*
BCB	123.82	126.76	2.343	48	0.023	*
SH	34.91	37.94	4.508	48	0.000	*
BA	103.73	104.18	0.321	48	0.750	
RL	34.52	35.00	0.755	48	0.454	
Facial angles						
G$\angle$	117.73	116.53	- 0.871	48	0.388	

Table 237

"t" SCORES FOR INDICES OF:
ISWANID-ILINID MALE VARIETIES

(N = Iswanid 33; Ilinid 17)

	$\bar{X}_{Isw}$	$\bar{X}_{Ili}$	t-ratio	DF	t-prob.	Sig. diff.
Cranial vault						
B/L	76.25	77.12	1.173	48	0.246	
H/L	78.47	78.20	0.378	48	0.707	
H/B	102.96	101.44	1.668	48	0.101	
H/L+B/2	89.04	88.30	1.096	48	0.278	
PAH/L	65.55	65.41	0.237	48	0.813	
BPH/H	------	17.71	-------	---	-----	
MF/B	67.20	67.73	- 0.512	22	0.613	
Face						
TFH/TFB	86.90	88.50	- 1.761	48	0.085	
UFH/TFB	52.17	52.52	- 0.549	48	0.586	
UFH/MFB	72.16	72.17	- 0.010	48	0.992	
TFB/B	100.80	100.20	0.593	48	0.556	
MF/TFB	66.71	67.61	- 1.055	48	0.297	
BA/MF	114.66	110.00	2.685	43	0.010	*
BA/TFB	76.39	74.30	1.730	48	0.090	
SIOB/IOB	17.84	18.73	- 1.475	20	0.155	
AIB/BOB	18.54	19.56	- 2.022	48	0.049	
Nasal structure						
NB/NH	46.78	49.31	- 2.091	48	0.042	
DS/DC	52.60	61.66	- 3.329	48	0.002	*
SMN/MN	39.59	58.21	- 6.345	48	0.000	*
Orbit						
LOH/LOBM	77.78	78.41	- 0.465	48	0.644	
LOH/LOBD	83.09	84.03	- 0.656	48	0.515	
Dental arch						
MB/ML	122.99	119.54	2.261	48	0.032	*
Mandible						
LM/BCB	80.25	83.78	- 3.012	48	0.004	*

APPENDIX E

Table 238
"t" SCORES FOR MEASUREMENTS OF: ISWANID-MUSKOGID MALE VARIETIES

(N = Iswanid 33; Muskogid 48)

	$\bar{X}_{Isw}$	$\bar{X}_{Mus}$	t-ratio	DF	t-prob.	Sig. diff.
Cranial vault						
CM	150.21	154.96	- 6.846	76	0.000	*
TP	4.97	4.73	1.451	79	0.151	
L	176.97	181.15	- 3.887	79	0.000	*
B	134.88	139.58	- 4.578	79	0.000	*
MF	90.61	94.77	- 4.438	79	0.000	*
H	138.79	144.15	- 6.756	79	0.000	*
PAH	115.94	------	-------	---	-----	
BPH	------	25.81	-------	---	-----	
LB	99.97	105.83	- 7.518	79	0.000	*
Face						
TFH	118.03	125.77	- 8.002	79	0.000	*
UFH	70.88	75.65	- 6.565	79	0.000	*
TFB	135.88	139.65	- 3.792	79	0.000	*
MFB	98.36	103.27	- 5.519	79	0.000	*
IOB	96.00	100.04	- 5.808	79	0.000	*
SIOB	17.12	19.06	- 4.739	76	0.000	*
BOB	96.18	100.85	- 7.058	79	0.000	*
AIB	17.85	20.19	- 5.366	79	0.000	*
Nasal structure						
NB	23.91	26.23	- 5.777	79	0.000	*
NH	51.21	53.79	- 4.176	79	0.000	*
DC	19.61	22.12	- 5.126	79	0.000	*
DS	10.21	11.29	- 3.819	79	0.000	*
MN	8.18	9.96	- 4.832	79	0.000	*
SMN	3.21	4.17	- 5.405	79	0.000	*
Orbit						
LOH	32.67	34.52	- 4.967	79	0.000	*
LOBM	42.03	43.35	- 4.045	77	0.000	*
LOBD	39.33	40.79	- 4.600	77	0.000	*
Dental arch						
MB	63.70	68.60	- 8.058	77	0.000	*
ML	51.85	56.79	- 8.875	77	0.000	*
FL	94.61	101.71	-11.105	79	0.000	*
FLA	92.94	100.00	-10.372	79	0.000	*
Mandible						
LM	99.27	108.08	- 7.648	79	0.000	*
BCB	123.82	126.46	- 2.439	79	0.017	*
SH	34.91	38.21	- 6.177	79	0.000	*
BA	103.73	104.60	- 0.687	79	0.494	
RL	34.52	35.96	- 2.450	79	0.017	*
Facial angles						
GL	117.73	116.25	1.381	79	0.171	

Table 239

"t" SCORES FOR INDICES OF:
ISWANID-MUSKOGID MALE VARIETIES

(N = Iswanid 38; Muskogid 48)

	$\bar{x}_{Isw}$	$\bar{x}_{Mus}$	t-ratio	DF	t-prob.	Sig. diff.
Cranial vault						
B/L	76.25	77.08	- 1.447	79	0.152	
H/L	78.47	79.62	- 2.028	79	0.046	
H/B	102.96	103.36	- 0.505	79	0.614	
H/L+B/2	89.04	89.92	- 1.575	79	0.119	
PAH/L	65.55	------	-------	---	-----	
BPH/H	0.00	17.90	-------	---	-----	
MF/B	67.20	67.97	- 1.059	77	.0.293	
Face						
TFH/TFB	86.90	88.05	- 0.590	52	0.557	
UFH/TFB	52.17	54.21	- 3.929	79	0.000	*
UFH/MFB	72.16	73.35	- 1.262	79	0.211	
TFB/B	100.80	100.10	0.932	79	0.354	
MF/TFB	66.71	67.92	- 1.751	77	0.080	
BA/MF	114.66	110.65	2.164	79	0.034	*
BA/TFB	76.39	74.94	1.529	79	0.130	
SIOB/IOB	17.84	19.04	- 3.134	77	0.002	*
AIB/BOB	18.54	20.01	- 3.681	79	0.000	*
Nasal structure						
NB/NH	46.78	48.85	- 2.406	79	0.018	*
DS/DC	52.60	51.52	0.606	79	0.546	
SMN/MN	39.59	43.02	- 1.502	79	0.137	
Orbit						
LOH/LOBM	77.78	79.67	- 2.134	79	0.036	*
LOH/LOBD	83.09	84.70	- 1.679	79	0.097	
Dental arch						
MB/ML	122.99	121.02	1.449	76	0.152	
Mandible						
LM/BCB	80.25	85.59	- 5.075	76	0.000	*

APPENDIX E

Table 240
"t" SCORES FOR MEASUREMENTS OF:
ILINID-DAKOTID MALE VARIETIES

(N = Ilinid 17; Dakotid 58)

	$\bar{X}_{Ili}$	$\bar{X}_{Dak}$	t-ratio	DF	t-prob.	Sig. diff.
Cranial vault						
CM	154.65	151.71	3.572	37	0.001	*
TP	4.82	4.62	0.999	40	0.324	
L	181.76	178.40	2.073	73	0.042	
B	140.12	145.67	- 4.563	45	0.000	*
MF	94.82	94.28	0.478	73	0.634	
H	142.06	131.05	10.854	65	0.000	*
PAH	118.82	------	-------	---	-----	
BPH	25.18	19.62	11.544	55	0.000	*
LB	107.18	101.31	8.239	58	0.000	*
Face						
TFH	124.12	124.97	- 0.755	43	0.454	
UFH	73.65	75.69	- 2.208	52	0.032	*
TFB	140.35	141.33	- 0.662	73	0.510	
MFB	102.18	102.86	- 0.516	73	0.608	
IOB	99.94	98.48	1.863	38	0.070	
SIOB	18.71	18.98	- 0.444	73	0.658	
BOB	101.00	99.07	2.312	38	0.026	*
AIB	19.76	19.76	0.012	73	0.991	
Nasal structure						
NB	26.41	26.10	0.575	73	0.567	
NH	53.65	54.03	- 0.562	45	0.577	
DC	21.76	20.36	2.450	73	0.017	*
DS	13.24	12.53	1.800	73	0.076	
MN	8.71	9.00	- 0.892	38	0.378	
SMN	5.00	4.64	1.346	73	0.182	
Orbit						
LOH	33.88	35.21	- 2.482	73	0.015	*
LOBM	43.24	42.47	1.453	73	0.151	
LOBD	40.35	40.74	- 1.014	38	0.317	
Dental arch						
MB	66.06	65.97	0.104	73	0.917	
ML	55.29	54.17	1.984	36	0.055	
FL	101.06	97.52	2.920	73	0.005	*
FLA	99.24	101.24	- 0.381	60	0.705	
Mandible						
LM	106.12	106.83	- 0.568	73	0.572	
BCB	126.76	125.09	1.197	73	0.235	
SH	37.94	36.74	1.780	73	0.079	
BA	104.18	104.50	- 0.261	73	0.794	
RL	35.00	36.81	- 2.904	73	0.005	*
Facial angles						
G∠	116.53	115.97	0.458	36	0.650	

Table 241

"t" SCORES FOR INDICES OF:
ILINID-DAKOTID MALE VARIETIES

(N = Ilinid 17; Dakotid 58)

	$\bar{x}_{Ili}$	$\bar{x}_{Dak}$	t-ratio	DF	t-prob.	Sig. diff.
Cranial vault						
B/L	77.12	81.78	- 5.369	56	0.000	*
H/L	78.20	73.47	6.490	73	0.000	*
H/B	101.44	90.17	10.634	62	0.000	*
H/L+B/2	88.30	80.90	10.613	47	0.000	*
PAH/L	65.41	------	------	---	-----	
BPH/H	17.71	14.94	6.223	67	0.000	*
MF/B	67.73	64.80	3.110	73	0.003	*
Face						
TFH/TFB	88.50	88.54	- 0.034	40	0.973	
UFH/TFB	52.52	53.61	- 1.415	41	0.165	
UFH/MFB	72.17	73.66	- 1.174	73	0.244	
TFB/B	100.20	97.11	2.997	73	0.004	*
MF/TFB	67.61	66.77	0.952	73	0.344	
BA/MF	110.00	111.03	- 0.601	73	0.549	
BA/TFB	74.30	74.01	0.294	73	0.769	
SIOB/IOB	18.73	19.29	- 0.898	73	0.372	
AIB/BOB	19.56	19.75	- 0.790	73	0.432	
Nasal structure						
NB/NH	49.31	48.53	0.727	37	0.472	
DS/DC	61.66	61.97	- 0.125	73	0.901	
SMN/MN	58.21	52.61	1.621	73	0.109	
Orbit						
LOH/LOBM	78.41	81.34	- 1.482	63	0.143	
LOH/LOBD	84.03	84.80	- 0.374	57	0.710	
Dental arch						
MB/ML	119.54	121.93	- 1.388	73	0.169	
Mandible						
LM/BCB	83.70	83.82	- 0.018	71	0.986	

APPENDIX E

Table 242

"t" SCORES FOR MEASUREMENTS OF: ILINID-DAKOTID

FEMALE VARIETIES

(N = Ilinid 19; Dakotid 6)

	$\bar{X}_{Ili}$	$\bar{X}_{Dak}$	t-ratio	DF	t-prob.	Sig. diff.
Cranial vault						
CM	147.61	145.72	1.592	21	0.126	
TP	4.47	5.17	- 2.086	23	0.048	
L	174.05	175.17	- 0.596	21	0.557	
B	135.53	134.50	0.548	23	0.589	
MF	90.95	92.17	- 0.649	23	0.523	
H	133.26	127.50	2.856	23	0.009	*
PAH	113.89	------	-------	--	-----	
BPH	22.63	21.17	1.160	23	0.258	
LB	96.89	98.67	- 1.154	23	0.260	
Face						
TFH	112.05	122.17	- 8.635	23	0.0	*
UFH	66.74	74.83	- 9.240	23	0.0	*
TFB	131.74	132.17	- 0.189	23	0.852	
MFB	95.05	101.50	- 2.271	4	0.086	
IOB	94.79	94.83	- 0.025	23	0.980	
SIOB	15.32	18.00	- 3.034	23	0.006	*
BOB	95.79	96.00	- 0.127	23	0.900	
AIB	17.47	19.67	- 2.898	23	0.008	*
Nasal structure						
NB	24.68	24.33	0.393	23	0.698	
NH	49.89	51.83	- 2.298	23	0.031	*
DC	20.42	19.67	0.911	23	0.372	
DS	11.32	11.67	- 0.389	23	0.701	
MN	7.84	8.17	- 0.623	19	0.541	
SMN	3.89	4.00	- 0.212	23	0.834	
Orbit						
LOH	32.95	33.67	0.905	23	0.375	
LOBM	41.37	40.67	0.767	23	0.451	
LOBD	38.95	39.33	- 0.459	23	0.651	

Table 242 - continued

Dental arch						
MB	60.11	64.00	- 2.553	4	0.063	
ML	51.11	54.00	- 2.406	23	0.025	*
FL	94.95	97.00	- 0.923	4	0.408	
FLA	92.89	95.50	- 1.507	23	0.145	
Mandible						
LM	99.21	105.67	- 4.976	23	0.000	*
BCB	118.89	118.50	- 0.175	23	0.863	
SH	34.11	36.50	- 2.790	23	0.010	*
BA	95.16	98.83	- 1.218	23	0.236	
RL	30.79	35.33	- 5.003	23	0.000	*
Facial angles						
G/	123.63°	120.83°	1.464	23	0.157	

APPENDIX E

Table 243

"t" SCORES FOR INDICES OF: ILINID-DAKOTID FEMALE VARIETIES

(N = Ilinid 19; Dakotid 6)

	$\bar{X}_{Ili}$	$\bar{X}_{Dak}$	t-ratio	DF	t-prob.	Sig. diff.
Cranial vault						
B/L	77.93	76.80	0.921	23	0.367	
H/L	76.60	72.78	6.244	17	0.0	*
H/B	98.37	94.83	2.380	23	0.026	*
H/L+B/2	86.11	82.35	4.099	23	0.000	*
PAH/L	65.48	------	-------	--	-----	
BPH/H	------	------	-------	--	-----	
MF/B	67.14	68.56	- 1.002	23	0.327	
Face						
TFH/TFB	85.15	92.51	- 4.785	23	0.000	*
UFH/TFB	50.72	56.69	- 5.532	23	0.000	*
UFH/MFB	70.29	73.96	- 1.754	4	0.154	
TFB/B	97.24	98.29	- 0.655	23	0.519	
MF/TFB	69.07	69.81	- 0.506	23	0.618	
BA/MF	104.79	107.39	- 0.688	23	0.498	
BA/TFB	72.23	74.88	- 1.250	23	0.224	
SIOB/IOB	16.14	18.96	- 5.087	17	0.000	*
AIB/BOB	18.26	20.49	- 2.833	23	0.009	*
Nasal structure						
NB/NH	49.56	46.99	1.237	23	0.229	
DS/DC	55.60	59.43	- 0.883	23	0.386	
SMN/MN	46.50	48.87	- 0.357	23	0.724	
Orbit						
LOH/LOBM	79.76	82.95	- 1.355	23	0.189	
LOH/LOBD	84.71	85.78	- 0.436	23	0.667	
Dental arch						
MB/ML	117.83	118.55	- 0.301	23	0.766	
Mandible						
LM/BCB	83.57	89.31	- 2.986	23	0.007	*

Table 244

"t" SCORES FOR MEASUREMENTS OF: ILINID-MUSKOGID MALE VARIETIES

(N = Ilinid 17; Muskogid 48)

	$\bar{X}_{Ili}$	$\bar{X}_{Mus}$	t-ratio	DF	t-prob.	Sig. diff.
Cranial vault						
CM	154.65	154.96	- 0.329	63	0.743	
TP	4.82	4.73	0.443	63	0.660	
L	181.76	181.15	0.446	63	0.657	
B	140.12	139.58	0.411	63	0.683	
MF	94.82	94.77	0.041	63	0.967	
H	142.06	144.15	- 2.594	41	0.013	*
PAH	118.82	------	-------	---	-----	
BPH	25.18	25.81	- 0.979	63	0.331	
LB	107.18	105.83	1.302	63	0.198	
Face						
TFH	124.18	125.77	- 1.418	63	0.161	
UFH	73.65	75.65	- 2.378	63	0.020	*
TFB	140.35	139.65	0.534	63	0.596	
MFB	102.18	103.27	- 0.936	63	0.352	
IOB	99.94	100.04	- 0.121	63	0.904	
SIO B	18.71	19.06	- 0.559	63	0.578	
BO B	101.00	100.85	0.181	63	0.857	
AIB	19.76	20.19	- 0.770	63	0.444	
Nasal structure						
NB	26.41	26.23	0.410	63	0.683	
NH	53.65	53.79	- 0.195	63	0.846	
DC	21.76	22.12	- 0.570	63	0.571	
DS	13.24	11.29	5.386	63	0.000	*
MN	8.71	9.96	- 3.473	46	0.001	*
SMN	5.00	4.17	3.675	63	0.000	*
Orbit						
LOH	33.88	34.52	- 1.283	63	0.204	
LO BM	43.24	43.35	- 0.256	63	0.798	
LO BD	40.35	40.79	- 0.995	63	0.324	
Dental arch						
MB	66.06	68.60	- 2.851	63	0.006	*
ML	55.29	56.79	- 2.454	43	0.018	*
FL	101.06	101.71	- 0.548	18	0.591	
FLA	99.24	100.00	- 0.640	19	0.530	
Mandible						
LM	106.12	108.08	- 1.685	44	0.100	
BCB	126.76	126.46	0.222	63	0.825	
SH	37.94	38.21	- 0.403	63	0.688	
BA	104.18	104.60	- 0.331	41	0.742	
RL	35.00	35.96	- 1.559	40	0.127	
Facial angles						
G$\angle$	116.53	116.25	0.222	63	0.825	

APPENDIX E

Table 245

"t" SCORES FOR INDICES OF:
ILINID-MUSKOGID MALE VARIETIES

(N = Ilinid 17; Muskogid 48)

	$\bar{X}_{Ili}$	$\bar{X}_{Mus}$	t-ratio	DF	t-prob.	Sig. diff.
Cranial vault						
B/L	77.12	77.08	0.063	63	0.905	
H/L	78.20	79.62	- 2.024	63	0.047	
H/B	101.44	103.36	- 2.026	63	0.047	
H/L+B/2	88.30	89.92	- 2.352	63	0.022	*
PAH/L	65.41	------	-------	---	-----	
BPH/H	17.71	17.90	- 0.557	41	0.580	
MF/B	67.73	67.97	- 0.222	63	0.825	
Face						
TFH/TFB	88.50	88.05	0.223	57	0.824	
UFH/TFB	52.52	54.21	- 2.448	63	0.017	*
UFH/MFB	72.17	73.35	- 1.083	63	0.283	
TFB/B	100.20	100.10	0.106	63	0.916	
MF/TFB	67.61	67.92	- 0.311	63	0.757	
BA/MF	110.00	110.65	- 0.375	49	0.709	
BA/TFB	74.30	74.94	- 0.551	63	0.584	
SIOB/IOB	18.73	19.04	- 0.520	63	0.605	
AIB/BOB	19.56	20.01	- 0.887	63	0.379	
Nasal structure						
NB/NH	49.31	48.85	0.483	63	0.631	
DS/DC	61.66	51.52	3.608	20	0.002	*
SMN/MN	58.21	43.02	4.914	63	0.000	*
Orbit						
LOH/LOBM	78.41	79.67	- 0.973	20	0.342	
LOH/LOBD	84.03	84.70	- 0.525	63	0.602	
Dental arch						
MB/ML	119.54	121.02	- 0.800	63	0.427	
Mandible						
LM/BCB	83.78	85.59	- 1.551	40	0.129	

Table 246

"t" SCORES FOR MEASUREMENTS OF:
MUSKOGID-DAKOTID MALE VARIETIES

(N = Muskogid 48; Dakotid 58)

	$\bar{x}_{Mus}$	$\bar{x}_{Dak}$	t-ratio	DF	t-prob.	Sig. diff.
Cranial vault						
CM	154.96	151.71	4.442	104	0.000	*
TP	4.73	4.62	0.621	102	0.536	
L	181.15	178.40	2.489	104	0.014	*
B	139.58	145.67	- 5.553	101	0.000	*
MF	94.77	94.28	0.591	104	0.556	
H	144.15	131.05	13.346	93	0.000	*
PAH	------	------	-------	---	-----	
BPH	25.81	19.62	9.856	95	0.000	*
LB	105.83	101.31	5.506	104	0.000	*
Face						
TFH	125.77	124.97	0.820	101	0.414	
UFH	75.65	75.69	- 0.054	94	0.957	
TFB	131.65	141.33	- 1.682	104	0.096	
MFB	103.27	102.86	0.448	104	0.655	
IOB	100.04	98.48	2.289	104	0.024	*
SIOB	19.06	18.98	0.180	104	0.857	
BOB	100.85	99.07	2.617	100	0.010	*
AIB	20.19	19.67	1.138	104	0.258	
Nasal structure						
NB	26.23	26.10	0.352	102	0.725	
NH	53.79	54.03	- 0.390	102	0.697	
DC	22.12	20.36	4.274	104	0.000	*
DS	11.29	12.53	- 4.708	104	0.000	*
MN	9.96	9.00	2.921	104	0.004	*
SMN	4.17	4.64	- 2.653	102	0.009	*
Orbit						
LOH	34.52	35.21	- 1.975	104	0.051	
LOBM	43.35	42.47	2.403	104	0.018	*
LOBD	40.79	40.74	0.146	104	0.884	
Dental arch						
MB	68.60	65.97	4.068	104	0.000	*
ML	56.79	54.17	4.833	104	0.000	*
FL	101.71	97.52	6.067	95	0.000	*
FLA	100.00	101.24	- 0.240	56	0.811	
Mandible						
LM	108.08	106.83	1.247	104	0.215	
BCB	126.46	125.09	1.344	104	0.181	
SH	38.21	36.74	3.047	104	0.003	*
BA	104.60	104.50	0.098	85	0.922	
RL	35.96	36.81	- 1.699	104	0.092	
Facial angles						
G∠	116.25	115.97	0.275	104	0.784	

APPENDIX E 603

Table 247

"t" SCORES FOR INDICES OF: MUSKOGID-DAKOTID MALE VARIETIES

(N = Muskogid 48; Dakotid 58)

	$\bar{x}_{Mus}$	$\bar{x}_{Dak}$	t-ratio	DF	t-prob.	Sig. diff.
Cranial vault						
B/L	77.08	81.78	- 6.293	86	0.000	*
H/L	79.62	73.47	11.808	104	0.000	*
H/B	103.36	90.17	13.393	90	0.000	*
H/L+B/2	89.92	80.90	14.678	99	0.000	*
PAH/L	------	------	-------	---	-----	
BPH/H	17.90	14.94	6.841	90	0.000	*
MF/B	67.97	64.80	4.510	104	0.000	*
Face						
TFH/TFB	88.05	88.54	- 0.245	57	0.807	
UFH/TFB	55.21	53.61	0.969	96	0.335	
UFH/MFB	73.35	73.66	- 0.348	104	0.728	
TFB/B	100.10	97.11	4.278	104	0.000	*
MF/TFB	67.92	66.77	1.744	104	0.084	
BA/MF	110.65	111.03	- 0.250	83	0.803	
BA/TFB	74.94	74.01	1.228	104	0.222	
SIOB/IOB	19.04	19.29	- 0.577	104	0.565	
AIB/BOB	20.01	19.95	0.171	104	0.865	
Nasal structure						
NB/NH	48.85	48.53	0.381	98	0.704	
DS/DC	51.52	61.97	- 6.783	104	0.000	*
SMN/MN	43.02	52.61	- 4.114	104	0.000	*
Orbit						
LOH/LOBM	79.67	81.34	- 1.005	67	0.319	
LOH/LOBD	84.70	84.80	- 0.058	71	0.954	
Dental arch						
MB/ML	121.02	121.93	- 0.695	104	0.489	
Mandible						
LM/BCB	85.59	83.82	1.003	80	0.319	

Table 248

POPULATION DISTANCE RATIOS, VARIETAL LEVEL
(Significantly differing t-probabilities at 0.04 level)

Varietal Comparisons	Ratio Measurements	Coeff. Measurements	Ratio Indices	Coeff. Indices	Ratios Combined
Lenid-Dakotid - M	19/35	54	10/22	45	29/57
Lenid-Dakotid - F	6/35	17	7/21	33	13/56
Lenid-Ilinid - M	17/35	49	8/22	36	25/57
Lenid-Ilinid - F	5/36	14	2/22	9	7/58
Lenid-Iswanid* - M	22/34	65	13/21	62	35/55
Lenid-Muskogid* - M	18/35	51	10/22	45	28/57
Iswanid-Ilinid - M	30/35	86	5/22	23	35/57
Iswanid-Muskogid - M	31/34	91	7/21	33	38/55
Ilinid-Dakotid - M	11/35	31	7/22	32	18/57
Ilinid-Dakotid - F	10/35	29	8/21	38	18/56
Ilinid-Muskogid - M	7/35	20	4/22	18	11/57
Muskogid-Dakotid - M	17/35	49	9/22	41	26/57

*Iswanid and Muskogid female series unavailable.

APPENDIX E

Table 249
"t" SCORES FOR MEASUREMENTS OF:
FORT ANCIENT ILINID-FORT ANCIENT MUSKOGID MALE VARIETY

(N = F. A. Ilinid 84; F. A. Muskogid 50)

	$\bar{x}_{FAI}$	$\bar{x}_{FAM}$	t-ratio	DF	t-prob.	Sig. diff.
Cranial vault						
CM	153.85	152.85	1.476	131	0.142	
TP	4.90	4.98	- 0.446	83	0.657	
L	181.46	178.18	2.110	82	0.038	*
B	138.88	144.36	- 5.420	132	0.000	*
MF	94.00	95.12	- 0.843	126	0.401	
H	141.20	136.12	6.974	132	0.000	*
PAH	118.44	116.62	2.505	128	0.013	*
BPH	------	------	-------	---	-----	
LB	104.13	103.52	0.707	78	0.481	
Face						
TFH	124.86	123.84	0.833	65	0.408	
UFH	75.18	73.26	3.319	132	0.001	*
TFB	141.38	141.42	- 0.060	122	0.952	
MFB	102.13	102.40	- 0.408	132	0.684	
IOB	100.11	99.98	0.209	132	0.835	
SIOB	18.01	17.38	1.854	132	0.066	
BOB	100.77	101.00	- 0.478	120	0.633	
AIB	19.87	20.72	- 2.672	132	0.008	*
Nasal structure						
NB	26.76	27.06	- 0.947	132	0.345	
NH	54.11	53.06	2.620	132	0.010	*
DC	20.88	22.42	- 4.405	132	0.000	*
DS	10.95	11.64	- 3.440	132	0.001	*
MN	8.79	9.76	- 3.697	132	0.000	*
SMN	3.94	4.08	- 1.014	132	0.313	
Orbit						
LOH	34.68	33.88	2.716	132	0.007	*
LOBM	43.82	43.54	1.180	128	0.240	
LOBD	41.49	40.80	2.941	127	0.004	*
Dental arch						
MB	68.35	64.32	4.562	81	0.000	*
ML	54.37	55.08	- 1.944	132	0.054	
FL	97.52	98.68	- 2.093	132	0.038	*
FLA	95.62	97.38	- 3.843	132	0.002	*
Mandible						
LM	105.68	105.36	0.422	132	0.673	
BCB	129.13	129.26	- 0.173	132	0.863	
SH	36.33	36.00	0.843	132	0.401	
BA	103.67	105.32	- 1.961	121	0.052	
RL	35.17	35.42	0.336	132	0.737	
Facial angles						
G∠	114.61	119.60	- 5.464	132	0.000	*

Table 250

"t" SCORES FOR INDICES OF:
FORT ANCIENT ILINID-FORT ANCIENT MUSKOGID MALE VARIETY

(N = F. A. Ilinid 84; F. A. Muskogid 50)

	$\bar{x}_{FAI}$	$\bar{x}_{FAM}$	t-ratio	DF	t-prob.	Sig. diff.
Cranial vault						
B/L	76.70	79.27	- 1.679	62	0.098	
H/L	77.92	74.69	2.090	52	0.042	
H/B	101.81	94.44	9.640	131	0.000	*
H/L+B/2	88.18	84.58	5.605	65	0.000	*
PAH/L	65.37	65.74	- 0.488	131	0.626	
BPH/H	------	------	-------	---	-----	
MF/B	67.74	65.92	1.895	125	0.060	
Face						
TFH/TFB	87.18	85.51	0.925	131	0.356	
UFH/TFB	53.22	51.82	3.005	131	0.003	*
UFH/MFB	73.67	71.65	3.281	131	0.001	*
TFB/B	101.91	91.13	5.844	131	0.000	*
MF/TFB	66.55	67.20	- 0.691	122	0.491	
BA/MF	109.35	111.10	- 1.394	131	0.166	
BA/TFB	73.39	74.51	- 1.706	123	0.090	
SIOB/IOB	17.98	17.31	2.083	83	0.040	
AIB/BOB	19.72	20.42	- 2.438	131	0.016	*
Nasal structure						
NB/NH	49.58	51.04	- 2.202	131	0.029	*
DS/DC	52.94	52.40	0.414	131	0.679	
SMN/MN	45.29	42.60	1.862	131	0.065	
Orbit						
LOH/LOBM	79.20	77.91	1.841	131	0.068	
LOH/LOBD	83.67	83.11	0.719	131	0.474	
Dental arch						
MB/ML	125.83	116.86	5.408	82	0.000	*
Mandible						
LM/BCB	81.95	81.46	0.712	120	0.478	

APPENDIX E

Table 251

"t" SCORES FOR MEASUREMENTS OF: FORT ANCIENT ILINID-FORT ANCIENT MUSKOGID

FEMALE VARIETY

(N = F. A. Ilinid 66; F. A. Muskogid 54)

	$\bar{X}_{FAI}$	$\bar{X}_{FAM}$	t-ratio	DF	t-prob.	Sig. diff.
Cranial vault						
CM	148.31	139.25	2.972	53	0.004	*
TP	4.82	5.17	-2.070	118	0.041	
L	176.14	171.81	4.724	118	0.000	*
B	133.73	139.94	-8.159	118	0.0	*
MF	89.52	91.93	-1.625	80	0.108	
H	134.67	132.81	1.818	80	0.073	
PAH	113.71	113.44	0.422	118	0.674	
BPH	------	------	-------	---	-----	
LB	96.39	100.04	-1.665	68	0.100	
Face						
TFH	114.71	111.80	5.689	118	0.000	*
UFH	69.97	68.17	4.030	118	0.000	*
TFB	129.92	130.63	-1.021	118	0.309	
MFB	93.82	98.00	-2.086	68	0.041	
IOB	94.29	95.33	-2.149	118	0.034	*
SIOB	16.59	16.06	1.747	116	0.083	
BOB	96.82	97.65	-21.05	94	0.038	*
AIB	18.45	19.31	-3.113	96	0.002	*
Nasal structure						
NB	25.82	26.35	-2.340	98	0.021	*
NH	50.29	49.70	1.846	118	0.067	
DC	20.14	21.00	-2.914	118	0.004	*
DS	10.06	10.93	-4.785	112	0.000	*
MN	8.21	8.83	-2.314	118	0.022	*
SMN	3.35	3.56	-1.483	118	0.141	
Orbit						
LOH	33.53	33.04	1.941	118	0.055	
LOBM	41.82	42.30	-1.966	93	0.052	
LOBD	39.50	39.20	1.445	118	0.151	

Table 251 - continued

Dental arch						
MB	64.58	62.76	1.451	56	0.152	
ML	52.86	52.65	0.206	55	0.838	
FL	94.83	96.78	- 1.350	73	0.181	
FLA	93.15	95.57	- 1.677	73	0.098	
Mandible						
LM	101.82	101.19	1.037	98	0.302	
BCB	121.85	124.87	- 3.982	118	0.000	*
SH	33.35	32.81	1.653	118	0.101	
BA	96.77	97.61	- 1.193	115	0.235	
RL	32.83	33.24	- 1.123	118	0.264	
Facial angles						
G/	122.44°	123.37°	- 1.119	118	0.265	

APPENDIX E

Table 252

"t" SCORES FOR INDICES OF: FORT ANCIENT ILINID-FORT ANCIENT MUSKOGID

FEMALE VARIETY

(N = F. A. Ilinid 66; F. A. Muskogid 54)

	$\bar{X}_{FAI}$	$\bar{X}_{FAM}$	t-ratio	DF	t-prob.	Sig. diff.
Cranial vault						
B/L	76.00	77.25	- 0.826	57	0.412	
H/L	76.46	76.09	0.500	76	0.619	
H/B	100.69	94.70	6.752	90	0.0	*
H/L+B/2	86.89	82.87	3.934	64	0.000	*
PAH/L	64.55	57.61	2.455	52	0.017	*
BPH/H	------	------	-------	--	-----	
MF/B	66.90	58.46	3.200	71	0.002	*
Face						
TFH/TFB	88.29	75.78	3.859	52	0.000	*
UFH/TFB	53.89	52.37	3.520	98	0.000	*
UFH/MFB	71.66	67.24	3.211	118	0.002	*
TFB/B	97.13	85.83	4.396	53	0.000	*
MF/TFB	68.92	72.00	- 2.409	105	0.018	*
BA/MF	114.14	102.78	1.491	67	0.141	
BA/TFB	74.47	66.48	2.937	54	0.005	*
SIOB/IOB	17.15	26.54	- 2.826	52	0.007	*
AIB/BOB	19.08	23.78	- 3.434	52	0.001	*
Nasal structure						
NB/NH	50.92	56.25	- 2.709	61	0.009	*
DS/DC	50.33	56.04	- 3.358	89	0.001	*
SMN/MN	40.82	48.27	- 2.649	67	0.010	*
Orbit						
LOH/LOBM	80.09	78.96	1.562	98	0.121	
LOH/LOBD	84.86	82.05	2.689	77	0.009	*
Dental arch						
MB/ML	122.16	99.41	3.686	52	0.001	*
Mandible						
LM/BCB	83.66	78.26	4.779	69	0.000	*

Table 253

"t" SCORES FOR MEASUREMENTS OF: FORT ANCIENT ILINID-LENID MALE VARIETY

(N = F. A. Ilinid 84; Lenid 45)

	$\bar{x}_{FAI}$	$\bar{x}_{Len}$	t-ratio	DF	t-prob.	Sig. diff.
Cranial vault						
CM	153.85	153.11	0.796	61	0.429	
TP	4.90	4.91	- 0.042	127	0.967	
L	181.46	185.62	- 1.794	54	0.078	
B	138.88	136.29	2.773	111	0.007	*
MF	94.00	93.96	0.035	117	0.972	
H	141.20	137.42	5.117	127	0.000	*
PAH	118.44	-----	-------	---	-----	
BPH	-----	23.11	-------	---	-----	
LB	104.13	104.60	- 0.558	72	0.578	
Face						
TFH	124.86	123.13	2.024	127	0.045	
UFH	75.18	73.76	2.357	127	0.020	*
TFB	141.38	137.60	4.719	127	0.000	*
MFB	102.13	99.82	3.307	127	0.001	*
IOB	100.11	97.44	4.181	127	0.000	*
SIOB	18.01	18.67	- 1.678	71	0.098	
BOB	100.77	98.89	3.334	127	0.001	*
AIB	19.87	20.22	- 1.002	74	0.319	
Nasal structure						
NB	26.79	25.29	6.197	111	0.000	*
NH	54.10	53.76	0.618	60	0.539	
DC	20.88	22.47	- 4.242	127	0.000	*
DS	10.95	12.38	- 6.404	127	0.000	*
MN	8.79	8.56	0.900	127	0.370	
SMN	3.94	4.07	- 0.886	127	0.377	
Orbit						
LOH	34.68	34.04	2.189	127	0.030	*
LOBM	43.82	42.00	5.029	71	0.000	*
LOBD	41.49	39.36	6.254	73	0.000	*
Dental arch						
MB	68.35	65.58	4.922	125	0.000	*
ML	54.37	56.98	- 5.988	72	0.000	*
FL	97.52	101.98	- 5.883	66	0.000	*
FLA	95.62	100.56	- 6.431	67	0.000	*
Mandible						
LM	105.68	110.16	- 5.533	127	0.000	*
BCB	129.13	122.11	9.976	125	0.000	*
SH	36.33	36.44	- 0.285	127	0.776	
BA	103.67	104.56	- 0.695	67	0.489	
RL	35.57	35.22	0.725	127	0.470	
Facial angles						
G∠	114.61	120.60	- 6.977	109	0.000	*

APPENDIX E

Table 254

"t" SCORES FOR INDICES OF: FORT ANCIENT ILINID-LENID MALE VARIETY

(N = F. A. Ilinid 84; Lenid 45)

	$\bar{X}_{FAI}$	$\bar{X}_{Len}$	t-ratio	DF	t-prob.	Sig. diff.
Cranial vault						
B/L	76.70	71.91	4.073	69	0.000	*
H/L	77.92	72.53	5.669	58	0.000	*
H/B	101.81	100.93	1.117	127	0.266	
H/L+B/2	88.18	83.39	3.101	45	0.003	*
PAH/L	65.37	------	-------	---	-----	
BPH/H	------	------	-------	---	-----	
MF/B	67.74	68.97	- 1.340	114	0.183	
Face						
TFH/TFB	87.18	87.32	- 0.057	69	0.955	
UFH/TFB	53.22	53.63	- 0.855	127	0.394	
UFH/MFB	73.67	73.95	- 0.455	127	0.650	
TFB/B	101.91	101.05	1.187	127	0.238	
MF/TFB	66.56	68.31	- 1.928	116	0.056	
BA/MF	109.35	111.39	- 1.457	127	0.148	
BA/TFB	73.39	75.98	- 3.071	127	0.003	*
SIOB/IOB	17.98	19.15	- 3.116	65	0.003	*
AIB/BOB	19.72	20.46	- 2.104	71	0.039	*
Nasal structure						
NB/NH	49.58	47.22	3.621	127	0.000	*
DS/DC	52.94	55.58	- 1.857	127	0.066	
SMN/MN	45.29	48.41	- 1.761	72	0.082	
Orbit						
LOH/LOBM	79.20	81.21	- 2.594	127	0.011	*
LOH/LOBD	83.67	84.45	- 0.373	47	0.711	
Dental arch						
MB/ML	125.83	115.26	8.913	117	0.000	*
Mandible						
LM/BCB	81.95	90.21	-12.688	121	0.000	*

Table 255

"t" SCORES FOR MEASUREMENTS OF: FORT ANCIENT ILINID-LENID

FEMALE VARIETY

(N = F. A. Ilinid 66; Lenid 5)

	$\bar{X}_{FAI}$	$\bar{X}_{Len}$	t-ratio	DF*	t-prob.	Sig. diff.
Cranial vault						
CM	148.31	150.47	- 1.530	69	0.131	
TP	4.82	4.40	0.959	69	0.341	
L	176.15	181.20	- 2.068	69	0.042	
B	133.73	135.20	- 0.780	69	0.438	
MF	89.52	88.20	0.602	9	0.562	
H	134.67	135.00	- 1.189	69	0.851	
PAH	113.71	116.00	- 1.497	69	0.139	
BPH	------	------	--------	--	-----	
LB	96.39	99.00	- 0.706	7	0.503	
Face						
TFH	114.71	113.40	0.963	69	0.339	
UFH	69.97	69.60	0.331	69	0.741	
TFB	129.92	132.00	- 1.873	69	0.065	
MFB	93.82	95.40	- 0.713	45	0.480	
IOB	94.29	92.80	0.841	2	1.000	
SIOB	16.59	16.00	0.692	69	0.491	
BOB	96.82	92.20	0.723	69	0.472	
AIB	18.45	18.60	0.147	2	1.000	
Nasal structure						
NB	25.82	23.20	5.288	69	0.000	*
NH	50.29	49.20	0.774	2	1.000	
DC	20.14	23.00	- 4.307	69	0.000	*
DS	10.06	12.80	-11.098	7	0.0	*
MN	8.21	8.40	- 0.119	2	1.000	
SMN	3.35	2.80	1.452	69	0.151	
Orbit						
LOH	33.53	33.60	- 0.110	69	0.912	
LOBM	41.82	41.00	0.811	2	1.000	
LOBD	39.50	38.80	0.804	2	1.000	

Table 255 - continued

Dental arch						
MB	64.58	60.60	3.972	69	0.000	*
ML	52.86	53.00	- 0.118	2	1.000	
FL	94.83	98.40	- 1.566	8	0.156	
FLA	93.15	97.00	- 1.768	9	0.111	
Mandible						
LM	101.82	99.60	0.827	2	1.000	
BCB	121.85	121.00	1.200	20	0.244	
SH	33.35	34.60	- 1.446	69	0.153	
BA	96.77	97.80	- 0.490	69	0.626	
RL	32.83	32.00	0.838	69	0.405	
Facial angles						
G/	122.44°	124.00°	- 0.683	69	0.497	

*DF $\leq$ 3, t-prob. = 1

Table 256

"t" SCORES FOR INDICES OF: FORT ANCIENT ILINID-LENID

FEMALE VARIETY

(N = F. A. Ilinid 66; Lenid 5)

	$\overline{X}_{FAI}$	$\overline{X}_{Len}$	t-ratio	DF*	t-prob.	Sig. diff.
Cranial vault						
B/L	76.00	74.63	2.114	6	0.079	
H/L	76.46	74.56	1.564	69	0.123	
H/B	100.69	99.92	0.436	69	0.664	
H/L+B/2	86.89	85.39	1.192	69	0.237	
PAH/L	64.55	64.04	0.545	69	0.587	
BPH/H	------	------	-------	--	-----	
MF/B	66.90	65.23	1.427	50	0.160	
Face						
TFH/TFB	88.29	85.33	2.134	69	0.036	*
UFH/TFB	53.89	52.36	1.617	69	0.110	
UFH/MFB	71.66	72.96	- 1.167	34	0.251	
TFB/B	97.13	98.48	- 0.639	2	1.000	
MF/TFB	68.92	66.35	1.401	7	0.204	
BA/MF	114.14	110.99	0.387	59	0.700	
BA/TFB	74.47	73.62	0.494	69	0.623	
SIOB/IOB	17.15	17.25	0.363	69	0.718	
AIB/BOB	19.08	19.34	- 0.231	2	1.000	
Nasal structure						
NB/NH	50.92	47.28	1.718	69	0.090	
DS/DC	50.33	55.73	- 3.061	5	0.028	*
SMN/MN	40.82	33.79	1.865	69	0.066	
Orbit						
LOH/LOBM	80.09	82.12	- 0.798	2	1.000	
LOH/LOBD	84.86	86.75	- 1.031	69	0.306	
Dental arch						
MB/ML	122.16	114.49	2.519	2	1.000	
Mandible						
LM/BCB	83.66	82.36	0.788	69	0.433	

*DF $\leq$ 3, t-prob. = 1

APPENDIX E

Table 257
"t" SCORES FOR MEASUREMENTS OF:
FORT ANCIENT ILINID-ISWANID MALE VARIETY

(N = F. A. Ilinid 84; Iswanid 33)

	$\bar{X}_{FAI}$	$\bar{X}_{Isw}$	t-ratio	DF	t-prob.	Sig. diff.
Cranial vault						
CM	153.85	150.21	6.014	74	0.000	*
TP	4.90	4.97	- 0.417	115	0.678	
L	181.46	176.97	4.055	94	0.000	*
B	138.88	134.88	4.211	85	0.000	*
MF	94.00	90.61	2.659	112	0.009	*
H	141.20	138.79	3.183	115	0.002	*
PAH	118.44	115.94	3.376	99	0.001	*
BPH	------	------	-------	---	-----	
LB	104.13	99.97	5.523	115	0.000	*
Face						
TFH	124.86	118.03	7.664	115	0.000	*
UFH	75.18	70.88	6.293	115	0.000	*
TFB	141.38	135.88	6.391	115	0.000	*
MFB	102.13	98.36	4.933	115	0.000	*
IOB	100.11	96.00	5.964	115	0.000	*
SIOB	18.01	17.12	2.589	115	0.011	*
BOB	100.77	96.18	7.434	115	0.000	*
AIB	19.87	17.85	5.755	115	0.000	*
Nasal structure						
NB	26.79	23.91	7.467	46	0.000	*
NH	54.10	51.21	6.130	115	0.000	*
DC	20.88	19.61	3.107	115	0.002	*
DS	10.95	10.21	3.121	115	0.002	*
MN	8.79	8.18	2.101	115	0.038	*
SMN	3.94	3.21	4.603	115	0.000	*
Orbit						
LOH	34.68	32.67	6.066	115	0.000	*
LOBM	43.82	42.03	6.390	75	0.000	*
LOBD	41.49	39.33	7.964	76	0.000	*
Dental arch						
MB	68.35	63.70	7.899	102	0.000	*
ML	54.37	51.85	6.031	115	0.000	*
FL	97.52	94.61	4.545	115	0.000	*
Fla	95.62	92.94	4.097	115	0.000	*
Mandible						
LM	105.68	99.27	7.137	115	0.000	*
BCB	129.13	123.82	5.246	115	0.000	*
SH	36.33	34.91	3.172	115	0.002	*
BA	103.67	103.73	- 0.055	115	0.956	
RL	35.57	34.52	2.132	115	0.035	*
Facial angles						
G∠	114.61	117.73	- 2.876	115	0.005	*

Table 258

"t" SCORES FOR INDICES OF:
FORT ANCIENT ILINID-ISWANID MALE VARIETY

(N = F. A. Ilinid 84; Iswanid 33)

	$\bar{X}_{FAI}$	$\bar{X}_{Isw}$	t-ratio	DF	t-prob.	Sig. diff.
Cranial vault						
B/L	76.70	75.25	0.618	107	0.538	
H/L	77.92	78.47	- 0.979	79	0.331	
H/B	101.81	102.96	- 1.575	74	0.120	
H/L+B/2	88.18	89.04	- 1.746	115	0.083	
PAH/L	65.37	65.55	- 0.313	104	0.755	
BPH/H	------	------	-------	---	-----	
MF/B	67.74	67.20	0.577	112	0.565	
Face						
TFH/TFB	87.18	86.90	0.233	108	0.816	
UFH/TFB	53.22	52.17	2.261	77	0.027	*
UFH/MFB	73.67	72.16	1.733	44	0.090	
TFB/B	101.91	100.80	1.513	115	0.133	
MF/TFB	66.56	66.71	- 0.168	112	0.867	
BA/MF	109.35	114.66	- 3.583	115	0.000	*
BA/TFB	73.39	76.39	- 3.374	115	0.001	*
SIOB/IOB	17.98	17.84	0.478	115	0.634	
AIB/BOB	19.72	18.54	3.557	115	0.001	*
Nasal structure						
NB/NH	49.58	46.78	3.662	115	0.000	*
DS/DC	52.95	52.60	0.213	115	0.832	
SMN/MN	45.29	39.59	3.318	115	0.001	*
Orbit						
LOH/LOBM	79.20	77.78	1.722	115	0.088	
LOH/LOBD	83.67	83.09	0.655	115	0.514	
Dental arch						
MB/ML	125.83	122.99	2.252	85	0.027	*
Mandible						
LM/BCB	81.95	80.25	1.893	115	0.061	

APPENDIX E

Table 259

"t" SCORES FOR MEASUREMENTS OF:
FORT ANCIENT ILINID-MUSKOGID MALE VARIETY

(N = F. A. Ilinid 84; Muskogid 48)

	$\bar{x}_{FAI}$	$\bar{x}_{Mus}$	t-ratio	DF	t-prob.	Sig. diff.
Cranial vault						
CM	153.85	154.96	- 1.740	130	0.084	
TP	4.90	4.73	1.217	130	0.226	
L	181.46	181.15	0.297	124	0.767	
B	138.88	139.58	- 0.692	130	0.490	
MF	94.00	94.77	- 0.594	122	0.553	
H	141.20	144.15	- 4.246	130	0.000	*
PAH	118.44	------	-------	---	-----	
BPH	------	25.81	-------	---	-----	
LB	104.13	105.83	- 2.474	130	0.015	*
Face						
TFH	124.86	125.77	- 1.154	130	0.251	
UFH	75.18	75.65	- 0.799	130	0.426	
TFB	141.38	139.65	2.172	130	0.032	*
MFB	102.13	103.27	- 1.594	130	0.133	
IOB	100.11	100.04	0.109	130	0.913	
SIOB	18.01	19.06	- 2.761	78	0.007	*
BOB	100.77	100.85	- 0.148	130	0.883	
AIB	19.87	20.19	- 0.992	130	0.323	
Nasal structure						
NB	26.79	26.23	1.959	130	0.052	
NH	54.11	53.79	0.677	77	0.501	
DC	20.88	22.12	- 3.336	130	0.001	*
DS	10.95	11.29	- 1.604	130	0.111	
MN	8.79	9.96	- 3.928	79	0.000	*
SMN	3.94	4.17	- 1.580	130	0.116	
Orbit						
LOH	34.68	34.52	0.542	130	0.589	
LOBM	43.82	43.35	1.549	130	0.124	
LOBD	41.49	40.79	2.377	130	0.019	*
Dental arch						
MB	68.34	68.60	- 0.398	114	0.691	
ML	54.37	56.79	- 5.126	71	0.000	*
FL	97.52	101.71	- 7.667	130	0.000	*
FLA	95.62	100.00	- 7.560	130	0.000	*
Mandible						
LM	105.68	108.08	- 2.564	79	0.012	*
BCB	129.13	126.46	2.866	130	0.005	*
SH	36.33	38.21	- 4.625	130	0.000	*
BA	103.67	104.60	- 0.915	130	0.362	
RL	35.57	35.96	- 0.823	130	0.412	
Facial angles						
G∠	114.61	116.25	- 1.764	130	0.080	

Table 260
"t" SCORES FOR INDICES OF:
FORT ANCIENT ILINID-MUSKOGID MALE VARIETY

(N = F. A. Ilinid 84: Muskogid 48)

	$\bar{X}_{FAI}$	$\bar{X}_{Mus}$	t-ratio	DF	t-prob.	Sig. diff.
Cranial vault						
B/L	76.70	77.08	- 0.566	125	0.573	
H/L	77.92	79.62	- 3.256	118	0.001	
H/B	101.81	103.36	- 2.124	130	0.036	
H/L+B/2	88.18	89.92	- 3.914	130	0.000	*
PAH/L	65.37	-----	-------	---	-----	
BPH/H	------	17.90	-------	---	-----	
MF/B	67.74	67.97	- 0.230	127	0.818	
Face						
TFH/TFB	87.18	88.05	- 0.395	78	0.694	
UFH/TFB	53.22	54.21	- 2.074	130	0.040	
UFH/MFB	73.67	73.35	0.481	130	0.632	
TFB/B	101.91	100.10	2.825	130	0.005	*
MF/TFB	66.55	67.92	- 1.418	126	0.159	
BA/MF	109.35	110.65	- 0.922	130	0.358	
BA/TFB	73.39	74.94	- 1.985	130	0.049	
SIOB/IOB	17.98	19.04	- 3.066	76	0.003	*
AIB/BOB	19.72	20.01	- 0.958	130	0.340	
Nasal structure						
NB/NH	49.58	48.85	1.179	130	0.240	
DS/DC	52.94	51.52	1.036	130	0.302	
SMN/MN	45.29	43.02	1.266	76	0.209	
Orbit						
LOH/LOBM	79.20	79.67	- 0.691	130	0.491	
LOH/LOBD	83.67	84.70	- 1.362	130	0.176	
Dental arch						
MB/ML	125.83	121.02	3.502	130	0.001	*
Mandible						
LM/BCB	81.95	85.59	- 4.167	130	0.000	*

APPENDIX E

Table 261

"t" SCORES FOR MEASUREMENTS OF:
FORT ANCIENT ILINID-SENECA MALE SERIES

(N = F. A. Ilinid 84: Seneca 31)

	$\bar{x}_{FAI}$	$\bar{x}_{Sen}$	t-ratio	DF	t-prob.	Sig. diff.
Cranial vault						
CM	153.85	154.63	- 1.101	113	0.273	
TP	4.90	4.55	2.171	113	0.032	*
L	181.46	186.48	- 4.489	88	0.000	*
B	138.88	135.61	3.187	70	0.002	*
MF	94.00	94.19	- 0.140	108	0.889	
H	141.20	141.81	- 0.690	113	0.492	
PAH	118.44	------	--------	---	-----	
BPH	------	26.94	--------	---	-----	
LB	104.13	108.58	- 5.425	113	0.000	*
Face						
TFH	124.86	124.77	0.090	113	0.928	
UFH	75.18	75.55	- 0.534	113	0.594	
TFB	141.38	136.68	5.300	113	0.000	*
MFB	102.13	99.81	3.004	113	0.003	*
IOB	100.11	98.39	2.475	113	0.015	*
SIOB	18.01	20.35	- 5.216	42	0.000	*
BOB	100.77	98.48	3.722	113	0.000	
AIB	19.87	20.06	- 0.452	41	0.654	
Nasal structure						
NB	26.79	26.87	- 0.196	39	0.846	
NH	59.11	54.35	- 0.551	113	0.583	
DC	20.88	20.45	1.016	113	0.312	
DS	10.95	11.29	- 1.454	113	0.149	
MN	8.79	9.19	- 1.369	113	0.174	
SMN	3.94	4.10	- 0.899	113	0.371	
Orbit						
LOH	34.68	33.90	2.418	113	0.017	*
LOBM	43.83	42.87	2.864	113	0.005	*
LOBD	41.49	40.58	2.750	113	0.007	*
Dental arch						
MB	68.34	67.23	1.953	102	0.053	
ML	54.37	57.58	- 6.348	43	0.000	*
FL	97.52	104.29	- 9.802	113	0.000	*
FLA	95.62	102.97	-10.252	113	0.000	*
Mandible						
LM	105.68	109.48	- 3.969	113	0.000	*
BCB	129.13	124.10	5.695	71	0.000	*
SH	36.33	37.39	- 2.337	113	0.021	*
BA	103.67	102.71	0.874	113	0.384	
RL	35.57	35.97	0.973	76	0.334	*
Facial angles						
G∠	114.61	120.43	- 5.111	113	0.000	

Table 262
"t" SCORES FOR INDICES OF:
FORT ANCIENT ILINID-SENECA MALE SERIES

(N = F. A. Ilinid 84; Seneca 31)

	$\bar{x}_{FAI}$	$\bar{x}_{Sen}$	t-ratio	DF	t-prob.	Sig. diff.
Cranial vault						
B/L	76.70	72.76	5.154	95	0.000	*
H/L	77.92	76.07	2.741	113	0.001	*
H/B	101.81	104.65	- 3.136	113	0.002	*
H/L+B/2	88.18	88.07	0.214	113	0.831	
PAH/L	65.37	------	-------	---	-----	
BPH/H	------	18.97	-------	---	-----	
MF/B	67.74	69.47	- 1.808	111	0.073	
Face						
TFH/TFB	87.18	91.36	- 3.169	111	0.002	*
UFH/TFB	53.22	55.31	- 3.643	113	0.000	*
UFH/MFB	73.67	75.76	- 2.857	113	0.005	*
TFB/B	101.91	100.84	1.446	113	0.151	
MF/TFB	66.55	68.92	- 2.490	111	0.014	*
BA/MF	109.35	109.28	0.048	113	0.962	
BA/TFB	73.39	75.17	- 2.480	77	0.015	*
SIOB/IOB	17.98	20.68	- 6.412	40	0.000	*
AIB/BOB	19.72	20.35	- 1.780	113	0.078	
Nasal structure						
NB/NH	49.58	49.45	0.175	113	0.861	
DS/DC	52.94	55.62	- 1.752	113	0.083	
SMN/MN	45.29	44.86	0.234	113	0.816	
Orbit						
LOH/LOBM	79.20	79.14	0.081	113	0.935	
LOH/LOBD	83.67	83.61	0.069	113	0.945	
Dental arch						
MB/ML	125.83	116.88	7.809	97	0.000	*
Mandible						
LM/BCB	81.95	85.09	- 1.070	30	0.293	

APPENDIX E

Table 263

"t" SCORES FOR MEASUREMENTS OF: FORT ANCIENT ILINID-SENECA FEMALE SERIES

(N = F. A. Ilinid 66; Seneca 33)

	$\bar{X}_{FAI}$	$\bar{X}_{Sen}$	t-ratio	DF	t-prob.	Sig. diff.
Cranial vault						
CM	148.31	149.29	-1.532	97	0.129	
TP	4.82	4.42	2.326	80	0.022	*
L	176.15	179.67	-3.257	97	0.002	*
B	133.73	132.85	1.062	97	0.291	
MF	89.52	91.48	-1.284	86	0.203	
H	134.67	135.36	-0.778	97	0.438	
PAH	113.71	------	------	--	-----	
BPH	------	------	------	--	-----	
LB	96.39	102.03	-2.532	72	0.014	*
Face						
TFH	114.71	113.33	1.478	42	0.147	
UFH	69.97	69.58	0.635	50	0.528	
TFB	129.92	128.67	1.575	97	0.119	
MFB	93.82	95.94	-1.021	77	0.310	
IOB	94.29	94.97	-1.050	48	0.299	
SIOB	16.59	18.45	-4.601	97	0.000	*
BOB	96.82	95.64	1.762	38	0.086	
AIB	18.45	19.52	-3.646	97	0.000	*
Nasal structure						
NB	25.82	25.88	-0.203	46	0.840	
NH	50.29	50.15	0.320	47	0.750	
DC	20.14	20.21	-0.241	97	0.810	
DS	10.06	10.64	-2.455	97	0.016	*
MN	8.21	9.30	-3.429	97	0.001	*
SMN	3.35	3.48	-0.768	97	0.444	
Orbit						
LOH	33.53	33.52	0.051	97	0.959	
LOBM	41.82	40.76	3.392	45	0.001	*
LOBD	39.50	38.64	2.407	40	0.021	*

Table 263 - continued

Dental arch						
MB	64.58	63.88	1.458	97	0.148	
ML	52.86	54.88	- 4.282	45	0.000	*
FL	94.83	99.15	- 2.869	82	0.005	*
FLA	93.15	99.18	- 3.334	82	0.001	*
Mandible						
LM	101.82	103.76	- 2.509	48	0.016	*
BCB	121.85	116.36	5.923	97	0.000	*
SH	33.35	33.33	0.037	97	0.970	
BA	96.77	96.36	0.463	97	0.645	
RL	32.83	33.27	- 0.732	46	0.468	
Facial angles						
G/	122.44°	125.55°	- 2.813	97	0.006	*

APPENDIX E

Table 264

"t" SCORES FOR INDICES OF: FORT ANCIENT ILINID-SENECA FEMALE SERIES

(N = F. A. Ilinid 66; Seneca 33)

	$\bar{X}_{FAI}$	$\bar{X}_{Sen}$	t-ratio	DF	t-prob.	Sig. diff.
Cranial vault						
B/L	76.00	73.98	3.490	97	0.001	*
H/L	76.46	75.38	1.812	97	0.073	
H/B	100.69	101.93	-1.544	97	0.126	
H/L+B/2	86.89	86.65	0.407	97	0.685	
PAH/L	64.55	-----	------	--	-----	
BPH/H	-----	-----	------	--	-----	
MF/B	66.90	68.90	-1.702	88	0.092	
Face						
TFH/TFB	88.29	88.14	0.194	48	0.847	
UFH/TFB	53.89	54.11	-0.433	50	0.667	
UFH/MFB	71.66	72.63	-0.808	94	0.421	
TFB/B	97.13	96.89	0.387	97	0.700	
MF/TFB	68.92	71.12	-1.916	78	0.059	
BA/MF	114.14	105.46	1.147	65	0.255	
BA/TFB	74.47	74.93	-0.716	82	0.476	
SIOB/IOB	17.15	19.43	-4.710	97	0.000	*
AIB/BOB	19.08	20.41	-4.645	97	0.000	*
Nasal structure						
NB/NH	50.92	51.73	-0.842	97	0.402	
DS/DC	50.33	52.90	-1.744	97	0.084	
SMN/MN	40.82	37.80	1.658	97	0.100	
Orbit						
LOH/LOBM	80.09	82.36	-2.395	46	0.021	*
LOH/LOBD	84.86	86.93	-1.963	46	0.056	
Dental arch						
MB/ML	122.16	116.58	4.690	46	0.000	*
Mandible						
LM/BCB	83.66	89.27	-6.273	50	0.0	*

Table 265

"t" SCORES FOR MEASUREMENTS OF:
FORT ANCIENT ILINID-SHAWNEE MALE SERIES

(N = F. A. Ilinid 84; Shawnee 4)

	$\bar{X}_{FAI}$	$\bar{X}_{Sha}$	t-ratio	DF**	t-prob.	Sig. diff.
Cranial vault						
CM	153.85	153.50	0.193	86	0.847	
TP	4.90	4.50	0.996	86	0.322	
L	181.46	180.50	0.255	86	0.799	
B	138.88	141.00	- 0.683	86	0.496	
MF	94.00	96.00	- 1.205	8	0.263	
H	141.20	139.00	0.496	1	1.000	
PAH	118.44	118.50	- 0.023	86	0.982	
BPH	------	------	-------	---	-----	
LB	104.13	104.50	- 0.118	1	1.000	
Face						
TFH	124.86	132.00	- 3.129	86	0.002	*
UFH	75.18	73.00	0.639	1	1.000	
TFB	141.38	140.75	0.291	86	0.772	
MFB	102.13	101.25	0.458	86	0.648	
IOB	100.11	101.50	- 0.793	86	0.430	
SIOB	18.01	19.00	- 1.092	86	0.278	
BOB	100.77	101.50	- 0.469	86	0.640	
AIB	19.87	20.00	- 0.154	86	0.878	
Nasal structure						
NB	26.79	25.25	1.158	1	1.000	
NH	59.11	53.25	0.342	1	1.000	
DC	20.88	21.50	- 1.723	5	0.145	
DS	10.95	11.25	- 0.508	86	0.613	
MN	8.79	8.00	1.105	86	0.272	
SMN	3.94	3.50	0.677	1	1.000	
Orbit						
LOH	34.68	33.25	1.733	86	0.087	
LOBM	43.82	45.00	- 1.413	86	0.161	
LOBD	41.49	41.75	- 0.322	86	0.749	
Dental arch						
MB	68.34	62.75	2.702	86	0.008	*
ML	54.37	56.00	- 0.961	1	1.000	
FL	97.52	101.25	- 2.256	86	0.027	*
FLA	95.62	99.75	- 2.446	86	0.016	*
Mandible						
LM	105.68	107.00	- 0.593	86	0.555	
BCB	129.13	128.75	0.451	8	0.664	
SH	36.33	36.00	0.297	86	0.767	
BA	103.67	107.00	- 1.207	86	0.231	
RL	35.57	34.00	1.260	86	0.211	
Facial angles						
G∠	114.61	119.75	- 1.837	86	0.070	

** DF ≤ 3, t-prob. = 1

APPENDIX E

Table 266

"t" SCORES FOR INDICES OF:
FORT ANCIENT ILINID-SHAWNEE MALE SERIES

(N = F. A. Ilinid 84; Shawnee 4)

	$\overline{X}_{FAI}$	$\overline{X}_{Sha}$	t-ratio	DF**	t-prob.	Sig. diff.
Cranial vault						
B/L	76.70	78.40	- 0.622	86	0.535	
H/L	77.92	76.99	0.538	86	0.592	
H/B	101.81	98.92	0.585	1	1.000	
H/L+B/2	88.18	86.43	0.807	1	1.000	
PAH/L	65.37	65.71	- 0.170	86	0.865	
BPH/H	------	------	------	---	-----	
MF/B	67.74	68.20	- 0.267	3	1.000	
Face						
TFH/TFB	87.18	93.84	- 1.286	86	0.202	
UFH/TFB	53.22	51.84	0.953	86	0.343	
UFH/MFB	73.67	72.15	0.413	1	1.000	
TFB/B	101.91	100.02	0.983	86	0.328	
MF/TFB	66.55	68.23	- 1.142	4	0.317	
BA/MF	109.35	111.58	- 0.609	86	0.544	
BA/TFB	73.39	76.02	- 1.188	86	0.238	
SIOB/IOB	17.98	18.74	- 0.934	86	0.353	
AIB/BOB	19.72	19.69	0.036	86	0.972	
Nasal structure						
NB/NH	49.58	47.45	1.210	86	0.230	
DS/DC	52.94	52.38	0.145	86	0.885	
SMN/MN	45.29	43.36	0.288	1	1.000	
Orbit						
LOH/LOBM	79.20	73.86	2.702	86	0.008	*
LOH/LOBD	83.67	79.64	1.863	86	0.066	
Dental arch						
MB/ML	125.83	112.30	3.352	86	0.001	*
Mandible						
LM/BCB	81.95	83.13	- 0.517	86	0.607	

** DF ≤ 3, t-prob. = 1

Table 267

"t" SCORES FOR MEASUREMENTS OF:
FORT ANCIENT MUSKOGID-LENID MALE VARIETY

(N = F. A Muskogid 50; Lenid 45)

	$\bar{x}_{FAM}$	$\bar{x}_{LEN}$	t-ratio	DF	t-prob.	Sig. diff.
Cranial vault						
CM	152.85	153.11	- 0.251	78	0.801	
TP	4.98	4.91	0.356	93	0.723	
L	178.18	185.62	- 2.915	72	0.005	*
B	144.36	136.28	8.152	93	0.000	
MF	95.12	93.96	1.235	93	0.220	
H	136.12	137.42	- 1.472	93	0.144	
PAH	116.62	-----	-------	---	-----	
BPH	------	23.11	-------	---	-----	
LB	103.52	104.60	- 1.207	93	0.307	
Face						
TFH	123.84	123.13	0.525	83	0.601	
UFH	73.26	73.76	- 0.766	93	0.446	
TFB	141.42	137.60	4.723	78	0.000	*
MFB	102.40	99.82	3.474	93	0.001	*
IOB	99.98	97.44	3.641	93	0.000	*
SIOB	17.38	18.67	- 2.847	93	0.005	*
BOB	101.00	98.89	3.692	80	0.000	*
AIB	20.72	20.22	1.205	93	0.231	
Nasal structure						
NB	27.06	25.29	5.882	84	0.000	*
NH	53.06	53.76	- 0.111	93	0.912	
DC	22.42	22.47	- 0.111	93	0.912	
DS	11.64	12.38	- 2.905	93	0.005	*
MN	9.76	8.56	3.975	93	0.000	*
SMN	4.08	4.07	0.086	93	0.931	
Orbit						
LOH	33.88	34.04	- 0.489	93	0.626	
LOBM	43.54	42.00	4.379	63	0.000	*
LOBD	40.80	39.36	4.345	66	0.000	*
Dental arch						
MB	64.32	65.58	- 1.508	66	0.136	
ML	55.08	56.98	- 3.980	93	0.000	*
FL	98.68	101.98	- 4.166	72	0.000	*
FLA	97.38	100.56	- 3.977	72	0.000	*
Mandible						
LM	105.36	110.16	- 5.674	93	0.000	*
BCB	129.26	122.11	11.001	93	0.000	*
SH	36.00	36.44	- 0.982	93	0.329	
BA	105.32	104.56	0.597	65	0.553	
RL	35.42	35.22	0.352	93	0.725	
Facial angles						
G∠	119.60	120.60	- 1.113	93	0.269	

Table 268

"t" SCORES FOR INDICES OF:
FORT ANCIENT MUSKOGID-LENID MALE VARIETY

(N = F. A. Muskogid 50; Lenid 45)

	$\bar{X}_{FAM}$	$\bar{X}_{LEN}$	t-ratio	DF	t-prob.	Sig. diff.
Cranial vault						
B/L	79.27	71.91	4.192	84	0.000	*
H/L	74.69	72.53	1.244	75	0.217	
H/B	94.44	100.93	- 7.347	93	0.000	*
H/L+B/2	84.58	83.39	0.730	55	0.469	
PAH/L	65.74	38.65	6.010	44	0.000	*
BPH/H	------	16.81	-------	---	-----	
MF/B	65.92	68.97	- 4.679	88	0.000	*
Face						
TFH/TFB	85.51	87.32	- 0.734	77	0.465	
UFH/TFB	51.82	53.63	- 3.807	93	0.000	*
UFH/MFB	71.65	73.95	- 3.134	93	0.002	*
TFB/B	98.13	101.05	- 3.656	93	0.000	*
MF/TFB	67.20	68.31	- 1.736	93	0.086	
BA/MF	111.10	111.39	- 0.184	93	0.854	
BA/TFB	74.51	75.98	- 1.717	72	0.090	
SIOB/IOB	17.31	19.15	- 4.287	93	0.000	*
AIB/BOB	20.42	20.46	- 0.115	81	0.909	
Nasal structure						
NB/NH	51.04	74.23	4.788	93	0.000	*
DS/DC	52.40	55.58	- 2.073	93	0.041	
SMN/MN	42.60	48.41	- 3.054	80	0.003	*
Orbit						
LOH/LOBM	77.91	81.21	- 3.671	93	0.000	*
LOH/LOBD	83.11	84.45	- 0.627	51	0.534	
Dental arch						
MB/ML	116.86	115.26	0.979	74	0.331	
Mandible						
LM/BCB	81.46	90.21	-13.376	93	0.000	*

PREHISTORIC PEOPLE OF FORT ANCIENT

Table 269

"t" SCORES FOR MEASUREMENTS OF: FORT ANCIENT MUSKOGID-LENID FEMALE VARIETY

(N = F. A. Muskogid 54; Lenid 5)

	$\bar{X}_{FAM}$	$\bar{X}_{Len}$	t-ratio	DF*	t-prob.	Sig. diff.
Cranial vault						
CM	139.25	150.47	- 3.132	31	0.004	*
TP	5.17	4.40	1.852	57	0.069	
L	171.81	181.20	- 4.046	57	0.000	*
B	139.94	135.20	2.338	57	0.023	*
MF	91.93	88.20	2.098	57	0.040	
H	132.81	135.00	- 1.672	12	0.120	
PAH	113.44	116.00	- 1.471	57	0.146	
BPH	------	------	-------	--	-----	
LB	100.04	99.00	0.342	2	1.000	
Face						
TFH	111.80	113.40	- 1.365	57	0.178	
UFH	68.17	69.60	- 1.269	57	0.210	
TFB	130.63	132.00	- 1.262	57	0.212	
MFB	98.00	95.40	1.947	57	0.056	
IOB	95.33	92.80	1.828	57	0.073	
SIOB	16.06	16.00	0.081	57	0.936	
BOB	97.65	92.20	1.281	57	0.205	
AIB	19.31	18.60	0.894	57	0.375	
Nasal structure						
NB	26.35	23.20	5.062	57	0.000	*
NH	49.70	49.20	0.356	2	1.000	
DC	21.00	23.00	- 5.020	8	0.001	*
DS	10.93	12.80	- 5.153	57	0.000	*
MN	8.83	8.40	0.274	2	1.000	
SMN	3.56	2.80	2.153	57	0.036	*
Orbit						
LOH	33.04	33.60	- 0.826	57	0.412	
LOBM	42.30	41.00	1.787	57	0.079	
LOBD	39.20	38.80	0.461	2	1.000	

Table 269 - continued

Dental arch						
MB	62.76	60.60	1.214	12	0.248	
ML	52.65	53.00	- 0.229	11	0.822	
FL	96.78	98.40	- 1.188	57	0.240	
FLA	95.57	97.00	- 1.059	57	0.294	
Mandible						
LM	101.19	99.60	0.587	2	1.000	
BCB	124.87	121.00	5.733	16	0.000	*
SH	32.81	34.60	- 2.256	57	0.028	*
BA	97.61	97.80	- 0.073	2	1.000	
RL	33.24	32.00	1.511	57	0.136	
Facial angles						
G/	123.37°	124.00°	- 0.331	57	0.742	

*DF $\leq$ 3, t-prob. = 1

Table 270

"t" SCORES FOR INDICES OF: FORT ANCIENT MUSKOGID-LENID

FEMALE VARIETY

(N = F. A. Muskogid 54; Lenid 5)

	$\bar{X}_{FAM}$	$\bar{X}_{Len}$	t-ratio	DF	t-prob.	Sig. diff.
Cranial vault						
B/L	77.25	74.63	1.665	53	0.102	
H/L	76.09	74.56	1.317	7	0.230	
H/B	94.70	99.92	- 3.769	6	0.009	*
H/L+B/2	82.87	85.39	- 1.811	12	0.095	
PAH/L	57.61	64.04	- 2.193	55	0.033	*
BPH/H	------	------	-------	--	-----	
MF/B	58.46	65.23	- 2.740	54	0.008	*
Face						
TFH/TFB	75.78	83.33	- 2.693	47	0.010	*
UFH/TFB	52.37	52.36	0.009	57	0.993	
UFH/MFB	67.24	72.96	- 4.948	35	0.000	*
TFB/B	85.83	98.48	- 3.847	19	0.001	*
MF/TFB	72.00	66.35	2.438	57	0.018	*
BA/MF	102.78	110.99	- 1.895	77	0.063	
BA/TFB	66.48	73.62	- 1.967	16	0.067	
SIOB/IOB	26.54	17.25	2.886	54	0.006	*
AIB/BOB	23.78	19.34	2.611	23	0.016	*
Nasal structure						
NB/NH	56.25	47.28	3.858	25	0.001	*
DS/DC	56.04	55.73	0.150	12	0.884	
SMN/MN	48.27	33.79	4.493	25	0.000	*
Orbit						
LOH/LOBM	78.96	82.12	- 1.524	57	0.133	
LOH/LOBD	82.05	86.75	- 1.480	57	0.145	
Dental arch						
MB/ML	99.41	114.49	- 2.204	44	0.033	*
Mandible						
LM/BCB	78.26	82.36	- 1.159	57	0.251	

APPENDIX E

Table 271

"t" SCORES FOR MEASUREMENTS OF:
FORT ANCIENT MUSKOGID-ISWANID MALE VARIETY

(N = F. A. Muskogid 50; Iswanid 33)

	$\bar{X}_{FAM}$	$\bar{X}_{ISW}$	t-ratio	DF	t-prob.	Sig. diff.
Cranial vault						
CM	152.85	150.21	3.481	78	0.001	*
TP	4.98	4.97	0.057	79	0.955	
L	178.18	176.97	0.785	72	0.435	
B	144.36	134.88	9.029	81	0.000	*
MF	95.12	90.61	4.792	79	0.000	*
H	136.12	138.79	-3.224	78	0.002	*
PAH	116.62	115.94	0.962	81	0.339	
BPH	------	------	-------	---	-----	
LB	103.52	99.97	3.841	78	0.000	*
Face						
TFH	123.84	118.03	4.343	76	0.000	*
UFH	73.26	70.88	3.302	81	0.001	*
TFB	141.42	135.88	6.943	81	0.000	*
MFB	102.40	98.36	5.154	81	0.000	*
IOB	99.98	96.00	5.475	81	0.000	*
SIOB	17.38	17.12	0.667	79	0.507	
BOB	101.00	96.18	8.236	81	0.000	*
AIB	20.72	17.85	6.605	81	0.000	*
Nasal structure						
NB	27.06	23.91	7.617	81	0.000	*
NH	53.06	51.21	3.315	81	0.001	*
DC	22.42	19.61	6.253	81	0.000	*
DS	11.64	10.21	5.438	81	0.000	*
MN	9.76	8.18	4.668	81	0.000	*
SMN	4.08	3.21	5.180	81	0.000	*
Orbit						
LOH	33.88	32.67	3.165	81	0.002	*
LOBM	43.54	42.03	5.792	81	0.000	*
LOBD	40.80	39.33	5.734	81	0.000	
Dental arch						
MB	64.32	63.70	0.731	68	0.467	
ML	55.08	51.85	6.816	81	0.000	*
FL	98.68	94.61	6.131	81	0.000	*
FLA	97.38	92.94	6.707	81	0.000	*
Mandible						
LM	105.36	99.27	6.693	81	0.000	*
BCB	129.26	123.82	6.421	81	0.000	*
SH	36.00	34.91	2.100	81	0.039	*
BA	105.32	103.73	1.557	81	0.123	
RL	35.42	34.52	1.623	81	0.108	
Facial angles						
G∠	119.60	117.73	1.783	81	0.078	

Table 272

"t" SCORES FOR INDICES OF:
FORT ANCIENT MUSKOGID-ISWANID MALE VARIETY

(N = F. A. Muskogid 50; Iswanid 33)

	$\bar{X}_{FAM}$	$\bar{X}_{ISW}$	t-ratio	DF	t-prob.	Sig. diff.
Cranial vault						
B/L	79.27	76.25	2.025	55	0.048	
H/L	74.69	78.47	- 2.424	53	0.019	*
H/B	94.44	102.96	- 9.781	81	0.000	*
H/L+B/2	84.58	89.04	- 6.218	76	0.000	*
PAH/L	65.74	65.55	0.258	68	0.797	
BPH/H	------	------	-------	---	-----	
MF/B	65.92	67.20	- 1.895	77	0.062	
Face						
TFH/TFB	85.51	86.90	- 0.934	59	0.354	
UFH/TFB	51.82	52.17	- 0.700	81	0.486	
UFH/MFB	71.65	72.16	- 0.573	81	0.568	
TFB/B	98.13	100.80	- 3.481	81	0.001	*
MF/TFB	67.20	66.71	0.718	81	0.475	
BA/MF	111.10	114.66	- 2.271	81	0.026	*
BA/TFB	74.51	76.39	- 2.199	54	0.032	*
SIOB/IOB	17.31	17.84	- 1.434	78	0.155	
AIB/BOB	20.42	18.54	5.127	81	0.000	*
Nasal structure						
NB/NH	51.04	46.78	4.542	81	0.000	*
DS/DC	52.40	52.60	- 0.123	81	0.902	
SMN/MN	42.60	39.60	1.612	81	0.111	
Orbit						
LOH/LOBM	77.91	77.78	0.140	81	0.890	
LOH/LOBD	83.11	83.09	0.013	81	0.990	
Dental arch						
MB/ML	116.86	122.99	- 3.636	75	0.001	*
Mandible						
LM/BCB	81.46	80.25	1.454	81	0.150	

APPENDIX E

Table 273

"t" SCORES FOR MEASUREMENTS OF:
FORT ANCIENT MUSKOGID-MUSKOGID MALE VARIETY

(N = F. A. Muskogid 50; Muskogid 48)

	$\bar{X}_{FAM}$	$\bar{X}_{Mus}$	t-ratio	DF	t-prob.	Sig. diff.
Cranial vault						
CM	152.85	154.96	- 2.680	95	0.009	*
TP	4.98	4.73	1.363	90	0.176	
L	178.18	181.15	- 1.956	73	0.054	
B	144.36	139.58	4.732	96	0.000	*
MF	95.12	94.77	0.359	96	0.720	
H	136.12	144.15	- 9.725	96	0.000	*
PAH	116.62	------	-------	---	-----	
BPH	------	25.81	-------	---	-----	
LB	103.52	105.83	- 2.510	85	0.014	*
Face						
TFH	123.84	125.77	- 1.502	75	0.137	
UFH	73.26	75.65	- 3.804	96	0.000	*
TFB	141.42	139.65	2.177	82	0.032	*
MFB	102.40	103.27	- 1.117	96	0.267	
IOB	99.98	100.04	- 0.095	96	0.925	
SIOB	17.38	19.06	- 3.785	96	0.000	*
BOB	101.00	100.85	0.271	96	0.787	
AIB	20.72	20.19	1.329	96	0.187	
Nasal structure						
NB	27.06	26.23	2.446	96	0.016	*
NH	53.06	53.79	- 1.399	96	0.165	
DC	22.42	22.12	0.698	96	0.487	
DS	11.64	11.29	1.451	96	0.150	
MN	9.76	9.96	- 0.584	96	0.560	
SMN	4.08	4.17	- 0.550	96	0.584	
Orbit						
LOH	33.88	34.52	- 1.880	96	0.063	
LOBM	43.54	43.35	0.636	78	0.527	
LOBD	40.80	40.79	0.029	79	0.977	
Dental arch						
MB	64.32	68.60	- 4.780	80	0.000	*
ML	55.08	56.79	- 3.324	84	0.001	*
FL	98.68	101.71	- 5.288	96	0.000	*
FLA	97.38	100.00	- 4.297	96	0.000	*
Mandible						
LM	105.36	108.08	- 2.790	82	0.007	*
BCB	129.26	126.46	3.165	80	0.002	*
SH	36.00	38.21	- 4.617	96	0.000	*
BA	105.32	104.60	0.678	82	0.500	
RL	35.42	35.96	- 0.981	96	0.329	
Facial angles						
G∠	119.60	116.25	3.619	96	0.000	*

Table 274

"t" SCORES FOR INDICES OF:
FORT ANCIENT MUSKOGID-MUSKOGID MALE VARIETY

(N = F. A. Muskogid 50; Muskogid 48)

	$\bar{X}_{FAM}$	$\bar{X}_{Mus}$	t-ratio	DF	t-prob.	Sig. diff.
Cranial vault						
B/L	79.27	77.08	1.492	52	0.142	
H/L	74.69	79.62	- 3.191	52	0.002	*
H/B	94.44	103.36	-11.210	96	0.000	*
H/L+B/2	84.58	89.92	- 7.691	79	0.000	*
PAH/L	65.74	------	-------	---	-----	
BPH/H	------	17.90	-------	---	-----	
MF/B	65.92	67.97	- 2.700	96	0.008	*
Face						
TFH/TFB	85.51	88.05	- 1.086	85	0.281	
UFH/TFB	51.82	54.21	- 4.981	96	0.000	*
UFH/MFB	71.65	73.35	- 2.245	96	0.027	*
TFB/B	98.13	100.10	- 2.891	96	0.005	*
MF/TFB	67.20	67.92	- 1.017	96	0.312	
BA/MF	111.10	110.65	0.288	86	0.774	
BA/TFB	74.51	74.94	- 0.572	85	0.569	
SIOB/IOB	17.31	19.04	- 4.260	96	0.000	*
AIB/BOB	20.42	20.01	1.168	96	0.246	
Nasal structure						
NB/NH	51.04	48.85	2.887	96	0.005	*
DS/DC	52.40	51.52	0.592	96	0.555	
SMN/MN	42.60	43.01	- 0.215	84	0.830	
Orbit						
LOH/LOBM	77.91	79.67	- 2.300	96	0.024	*
LOH/LOBD	83.11	84.70	- 1.808	96	0.074	
Dental arch						
MB/ML	116.86	121.02	- 2.393	84	0.019	*
Mandible						
LM/BCB	81.46	85.59	- 4.508	77	0.000	*

Table 275
"t" SCORES FOR MEASUREMENTS OF:
FORT ANCIENT MUSKOGID-HISTORIC MUSKOGID MALE SERIES

(N = F. A. Muskogid 50; Hist. Musk. Ser. 18)

	$\bar{X}_{FAM}$	$\bar{X}_{HMS}$	t-ratio	DF	t-prob.	Sig. diff.
Cranial vault						
CM	152.85	153.43	- 0.524	65	0.602	
TP	4.98	5.17	- 0.847	42	0.402	
L	178.18	179.28	- 0.541	42	0.591	
B	144.36	140.39	3.978	50	0.000	*
MF	95.12	92.83	1.746	66	0.085	
H	136.12	140.61	- 3.574	66	0.001	*
PAH	116.62	------	-------	---	-----	
BPH	------	23.17	-------	---	-----	
LB	103.52	102.72	0.573	66	0.569	
Face						
TFH	123.84	125.00	- 0.825	60	0.413	
UFH	73.26	75.16	- 2.097	66	0.039	*
TFB	141.42	139.72	1.277	20	0.216	
MFB	102.40	103.17	- 0.571	21	0.574	
IOB	99.98	98.00	2.135	66	0.036	*
SIOB	17.38	19.28	- 3.119	66	0.003	*
BOB	101.00	98.72	2.625	21	0.016	*
AIB	20.73	19.17	2.889	66	0.005	*
Nasal structure						
NB	27.06	25.72	2.911	66	0.005	*
NH	53.06	53.78	- 1.161	66	0.250	
DC	22.42	20.78	3.205	66	0.002	*
DS	11.64	12.11	- 1.412	66	0.163	
MN	9.76	10.17	- 0.650	20	0.523	
SMN	4.08	4.44	- 1.621	66	0.110	
Orbit						
LOH	33.88	34.11	- 0.622	42	0.537	
LOBM	43.54	42.72	1.829	20	0.082	
LOBD	40.80	40.00	1.679	19	0.110	
Dental arch						
MB	64.32	67.22	- 2.525	42	0.015	*
ML	55.08	57.67	- 3.497	22	0.002	*
FL	98.68	101.67	- 2.898	22	0.008	*
FLA	97.38	100.06	- 2.542	22	0.019	*
Mandible						
LM	105.36	113.00	- 7.107	66	0.000	*
BCB	129.26	122.44	6.570	66	0.000	*
SH	36.00	37.89	- 4.230	53	0.000	*
BA	105.32	103.00	2.019	66	0.048	
RL	35.42	35.78	- 0.524	66	0.602	
Facial angles						
G∠	119.60	123.83	- 3.578	66	0.001	*

Table 276

"t" SCORES FOR INDICES OF:
FORT ANCIENT MUSKOGID-HISTORIC MUSKOGID MALE SERIES

(N = F. A Muskogid 50; Hist. Musk. Ser. 18)

	$\bar{X}_{FAM}$	$\bar{X}_{HMS}$	t-ratio	DF	t-prob.	Sig. diff.
Cranial vault						
B/L	79.27	78.39	0.560	61	0.578	
H/L	74.69	78.51	- 2.226	63	0.030	*
H/B	94.44	100.18	- 5.083	66	0.000	*
H/L+B/2	84.58	88.00	- 3.173	66	0.002	*
PAH/L	65.74	------	-------	---	-----	
BPH/H	------	16.47	-------	--	-----	
MF/B	65.92	66.16	- 0.255	66	0.799	
Face						
TFH/TFB	85.51	89.55	- 2.499	63	0.015	*
UFH/TFB	51.82	53.82	- 3.158	66	0.002	*
UFH/MFB	71.65	72.96	- 1.319	66	0.192	
TFB/B	98.13	99.57	- 1.409	66	0.164	
MF/TFB	67.20	66.55	0.680	66	0.499	
BA/MF	111.10	111.17	- 0.034	66	0.973	
BA/TFB	74.51	73.82	0.730	66	0.468	
SIOB/IOB	17.31	19.65	- 4.241	66	0.000	*
AIB/BOB	20.42	19.41	2.270	66	0.027	*
Nasal structure						
NB/NH	51.04	47.84	3.902	48	0.000	*
DS/DC	52.40	58.63	- 3.077	66	0.003	*
SMN/MN	42.60	45.54	- 0.976	21	0.340	
Orbit						
LOH/LOBM	77.91	79.95	- 1.875	66	0.065	
LOH/LOBD	83.11	85.46	- 1.832	66	0.072	
Dental arch						
MB/ML	116.86	116.66	0.104	53	0.918	
Mandible						
LM/BCB	81.46	86.79	- 1.055	15	0.308	

APPENDIX E

Table 277

"t" SCORES FOR MEASUREMENTS OF: FORT ANCIENT MUSKOGID-

HISTORIC MUSKOGID

FEMALE SERIES

(N = F. A. Muskogid 54; Hist. Muskogid 3)

	$\bar{X}_{FAM}$	$\bar{X}_{HMS}$	t-ratio	DF*	t-prob.	Sig. diff.
Cranial vault						
CM	139.25	146.78	-2.440	53	0.018	*
TP	5.17	4.67	0.963	55	0.340	
L	171.81	167.00	1.716	55	0.092	
B	139.94	134.00	2.342	55	0.023	*
MF	91.93	91.00	0.412	55	0.682	
H	132.81	139.33	-5.824	12	0.000	*
PAH	113.44	------	-------	--	-----	
BPH	------	------	-------	--	-----	
LB	100.04	99.67	0.692	10	0.505	
Face						
TFH	111.80	------	-------	--	-----	
UFH	68.17	68.67	-0.117	0	1.000	
TFB	130.63	129.67	0.398	55	0.693	
MFB	98.00	98.33	-0.112	0	1.000	
IOB	95.33	95.33	0.0	9	1.000	
SIOB	16.06	17.67	-0.907	0	1.000	
BOB	97.65	97.33	0.223	55	0.824	
AIB	19.31	16.67	2.719	55	0.009	*
Nasal structure						
NB	26.35	34.00	-1.166	0	1.000	
NH	49.70	51.00	-1.120	55	0.267	
DC	21.00	20.33	1.618	3	1.000	
DS	10.93	11.33	-0.869	55	0.389	
MN	8.83	7.67	1.365	55	0.178	
SMN	3.56	3.67	-0.263	55	0.794	
Orbit						
LOH	33.04	33.00	0.043	55	0.966	
LOBM	42.30	43.00	-0.805	55	0.424	
LOBD	39.20	39.33	-0.189	55	0.851	

Table 277 - continued

Dental arch					
MB	62.76	64.00	- 0.916	32	0.366
ML	52.65	51.00	0.375	55	0.709
FL	96.78	98.00	- 0.737	55	0.464
FLA	95.57	96.33	- 0.462	55	0.646
Mandible					
LM	101.19	------	-------	--	-----
BCB	124.87	------	-------	--	-----
SH	32.81	------	-------	--	-----
BA	97.61	------	-------	--	-----
RL	33.24	------	-------	--	-----
Facial angles					
G/	123.37°	------	-------	--	-----

*DF $\leq$ 3, t-prob. = 1

APPENDIX E

Table 278

"t" SCORES FOR INDICES OF: FORT ANCIENT MUSKOGID-HISTORIC MUSKOGID

FEMALE SERIES

(N = F. A. Muskogid 54; Hist. Muskogid 3)

	$\bar{X}_{FAM}$	$\bar{X}_{HMS}$	t-ratio	DF*	t-prob.	Sig. diff.
Cranial vault						
B/L	77.25	80.25	- 1.515	8	0.168	
H/L	76.09	83.44	- 7.557	5	0.0	*
H/B	94.70	104.04	- 2.891	55	0.006	*
H/L+B/2	82.87	92.06	- 6.588	4	0.0	*
PAH/L	57.61	------	-------	--	-----	
BPH/H	------	------	-------	--	-----	
MF/B	58.46	67.92	- 3.422	24	0.002	*
Face						
TFH/TFB	75.78	------	-------	--	-----	
UFH/TFB	52.37	53.01	- 0.186	0	1.000	
UFH/MFB	67.24	69.70	- 0.576	55	0.567	
TFB/B	85.83	96.87	- 2.519	3	1.000	
MF/TFB	72.00	70.27	0.579	55	0.565	
BA/MF	102.78	------	-------	--	-----	
BA/TFB	66.48	------	-------	--	-----	
SIOB/IOB	26.54	18.52	2.203	23	0.038	*
AIB/BOB	23.78	17.12	4.739	52	0.000	*
Nasal structure						
NB/NH	56.25	53.75	0.309	55	0.758	
DS/DC	56.04	55.79	0.040	55	0.968	
SMN/MN	48.27	49.54	- 0.112	55	0.912	
Orbit						
LOH/LOBM	78.96	76.83	0.817	55	0.417	
LOH/LOBD	82.05	83.87	- 0.451	55	0.653	
Dental arch						
MB/ML	99.41	125.49	- 4.171	53	0.000	*
Mandible						
LM/BCB	78.26	------	-------	--	-----	

*DF $\leq$ 3, t-prob. = 1

Table 279

"t" SCORES FOR MEASUREMENTS OF: FORT ANCIENT MUSKOGID-ILINID FEMALE VARIETY

(N = F. A. Muskogid 54; Ilinid 19)

	$\bar{X}_{FAM}$	$\bar{X}_{Ili}$	t-ratio	DF	t-prob.	Sig. diff.
Cranial vault						
CM	139.25	147.61	- 2.606	62	0.011	*
TP	5.17	4.47	3.089	71	0.003	*
L	171.81	174.05	- 1.288	22	0.211	
B	139.94	135.53	3.833	71	0.000	*
MF	91.93	90.95	0.935	71	0.353	
H	132.81	133.26	- 0.320	43	0.750	
PAH	113.44	113.89	- 0.431	71	0.668	
BPH	------	------	-------	--	-----	
LB	100.04	96.89	3.779	71	0.000	*
Face						
TFH	111.80	112.05	- 0.378	71	0.707	
UFH	68.17	66.74	2.825	45	0.007	*
TFB	130.63	131.74	- 0.981	71	0.330	
MFB	98.00	95.05	3.522	71	0.001	*
IOB	95.33	94.79	0.650	71	0.518	
SIOB	16.06	15.32	1.475	23	0.154	
BOB	97.65	95.79	2.175	22	0.041	
AIB	19.31	17.47	4.237	71	0.000	*
Nasal structure						
NB	26.35	24.68	3.589	23	0.002	*
NH	49.70	49.89	- 0.390	71	0.698	
DC	21.00	20.42	1.204	71	0.232	
DS	10.93	11.32	- 0.805	18	0.431	
MN	8.83	7.84	2.401	71	0.019	*
SMN	3.56	3.89	- 1.306	22	0.205	
Orbit						
LOH	33.04	32.95	0.221	71	0.726	
LOBM	42.30	41.37	2.237	71	0.028	*
LOBD	39.20	38.95	0.647	23	0.524	

APPENDIX E

Table 279 - continued

Dental arch						
MB	62.76	60.11	2.079	59	0.042	
ML	52.65	51.11	1.290	69	0.201	
FL	96.78	94.95	2.388	71	0.020	*
FLA	95.57	92.89	3.402	71	0.001	*
Mandible						
LM	101.19	99.21	2.128	71	0.037	*
BCB	124.87	118.89	5.581	71	0.000	*
SH	32.81	34.11	-2.942	71	0.004	*
BA	97.61	95.16	1.480	19	0.155	
RL	33.24	30.79	5.117	71	0.000	*
Facial angles						
G/	123.37°	123.63°	-0.239	71	0.811	

Table 280

"t" SCORES FOR INDICES OF: FORT ANCIENT MUSKOGID-ILINID

FEMALE VARIETY

(N = F. A. Muskogid 54; Ilinid 19)

	$\bar{x}_{FAM}$	$\bar{x}_{Ili}$	t-ratio	DF	t-prob.	Sig. diff.
Cranial vault						
B/L	77.25	77.93	- 0.422	66	0.674	
H/L	76.09	76.60	- 0.625	66	0.534	
H/B	94.70	98.37	- 3.504	53	0.000	*
H/L+B/2	82.87	86.11	- 3.022	67	0.004	*
PAH/L	57.61	68.48	- 2.738	55	0.008	*
BPH/H	------	------	-------	--	-----	
MF/B	58.46	67.14	- 3.448	59	0.001	*
Face						
TFH/TFB	75.78	85.15	- 2.827	57	0.006	*
UFH/TFB	52.37	50.72	2.513	71	0.014	*
UFH/MFB	67.24	70.29	- 2.610	69	0.011	*
TFB/B	85.83	97.24	- 4.313	59	0.000	*
MF/TFB	72.00	69.07	2.958	50	0.005	*
BA/MF	102.78	104.79	- 0.822	71	0.414	
BA/TFB	66.48	72.23	- 1.995	64	0.050	
SIOB/IOB	26.54	16.14	3.247	53	0.002	*
AIB/BOB	23.78	18.26	3.921	58	0.000	*
Nasal structure						
NB/NH	56.25	49.56	3.117	69	0.003	*
DS/DC	56.04	55.60	0.159	71	0.874	
SMN/MN	48.27	46.50	0.363	71	0.717	
Orbit						
LOH/LOBM	78.96	79.76	- 0.662	71	0.510	
LOH/LOBD	82.05	84.71	- 1.529	71	0.131	
Dental arch						
MB/ML	99.41	117.83	- 2.944	55	0.005	*
Mandible						
LM/BCB	78.26	83.57	- 3.806	58	0.000	*

APPENDIX E 643

Table 281
"t" SCORES FOR MEASUREMENTS OF:
FORT ANCIENT MUSKOGID-SHAWNEE MALE SERIES

(N = F. A. Muskogid 50; Shawnee 4)

	$\bar{X}_{FAM}$	$\bar{X}_{Sha}$	t-ratio	DF**	t-prob.	Sig. diff.
Cranial vault						
CM	152.58	153.50	- 0.297	51	0.768	
TP	4.98	4.50	0.924	52	0.360	
L	178.18	180.50	- 0.474	52	0.638	
B	144.36	141.00	0.811	1	1.000	
MF	95.12	96.00	- 0.342	52	0.734	
H	136.12	139.00	- 0.646	1	1.000	
PAH	116.62	118.50	- 0.680	1	1.000	
BPH	------	------	------	---	-----	
LB	103.52	104.50	- 0.351	52	0.727	
Face						
TFH	123.84	132.00	- 2.004	52	0.050	
UFH	73.26	73.00	- 0.076	1	1.000	
TFB	141.42	140.75	0.395	52	0.695	
MFB	102.40	101.25	0.645	52	0.522	
IOB	99.98	101.50	- 0.882	52	0.382	
SIOB	17.38	19.00	- 1.477	52	0.146	
BOB	101.00	101.50	- 0.403	52	0.689	
AIB	20.73	20.00	0.696	52	0.490	
Nasal structure						
NB	27.06	25.25	1.929	52	0.059	
NH	53.06	53.25	- 0.075	1	1.000	
DC	22.42	21.50	2.305	8	0.050	
DS	11.64	11.25	0.646	52	0.521	
MN	9.76	8.00	2.184	52	0.034	*
SMN	4.08	3.50	0.887	1	1.000	
Orbit						
LOH	33.88	33.25	0.691	52	0.493	
LOBM	43.54	45.00	- 2.524	52	0.015	*
LOBD	40.80	41.75	- 1.614	52	0.113	
Dental arch						
MB	64.32	62.75	0.575	52	0.568	
ML	55.08	56.00	- 0.802	52	0.427	
FL	98.68	101.25	- 1.622	52	0.111	
FLA	97.38	99.75	- 1.506	52	0.138	
Mandible						
LM	105.36	107.00	- 0.822	52	0.415	
BCB	129.26	128.75	0.641	5	0.550	
SH	36.00	35.00	0.000	52	1.000	
BA	105.32	107.00	- 0.767	52	0.447	
RL	35.42	34.00	1.065	52	0.292	
Facial angles						
G∠	119.60	119.75	- 0.062	52	0.951	

** DF ≤ 3, t-prob. = 1

Table 282

"t" SCORES FOR INDICES OF:
FORT ANCIENT MUSKOGID-SHAWNEE MALE SERIES

(N = F. A. Muskogid 50; Shawnee 4)

	$\overline{X}_{FAM}$	$\overline{X}_{Sha}$	t-ratio	DF**	t-prob.	Sig. diff.
Cranial vault						
B/L	79.27	78.40	0.170	52	0.866	
H/L	74.69	76.99	- 1.203	15	0.248	
H/B	94.44	98.92	- 0.904	1	1.000	
H/L+B/2	84.58	86.43	- 0.865	52	0.391	
PAH/L	65.74	65.71	0.014	52	0.989	
BPH/H	------	------	-------	---	-----	
MF/B	65.92	68.20	- 1.250	52	0.217	
Face						
TFH/TFB	85.51	93.84	- 1.682	52	0.099	
UFH/TFB	51.82	51.84	- 0.009	1	1.000	
UFH/MFB	71.65	72.15	- 0.137	1	1.000	
TFB/B	98.13	100.02	- 1.020	52	0.312	
MF/TFB	67.20	68.23	- 0.606	52	0.547	
BA/MF	111.10	111.58	- 0.137	52	0.891	
BA/TFB	74.51	76.02	- 0.939	52	0.352	
SIOB/IOB	17.31	18.74	- 1.425	52	0.160	
AIB/BOB	20.42	19.69	0.877	52	0.385	
Nasal structure						
NB/NH	51.04	47.45	1.726	52	0.090	
DS/DC	52.40	52.38	0.005	52	0.996	
SMN/MN	42.60	43.36	- 0.112	1	1.000	
Orbit						
LOH/LOBM	77.91	73.86	1.965	52	0.055	
LOH/LOBD	83.11	79.64	1.478	52	0.146	
Dental arch						
MB/ML	116.86	112.30	0.898	52	0.373	
Mandible						
LM/BCB	81.46	83.13	- 0.946	52	0.348	

** DF ≤ 3, t-prob. = 1

APPENDIX E

Table 283

"t" SCORES FOR MEASUREMENTS OF:
SHAWNEE-HISTORIC MUSKOGID MALE SERIES

(N = Shawnee 4; Hist. Musk. 18)

	$\bar{x}_{Sha}$	$\bar{x}_{HMS}$	t-ratio	DF**	t-prob.	Sig. diff.
Cranial vault						
CM	153.50	153.43	0.035	20	0.972	
TP	4.50	5.17	- 1.750	20	0.095	
L	180.50	179.28	0.319	20	0.753	
B	141.00	140.39	0.148	1	1.000	
MF	96.00	92.83	1.587	20	0.128	
H	139.00	140.61	- 0.352	1	1.000	
PAH	118.50	------	-------	---	-----	
BPH	------	23.17	-------	---	-----	
LB	104.50	102.72	0.703	20	0.490	
Face						
TFH	132.00	125.00	3.127	20	0.005	*
UFH	73.00	76.16	- 0.617	1	1.000	
TFB	140.75	139.72	0.368	20	0.717	
MFB	101.25	103.17	- 0.700	20	0.492	
IOB	101.50	98.00	1.871	20	0.076	
SIOB	19.00	19.28	- 0.213	20	0.834	
BOB	101.50	98.72	1.534	20	0.141	
AIB	20.00	19.17	0.803	20	0.431	
Nasal structure						
NB	25.25	25.72	- 0.348	1	1.000	
NH	53.25	53.78	- 0.208	1	1.000	
DC	21.50	20.78	1.525	12	0.153	
DS	11.25	12.11	- 1.044	20	0.309	
MN	8.00	10.17	- 3.039	14	0.009	*
SMN	3.50	4.44	- 1.650	20	0.115	
Orbit						
LOH	33.25	34.11	- 0.806	1	1.000	
LOBM	45.00	42.72	2.428	20	0.025	*
LOBD	41.75	40.00	1.708	20	0.103	
Dental arch						
MB	62.75	67.22	- 2.317	20	0.031	*
ML	56.00	57.67	- 1.022	20	0.319	
FL	101.25	101.67	- 0.185	20	0.855	
FLA	99.75	100.06	- 0.136	20	0.893	
Mandible						
LM	107.00	113.00	- 2.870	20	0.009	*
BCB	128.75	122.44	5.026	17	0.000	*
SH	36.00	37.89	- 1.137	1	1.000	
BA	107.00	103.00	1.803	20	0.086	
RL	34.00	35.78	- 1.638	20	0.117	
Facial angles						
G∠	119.75	123.83	- 1.200	1	1.000	

** DF ≤ 3, t-prob. = 1

Table 284

"t" SCORES FOR INDICES OF:
SHAWNEE-HISTORIC MUSKOGID MALE SERIES

(N = Shawnee 4; Hist. Musk. 18)

	$\bar{x}_{Sha}$	$\bar{x}_{HMS}$	t-ratio	DF**	t-prob.	Sig. diff.
Cranial vault						
B/L	78.40	78.39	0.002	1	1.000	
H/L	76.99	78.51	- 0.809	20	0.428	
H/B	98.92	100.18	- 0.252	1	1.000	
H/L+B/2	86.43	88.00	- 0.819	20	0.423	
PAH/L	65.71	------	------	---	-----	
BPH/H	------	16.47	------	---	-----	
MF/B	68.20	66.16	1.174	20	0.254	
Face						
TFH/TFB	93.84	89.55	2.023	20	0.057	
UFH/TFB	51.84	53.82	- 0.906	1	1.000	
UFH/MFB	72.15	72.96	- 0.215	1	1.000	
TFB/B	100.02	99.57	0.182	20	0.857	
MF/TFB	68.23	66.55	0.809	20	0.428	
BA/MF	111.58	111.17	0.108	20	0.915	
BA/TFB	76.02	73.82	1.041	20	0.310	
SIOB/IOB	18.74	19.65	- 0.755	20	0.459	
AIB/BOB	19.69	19.41	0.305	20	0.763	
Nasal structure						
NB/NH	47.45	47.84	- 0.282	20	0.781	
DS/DC	52.38	58.63	- 1.340	20	0.195	
SMN/MN	43.36	45.54	- 0.328	20	0.747	
Orbit						
LOH/LOBM	73.86	79.95	- 2.893	20	0.009	*
LOH/LOBD	79.64	85.46	- 2.156	20	0.043	
Dental arch						
MB/ML	112.30	116.66	- 1.401	20	0.177	
Mandible						
LM/BCB	83.13	86.79	- 0.700	17	0.494	

** DF $\leq$ 3, t-prob. = 1

APPENDIX E 647

Table 285

POPULATION DISTANCE RATIOS,
FORT ANCIENT "VARIETAL" COMPARISONS
(Significantly differing t-probabilities on 0.04 level)

Series Compared	Ratio Measurements	Coeff. Measurements	Ratio Indices	Coeff. Indices	Ratios Combined
Fort Ancient Ilinid- Fort Ancient Muskogid - M	16/35	46	8/22	36	24/57
Fort Ancient Ilinid- Fort Ancient Muskogid - F	13/35	37	18/22	82	31/57
Fort Ancient Ilinid-Lenid - M	20/34	59	10/21	48	30/55
Fort Ancient Ilinid-Lenid - F	4/35	11	2/22	9	6/57
Fort Ancient Ilinid-Iswanid - M	33/35	94	7/22	32	40/57
Fort Ancient Ilinid-Muskogid - M	13/34	38	7/21	33	20/55
Fort Ancient Ilinid-Seneca - M	20/34	59	10/21	48	30/55
Fort Ancient Ilinid-Seneca - F	15/34	43	6/21	29	21/55
Fort Ancient Ilinid-Shawnee - M	4/34	12	2/22	9	6/56

Table 285 - continued

Fort Ancient Muskogid-Lenid - M	17/34	50	12/22	55	29/56
Fort Ancient Muskogid-Lenid - F	9/35	26	12/22	55	21/57
Fort Ancient Muskogid-Iswanid - M	27/34	79	9/21	43	36/55
Fort Ancient Muskogid-Muskogid - M	16/34	47	12/21	57	28/55
Fort Ancient Muskogid-Hist. Muskogid - M	17/34	50	9/21	43	26/55
Fort Ancient Muskogid-Hist.' Muskogid - F	4/27	15	7/17	41	11/44
Fort Ancient Muskogid-Ilinid - F	16/35	46	14/22	64	30/57
Fort Ancient Muskogid-Shawnee - M	2/35	6	0/22	--	2/57
Shawnee-Hist. Muskogid - M	6/34	18	1/22	5	7/56

APPENDIX F

DRAWINGS OF SAMPLE CRANIA FROM
EACH FOCUS AND VARIETY

Examples of Lenid, Ilinid,
Iswanid, Dakotid, and Muskogid varieties

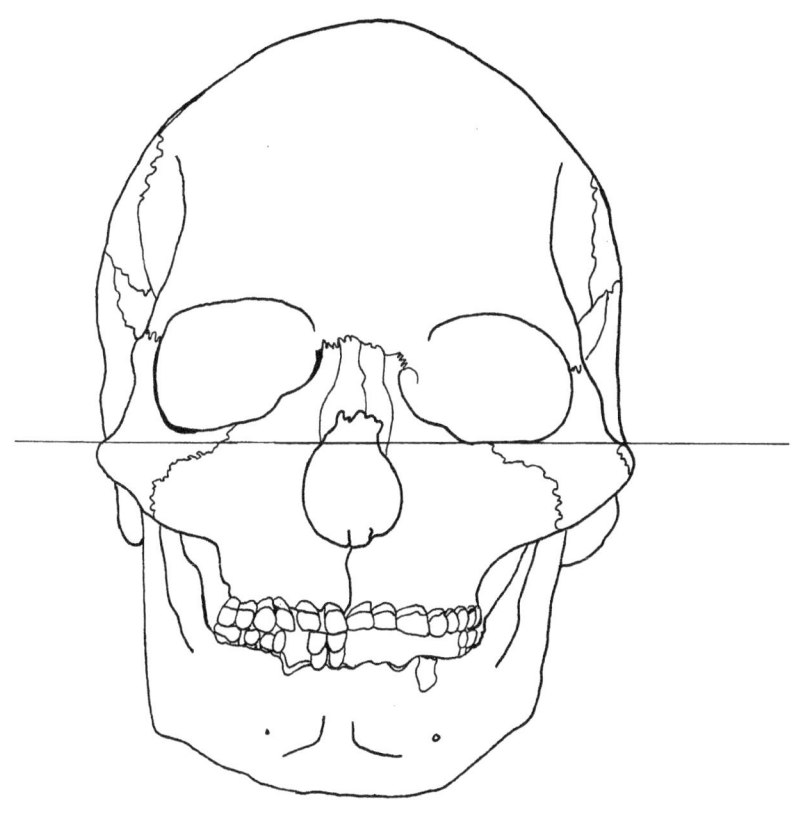

PLATE I - A

LENID VARIETY -- MALE
(FRONT VIEW)

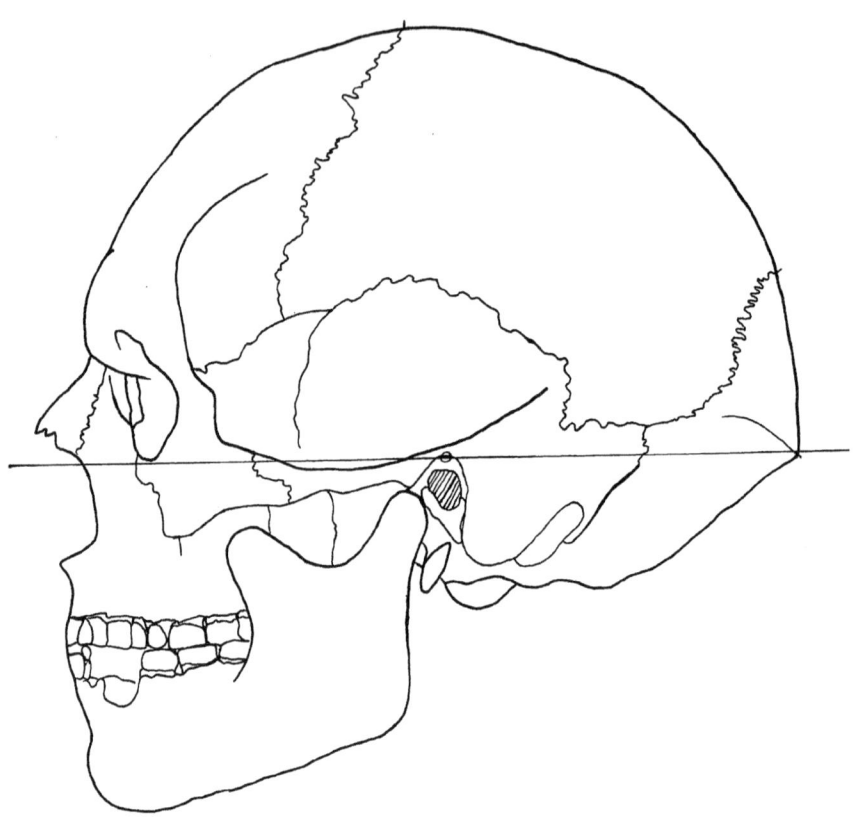

PLATE I - B

LENID VARIETY -- MALE

(LATERAL VIEW)

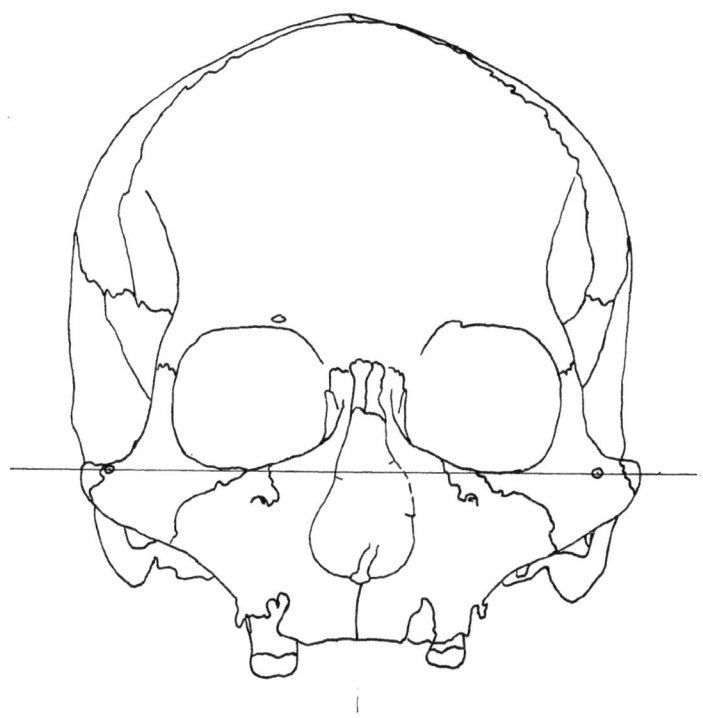

PLATE II - A

ILINID VARIETY -- MALE
(FRONT VIEW)

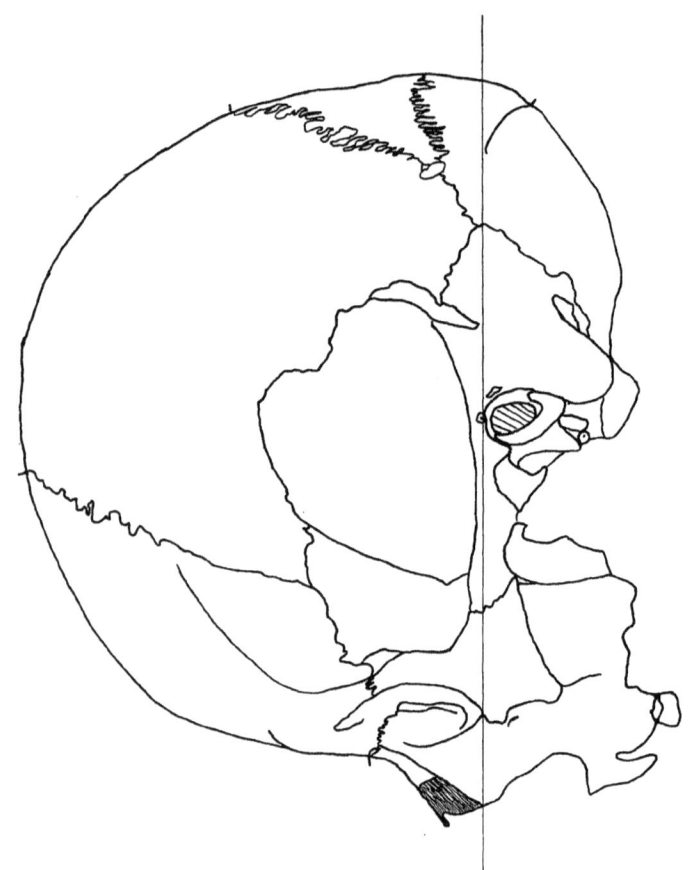

PLATE II - B

ILINID VARIETY -- MALE
(LATER VIEW)

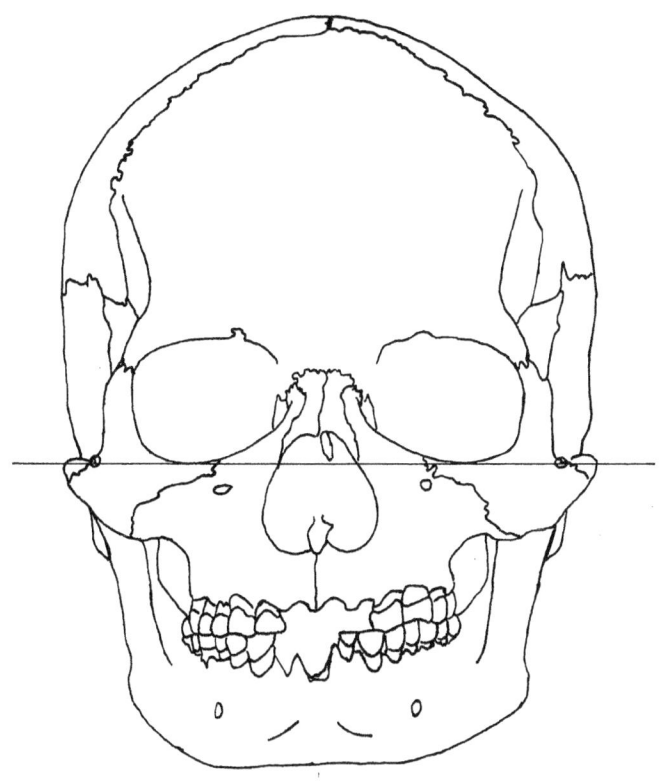

PLATE II - C

ILINID VARIETY -- FEMALE
(FRONT VIEW)

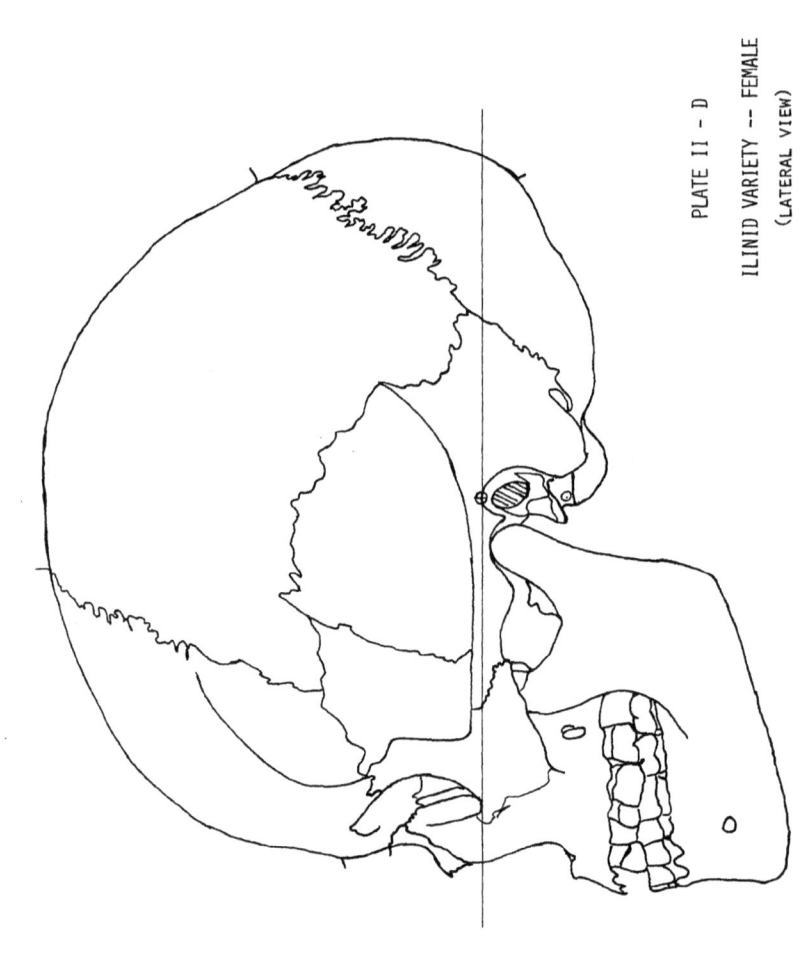

PLATE II - D

ILINID VARIETY -- FEMALE
(LATERAL VIEW)

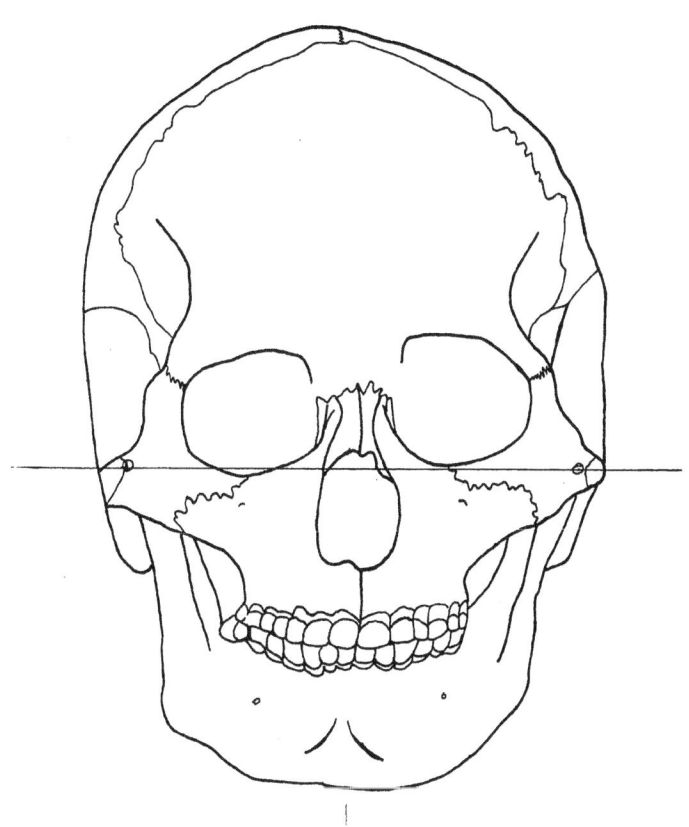

PLATE III - A

ISWANID VARIETY -- MALE
(FRONT VIEW)

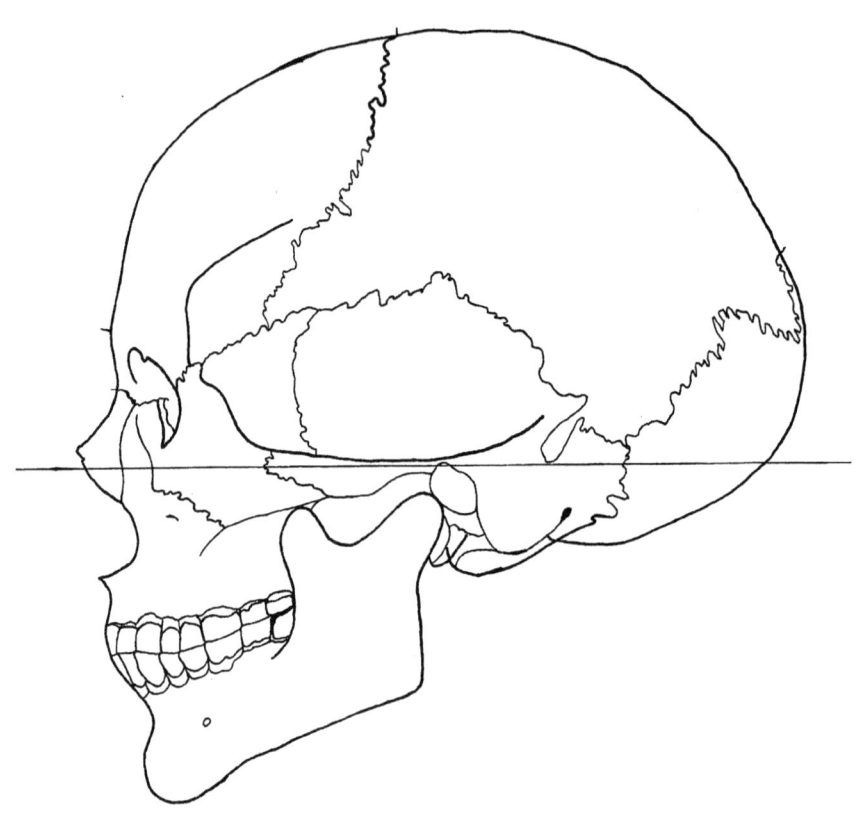

PLATE III - B

ISWANID VARIETY -- MALE

(LATERAL VIEW)

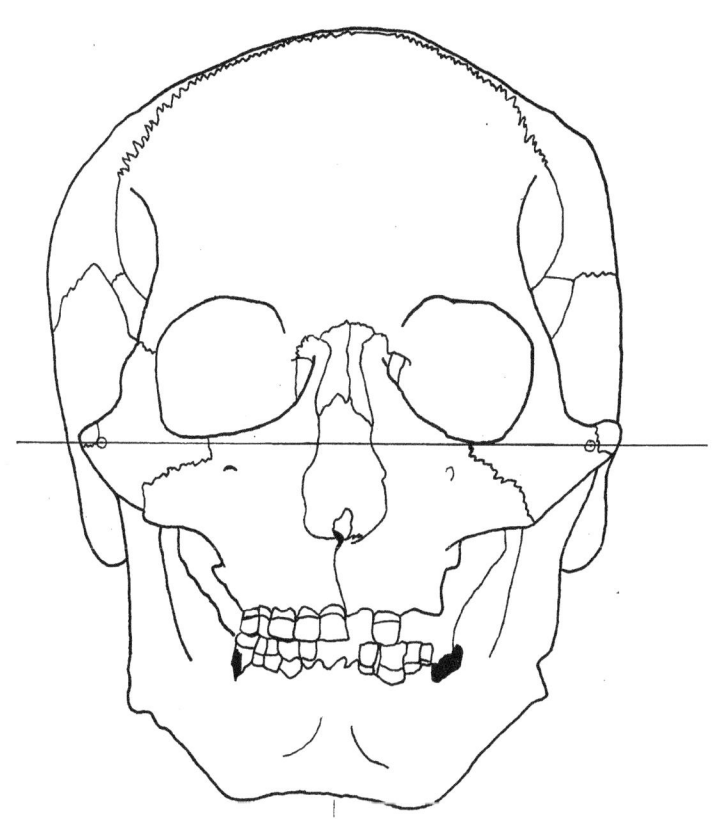

PLATE IV - A

DAKOTID VARIETY -- MALE
(FRONT VIEW)

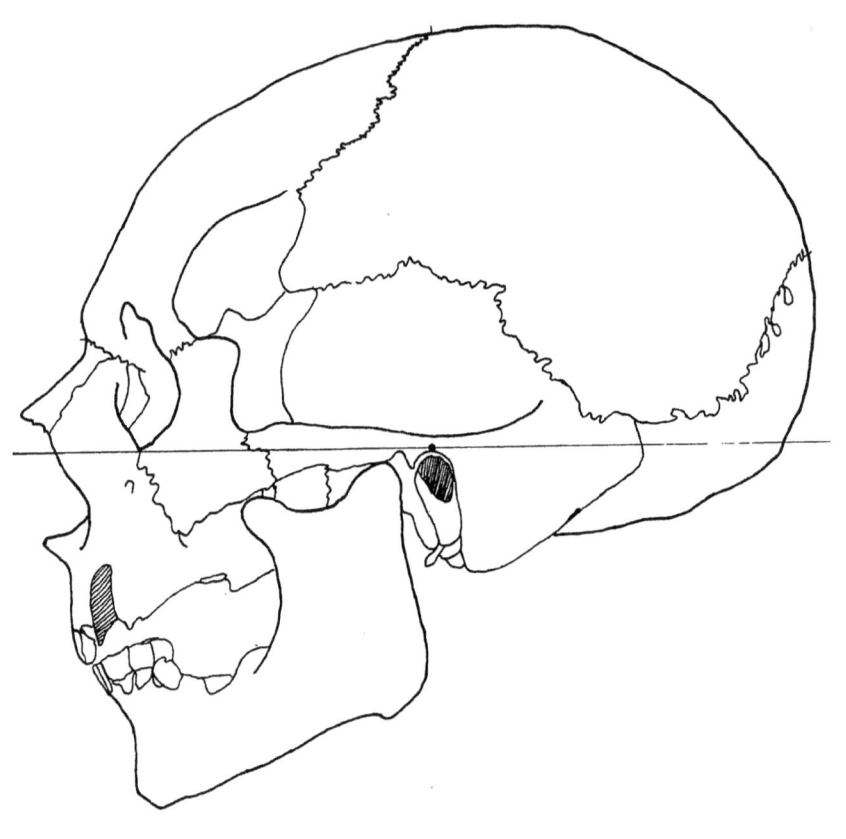

PLATE IV - B

DAKOTID VARIETY -- MALE

(LATERAL VIEW)

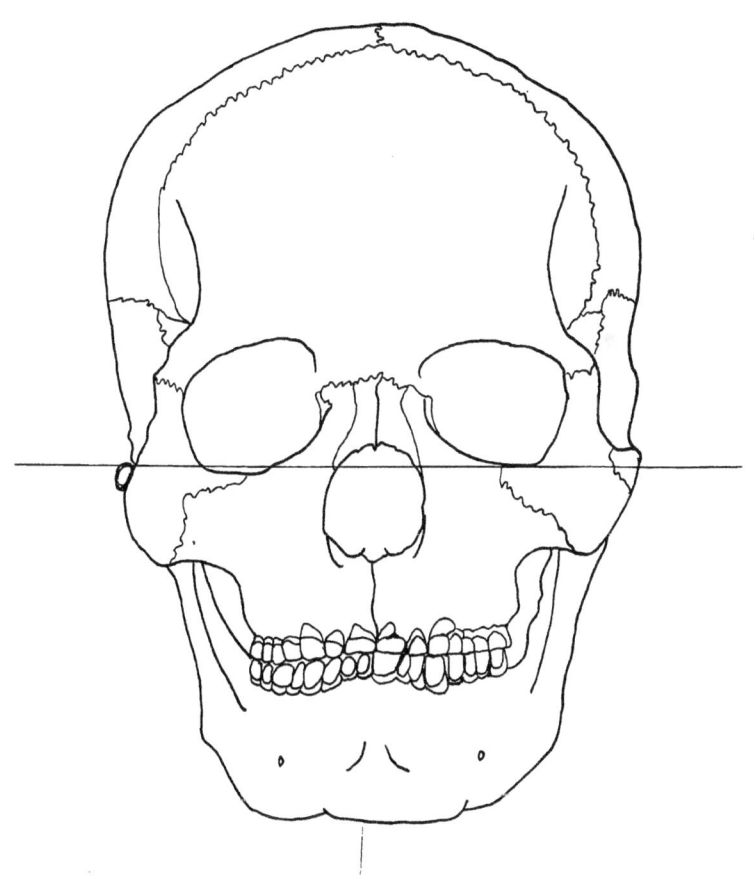

PLATE V - A

MUSKOGID VARIETY -- MALE
(FRONT VIEW)

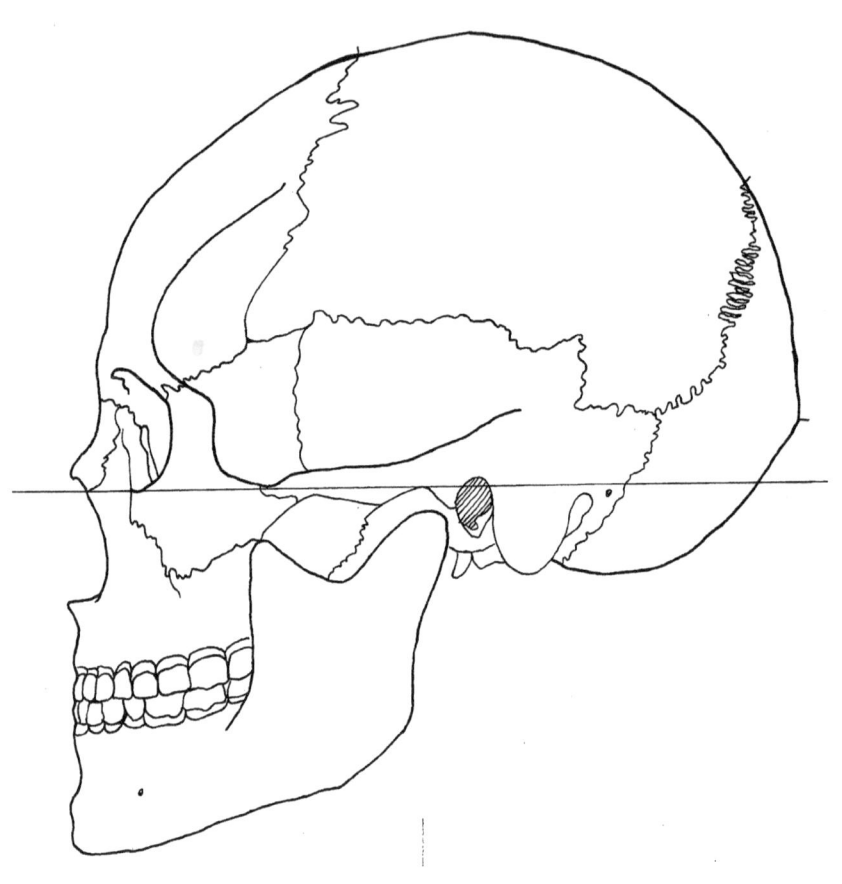

PLATE V - B

MUSKOGID VARIETY -- MALE

(LATERAL VIEW)

Baum Focus

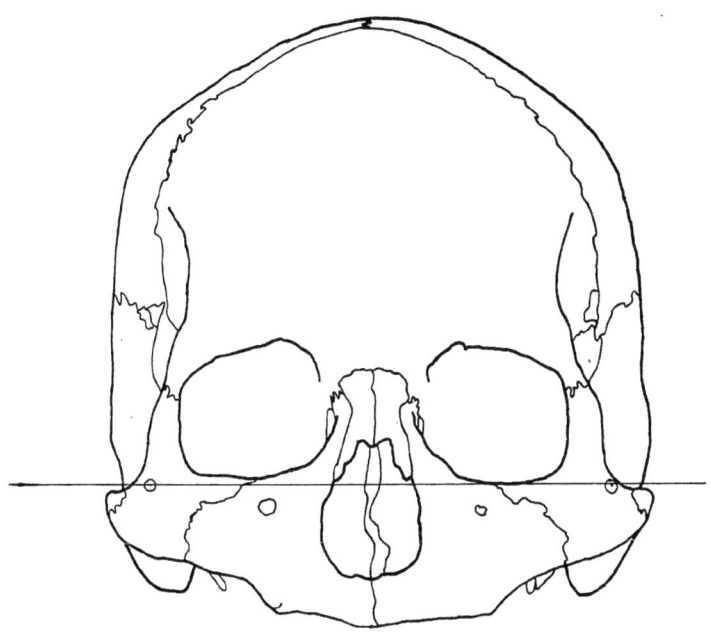

PLATE VI - A: BAUM VILLAGE SITE

UNDEFORMED ILINID TYPE MALE (USNM #134,733)

(FRONT VIEW)

PLATE VI - B: BAUM VILLAGE SITE

UNDEFORMED ILINID TYPE MALE (USNM #134,733)

(LATERAL VIEW)

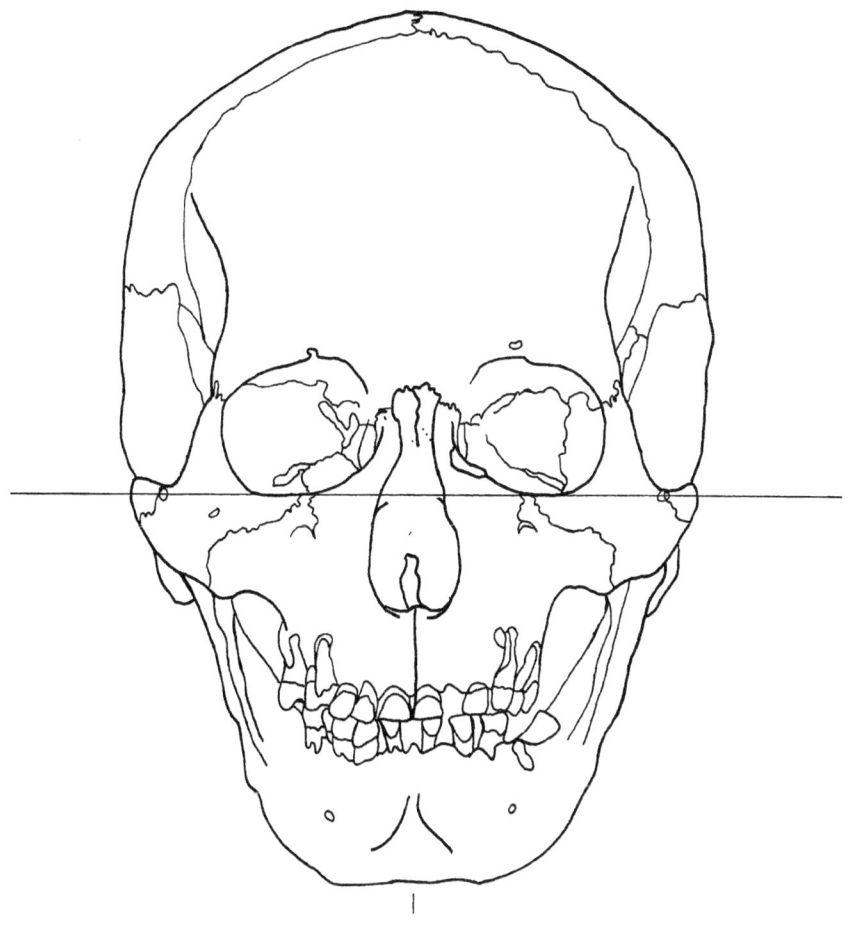

PLATE VI - C: GARTNER MOUND
UNDEFORMED ILINID TYPE MALE (USNM #328,785)
(FRONT VIEW)

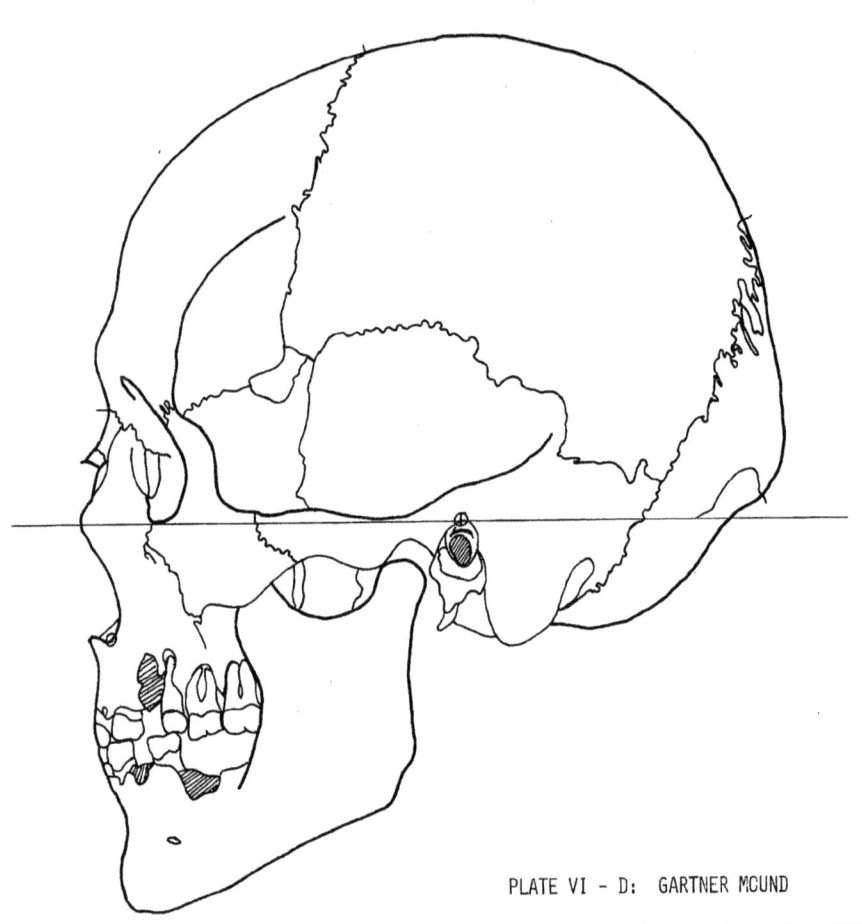

PLATE VI - D: GARTNER MOUND
UNDEFORMED ILINID TYPE MALE (USNM #328,785)
(LATERAL VIEW)

Feurt Focus

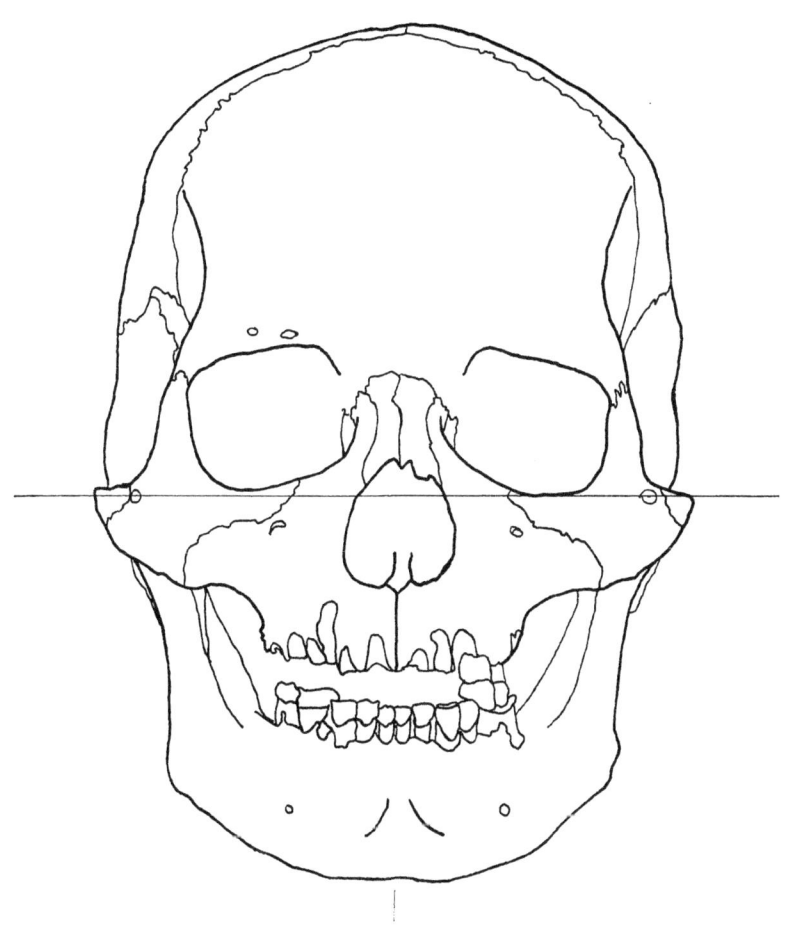

PLATE VII - A: FEURT MOUND
UNDEFORMED ILINID TYPE MALE (USNM #328,818)
(FRONT VIEW)

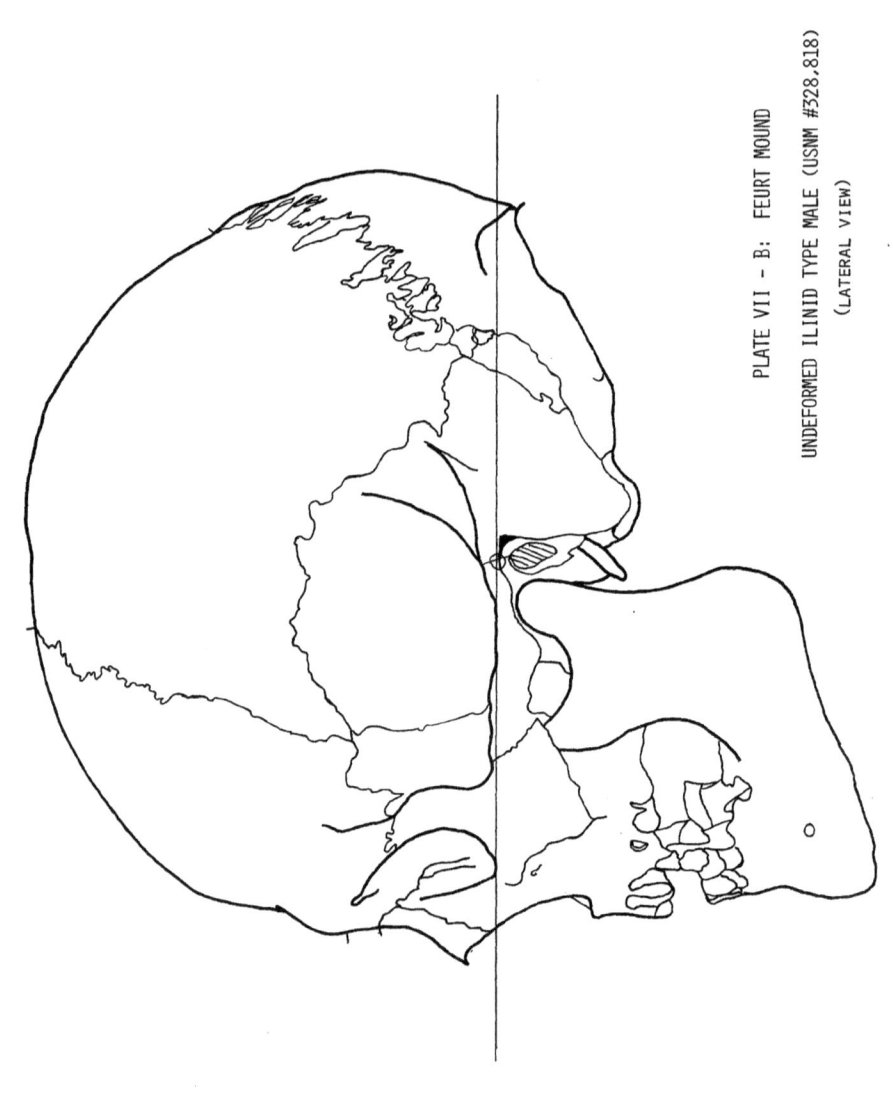

PLATE VII - B: FEURT MOUND
UNDEFORMED ILINID TYPE MALE (USNM #328,818)
(LATERAL VIEW)

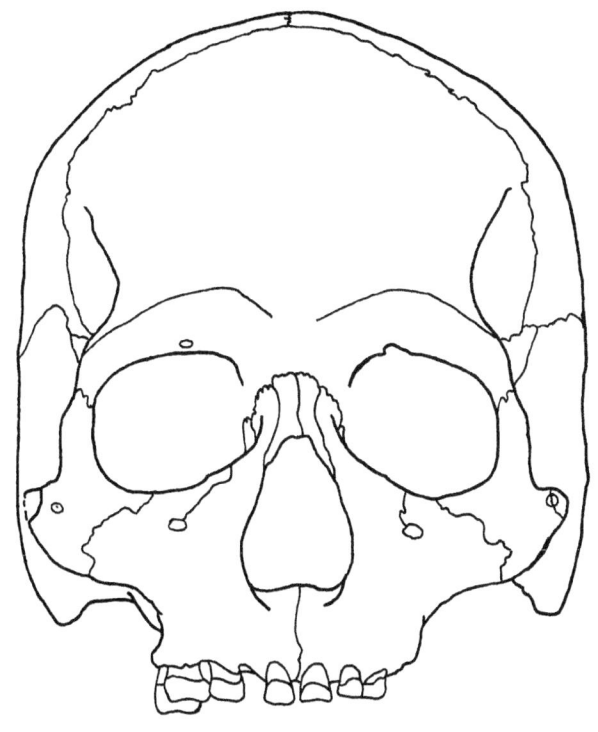

PLATE VII - C: FEURT MOUND

SL. DEFORMED MUSKOGID TYPE MALE (USNM #328,812)
(FRONT VIEW)

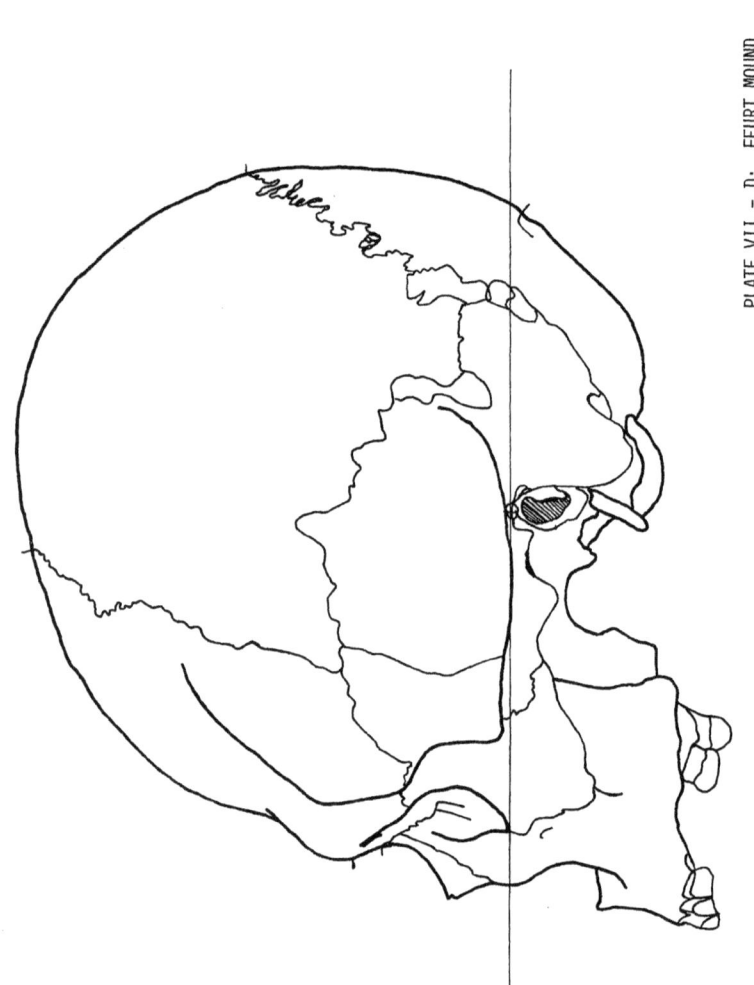

PLATE VII - D: FEURT MOUND
SL. DEFORMED MUSKOGID TYPE MALE (USNM #328,812)
(LATERAL VIEW)

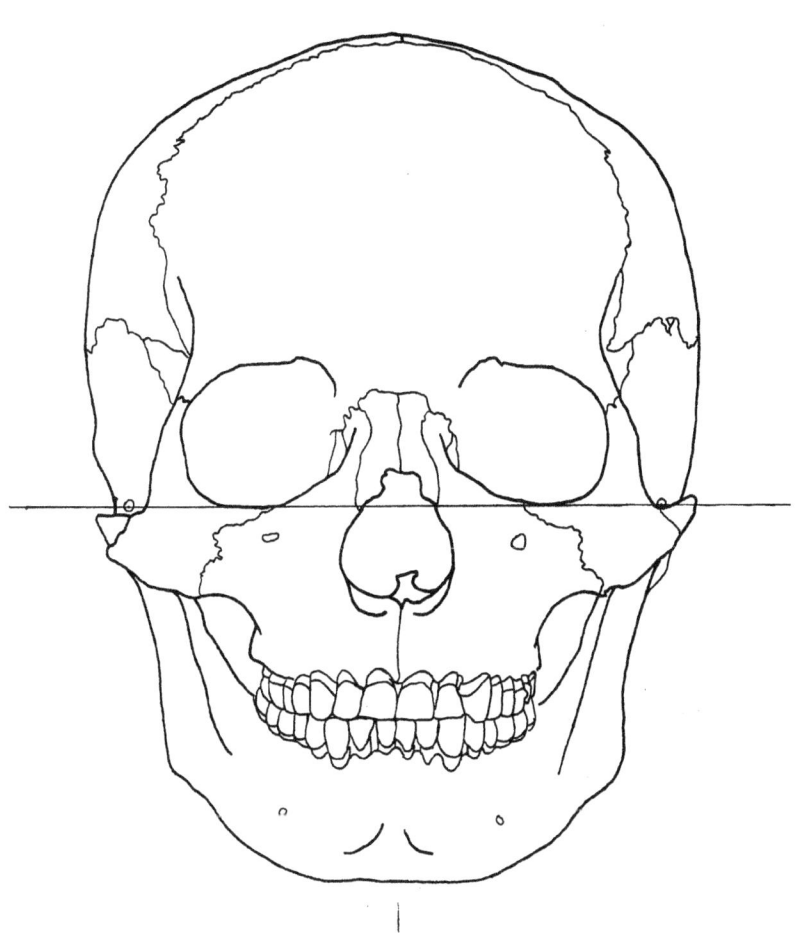

PLATE VII - E: GP 1 "OLD FORT" SITE
SL. DEFORMED MUSKOGID TYPE MALE (UKMA 21-10)
(FRONT VIEW)

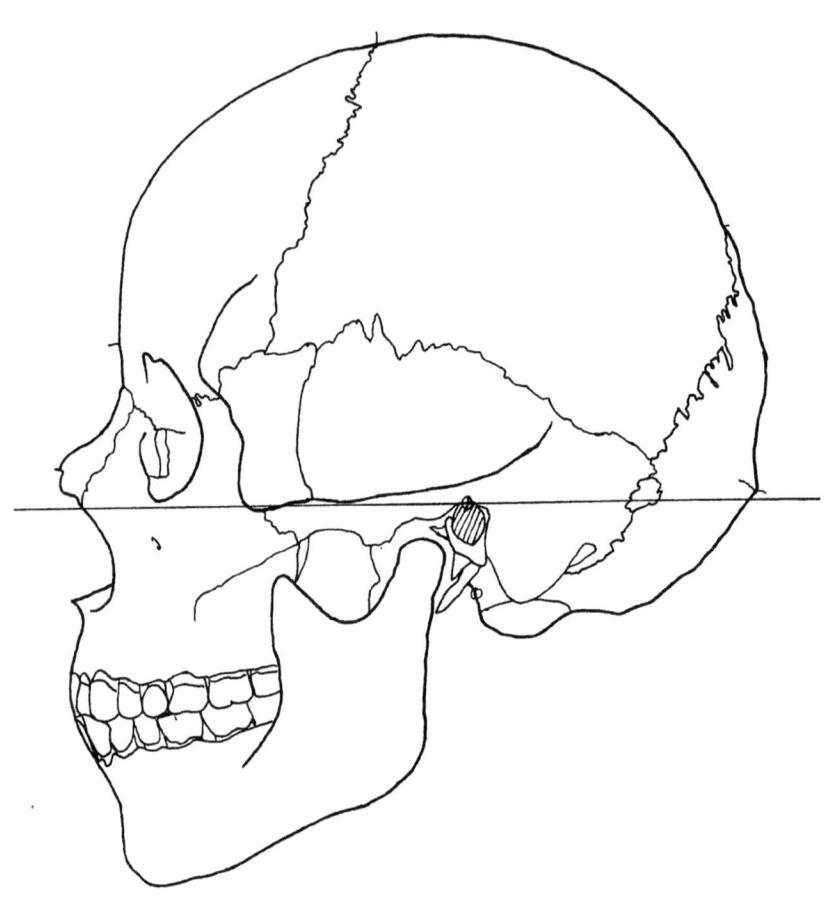

PLATE VII - F: GP 1 "OLD FORT" SITE
SL. DEFORMED MUSKOGID TYPE MALE (UKMA 21-10)
(LATERAL VIEW)

Anderson Focus

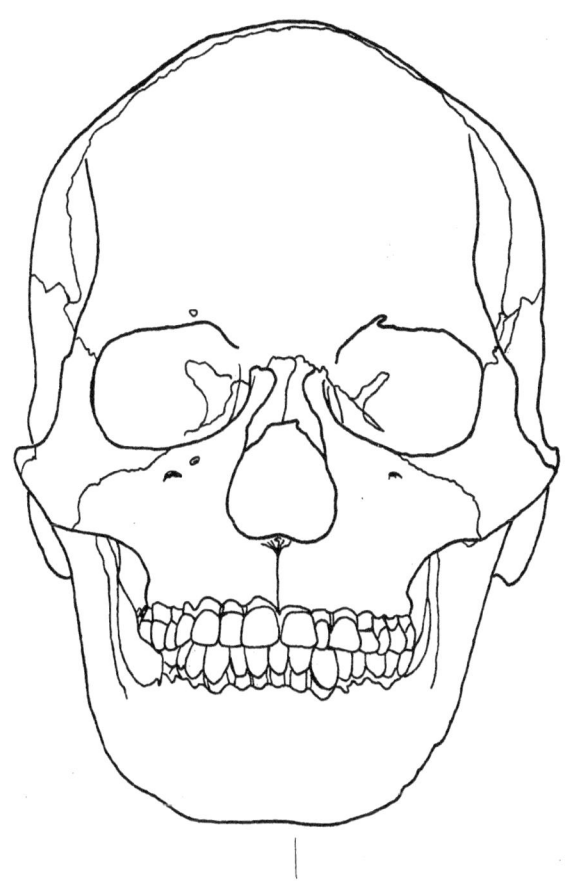

PLATE VIII - A: FORT ANCIENT VILLAGE SITE
UNDEFORMED ILINID TYPE MALE (FAM #A91)
(FRONT VIEW)

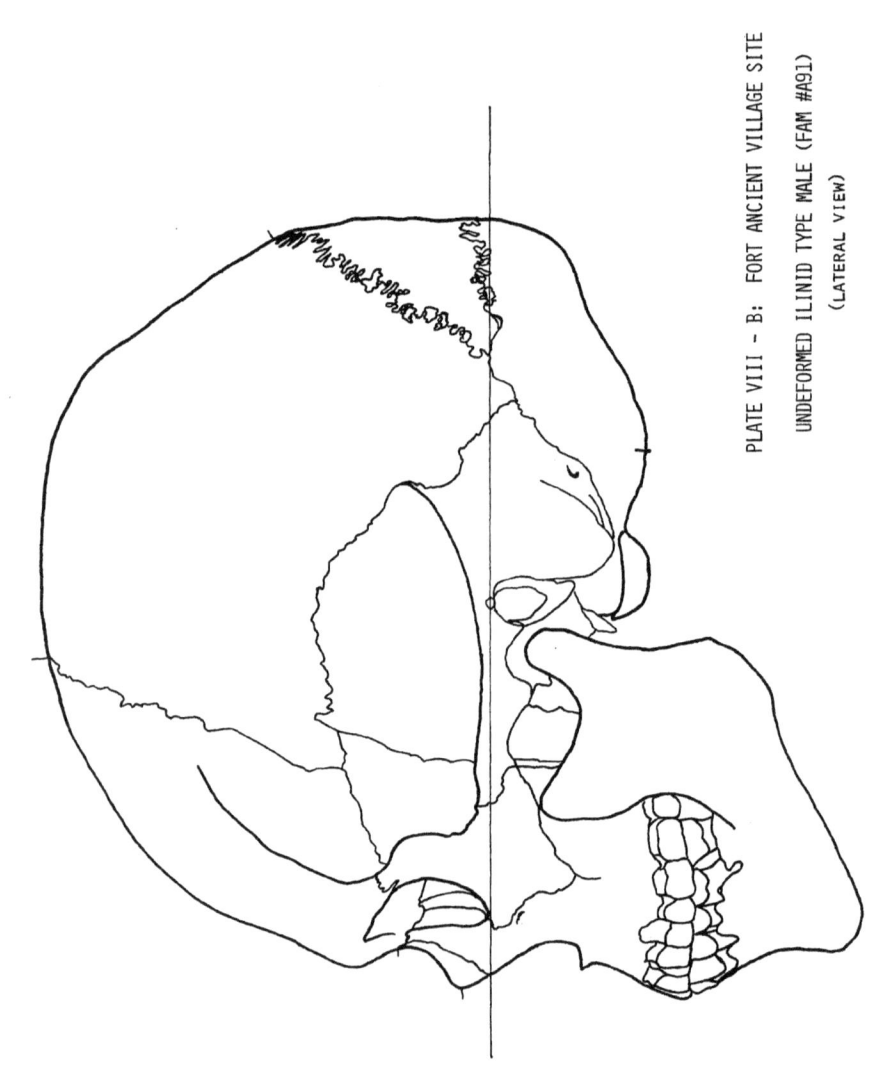

PLATE VIII - B: FORT ANCIENT VILLAGE SITE
UNDEFORMED ILINID TYPE MALE (FAM #A91)
(LATERAL VIEW)

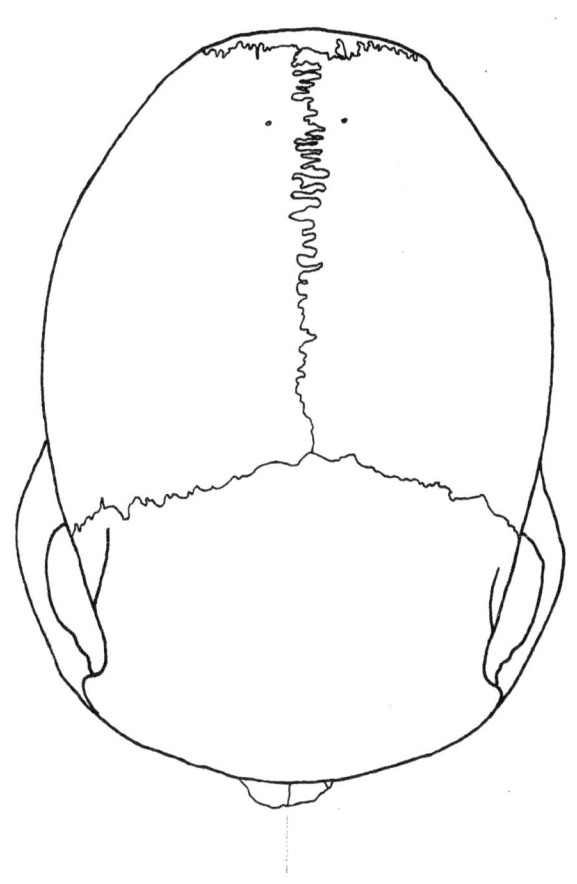

PLATE VIII - C: FORT ANCIENT VILLAGE SITE
UNDEFORMED ILINID TYPE MALE (FAM #A91)
(SUPERIOR VIEW)

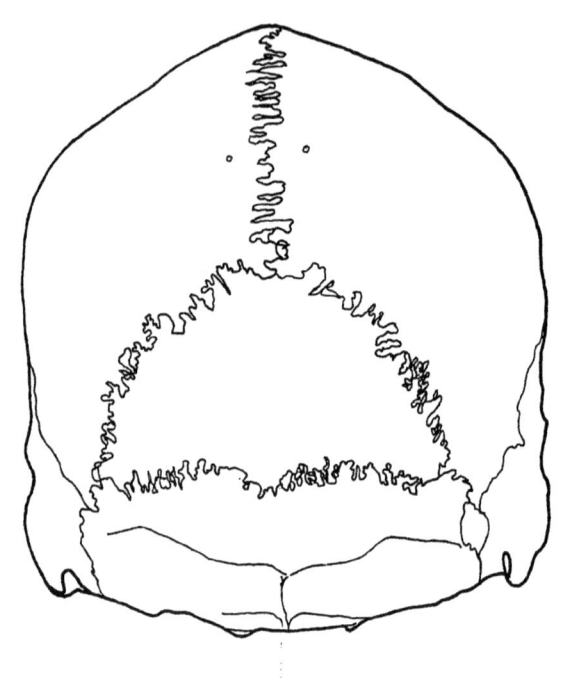

PLATE VIII - D: FORT ANCIENT VILLAGE SITE
UNDEFORMED ILINID TYPE MALE (FAM #A91)
(POSTERIOR VIEW)

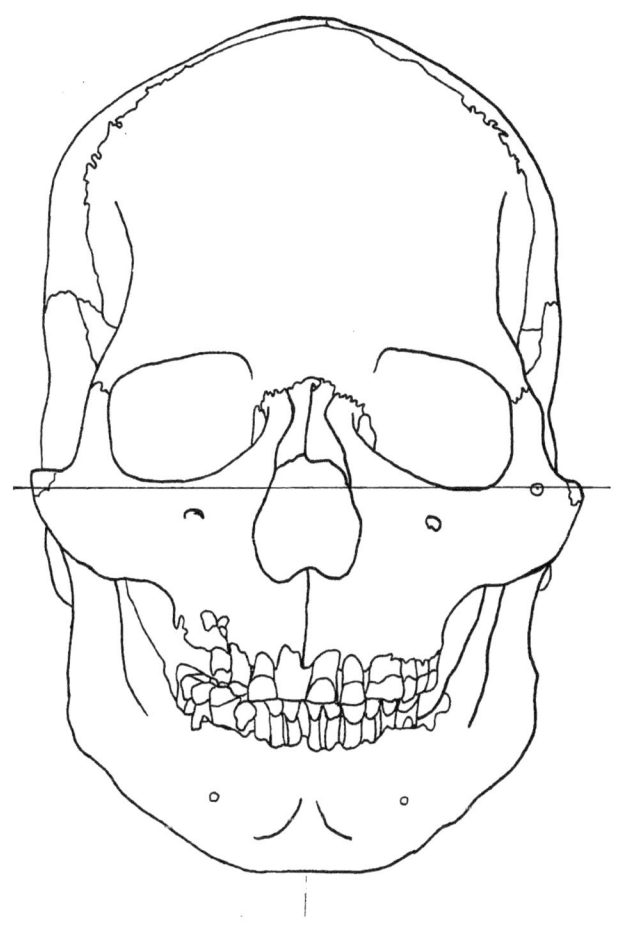

PLATE VIII - E: FORT ANCIENT VILLAGE SITE
UNDEFORMED LENID-LIKE TYPE MALE (FMNH #41517)
(FRONTAL VIEW)

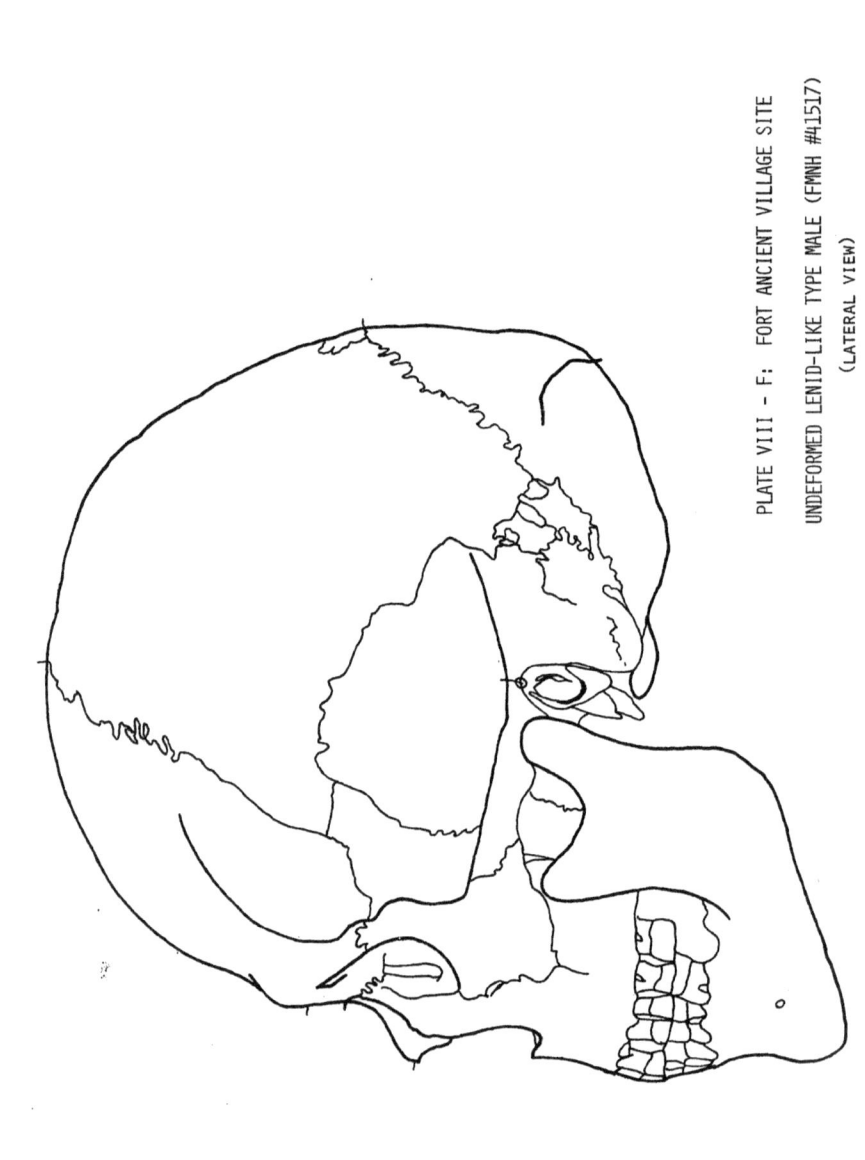

PLATE VIII - F: FORT ANCIENT VILLAGE SITE
UNDEFORMED LENID-LIKE TYPE MALE (FMNH #41517)
(LATERAL VIEW)

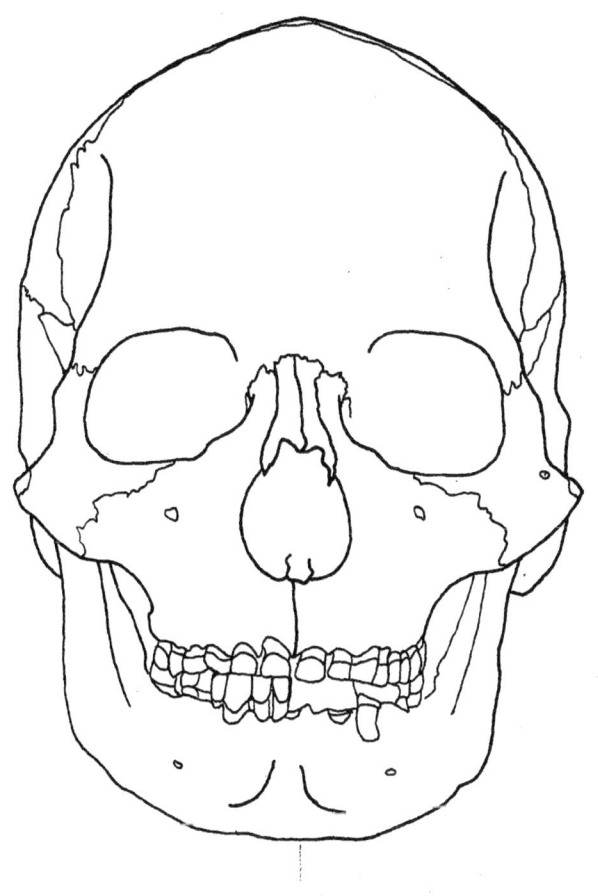

PLATE VIII - G: TAYLOR SITE
UNDEFORMED ILINID TYPE MALE (FMNH #41578B)
(FRONT VIEW)

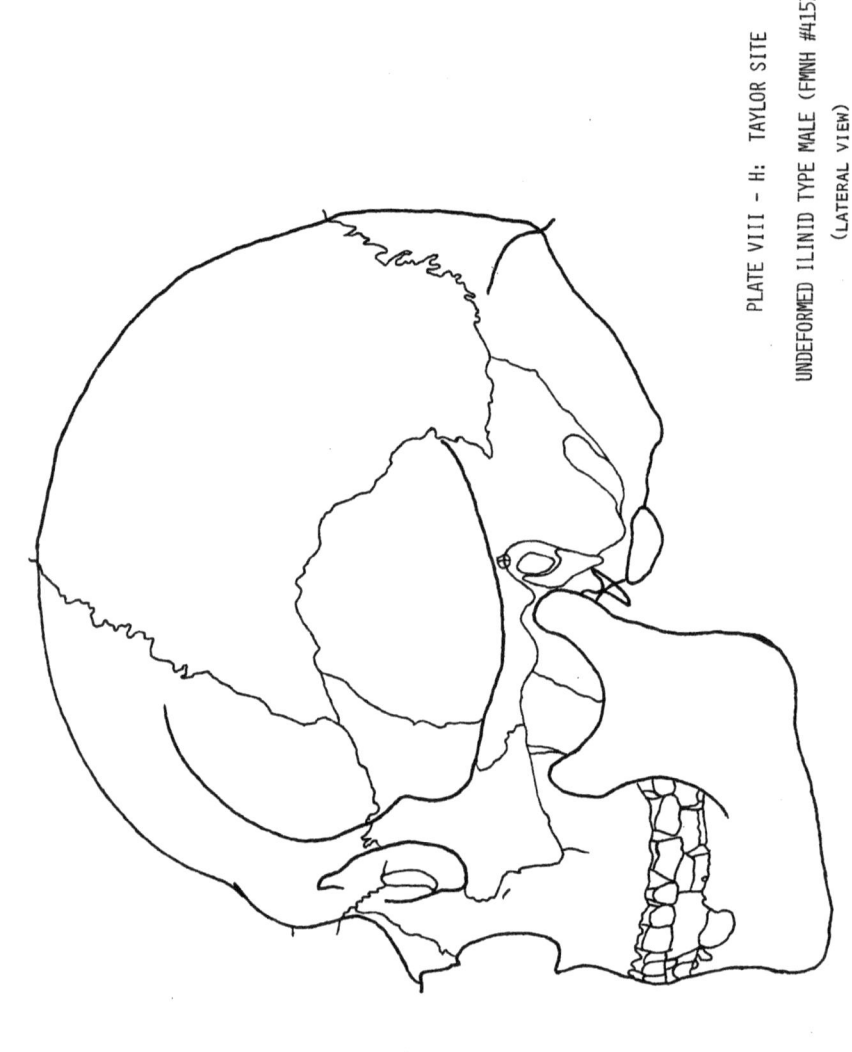

PLATE VIII - H: TAYLOR SITE
UNDEFORMED ILINID TYPE MALE (FMNH #41578B)
(LATERAL VIEW)

Madisonville Focus

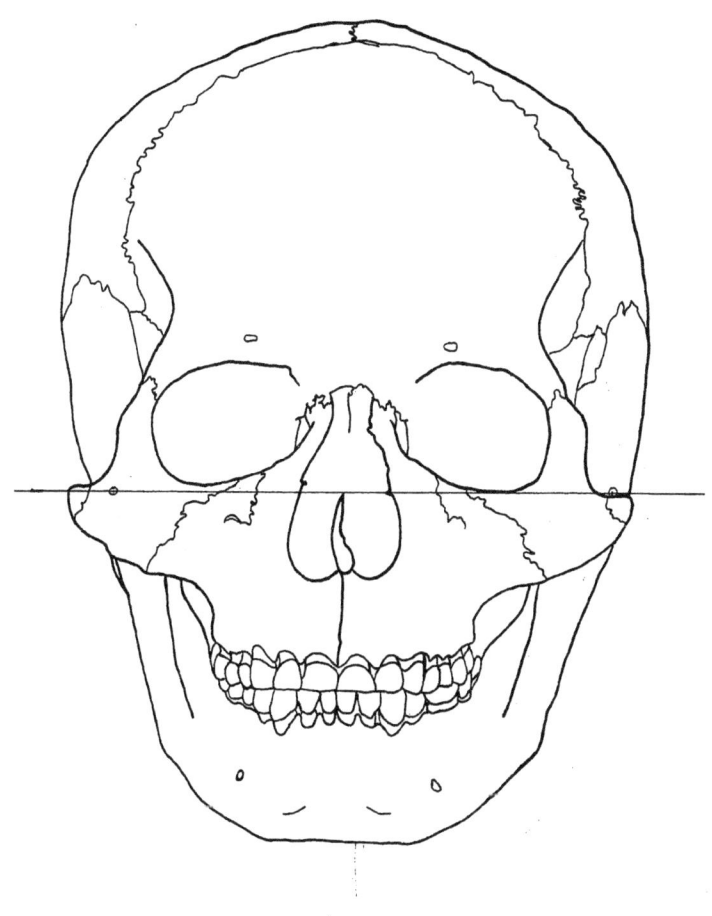

PLATE IX - A: TURPIN FARM SITE
UNDEFORMED MUSKOGID TYPE MALE (PMHU #N587)
(FRONT VIEW - NO LATERAL VIEW MADE)

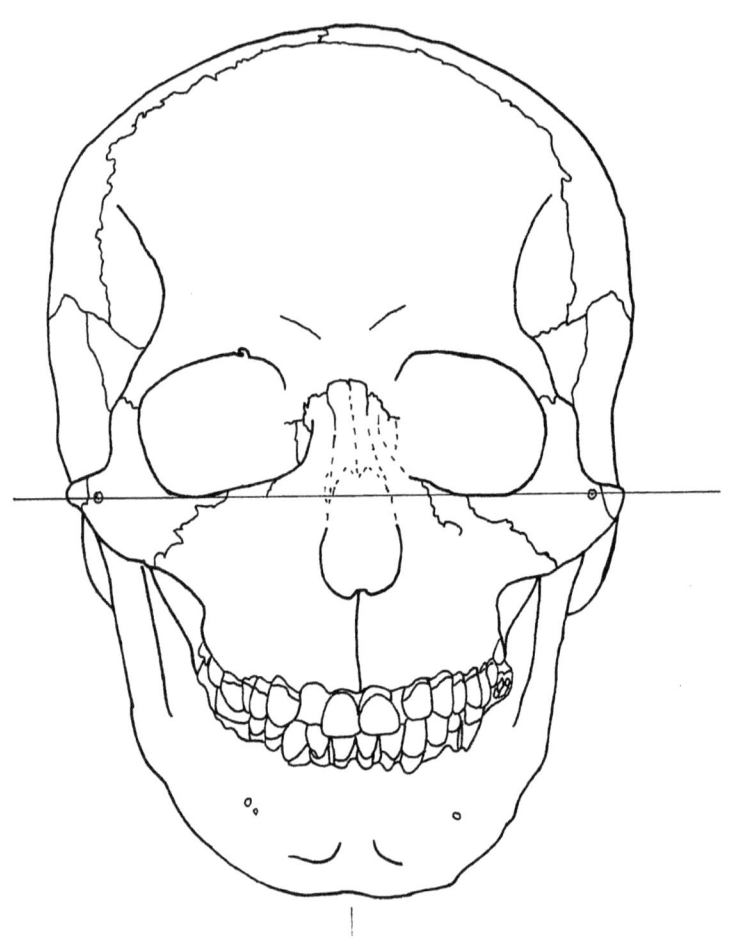

PLATE IX - B: TURPIN FARM SITE
UNDEFORMED MUSKOGID TYPE MALE (PMHU #N561)
(FRONTAL VIEW)

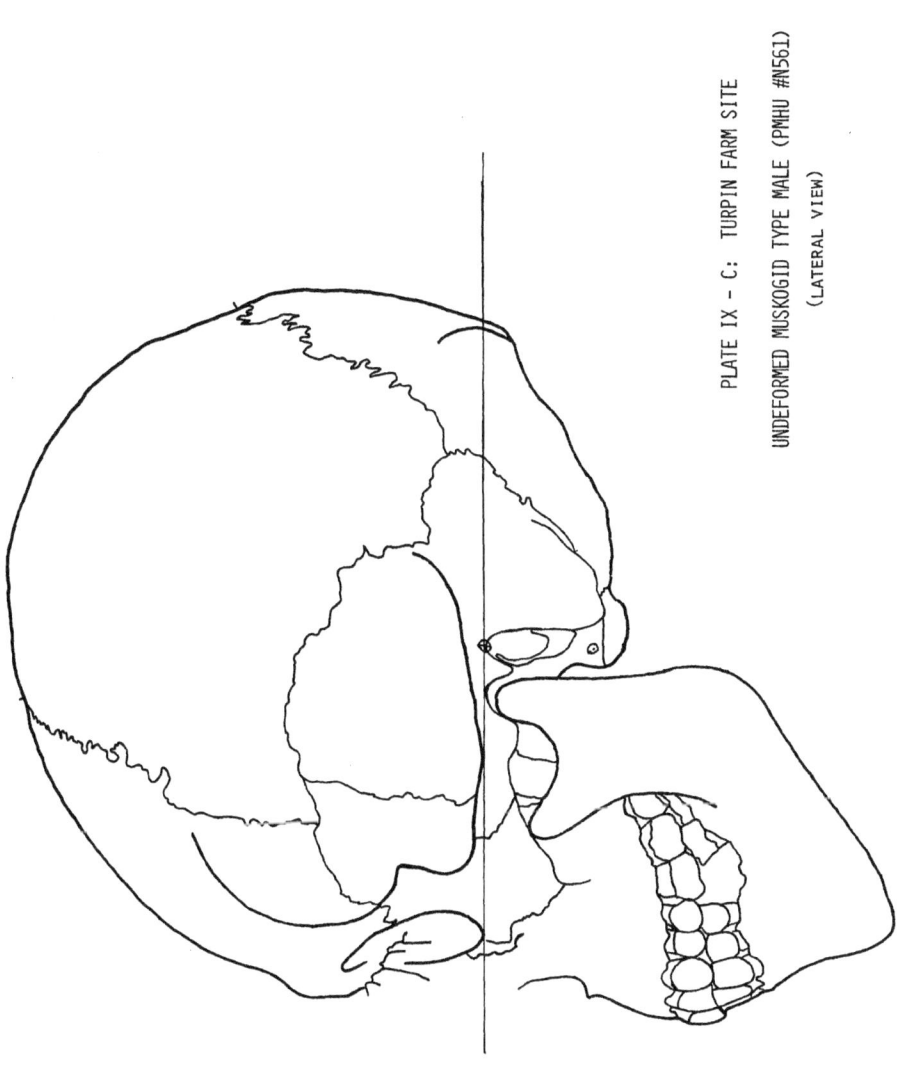

PLATE IX - C: TURPIN FARM SITE
UNDEFORMED MUSKOGID TYPE MALE (PMHU #N561)
(LATERAL VIEW)

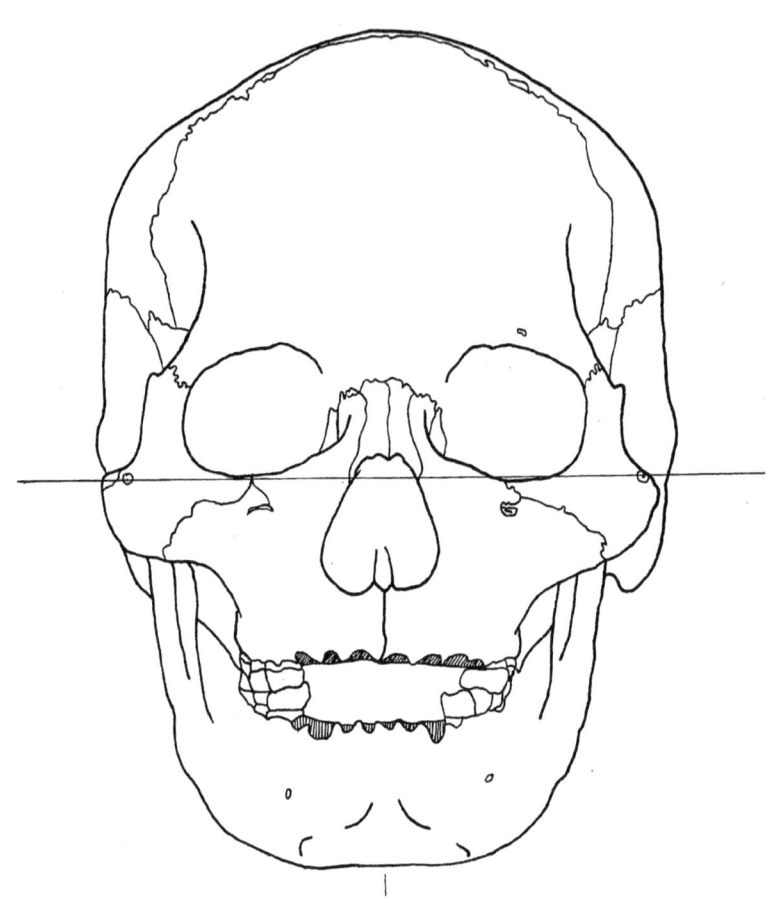

PLATE IX - D: CAMPBELL ISLAND SITE
UNDEFORMED ILINID TYPE MALE (USNM #328,828)
(FRONTAL VIEW)

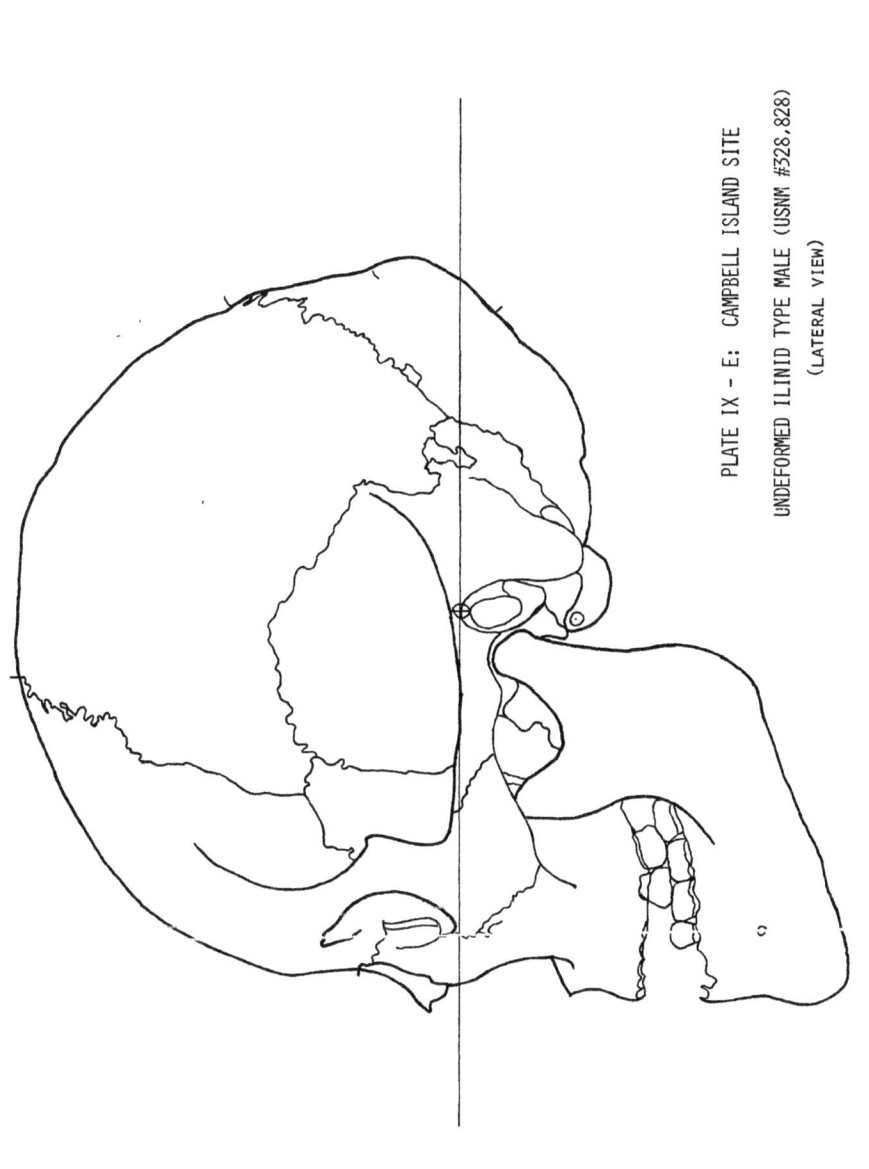

PLATE IX - E: CAMPBELL ISLAND SITE
UNDEFORMED ILINID TYPE MALE (USNM #328,828)
(LATERAL VIEW)

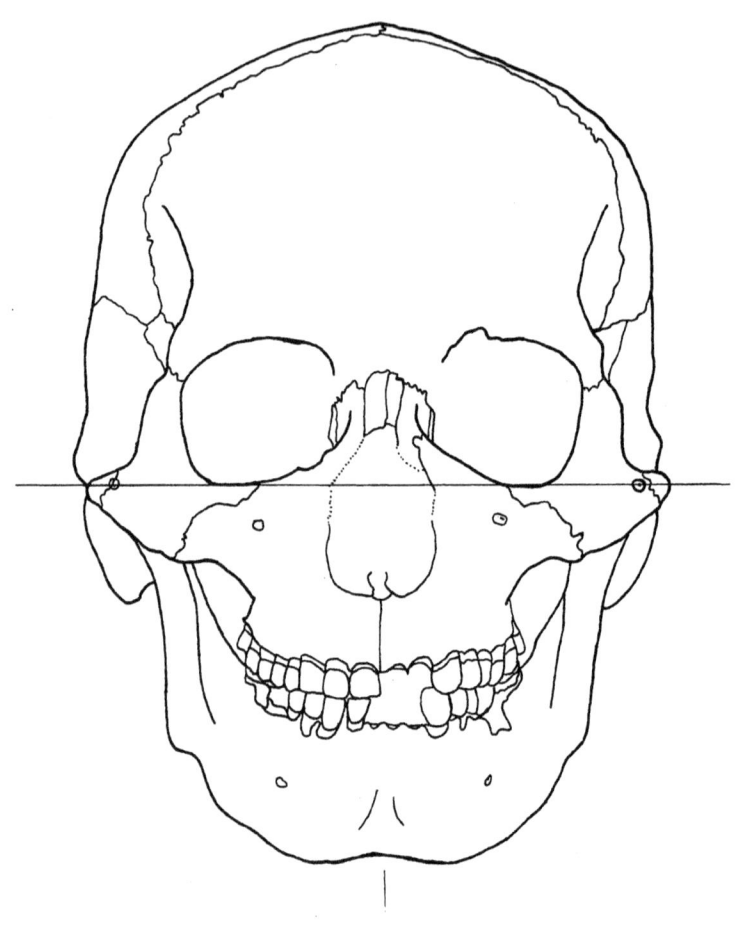

PLATE IX - F: CAMPBELL ISLAND SITE
UNDEFORMED MUSKOGID TYPE MALE (USNM #328,827)
(FRONT VIEW)

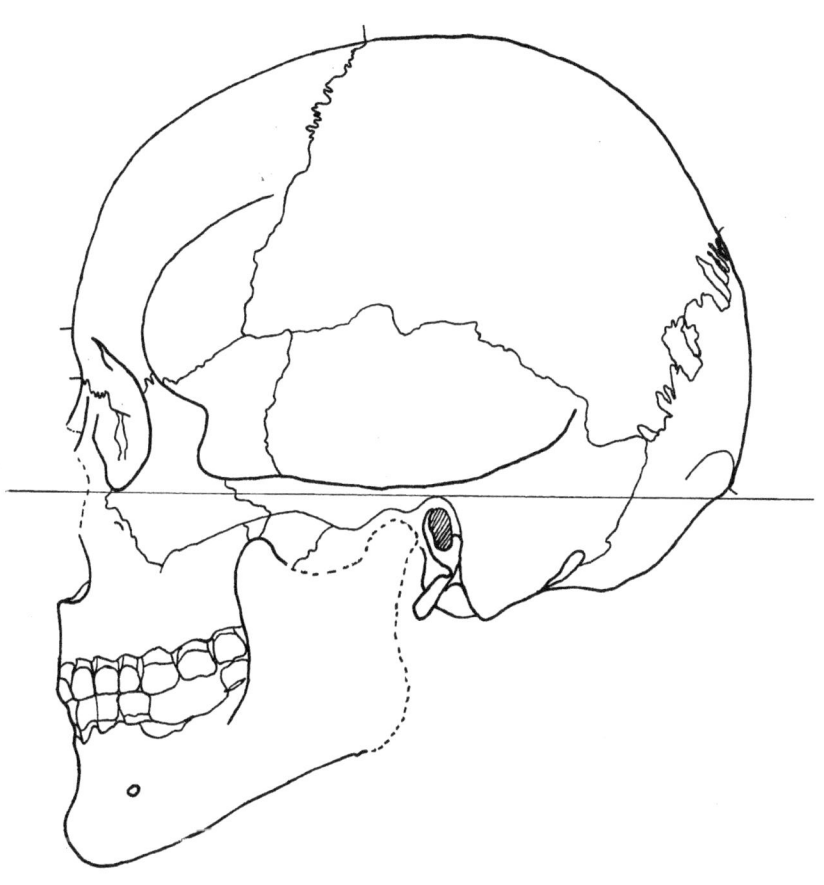

PLATE IX - G: CAMPBELL ISLAND SITE

UNDEFORMED MUSKOGID TYPE MALE (USNM #328,827)

(LATERAL VIEW)

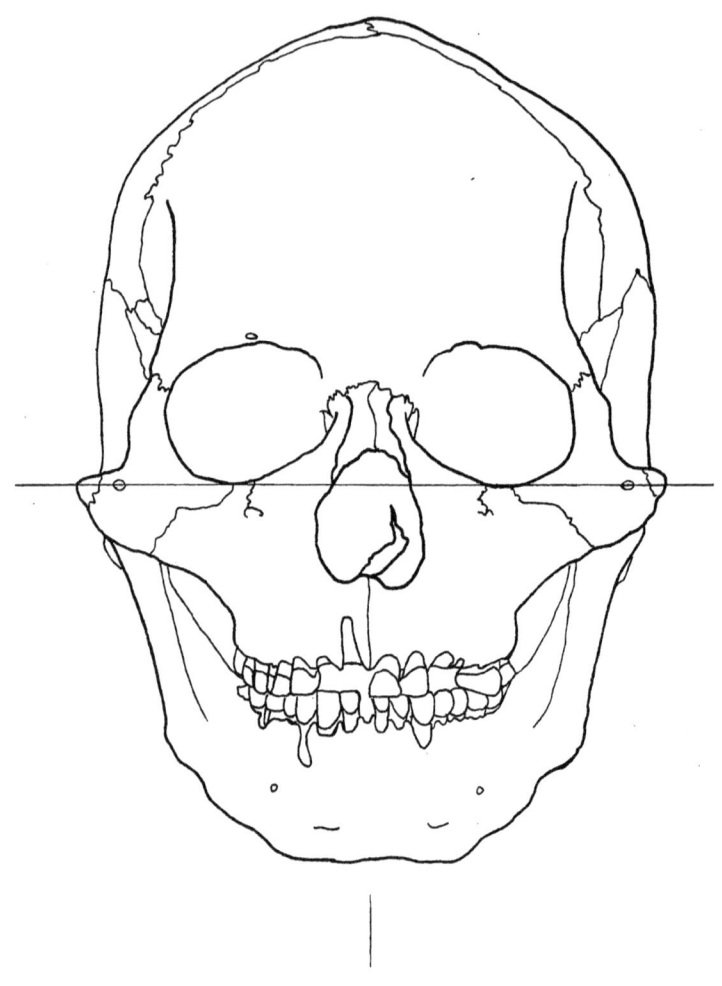

PLATE IX - H: MADISONVILLE SITE
UNDEFORMED ILINID TYPE MALE (PMHU #35524)
(FRONT VIEW)

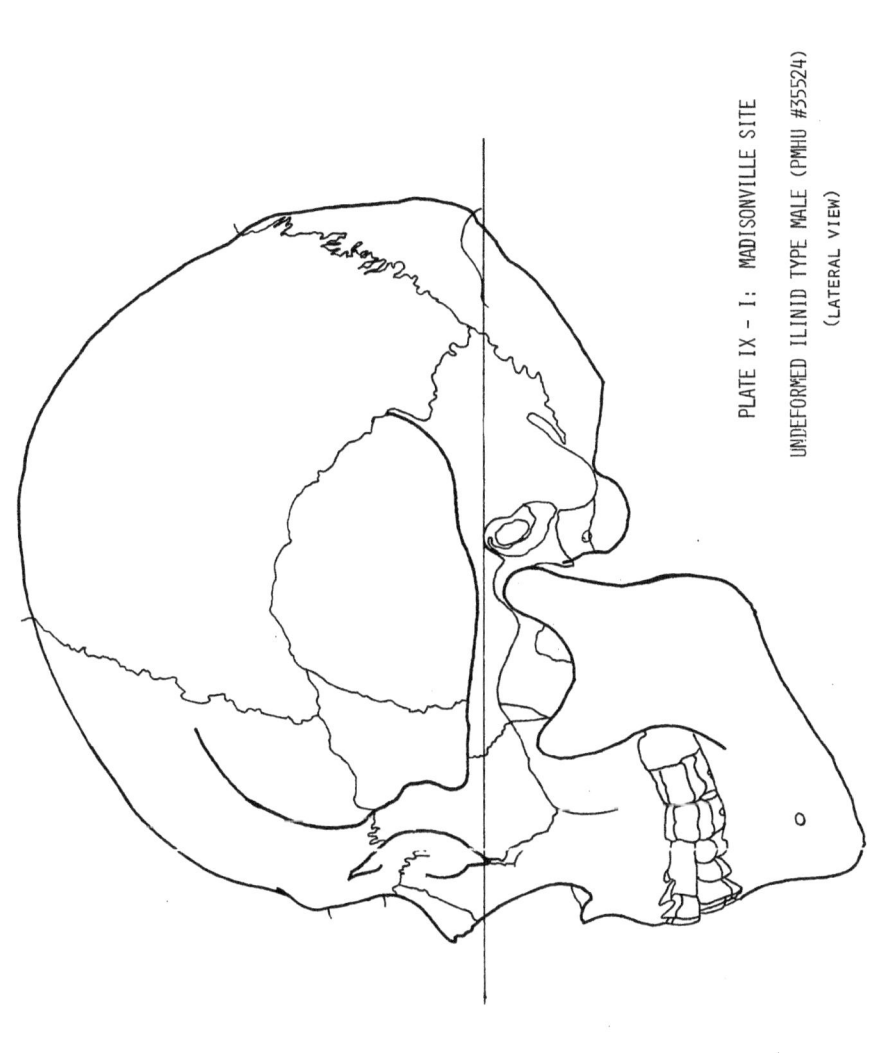

PLATE IX - 1: MADISONVILLE SITE
UNDEFORMED ILINID TYPE MALE (PMHU #35524)
(LATERAL VIEW)

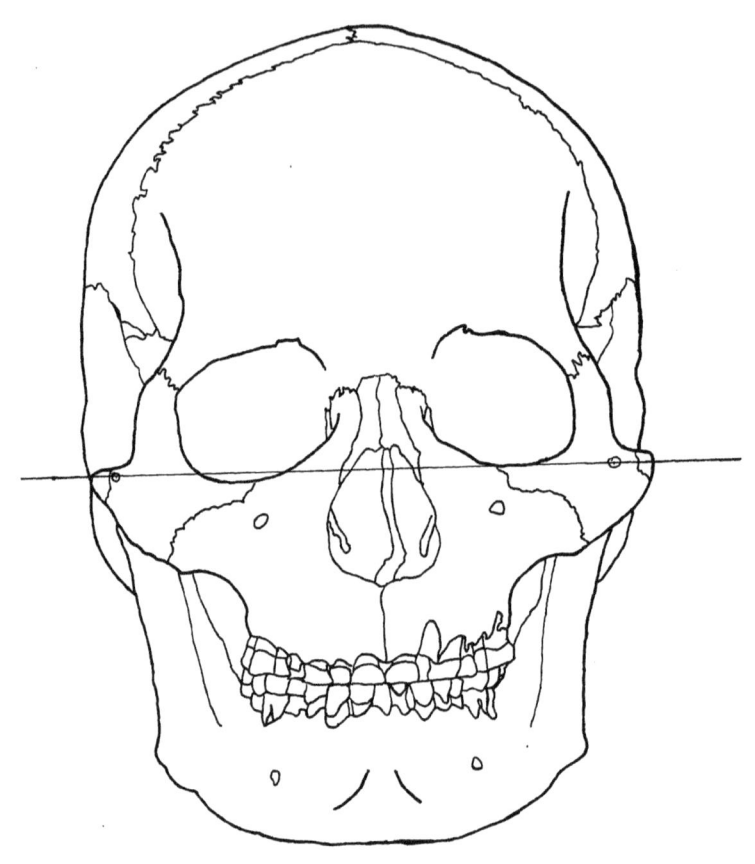

PLATE IX - J: MADISONVILLE SITE
UNDEFORMED ILINID TYPE MALE (AMNH #20/3669)
(FRONT VIEW)

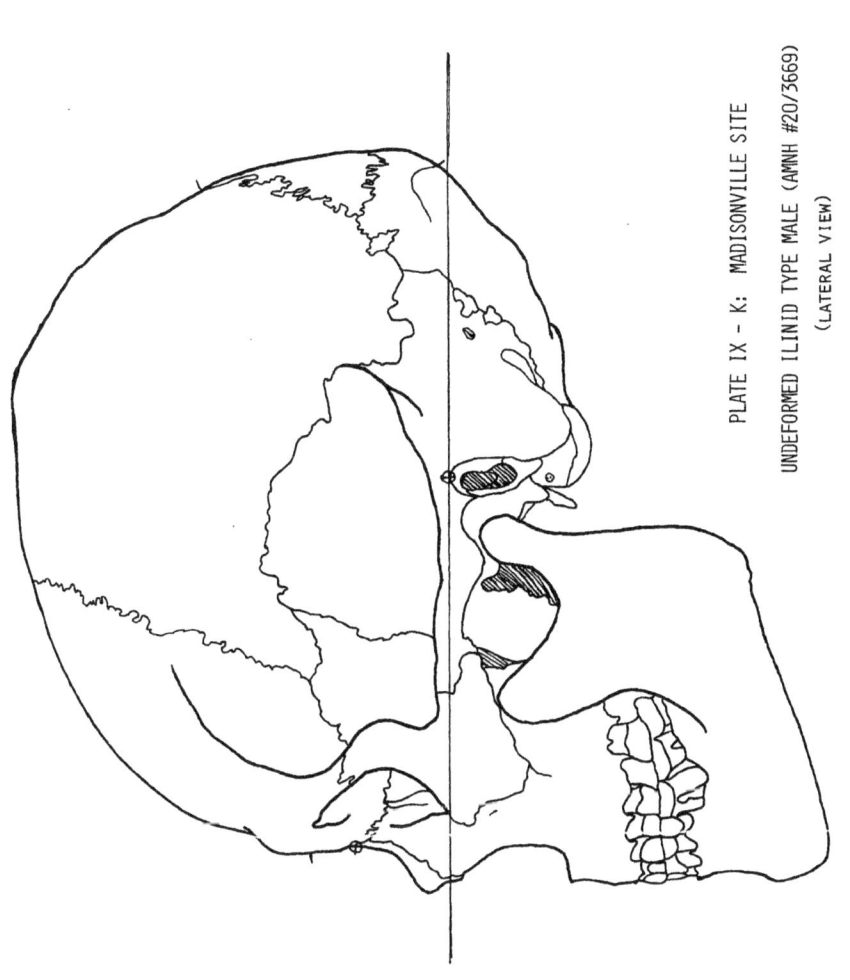

PLATE IX - K: MADISONVILLE SITE
UNDEFORMED ILINID TYPE MALE (AMNH #20/3669)
(LATERAL VIEW)

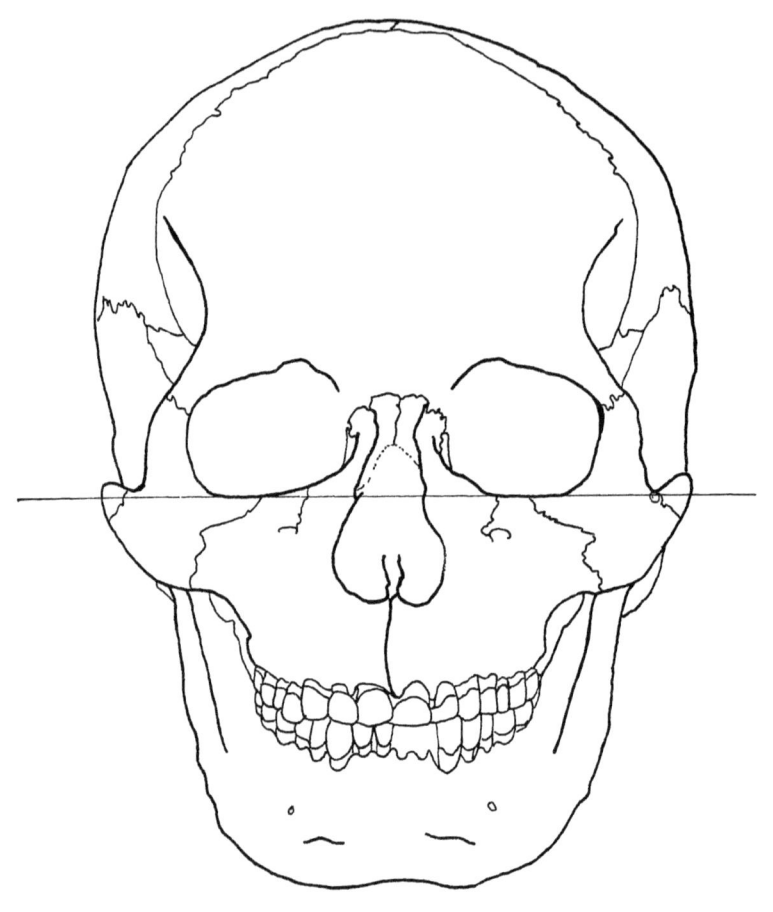

PLATE IX - L: MADISONVILLE SITE
UNDEFORMED MUSKOGID TYPE MALE (PMHU #25130)
(FRONT VIEW)

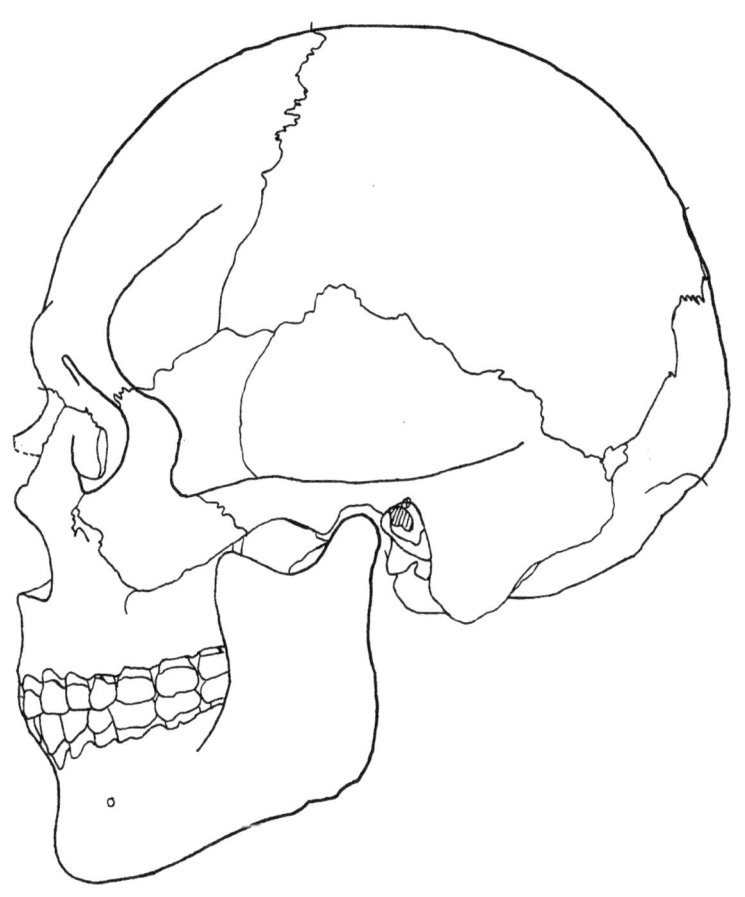

PLATE IX - M: MADISONVILLE SITE
UNDEFORMED MUSKOGID TYPE MALE (PMHU #25130)
(LATERAL VIEW)

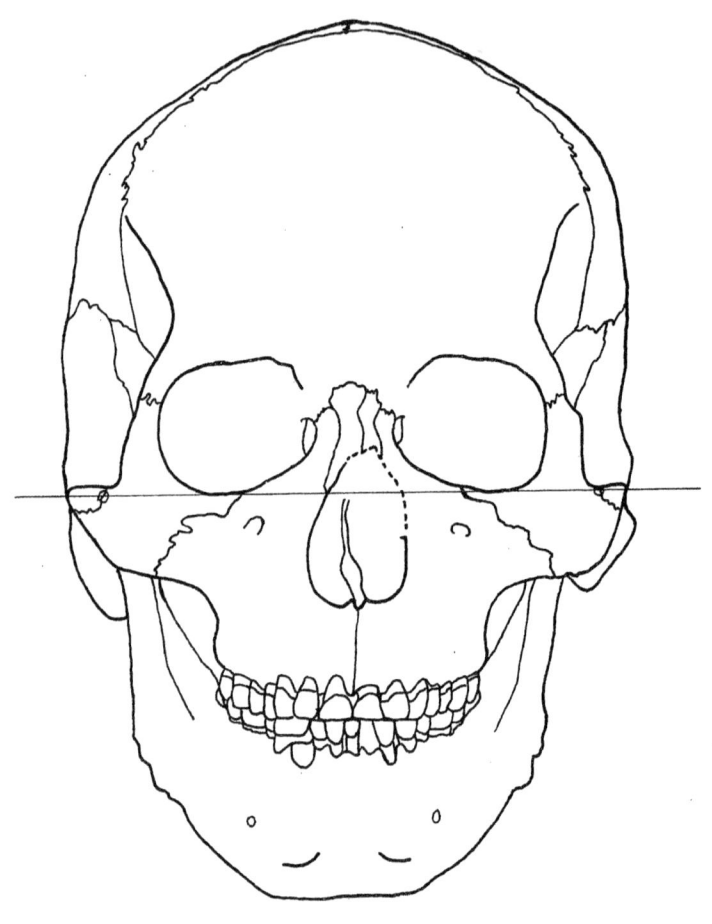

PLATE IX - N: MADISONVILLE SITE

UNDEFORMED STONE GRAVE MUSKOGID TYPE MALE (PMHU #58541)

(FRONT VIEW)

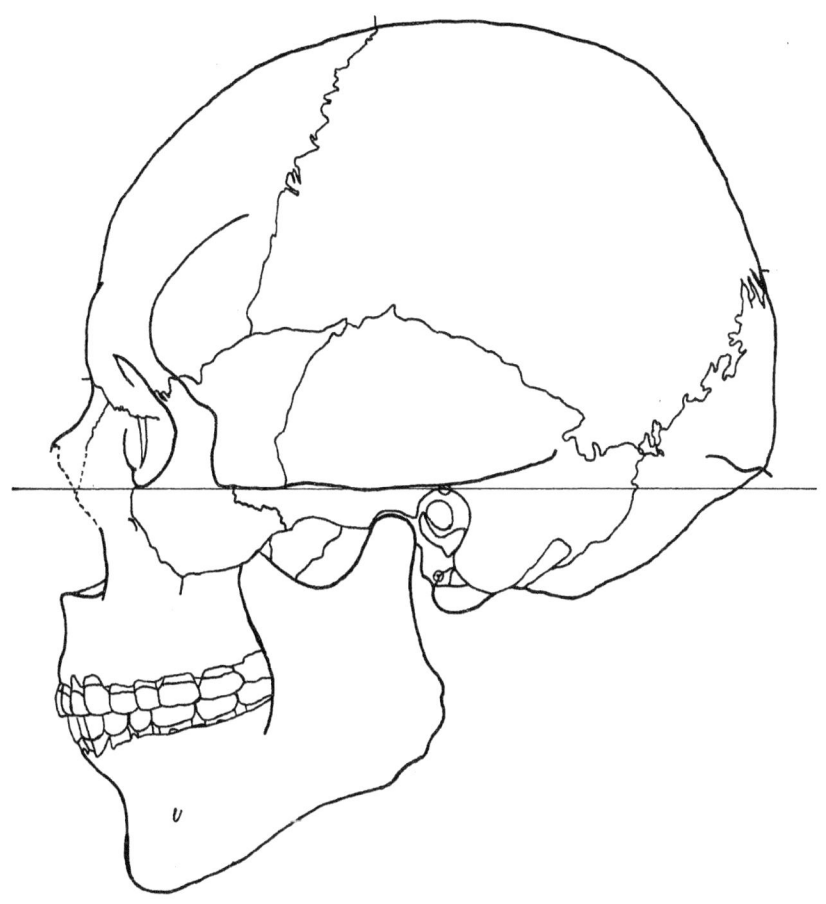

PLATE IX - O: MADISONVILLE SITE

UNDEFORMED STONE GRAVE MUSKOGID TYPE MALE (PMHU #58541)

(LATERAL VIEW)

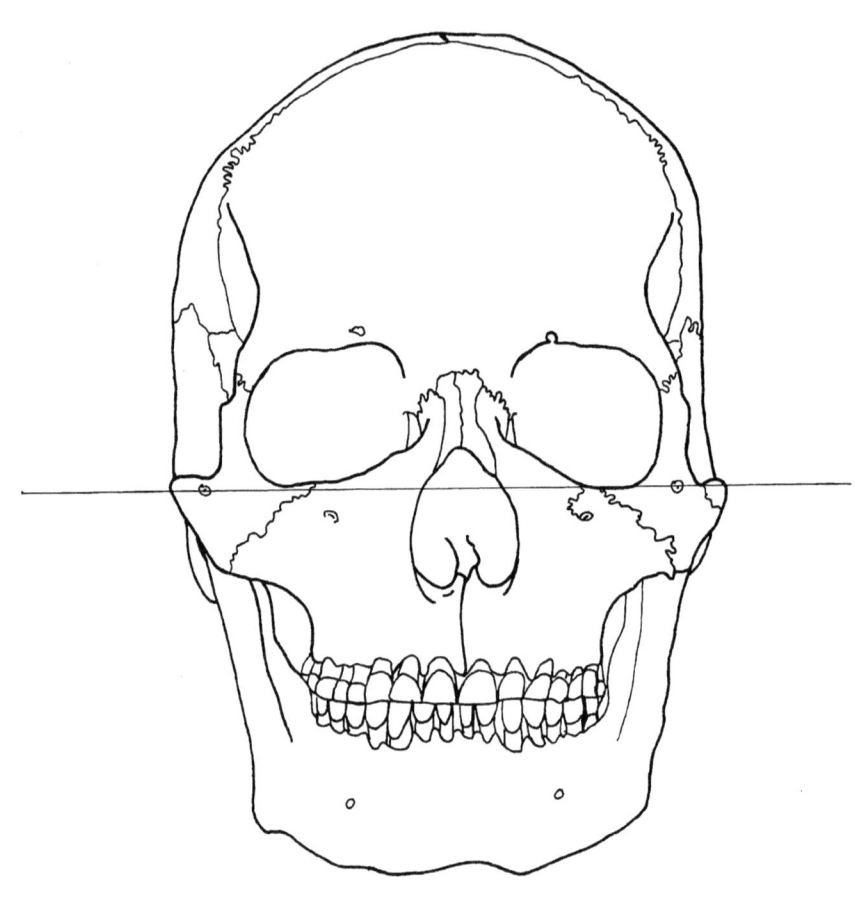

PLATE IX - P: FOX FARM SITE
UNDEFORMED ILINID TYPE MALE (BLM -B1)
(FRONT VIEW)

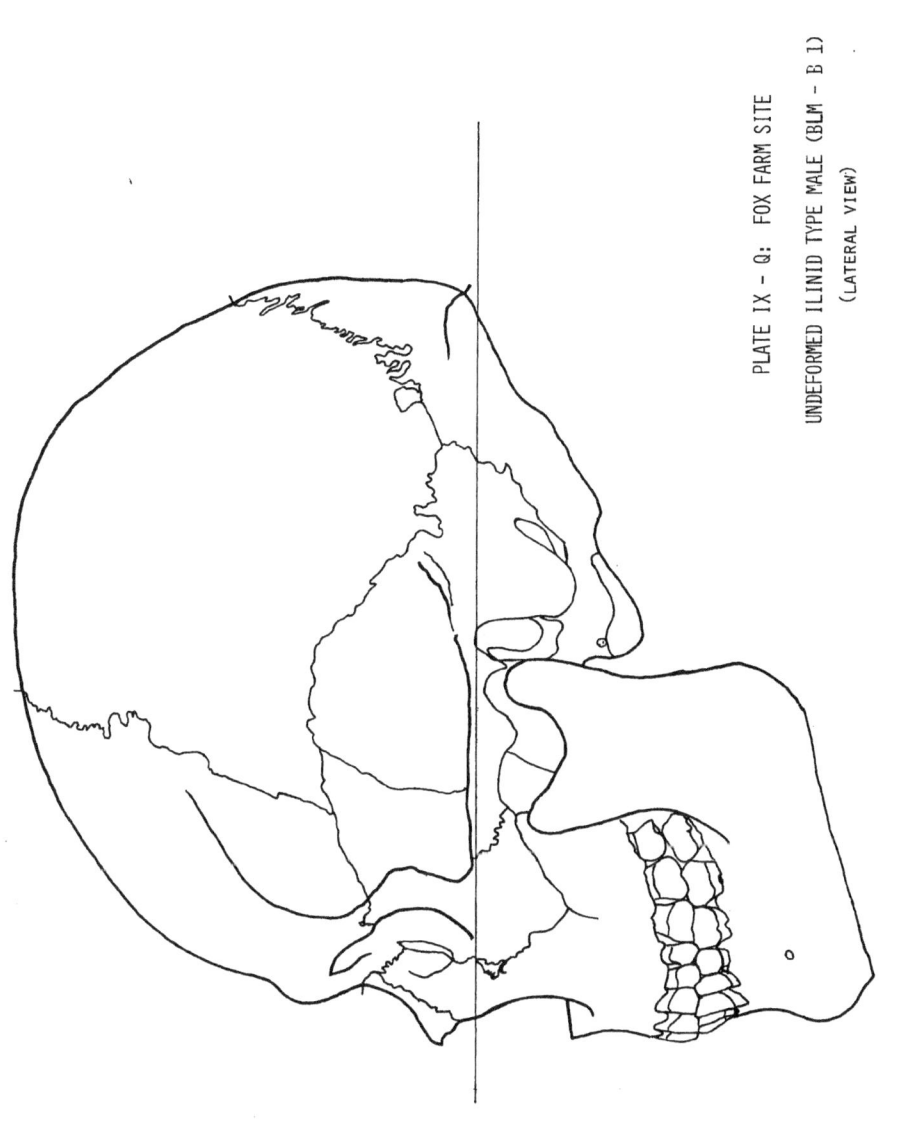

PLATE IX - Q: FOX FARM SITE
UNDEFORMED ILINID TYPE MALE (BLM - B 1)
(LATERAL VIEW)

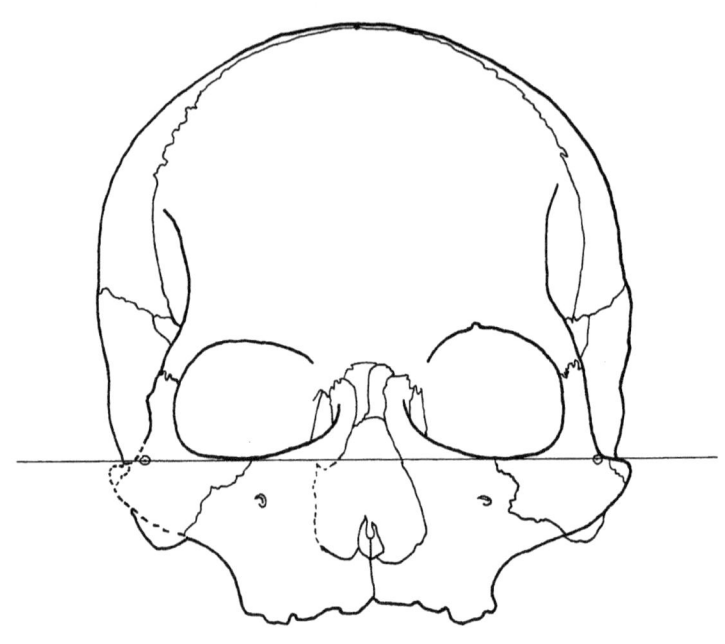

PLATE IX - R: FOX FARM SITE

UNDEFORMED ILINID TYPE FEMALE (AMNH #20/441)

(FRONT VIEW)

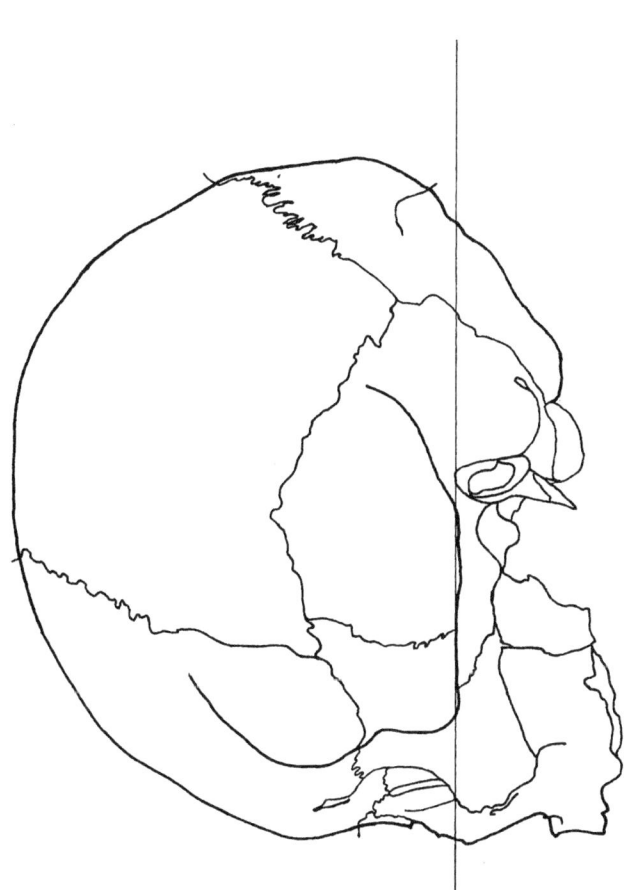

PLATE IX - S: FOX FARM SITE

UNDEFORMED ILINID TYPE FEMALE (AMNH #20/441)
(LATERAL VIEW)

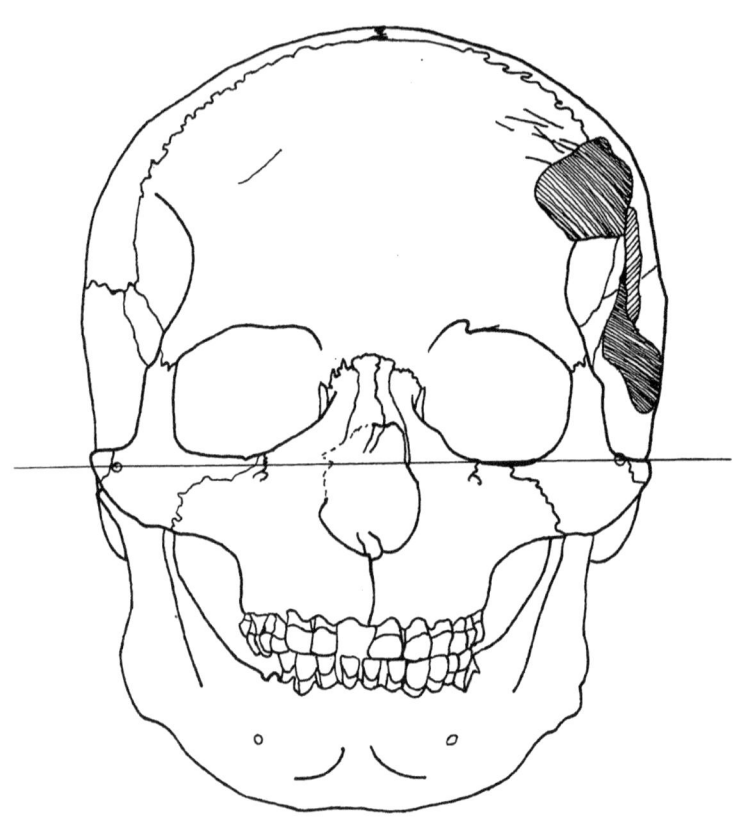

PLATE IX -T: FOX FARM SITE

UNDEFORMED MUSKOGID TYPE MALE (AMNH #20/1268)

(FRONT VIEW)

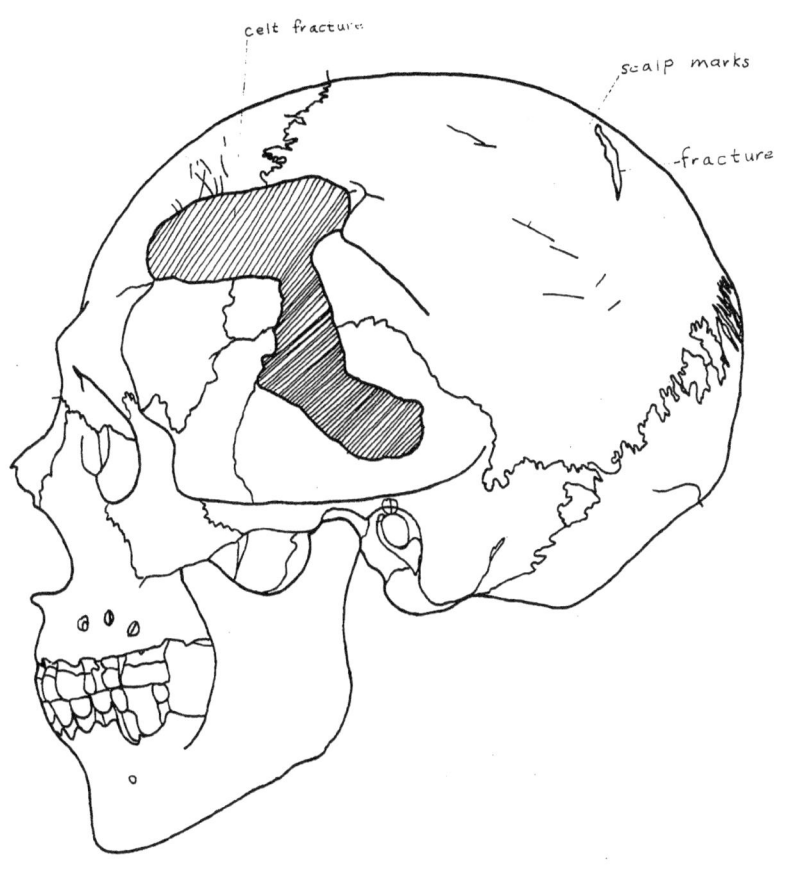

PLATE IX - U: FOX FARM SITE
UNDEFORMED MUSKOGID TYPE MALE (AMNH #20/1268)
(LATERAL VIEW)

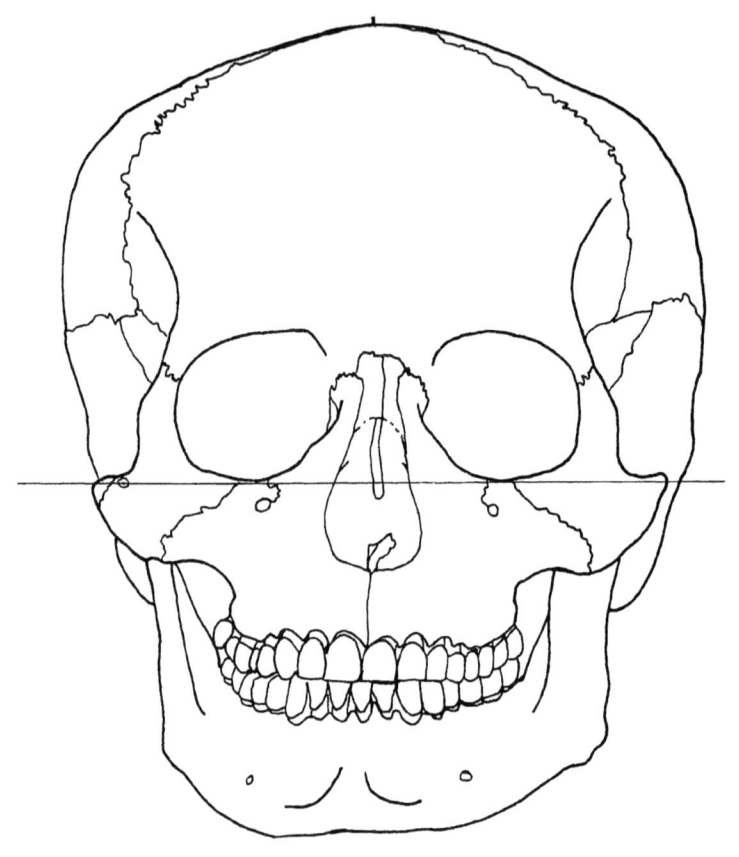

PLATE IX - V: FOX FARM SITE

DEFORMED MUSKOGID TYPE MALE (AMNH #20/758)
(FRONTO-VERTICO-OCCIPITAL DEFORMATION)
(FRONT VIEW)

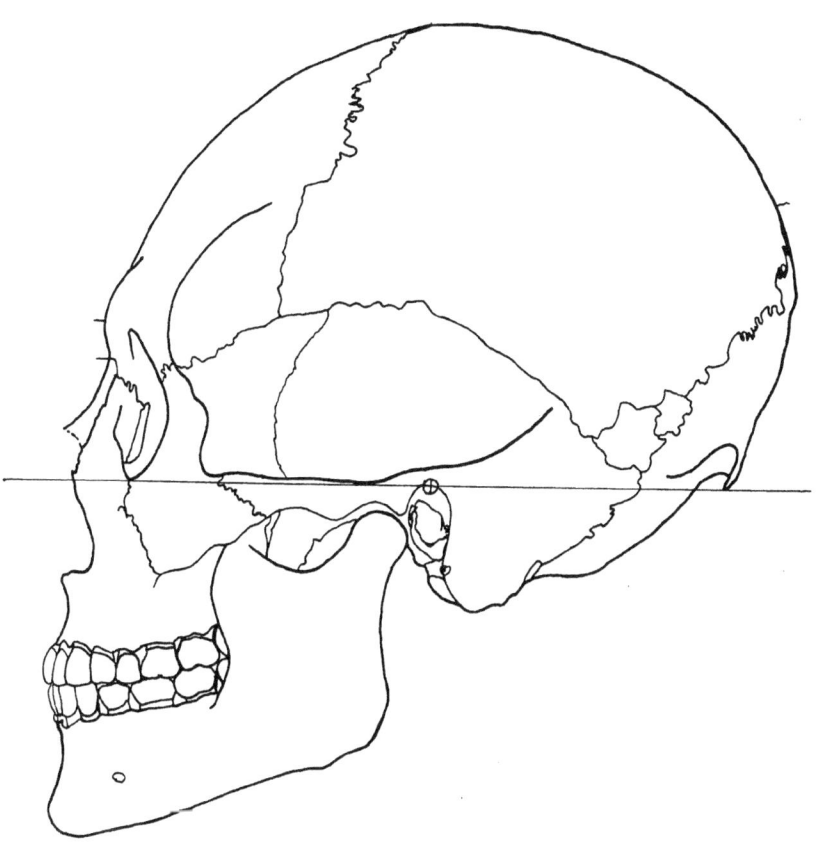

PLATE IX - W: FOX FARM SITE

DEFORMED MUSKOGID TYPE MALE (AMNH #20/758)
(FRONTO-VERTICO-OCCIPITAL DEFORMATION)
(LATERAL VIEW)

www.ingramcontent.com/pod-product-compliance
Lightning Source LLC
Jackson TN
JSHW070312120426
100741JS00007B/31